MAJOR AIRLINE FLEET LISTS

As at Summer 1978 (including aircraft on order for later delivery).

Airline	Airbus A300	Boeing 707/720	Boeing 727	Boeing 737	Boeing 747	Aérospatiale Caravelle	Aérospatiale/BAC Concorde	McDonnell Douglas DC-8 Srs 10-50	McDonnell Douglas DC-8 Si	McDonnell Douglas D	McDonnell Do	Fokker F27 Fr	Fokker-VFW F	BAC One-Ele	Hawker Sidde	Lockheed L-1	BAC (Vickers	NAMC YS-11	Helicopters	Miscellaneo
Lufthansa Germany	11	12	37	28	15						11									
Malaysian AS Malaysia		3		8							2	9								4 Islander
MEA Lebanon		17			3															
National Airlines USA			38								15									
Northwest Airlines USA		2	69		27						22									
Olympic Airways Greece	2	13	6	4	2													6		
Pakistan International Pakistan		12			3						4	8								
Pan American USA		46	13		44											12				
Qantas Australia		7			17															1 HS.125
Sabena Belgium		6		14	2	1					3									6 Cessna 310
Saudia Saudi Arabia		12		19	2							3				13				3 Gulfstream 6 others
SAS Scandinavia	2				4				12	60	5									
Singapore Airlines Singapore		10	10	5	12						4									
South African Airways South Africa	4	5	9	6	11															3 HS.748
Swissair Switzerland					2				6	48	10									
Trans-Australia Australia			12							12		14								3 Twin Otter
TAP Portugal		12	8		2															
TWA USA		96	88		11					14						26				
THY Turkey		4	5							9	2		3							
United Airlines USA			189	59	18			59	39		42									
Varig Brazil		16	9	10							4									10 Electra
Western Airlines USA		18	37	23							11									

The Illustrated Encyclopedia of the World's

COMMERCIAL AIRCRAFT

air new zeala

The Illustrated Encyclopedia of the World's

COMMERCIAL AIRCRAFT

William Green and Gordon Swanborough

a Salamander book

Published by
CRESCENT BOOKS
New York

A Salamander Book

Library of Congress Catalog Card Number:
78-59196
This edition is published by Crescent Books,
a division of Crown Publishers, Inc.
by arrangement with Salamander Books Ltd.
a b c d e f g h

Crescent Books,
a division of Crown Publishers, Inc.
One Park Avenue, New York,
New York 10016

ISBN 0-517-26287-8

All correspondence concerning the content of this volume should be addressed to Salamander Books Limited.

This book may not be sold outside the United States and Canada.

Authors' Note

Entries in this book are arranged alphabetically according to name of manufacturer and aircraft designation, although in certain cases layout considerations have forced us to slightly modify this arrangement.

The first section of this book is devoted to aircraft that are used exclusively or principally by the world's airlines, while those types in the second section are used mainly for business and executive flying. There is no hard and fast rule dividing these types, however; some aircraft in part two are operated on scheduled services by the smaller airlines, while some of the larger airliners—even Boeing 707s and 747s—have been bought for private use by large corporations and as the personal transports of kings and presidents. The airliners section of the book also includes a single helicopter—the Sikorsky S-61—because it is the only helicopter in use in 1978 for *scheduled* airline service. Other helicopter types are used for air taxi, contract and business flying, and are described in the third section of the book.

Credits

Introduction material by Bill Gunston

Editors: Veronica Pratt and Trisha Palmer
Designer: Nick Buzzard

Cutaway and line drawings © Pilot Press Ltd
Color artwork drawn by Keith Fretwell,
© Salamander Books Ltd

Filmset by SX Composing, Essex, England
Color reproduction by Paramount Litho,
Essex, England
Tenreck Ltd, London, England

Printed in Belgium by
Henri Proost & Cie, Turnhout, Belgium

Contents

A HISTORY
The first fifty years

Passengers travelled by air as early as November 1783. But that was by balloon, and—although a few aeronauts strove to paddle themselves along with oars—the balloon could never be very useful as a transport vehicle because it is at the mercy of the wind. It needed the addition of propulsion and a rudder to turn it into the airship, or dirigible (from a French word meaning steerable), which gradually became a practical proposition in the second half of the 19th century. At the turn of the 20th century the stage was set for Count von Zeppelin, a former general in the German army and a brilliant engineer, to build the first useful airships.

By the summer of 1908 his large but flimsy craft could fly for 12 hours, covering more than 100 miles (160km). By the end of 1909 a Zeppelin airline, called Delag, had been formed to build and operate bigger and better ships. It was still a terribly chancy business, because engines were rather unreliable, and if a ship hit trees or any other obstructions it was probably doomed. Even a sudden gust of wind could smash a Zeppelin if it was badly moored or half out of its giant shed. One innovation, masterminded by the greatest of all Zeppelin commanders, Hugo Eckener, was a nationwide meteorological forecasting service, the first ever. By 1912 passenger services were criss-crossing central Europe, and seven airships had very successfully carried 33,722 passengers by the time World War I broke out in August 1914.

Subsequently, in September 1928, the most successful airship in history, the *Graf Zeppelin*, made a completely trouble-free maiden flight. Over the next nine years she flew all over the world, frequently operating regular transatlantic services, and carrying over 18,000 passengers. In March 1936 she was joined by an even bigger airship, the *Hindenburg*, but in May 1937 this was consumed by fire as it was landing in New Jersey, and that was the end of civil airship transport. Today several people are convinced airship freight operations make sense, with totally new technology, but it has yet to be proved.

After the Delag airship services, the first regular airline was operated with a small Benoist flying boat across Tampa Bay, Florida, in 1914. It linked Tampa to the smaller resort of St Petersburg, which helped subsidize the operation, but it failed to start a permanent air transport industry. This had to wait until technology had been forced ahead in World War I, when several countries used military aircraft as VIP and staff transports. Military "airliners" shuttled to and from the Versailles Peace Conference in 1919, while aircraft constructors set about converting warplanes for civil use. Four of the most important had been bombers: the British de Havilland D.H.4, Vickers Vimy and Handley Page O/400, and the French Breguet XIV. All were readily available and reasonably reliable, and such machines were the foundation of the first permanent air services in 1919–20. Former fighters and trainers, such as the Curtiss JN-4 "Jenny" in the USA and Bristol Fighters and Martinsyde F.4 scouts in Britain, were used to carry mails.

Air transport gradually staggered off the ground, mainly in Europe, in 1919–20. The aircraft could only just maintain a semblance of a regular service; passengers had to dress in leather coats and gauntlets and suck barley sugar, with earplugs "strongly recommended", and even hot-water bottles

were not uncommon in winter. Engine failures and forced landings were frequent; one flight managed to suffer 11 forced landings on the short journey from Kent in Southern England to Paris. With quite large aircraft seating only from two to six passengers the cost per seat-mile (a basic yardstick for transport aircraft) was inordinately high, and passengers almost never flew as routine but only as a costly once-only experience, or because they wanted to get into the papers. Progress was bound to be slow and halting, and most of the early services had to be terminated.

Aircraft manufacturers struggled as hard as the young airlines. They could build better civil airliners, but only at a prohibitive price. A D.H.16 with a proper cabin for four passengers cost almost four times as much as the surplus military two-passenger D.H.4A; a little later, in March 1920,

Main picture: The world's first commercial air vehicle was the Zeppelin airship LZ.7 Deutschland. She made her first passenger flight on June 22, 1910, from Friedrichshafen to Dusseldorf with 32 people on board. The Zeppelin airline, Delag, made 1,588 flights by August 1914, mostly pleasure trips in the summer with passengers treated to a sumptuous meal on board.

Top inset: Departure of a Curtiss R-4 of the US Army Signal Corps from Potomac Park, Washington on May 15, 1918; the start of the World's first sustained commercial airmail service, linking the capital with Philadelphia and New York.

Above inset: On February 5, 1919 the new German airline Deutsche Luftreederei opened an airmail service between Berlin and Weimar (the seat of government). Soon it was extended to other cities; here an LVG C VI is being loaded at Gelsenkirchen.

Right: On August 25, 1918 Aircraft Transport & Travel opened the world's first daily international passenger service, flying D.H.16s between London and Paris.

de Havilland's slightly larger D.H.18, with a cabin for eight, sold only six aircraft. Likewise, the early converted-bomber Handley Pages seated six passengers, while the purpose-designed W/8 and W/8B seated 12 but at more than double the price. One of the few true airliners to be sold in fair numbers over a long period was the French Farman Goliath; this was quite large and seated 12, but as it had only two 260hp engines it was cheaper to buy and to run—though very slow and unable to make much progress in a stiff headwind.

While established builders in Britain, France and other countries completely failed to produce any successful civil transport—success naturally being defined by how many were sold—two manufacturers did achieve success in adverse circumstances. The first was the German Dr Hugo Junkers, who had patented extremely advanced cantilever monoplane airliners as early as 1910 and who had from the start concentrated upon monoplanes with efficient structures made and skinned in light alloy. Such structures were challenging, and Junkers was one of the great pioneers. He used tubes and angle-girder strips joined together by rivets and bolts, and then applied a skin of light alloy with corrugations running fore and aft. This skin was much more robust than flat sheet, but the drag was greater than Junkers expected, partly because the air did not often flow exactly along the direction of the corrugations. But the Junkers monoplanes were far superior in general serviceability to their wood, wire and fabric competitors. The concept had been proven in front-line machines in the final two years of World War I, and when the Junkers F.13 flew on 25 June 1919 it was a winner from the start. Unlike almost all other civil machines it was a low-wing cantilever monoplane, and though it cruised at only 75mph (120kph) it carried four passengers in a comfortable cabin on an engine of only 240hp, roughly half that of rival machines. It was tough enough to last 30 years in such harsh environments as the Soviet Arctic, the jungles of the Amazon or the goldfields of the interior of New Guinea.

Only one other transport showed the promise of the single-engined Junkers, and this was the Fokker F.II, again a modest cantilever monoplane with the same 240hp engine. Fokker had built combat aircraft for the Germans, but in 1919—amidst frightening civil disorder and a near-total breakdown of law in Germany—he managed to load his entire factory of

Opposite top: With the appearance of the Handley Page W.8, which was first flown on December 4, 1919, the airliner was beginning to emerge into full adulthood. Though identical in technology to the wartime O/400 bomber, the W.8 had space for 12 passengers and cut DOC (direct operating cost) from 24 to only 13 pence per passenger mile.

Opposite below: By far the most important French airliner of the early post-war period was the Farman Goliath – with wings which were said to be made by the kilometre and chopped off as needed! On March 22, 1919 a Goliath took off from Paris with a number of passengers and flew to Brussels, thereby initiating the very first international passenger service. Despite its auspicious beginnings, however, the operation was not sustained. These Air Union Goliaths were pictured at Le Bourget after 1920.

Top left: First flown on June 25, 1919, the Junkers F.13 was inherently more advanced than all other airliners of its day, with a low-mounted cantilever monoplane wing and stressed-skin structure of the new alloy Duralumin. Dr Junkers believed in using a corrugated exterior skin to increase stiffness and strength, and did not appreciate that this noticeably reduced cruising speed.

Left: First of a highly successful family of airliners, the Fokker F.VII first flew in late 1923. This (as yet unregistered) example has a Napier Lion engine; most had a Rolls-Royce Eagle of 360hp and the much superior F.VIIA had the 435hp Bristol Jupiter radial and eight instead of six passenger seats.

Below: In 1925, Fokker flew the first three-engined F.VII/3m. These became instantly popular and not only outsold all other transports of the 1920s but also set a standard which was widely copied by other airlines. This particular example was used on the Amsterdam–Batavia (Netherlands East Indies) service, then the world's longest air route.

tools, engines, aircraft parts and raw material on to six private trains which were smuggled into his native Holland under the noses of the Allied Control Commission. At Amsterdam, he set up what became for a time the world's most successful aircraft factory, building every kind of civil and military aircraft for world markets. Nearly all had fuselages of welded steel tube and wings with an all-wood construction based on two large box spars (each spar was in the form of a stiff but slender box running from tip to tip). These wings, like those of Junkers, needed no exterior bracing.

Though the Fokkers paralleled the Junkers transports in size and power, they had wings mounted on the top of the fuselage. The F.II was a neat four-passenger machine, and while producing this in quantity Fokker fitted a Siddeley Puma engine and a fifth passenger seat to give the F.III of 1921. About 60 of both types were built. Two years later a considerably larger machine emerged, the F.VII six-seater with a Rolls-Royce Eagle, which led to the F.VIIA with eight seats. The VIIA had a new engine, the 400hp Bristol Juniper. This aircooled radial was the first post-war engine to hit the market in a big way, and it gradually swept away the wartime leftovers. With its rivals from the United States, the 220hp Wright Whirlwind and 400hp Pratt & Whitney Wasp, it established a completely new order of reliability, long life and reduced operating cost, and transformed air transport into a dependable and at least a desirable and serious business, even if not yet a commercially viable one without government subsidy.

Fokker made 45 F.VIIAs and then in 1925 flew a three-engined version, the F.VIIA/3m. With the larger F.VIIB/3m this sold to major operators all over the world, more than 150 being delivered. One was chosen by a famous Australian, Sir Charles Kingsford Smith, who did more than anyone except Lindbergh to survey new long-distance civil air routes. The three-engined F.VII versions were usually still only eight-seaters but they considerably reduced the cost per seat-mile and had the stamina to fly such extremely long routes as Amsterdam to Batavia (now Djakarta, Indonesia). In the early 1930s this took about two weeks end-to-end, with numerous stops and flying only by day. Night flying was still rare, and services were often disrupted by bad weather and even by strong winds. A gale could easily tip over the airliners at an airport, because wing loading (aircraft weight divided by the area of the wings) was quite low and the wings could lift the aircraft off the ground in a wind of about 50mph (80kph). Airline fleets were small, often numbering only two or three machines of each type, so one casualty caused major disruption.

Early American services were concerned almost wholly with mail. Relatively small single-engined single-seat biplanes droned hour after gruelling hour across some of the toughest regions—the endless midwest plains, the rugged Rockies and the waterless desert—to get the mail through. Not until the end of the 1920s did the situation change, partly through legislation and partly through the emergence of better transports. In September 1928 the Ford Tri-Motor went into service. This was like an F.VIIB/3m but made entirely of metal, and it seated 10 to 14 passengers. Boeing's 80A was a twin-engined biplane seating 18. Curtiss built the very similar Condor, which later had retractable landing gear and supercharged engines. Such machines laid a foundation on which the US airlines grew to outdistance all others.

Britain had unrivalled expertise but produced only somewhat outdated fabric-covered biplane airliners, reflecting the reactionary view of Imperial Airways, and as these seldom sold abroad the production runs were uneconomically short. Landplanes included the D.H.66 with three Jupiters, the A.W. Argosy with three Jaguars and the stately H.P.42 with four Jupiters, with Vickers and Boulton & Paul supplying twin-Jupiter mailplanes. Short supplied the Calcutta and Kent flying boats, with three and four Jupiters respectively, and two examples of a landplane Kent (the Scylla) seating up to 39 on short sectors. These British leviathans were the largest and most luxurious airliners of their day, but at 95–100mph (152–160kph) were about to be hit between the eyes by new technology.

In World War I German designers had built stressed-skin machines of the new light alloy Duralumin. The metal skin was not just a covering but a major part of the structure, carrying basic loads in what was called the monocoque way (a monocoque structure has its strength in the shell, like a lobster claw, instead of in a supporting framework underneath). One of the pioneers of monocoque airliners was Lockheed in the United States, whose Vega of 1927 was almost perfectly streamlined and not only went faster than rivals with the same power but hit the headlines with two great flights around the world. The Vega was wooden, and so was the Orion of 1931, which moved the wing from high to low and retracted the landing gear. Swissair put the Orion into use in Europe and no rival operator could come near it; the swift American aircraft cut 50 per cent off the flight schedules. But other Americans were combining the monocoque construction with light alloy, as did Lockheed. Northrop was one of the pioneers, but the first of all was Boeing, whose Monomail of May 1930 carried six or eight passengers plus a heavy load of mail at about 140mph (225kph) on a single 575hp Hornet engine. It was a clean cantilever monoplane built entirely of light alloy and with retractable landing gear.

On 8 February 1933 Boeing flew the first model 247, often regarded as "the first modern airliner". Powered by two 550hp Wasps, it seated 10 plus a stewardess, had metal stressed-skin structure and such refinements as cowled engines, retractable landing gear, variable-pitch propellers and pulsating-rubber de-icers along the leading edges of the wings and tail. At a price of $50,000 (then about £12,500) the Boeing gained a massive order for 60 from a new airline, United, half the order being delivered by June 1933. This immensely powerful competition caused a reaction by rivals, and within two years put the American manufacturing industry

Top left: *The pride of Imperial Airways were the great four-engined Handley Page H.P.42 class, the first of which flew in November 1930. Like silver galleons they cruised majestically at 95mph (152kph), holding their own despite a concept that was completely obsolete – strut-based biplane wings, fixed-pitch wooden propellers swung by uncowled engines, fixed landing gear and even a biplane tail.*

Top centre: *In 1927 Lockheed flew the radical Vega, a small high-winger with wooden monocoque (single-shell) structure and unbraced monoplane wing. In the autumn of 1931 this low-wing development, the Orion, entered service between New York and Washington. It had a retractable landing gear, and was almost twice as fast as some rivals. This really shook an industry that was essentially conservative in outlook.*

Above: *On February 8, 1933 Boeing flew the first 247, which took the Orion philosophy much further and translated it into metal-stressed skin. The newly-formed giant United Air Lines had 30 of the radical monoplanes in service by the end of June 1933. This museum piece belongs to Pacific Air Transport, which has virtually duplicated the original United livery.*

Top right: Christmas aboard a Handley Page W.10 after the formation of Imperial Airways (probably in 1926). Virtually all airliners of the day had wickerwork chairs, structural members inside the cabin and railway-type baggage racks.

Above centre: Short Brothers, which built all Imperial's flying boats, also delivered two L.17 landplanes, named Scylla and Syrinx, in 1934. Seating 39, they were the biggest airliners then in use, and they even boasted a steward's pantry.

Above right: Gradually Deutsche Lufthansa became the biggest civil airline in the world, and even before the rise to power of the Nazi party German aviation was characterized by impressively grand design. This was the passenger check-in hall at Berlin Tempelhof in 1928, when most airports were still using primitive wooden huts or tents.

Right: Sometimes Teutonic grandeur over-reached itself. The Dornier Do X flying boat of 1929 had 12 engines and once flew with 169 people on board (nine were stowaways), but never entered revenue service. Though far bigger than all contemporaries, its cabins were narrow by later standards.

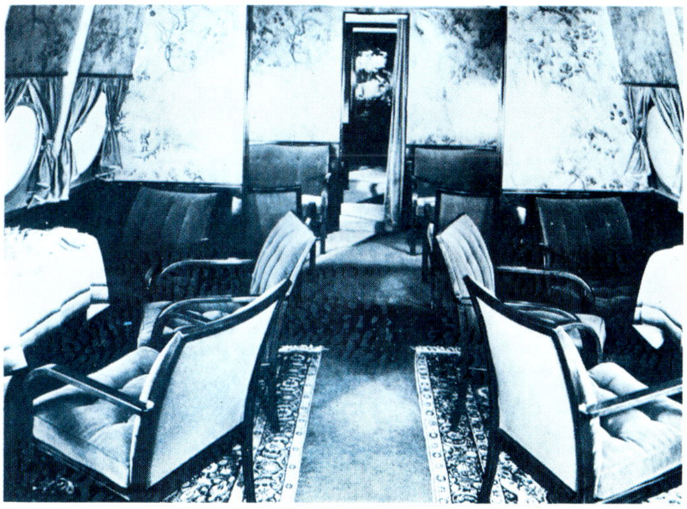

into a completely unprecedented position from which it dominated Europe and other world markets.

Biggest and fastest of the rivals was Douglas, which had been asked to build a new all-metal tri-motor for TWA. Instead, the company schemed a modern twin, with all the features of the 247 plus better engine cowlings, flaps, a roomier and unobstructed fuselage seating 12, and a better aerodynamic shape. The DC-1 (Douglas Commercial 1) flew on 1 July 1933. From it stemmed the strikingly attractive DC-2, seating 14, with 710hp Wright Cyclone engines. A DC-2 of the Dutch airline KLM came second (behind a special racer) in the 1934 England–Australia air race, while carrying a full load of passengers and mail. No other transport was in the same class, and despite its speed of over 170mph (274kph) it had a world-beating DOC (direct operating cost). About 220 were soon sold, and when the similar but enlarged DC-3 was produced in 1935 the stage was set for air transport really to take off. The DC-3 had a wider and better-shaped fuselage seating 21, and improved Cyclone or Twin Wasp engines in the 1,000hp class increased the speed despite the great increase in weight. The DC-3 had extended wings of unprecedented efficiency, and thanks to their multi-spar structure proved resistant to fatigue —then a virtually ignored phenomenon—and thus opened the way to a new era of longevity. Today some DC-3s have flown 70,000 or more hours without cracking. By 1936 the DC-3 was fast becoming the world standard transport, even in the Soviet Union and Japan. Including models made in those countries, and the vast armadas built in World War II, about 13,300 of the basic DC-3 type were delivered, many times more than any other airliner in history.

In the late 1930s there were only two rivals worth bothering about. Lockheed flew the Model 10 Electra in February 1934, a trim all-metal eight-seater with twin fins. From it stemmed the Models 12, 14 and 18, of which well over 1,000 were made in all. They grew in size and power and were the fastest airliners of the pre-war era with cruising speeds exceeding 200mph (322kph). The models 14 and 18 featured a dramatically effective Fowler flap, which slid backwards out of the wing to increase area, before finally depressing in the landing setting, and this type of flap is still used on the latest airliners. In

Below left: *The crucial decision of Boeing to refuse to sell any 247s until it had completed delivery of all 60 ordered by United opened the way to the DC (Douglas Commercial) series. The first built in quantity was the DC-2, which knocked the 247 for six. This DC-2 for Swissair was photographed just before delivery in 1934. Today Swissair is chief sponsor for the newest Douglas, the Super 80.*

Bottom: *Despite the Depression and near-bankruptcy Lockheed forged ahead under new management, and made the transition from wood to light alloy. Smaller than the Douglases, their airliners were the fastest in the world. This was the Lockheed 14, first flown on July 29, 1937.*

Below right: *Best-selling European airliner of the 1930s (before the advent of the all-time popular DC-3) was the corrugated-skin Junkers Ju 52/3m, seen in Sabena livery. This extremely robust aircraft first flew in April 1932.*

Germany, Junkers conceived a "double wing" flap, forming a separate surface hinged behind the trailing edge, and used it on the Ju 52, the other great transport of the 1930s. Junkers had been building tri-motors since 1924, but it was not until the Ju 52/3m was introduced in April 1932 that it became No 1 in Europe. Thanks to the German Deutsche Luft Hansa, the top European airline, the efficient Junkers outsold all other European transports. Including wartime military production about 4,800 were built.

In June 1938 Douglas flew a giant transport with four engines, three fins and a tricycle landing gear. There had been numerous four-engined airliners, notably long-range flying boats such as the Sikorsky S-42 and Martin 130 for PanAm and the Short C-class for Imperial, but this DC-4 was clearly of a new generation. During World War II a simplified version went into military service, and in 1945 DC-4 Skymasters reached the airlines, carrying 42 passengers in comfort over long ranges at over 200mph (322kph). Pratt & Whitney Twin Wasps of 1,350hp were used, but Double Wasps of 2,000 to 2,500hp had been developed during the war and these made possible the DC-6, 6A and 6B. With lengthened and pressurized fuselages seating up to 90, these were the leading long-range aircraft of 1947–55, and well over 500 were delivered. Substitution of the 3,250hp Turbo-Compound led to the DC-7 and long-range 7B, the final piston-engined "DC" being the DC-7C Seven Seas of 1955, the first airliner able to carry a full payload (about 100 passengers) non-stop across the North Atlantic.

Lockheed flew a strikingly advanced airliner in January 1943, the Constellation, and over the next 15 years made over 850 in many versions which tended to become ever longer, more capacious and more powerful. Boeing had pioneered the pressure cabin with the four-engined 307 Stratoliner of 1938, the idea being to pump fresh air into the interior to try to maintain the atmosphere as nearly as possible like that at sea level, as the aircraft climbed into thinner air at high altitude. Its use meant a great increase in weight, complexity and cost. Early pressurization systems worked at maximum differential pressures (the difference in pressure between inside and outside) of only about 2 lb per square inch (0.14kg/cm^2).

***Below left:** In the 1930s flying boats often surpassed landplanes in size and range, but this was mainly because no comparable landplanes were built (the problem being that sheltered water areas were larger than "airports", which were little better than football pitches). A pioneer on both the Atlantic and Pacific routes was Pan American, whose Sikorsky S-42 of 1934 established the pattern for many of its successors.*

***Bottom:** In July 1936 Short Brothers showed that Britain had, after all, heard of the modern stressed-skin monoplane. While the RAF used fabric-covered biplane fighters, this splendid new C-class Empire boat introduced a long overdue improvement in aerial technology.*

***Below right:** This interior of an Armstrong Whitworth Ensign, the biggest airliner in service anywhere in 1938, shows that by this time it was realized that passenger cabins were for transport and not meant to duplicate the lounges of houses.*

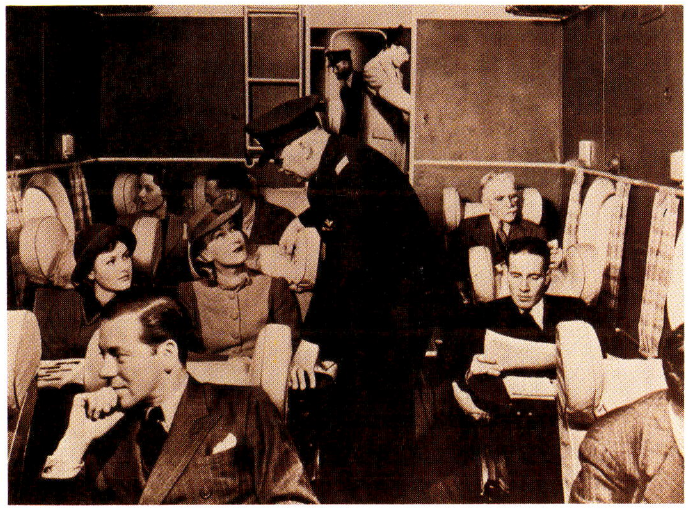

Top: Lockheed flew the first Constellation on January 9, 1943 (at the time, taken over as the Army Air Force C-69). After the war, despite prolonged groundings due to severe technical snags, this shapely airliner became "Queen of the airways" and was extensively developed to seat more passengers and extend its range.

Above: Considerably larger and heavier than the DC-6 or Constellation, the Boeing 377 Stratocruiser rode on the back of the B-29 Superfortress strategic bomber, which broke as much new engineering ground as any aircraft in history. Yet only 55 civil examples were sold and the type is chiefly remembered because it usually had a downstairs bar.

Top right: On May 2, 1952 BOAC leaped far ahead of all other operators by introducing the jet-propelled Comet. Gradually its fantastic passenger appeal won over a previously scornful airline industry but a structural fault threw away the most significant lead in airline history.

Middle: The Vickers-Armstrongs Viscount entered passenger service in April 1953 and, despite the fact that it was not

The post-war generation, such as the DC-6 and Constellation, more than doubled this pressure differential, and today it is quadrupled. The best early post-war short-haul transport, similarly pressurized, was the Convair 240, with two 2,100hp Double Wasps and cruising speed nudging 300mph (483kph), which was developed into the 340 and 440 and today is still occasionally found as the Convair 580, 600 or 640 re-engined with turboprops. Biggest of the immediately post-war transports was the Boeing 377 Stratocruiser, derived from the B-29 bomber, with four 3,500hp Wasp Majors and two pressurized decks seating up to 100 on transatlantic routes.

During World War II Britain had pioneered gas-turbine engines, and the Brabazon Committee had deliberated on what types of airliner to build once peace was won. Some of its proposals, such as the monster Brabazon airliner, were mistaken, but two proved to be of immense significance. The Brabazon IIB specification for a short-haul turboprop resulted in the Vickers-Armstrong Viscount, flown on 16 July 1948. Its 990hp Rolls-Royce Dart engines were extremely simple and robust and by 1950 the prototype was carrying 32 passengers at a time on routes from London to Paris or Edinburgh. Never before had passengers travelled so

American, gradually won customers all over the world because of its demonstrable superiority. Of 444 built, about 118 are still in scheduled service.

Above: Even had the Comet I been free from structural trouble, it would not have seriously delayed the introduction of the jet age – an era largely brought about by aircraft of later concept. The French deserve particular credit for using Comet technology – flight deck, engines, flight-controlled power units and systems – in a much better short-haul transport, the Caravelle, which also introduced the rear-engine configuration.

fast, so quietly or so smoothly, nor had such panoramic windows. Rolls-Royce developed the Dart to produce over 1,500hp and made possible the 47-passenger V.701 Viscount which entered regular service in 1953. A still more powerful Dart powered the stretched V.802 with 65 seats and 320mph (515kph) cruising speed, and the final model with 1,990hp engines was the V.810 with 75 seats and 360mph (579kph) cruise. Some 440 Viscounts were sold, of which about 150 were still in use 25 years later.

The other important machine was the Brabazon IV, the de Havilland Comet. Planned as a tailless mailplane for transatlantic use, this was wisely recast as a more conventional passenger airliner, with four 5,000lb (2,260kg) thrust DH Ghost turbojets and capable of flying almost 2,000 miles (3,220km) at 480mph (722kph) with 36 passengers. Entering service in May 1952, the Comet I halved flight times and gave passengers speed, comfort and luxury never before approached. The pressure differential of $8\frac{1}{4}$lb per square inch ($0.58 kg/cm^2$) enabled the Comet to cruise almost silently at 40,000 feet where passengers could see vast distances. No more did they wallow in storm clouds, reaching for sick-bags. Riding the Comet was fantastic, and few passengers wanted to fly by any other aircraft once they had sampled it. Unfortunately the large pressure differential proved its undoing; the successive inflation and deflation of the thin-skinned fuselage caused gradual growth of fatigue cracks which by 1954 caused two Comets to break up as they were climbing into thin air. Britain could quickly have made the aircraft safe, but—stunned by a national tragedy—suspended production and scrapped the early examples. Not until four years later did a bigger and better Comet 4 emerge, and this was pressed into service, just ahead of the Boeing 707, on the North Atlantic, a long route for which it had not really been intended. The longer-body but shorter-winged Comet 4B for short routes was more successful, and a handful of these well-liked pioneer jets were still used by Dan-Air of Britain in 1978.

In 1947 an excellent Brabazon III project was cancelled and a totally uncompetitive "Medium Range Empire" project launched instead. Later this MRE was completely recast as the turboprop Britannia, flown in August 1952. A beautiful and wholly challenging machine that had no rival, it promised to carry about 100 in great comfort at nearly 400mph (646kph) over long routes. The Britannia 310-series had more seats, more power and more fuel, and could carry up to 130 passengers on transatlantic routes but Britain again failed to reap what should have been gigantic rewards, because it took five long years to get all the "bugs" out of this fine transport, and by 1957 the stage was set for long-range jets.

But from 15 July 1954 the writing was on the wall. On that day Boeing flew the 367–80, a company-funded prototype of a new breed of "big jet" characterized by swept wings and before and an impressive combination of speed and range. Underpinned by gigantic orders for military tanker versions Boeing offered an enlarged civil design, the 707. Soon an even bigger 707-320 Intercontinental was being built, and today there have been many variants taking civil 707 sales very close to 1,000. The 707 was a great technical advance in many areas, and performance and economy were improved later by replacing the original noisy, smoky and inefficient turbojets by turbofans of greater thrust (17,000–18,000lb—7,720–8,170kg). Douglas found it hard to counter the 707, but in late 1955 it boldly took the plunge with the DC-8, generally similar to the 707 with four engines in single pods under a wing with slightly less sweepback. Like Boeing, Douglas built heavier long-range versions and then fitted turbofans, and in 1965—when the 707 was definitely on top—managed to launch the Super-60 series of stretched or ultra-long-range DC-8 models which kept production going until the 556th and last in 1972.

Convair launched medium-haul jets of identical configuration in 1957, slightly smaller and carrying much less fuel to give less than half the gross weight. The CV-880 and larger CV-990 were attractive, but just failed to find a large market and, after some early technical difficulties, resulted in the biggest financial loss on any engineering product up to that time. But in France SNCASE won a government order for a prototype for a smaller short-range jet flown in May 1955 as the Caravelle. Novel in having its two engines hung on the sides of the rear

fuselage, this proved—to the surprise of many experts—to find an increasing world market, and 280 were sold. It proved the sense of the short-haul jet, which to some degree appealed because of comfort and image rather than the few minutes saved. The Caravelle is still in wide service, whereas two contemporary turboprops, the American Lockheed Electra and British Vickers-Armstrongs Vanguard, proved commercial mistakes to their builders and are seldom seen in mainline passenger service today. Canadair similarly failed to break even with a stretched version of the Britannia which is still used today as a freighter, some having a swing-tail for bulky loads. Airline freight generally goes under the floor of passenger jets, but there are many all-freight or quick-change (QC) versions and a few specialized freighters based on military types such as the Lockheed C-130.

In the Soviet Union a bold programme of large jets and turboprops has completely updated the vast Aeroflot fleet, though not without much technical trouble in some programmes and with relatively few export sales. By far the best-selling modern transport has been the Boeing 727, which appeared a year after an almost identical British airliner, the Trident (which has been outsold 15 to 1). Both have three engines at the back and highly swept wings with complex high-lift devices on leading and tailing edges. The Trident also has the world's pioneer Autoland system for blind landings, and both have T-tails and advanced lateral-control systems with spoilers. Other widely used short-haulers include the McDonnell Douglas DC-9, BAC One-Eleven and Boeing 737 jets and the Fokker/Fairchild F27 Friendship and Hawker Siddeley 748 turboprops, the jets being more than twice as capacious and roughly three times as heavy.

In the past decade the main developments have been the SST and the wide bodies. The SST (SuperSonic Transport) appeared to be just round the corner in the 1950s, and was launched in the Soviet Union and in a joint Franco-British programme in 1962. Such a transport has to have a very small frontal area, and the result is a slender but extremely long fuselage, pressurized to 10$\frac{3}{4}$lb per square inch (0.76kg/cm) and with small windows, carried on a slender delta-wing utterly unlike anything seen before at airports, propelled by four powerful but slim engines. The two types of aircraft in service, the Concorde and Tu-144, also have unique drooping noses to improve forward view from the flight deck in the takeoff and landing regimes. Fuel is pumped to front or rear in the Concorde to counter transonic change of trim, and the Tu-144 has retractable foreplanes to lift the nose in the takeoff and landing configuration. Both are made principally of aluminium alloy which cannot be used with cruising speeds much in excess of Mach 2 (1,320mph (2,124kph)) because of kinetic heating. A further innovation for the airlines is a fully variable

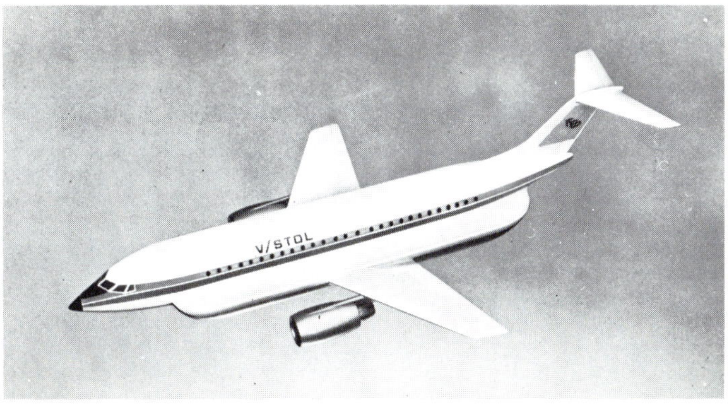

Left: By 1971 the United States had expended more funds on the SST (SuperSonic transport) than Britain and France had spent on the Concorde, yet a unique alliance of conservationists, anti-technologists and other pressure groups succeeded in killing off the Boeing programme that had finally been selected. But in 1976 Lockheed proposed this supposedly much better SST.

Above left: In 1970 Hawker Siddeley wanted to build this V/STOL airliner, which would have linked short city-centre airstrips at jet speed. The four sets of doors on each side ahead of and behind the wing cover fans capable of lifting the laden HS.141 vertically. Lack of city-centre airstrips killed its prospects.

Top: A year after the HS.141 a rash of "Quiet STOL" projects appeared, with unswept wings and very quiet geared-fan engines. These, too, failed to become practical realities, though the Canadian Dash-7 is a slower turboprop form of the same concept.

Above right: The Boeing 7N7 and 7X7, shown here in 1976 form, represented the distillation of millions of items of data culled from almost all the world's major airlines. Boeing had already spent over ten years looking for a market slot for a new jetliner, and in 1978 both proposals had been overtaken by such later projects as the 777 and 767. Boeing was hoping to launch at least one of these as this book went to press.

propulsion installation with power-driven inlet valves, ramps and doors and variable-profile nozzles. Like most current subsonic jets, the SST has nozzles that are designed to reduce noise and to fold in inwards to reverse thrust after landing, greatly reducing wear on the wheel brakes.

Boeing took the decision to build the first wide-body, the 747, in 1966. The gamble called for investment of much more than the net worth of the company, but it came off handsomely with 350 already sold. Far bigger than any previous airliner, the 747 rested squarely on the development (originally for military purposes) of enormous turbofans of a new type offering much increased thrust with dramatically reduced noise and specific fuel consumption. Sticking to the 707-type layout, four JT9D engines of 43,000lb (19,520kg) thrust were matched to a fuselage 20 feet (6.4m) wide seating up to 500 at one level, or carrying 100 tons (101 tonnes) of cargo loaded through a hinged nose and large side doors. Like the 707 the 747 was strongly innovative, but troubles were never critical and this aircraft heralded a new era in which vastly increased traffic is matched with greatly reduced social disturbance. Today the JT9D, CF6 and RB.211 engines all fly on the 747 at ratings up to 54,000lb (24,516kg), and the 747SP is a shorter variant able to fly non-stop on the longest routes anyone could wish such as London–Johannesburg, New York–Tokyo and Sydney–San Francisco.

In 1968 McDonnell Douglas launched the DC-10 and Lockheed the L-1011 TriStar, slightly smaller than the 747 and with two wing pods and a third engine at the tail. A consortium of European builders formed Airbus Industrie to build the A300B, a short-haul twin in the same class. As the trijets are American they have at present greatly outsold the A300B, despite the fact that the latter has a technically superior wing (with less sweep and a near-supercritical profile which greatly improves efficiency) and is matched to a vastly bigger world market. In early 1978 there were signs that, after having a hard struggle even for acceptance since it entered service in 1973, the A300B was at last on its way to becoming a major commercial success, perhaps to become the best-selling transport of all time. The only way to beat it is to copy it, and it is hard to do this at a competitive price after ten years of inflation (the time difference between Airbus and any rival).

In the small local-service class there are more options. Some operators have selected the trim 30-seat Shorts 330 twin-turboprop. Others use the less-capactious Nord 262, which cost more and has less room because it is pressurized. A few need the very STOL (Short Take-Off and Landing) performance of the ultra-quiet DHC-7, despite its high costs with four turboprops driving large gearboxes and slow-running propellers. The Soviets prefer the simple Yak-40 with three turbofans but a completely unswept wing.

Since World War II the world market for large and medium civil transport aircraft has been dominated (currently to the tune of about 90 per cent) by the United States. This situation arose in the 1930s when American airliners demonstrated technical superiority, higher performance, better economy and greater reliability than those from the long-established but fragmented European firms. In the 1950s, despite British pioneering with turbojet and turboprop engines, the American lead became increasingly unchallenged. Today only the Soviet Union attempts to maintain an on-going capability "across the board" with civil transports, and Soviet aircraft have not yet succeeded either in inspiring confidence in purchasers or in selling widely as exports, despite low prices subsidised by the Soviet government.

Yet one aircraft alone shows that the future may not be wholly an American monopoly. In 1970 Airbus Industrie was set up by European governments to manage a programme to build a new kind of airliner, a wide-body short-hauler. The wide-body concept, though it was studied in many places in the early 1960s, was given its first partial application in the United States. Making use of technical developments funded by the US Air Force in its search for a monster logistic freighter (which is in service today as the Lockheed C-5A, but did not find a civil market), the engine companies General Electric and Pratt & Whitney produced extremely large and efficient turbofan propulsion systems which offered not only two to three times the thrust of previous engines, with much lower specific fuel consumption but also greatly reduced noise and pollution. Boeing built the first, and biggest, wide-body, the 747 "Jumbo", around four such engines. Subsequently Lockheed and McDonnell Douglas built only slightly smaller trijets, Lockheed choosing an even newer engine from Britain, the RB.211.

Yet none of these aircraft is properly matched to the biggest market of all, the shorter sectors of less than 2,500 miles. For highest efficiency on the mass-market shorter routes an airliner needs only two engines and a smaller wing, with more slender plan-shape, less sweep and a different profile

(cross section) called the "supercritical" type. Airbus Industrie combined these features with the established technology and systems of the other wide-body airliners and, after a slow struggle even to be taken seriously, has gradually won worldwide sales of a product dramatically superior to what have been called "the noisy, smoky, fuel-hungry narrow-bodies" which are the only alternative on the world's shorter routes.

On the face of it, there would appear to be no contest in future. How could "noisy, smoky, fuel-hungry" aircraft even be considered ? The answer lies in the extremely conservative nature of the world airline industry, an industry that operates with gigantic sums of money (and thus potentially gigantic risks) yet very small profit-margins. It strongly resists anything new, no matter how well proven it may be claimed to be. New airliners, or new manufacturers (even if they are a consortium formed by people who have been in business 50 years), thus have a very hard struggle for a toehold. The housewife at the supermarket can afford to try an unknown product with small risk, but the unknown planemaker has no chance of selling anything. Today big civil transports require an investment of a billion dollars just to sell No 1 off the line, and the credibility of the supplier is at least as important as anything written in a brochure.

Aero Spacelines Guppy
USA

Power Plant: Four 4,912shp Allison 501-D22C turboprops.
Performance: Max speed, Mach = 0·413 IAS above 14,800ft (4510m); max cruising speed, 288mph (463km/h) at 20,000ft (6100m); economical cruising speed, 253mph (407km/h) at 20,000ft (6100m); initial rate of climb, 1,500ft/min (7·6m/sec); service ceiling, 25,000ft (7620m); range with max payload, 505mls (813km); range with max fuel, 2,920mls (4700km).
Weights: Empty, 100,000lb (45,359kg); max payload, 54,000lb (24,494kg); max take-off, 170,000lb (77,110kg); max landing, 160,000lb (72,570kg).
Dimensions: Span, 156ft 3in (47·62m); length, 143ft 10in (43·84m); height, 48ft 6in (14·78m); wing area, 1,965sq ft (182·52m^2).

Between 1962 and 1972, the Aero Spacelines company in the USA produced six outsize cargo carriers by converting Boeing 377 Stratocruiser airframes to varying specifications. The original conversion was known as the Pregnant Guppy, first flown on 19 September 1962, being a Stratocruiser with the fuselage lengthened and a new upper lobe, of large diameter, fitted. The entire rear fuselage and tail unit could be detached, to permit straight-in loading of booster rockets used in the US space programme. The Super Guppy, first flown on 31 August 1965, was even larger and had T34 turboprop engines, while the Mini Guppy had piston engines and a longer, wider fuselage than the basic Stratocruiser's; it was first flown on 24 May 1967. Two Guppy 201s, initially flown on 24 August 1970 and 24 August 1971, respectively, were dimensionally similar to the Super Guppy but had Allison 501-D22C turboprops.

Both Guppy 201s were acquired by Aérospatiale in France to be used in support of the Airbus and Concorde programmes and were still being operated in 1977 in this rôle by Aéromaritime. During 1974, the original Pregnant Guppy and Mini-Guppy were acquired by American Jet Industries to be used as "pick-up trucks" for damaged aircraft, or for cargo-carrying charter flights.

***Below:** The AS Guppy 201, one of several variants of outsize transports based on the Boeing 377.*

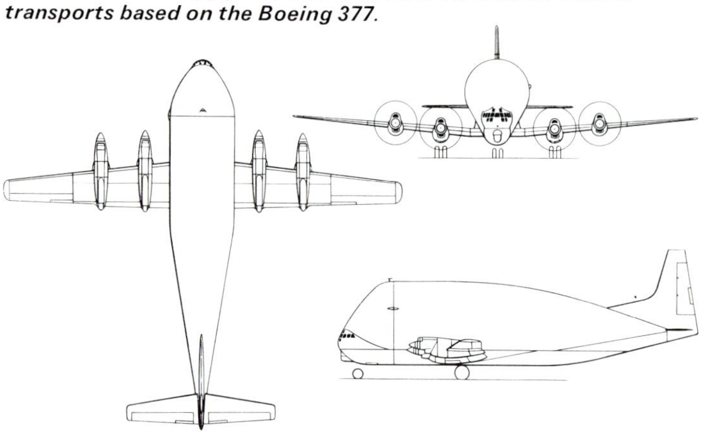

Aérospatiale Caravelle
France

Power Plant: Two 12,600lb st (5725kgp) Rolls-Royce Avon 532R or 533R turbojets.
Performance: Max cruising speed at 25,000ft (7620m), 525mph (845km/h); best economy cruise, 488mph (785km/h); range with max payload typical reserves, 1,430mls (2300km).
Weights: Basic operating 63,175lb (28,655kg); max payload, 18,080lb (8200kg); max take-off, 110,230lb (50,000kg).
Dimensions: Span, 112ft 6in (34·30m); length, 105ft 0in (32·01m); height, 28ft 7in (8·72m); wing area, 1,579sq ft (146·7m^2).

The origins of the Caravelle, which was the world's first short-to-medium range transport designed to be powered by turbojet engines, lay in a specification drawn up in 1951 by the French government civil aviation agency, SGACC. The purpose of the specification was to encourage the development in France of a commercial aircraft having export appeal and matching in technical excellence the new generation of post-war airliners that was emerging in the USA and the UK. Since the types of jet airliner already then being developed were for use over medium-to-long ranges, the SGACC decided to focus the attention of the French industry on a medium-to-short range aircraft, and the specification issued on 6 November 1951 suggested a payload of 6–7 tonnes to be carried over a range of 1,000–1,200mls (1930km) at an average speed of more than 380mph (700km/h).

From numerous projects submitted, the SGACC eventually selected – in September 1952 – the X210 design by the state-owned SNCASE company (later merged with SNCASO to form Sud Aviation, and then with Nord to form Aérospatiale). This was at first proposed with three locally-developed Atar turbojets grouped in and on the rear fuselage, but the Rolls-Royce Avon was chosen as being more reliable for early operation and as this offered considerably more power, only two were required, giving the Caravelle its unique (at the time of introduction) rear-engined layout. The aerodynamic disadvantages of T-tail arrangements were avoided by locating the tailplane just above the fuselage, and the wing was given modest sweepback. A seating capacity of 52 was projected at this early stage, with five-abreast seating.

Design and construction of the SNCASE transport was wholly financed by the French government, a contract being placed on 3 January 1953 for two flying prototypes and two structural test airframes. The designation became SE210 and the name Caravelle was adopted in due course. First flights were made by the two prototypes on 25 May 1955 and 6 May 1956 respectively, both having Avon RA.26 engines compared with the Avon RA.29 intended for production models. Meanwhile, the order book had been opened with a contract from Air France for 12 placed on 16 November 1955, and other European operators were beginning to join the queue.

French certification of the Caravelle was obtained on 2 April 1958 (followed by US type approval six days later) and the first production Caravelle I flew on 18 May 1958. Deliveries to Air France began on 19 March 1959 and the first regular service was operated by the national airline on 6 May 1959, while SAS became the first to use an exported Caravelle, on 15 May. The Caravelle Is had Avon RA.29 Mk 522 engines and differed from the prototype in that the fuselage was lengthened by 4ft $7\frac{1}{2}$in (1·5m) and a long extension of the dorsal fin along the top of the fuselage housed communications antennae. Various layouts were evolved, for up to a maximum of 99 passengers, 64 being a more typical figure in mixed-class arrangements.

Twenty Caravelle Is were followed by 12 Caravelle IAs (the first of which flew on 11 February 1960) which had RA.29/1 Mk 526 engines, and all these early aircraft were later uprated to Caravelle IIIs with RA.29/3 Mk 527 engines, permitting the use of higher operating weights and cruising speeds. In addition, 78 Caravelle IIIs were built as such, the first flight being made on 30 December 1959.

Caravelle designations were linked at this stage with the engine designations, so that the next to appear, based on the Avon RA.29/6 Mk 531, was the Caravelle VI, again with a step-up in weights and performance, but no change of dimensions. The first Caravelle VI (the Mk III prototype converted) flew on 10 September 1960, and Sabena was the first to operate this variant, starting on 18 February 1961. A significant order for 20 Caravelles placed by United Airlines in February 1960 led to the development of the Caravelle VI-R, which had Avon 532R or 533R engines with thrust reversers and certain other features to meet US requirements, including additional wing spoilers and more powerful brakes. The first VI-R flew on 6 February 1961 and deliveries to United began in June, the first service being flown on 14 July. The designation Caravelle VI-N was then adopted to distinguish the earlier standard of aircraft without thrust reversers, production of the VI-N totalling 53 and of the VI-R, 56, this completing production of Avon-engined versions of the airliner.

The use of alternative power plants was studied by Sud Aviation for some time, and during 1960 a Caravelle III was sold to General Electric and fitted in the USA with CJ805-23C turbofans. First flown on 29 December 1960, it was known as the Caravelle VII. The same engines were specified for the projected Caravelle 10, which would have had a 3ft 4in (1-m) fuselage extension, and for the Caravelle 10A (also known as the Caravelle Horizon and then as the Caravelle Super A) which was intended specifically to meet TWA requirements, having a wing root leading edge extension, raised window line, double-slotted flaps and fin/tailplane acorn fairing. TWA ordered 20 in 1961 but cancelled in 1962 and only a prototype was flown, on 31 August 1962. In parallel, Sud developed the Caravelle 10B (later, Super B or just Super Caravelle) with 14,000lb st (6350kgp) Pratt & Whitney JT8D-1 turbofans. A prototype flew on 3 March 1964 and production of this variant totalled 22, the first of which entered service with Finnair on 16 August 1964. This had a gross weight of 114,640lb (52,000kg), but Sterling Airways introduced the Super B at a weight of 119,050lb (54,000kg)

***Below:** Three-view of the Aérospatiale Caravelle VI-R, the suffix indicating the use of thrust reversers on the Avon engines.*

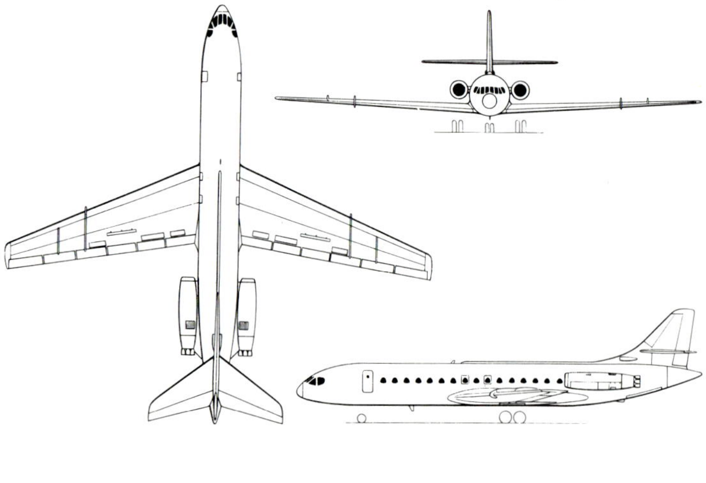

Below: The Mini-Guppy, which retained the Boeing 377 wing and power plant and had a hinged rear fuselage.

on 23 February 1968 and the final examples, also for Sterling, had a max take-off weight of 123,460lb (56,000kg). Seating arrangements in the Super B provided for 68 to 105 passengers.

Use of the JT8D-7 engines in what was basically the Caravelle VI air-frame, with Sud-designed cascade thrust reversers, led to the introduction of the Caravelle 10R, first flown on 18 January 1965. While passenger capacity remained unchanged, the payload/range and speed performance was improved; 20 were built, the first operator being Royal Jordanian Airlines (Alia) on 31 July 1965. Closely related to the 10R, the Caravelle 11R was developed for mixed passenger/cargo operations, having a large side-loading freight door and a movable bulkhead to separate freight and passenger compartments. The fuselage was lengthened, compared with the 10R, by 3ft 0½in (0·93m). First flight of the prototype was made on 21 April 1967 and the first of six entered service on 22 September 1967, the only operators being Air Afrique, Air Congo and Transeuropa.

As the final Caravelle variant, Sud produced the Caravelle 12, a stretched-fuselage version of the Super B, lengthened by 10ft 7in (3·21m) and with structural reinforcement to permit operation at weights up to 127,870lb (58,000kg), the highest for any Caravelle version. The engines were 14,500lb st (6577kgp) JT8D-9 turbofans and the maximum seating was for 140 passengers in a high-density arrangement. The Caravelle 12 was developed primarily for the IT operations of Sterling Airways, which acquired seven, the first flight being made on 29 October 1970. In addition, Air Inter bought five Caravelle 12s, delivery of the last of these in 1972 bringing production of the type to a close at a grand total of 282, of which three were unsold prototypes.

The major users of the Caravelle were Air France, which acquired 46 in all, SAS and Alitalia with 21 each, United and Sterling with 20 apiece, Iberia with 19, Air Inter with 14 and Finnair with 12. Although the Caravelle had been displaced by larger and newer types on most primary routes by the mid'seventies, it remained in large scale service on secondary routes and for charter flights.

Below: An Air France Caravelle III, surrounded by some of the typical ground service vehicles that attend each airport arrival.

Aérospatiale Corvette
France

Power Plant: Two 2,310lb st (1048kgp) Pratt & Whitney (UACL) JT15D-4 turbofans.
Performance: Max cruising speed, 495mph (796km/h) at 30,000ft (9144m); best economy cruise, 391mph (630km/h) at 36,100ft (11,000m); initial rate of climb, 3,000ft/min (15·25m/sec); service ceiling, 38,000ft (11,580m); range with max payload, 1,022mls (1645km); range with max fuel (including tip tanks), 1,670mls (2690km).
Weights: Empty equipped, 7,985lb (3622kg); max payload, 2,248lb (1020kg); max take-off, 13,450lb (6100kg).
Dimensions: Span, 42ft 0in (12·80m); span (over tip tanks), 43ft 5¼in (13·24m); length, 45ft 4in (13·82m); height, 13ft 10in (4·23m); wing area, 236·8sq ft (22·00m²).

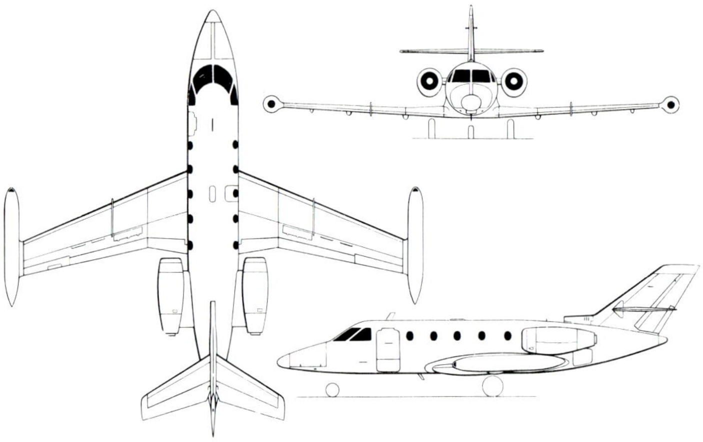

Above: Three-view drawing of the Aérospatiale Corvette short-haul airliner, production of which ended after 40 had been built.

Among the smallest jet aircraft developed with third-level airline operations in view, the Corvette was also marketed as an executive jet, and was evolved especially to meet North American requirements. It originated shortly before the Sud-Nord merger into Aérospatiale, initially as a joint project between the two State-owned companies – hence the original SN600 designation. The prototype flew on 16 July 1970 but was lost during flight development, small changes being made in the SN601 second and third prototypes flown on 20 December 1972 and 7 March 1973 respectively. The first full production standard aircraft flew on 9 November 1973 and French certification was achieved on 28 May 1974.

Production deliveries were delayed by a protracted strike at UACL, Canadian source of the JT15D turbofan engines, but Air Alpes, a French local service airline, had two in service by September 1974, one of these being in full Air France livery for operation on the Lyons–Brussels route while the other operated on Air Alpes' own routes out of Paris and was joined by two more early in 1975. The Corvette 100, as the initial production version was known, had a crew of two and up to 12 individual passenger seats in two rows, and could be fitted with wing-tip tanks to extend range. The Corvette 200 was projected to have the fuselage lengthened by 6ft 7in (2·0m) to accommodate up to 18 passengers but this did not proceed beyond the design stage, and production of the Corvette 100 ended in 1977 at a total of 40.

Right: The Corvette in Air Alsace markings, with optional wing-tip tanks fitted. Seating 12, the Corvette proved a little too small for the market it was designed to fulfill.

Below: Dual markings indicate its operation by Air Alpes on behalf of Air France on the Lyons-Brussels route.

Aérospatiale (Nord) 262 Frégate and Mohawk 298

France

Power Plant: Two 1,145ehp Turboméca Bastan VII turboprops.
Performance (N 262A): Max speed, 239mph (385km/h); typical cruising speed, 233mph (375km/h); initial rate of climb, 1,200ft/min (6·1m/sec); service ceiling, 23,500ft (7160m); range with max payload, 605mls (975km); range with max fuel, 1,095mls (1760km).
Weights: (N 262A): Basic operating weight, 15,496lb (7029kg); max payload, 7,209lb (3270kg); max take-off weight, 23,370lb (10,600kg); max landing, 22,710lb (10,300kg).
Dimensions: Span: (N 262A): 71ft 10in (21·90m); (Fregate), 74ft $1\frac{3}{4}$in (22·60m); length, 63ft 3in (19·28m); height, 20ft 4in (6·20m); wing area (N 262A), 592sq ft (55.0m^2); (Fregate), 601sq ft (55·79m^2).

Sometimes referred to as the Aérospatiale Frégate but in fact better known as the Nord 262, this commuter transport had its origins in a design by the well-known French engineer Max Holste. His company, Avions Max Holste, built a prototype known as the MH-250, with Pratt & Whitney Wasp piston radial engines, as a small utility transport, and followed this with a second prototype, the MH-260, in which Turboméca Bastan turboprops were substituted for the Wasps. First flight dates for these two prototypes were 20 May 1959 and 29 July 1960 respectively. Nord Aviation (state owned and subsequently merged with Sud to form Aérospatiale) participated in production of a batch of 10 MH-260s, which were operated by Widerøes Flyveselskap and Air Inter, and at the same time undertook development of the improved Nord 262, with a pressurized, circular-section fuselage replacing the square-section unpressurized fuselage of the MH-260.

With seating for 24–26 passengers in typical airline layouts, arranged three-abreast, the Nord 262 was aimed at the regional or third-level operator with only short sectors (up to about 600mls/970km) to serve. The prototype first flew on 24 December 1962 and was joined by three pre-production Nord 262s in certification flying, these being constructed at Châtillon-sous-Bagneux and assembled for flight testing at Melun-Villaroche. French certification was awarded on 16 July 1964, by which time the first production aircraft was ready to enter service with Air Inter, having made its first flight on 8 July 1964. Further small improvements established the full production standard with effect from the fifth airframe, the first four being designated Nord 262Bs and the main production run of 67 aircraft that followed being Nord 262As. The A model first flew early in 1965, was certificated in March and entered service in August. All production aircraft were constructed and flown at Bourges.

An early customer for the Nord 262A was Lake Central in the US, which purchased a fleet of 12 for a commuter-type operation typical of that for which the aircraft had been designed. After Lake Central had been acquired by Allegheny Airlines, the Nord 262s continued in service in the latter's colours, and in 1974 the airline embarked on a programme to fit 1,180shp Pratt & Whitney PT6A-45 turboprops in place of Bastans in nine aircraft still in the company's service. The conversion work was undertaken by Mohawk Air Services and the modified aircraft were to become known as Mohawk 298s, taking the number from FAR 298, the airworthiness regulation covering third-level operations in the USA. The first flight of a converted example was made on 7 January 1975 and after FAA certification on 19 October 1976 the Mohawk 298 entered service on the Allegheny commuter network early in 1977.

After the Nord/Sud merger into Aérospatiale, a version of the 262 with 1,145ehp Bastan VII engines in place of 1,080ehp Bastan VICs was developed, this new model also featuring wing-tips of revised design that added 2ft $3\frac{3}{4}$in (0·70m) to the overall span. First flown in July 1968, this N.262C version was named Frégate, its military equivalent being the N.262D. Certification was obtained on 24 December 1970, but the only major order for the improved Frégate came from the French Armée de l'Air, which bought 18 to join six Nord 262As acquired earlier. The Aéronavale had also bought 15 Nord 262As. Other sales were mostly in twos and threes to airlines in Europe, North Africa and Asia.

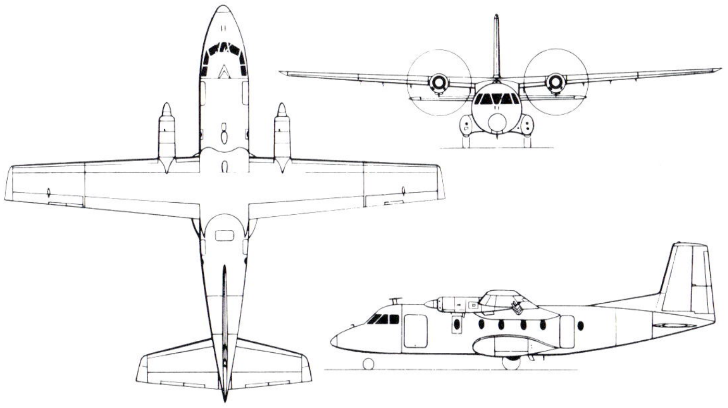

***Above:** The Aérospatiale (Nord) N.262C Frégate, with Turboméca Bastan engines, showing the extended wing-tips of this version.*

***Below:** One of the Nord 262s converted in the USA to Mohawk 298 standard for operation on the Allegheny Commuter network, with Pratt & Whitney PT6A engines replacing the Bastans.*

Antonov An-12
Soviet Union

The following specification relates to the late production An-12V:
Power Plant: Four 4,000ehp Ivchenko AI-20K turboprops.
Performance: Max speed, 444mph (715km/h); max cruise, 373mph (600km/h); normal cruise, 342mph (550km/h) at 25,000ft (7500m); initial climb rate, 1,970ft/min (10·0m/sec); service ceiling, 33,500ft (10,200m); range (with 22,050-lb/10,000-kg payload and one hour reserves), 2,110mls (3400km).
Weights: Empty 61,730lb (28,000kg); normal loaded, 119,050lb (54,000kg); max take-off, 134,480lb (61,000kg).
Dimensions: Span, 124ft 8in (38·00m); length, 121ft $4\frac{1}{2}$in (37·00m); height, 32ft 3in (9·83m); wing area, 1,286sq ft (119·5m^2).

Although evolved from the commercial An-10A primarily for the military rôle, the An-12 has been operated extensively as a commercial freighter by Aeroflot, Polish Air Lines, Air Guinee, Iraqi Airways, Bulair and Egyptair. Differing from the An-10A (which is no longer in service) primarily in having a redesigned rear fuselage embodying an integral loading ramp, a defensive tail gun position and revised tail surfaces, the An-12 had a heavy-duty freight floor designed for loadings of up to 307lb/sq ft (1500kg/m^2) and a maximum payload of the order of 44,090lb (20,000kg).

Early examples of the commercial model, the An-12V, retained the tail turret glazing, but later aircraft have a fairing replacing the complete turret. One of the An-12Vs operated by Aeroflot was tested with broad skis with shallow curved-vee planing surfaces and equipped with heating and braking devices. This form of undercarriage was intended to enable the An-12V to operate from unprepared snow-covered surfaces. More than 900 An-12s are believed to have been built of which approximately one-third were intended for commercial operation.

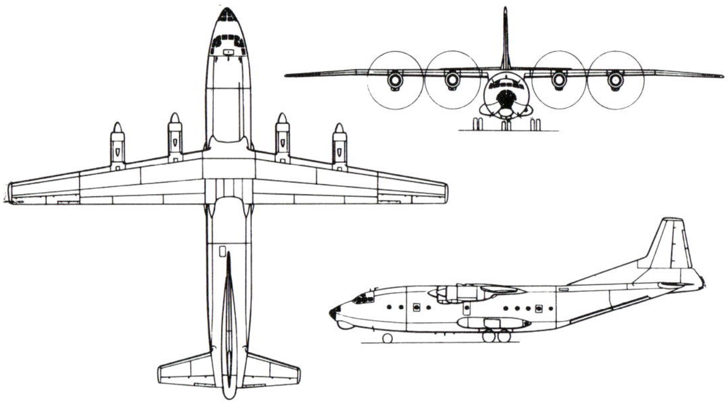

***Above:** Three-view drawing of the Antonov An-12, a specialized cargo transport derivative of the An-10.*

***Below:** The An-12 freighter has been extensively used within the Soviet Union by Aeroflot since the 'sixties.*

Antonov An-14 and An-28
Soviet Union

The following data is for the An-14:
Power Plant: Two 300hp Ivchenko AI-14RF nine-cylinder radial air-cooled engines.
Performance: Max speed, 138mph (222km/h) at 3,280ft (1000m); normal cruise, 112mph (180km/h); initial climb, 1,000ft/min (5·08m/sec); service ceiling, 17,060ft (5200m); range (max payload), 404mls (650km), (with 1,212lb/550kg payload), 444mls (715km), (with max fuel), 497mls (800km).
Weights: Empty, 4,409lb (2000kg); max take-off, 7,935lb (3600kg).
Dimensions: Span, 72ft 2in (21·99m); length, 37ft 6in (11·44m); height, 15ft $2\frac{1}{2}$in (4·63m); wing area, 427·5sq ft (39·72m^2).

Developed to meet an Aeroflot requirement for a small utility transport offering a higher performance and standard of comfort than the general-purpose An-2 but with comparable short take-off and landing characteristics, the An-14 *Pchelka* (Little Bee) was flown for the first time on 15 March 1958 but suffered extremely protracted development. Series manufacture did not begin until 1965, and the definitive production model bore little similarity to the prototypes, a new long-span wing with tapered trailing edges outboard of the engine nacelles having superseded the original shorter untapered wing, the fuselage contours having been refined, passenger capacity being increased, and updated engines being introduced.

A braced high-wing monoplane with an all-metal semi-monocoque pod-and-boom fuselage and two-spar wing carrying full-span leading-edge slats and double-slotted trailing-edge flaps, the An-14 was intended for single-pilot operation. There was provision for a passenger beside the pilot and the main cabin normally accommodated six passengers in individual forward-facing seats with a central aisle, but a seven-seat cabin arrangement has also been offered.

Several hundred examples of the An-14 were built, primarily for use by Aeroflot, versions including a five-seat executive transport, a light freighter, geological survey and photographic models, and an ambulance capable of accommodating six casualty stretchers and a medical attendant.

Essentially a scaled-up, turboprop-powered derivative of the An-14, the An-28 was flown in prototype form for the first time in September 1969, but also suffered a protracted gestation, State trials not being completed until the summer of 1972 and the definitive model not appearing until early 1974 when it was publicly displayed at Sheremetyevo International Airport, Moscow.

Initially referred to as the An-14M, the An-28 retained little more than a similarity of basic configuration to the An-14 and possessed twice the capacity. During the course of development, progressive changes were made to the wing and its high-lift devices, to the tail assembly and to the stub wings carrying the main units of the non-retractable levered-suspension undercarriage. Originally, all three members of the undercarriage were retractable, the main members retracting into fairings at the base of the fuselage and the nosewheel retracting aft into the fuselage nose, but it was concluded that the marginal performance improvement provided by retractable gear was outweighed by the added weight and complication in which it resulted, and all examples of the An-28 subsequent to the first aeroplane featured fixed gear. The prototypes were powered by 810shp Isotov TVD-850 engines, replaced in production models by 960shp TVD-10As.

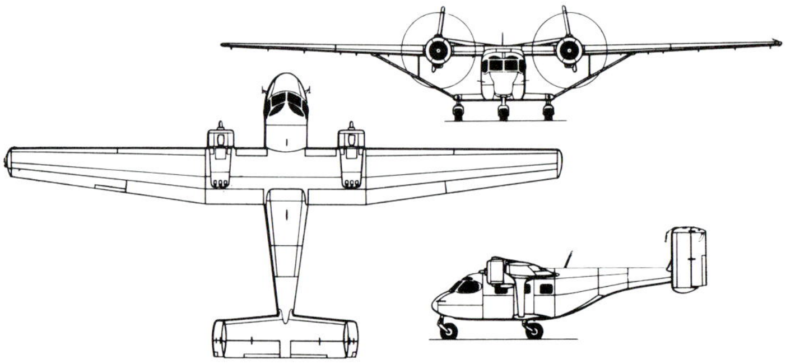

***Above:** Three-view drawing of the Antonov An-14, a small multi-purpose transport that is widely used by Aeroflot.*

Features shared by the An-28 with the An-14 included hinged wing trailing edges comprising double-slotted flaps extending to the wingtips and incorporating single-slotted ailerons, and wide-tread low-pressure balloon tyres to permit operation of the aircraft at its normal loaded weight from unimproved strips of 600–650 yards (550–600m) length. The passenger cabin was arranged with 15 seats three-abreast (two to starboard and one to port), the seats folding back against the walls when the aircraft was operated in the freighter or mixed passenger/cargo rôles. Access to the main cabin was provided by clamshell-type doors under the upswept rear fuselage.

The An-28 was expected to be operated over Aeroflot's shortest routes and particularly those operated by An-2 biplanes. The An-28 was also proposed for parachute training, geological survey, fire fighting, rescue operations and agricultural tasks (with a 1,760lb/800kg capacity hopper in the fuselage), but its primary task was third-level passenger services from short, semi-prepared strips. Standard equipment included a 550-lb (250-kg) capacity cargo-handling winch.

Antonov An-22
Soviet Union

Power Plant: Four 15,000shp Kuznetsov NK-12MA turboprops.
Performance: Max speed, 460mph (740km/h); max cruise, 422mph (679km/h); range (with max payload – 176,350lb/80,000kg) 3,107mls (5000km), (with max fuel and 99,200-lb/45,000-kg payload), 6,800mls (10,950km); cruising altitude, 26,250–32,800ft (8000–10,000m).
Weights: Empty equipped, 251,327lb (114,000kg); max take-off 551,156lb (250,000kg).
Dimensions: Span, 211ft $3\frac{1}{2}$in (64·40m); length, 189ft 8in (57·80m); height, 41ft 1in (12·53m); wing area, 3,713·6sq ft (345m²).

The world's largest aircraft at the time of its appearance but subsequently surpassed in size by the Lockheed C-5A Galaxy and Boeing 747, the An-22 *Antei* (Antheus) was developed in the Soviet Union as a heavy military and commercial freighter.

The first of five prototypes of the An-22 was flown on 27 February 1965, two of these prototypes being used by Aeroflot on experimental freight services in 1967, and a commercial production version was subsequently placed in service by the airline primarily to undertake special supply operations in the more remote and underdeveloped regions of the Soviet Union and elsewhere.

The An-22 carries a crew of five–six and there is a compartment for 28–29 passengers immediately aft of the flight deck and separated from the main hold by a bulkhead. There are rails in the roof of the hold for four travelling gantries, these continuing rearward on the underside of the large door, which, forming the underside of the rear fuselage, is raised upward inside the fuselage to facilitate the loading of large vehicles over the ramp. Two winches, used in conjunction with the gantries, each have a 5,500 lb (2500 kg) capacity. Approximately 100 transports of this type were believed to have been delivered for military and civil use by late 1974, when production ended.

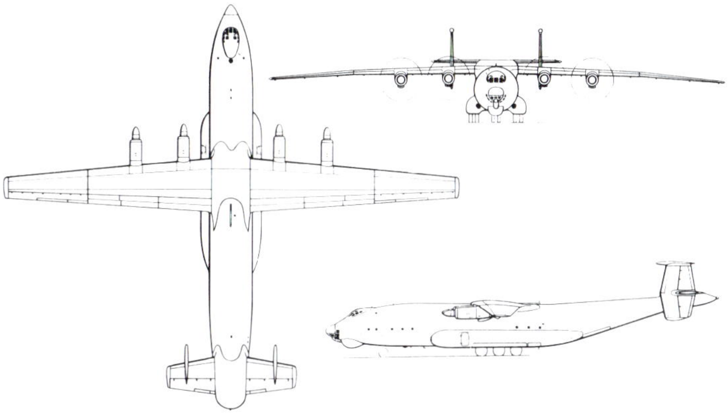

***Above:** Three-view drawing of the Antonov An-22, largest transport in the range developed by the Antonov design bureau.*

***Below:** The An-22 was first flown in 1965, and this outsize transport is used in small numbers in both military and civil guise.*

***Below:** The Antonov An-28 was developed as a derivative of the An-14, but in production form is virtually a new aircraft.*

Antonov An-24, An-26, An-30 and An-32

Soviet Union

The following specification relates to the An-24V *Seriiny II*:
Power Plant: Two 2,500ehp Ivchenko AI-24 Seriiny II turboprops.
Performance: Max cruise, 310mph (498km/h); best-range cruise, 280mph (450km/h) at 19,700ft (6000m); initial climb, 1,515ft/min (7·7m/sec); service ceiling, 27,560ft (8400m); range (max payload and reserves), 341mls (550km), (max fuel and 45 min reserves), 1,490mls (2400km).
Weights: Empty, 29,320lb (13,300kg); max take-off, 46,300lb (21,000kg).
Dimensions: Span, 95ft 9½in (29·20m); length, 77ft 2½in (23·53m); height, 27ft 3½in (8·32m); wing area, 807·1sq ft (74·98m²).

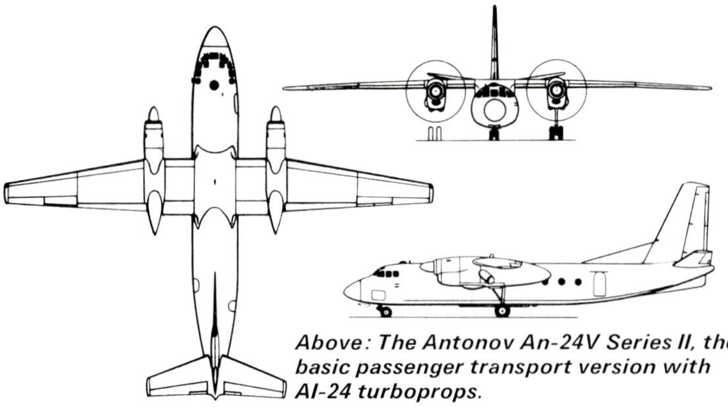

***Above:** The Antonov An-24V Series II, the basic passenger transport version with AI-24 turboprops.*

Among the most widely used and most-exported of Soviet commercial transport, having been in continuous production for some 15 years with more than 1,000 delivered in a variety of versions, the An-24 short-range transport is numerically the most important airliner in the Aeroflot inventory in which it has succeeded the piston-engined Ilyushin Il-14. It also serves with, or has been delivered to, such airlines as Air Guinée, Air Mali, Balkan Bulgarian, Cubana, the Civil Aviation Administration of China, Egyptair, Iraqi Airways, Interflug, Mongolian Airlines, Polish Air Lines Lot and Tarom, and small numbers have been delivered for military service.

Flown for the first time in April 1960, the An-24 was intended originally to accommodate 32–40 passengers but during the course of prototype construction a change in the Aeroflot requirement resulted in the aircraft being developed as a 44-seater. A second prototype and five pre-production aircraft, including two for static and fatigue testing, were employed for manufacturer's and State trials, and Aeroflot inaugurated services with the An-24 over the routes between Moscow, Voronezh and Saratov in September 1963. The initial production 44-seater was supplanted at an early stage by the 50-seat An-24V which gave place in turn, in 1968, to the An-24V *Seriiny II* embodying various refinements including an extended centre section chord with enlarged flaps, increasing gross wing area to 807·1sq ft (74·98m²) from 779·9sq ft (72·46m²). This version also used AI-24 *Seriiny II* turboprops, which, having water injection and a similar rating to the initial AI-24 engines, could be replaced by 2,820ehp AI-24T turboprops to meet specific hot-and-high operating requirements. The *Seriiny II* aircraft had a normal flight crew of three and standard accommodation for 50 passengers in one-class four-abreast seating, but various optional mixed passenger/freight and convertible cargo/passenger arrangements were offered.

Specialized freighters generally similar to the An-24V *Seriiny II* are the An-24T and An-24RT, the latter having a Tumansky RU-19-300 auxiliary turbojet of 1,984lb (900kg) thrust in the starboard engine nacelle for use under hot-and-high conditions, permitting take-off with full payload from airfields at altitudes up to 9,840ft (3000m) above sea level and in temperatures up to ISA+30°C. Both models had provision for five crew members and the normal passenger door at the rear of the cabin deleted and replaced by a ventral freight door which hinged upward and aft for cargo loading. A 3,300lb (1500kg) capacity electric winch was fitted to hoist cargo through the ventral door and an electrically- or manually-operated 9,920lb (4500kg) capacity conveyor was installed in the cabin floor. The An-24RV was similar to the *Seriiny II* passenger transport apart from having a similar auxiliary turbojet to that installed in the An-24RT.

A further specialized version was the An-24P (*Protivopozharny* or, simply, *Pozharny*) intended for fighting forest fires. First tested in October 1971, the An-24P carried parachutists and fire-fighting equipment which could be dropped in the vicinity of a fire.

Derived from the An-24RT and intended for both military and civil applications, the An-26 was evolved during the late 'sixties with production deliveries commencing in 1969. Its principal new feature was a redesigned rear fuselage of "beaver-tail" configuration incorporating a two-position door which could be lowered to form a conventional ramp for the loading of vehicles, or swung down and forward beneath the fuselage to permit straight-in loading of freight from ground vehicles at truck-bed height. The An-26 standardized on the uprated AI-24T turboprops offered as an option on the An-24V *Seriiny II* and the basic structure of the two aircraft was similar, although that of the An-26 was re-stressed to cater for higher weights. The An-26 is primarily used in military guise but can be easily adapted for passenger-carrying.

A specialized aerial survey derivative of the An-24RT, the An-30 initiated its test programme during the summer of 1973 and has entered service with Aeroflot for mapping tasks in the remoter areas of the Soviet Union. The An-30 is structurally identical with the An-24RT apart from the forward fuselage which has been entirely redesigned. The nose is extensively glazed to provide the navigator with a wide field of vision and the size of the navigator's compartment is increased by raising the flight deck, simultaneously improving the pilots' view.

For its primary task of aerial photography for map-making, the An-30 is provided with four large survey cameras mounted in the cabin and operated by remote control by the crew photographer. Equipment includes a pre-programmed computer to control aircraft speed, altitude and direction throughout the mission. Five camera hatches are provided as well as hatches permitting the use of laser, thermographic, gravimetric, magnetic and geophysical sensors. A crew of seven is normally carried and sufficient oxygen to permit a high-altitude mission of eight hours endurance.

A further derivative of the basic aircraft appeared in 1977 as the An-32, this being the An-26 powered by two 4,250shp AI-20M engines and having some aerodynamic changes to handle the large increase in power. The An-32 was intended to enter production for Aeroflot use, primarily as a freighter, at high altitude and high ambient temperature airfields.

***Above left:** The Antonov An-32 is a derivative of the An-24, with the same basic wing and fuselage but AI-20 turboprops to improve take-off in difficult conditions.*

***Left:** The Antonov An-24V has a number of later variants and has also proved one of the most successful Soviet airliners in terms of exports.*

Antonov An-72
Soviet Union

A product of the well-known Antonov design bureau in Kiev, the An-72 emerged at the end of 1977 to begin its flight test programme on 22 December and is a small twin-engined transport of completely original design. The prototype carries Aeroflot markings and it is likely that the An-72 is projected in both civil and military versions, but its special features make it of particular use in difficult and remote areas where take-off and landing distances are restricted and runways are poor. Primarily intended to carry freight, the An-72 is reported to have a payload of about 11,000lb (5000kg) and a cruising speed of 375–435mph (600–700km/h); no other data were published when the An-72 was first publicised in the Soviet Union, just before this book went to press.

In its overall configuration, the An-72 closely resembles the much larger Boeing YC-14, a military transport built to the requirements of the USAAF's AMST specification. A feature of the YC-14, and apparently of the An-72 also, is the "upper surface blowing" system, in which the two turbofan engines are located above and ahead of the wing, so that the exhaust efflux passes over the upper wing surfaces. The design of the wing trailing edge flaps behind the engine is such that lift is substantially increased, allowing the aircraft to fly with safety at lower speeds than would otherwise be possible. In the Boeing USB system, the exhaust gases are deflected downwards when the flaps are extended, to give an upward thrust component in addition to the purely aerodynamic lift; it is not clear whether the An-72's system is similar in this respect or if a simpler flap design is used.

The An-72 has two engines of about 14,300lb st (6500kgp) thrust each, believed to be versions of the Lotarev D-36 that powers the Yak-42. The undercarriage includes two independent main legs each side in the fuselage fairings, rather than tandem wheels on a single leg; this arrangement facilitates operation of the aircraft on rough and uneven field surfaces. Production deliveries of the An-72, which may be intended to replace part of the An-24 fleet in use with Aeroflot, are unlikely to begin earlier than 1980–81.

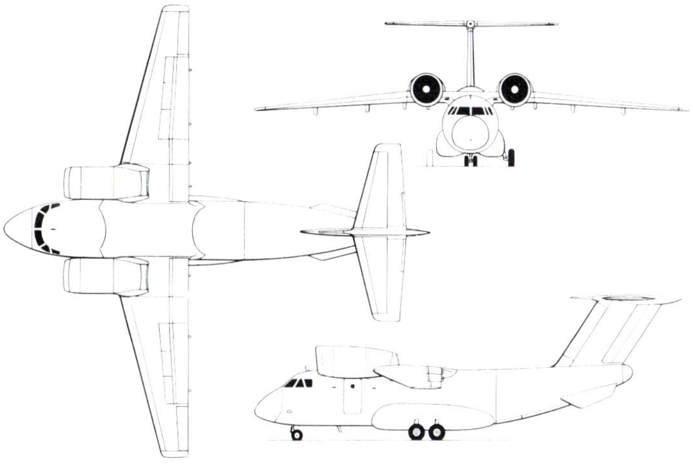

***Above:** Provisional three-view drawing of the Antonov An-72, the prototype of which flew at Kiev at the end of 1977.*

***Below:** The Antonov An-72, for military as well as civil use, has "upper surface blowing" to reduce its take-off run.*

BAC (Vickers) VC10 and Super VC10

United Kingdom

The following specification refers to the Super VC10, except as indicated:
Power Plant: Four 20,370lb st (9240kgp) Rolls-Royce Conway RCo 42 Mk 540 (VC10) or 21,800lb st (9888kgp) RCo 43D Mk 550 (Super VC10) turbofans.
Performance: High speed cruise, 581mph (935km/h) at 31,000ft (9450m); long range cruise, 550mph (886km/h) at 38,000ft (11,600m); range with max payload, 4,720mls (7600km), range with max fuel, 7,128mls (11,470km).
Weights: Operating weight empty, 158,594lb (71,940kg); max take-off, 335,000lb (151,950kg), max payload, 60,321lb (27,360kg), max landing, 237,000lb (107,500kg).
Dimensions: Span, 146ft 2in (44·55m); length (VC10), 158ft 8in (48·36m); length (Super VC10), 171ft 8in (52·32m); height, 39ft 6in (12·04m); wing area (VC10), 2,851sq ft (264·9m^2); wing area (Super VC10) 2,932sq ft (272·4m^2).

The VC10 was the World's first long-range intercontinental jet transport to make use of the rear-engined, clean-wing layout that characterized a whole generation of smaller airliners and business jet aircraft entering service in the mid 'sixties. It was conceived in 1956 by the design team of Vickers Armstrongs at Weybridge, where the Viscount and Vanguard were in production and development, and the VC10 remained essentially a Vickers project even after the formation of BAC, in which Vickers held a 40 per cent stake.

The initial impetus leading to development of the VC10 was provided by BOAC, which required an aircraft to operate over the Commonwealth routes served by the Corporation: in general, these were routes from the UK eastwards to Africa, the Far East and Australasia. They involved operations at aerodromes in hot climates, often located at high altitudes and with relatively short runways. BOAC required an aeroplane that would carry a 32,000-lb (14,515kg) payload over ranges of up to 2,500mls (4023km) at speeds above Mach = 0·8, with an airfield performance compatible with the requirements on the routes to be served.

BOAC announced on 22 May 1957 that, after considering various alternatives, it had decided that the VC10 as then projected by Vickers would best meet its needs, and that it was starting negotiations to purchase 35 aircraft for entry into service from 1963, at a cost of about £68m. The contract was signed on 14 January 1958, and included an option on 20 more VC10s, which were to be powered by four Rolls-Royce Conway turbofans and to seat 135–152 passengers. It was at that time the largest airliner order ever placed with the British aircraft industry.

Subsequent evolution of the VC10 made it possible to provide sufficient range for transatlantic operation, and to increase the payload to 40,000lb (18,143kg); it also led to development of the Super VC10 with a lengthened fuselage for up to 187 passengers, higher operating weights, 58,000-lb (26,300-kg) payload, uprated Conways and an integral fuel tank in the fin.

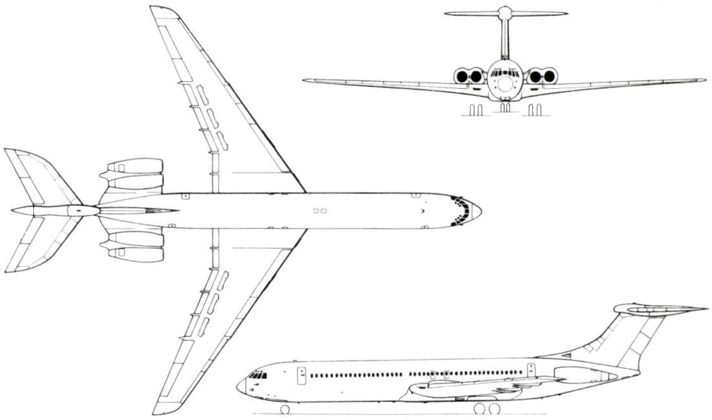

Above: Three-view of the BAC Super VC10, the final development of this four-jet transport first flown in June 1962.

BOAC ordered 10 Supers on 23 June 1960, for North Atlantic operation, and in 1961 changed its order to 12 Standard VC10s and 30 Supers, with a further change in 1963 to provide for eight of the latter to be convertible passenger/freighters with side-loading freight doors. After the Standard VC10 had entered service, the order for Supers was again reduced, to a final total of 17, all as passenger carriers.

First flight of the VC10 prototype was made from Weybridge on 29 June 1962 and the first production aircraft flew on 8 November 1962. Full British certification was gained in April 1964 and BOAC operated its first VC10 service, to Lagos, on 29 April 1964. The first Super flew from Weybridge on 7 May 1964 and entered service with BOAC on 1 April 1965.

In conformity with standard Vickers drawing office procedure, VC10 variants were identified by Type numbers in blocks commencing at 1100 for the basic Standard VC10 (and the prototype) and 1150 for the basic Super VC10. The BOAC Standard was Type 1101, the BOAC Super was Type 1151 and the projected BOAC passenger/freight convertible was the 1152. After conversion for airline use, the prototype became Type 1109 and was sold to Laker Airways. Other VC10 customers and variants were Ghana Airways (two Type 1102), BUA (three Type 1103), East African Airways (five Type 1154) and the RAF (14 Type 1106). The Type 1153 was a projected all-freight Super, Types 1110 and 1111 were basic and BOAC versions of a projected VC10A and Type 1125 was a projected hybrid with Standard dimensions and the uprated Super engines.

By 1975, British Airways Overseas Division (previously BOAC) had phased out its Standard VC10s, five going to Gulf Air and others to non-airline users. British Caledonian, which had acquired the BUA and Laker aircraft, had sold one to Air Malawi and withdrawn the others, and East African had also withdrawn its Supers. The British Airways fleet of Super VC10s remained fully operational in the late 'seventies.

Below: A Super VC10 gets airborne on the thrust of its four Rolls-Royce Conway turbofan engines.

Aérospatiale/BAC Concorde
International

Power Plant: Four 38,050lb st (17,260kgp) Rolls-Royce/SNECMA Olympus 593 Mk 610 turbojets with silencers and reversers.
Performance: Max cruising speed, 1,450mph (2333km/h) at 54,500ft (16,600m); best range cruise, Mach = 2·05; service ceiling about 60,000ft (18,288m); range with max payload, 3,050mls (4900km); range with max fuel, 4,490mls (7215km).
Weights: Basic operating, 170,000lb (77,110kg); typical payload, 25,000lb (11,340kg); max take-off, 400,000lb (181,400kg); max landing, 240,000lb (108,860kg).
Dimensions: Span, 84ft 0in (25·60m); length, 203ft 11½in (62·17m); height, 40ft 0in (12·19m); wing area, 3,856sq ft (358·25m²).

Although the Tupolev Tu-144 was first to fly and first to reach supersonic speed during its flight test programme, the Concorde was the world's first supersonic airliner to enter regular service carrying revenue passengers. When that milestone was reached early in 1976, just over 20 years had elapsed since the first steps were taken in Britain that were to lead to development of an SST (supersonic transport) and the creation of an Anglo-French programme to build and test such an aircraft.

Preliminary design work undertaken by British companies and government agencies in 1955 led to the setting up in 1956 of a Supersonic Transport Aircraft Committee (STAC) to study the feasibility of an SST. Among the specific project studies looked at by STAC was the Bristol Type 198 – a design number covering several different aircraft configurations of which the most favoured came to be a slender delta-winged layout with eight engines and able to operate across the North Atlantic at Mach = 2·0. Through a process of continuous refinement, this evolved into the smaller Bristol 223, with four engines and 110 seats for London–New York operation.

While this work went on in Britain, a similar process was under way in France, leading by 1961 to evolution of a project called the Super Caravelle that was strikingly similar to the Bristol 223. This similarity of project and objective facilitated a merging of the designs, at government behest, and a protocol of agreement was signed between Britain and France on 29 November 1962, since which time Concorde has been a joint project, costs and work being equally shared. Principal airframe companies were BAC (which had absorbed Bristol) and Aérospatiale (incorporating Sud), and the engine companies were Rolls-Royce (which had meanwhile acquired the Bristol Siddeley engine company in which Concorde's Olympus engines originated) and SNECMA.

continued on page 30 ▸

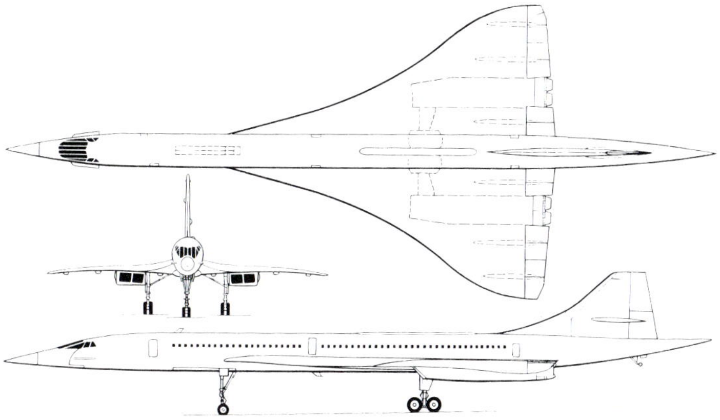

Above: Three-view of the Aérospatiale/BAC Concorde in its final production configuration; the prototypes had a shorter fuselage.

Above: Viewed through the heat haze on the runway, a Concorde prepares for take-off, its nose drooped to improve the pilots' view.

Below: Concorde 206, the second example to join British Airways' fleet, climbs towards the cruising altitude, with nose raised.

► The Concorde programme has been handled in a number of stages, embracing the construction and testing of two prototypes, known as Concorde 001 and Concorde 002; two pre-production aircraft, originally known as Concorde 01 and 02 and subsequently as Concorde 101 and 102; and a production sequence commencing with Concorde 201. Production of an initial batch of 16 aircraft was authorized by the two governments and production of major airframe and engine components was divided between companies in Britain and France without duplication. Separate final assembly lines were set up at Toulouse and Filton, alternate aircraft being assembled in Britain and France.

Concorde 001 made its first flight from Toulouse on 2 March 1969, its first supersonic flight on 1 October 1969 and the first excursion to Mach = 2 on 4 November 1970 (on its 102nd flight). Concorde 002 joined the programme from Filton on 9 April 1969 and these two aircraft built up hours and experience steadily throughout 1970, 1971, 1972 and 1973. With a design gross weight of 326,000lb (148,000kg), these prototypes were slightly smaller than the production standard, which introduced lengthened front and rear fuselages, revised nose visor, changes to the wing geometry and uprated engines.

These new features appeared progressively on Concorde 101, first flown from Toulouse on 17 December 1971, and Concorde 102, flown from Filton on 10 January 1973. Design gross weight was 385,000lb (174,640kg) and versions of the Olympus 593 engine fitted were rated at 38,050lb st (17,260kgp) compared with the 38,285lb st (14,890kgp) at which the prototypes had begun. Production aircraft, represented by Concorde 201 flown from Toulouse on 6 December 1973 and Concorde 202 flown from Filton on 13 February 1974, have Olympus 593 Mk 610 engines and 400,000 lb (181,400kg) gross weight. The cabin permits 128 passengers to be carried in a 2+1 arrangement, or up to 144 in high density layouts.

Concordes 203 and 204 flew on 31 January and 27 February 1975 respectively and were extensively used for development flying and route-proving, leading to the certification of the Concorde for full passenger-carrying operation on 13 October 1975 (in France) and 5 December 1975 (in the UK). Concordes 205 and 206 flew on 25 October and 5 November 1975 and were used to inaugurate SST scheduled services on 21 January 1976, by British Airways from London to Bahrein and by Air France from Paris to Dakar and Rio de Janeiro. Operations from London and Paris across the North Atlantic to Washington (Dulles) began on 24 May 1976, and on the important routes to New York from Paris and London in December 1977. In the same month, a joint British Airways/Singapore Airlines service from London to Singapore via Bahrein was also launched.

Above: One of the Air France fleet of four Concordes climbs away from the runway at the final assembly centre at Toulouse.

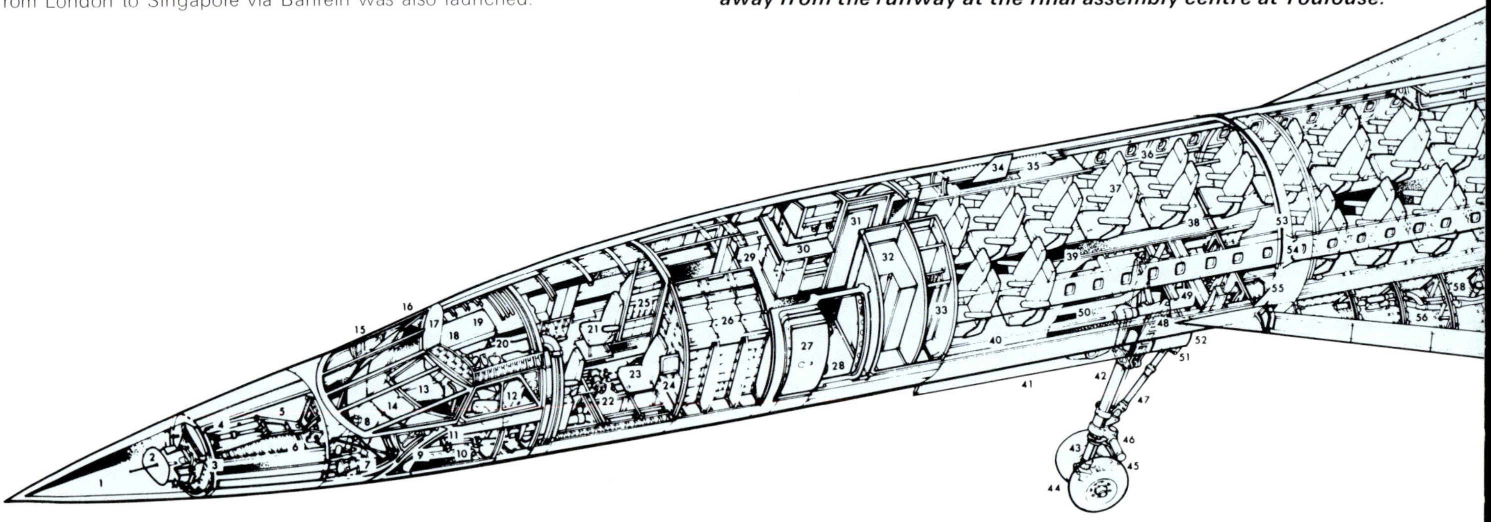

Above: The cutaway drawing shows the principal structural features of Concorde, which incorporates many advanced techniques. Fuel is carried in the fin as well as in tanks in the wings, and is transferred between tanks as required to keep the aircraft's centre of gravity within required limits during the cruise at supersonic speed.

Above: British Airways operates a fleet of five Concordes, all assembled at the UK production centre at Filton, Bristol. The registrations are G-BOAA, G-BOAB, G-BOAC, G-BOAD and G-BOAE. The first to enter service was G-BOAC, but by the time the Concorde was introduced, the former BOAC had already become British Airways.

BAC One-Eleven
United Kingdom

The following specification refers to the One-Eleven 500:
Power Plant: Two 12,550lb st (5692kgp) Rolls-Royce Spey 512-DW turbofans.
Performance: Max cruising speed: 541mph (871km/h) at 21,000ft (6400m); best economy cruise, 461mph (742km/h) at 25,000ft (7620m); initial rate of climb, 2,400ft/min (12·2m/sec); range with typical capacity payload, 1,480mls (2380km); range with max fuel, 2,149mls (3458km).
Weights: Basic operating, 54,582lb (24,758kg); max payload, 26,418lb (11,983kg); max take-off, 104,500lb (47,400kg).
Dimensions: Span, 92ft 6in (28·50m); length, 107ft 0in (32·61m); height, 24ft 6in (7·47m); wing area, 1,031sq ft (95·78m^2).

As a jet successor to the turboprop Viscount, the BAC One-Eleven proved somewhat less successful than its illustrious forebear, although by 1970 the sale of some 200 One-Elevens had established the type as largest earner of foreign exchange among the British civil aircraft then being exported. Deliveries had exceeded 220 by mid-1978, at which time further developments of the basic One-Eleven design were under discussion.

The One-Eleven had its origins in a project study by the Hunting Aircraft Ltd design team at Luton, which was working on a small jet airliner as early as 1956. Identified as the Hunting H-107, the early project was for a 48-seat (four-abreast) aircraft with a range of up to 1,000mls (1610km); the layout, following the style set by the Sud Caravelle, featured a low wing with modest sweepback, a T-tail and engines on the rear fuselage. The choice of suitable engines was severely restricted in 1956 and Hunting designers based their project upon two Bristol Orpheus turbojets. Wind tunnel tests were made and a mock-up was built, and in September 1958 the design was revised around two BS.61 or BS.75 turbofans.

During 1960, the Hunting company was acquired by the British Aircraft Corporation, which was set up at the beginning of that year to merge Vickers, Bristol and English Electric, and work proceeded on the H-107 as a joint effort between the Vickers-Weybridge and Hunting design teams. By early 1961, following an assessment of potential airline interest, the design had been enlarged to provide five-abreast seating for about 65 passengers and an optimum range of about 600mls (272km), using two of the commercial Rolls-Royce Spey turbofans that had been specified for the D.H.121 Trident. In this enlarged form the airliner was known as the BAC-111 (One-Eleven).

An order for 10 One-Elevens was placed with BAC by British United Airways and announced on 9 May 1961, a few weeks after the company had decided to lay down a batch of 20 aircraft in order to achieve the target delivery date of autumn 1964. The order book grew rapidly and by the time the first aircraft (intended for use as a company demonstrator and development machine) flew from Hurn on 20 August 1963, it stood at a total of 60. By that date, the aircraft had grown to have a gross weight of 73,500lb (33,340kg) and its maximum seating capacity was put at 79 in a high-density layout.

The North American market, in which the Viscount had always done so well, was regarded as a prime outlet for the One-Eleven, and orders were soon accepted from Braniff (a trunk operator) and Mohawk (a local service airline). The seal was put on the success of the One-Eleven in the US in July 1963, however, when American Airlines, one of the "big five" US operators, ordered 15, with options on 15 more to be taken up later.

***Right:** A Series 475 BAC One-Eleven, combining the original fuselage with the lengthened wing and uprated engines of the Series 500.*

***Below:** The BAC One-Eleven 500, the largest of the variants built to date, with longer fuselage and increased span.*

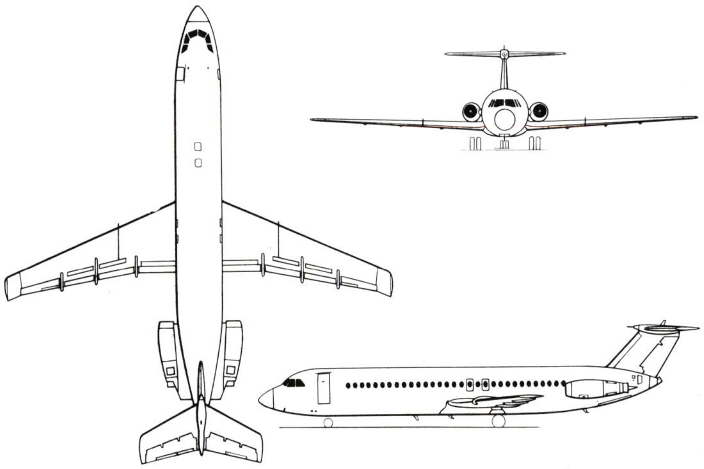

The American Airlines order was the first for the One-Eleven Series 400, a specially "Americanized" version with some features required to meet the then-applicable FAA certification requirements. In May 1963, BAC had adopted the designation One-Eleven 200 for the initial production standard and had introduced the Series 300 with uprated Spey engines, a centre-section fuel tank and higher gross weights – up to 87,000lb (39,463kg) – to provide a better range with full payload. The Series 400 had the same engines as the Srs 300, and the same structure, but was initially restricted to a gross weight of 79,000lb (35,834kg) to permit two crew operation in the USA (this limit being lifted subsequently).

Flight development of the BAC One-Eleven was ill-fated, the first aircraft being lost, with a highly experienced crew, on 22 October 1963 when a hitherto unsuspected deep-stall problem was encountered, related to the T-tail, rear-engined layout. The subsequent investigation and corrective action, including installation of a stick-pusher to prevent excessive (nose-high) angles of incidence being achieved inadvertently, was of great value to all manufacturers, including those competing with BAC for the same airline orders. Certification was achieved on 6 April 1965. British United flew the first One-Eleven services on 9 April, and Braniff flew the first in the US on 25 April, following the granting of FAA Type Approval on 15 April.

The next One-Eleven milestone was reached on 13 July 1965, when the first of American's fleet – distinctive in that airline's natural metal finish without the usual white upper surfaces to the fuselage – made its first flight. FAA Type Approval was obtained on 22 November 1965, and this type was to become one of the numerically most important One-Eleven variants (the other being the Series 500 which emerged in 1966) with 69 examples being built. Only nine Series 300 were built, and 56 Series 200s were delivered.

Whereas the Series 200, 300 and 400 were all dimensionally similar, the Series 500 introduced a lengthened fuselage to increase maximum passenger accommodation to 97 – and eventually, when higher weights were certificated, to 119. Stretched One-Elevens had been studied by BAC since before the first flight, but it was not until BEA decided to order the Series 500 that a go-ahead was given.

The fuselage of the Series 500 was lengthened by 13ft 6in (4·11m), and the wing span was increased by 5ft (1·2m) to cope with the increased weights, which also required a further uprating of the engine thrust, to 12,000lb st (4443kg) in the Spey 512-14 version. A company-owned Series 400 demonstrator was converted to the new configuration and flew as the prototype Series 500 on 30 June 1967 (initially retaining Spey 511 engines). The first production Series 500 flew on 7 February 1968 and was certificated on 18 August for BEA at a max weight of 92,483lb (41,950kg). Subsequently, the Series 500 was recertificated with 12,550lb st (5562kgp) Spey 512-14DW engines (with water injection) and the max weight went up to 99,650lb (45,200kg) or, to permit the use of a supplementary fuel tank in the aft end of the rear freight hold, 104,400lb (47,400kg). Orders for the Series 500 totalled 80 by the end of 1976, major users being British Airways, British Caledonian, Philippine Air Lines, Tarom and several IT operators.

Final One-Eleven variant to emerge up to 1976 was the Series 475, a "hot and high" version using the Spey 512-14DW engine and the extended span of the Series 500 with the original fuselage length, plus large-diameter low-pressure tyres which called for some modification of the wheel bays in the fuselage. The original Series 400/500 development aircraft was converted back to have the short fuselage and made its first flight as the Srs 475 prototype on 27 August 1970. The first production 475 flew on 5 April 1971 and certification was completed in July, when the first delivery was also made – to Faucett of Peru. The specialized characteristics of the One-Eleven Srs 475 proved, however, to be of rather limited airline interest and only a few examples were built.

In an effort to extend the useful life of the One-Eleven, BAC developed a "hush kit" for application to its Rolls-Royce Spey 512 engines, comprising an intake duct lining, a by-pass duct lining, an extended acoustically-lined jet pipe and a six-chute jet mixing exhaust silencer. The Srs 475 prototype fitted with these hush-kits made its first flight on 14 June 1974. Also during 1974, a freight door installation was designed for the One-Eleven for retrospective installation. Stretched versions of the aircraft have been under continuous study by BAC, including the Series 700, based on the use of the projected 16,900lb st (7665kgp) Rolls-Royce Spey 605 (with a new front fan), and a fuselage lengthened by 12ft (3·66m) compared with the Series 500, to carry up to 134 passengers. The Series 800 was planned to use CFM-56 engines of about 22,000lb st (10,000kgp) and the X-Eleven, a 1976 project, introduced a new fuselage of larger diameter with these or other engines of similar power.

Above: Principal operator of the BAC One-Eleven 500 is British Airways, for whom this stretched version was developed in 1967.

Beech 18
USA

The following specification refers to the Beech Super H 18:
Power Plant: Two 450hp Pratt & Whitney R-985AN-14B Wasp Jr piston radial engines.
Performance: Max cruising speed, 220mph (354km/h) at 10,000ft (3050m); best economy cruise, 185mph (298km/h) at 10,000ft (3050m); initial rate of climb, 1,400ft/min (7·1m/sec); service ceiling, 21,400ft (6520m); range with max fuel, 1,530mls (2460km).
Weights: Basic operating, 5,845lb (2651kg); max take-off, 9,900lb (4490kg).
Dimensions: 49ft 8in (15·14m); length, 35ft 2½in (10·70m); height, 9ft 4in (2·84m); wing area, 360·7sq ft (33·54m²).

More than 9,000 examples of the Beech 18 light twin were built between 1937 and 1969, of which nearly 2,000 were post-war commercial models. A substantial number remains in use with third-level airline and air taxi operators throughout the world including ex-military examples as well as the C18, D18, E18, G18 and H18 models, typical layouts providing for 7–9 passengers. Some H18 variants had a nosewheel undercarriage.

The Beech 18 also provided the basis for several conversion schemes, some examples of these being in airline use. Examples included the Dumodliner with lengthened fuselage to seat up to 14 passengers and the Pacific Tradewind, with a single fin and rudder. The Hamilton Westwind II and Westwind III have Pratt & Whirney PT6A turboprops and the Volpar Turbo 18 and Turboliner have TPE 331 turboprops, the latter with lengthened fuselage and up to 15 passengers. The Aerocom Skyliner is an even more radical derivative in which little of the original Beech 18 remains other than the centre fuselage.

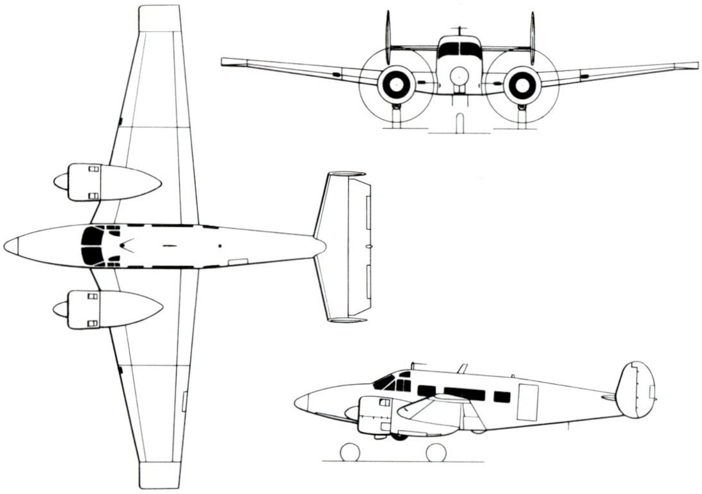

Above: Three-view drawing of the Beech 18, showing the Super H18 version that was the final production derivative of the light transport first flown in 1937.

Left: A Beech Super 18 for service in Sierra Leone, fitted with the Volpar-developed nosewheel undercarriage that was a late production option.

Beech 99 Airliner
USA

The following specification relates to the 99A:
Power Plant: Two 680shp Pratt & Whitney PT6A-27 turboprops.
Performance: Max cruising speed, 283mph (455km/h) at 8,000ft (2440m); initial rate of climb, 2,090ft/min (10·6m/sec); service ceiling, 26,313ft (8020m); range with max payload, 530mls (853km), range with max fuel, 838mls (1348km).
Weights: Empty equipped, 5,872lb (2663kg), max take-off, 10,900lb (4944kg).
Dimensions: Span, 45ft 10½in (14·00m); length, 44ft 6¾in (13·58m); height, 14ft 4¼in (4·38m); wing area, 279·7sq ft (25·98m²).

The Beech 99, largest of the company's range of twin-engined aircraft, was evolved from the original piston-engined Queen Air during 1965, primarily for commuter airline use. In this rôle, it carried up to 15 passengers in single seats each side of the central aisle, and an air-stair was incorporated in the main cabin door. A wide cargo-loading door in the fuselage adjacent to the main passenger door was offered as an option to facilitate the use of the Beech 99 in mixed passenger-cargo operations.

Beech flew a long-fuselage prototype of the Queen Air in December 1965, and PT6A-20 turboprops were fitted in this aircraft in July 1966, providing a basis for FAA Type Approval to be obtained on 2 May 1968, with production deliveries beginning at the same time. Initial aircraft were powered by 550shp PT6A-20 engines, with 680shp PT6A-27s introduced in the Model 99A. Over 150 Beech 99s had been delivered by the end of 1974, the great majority of these being for local operators in the USA, with small numbers sold overseas.

Above: A Beech 99 Airliner in the USA. Primarily operated as a third-level airliner, the type is also used as a business transport.

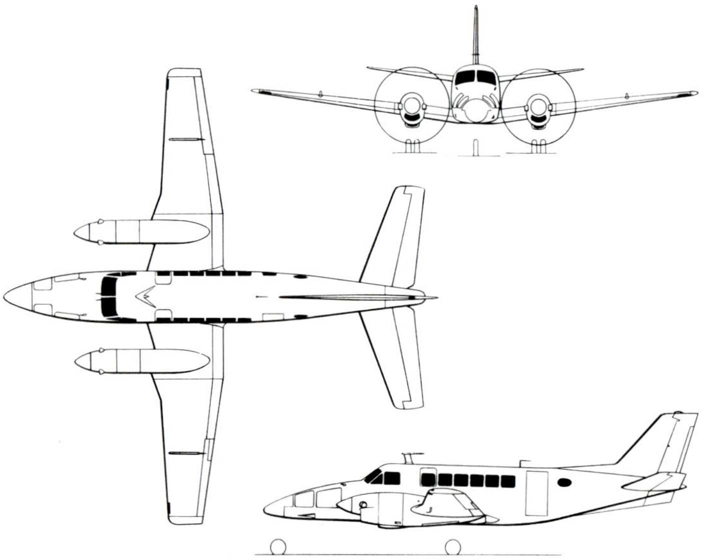

Above: Three-view of the Beech 99, developed as a 15-seat commuter airliner and widely used as such in the USA.

Boeing 707 (and 720)
USA

The following specification refers to the Boeing 707 320C:
Power Plant: Four 18,000lb st (8165kgp) Pratt & Whitney JT3D-3 or 19,000lb st (8618kgp) JT3D-7 turbofans.
Performance: Max cruising speed, 600mph (965km/h); best economy cruise, 550mph (886km/h); initial rate of climb, 4,000ft/min (20·3m/sec); service ceiling, 39,000ft (11,885m); range with max payload, 4,300mls (6920km); range with max fuel, 7,475mls (12,030km).
Weights: Basic operating, 136,610–146,000lb (62,872–66,224kg); max payload (passsenger), 84,000lb (38,100kg), (cargo), 91,390lb (41,453kg); max take-off, 333,600lb (151,315kg).
Dimensions: Span, 145ft 8½in (44·42m); length, 152ft 11in (45·6m); height, 42ft 5½in (12·94m); wing area, 3,050sq ft (283·4m^2).

The following specification refers to the Boeing 720B.
Power Plant: Four 17,000lb st (7718kgp) Pratt & Whitney JT3D-1 or 18,000lb st (8165kg) JT3D-3 turbofans.
Performance: Max cruising speed at 25,000ft (7620m), 608mph (978km/h); best economy cruise, 533mph (858km/h); initial rate of climb, 3,700ft/min ·(18·7m/sec); service ceiling, 40,500ft (12,344m); no-reserves range with max payload, 4,110mls (6614km); range with max fuel, 6,450mls (10,380km).
Weights: Basic operating, 115,000lb (52,163kg); max payload, 41,000lb (18,600kg); max take-off, 234,000lb (106,140kg).
Dimensions: Span, 130ft 10in (39·87m); length, 136ft 9in (41·68m); height, 41ft 7in (12·67m); wing area, 2,521sq ft (234·2m^2).

Through its production in the late 'forties of the C-97 and KC-97 family of transports and tankers for the USAF, the Boeing company was well placed to assess the future requirement for aircraft of this type; and production of 56 Stratocruisers for the airlines in the same timescale had given the company a feel for the commercial market too. With both these future possibilities in mind, Boeing had project studies under way before 1950 to investigate a turboprop- or turbojet-powered successor to the KC-97/Stratocruiser family. The studies were conducted under the C-97 Model number of 367 and by the beginning of 1952, the 367-80 study had emerged as the most promising, this being for a large transport with a swept-back wing, four turbojet engines in individual underwing pods and a large-diameter fuselage.

On 20 May 1952, the Boeing company decided to proceed to prototype construction of the 367-80, and the first flight was made at Renton, near Seattle, Washington, on 15 July 1954, opening the era of the Boeing jet transports which by 1977 had achieved sales of more than 3,000. Powered by 10,000lb st (4540kgp) Pratt & Whitney JT3C turbojets, this prototype, which became known in later years as the Dash 80, emerged as the prototype Boeing 707. This new model number had been assigned to the projected commercial jet transport based on the prototype, and was allocated in sequence (numbers up to 499 having been assigned to earlier Boeing aircraft, and 500 to 699 being reserved meanwhile for industrial products and gas turbines, with the aircraft types resuming at 700). The number 707 proved to be especially felicitous from a marketing point of view, however, and the Model 727, 737, 747 sequence used for later Boeing jet airliners followed as a direct result of this, and not by chance.

The Boeing 707 prototype, with the appropriate civil registration N70700, was extensively demonstrated to airlines and the USAF, and the latter placed an initial order for production of a tanker/transport version on 5 October 1954, this appearing in due course as the KC-135A (Boeing Model 717). Another year was to elapse before an airline order was to be placed for the Boeing transport, however, this order being from Pan American, which contracted to buy 20 Boeing 707s on 13 October 1955, a similar contract being placed with Douglas for 20 DC-8s at the same time. For the airlines, Boeing had meanwhile redesigned the fuselage of the Dash 80 to be 4in (10cm) wider to permit six-abreast seating, and alternative short-body and long-body versions were offered, this being an early indication of the Boeing philosophy to offer many different variants of the basic design to meet different airline requirements. The engines were to be 13,000lb st (5896kgp) JT3C-6s and with a gross weight of about 240,000lb (108,860kg), the new airliner would carry up to 179 passengers (one class, high density) and have sufficient range for US transcontinental operation.

The Pan American order triggered off a "jet buying spree" by the world's airlines that allowed Boeing (and other manufacturers which had meanwhile proposed their own jet airliners) to launch full-scale production, and the first two 707s off the line flew on 20 December 1957 and 3 February 1958 respectively. Full Type Approval was obtained on 23 September 1958 and the Boeing 707 entered service with Pan American on 26 October – this marking the introduction of the first US commercial jet transport and the world's third (after the Comet and Tu-104). Under the impetus of competition from BOAC with the Comet 4, Pan American used its first Boeing 707s on the New York–London route, although they had insufficient range for consistent non-stop operation over so long a sector. Domestic US operation of the Boeing 707 began on 10 December 1958, National Airlines using aircraft leased from Pan American, and American Airlines began using its own 707s within the USA on 25 January 1959.

All these early Boeing 707s were of the long-body type, only one operator, Qantas, choosing the short-body alternative – respective lengths were 144ft 6in (44·04m) and 134ft 6in (41·00m). Each customer variant was identified by a dash number, commencing at –121 for the JT3C-powered aircraft, which were known generically as 707-120s; several different fuel capacities were available, depending on the number of flexible bag tanks in the centre section, and weights up to 256,000lb (116,120kg) were eventually approved. To provide improved take-off performance, Boeing also produced a version of the basic domestic model as the 707-220 with 15,800lb st (7166kgp) JT4A-3 or -5 turbojets and gross weight of 257,000lb (116,573kg), but this was purchased by only one airline, Braniff. The first example flew on 11 June 1959 and Type Approval was obtained on 5 November, permitting service to begin on 20 December.

continued on page 42 ▶

Below: The Boeing 707-320B version, with turbofan engines. The 707 is the most successful four-jet airliner to date.

► Boeing offered a long-range version of the 707, as the Intercontinental, from the outset of the programme, this having increased wing span and area, lengthened fuselage to seat up to 189 passengers, more fuel, higher weights and either JT4A or Rolls-Royce Conway engines. Depending on engine type, these were designated 707-320 or 707-420 respectively. The first 707-320 flew on 11 January 1959 and certification was obtained on 15 July 1959, with 15,800lb st (7167kgp) JT4A engines and a gross weight of 302,000lb (136,985kg); subsequently, the 16,800lb st (7620kgp) JT4A-9 and -10, and the 17,500lb st (7940kgp) JT4A-11 and -12 became available, alternative fuel capacities were introduced and gross weights up to 316,000lb (143,335kg) were certificated. Pan American put the 707-320 into service on 26 August 1959 on routes out of the US West Coast, and across the North Atlantic on 10 October 1959.

With the same overall features as the -320, the 707-420 first flew on 20 May, being one of a fleet ordered by BOAC with 16,500lb st (7480kgp) Conway 505 engines. Considerable flight testing was required to achieve British certification, leading to the introduction of several new features concerned with aircraft handling, including a taller fin and rudder and a ventral fin, which became applicable to all 707 variants in due course. The 707-420 was type approved on 12 February 1960, with British ARB certification on 27 April and BOAC began services in May. The 17,500lb st (7940kgp) Conway 508 was introduced later and weights up to 316,000lb (143,335kg) were approved.

In addition to BOAC, four airlines specified the Conway-engined 707-420, and 37 were built. Production of the 707-320 totalled 69, and 60 707-120s were built for airlines. These, with the five 707-220s, represented the first phase of Boeing jetliner development and production; aerodynamic refinements, and the introduction of turbofan engines, were to bring major improvements in subsequent models, and consequently many of the earlier aircraft have now been retired as being at the end of their useful life, or have been modified to later standards.

The first aerodynamic refinements introduced by Boeing were applied to a short-to-medium range variant offered in 1957 under the designation 707-020. Also known for a time as the Model 717 (this being the type number already allocated to the military KC-135) it was eventually marketed as the Boeing 720. It shared a common fuselage length with the short-body 707-120 as first offered (but the latter, as built, was shortened by another 1ft 8in (0·51m) and it was designed to operate at lower gross weights, carrying less fuel, having a lightened structure in certain respects and using lighter, lower-powered JT3C engines. To achieve an increase of 0·02 in cruising Mach number, the effective thickness/chord ratio on the inner wing sections was reduced by adding an inner wing "glove" that extended the leading edge forwards between the fuselage and inner pylons, and leading edge flaps were added on the outer wings. The Boeing 720 first flew on 23 November 1959 and was type approved on 30 June 1960; first services were flown by United on 5 July and by American on 31 July 1960. The engines were 12,000lb st (5443kgp) JT3C-7 or -12, and weights up to 229,000lb (103,873kg) were eventually approved; the maximum passenger

continued on page 44 ►

Boeing 707-320C Cutaway Key:
1 Nose cone
2 Weather radar scanner
3 Glide-slope aerial
4 Forward pressure bulkhead
5 Pitot head
6 Nose frames
7 Windscreen panels
8 Eyebrow windows
9 Overhead console
10 First Officer's seat
11 Captain's seat
12 Forward frame
13 Twin nosewheels
14 Nosewheel doors
15 Nosewheel box
16 Drag struts
17 Navigator's table
18 Observer's seat
19 Navigator's seat
20 Navigator's overhead panel
21 Flight Engineer's seat
22 Flight Engineer's instrument panels
23 Flight deck entry door
24 Crew coat closet
25 Crew toilet
26 Crew galley/buffet
27 Spare life vest stowage
28 Radio (emergency) transmitter
29 Life raft stowage (2)
30 VHF aerial
31 Smoke and fume-proof curtain
32 Forward entry door (24in x 72in)
33 Escape slide stowage
34 Forward underfloor freight hold
35 Cabin floor level
36 Six cargo pallets (total 4,424cu ft)
37 Ball transfer mat (five segments)
38 Door actuator rams
39 Main cargo door (raised)
40 Engine intakes
41 Secondary inlet doors
42 Turbocompressor intakes
43 Turbocompressor outlets
44 Nacelle pylons
45 Leading-edge wing flaps
46 Main tank No 3 (4,069 US gals)
47 Fuel system dry bay
48 Vortex generators
49 Main tank No 4 (2,323 US gals)
50 Reserve tank (439 US gals)
51 Vent surge tank
52 Starboard wingtip
53 Starboard outboard aileron
54 Aileron balance tab
55 Starboard outboard spoiler (extended)
56 Starboard outboard flap
57 Flap tracks
58 Aileron/spoiler actuator linkage
59 Starboard inboard aileron
60 Control tab
61 Starboard inboard flap
62 Starboard inboard spoiler (extended)
63 Life raft stowage (4)
64 Escape straps
65 Escape hatches/emergency exits (20in x 38in) (4)
66 Life raft attachment clips
67 Inter-cabin movable bulkhead
68 Access door (port walkway)
69 Fuselage frames
70 87-passenger Tourist Class cabin configuration (34in seat pitch)

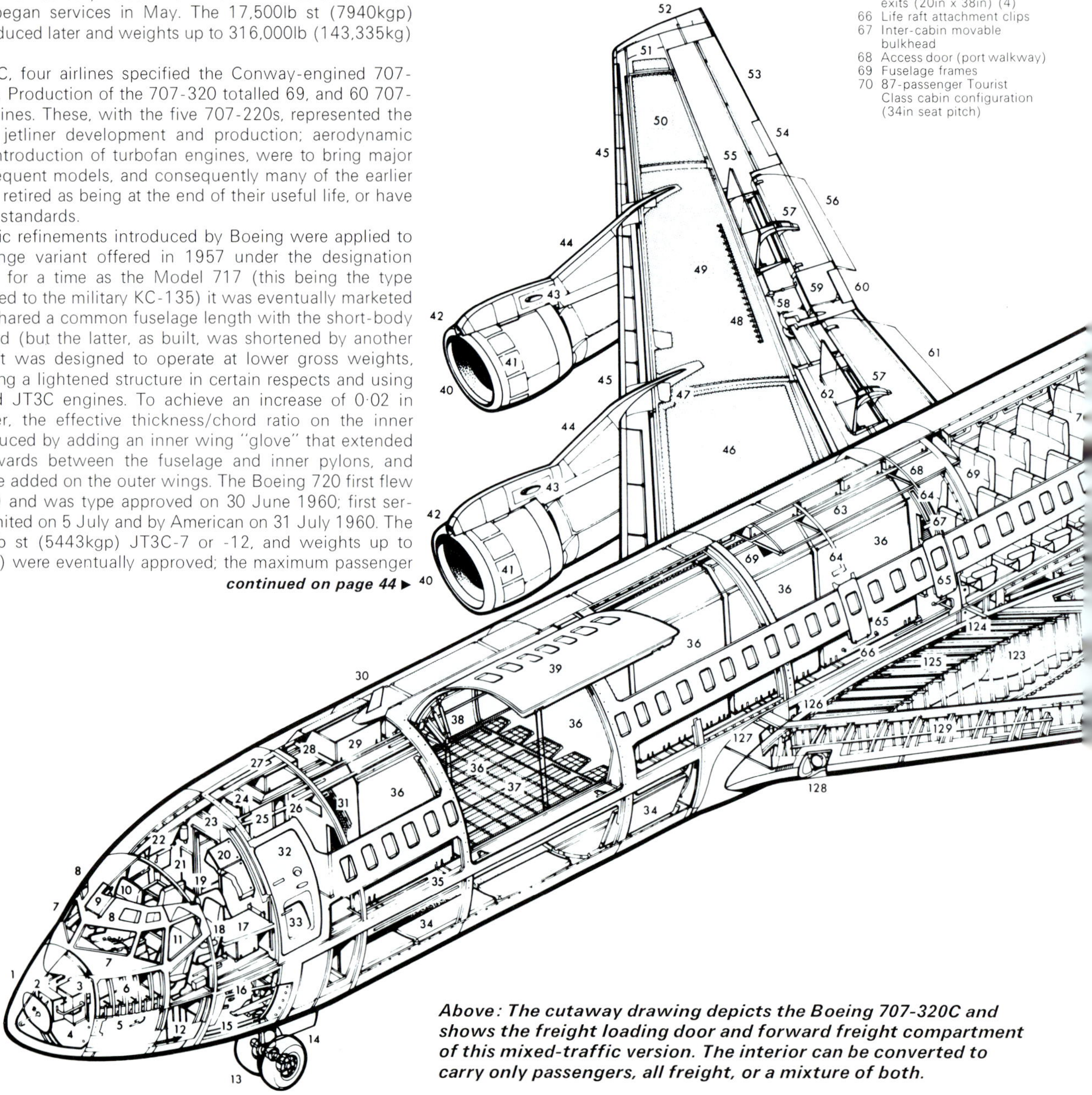

Above: The cutaway drawing depicts the Boeing 707-320C and shows the freight loading door and forward freight compartment of this mixed-traffic version. The interior can be converted to carry only passengers, all freight, or a mixture of both.

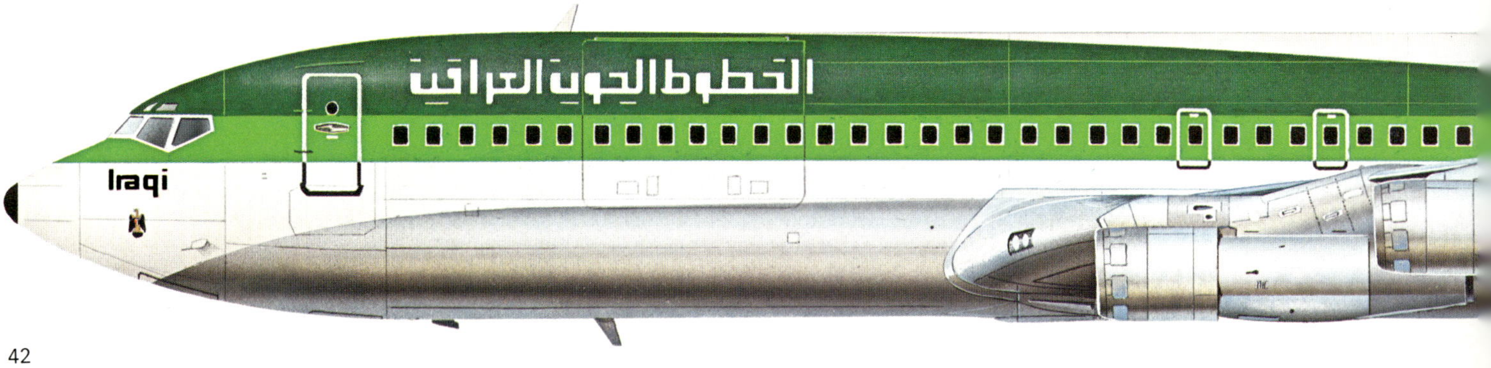

71 4-abreast seating row (emergency exit stations)
72 Ceiling air-conditioning
73 Passenger amenities
74 Rear cabin single-row seating
75 Cabin windows
76 Coat closet
77 Life raft stowage (2)
78 Spare life vests (and machete)
79 First-aid kit
80 Aft service door (starboard) 24in x 48in
81 Fin fillet
82 Starboard tailplane
83 VOR antenna
84 Removable fin leading edge
85 Rudder control linkage
86 Tailfin construction
87 Rudder 'Q' bellows
88 HF probe antenna
89 LORAN antenna
90 Rudder
91 Rudder control tab
92 Rudder anti-balance tab
93 Internal balance panel
94 Rudder flutter damper
95 Elevator torque tube
96 Rudder trim tab
97 Tail cone
98 Tailplane actuator tab
99 Elevator control tab
100 Port elevator
101 Port tailplane
102 Internal balance panel
103 Elevator linkage
104 Crank assembly
105 Elevator quadrant
106 Autopilot elevator servo
107 Tailfin spar/fuselage joints
108 Rear pressure bulkhead
109 Aft toilets (2)
110 Coat closet
111 Aft entry door
112 Escape slide stowage
113 Vestibule
114 Fuselage skinning
115 Aft underfloor freight hold
116 Wingroot fairing
117 Fillet flap
118 Landing gear trunnion
119 Undercarriage shock strut
120 Main undercarriage well
121 Side strut
122 Torsion links
123 Fuel tank end rib
124 Wing rear spar/fuselage pick-up point
125 Inboard wing stringers
126 Wing front spar/fuselage pick-up point
127 Fuselage centre tank forward face
128 Landing lights
129 Front spar
130 Four-wheel main landing gear
131 Port inboard spoilers
132 Port inboard flap
133 Vortex generators
134 Nacelle pylon
135 Turbocompressor
136 Engine intake
137 Pratt & Whitney TF33 turbofan
138 Fan thrust reverser doors
139 Engine fuel pump
140 Starter
141 Primary thrust reverser cascade vanes
142 Wing anti-ice check valve
143 Wing anti-ice shut-off valve
144 Duct temperature sensor
145 Leading-edge wing flap
146 Dimpled inner skin
147 Rear spar
148 Leading-edge thermal anti-icing duct
149 Integral wing fuel tanks
150 Port inboard aileron
151 Control tab
152 Port outboard spoilers
153 Port outboard flap
154 Engine access doors (port and starboard)
155 Nacelle nose cowl
156 Nacelle structure
157 Strut/pylon attachment
158 Exhaust
159 Pylon/wing joint
160 Tab
161 Leading-edge anti-ice supply manifold
162 Port outboard aileron
163 Wing skinning
164 Port wingtip

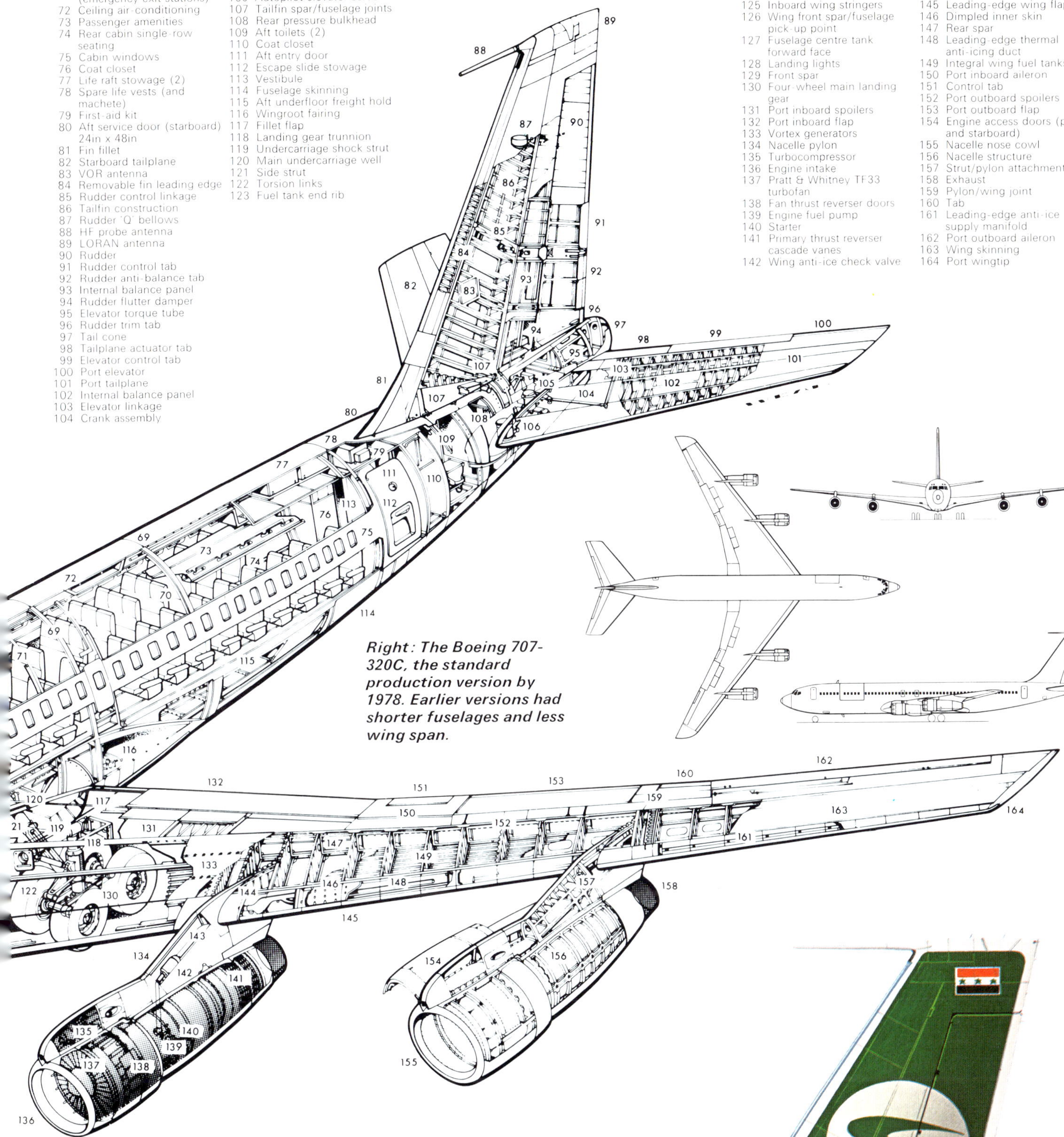

Right: The Boeing 707-320C, the standard production version by 1978. Earlier versions had shorter fuselages and less wing span.

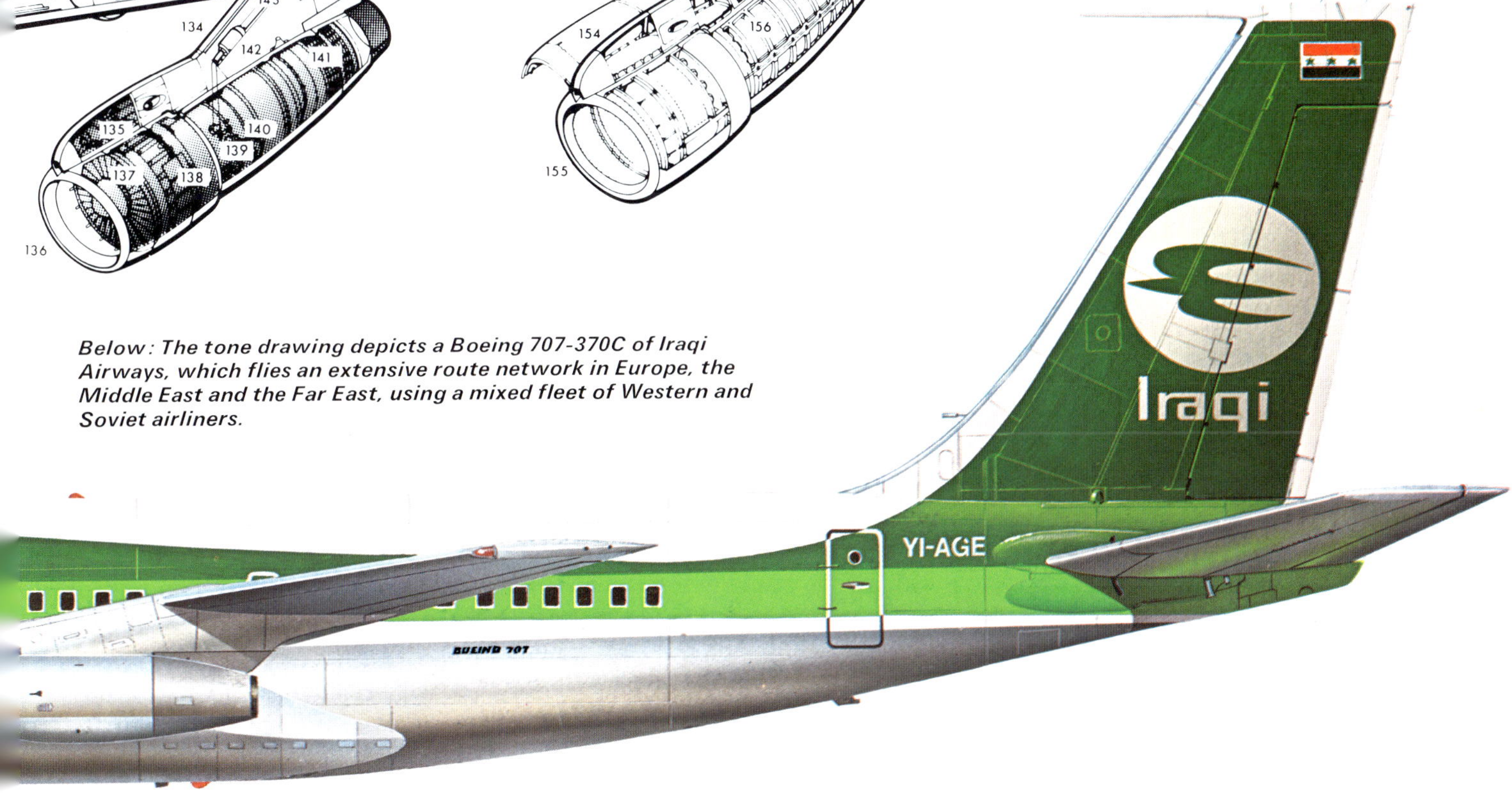

Below: The tone drawing depicts a Boeing 707-370C of Iraqi Airways, which flies an extensive route network in Europe, the Middle East and the Far East, using a mixed fleet of Western and Soviet airliners.

►capacity was 149, although Eastern Air Lines later obtained approval to carry 165 passengers in their aircraft. Production of the Boeing 720 totalled 65, of which many were later converted to have turbofan engines.

Development of a front fan version of the JT3C engine by Pratt & Whitney brought the promise of greater power and reduced specific fuel consumption, and versions of the Boeing 707-120, 707-320 and 720 were all quickly offered with the new power plant, which entered production as the 17,000lb st (7710kgp) JT3D-1. These versions were identified by the addition of a letter "B" as a suffix to the type designation. First to fly was a Boeing 707-120B, on 22 June 1960; in addition to the fan engines, distinguished by new cowlings with an annular exhaust for the front fan, it had the inner wing glove and extra leading edge flaps of the 720, and taller fin and ventral fin as already introduced on 707-320s in production. Type approval was obtained on 1 March 1961 and American Airlines put the type into service on 12 March 1961. Boeing built 78 Model 707-120Bs, and several airlines had their -120s modified; these included Qantas, with the result that the short-body version of the -120 also appeared with fan engines. Gross weights up to 258,000lb (117,027kg) were approved and the 18,000lb st (8164kgp) JT3D-3 or -3B engines were also used.

The first Boeing 720B flew on 6 October 1960 and certification followed on 3 March 1961, American Airlines starting service with this type alongside its -120Bs on 12 March 1961. Only JT3D-1 engines were used, and the gross weight was 234,000lb (106,141kg). Production totalled 89, plus some 720s converted.

Fitting turbofan engines to the Boeing 707-320 produced what was to become the most universally used version, in all-passenger (-320B) and passenger/cargo convertible (-320C) variants, the latter having a large side-loading freight door in the forward fuselage and associated freight floor and handling equipment. As well as the turbofan engines, these models featured new low-drag wing tips that extended the span by 3ft 3½in (1·0m), slotted leading-edge flaps and improved trailing-edge flaps, but the inner wing "glove" and ventral fin were not used. Boeing flew the first 707-320B on 31 January 1962 and after type approval on 31 May, this version entered service with Pan American in June. It could use JT3D-1, -3 or -7 engines and was initially approved to operate at 327,000lb (148,325kg) but all aircraft built after February 1964 had structural provision for weights up to 335,000lb (151,953kg).

The first 707-320C flew on 19 February 1963 and was type approved on 30 April, entering service with Pan American in June. A few examples, such as those used by American Airlines, operated as pure freighters, with the cabin windows blanked off. The same engine choice was available as for the 707-320B but the maximum flight weight was slightly reduced.

By early 1977, Boeing had sold 183 -320Bs and 331 -320Cs, including several for military use, and the grand total of all 707/720 variants then sold was 920, with production continuing. The long-range versions of the Boeing jetliner had been purchased by over 70 of the world's major airlines and as a result of lease or second-hand purchase deals, another 50 or so operators were using or had used the type. Boeing was also working, in 1977, on a prototype conversion of a 707 to have CFM-56 engines and a fuselage-stretched production version was projected as the 707-500.

***Below:** The flight deck of the 707 has not changed significantly in 25 years, and it has served as the basis for two other extremely numerous Boeing jetliners, the 727 and 737. As it was itself based upon the experience, practice and actual instruments of the 1952–53 period it is today visibly outdated. It was logical to make the 707 cockpit as little different as possible from those of existing piston-engined transports, and in fact the first 707 was much less radical than the company's earlier 377 Stratocruiser or the British Comet. The flight crew comprises a captain and first officer, supernumerary at rear left and flight engineer at rear right. Seats all slide on floor tracks, the engineer's being arranged to face sideways so that he can manage the large panel on the right wall controlling such systems as fuel and cabin pressurization. Early versions of the 707, especially the original Dash-121 used on the North Atlantic, were some of the most "marginal" transports of modern times when operated at gross weight. Full available runway lengths were needed, and captains had to learn a new style of flying requiring far greater amounts of airspace to manoeuvre the large, heavy and fast-moving aircraft. Later the 707 was transformed by engines of much greater power, high-lift leading-edge systems, larger vertical tails (often with an underfin) and more efficient long-span curved wingtips. The flight and system instruments have also been greatly developed.*

Boeing 727
USA

The following specification relates to the Advanced 727-200:
Power Plant: Three 15,000lb st (6804kgp) Pratt & Whitney JT8D-11 or 15,500 lb st (7030kgp) JT8D-15 or 16,000lb st (7257kgp) JT8D-17 turbofans.
Performance: Max cruising speed, 599mph (964km/h) at 24,700ft (7530m); economy cruise, 570mph (917km/h) at 30,000ft (9145m); initial rate of climb, 2,600ft/min (13·2m/sec); service ceiling, 33,500ft (10,210m); range with max payload over 2,800mls (4500km).
Weights: Operating weight empty, 100,000lb (45,360kg); max payload, 42,800lb (19,414kg); max take-off, 209,500lb (95,027kg).
Dimensions: Span, 108ft 0in (32·92m); length, 153ft 2in (46·69m); height, 34ft 0in (10·36m); wing area, 1,700sq ft (157·9m^2).

Design studies to evolve a medium-to-short range partner for the Model 707 were begun by Boeing as early as February 1956, two years before the first 707 entered service. Many configurations were studied, with nearly 70 alternatives actually reaching the stage of wind-tunnel testing, but maximum commonality with the 707 was one of the major design objectives, in order to achieve economy in first cost and operating cost. Boeing designers eventually concluded that a three-engined configuration best suited the size and performance requirements, and the new type therefore evolved along lines closely resembling those of the de Havilland 121 Trident which was intended for the same segment of the airline market.

After three years in Preliminary Design, during which time the designation 727 was adopted to continue the family series begun with the 707, the new transport became an active project early in 1959 and all major design decisions had been finalized by 18 September in that year. For another twelve months or so the favoured engine was the Allison-built version of the Rolls-Royce Spey, but the Pratt & Whitney JT8D was eventually chosen, and in this form the Boeing 727 moved from project to production on 5 December 1960 when United Airlines and Eastern Air Lines each ordered 40 examples. Boeing expressed its confidence in the future market for medium-sized aircraft of the 727 type with an estimate of sales totalling at least 300; by early 1978, however, the sales total stood at exactly 1,500, making the 727 the world's best-selling jet airliner by a substantial margin, and with sales continuing steadily. Some 85 airlines had by then purchased examples of the 727 from Boeing, three of these each having acquired fleets of more

continued on page 54 ▶

***Below:** The world's best-selling jet airliner, the Boeing 727. This is a 727-243 in service with Alitalia.*

***Bottom:** Icelandair's Boeing 727-108C, a passenger/cargo convertible version of the original short-fuselage model.*

►than 100, and many other operators had acquired examples on lease or through second-hand purchases.

Commonality with the Boeing 707 included the entire upper lobe of the fuselage, based on a cabin floor of identical width and therefore permitting the use of the same interior arrangements, and similar flight decks. Special attention was paid to the field performance, and the wing design incorporated the most advanced high lift devices ever adopted for a commercial transport at the time the 727 was launched. With a sweepback of 32 deg, the 727's wing had leading-edge slats and flaps, triple-slotted trailing edge flaps, inboard (high-speed) and outboard (low-speed) ailerons and flight and ground spoilers. With accommodation for up to 125 passengers (high-density) the 727 was designed to operate over stage lengths of up to 1,700mls (2736km) and to be able to fly from 5,000ft (1524m) runways.

The first Boeing 727, in United colours, flew on 9 February 1963 from Seattle, followed by a company demonstrator in Boeing's canary yellow and brown house colours on 12 March. With two more production aircraft soon joining the flight test programme, FAA Type Approval was obtained on 24 December 1963 and the first commercial service was operated on 1 February 1964 by Eastern between Miami, Washington and Philadelphia, followed by United's first service on 6 February. Later in the same month, the first export delivery was made, to Lufthansa, and the German airline flew its first service with the type on 16 April. Thus, the Boeing 727 completely eroded the lead that the D.H.121 Trident had gained with its go-ahead in 1958, and was quickly to achieve ascendance in the sales battles that were to follow, not least because of the larger capacity and greater range offered by Boeing from the outset.

Following the precedent set with the 707, Boeing offered the 727 in a number of variants. At first, these were concerned primarily with fuel capacity and operating weights, the original certificated gross weight of 152,000lb (68,950kg) soon being increased to 160,000lb (72,575kg) and then, in the 727C version, to 169,000lb (76,655kg). Progressive increases in engine thrust also became available, starting with the 14,000lb st (6350kgp) JT8D-1 or -7, followed by the 14,500lb st (6577kgp) JT8D-9. The 727C was announced in July 1964 as a convertible passenger/cargo version, with the same side-loading freight door and cargo handling systems already developed for the Boeing 707-320C. Northwest Orient was the first to order the 727C; the first example flew on 30 December 1965, Type Approval was obtained on 13 January 1966 and Northwest flew the first service with the type on 23 April. A further refinement of the convertible idea was to mount passenger seats and galleys on pallets to achieve fast conversions, allowing the same aircraft to fly passengers by day and freight by night, although there was a weight penalty. This became known as the QC (Quick Change) version and was in service by May 1966, with United.

Meanwhile, in August 1965, Boeing had announced a "stretched' version as the 727-200 (the original production version then becoming the 727-100, or 727-100C in convertible form). The "stretch" comprised exactly 20ft (6·10m) in two equal sections fore and aft of the wing, which remained

continued on page 48►

Boeing Advanced 727-200,

1 Radome
2 Radar dish
3 Radar scanner mounting
4 Pressure bulkhead
5 Windscreen panels
6 Instrument panel shroud
7 Back of instrument panel
8 Rudder pedals
9 Radar transmitter and receiver
10 Pitot tube
11 Cockpit floor control ducting
12 Control column
13 Pilot's seat
14 Cockpit eyebrow windows
15 Co-pilot's seat
16 Engineers control panel
17 Flight engineers seat
18 Cockpit door
19 Observers seat
20 Nosewheel bay
21 Nosewheel doors
22 Twin nosewheels
23 Retractable airstairs (optional)
24 Handrail
25 Escape chute pack
26 Front entry door
27 Front toilet
28 Galley
29 Starboard galley service door
30 Cabin bulkhead
31 Closet
32 Window frame panel
33 Radio and electronics bay
34 First class passenger cabin, 18 seats in mixed layout
35 Cabin roof construction
36 Seat rails
37 Cabin floor beams
38 Cargo door
39 Anti-collision light
40 Air conditioning supply ducting
41 Forward cargo hold
42 Cargo hold floor
43 Baggage pallet container
44 Tourist class passenger cabin, 119 seats in mixed layout
45 Communications antenna
46 Fuselage frame and stringer construction
47 Cabin window frame panels
48 Air conditioning system intake
49 Air conditioning plant
50 Overhead air ducting
51 Main fuselage frames
52 Escape hatches, port and starboard
53 Wing centre section No. 2 fuel tank
54 Centre section stringer construction
55 Cabin floor construction
56 Starboard wing No. 3 fuel tank
57 Inboard Krueger flaps
58 Krueger flap hydraulic jack
59 Leading edge fence
60 Outboard leading edge slat segments
61 Slat hydraulic jacks
62 Fuel vent surge tank
63 Navigation lights
64 Starboard wing tip
65 Fuel jettison pipe
66 Static dischargers
67 Outboard, low speed, aileron
68 Aileron balance tab
69 Outboard spoilers
70 Outboard slotted flap
71 Flap screw jack mechanism
72 Inboard, high speed, aileron
73 Trim tab
74 Inboard spoilers
75 Inboard slotted flap
76 Fuselage centre section construction
77 Pressurised floor over starboard main undercarriage bay
78 Auxiliary power unit (APU)
79 Port main undercarriage bay
80 Tourist class, six-abreast, passenger seating
81 Overhead hand baggage stowage bins
82 Cabin trim panels
83 Rear cargo door
84 Aft cargo compartment floor

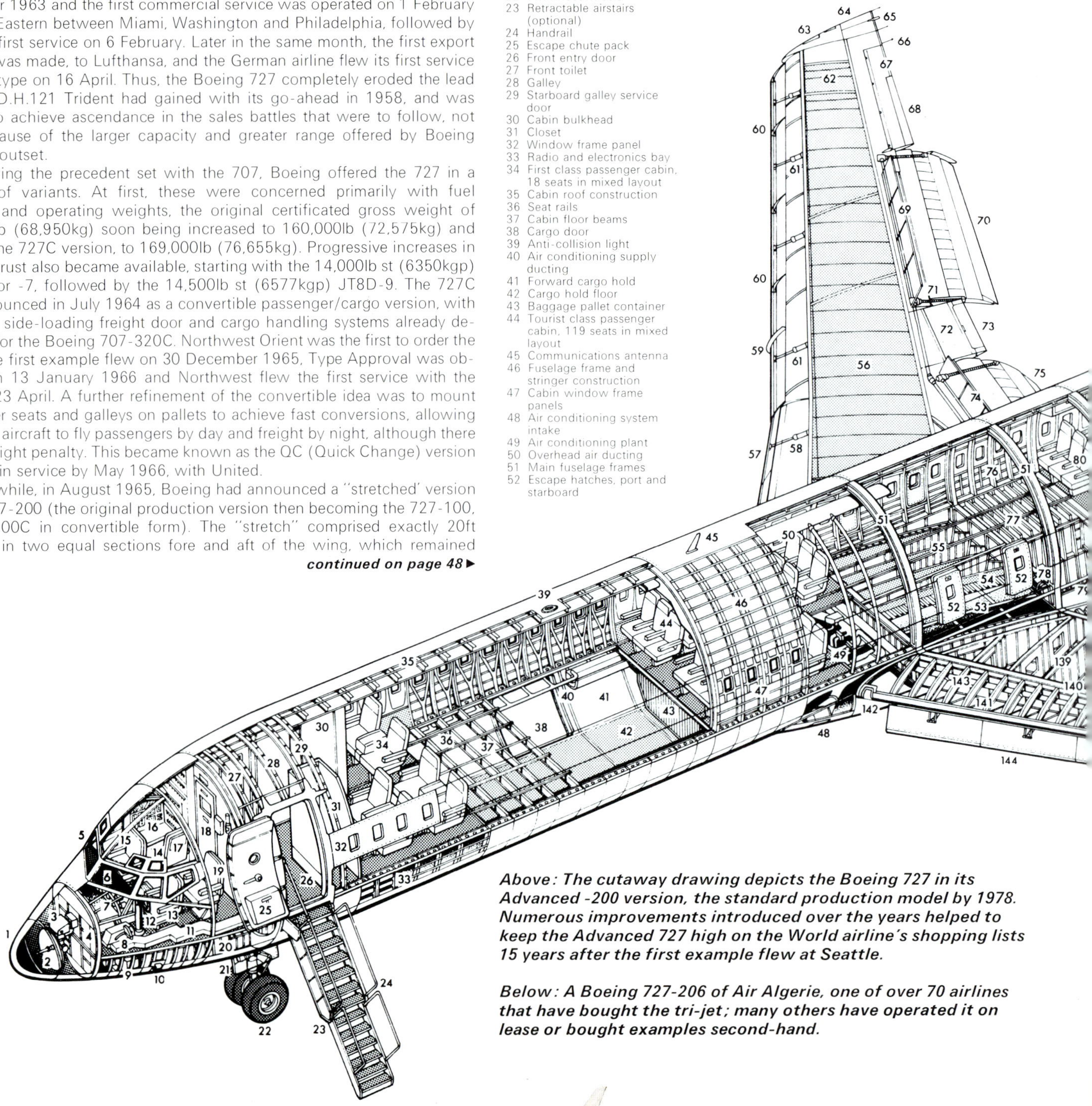

Above: The cutaway drawing depicts the Boeing 727 in its Advanced -200 version, the standard production model by 1978. Numerous improvements introduced over the years helped to keep the Advanced 727 high on the World airline's shopping lists 15 years after the first example flew at Seattle.

Below: A Boeing 727-206 of Air Algerie, one of over 70 airlines that have bought the tri-jet; many others have operated it on lease or bought examples second-hand.

85 Passenger overhead service panels
86 Starboard service door/ rear emergency exit
87 Aft galleys
88 Closet
89 Toilets, port and starboard
90 Cabin rear entry door
91 Starboard engine cowling
92 Centre engine intake
93 Noise attenuating intake lining
94 Intake S-duct
95 Duct de-icing
96 Fin root fairing construction
97 Fin construction
98 VOR aerial
99 Elevator control cables
100 Tailplane trim jack
101 Starboard tailplane
102 Elevator horn balance
103 Static dischargers
104 Starboard elevator
105 Elevator tab
106 Fin bullet fairing
107 VHF aerial boom
108 Elevator control jack
109 Port elevator
110 Tailplane construction
111 Port tailplane
112 Rudder upper section
113 Rudder control jacks
114 Rudder lower section
115 Lower section trim jack
116 Centre engine mounting pylon
117 Centre engine exhaust pipe
118 Thrust reverser
119 Centre engine
120 Rear fuselage construction
121 Side engine thrust reverser
122 Engine pylon fairing
123 Rear pressure bulkhead
124 Bleed air system pipes
125 Pratt & Whitney JT8D-9A turbofan engine
126 Detachable cowlings
127 Rear entry ventral airstairs
128 Engine air intake
129 Port rear service door/ emergency exit
130 Lower lobe fuselage frame construction
131 Trailing edge fillet
132 Inboard flap
133 Flap track fairings
134 Flap trap mechanism
135 Inboard spoilers
136 Main undercarriage leg pivot
137 Retraction mechanism
138 Rear spar
139 Wing rib construction
140 Front spar
141 Leading edge construction
142 Landing and taxying lamp
143 De-icing air duct
144 Inboard Krueger flap segments
145 Landing lamp
146 Main undercarriage leg
147 Twin mainwheels
148 Wing stringer construction
149 Inboard, high speed, aileron
150 Aileron trim tab
151 Flaps down position
152 Outboard spoilers
153 No. 1 wing integral fuel tank, total capacity 8,186 US gal (30,984 litres)
154 Re-fuelling connectors
155 Leading edge fence
156 Leading edge slat segments
157 Slat hydraulic jacks
158 Slat track mechanism
159 Outboard slotted trailing edge flap
160 Flap track fairings
161 Outboard flap track mechanism
162 Aileron balance tab
163 Outboard, low speed, aileron
164 Aileron control jack
165 Fuel vent surge tank
166 Port navigation lights
167 Static dischargers
168 Fuel jettison pipe

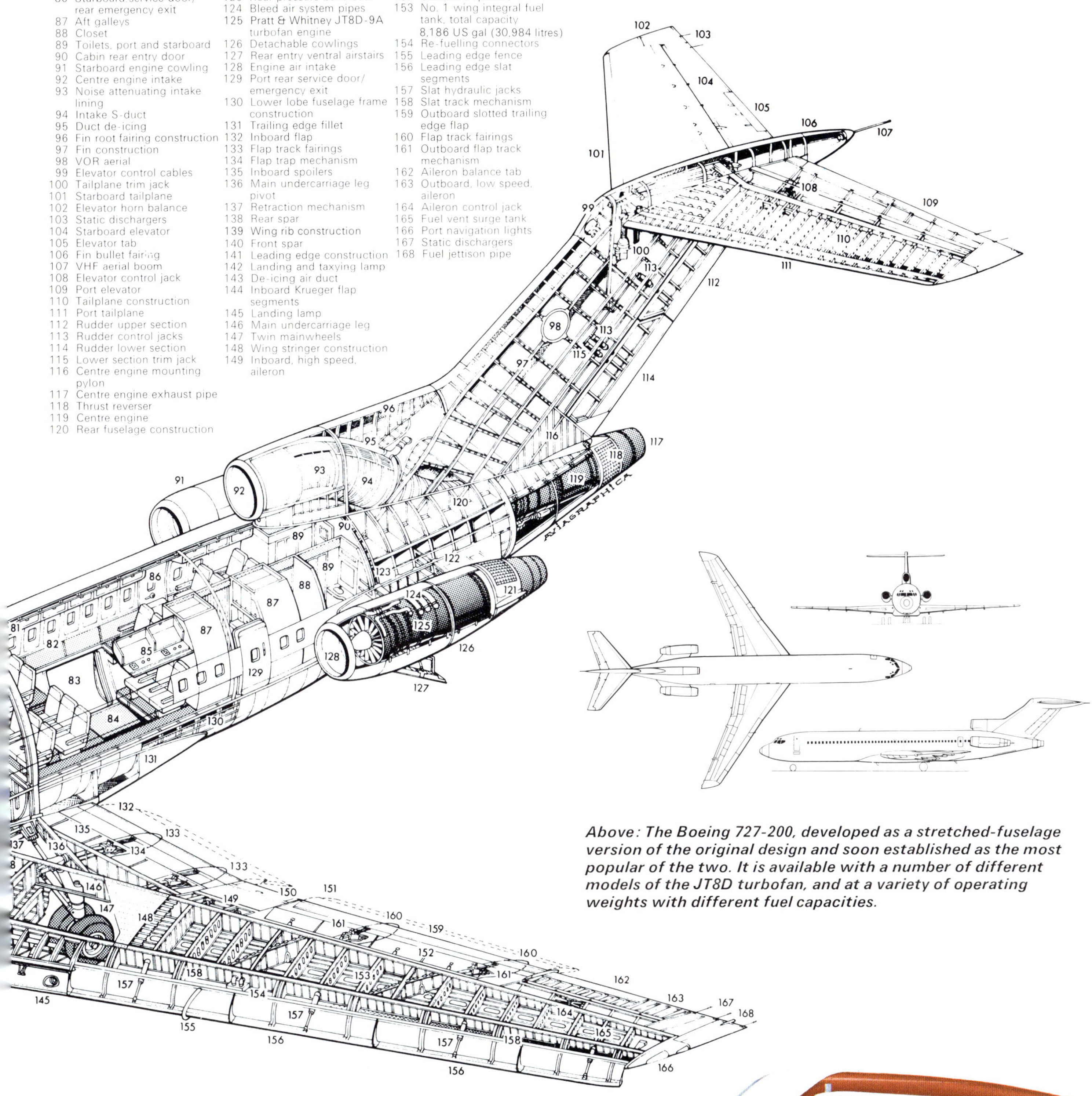

Above: The Boeing 727-200, developed as a stretched-fuselage version of the original design and soon established as the most popular of the two. It is available with a number of different models of the JT8D turbofan, and at a variety of operating weights with different fuel capacities.

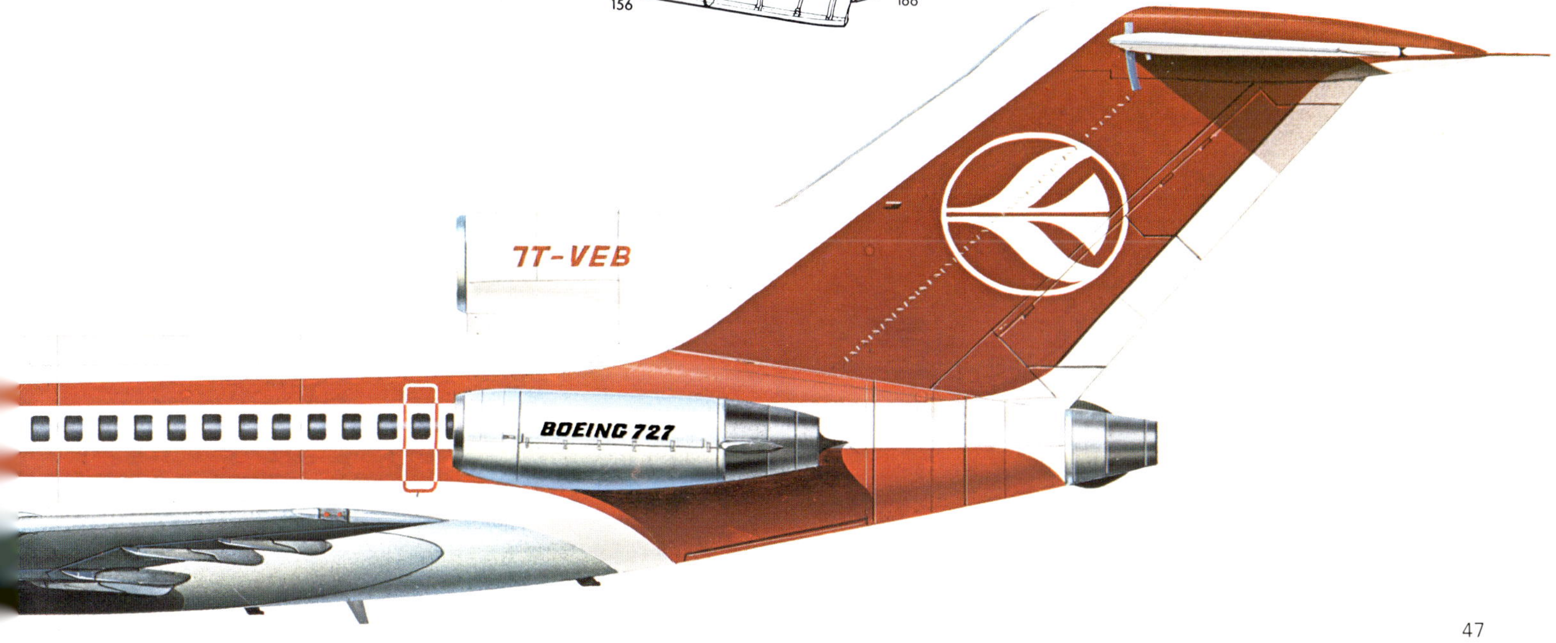

►unchanged, and maximum accommodation increased to 189. The JT8D-7 or -9 engines were specified at first, the gross weight being 169,000lb (76,655kg), but 15,000lb st (6804kgp) JT8D-11s became available in 1972 and the 15,500lb st (7030kgp) JT8D-15 was offered as a further alternative in later models. The first customer for the Boeing 727-200, which was to become the most important variant, was Northeast Airlines, with an order placed on 10 August 1965; the first example flew on 27 July 1967, Type Approval was obtained on 29 November and the first service was flown on 14 December 1967.

During 1970, when sales of the 727 were temporarily at a low ebb, Boeing began to plan a series of additional improvements, which led to introduction of the Advanced 727 with a wide option of gross weights, fuel capacities, engine powers and other features. Basic to the Advanced model were an increase in fuel capacity, new and improved aircraft systems, a "wide-body look" interior modelled on that of the Boeing 747 and additional noise reduction features to comply with new FAA regulations. First orders for the Advanced 727 were placed in December 1970 by TAA and Ansett of Australia, and the first example, destined for All-Nippon Airways, flew on 3 March 1972, with JT8D-15 engines and a gross weight of 191,000lb (86,636kgp). Type Approval was obtained on 14 June and All-Nippon flew the first service in July 1972.

On 26 July 1973, Boeing made the first flight of an Advanced 727 at a new gross weight of 207,500lb (94,120kg), this being destined for delivery to Sterling Airways before the end of 1973, with sufficient range to fly a full 189-passenger payload on routes from Scandinavia to the Canary Islands. Yet another option became available in 1974 with the introduction of 16,000lb st (7260kgp) JT8D-17 engines, first flown in a 727 in March of that year and first delivered, on 24 June, to Mexicana. Boeing also introduced, in 1976, the JT8D-17R engine with automatic thrust reserve, operating normally at 16,400lb st (7440kgp) with an extra 1,000lb (454kg) available from the remaining engines in the event of one engine failing during a critical stage of the flight. The first 727 with ATR flew on 27 May 1976 and was later delivered to Hughes Airwest.

Below: The flight deck of the 727 is virtually a 707 reconfigured for three engines. Any 707 captain would feel immediately at home, though of course the whole middle parts of the panels are arranged in threes, not fours: three engine-speed indicators, three pressure-ratio indicators, three fire/shut-down buttons, three throttles and three sets of fuel cocks and starting panels. The structure of what Boeing call the "can section" is identical to that of the earlier 707/720, but the general philosophy of the 727 was markedly different. The original 707 was planned merely as a pioneer four-jet transport for long-haul routes, whereas the 727 was intended for all-weather operation on short routes where flight crews might make ten take-offs and landings in a day. Intense effort went into all kinds of studies on airplane configuration, autopilot, flight-control and on many other areas, not least of which was wing lift. In the 727 the research and development team went to the limits and incorporated leading-edge slats, Krugers and unprecedented triple-slotted flaps, to fit the fast and heavy jetliner to small runways. They then spent over 20,000 man-hours on the autopilot, which became a Sperry product, and insisted (for the first time) that this be developed and certificated as an integral part of the 727. The dramatically simple manual flight controls of the 707 were replaced by fully powered systems to give the brute-force precision needed for accurate arrivals in the worst weather. Artificial feel was built in, together with multi-channel signalling and self-test features. After entry to service an unexpected series of crashes highlighted the problem of allowing speed to decline on the approach and, with pressure from Britain's certification authority, a complete stall-warning system was fitted. This first shakes the pilot's yoke front/rear and, if he keeps pulling back, bodily forces forces it forward to push the nose down (stall-warning panel visible in the roof).

Bristol 175 Britannia

United Kingdom

The following specification refers to the Series 310:
Power Plant: Four 4,450shp Bristol Proteus 765 turboprops.
Performance: Max cruising speed, 397mph (639km/h), best economy cruise, 357mph (575km/h), range with max payload, 3,100st mls (4990km); range with max fuel, 3,310st mls (5327km).
Weights: Empty equipped, 93,500lb (42,410kg); max payload, 34,500lb (15,650kg); max take-off, 185,000lb (83,915kg).
Dimensions: Span, 142ft 3in (43·36m); length, 124ft 3in (37·87m); height, 37ft 6in (11·43m); wing area, 2,074sq ft (192·76m²).

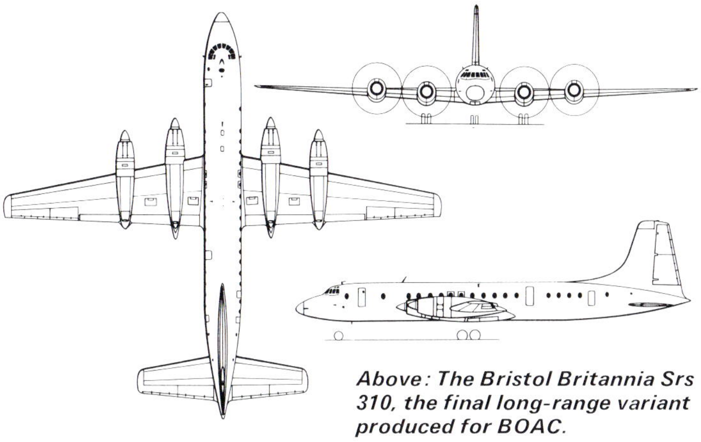

Above: The Bristol Britannia Srs 310, the final long-range variant produced for BOAC.

The Bristol Britannia was evolved to a BOAC specification for a Medium Range Empire (MRE) passenger transport, outlined soon after the end of the war. The prototype was flown on 16 August 1952 and was of the same configuration as the initial production Series 100; BOAC bought 15 of these but none now survive. The Series 300, first flown on 31 December 1956, had a longer fuselage and uprated Proteus turboprop engines and 45 of these were built (including the similar 305 and 310 versions), plus 23 for RAF use.

The BOAC fleet of Britannia 310s was sold off to British charter operators and a few went overseas; a few other airlines were among the original buyers of the Britannia, which in its long-fuselage variants could carry up to 139 passengers in one-class high-density layouts. By the end of 1974, fewer than a dozen Britannias remained in service and those mostly for cargo-carrying. During 1975, however, the RAF retired and offered for sale 22 Britannias that were generally similar to the commercial Srs 310s and a number of these were acquired for cargo carrying by small airlines in Europe, the Middle East and Africa.

Below: One of the last original Britannias in service with Air Turas. Ex-RAF Britannias also are in civil use.

Bristol 170 Freighter

United Kingdom

Power Plant: Two 1,950hp Bristol Hercules 734 piston radial engines.
Performance: Max cruising speed, 193mph (311km/h); best economy cruise, 163mph (262km/h); initial rate of climb, 1,380ft/min (7·0m/sec); service ceiling, 24,500ft (7467m); range with max payload, 820mls (1320km); range with max fuel, 1,730mls (2784km).
Weights: Basic operating, 27,229lb (12,380kg); max payload, 12,500lb (5670kg); max take-off, 44,000lb (19,958kg).
Dimensions: Span, 108ft 0in (32·92m); length, 68ft 4in (20·83m), height, 21ft 6in (6·56m); wing area, 1,487sq ft (138·0m²).

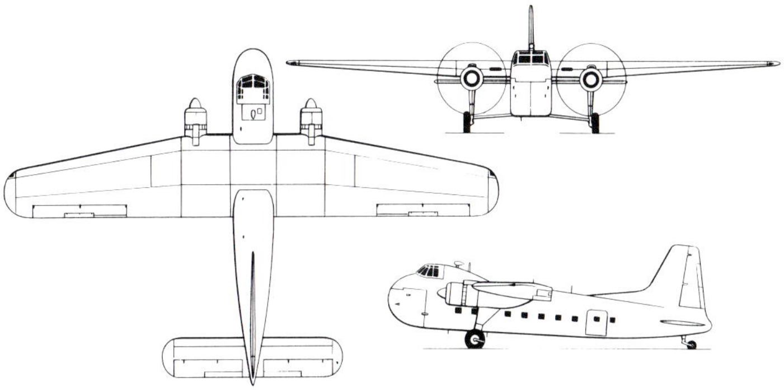

Above right: Three-view drawing of the Bristol 170, an early post-war attempt to produce an air-freighting "tramp".

The Bristol 170 was evolved during 1944 to meet an anticipated post-war demand for a utilitarian passenger and cargo transport, with possible military applications also in view. The prototype flew on 2 December 1945, with three more following on 30 April, 23 June and 15 September 1946, and a Certificate of Airworthiness was granted on 7 June 1946. Production of the Type 170 was launched in two basic series—the Freighter with nose opening doors and emphasis upon freight carrying; and the Wayfarer with fixed nose doors and all-passenger accommodation.

Production of the Type 170 totalled 214, including Mk I Freighter, Mk II Wayfarer; Mk XI with increased span, fuel and gross weight; Mk 21 with Hercules 672 and further weight increase; Mk 31 with Hercules 734, dorsal fin and higher weight and Mk 32 with lengthened nose to increase capacity on specialized car ferry services. At one time, large fleets of Bristol 170s were used on cross-Channel car ferry routes, finally by British Air Ferries, but by the mid-seventies the only major operator of the 170 was SAFE Air Ltd in New Zealand, which was using a fleet of 11 Mk 31s to carry freight between the islands.

Right: One of the few surviving Bristol 170s in 1978, the principal operator being SAFE Air Ltd in New Zealand.

Britten-Norman Trislander

United Kingdom

Power Plant: Three 260 Lycoming O-540-E4C5 piston engines.
Performance: Max speed, 183mph (294km/h) at sea level; max cruising speed (75 per cent engine power), 176mph (283km/h) at 6,500ft (1988m); typical cruise (67 per cent engine power), 174mph (280km/h) at 9,000ft (2750m); best economy cruise (59 per cent engine power), 168mph (270km/h) at 13,000ft (3960m); initial rate of climb, 980ft/min (4·98m/sec), service ceiling, 13,150ft (4010m); range with max payload (VFR reserves) 210mls (338km); range with max fuel, 860mls (1384km).
Weights: Basic operating, 6,178lb (2800kg); max payload, 3,550lb (1610kg); max take-off, 10,000lb (4536kg).
Dimensions: Span, 53ft 0in (16·15m); length, 43ft 9in (13·34m); length (extended nose), 47ft 6in (14·48m); height, 13ft $5\frac{3}{4}$in (4·11m); wing area, 337sq ft (31·25m^2).

Above: The Britten-Norman Trislander, used by a number of smaller airlines for "third-level" operation.

The uniquely configured Trislander was evolved directly from the best-selling Islander, having the same fuselage cross section and same mainplane and power plant. Its new features were increased fuselage length, and a third engine – necessary to cope with the higher operating weights – located in a nacelle carried on the fin. The tailplane – larger than that of the Islander – was located high on the fin instead of being on the fuselage.

Evolution of the Trislander began in 1968, when a long-fuselage Islander was test-flown (starting on 14 July). The prototype Trislander flew on 11 September 1970 and after some changes in tail unit shape and area, it entered small-scale production alongside the Islander; the first production model flew on 6 March 1971, British and US certification being obtained on 14 May and 4 August 1971 respectively. Up to 18 passengers are carried, two-abreast.

Deliveries began on 29 June 1971, and the assembly line was transferred from Bembridge, IoW, to Gosselies, Belgium, during 1973. The first Trislanders were known as BN-2A Mk IIIs at the gross weight of 9,350lb (4245kg) but this was soon increased to 10,000lb (4540kg) in the BN-2A Mk III-1. On 18 August 1974, the first Trislander with the lengthened nose of the BN-2S Islander made its first flight and this feature then became standard on the BN-2A Mk III-2. About 50 Trislanders had been sold by early 1978.

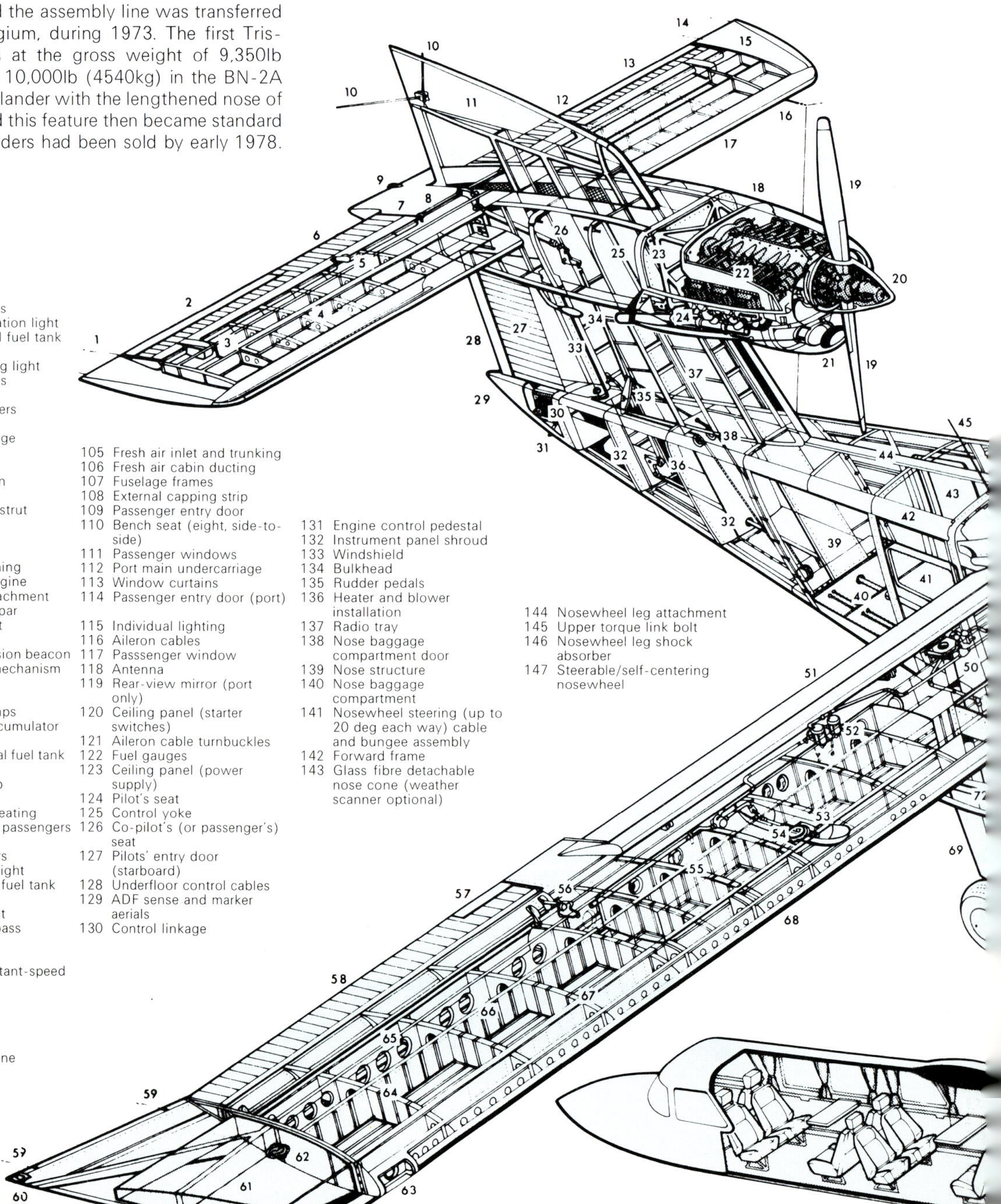

Britten-Norman Trislander Cutaway Drawing Key

1 Static dischargers
2 Elevator tab
3 Mass balance
4 Starboard tailplane structure
5 Elevator hinge
6 Starboard elevator
7 Glass fibre pylon tail cone
8 Elevator operating rod
9 Tail navigation light
10 VOR aerials
11 Upper fin structure
12 Port elevator
13 Elevator tab
14 Static dischargers
15 Tailplane tip
16 Aerial attachment
17 Port tailplane
18 Glass fibre engine cowling
19 Two-blade constant-speed propeller
20 Spinner
21 Intake
22 Lycoming IO-540-E4C5 engine
23 Steel-tube engine bearers
24 Exhaust
25 Firewall
26 Elevator control linkage
27 Rudder
28 Rudder trim tab
29 Glass fibre tail cone (detachable)
30 Battery
31 Vent pipe
32 Rear fuselage/fin attachment frames
33 Rudder post
34 Rudder mass balance
35 Control linkage
36 Elevator control rods
37 Pylon frames
38 Rudder cables
39 Aft bulkhead
40 Baggage compartment
41 Passenger aft entry door (starboard)
42 External joint straps
43 Baggage compartment door (port)
44 External fuel lines (to rear engine)
45 Antenna
46 Passenger window
47 Flap linkage
48 Fuselage/rear spar attachment point
49 Passenger window
50 Main-leg top attachment
51 Starboard flap
52 Electric fuel pumps
53 Fuel sump
54 Filler cap
55 Starboard wing integral fuel tank
56 Aileron control
57 Aileron servo tab
58 Starboard aileron
59 Static dischargers
60 Starboard navigation light
61 Wing-tip integral fuel tank
62 Gravity filler
63 Starboard landing light
64 Pressed wing ribs
65 Rear spar
66 Spar web stiffeners
67 Front spar
68 Wing leading-edge construction
69 Leg fairing
70 Twin-wheel main undercarriage
71 Shock-absorber strut
72 Exhaust
73 Intake
74 Spinner
75 Starboard Lycoming IO-540-E4C5 engine
76 Nacelle/spar attachment
77 Fuselage/front spar attachment point
78 Aileron cables
79 Dorsal anti-collision beacon
80 Flap actuating mechanism
81 Port flap
82 Fuel lines
83 Electric fuel pumps
84 Unfeathering accumulator
85 Fuel sump
86 Port wing integral fuel tank
87 Aileron actuator
88 Aileron servo tab
89 Portaleron
90 "Club" aircraft seating arrangement, 10 passengers
91 Aerial
92 Static dischargers
93 Port navigation light
94 Wingtip integral fuel tank
95 Gravity filler
96 Port landing light
97 Magnesyn compass
98 Two-spar wing construction
99 Two-blade constant-speed propeller
100 Spinner
101 Intake
102 Engine cowling
103 Oil filter access
104 Cowling hinge line
105 Fresh air inlet and trunking
106 Fresh air cabin ducting
107 Fuselage frames
108 External capping strip
109 Passenger entry door
110 Bench seat (eight, side-to-side)
111 Passenger windows
112 Port main undercarriage
113 Window curtains
114 Passenger entry door (port)
115 Individual lighting
116 Aileron cables
117 Passsenger window
118 Antenna
119 Rear-view mirror (port only)
120 Ceiling panel (starter switches)
121 Aileron cable turnbuckles
122 Fuel gauges
123 Ceiling panel (power supply)
124 Pilot's seat
125 Control yoke
126 Co-pilot's (or passenger's) seat
127 Pilots' entry door (starboard)
128 Underfloor control cables
129 ADF sense and marker aerials
130 Control linkage
131 Engine control pedestal
132 Instrument panel shroud
133 Windshield
134 Bulkhead
135 Rudder pedals
136 Heater and blower installation
137 Radio tray
138 Nose baggage compartment door
139 Nose structure
140 Nose baggage compartment
141 Nosewheel steering (up to 20 deg each way) cable and bungee assembly
142 Forward frame
143 Glass fibre detachable nose cone (weather scanner optional)
144 Nosewheel leg attachment
145 Upper torque link bolt
146 Nosewheel leg shock absorber
147 Steerable/self-centering nosewheel

Above: Loganair uses its Trislanders to fly an extensive network of local services in Scotland, including the Western Isles, Orkneys and Shetlands.

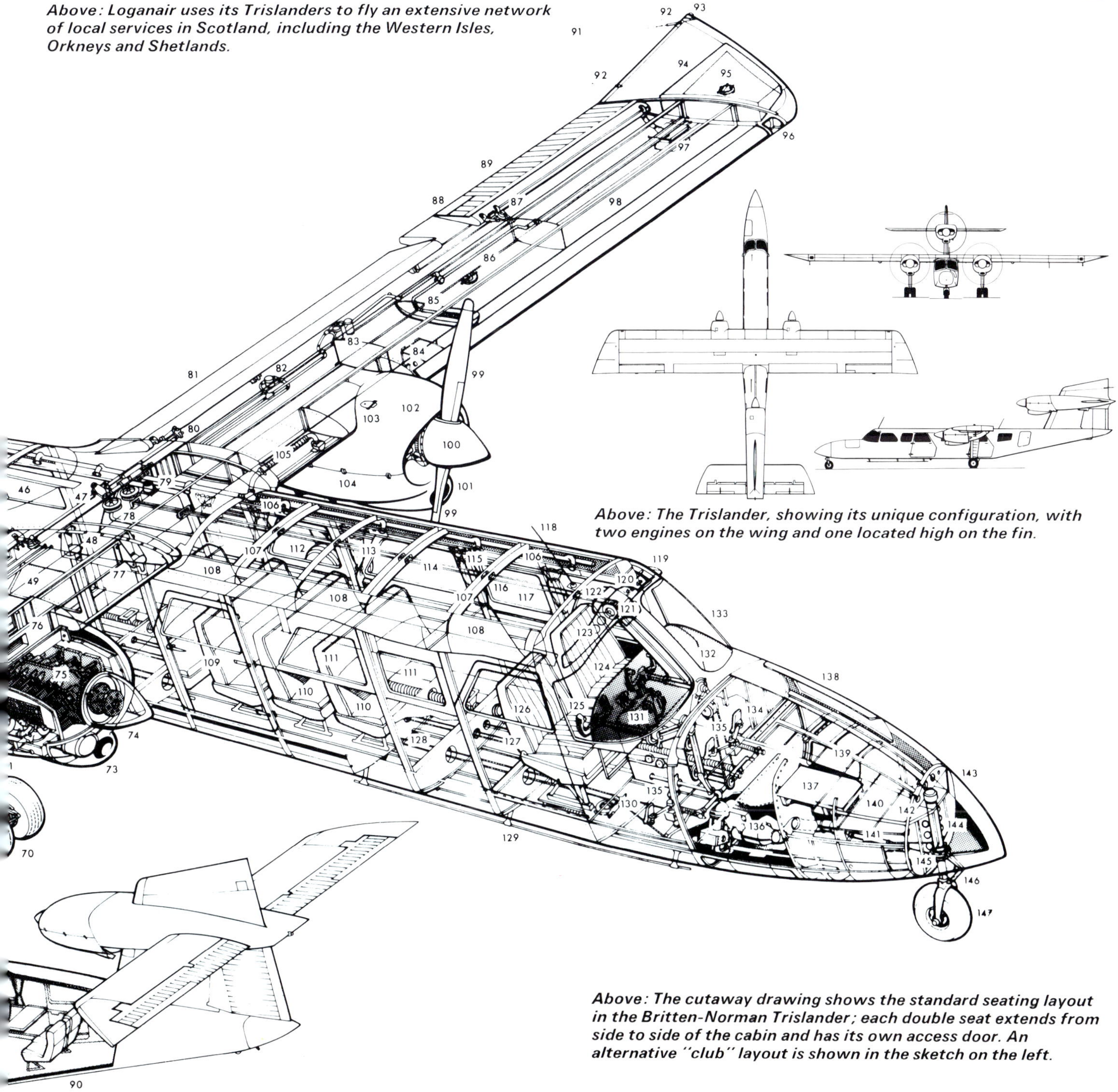

Above: The Trislander, showing its unique configuration, with two engines on the wing and one located high on the fin.

Above: The cutaway drawing shows the standard seating layout in the Britten-Norman Trislander; each double seat extends from side to side of the cabin and has its own access door. An alternative "club" layout is shown in the sketch on the left.

Britten-Norman Islander

United Kingdom

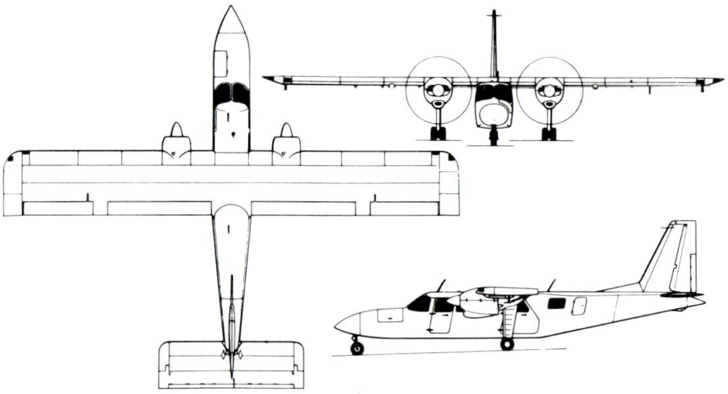

Above: *Islander with lengthened nose and standard wing-tips; extended tips, containing extra fuel, are often fitted.*

The following specification relates to the BN-2A-2:
Power Plant: Two 260hp Avco Lycoming O-540-E4C5 piston engines.
Performance: Max speed, 180mph (290km/h); typical cruise at 9,000ft (2750m), 168mph (270km/h); initial rate of climb, 1,250ft/min (6·35m/sec); service ceiling, 10,400ft (5013m); range at typical cruise speed, 800mls (1287km).
Weights: Basic operating, 3,738lb (1695kg); max take-off, 6,300lb (2857kg).
Dimensions: Span, 49ft 0in (14·94m); length, 35ft 7¾in (10·86m); height, 13ft 8¾in (4·18m); wing area, 325sq ft (30·19m²).

Launched into production in 1966 by one of Britain's smallest aircraft manufacturing companies, the Islander became, in mid-1974, the best-selling British multi-engined commercial aircraft when it surpassed the sales record of the de Havilland Dove. Announced sales of 550 Islanders at that time were supplemented by an order for 100 more for part-assembly by the embryonic aircraft industry in the Republic of the Philippines, leaving no doubt that the Islander would handsomely exceed the Dove's production total of 540 and by early 1978 the sales total had passed 750 with many more in prospect as the result of the introduction of new versions.

The concept of the Islander as an extremely simple, light twin-engined transport for the third-level and commuter airlines—a modern version of the D.H.89 Rapide, in fact — grew out of the requirements of one specific operator, Cameroon Air Transport, for a twin with "more than six seats", a good take-off performance, simple maintenance and low cost. The Britten-Norman company, with a 25 per cent interest in CAT, set about the design of a suitable aircraft, which was designated the BN-2 and, in its prototype form, was powered by two 210hp R-R Continental IO-360 engines, had a gross weight of 4,750lb (2155kg) and wing span of 45ft (13·7m). It first flew on 13 June 1965, being later modified to have 260hp Lycoming O-540-E engines, a span of 49ft (14·9m) and gross weight of 5,700lb (2585kg). In this revised form it flew on 17 December 1965 and was joined on 20 August 1966 by a second prototype of similar specification.

Production was launched at the company's Bembridge, Isle of Wight, factory, where the first production Islander flew on 24 April 1967. British certification was obtained on 10 August and initial deliveries were made on 13 and 15 August to Glosair and Loganair respectively. FAA Type Approval followed on 19 December with deliveries to the USA starting in January 1968. An unusual feature of the Islander was that "wall-to-wall" seating was adopted, access to the seat rows being obtained direct through doors alternating down each side of the fuselage; each seat accommodated two passengers, and one more could be carried alongside the pilot. Many optional interiors for cargo-carrying or special duties have also been developed.

Successive development of the Islander led to the introduction of a version with 300hp Lycoming IO-540K engines, first flown on 30 April 1970, a supercharged version with 270hp TIO-540-H engines, first flown on 30 April 1971, versions with Riley-Rajay superchargers on the standard O-540 engines, optional long-range versions with fuel carried in extended wing tips, increasing the span to 53ft (16·15m), and a so-called "stretched" version with a lengthened nose fairing to give extra baggage space and the cabin redesigned to carry two more passengers in the space previously used for baggage, this BN-2S version flying on 22 August 1972 but not being further developed.

Britten-Norman introduced a series of dash numbers to distinguish various of these developments, the basic BN-2A and the -1, -6, -7, -8 and -9 having 260hp engines, the -2 and -3 having 300hp engines and the -10 and -11 having the TIO engine (only a single BN-2A-10 being built, and no examples of the -11). The odd-numbered versions had the long-range wing-tip tanks, while the even-numbered variants did not. The -6 and -7 introduced new camber on the wing leading edges to meet US certification standards and the -8 and -9 had drooped flaps in addition, to meet FAR single-engined climb requirements at increased gross weights. An increase in gross weight to 6,600lb (2993kg) was noted by the allocation of 20-series numbers, the -20 to -23 having the 300hp IO-540-K1B5 engine and the -24 to -27 having the 260hp IO-540-E4C5. As with the earlier version, the odd-numbered types from -21 onwards have the long-range wing tips; the BN-2S-type lengthened nose is used on the -22 to -25 inclusive.

In 1967, Britten-Norman negotiated an agreement with the IRMA company in Rumania, permitting the latter to manufacture the Islander under licence and the first Rumanian-assembled example, using British-made components, flew on 4 August 1969 in Bucharest. Over 200 Islanders were to be built by IRMA initially, for sale through the Britten-Norman marketing organization. In August 1972, The Fairey Group acquired the whole share capital of Britten-Norman and in the course of 1973 production and assembly was progressively transferred from the UK to the Fairey factory at Gosselies in Belgium. However, the Fairey Group went into receivership late in 1977 and as the book went to press the receiver was negotiating the sale of the original Britten-Norman unit as a going concern.

In addition to developing new operational rôles for the Islander, such as crop spraying and fire fighting, Fairey Britten-Norman proceeded with the design of a version powered by 600shp Lycoming LTP101 turboprops and known as the BN-2A-40 (standard wing) or BN-2A-41 (long-range wing) Turbo-Islander. The prototype made its first flight on 6 April 1977 but a change of engine type was planned before the Turbo-Islander entered production. An amphibious version of the piston-engined Islander has been developed as the BN-2A-30 (standard) and BN-2A-31 (long-range).

Below: *A Britten-Norman Islander of Air Mahé, used to fly daily trips between Mahé and Praslin in the Seychelles.*

Boeing 747

USA

The following specification relates to the 747-200:

Power Plant: Four 43,500lb st (19,730kgp) Pratt & Whitney JT9D-3, 45,000lb st (20,410kgp) JT9D-3W, 45,500lb st (20,635kgp) JT9D-7, 47,000lb st (21,320kgp) JT9D-7W or 47,670lb st (21,620kgp) JT9D-7A turbofans.

Performance: Max speed, 608mph (978km/h) at 30,000ft (9150m); best economy cruise, 580mph (935km/h); cruise ceiling, 45,000ft (13,705m); no-reserves range with max payload, 4,985mls (8023km); range with max fuel, FAR reserves, 7,090mls (11,410km).

Weights: Basic operating, 367,900lb (166,876kg); max payload, 158,600lb (71,940kg); max take-off, 785,000lb (356,070kg).

Dimensions: Span, 195ft 8in (59·64m), length, 231ft 4in (70·51m); height, 63ft 5in (19·33m); wing area, 5,500sq ft (511m^2).

The first of the "wide-body" jet transports, and the largest airliner put into service to date, the Boeing 747 was developed as a logical extrapolation of the Boeing 707 concept, the basis of the design being Boeing's project work to meet a USAF requirement for a large logistics transport (eventually satisfied by the Lockheed C-5A). A number of possible configurations were studied, including mid-wing, double-bubble layouts, but the project eventually chosen as the most promising was essentially an enlargement of the 707, with a fuselage providing a long, single passenger deck with sufficient width to permit up to 10 seats across, and two aisles; the flight deck was located on a higher level, with space for a small passenger lounge behind.

By 1965, Boeing had defined the concept for this very large airliner, with accommodation for up to 500 passengers (but about 350 as a more typical load in mixed-class configuration) and a range of about 4,000 miles (6437km) with full payload. Gross weight was expected to be 680,000lb (308,440kg) and the new transport, which was inevitably designated Boeing 747 in continuation of the Boeing family of jet airliners, was to be powered by the completely new Pratt & Whitney JT9D turbofan rated initally at 41,000lb st (18,600kgp) and mounted in underwing pods.

The launching order for the 747, which quickly became known as the "Jumbo Jet", was placed by Pan American on 14 April 1966 and was for 25 aircraft with deliveries to start in 1969. Boeing waited for more orders to be placed before actually committing the type to production, however, this step being taken on 25 July after Lufthansa and JAL had each ordered three. Right from the start, Boeing planned to offer all-cargo and convertible versions, with upward-hinged nose to permit straight-in loading, but the introduction of these versions was, in the event, delayed because of difficulties encountered with the initial passenger versions, particularly related to structure weight growth and JT9D problems. The first flight of the 747 was made at Everett, where a new production facility for the "Jumbo" had been established, on 9 February 1969, by which time 27 airlines had ordered 160 examples of the new transport. FAA Type Approval was obtained on 30 December 1969 and Pan American launched service with the 747 across the North Atlantic on 21 January 1970; JT9D-3 engines rated at 43,500lb st (19,730kgp) had replaced the original -1 engines used at the start of flight tests and the certificated gross weight was 710,000lb (322,050kg). Considerable difficulties with the engine prevented the 747 from being fully exploited for some months, until the modified JT9D-3A engine was introduced; eventually, the 45,000lb st (20,410kgp) JT9D-3W, the 45,500lb st (20,635kgp) JT9D-7 and 47,000lb st (21,320kgp) JT9D-7W became available for use in the 747 and the permitted gross weight grew to 735,000lb (333,390kg) for some versions of the basic model.

A second variant had been announced, meanwhile, on 25 November 1967, to provide greater range but with no change in overall dimensions or passenger capacity. Extra fuel was carried in the wing centre section and structural changes were made, together with changes in the undercarriage design, to permit certification at a gross weight of 775,000lb (351,540kg), with JT9D-7 or -7W engines – later increased to 785,000lb (356,070kg) when the 47,670lb st (21,620kgp) JT9D-7A became available in 1973. The uprated 747 was introduced as the 747B but Boeing later adopted its customary designation system, the early models being 747-100 and the high gross weight version the 747-200. First flight of the Boeing 747-200 was made on 11 October 1970 and after certification on 23 December 1970 the type entered service with KLM early in 1971.

The first example of the 747 with hinged nose for freight loading flew on 30 November 1971 and entered service with Lufthansa on 19 April 1972 following certification on 7 March 1972, with the designation 747F as a pure freighter. A year later, on 23 March 1973, the first convertible variant, also with hinged nose, made its first flight and this entered service with World Airways after certification as the 747C on 24 April. Only Series 200 airframes were offered in F or C configurations. Another convertible/freighter option offered by Boeing comprises a side-loading freight door in the fuselage aft of the wing, usually without the nose-loading feature and known as the 747 Combi. The first such aircraft was delivered to Sabena in 1974 and by early 1977, more than 40 747s had been delivered with, or modified to have, the side freight door. The 200th 747 was delivered on 23 April 1973, this being a 747-200 for El Al with JT9D-7A engines which was also the first at a new high gross weight of 775,000lb (351,530kg).

Also in 1973, Boeing introduced the 747SR, a variant for high-density short-haul operations – primarily in Japan. Structural changes were made to permit a higher frequency of take-offs and landings, with restricted gross weight, JT9D-7AW engines and 747-100 fuel capacity. There was no dimensional change, and Japan Air Lines, the only airline to order this variant, had its aircraft arranged to accommodate 498 passengers – the largest capacity in use on a regular basis anywhere. Services began on the Tokyo–Okinawa route on 9 October 1973 and these aircraft operate at gross weights of 570,000lb (258,780kg) or (two aircraft only), 610,000lb (276,940kg).

To provide an aircraft suitable for use on very long ranges with only modest traffic, Boeing launched the 747SP (Special Performance) in August 1973, the first order being placed a month later by Pan American. The first variant to have different dimensions from the original 747, the SP has a fuselage shortened by 48ft (14·6m) to give a typical mixed-class

continued on page 54 ►

Below: The Boeing 747 is shown here in its -270C version, in the eye-catching livery of Iraqi Airways.

accommodation of 288 and maximum high-density layouts for 360. Other changes include lighter-weight structure in parts of the wing, fuselage and landing gear, a taller fin and rudder with double-hinged rudder and new trailing edge flaps. Gross weight is 663,000lb (301,000kg) and with JT9D-7A turbofans the 747SP offers improved take-off performance, higher cruising speeds and a full-payload range of nearly 6,900mls (11,000km). The first 747SP flew on 4 July 1975 and after certification on 4 February 1976, Pan American put the type into service in May. Six airlines had ordered 20 examples of the 747SP by early 1977.

To permit further weight growth of the 747, Pratt & Whitney, General Electric and Rolls-Royce offered advanced models of their respective large turbofans for use in variants delivered in 1975 and beyond. Boeing converted its orginal prototype to fly with 51,000lb st (32,135kgp) General Electric CF6-50D engines, flight testing starting on 26 June 1973, and the first airline order was announced in 1974 when KLM ordered two with 52,500lb st (23,850kgp) CF6 50Es and side loading freight doors and convertible interiors for up to 428 passengers, or 200 passengers plus 110,000lb (49,895kg) of freight. This variant was certificated at a gross weight of 800,000lb (362,874kg) and a similar weight was to become available in 1975 for variants powered by the 52,000lb st (23,586kgp) JT9D-70, the first examples of which were ordered by Seaboard World in 747F configuration.

During 1975, British Airways ordered the first examples of the 747 to be powered by 50,000lb st (22,700kgp) Rolls-Royce RB.211-524Bs and this variant made its first flight on 3 September 1976. The RB.211 version entered service with British Airways in 1977 at a gross weight of 800,000lb (363,200kg), to be increased to 817,000lb (372,918kg) when the 53,000lb st (24,062kg) RB.211-524D became available.

By early 1978, Boeing had sold some 364 Boeing 747s including 168 of the original Series 100s and four for the USAF.

Right: The cutaway drawing depicts the Boeing 747-200B with Rolls-Royce RB.211-524 engines, as used by British Airways. Alternative versions have JT9D or CF6-50 engines and there are numerous customer variants with different fuel capacities and gross weights.

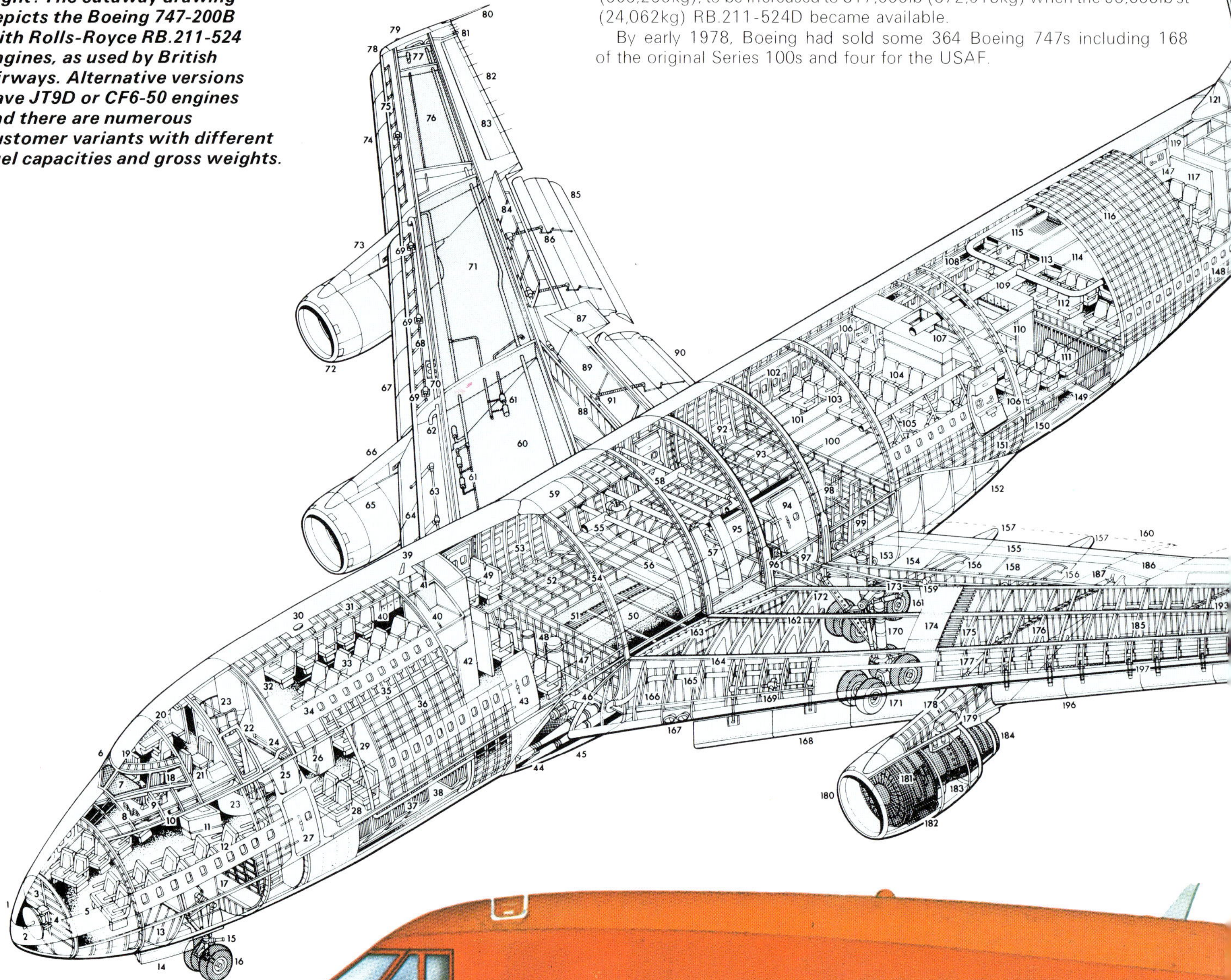

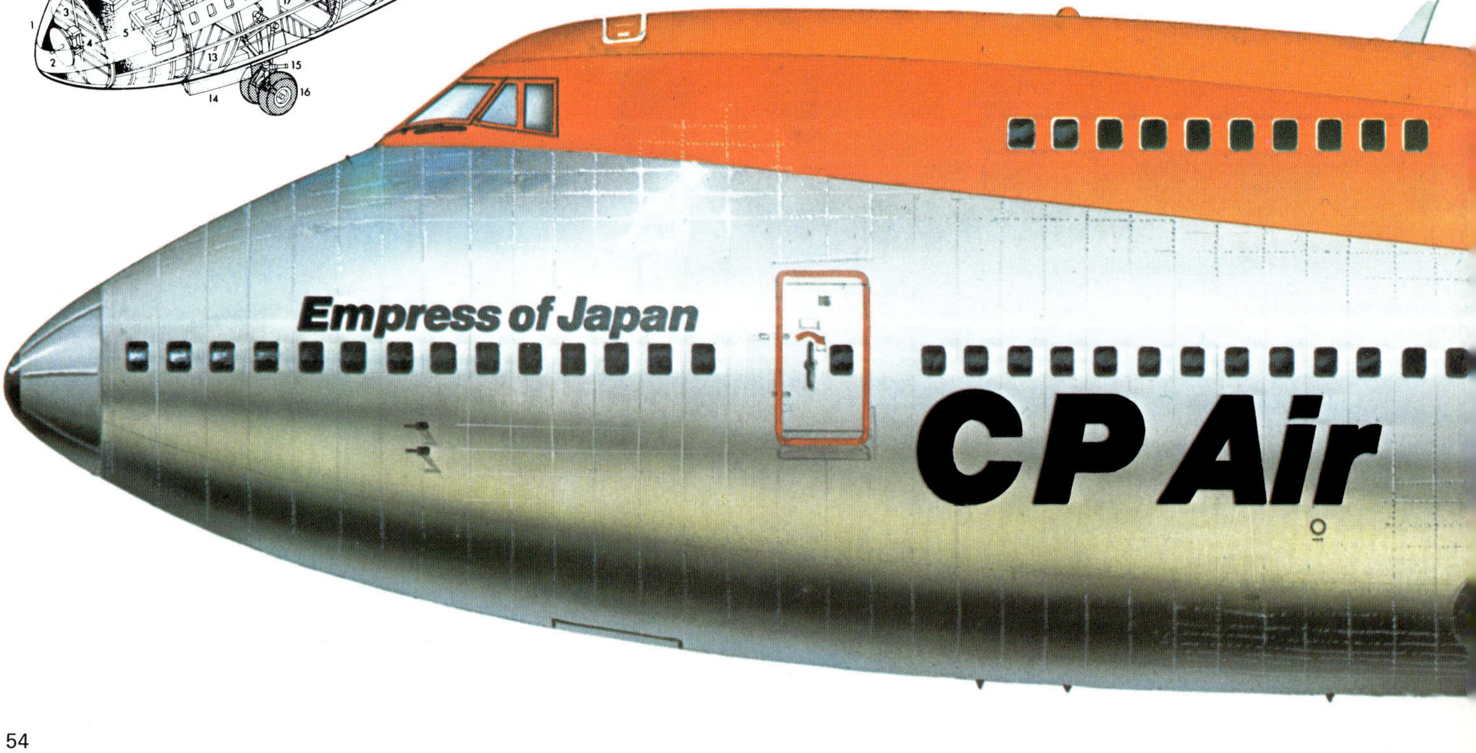

ype forward cabin
No 1
lass seats
dividing bulkhead
ollision light
roof construction
deck toilet
deck seating, up to
ssengers
w panel
nditioning supply ducts
rd fuselage
uction
ge pallet containers
rd under-floor
compartment
unications aerial
deck galley
rolley elevator
deck forward galley
passenger door, port
arboard
nditioning system

root fairing
nditioning plant
spar bulkhead
water tanks
rd economy-class
typically 141 seats
centre section fuel
capacity 17,000 US
4,345 l)
e section stringer
uction
floor construction
age frame and stringer
uction
fuselage frame
stribution duct
nditioning cross-feed

to distribution ducts
ned main frame
te navigation aerial
oard wing inboard
ank, capacity 12,300
al (46,555 l)
umps
e bleed-air supply
er flap operating

rd Krueger flap
oard inner engine
oard inner engine

ng edge Krueger flap
ents
er flap drive
anism
er flap motors
elling panel
oard wing outboard
ank, capacity 4,420
al (16,730 l)
oard outer engine
oard outer engine

oard Krueger flap
ents
er flap drive
anism
ded range fuel tank,
ity 800 US gal
3 l) each wing
tank
oard wing tip
ation light
aerial boom
vent
dischargers
oard, low-speed,
n

84 Outboard spoilers
85 Outboard slotted flaps
86 Flap drive mechanism
87 Inboard, high-speed aileron
88 Trailing edge beam
89 Inboard spoilers
90 Inboard slotted flap
91 Flap drive mechanism
92 Centre fuselage construction
93 Starboard undercarriage bay housing
94 No 3 passenger door
95 Wing-mounted main undercarriage bay
96 Flap drive motors
97 Undercarriage beam
98 Fuselage-mounted main undercarriage bay
99 Main undercarriage jack
100 Floor panels
101 Seat rails
102 Cabin window trim panels
103 Centre cabin economy class seating, typically 82 passengers
104 Nine-abreast seating
105 Air distribution ducts
106 No 4 passenger door, port and starboard
107 Centre cabin galley
108 Overhead baggage racks (with doors)
109 Main air supply duct
110 Rear cabin galley
111 Rear cabin seating, typically 114 passengers
112 Economy-class seating
113 Overhead baggage racks
114 Cabin roof panels
115 Control cable runs
116 Rear fuselage construction
117 Rear cabin seats
118 Rear cabin toilets
119 Wardrobes
120 Rear pressure dome bulkhead
121 Fin root fairing
122 Starboard tailplane
123 Static dischargers
124 Starboard elevator
125 Fin leading edge construction
126 Fin spar construction
127 Fin tip fairing
128 VOR aerial
129 Static dischargers
130 Upper rudder segment
131 Lower rudder segment
132 Rudder jacks
133 Tailcone fairing
134 APU exhaust
135 Auxiliary power unit (APU)
136 Port elevator inner segment
137 Port elevator outer segment
138 Static dischargers
139 Tailplane construction
140 Elevator jacks
141 Tailplane sealing plate
142 Aft fuselage frames
143 Fin attachment
144 Tailplane centre section
145 Moving tailplane jack
146 APU air duct
147 No 5 passenger door, port and starboard
148 Rear fuselage window panel
149 Rear under-floor freight hold
150 Freight and baggage pallet container

151
152
153
154
155
156
157
158
159
160
161
162
163
164
165
166
167
168
169
170
171
172
173
174
175
176
177
178
179
180
181
182
183
184
185
186
187
188
189
190
191
192
193
194
195
196
197
198
199
200
201
202
203
204
205
206
207
208
209
210
211
212
213
214

Above: The short-bodied Boeing 747SP provides very long range with reduced passenger accommodation.

Above: Cargo versions of the Boeing 747 have no windows in the fuselage, and a hinged nose for straight-in loading.

Left: Boeing has for many years placed the very greatest emphasis on flight-deck design, and it is no exaggeration to claim that the Boeing philosophy regarding up front area has made the company a leader in the actual design of new transport aircraft by many years. Jetliner builders, with Boeing in the forefront, have already spent many years in detailed design of flight decks for the airliners of 1985–2010. The 747 still bears a family resemblance to the flight deck of the 707, and the selected configuration of one vast main deck with a separate flight deck on an upper level resulted in a "cab section" no bigger than that of the earlier four-engined jetliner. The windshields, made in England, are totally new and have great size, acute sweepback and full electric anti-icing. In the roof are the expected hydraulics, fire, engine-start, lighting and similar panels, while the main pilot panels and consoles are as immaculate as the handling of the 747 itself. Prominent panels include the autopilot (with auto-set flight conditions) along the coaming, radar displays beside each pilot's outer knee, and the four throttles with stab-trim (tailplane) and speedbrakes on their left and flaps on the right.

Top: The Boeing 737, as smallest member of the family of Boeing jetliners, is used by some 71 operators worldwide. This is a Model 737-2M9 of Zambia Airways.

Above left: Southwest Airlines is an intrastate operator flying only within Texas; its Boeing 737-2H4s have an eye-catching orange, red and ochre livery.

Above right: One of Brazil's oldest airlines, Cruzeiro was founded in 1927; fifty years later its fleet included six of these Boeing 727-2C3 twin-jets.

3 Glide-slope aerial
4 Forward pressure bulkhead
5 Instrument panel shroud
6 Windscreen sections
7 Sliding side windows
8 Eyebrow windows
9 First officer's seat
10 Overhead panel
11 Centre console
12 Captain's seat
13 Flight kit stowage
14 Circuit breaker panel
15 Nosewheel doors
16 Towing lug
17 Twin nosewheels
18 Torsion links
19 Steering cylinders
20 Lock
21 Drag strut
22 Fixed side windows
23 Second observer's seat (optional)
24 First observer's seat (stowable)
25 Wall circuit breaker panel
26 Dome light
27 Flight deck door
28 Forward galley
29 Service door (starboard) 30in x 65in
30 Coat closet
31 Forward toilet
32 Forward entry door (port) 34in x 72in
33 Airstairs
34 Electrical/electronics bay
35 Underfloor forward freight hold
36 Cabin windows
37 14-seat First Class cabin configuration (38in seat pitch)
38 Inter-class bulkhead
39 Engine air intake
40 Air-conditioning pre-cooler
41 Integral wing fuel tank (Tank No. 2)
42 Dry bay
43 Overwing filler
44 Leading-edge slats (extended)
45 Vent surge tank
46 Starboard navigation light (flashing)
47 Starboard navigation light (white)
51 Ground spoiler/lift dumper (outer)
52 Wing spoilers (two segments)
53 Ground spoiler/lift dumper (inner)
54 Triple-slotted flap (inner section)
58 VHF communications antenna
59 HF communications antenna (optional)
60 Starboard escape hatch frame surround
61 Forged alloy fuselage main frames (3)
64 Centre-section fuel bladder cells (3)
65 Fuel pump
66 Centre-section floor beams
67 Port escape hatch frame
68 Hydraulics service bay (starboard mainwheel well)
69 Pressure-bearing floor structure
70 Insulation blankets
71 Overhead air distribution duct
72 Flat cabin ceiling sections
73 Passenger conditioned air
74 Overhead in-flight luggage stowage bins
75 Aerial
76 88-seat Tourist Class cabin configuration (34in seat pitch)
77 Aft bulkhead
78 Aft service door (starboard) 30in x 65in
79 Aft galley
80 Fin forward spar/pressure bulkhead attachment

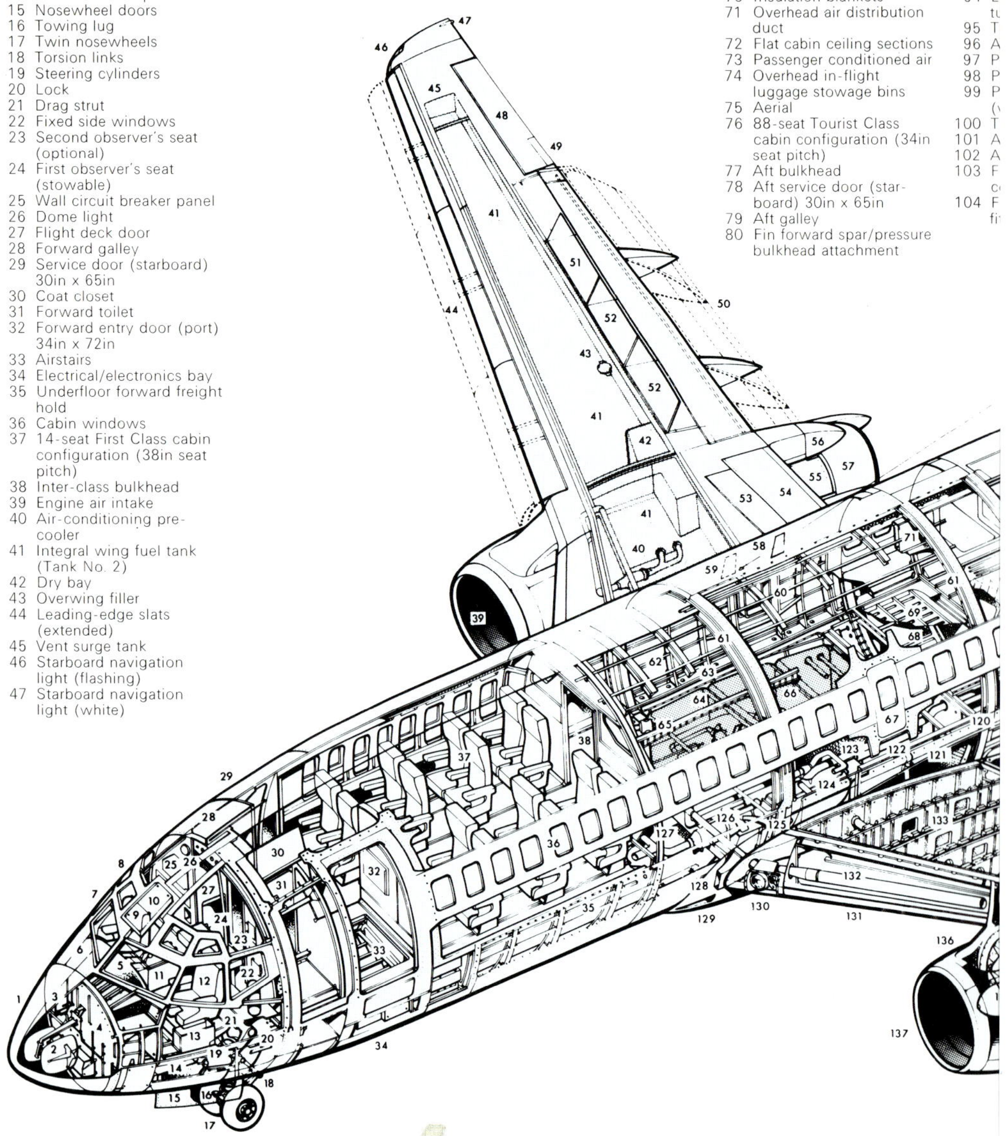

Spain

Power Plant: Two 776ehp Garrett-AiResearch TPE331-5-251C props.
Performance: Max speed, 230mph (370km/h) at 12,000ft (cruising speed, 196mph (315km/h) at 12,000ft (3660m); rate c 1,800ft/min (9·1m/sec); service ceiling, 26,700ft (8140m); range, (480km) with max payload.
Weights: Empty equipped, 8,609lb (3905kg); max payload, (2000kg); max take-off weight, 13,890lb (6300kg).
Dimensions: Span, 62ft 4in (19·0m); length, 49ft 10½in (15·20m) 20ft 8in (6·30m); wing area, 430·6sq ft (40·0m²).

The Aviocar was developed by the Spanish company Construccione nauticas SA (CASA) primarily to meet Spanish Air Force requirem a multi-rôle transport, and its initial construction and production wa guise, although civil applications were in prospect from the start of d high-wing monoplane of simple and rugged construction, the C.212 conventional lines for a light transport, with the cabin providing a uninterrupted box shape to which straight-in access can be obta means of a rear loading ramp.

Powered by 776shp Garrett-AiResearch TPE331 turboprops, tw types of the Aviocar were built, making their initial flights on 26 Ma 23 October 1971. Production was then launched against Spanish A contracts, the Aviocar being adopted to replace such elderly transp in service as the Junkers Ju 52/3m, Douglas DC-3 and CASA-20 As well as serving as a 16-paratroop carrier, the military C.212 c adapted as an ambulance, photo-survey aircraft, freighter or crew The first production aircraft flew on 17 November 1972.

As the C.212C, the Aviocar has been marketed as a 19-seat pa transport for civil operation, initial sales being made to Pertamin donesia for operation by its subsidiary Pelita Air Service. CASA a cluded an agreement with the PT Nurtania company in Djakarta the latter undertook to assemble Aviocars in Indonesia for supply t mers throughout the Far East. Initial civil Aviocars were of C standard, having a gross weight of 12,500lb (5675kg) but this creased to 13,890lb (6300kg) in the C.212CB for operators who have to observe the FAA weight limit for third-level services, and a increase to 14,332lb (6500kg) was in hand during 1977.

Below: First flown in 1971, the CASA Aviocar has sold steadily and, helped by military orders, the order book stood at about 130 by mid-1978. Initial civil sales were made to Pertamina and Pelita Air Service in Indonesia.

Below: The CASA 212 Aviocar, developed in Spain as a small general purpose transport, with particular applications in military rôles but some civil customers also.

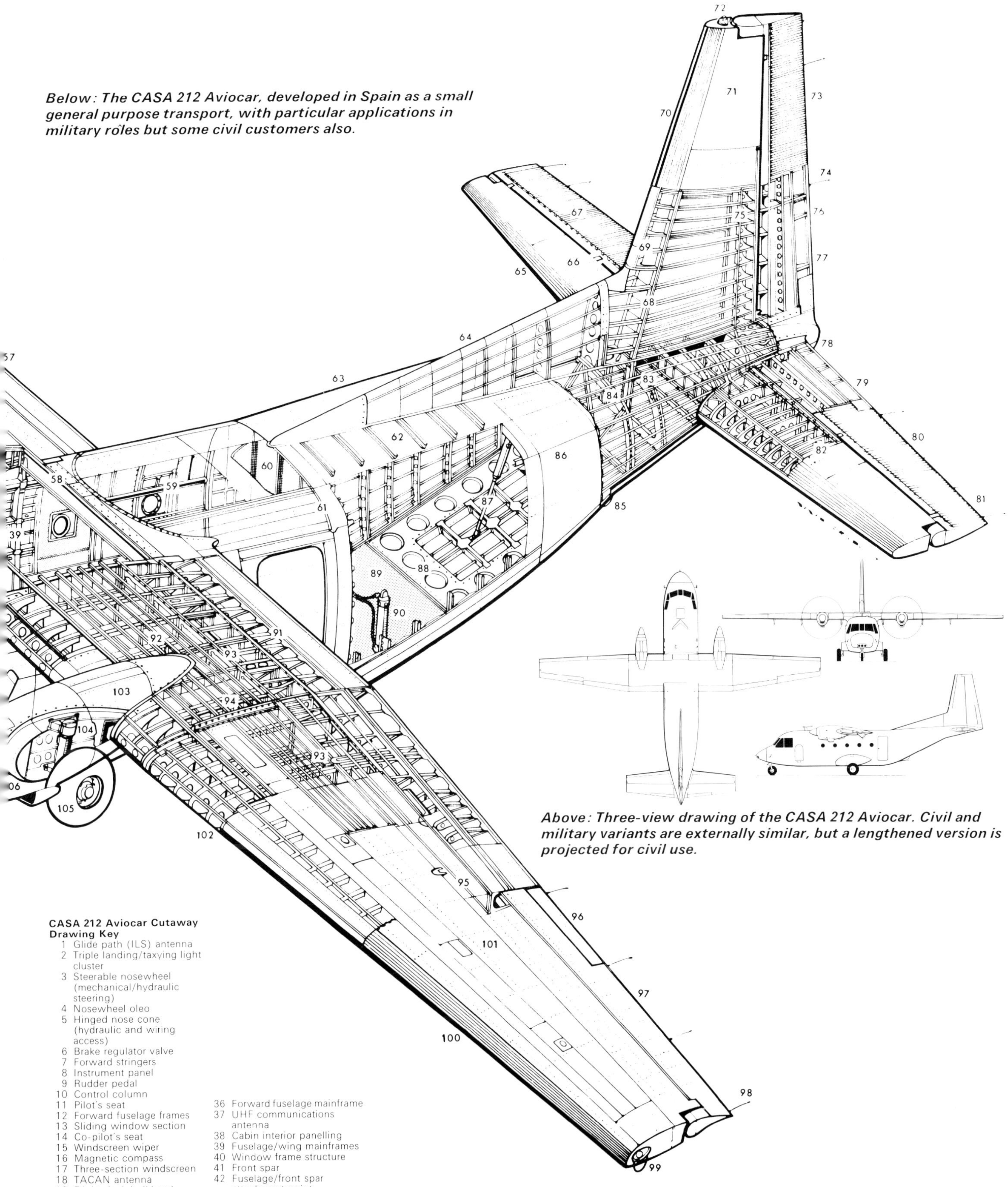

Above: Three-view drawing of the CASA 212 Aviocar. Civil and military variants are externally similar, but a lengthened version is projected for civil use.

CASA 212 Aviocar Cutaway Drawing Key

1 Glide path (ILS) antenna
2 Triple landing/taxying light cluster
3 Steerable nosewheel (mechanical/hydraulic steering)
4 Nosewheel oleo
5 Hinged nose cone (hydraulic and wiring access)
6 Brake regulator valve
7 Forward stringers
8 Instrument panel
9 Rudder pedal
10 Control column
11 Pilot's seat
12 Forward fuselage frames
13 Sliding window section
14 Co-pilot's seat
15 Windscreen wiper
16 Magnetic compass
17 Three-section windscreen
18 TACAN antenna
19 Flight deck bulkhead
20 Upper forward emergency exit
21 VHF communications/navigation antenna
22 Toilet compartment
23 Forward cabin door
24 Electronics bay
25 Flight deck door
26 External electrical connection
27 Anti-collision beacon
28 Marker (ILS) and ADF antenna under fuselage
29 Fuselage frames
30 Seat rail
31 Cabin windows
32 Cabin air intake
33 Main compartment
34 Sandwich panel floor with honeycomb core
35 Fuselage stringers
36 Forward fuselage mainframe
37 UHF communications antenna
38 Cabin interior panelling
39 Fuselage/wing mainframes
40 Window frame structure
41 Front spar
42 Fuselage/front spar attachment point
43 Rear spar
44 Main wing torsion box
45 Oil cooler intake
46 Hartzell LHC B3TN-5C three-blade constant-speed airscrew
47 Garrett-AiResearch TPE 331-5 251C turboprop
48 Wing skin support stringers
49 Wing centre/outer section joint
50 Gravity fuel fillers
51 Integral fuel tanks in outer wing boxes (296 Imp gal—1345 l total capacity)
52 De-icing boot
53 All-metal cantilever wing
54 Static dischargers
55 Starboard aileron
56 Starboard outer double-slotted flap
57 Starboard inner double-slotted flap
58 Auxiliary rear spar
59 Emergency exit
60 Rear cabin bulkhead (passenger configuration)
61 Aft fuselage mainframe
62 Fuselage frames
63 Aluminium alloy skinning
64 Dorsal fin
65 De-icing boot
66 Starboard tailplane
67 Corrugated-skin elevator
68 Tailfin forward spar
69 HF communications antenna
70 De-icing boot
71 Tailfin skinning
72 Anti-collision beacon
73 Corrugated-skin rudder
74 Static dischargers
75 Tailfin rear spar
76 Rudder construction
77 Rudder tab
78 Rear navigation light
79 Elevator tab
80 Corrugated-skin elevator
81 Static dischargers
82 Two-spar tailplane construction
83 Canted fuselage frame (in alignment with fin spar)
84 Fuselage/tail section frame
85 IFF antenna
86 Aluminium alloy skinning
87 Ventral ramp/door actuator
88 Ventral loading ramp/door
89 Cargo ramp
90 Cargo ramp actuator
91 Flap construction
92 Main wing torsion box
93 Flap runners
94 Multibolt centre/outer section joint
95 Auxiliary rear spar (terminating at outer flap)
96 Aileron tab (port only)
97 Port aileron
98 Static dischargers
99 Port navigation light (with guard)
100 De-icing boot
101 All-metal cantilever wing
102 Leading-edge ribs
103 Hinged nacelle cowling
104 Mainwheel oleo
105 Port mainwheel
106 Fixed undercarriage sponson

Canadair CL-44 (and Yukon)

Canada

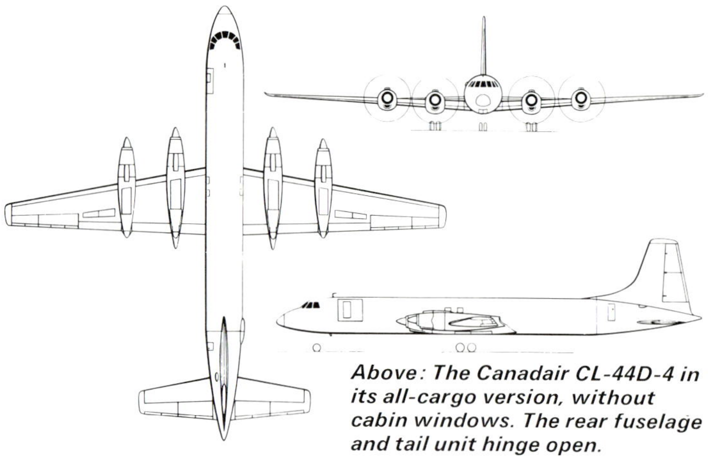

Above: The Canadair CL-44D-4 in its all-cargo version, without cabin windows. The rear fuselage and tail unit hinge open.

The following specification relates to the CL-44D-4:
Power Plant: Four 5,730hp Rolls-Royce Tyne 515/10 turboprops.
Performance: Cruising speed, 386mph (621km/h) at 20,000ft (6100m) at a weight of 190,000lb (86,180kg); range with max payload, 3,260mls (5245km); range with max fuel, 5,587mls (8990km) with payload of 35,564lb (16,132kg).
Weights: Operating weight empty, 88,952lb (40,348kg); max payload, 63,272lb (28,725kg); max take-off, 210,000lb (95,250kg); max landing, 165,000lb (74,843kg).
Dimensions: Span, 142ft $3\frac{1}{2}$in (43·37m); length, 136ft $10\frac{3}{4}$in (41·73m); height, 38ft 8in (11·80m); wing area, 2,075sq ft (192·76m²).

One of the largest turboprop transports in service, and among the largest ever developed specifically as a freighter, the Canadair CL-44 was a derivative of the Bristol Britannia design (previously described). Origin of the design was an RCAF requirement in 1956 for a long-range troop and freight transport, to meet which Canadair proposed several derivatives of the Britannia, for which the company already held a licence.

Among the alternatives proposed were versions with Wright R-3350 piston radials, Pratt & Whitney T34, Bristol Orion or Rolls-Royce Tyne turboprops, using a lengthened, Britannia-type fuselage and increased-span wing. The variant selected by the RCAF in 1958 was to have had Orion engines. When further work on this engine was cancelled in the UK a few months later, however, the Canadair transport was redesigned around four Tyne engines, then being designated CL-44D. The first of 12 built for military use was flown at Montreal on 15 November 1959, and deliveries were completed in 1961.

With the CL-44D established in production, Canadair marketed a variant specifically for commercial use, offering as a special feature in this version a hinged tail unit and rear fuselage. This permitted straight-in loading of large freight items or pallets and the CL-44D-4, as this version was known, became the first production aircraft to have this feature. A company-owned prototype flew on 16 November 1960 and initial orders were placed by Flying Tiger, Seaboard World and Slick, for a total of 17. The first commercial delivery was made to Flying Tiger on 31 May 1961; Seaboard received its first on 20 June 1961 and Slick its first on 17 January 1962. In the hands of these three companies, the CL-44D-4s operated scheduled and cargo flights carrying miscellaneous loads up to a maximum of 66,000lb (29,940kg), with the floor stressed for loads up to 300lb/sq ft (1465kg/m²).

Subsequent production brought the total of CL-44D-4s built to 27, with additional deliveries being made to the same three companies and to Loftleider of Iceland, which used the type as a 178-passenger transport on transatlantic services. To meet the latter's requirement for an aircraft of even larger capacity, Canadair developed the CL-44J with a 15-ft (4·6-m) fuselage extension and provision for up to 214 passengers. The last production CL-44D-4 was converted to the new standard and flew for the first time on 8 November 1965. Three others were converted subsequently, all for Loftleider, and were known as Canadair 400s in service. They were later transferred to the Luxembourg company Cargolux for use as pure freighters.

In second-hand deals, several other operators acquired CL-44s, and in 1977 one of the major users was Transmeridian, which also controlled British Air Ferries. Transmeridian then had seven CL-44Ds in service and had also acquired the sole example of the Canadair CL-44-O, an outsize cargo carrier comprising a CL-44D airframe with a modified fuselage having increased fuselage diameter, in style similar to the Aero Spacelines Guppy (separately described). This conversion, by Conroy Aircraft, first flew on 26 November 1969, and was produced by removing the upper half of the fuselage and building on a new pressurized structure that increased the maximum inside diameter to 13ft 11in (4·24m). The swing tail feature was retained.

The Canadian Armed Forces began to dispose of its CL-44D fleet in 1973 and several of these aircraft, sometimes known by their military name of Yukon, have been purchased for commercial use as freighters. They are distinguished from the CL-44D-4s by having large side-loading doors ahead of and aft of the wing, and they lack the swing tail feature.

Left: A Cargolux Canadair CL-44D, showing easy loading of freight through the hinged rear fuselage.

Below: Cargolux CL-44Ds had cabin windows and could carry over 200 passengers but were usually operated only as freighters.

Convair 240, 340, 440
USA

The following specification relates to the Convair 440:
Power Plant: Two 2,500hp Pratt & Whitney R-2800-CB16 or -CB17 piston radials.
Performance: Max cruising speed, 300mph (483km/h) at 13,000ft (3962m); best economy cruise, 289mph (465km/h) at 20,000ft (6100m); initial rate of climb, 1,260ft/min (6·4m/sec); service ceiling, 24,900ft (7590m); range with max payload, 285mls (459km); range with max fuel, 1,930mls (3106km).
Weights: Basic operating, 33,314lb (15,110kg); max payload, 12,836lb (5820kg); max take-off, 49,700lb (22,544kg).
Dimensions: Span, 105ft 4in (32·12m); length, 81ft 6in (24·84m); height, 28ft 2in (8·59m); wing area, 920sq ft (85·5m²).

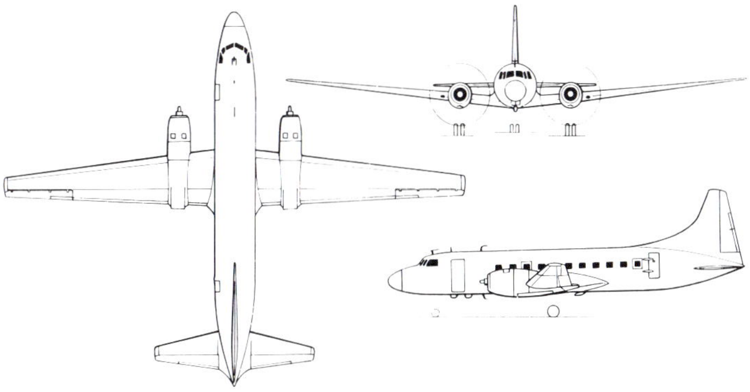

***Above:** A three-view of the Convair 440 in its standard production version, with weather radar in a lengthened nose.*

In view of the success enjoyed by the Douglas DC-3 in the years immediately preceding World War II, it was natural that airlines and manufacturers alike should be interested in the concept of a "DC-3 replacement" for use immediately after the war. A specification for such an aeroplane was set out by American Airlines early in 1945, for use on routes of up to about 1,000mls (1600km) in length to complement the four-engine types becoming available for the longer hauls.

Negotiations between American and Convair led the latter company to go ahead with construction of its first commercial airliner, the Model 110. Powered by 2,100hp Pratt & Whitney R-2800 radial engines, it provided accommodation for 30 passengers and was first flown on 8 July 1946 at San Diego. Before that event, however, American had decided that a somewhat larger aircraft was required, and placed an order with Convair for 75 of the Model 240 design, based on the prototype Model 110. No prototype of the 240 was built as such, production jigs and tools being used from the outset and the first aircraft being flown on 16 March 1947. The overall dimensions of the 240 – which retained the same power plant – were somewhat larger than those of the 110, and passenger accommodation was increased to a basic 40 in single class, although the fuselage diameter was actually reduced by 4in (10cm) to keep drag down.

American Airlines put the Model 240, often known as the Convairliner, into service on 1 June 1948 and the type quickly settled down as a modern companion to the four-engined generation represented by the DC-4 and early models of the Constellation. Although the availability of large numbers of surplus DC-3s probably restricted the market for Convair 240s to some extent, the type sold well, with sales totalling 176 for airline use and another 39 for other customers – primarily the USAF which acquired it for use both as a transport (C-131) and a trainer (T-29). Individual customer configurations were identified by dash numbers, such as Model 240-1, Western Airlines; 240-8, Ethiopian; 240-14, Mohawk and so on. A few Convair 240s are still used in various parts of the world, together with larger numbers of the improved Model 340 and 440.

Convair set about to improve the basic Model 240 in 1951, and on 5 October in that year flew the first Convair 340 at San Diego. This was a straightforward "stretch" of the original design, with the fuselage lengthened by 4ft 6in (1·38m) and the wing area also increased to cope with the higher operating weights. The passenger accommodation was increased by one seat row, to a basic 44, and the use of uprated engines – 2,500hp R-2800-CB16 or -CB17 – resulted in a slightly improved performance. The first airline service by Convair 340 was flown on 28 March 1952 and production totalled 212 for airline use, plus 99 non-airline.

Further refinement of the Model 340 led to the appearance of the Model 440 Metropolitan in 1955: the prototype flew on 6 October, and the first production model on 15 December in that year. Having the same overall dimensions as the Model 340, the 440 had redesigned engine nacelles and other refinements to improve performance and passenger comfort. Seating capacity was eventually increased to a maximum of 52 as high-density arrangements became more acceptable, and most Convair 440s had nose radar, lengthening the fuselage by another 2ft 4in (0·70m).

The Convair 440 entered airline service, with Continental Airlines, in February 1956 and production totalled 153 for the airlines and 26 for other users. The name Metropolitan was used primarily for Convair 440s supplied to European airlines, several of which used the Convair series in substantial quantities prior to the introduction of turboprop equipment. Considerable quantities of Convairliners were still in service in the mid-seventies, primarily in North and South America in the hands of smaller airlines. Many had also been converted to have turboprop engines, as described on the next page.

***Right:** Great Lakes Airlines flies scheduled services with a fleet of Convair 440s (illustrated) and turboprop-engined Convair 580s.*

***Below:** Built for operation on the US domestic air routes, the Convair twins now fly only on secondary routes.*

Convair 580, 600, 640
USA

The following specification relates to the Convair 580:
Power Plant: Two 3,750shp Allison 501-D13H turboprops.
Performance: Cruising speed, 342mph (550km/h); range with max fuel, 2,866mls (4611km).
Weights: Max payload 8,870lb (4023kg); max take-off, 58,140lb (26,371kg).
Dimensions: Span, 105ft 4in (32·12m), length, 81ft 6in (24·84m); height, 29ft 2in (8·89m); wing area, 920sq ft (85·5m²).
The following specification relates to the Convair 640:
Power Plant: Two 3,025eshp Rolls-Royce Dart 542-4 turboprops.
Performance: Cruising speed, 300mph (482km/h); range with max payload, 1,230mls (1975km) at 15,000ft (4575m); range with max fuel, 1,950mls (3138km) at 15,000ft (4575m).
Weights: Basic operating, 30,275lb (13,732kg); max payload, 15,800lb (7167kg); max take-off, 55,000lb (24,950kg) or 57,000lb (25,855kg) if Model 440 with outer wing fuel and fuel dumping.
Dimensions: Span, 105ft 4in (32·12m); length, 81ft 6in (24·84m); height, 28ft 2in (8·59m); wing area, 920sq ft (85·5m²).

Over 230 examples of the Convair 240/340/440 family (see previous page) were later converted to have turboprop engines in one or other of three such programmes undertaken between 1955 and 1967. Although other piston-engined aircraft have also been converted to turboprop power, only the Convair achieved success on this scale – a tribute to the sound structural and engineering design of the basic aircraft that allowed it to be given a new lease of life.

The primary reason for converting Convair airframes in this way was to improve performance and operating economics and thus prolong the useful life of an ageing aircraft type. To investigate the possibilities, Convair flew a Model 240 with Allison T38 (501-A2) turboprops on 29 December 1950, this prototype being known as the Turboliner. The T38 was developed into the T56 for military use, and two Convair 340s were converted to have these engines (similar to the commercial 501-D13) as part of a USAF investigation into the value of turboprops for transport aircraft in general; designated YC-131C, the first of these flew on 29 June 1954.

The first conversion programme aimed specifically at airline applications was launched by the former UK engine company D Napier & Son, Ltd, in 1954. A Convair 340 with two of that company's 3,060ehp Eland NEl.1 turboprops flew on 9 February 1955, and six more conversions were made, entering service with Allegheny Airlines in the USA in July 1959 as Convair 540s. Production and development of the Eland was terminated in 1962, however, and these conversions reverted to their original piston-engined f or m. Canadair also built ten Canadair 540s (using Convair's original jigs) as CL-66B Cosmopolitans for the RCAF, with Eland engines and converted three others, two going into service for a time with Quebecair.

Next to appear was the Allison-Convair, sometimes also referred to as the Super Convair, and eventuall designated the Convair 580. This had two 3,750eshp Allison 501-D13 turboprops and the conversion work was done by Pacific Airmotive, first flight being made on 19 January 1960. FAA certification – started with one of the YC-131Cs – was obtained on 21 April 1960, followed by first delivery (to a corporate owner) on 6 May 1960 and first airline service (by Frontier) in June 1964. Of 130 Allison-Convairs converted, 110 were for airline use in the first instance, with Allegheny and Lake Central (subsequently merged under the former name) having a combined fleet of over 40 at one time. Other major airline users were Frontier,

Convair (General Dynamics) 990
USA

The following specification relates to the Convair 990A:
Power Plant: Four 16,050lb st (7280kgp) General Electric CJ805-23B turbofans.
Performance: Max level speed (M = 0·871), 615mph (990km/h) at 20,000ft (6100m) at a weight of 200,000lb (90,720kg); long-range cruising speed (Mach = 0·84), 556mph (895km/h) at 35,000ft (10,670m); service ceiling, 41,000ft (12,500m); range with max payload, 3,800mls (6115km); range with max fuel, 5,446mls (8770km).
Weights: Basic operating, 120,900lb (54,840kg); max payload, 26,440lb (11,992kg); max take-off, 253,000lb (114,760kg); max landing, 202,000lb (91,625kg).
Dimensions: Span, 120ft 0in (36·58m); length, 139ft 2½in (42·43m); height, 39ft 6in (12·04m); wing area, 2,250sq ft (209m²).

The Convair Division of General Dynamics became the third US manufacturer to enter the jet transport market when it launched the construction of a medium-range, high performance airliner in September 1956. By that date, Boeing and Douglas were already committed to the 707 and DC-8 respectively and Convair was seeking to retain a foothold in the commercial market, following its success with the Convair 240/340/440 family. The attempt proved an extremely expensive one for the company and after only limited development of the basic design, all civil aircraft production by Convair came to an end.

Market surveys during 1955 led Convair to choose an aircraft of smaller capacity (90 in mixed class, up to 124 high density), but higher performance than the Boeing and Douglas types, although of the same overall configuration. Powered by four General Electric CJ805 engines (versions of the military J79) it was intended to operate primarily on US domestic trunk routes, and the fuselage diameter was sufficient only for five-abreast seating, compared with the six-abreast arrangements in the 707 and DC-8.

Designed as the Model 22, the new transport was at first called the Convair Skylark, and then the Golden Arrow; when this name was in turn dropped, the appellation Convair 600 was chosen, derived from the cruising speed of 600mph plus: this speed expressed as feet per second led to the definitive name of Convair 880. The first flight was made on 27 January 1959 at San Diego, certification being obtained on 1 May 1960 and Delta inaugurating Convair 880 service later that month.

The Convair 880 achieved little sales success compared with the larger Boeing and Douglas jets and only 65 were built, including 17 Convair Model 31 or 880-M with extra fuel in the centre section and higher weights.

***Above:* This ex-airline Convair 990 is used by the American National Aeronautics and Space Agency as a flying laboratory.**

***Below:* Principal remaining operator of the Convair 990 by 1978 was Spantax, the Spanish holiday charter company.**

North Central and Avensa, all still using the Convair 580 in 1974, and SAHSA-Honduras, which acquired two second-hand.

Final turboprop programme for the Convair family comprised installation of the Rolls-Royce Dart 542 rated at 3,025eshp, this being the only programme in which Convair Division of General Dynamics was directly involved, offering kits or converted airframes. These conversions were at first referred to as the Convair 240D, 340D and 440D, but the 240D later became the Convair 600, while Dart-engined 340s or 440s became Convair 640s. Central Airlines initiated the programme by ordering 10 Convair 600s, first flight being made at San Diego on 20 May 1965; FAA certification was obtained on 18 November 1965 and the type entered service on 30 November. The Convair 640 was launched by orders placed by Caribair and Hawaiian Airlines; the type entered service with the former airline on 22 December 1965.

Texas International also bought a large fleet of Convair 600s and Air Algerie bought some Convair 640s. Through second-hand deals, Mandala in Indonesia acquired some 600s and Zantop and Pacific Western later acquired the Hawaiian and Caribair 640s. In all, 39 Convair 600s and 28 Convair 640s were converted and most were still in service in the mid 'seventies.

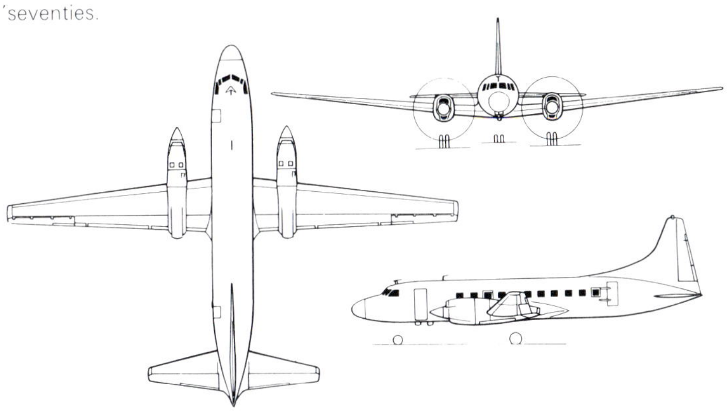

***Above:** The Convair 580, a conversion of the original piston-engined Convairliner with Allison 501D turboprops.*

***Left:** A Convair 580 of North Central Airlines, one of the US local-service airlines still operating substantial numbers in 1978.*

The last operator to use the 880-M regularly was Cathay Pacific in Hong Kong which had seven in service in 1974, but these are now out of use.

A growth version of the Convair 880 was first projected in 1958 as the Model 30, with a longer fuselage (of the same cross section), to seat up to 106 passengers, a longer wing, more fuel capacity and turbofan engines. An unusual feature was the use of four anti-shock fairings on the wing trailing edge to achieve higher cruising speeds for the same engine power. American Airlines placed a launching order for this new model on 30 July 1958, the name Convair 600 being used again for a time before it was changed to Convair 990.

First flight was made on 24 January 1961, but flight development proved to be protracted and expensive and a series of modifications had to be engineered and test-flown to allow the Convair 990A – as it became when fully modified – to meet its guaranteed speed and range performance.

American Airlines accepted its first (unmodified) aircraft on 8 January 1963 and modified 990As entered service later in the same year. Production ended after only 37 had been built, the original operators, other than American, being Swissair, SAS, Garuda Indonesian and Varig. Spantax, a Spanish charter company, and Modern Air Transport, a US supplemental airline, acquired fleets of Convair 990As from American, from 1967 onwards, and by 1977 Spantax was the last major operator of the Convair transport, with 12 in service.

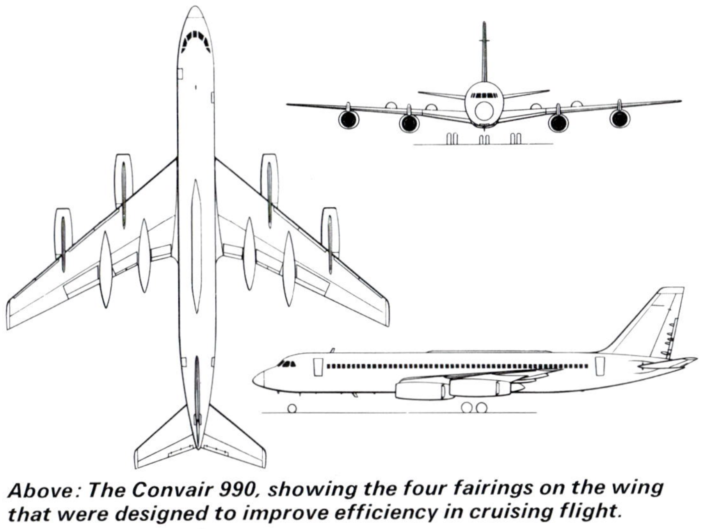

***Above:** The Convair 990, showing the four fairings on the wing that were designed to improve efficiency in cruising flight.*

Curtiss C-46
USA

Power Plants: Two 2,000shp Pratt & Whitney R-2800-34 piston engines.
Performance: Max speed, 269mph (433km/h); max cruising speed, 187mph (301km/h) at 7,000ft (2133m); initial rate of climb, 1,300ft/min (6·6m/sec); service ceiling, 27,600ft (8412m); range with max payload, 110mls (117km); range with max fuel, 1,170mls (1880km) with 5,700lb (2585kg) payload.
Weights: Empty equipped, 33,000lb (14,970kg); max payload, 11,630lb (5265kg); max take-off (passenger) 47,100lb (21,364kg), (freighter), 48,000lb (21,772kg).
Dimensions: Span, 108ft 0in (32·92m); length, 76ft 4in (23·27m); height, 21ft 8in (6·60m); wing area, 1,358sq ft (126m^2).

Among the most elderly transport aircraft still in regular use, the Curtiss C-46 was launched as a private venture in 1938 to compete with the Douglas DC-3 in the US market, and a prototype was flown on 26 March 1940. Of similar configuration to the DC-3, it differed primarily in having a larger fuselage, to seat up to 50 passengers (since increased to 62 in post-war high density layouts), more powerful engines and a shorter range. The intervention of the war prevented commercial exploitation of the type but as the C-46 Commando it was built in large quantities for the USAAF, a total of 3,141 being produced by 1945.

Post-war, large numbers of ex-military C-46s were acquired by civilian operators, at first for passenger use but subsequently more especially as freighters, for which purpose their large fuselages and military-style cargo loading doors made them particularly suitable. A few dozen were still being used in this capacity in the mid-sixties, mostly in North and South America, with smaller numbers in Asia.

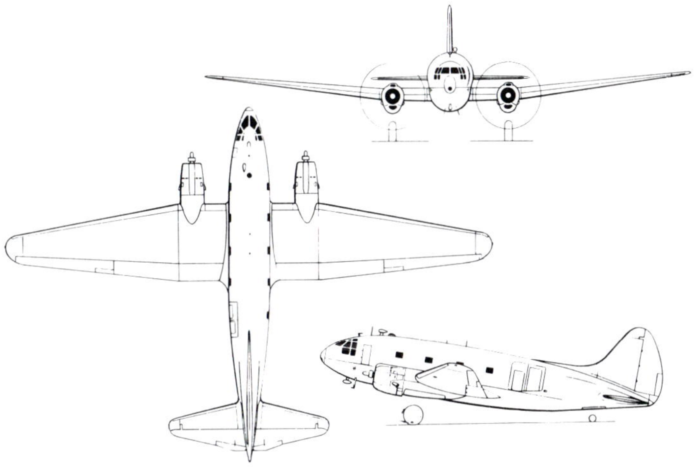

***Above:** The Curtiss C-46 showing the doors in the fuselage for loading large freight items, and the now outdated tailwheel undercarriage.*

***Below:** Built for military use in World War II, few C-46s survive in airline service; those that still fly are mostly in Central and South America, serving as freighters.*

Dassault-Breguet Mercure
France

Power Plant: Two 15,500lb st (7030kgp) Pratt & Whitney JT8D-15 turbofans.
Performance: Max cruising speed, 579mph (932km/h) at 20,000ft (6100m); best economy cruise, 533mph (858km/h) at 30,000ft (9145m); initial rate of climb, 3,300ft/min (16·76m/sec) at 100,000lb (45,359kg) weight; range with max payload, 466mls (750km); range with max fuel, 1,025mls (1650km).
Weights: Basic operating, 70,107lb (31,800kg); max payload, 35,715lb (16,200kg); max take-off, 124,560lb (56,500kg).
Dimensions: Span, 100ft 3in (30·55m); length, 114ft $3\frac{1}{2}$in (34·84m); height, 37ft $3\frac{1}{4}$in (11·36m); wing area, 1,249sq ft (116 0m²).

In a bold gamble to enter the airline market at a level considerably above the biz-jet field represented by the highly successful Falcon 20, the Dassault company launched the construction of a twin-jet transport in the Boeing 737 bracket in early 1969. This step followed a lengthy study of the potential market and the preparation of several smaller transport projects with the name Mystère 30 or Mercure, leading to the conclusion that there was a market for a very large capacity transport (up to 150 seats) optimized for ranges of up to 930mls (1500km). The market between 1973 and 1981 was estimated to be for as many as 1,500 aircraft, although Dassault was not so sanguine as to expect to capture the *whole* of the market with its new project.

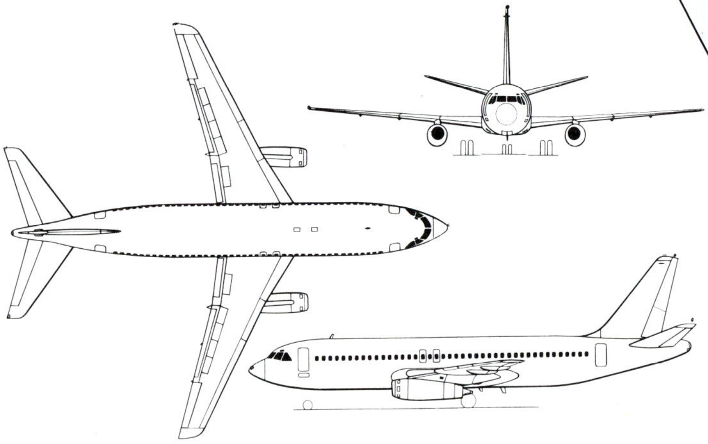

Above: Three-view drawing of the Dassault-Breguet Mercure 100, the initial production version and, in the event, only variant built.

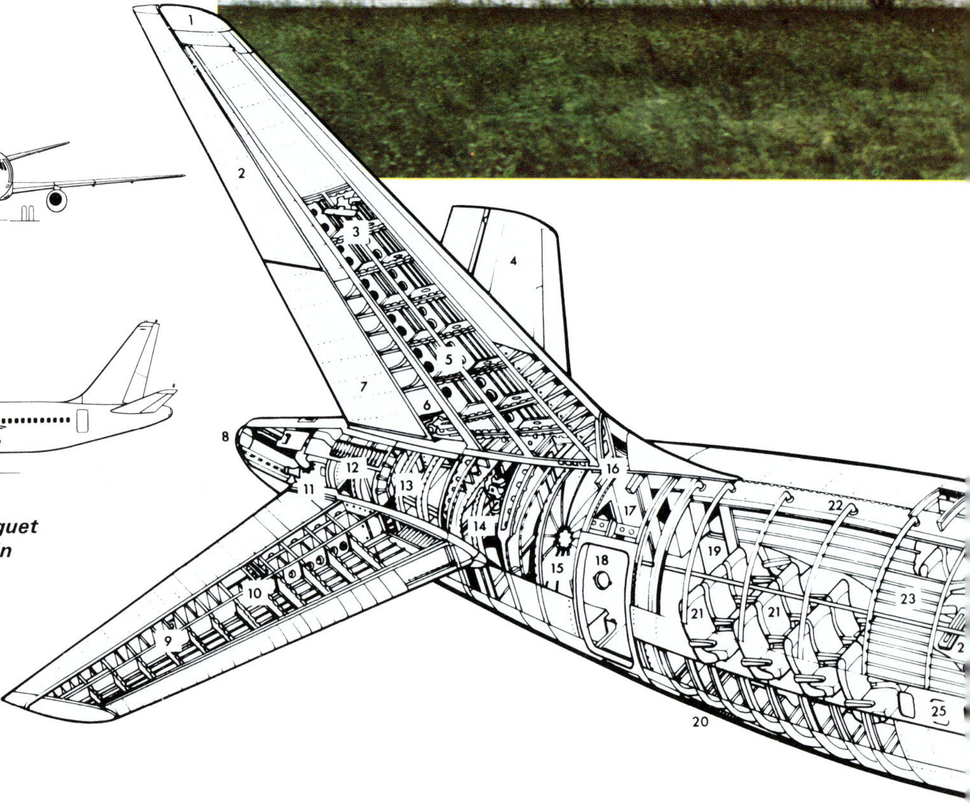

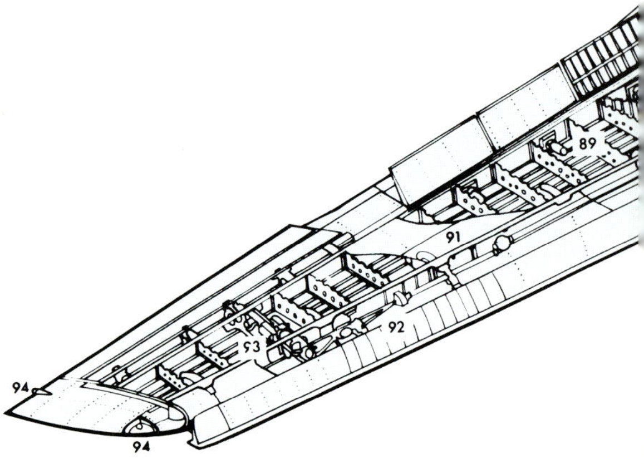

Dassault/Breguet Mercure cutaway drawing key
1 Detachable fin tip
2 Upper rudder
3 VOR antenna
4 Port tailplane
5 Two/three-spar fin box structure
6 Hydraulic rudder servo
7 Lower rudder
8 APU exhaust
9 Two-spar tailplane
10 Hydraulic servo unit
11 Garrett GTCP 85 auxiliary power unit in tail cone
12 APU intake grille
13 VI tailplane pivot frame
14 Horizontal tailplane trim motor and screw jack
15 Rear pressure dome
16 Front fin spar torque link
17 Two aft toilets
18 Aft cabin and service doors (starboard and port)
19 Cabin entry vestibule
20 Inward-opening door to underfloor baggage compartment
21 Rear two seat-rows staggered (three starboard, two port)
22 Flexible riser pipes for cabin ventilation
23 Constant pitch notched frame structure (fail safe)
24 Air conditioning diffusers
25 Polarised windows
26 Outward-opening rear freight hold door
27 Seat guide-rail
28 Cabin floor
29 Three machined fuselage/wing-spar pick-up frames
30 Floor-level ventilation outlet grille
31 Built-up floor grid
32 Integrally-machined window surround panels
33 Undercarriage and hydraulics bay
34 Central wing box
35 Over-wing longitudinal machined floor-support frame
36 Air-conditioning bay beneath wing centre box
37 Main air ducts
38 Air mixing chamber
39 Ceiling air distribution duct
40 Titanium flap-guide rails
41 Port wing spoilers
42 Triple-slotted flaps
43 Port aileron
44 Fore and aft port wingtip navigation lights
45 Wing leading-edge slats
46 Hot-air anti-icing ducts and telescopic links
47 Main hot air ducts from engine
48 Engine support bearer
49 Adjustable auxiliary intakes
50 Air intake
51 Enclosed overhead hand-baggage lockers
52 Six-abreast passenger seating
53 Forward galley (starboard)
54 Forward toilet (port)
55 Underfloor sealed avionics package
56 Forward cabin and service doors (starboard and port)
57 Flight-deck entry
58 Two-crew flight-deck layout
59 Single curvature front windscreen panels
60 Instrument panel central console
61 Forward pressure bulkhead
62 Nose cone
63 Weather radar and ILS antenna
64 Unpressurised nosewheel bay
65 Rudder pedals
66 Control column
67 Rearward-sliding clear-view panels
68 Electronics bay
69 Nosewheel retraction mechanism
70 Forward-retracting Messier twin nosewheels
71 Outward-opening forward freight hold door
72 Fuselage frames
73 Wing-root air-conditioning ram-air intakes
74 Multiple-bolt wing/fuselage attachment
75 Flap-drive hydraulic screw jacks
76 Wing spiler structure
77 Aft plate-and-angle built-up wing spar
78 Forward plate-and-angle built-up wing spar
79 Leading-edge slat structure
80 Hot-air anti-icing ducts and telescopic links
81 Anti-vibration engine mounting pad
82 Pratt and Whitney JT8D-15 engine
83 Hinged upward-opening engine cowling
84 Twin mainwheel undercarriage
85 Thrust-reverse cascades
86 Thrust-reverser cone
87 Mainwheel retraction jack
88 Integrally-machined wing-ribs
89 Hydraulic spoiler actuators
90 Hydraulic leading-edge slat actuator
91 Integrally-machined wing skin panels
92 Aileron cables to servo
93 Duplex hydraulic aileron servo
94 Fore and aft starboard wingtip navigation lights

The French government agreed to provide a loan – to be repaid by a levy on sales – of 56 per cent of the launching costs and Dassault contributed 14 per cent; the balance of 30 per cent was obtained from risk-sharing partners in Italy (Aeritalia); Spain (CASA), Belgium (SABCA), Switzerland (F+W) and Canada (Canadair). While two prototypes were put in hand, Dassault set about building up major new production facilities for the Mercure, which took shape as a conventional low-wing aeroplane with 25 deg sweepback and two podded Pratt & Whitney JT8D turbofan engines.

The first of two prototypes flew on 28 May 1971 from Bordeaux, powered by 15,000lb st (6800kgp) JT8D-11 engines. After 20 flights, the definitive JT8D-15 engines were fitted, flying in the prototype for the first time on 7 September 1971, and on 18 November the first flight was made with dihedral on the tailplane. The second prototype flew on 7 September 1972 from the new factory at Istres, with new leading edge slats fitted.

Although Dassault had originally indicated that it would put the Mercure into production only if reasonably firm orders for at least 50 were in prospect, the programme was in fact launched on the strength of a single order for 10 examples placed by the French domestic airline Air Inter on 29 January 1972. Operated by a flight crew of two, the Mercure was to be able to seat 155 passengers in a typical mixed class layout and would carry this maximum payload a distance of about 450mls (750km) – severely restricting its utility to airlines having route networks with a few longer sectors as well as many that might be suitable for the Mercure. Air Inter has remained the only Mercure customer despite Dassault attempts to launch an enlarged version as the Mercure 200, this project also being the basis of a joint Dassault-McDonnell Douglas design study and market survey in 1976/77.

The first production Mercure flew at Istres on 17 July 1973 and the French C of A was awarded on 12 February 1974, permitting operation in Cat II weather conditions. Delivery of the first two aircraft was made to Air Inter on 16 May and 11 June 1974 respectively, and the first commercial service was flown on 4 June.

Certification for Cat III operation was granted on 30 September 1974, by which time Air Inter had received four aircraft. The equipment for Cat III comprised a Bendix auto-pilot and a Thomson-CSF Head-up Display, permitting operations with a runway visual range of 500ft (150m) and a decision height of 50ft (15m). Two aircraft equipped to this standard (Nos 5 and 6) were delivered to Air Inter in 1974 and the remainder of the fleet entered service in 1975.

Above: A Dassault-Breguet Mercure – actually the second prototype – of France's Air Inter, the Mercure's only operator.

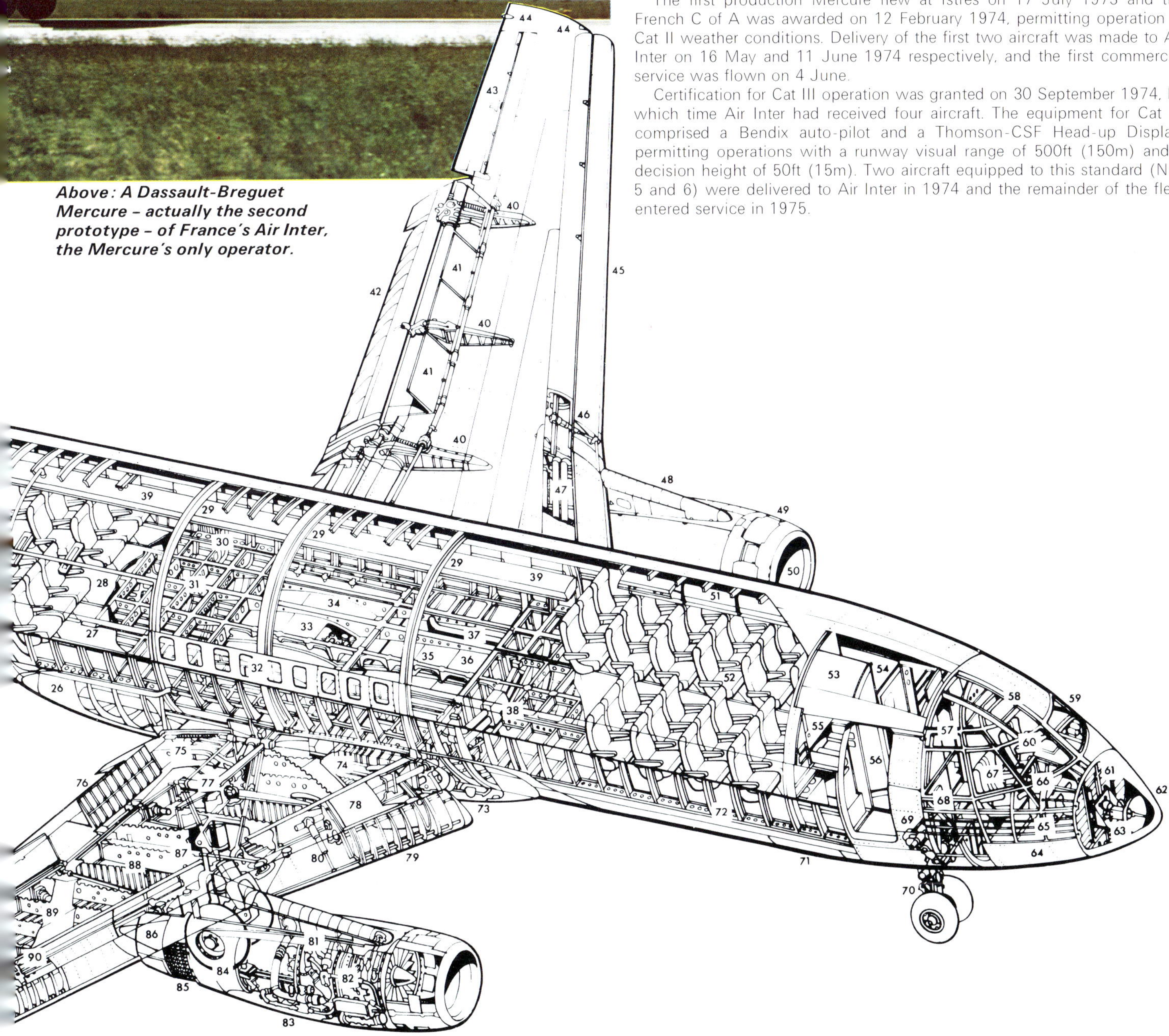

Above: Cutaway drawing of the Dassault-Breguet Mercure as operated by Air Inter. A "stretched" version was proposed by the manufacturer as the Mercure 200 and the possibility of joint development with McDonnell Douglas in the USA was explored, but not pursued.

De Havilland DHC-6 Twin Otter

Canada

The following specification refers to the Twin Otter Series 300:
Power Plant: Two 652eshp Pratt & Whitney PT6A-27 turboprops.
Performance: Max cruising speed, 210mph (338km/h); initial rate of climb, 1,600ft/min (8·1m/sec); service ceiling, 26,700ft (8140m); range with max payload, 115mls (160km); range with max fuel, 1,103mls (1775km).
Weights: Basic operating, 7,320lb (3320kg); max payload, 4,430lb (2010kg); max take-off, 12,500lb (5670kg).
Dimensions: Span, 65ft 0in (19·81m); length, 51ft 9in (15·77m); height, 18ft 7in (5·66m); wing area, 420sq ft (39·02m²).

The de Havilland Aircraft of Canada Ltd (originally a subsidiary of the British de Havilland company and until 1974 a member company of Hawker Siddeley Group) has specialized in the production of STOL utility aircraft and light transports since 1947, when the single-engined Beaver made its first flight. Continuing the Beaver theme, the company went on to produce the larger Otter (also single-engined, and known originally as the King Beaver) and then evolved the Twin Otter to use many of the wing and fuselage components of the Otter, but with two engines.

Whereas the company's earlier twin-engined types, the Caribou and the Buffalo, had been aimed primarily at the military user, the Twin Otter was intended specifically for commercial use, especially in the rôle of third-level airliner or commuter, operating from restricted areas. The Twin Otter used the same basic fuselage cross section as the Otter, with new nose and tail assemblies, and the cabin section extended in length to seat up to 20 passengers in individual seats with a central aisle. The basic wing section was also similar to that of the Otter, with the span increased from 58ft (17·68m) to 65ft (19·81m). STOL performance was achieved, as in the earlier DHC types, by aerodynamic lift only, using double-slotted full-span trailing edge flaps, the outer sections of which also operated differentially as ailerons. A fixed tricycle undercarriage was adopted, the small performance penalty that this involved being offset by the reduced first cost and simpler maintenance.

Turboprop power was chosen for the Twin Otter in the form of the then-new Pratt & Whitney PT6As developed in Canada by United Aircraft of Canada Ltd. The decision to proceed with development of the Twin Otter was taken early in 1964, and construction of an initial batch of five aircraft began in November of that year. Assembly proceeded rapidly, thanks to the commonality of many components with the Otter, and the first Twin Otter, appropriately registered CF-DHC, made its first flight at Downsview, near Ontario, on 20 May 1965. The first three examples had 579shp PT6A-6 turboprops, but the production standard incorporated the improved PT6A-20s of similar power. Type approval was obtained in May 1966 and deliveries began in July. When the Series 200 version of the Twin Otter was introduced in due course, the first production standard became known as the Series 100, production of this version totalling 115.

Delivery of the Twin Otter Series 200 began in April 1968, this version differing from the first in having a lengthened nose fairing with larger baggage capacity. Production of this variant also totalled 115.

About a year after the Twin Otter 200 appeared, de Havilland introduced the Series 300, which differed in having 652ehp PT6A-27 engines and an increase of nearly 1,000lb (454kg) in max take-off weight. By early 1978, over 370 Twin Otter 300s had been delivered, and production was continuing. The type was in use with many scheduled airlines throughout the world for commuter-style operations and for services on routes with low traffic densities. Floatplane and wheel/skiplane versions had also been delivered, all floatplanes having the original Series 100 short nose, irrespective of particular model concerned. Also available and used by a few operators was a ventral pod carrying up to 600lb (272kg) of baggage or freight.

During 1973, the Canadian government ordered six special Twin Otters to be used by a subsidiary of Air Canada known as Airtransit Canada in an inter-urban STOL demonstration service. This was undertaken – starting on 23 July 1974 – to evaluate the potential of STOL-type airliners operating from airports close to city centres: in this case, one in Montreal and one in Ottawa, both being within 15 minutes drive of the urban area they covered. The STOLports each comprised a single 2,000-ft (610-m) paved strip 100-ft (30-m) wide and the aircraft were specially modified to have upper wing spoilers, ahead of the flaps; high capacity brakes and an anti-skid braking system; emergency brakes; improved power-plant fire protection and other system changes. A sophisticated avionics package for IFR operation was fitted and these aircraft, designated Twin Otter Srs 300s, carried 11 passengers in airline-style seats.

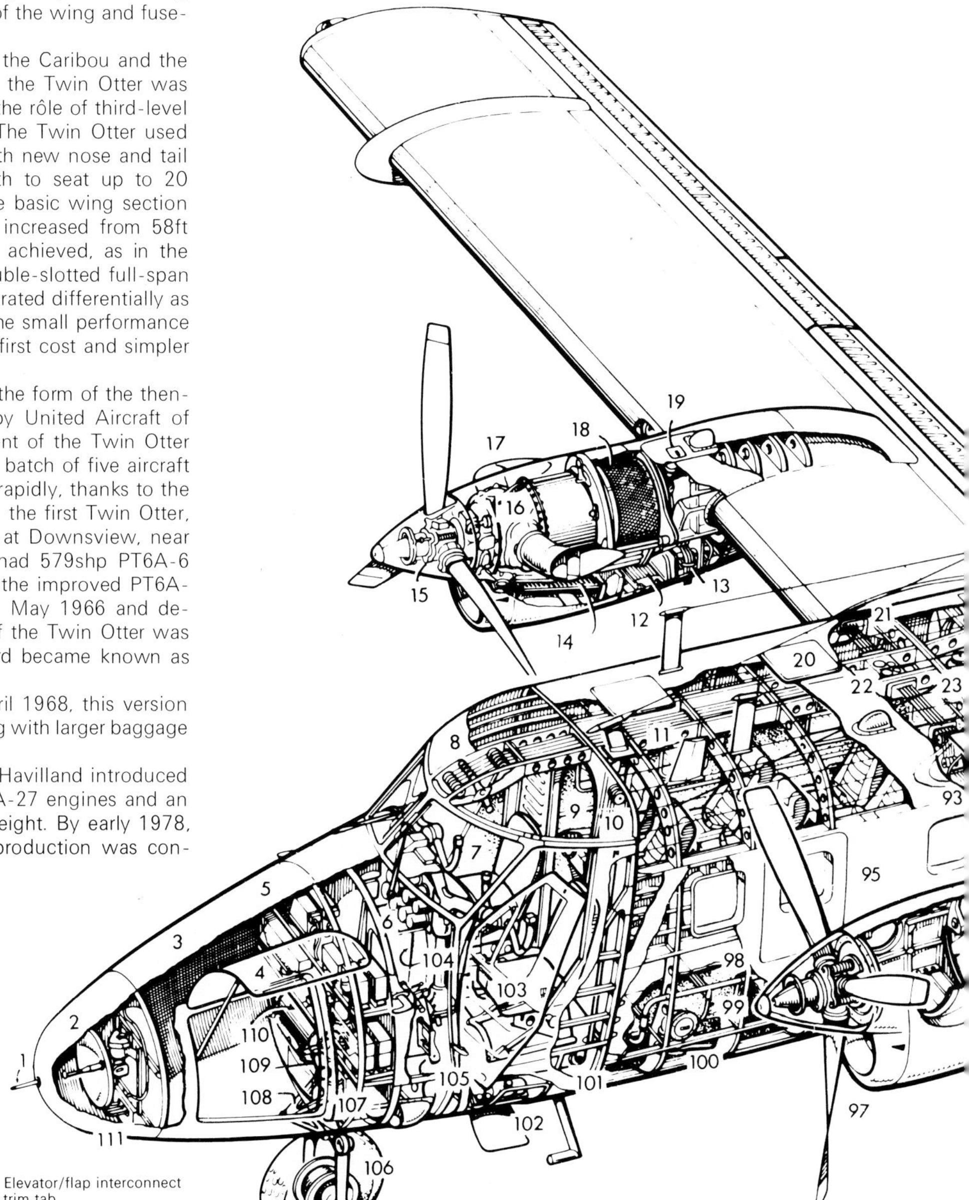

DHC-6 Twin Otter Cutaway Drawing Key

1 Lightning protection rod – not used when weather radar is fitted
2 Weather radar (customer option)
3 Baggage compartment – FWD
4 FWD baggage compartment door
5 Avionics equipment
6 Instrument panel – pilot & co-pilot
7 Control columns – pilot & co-pilot
8 Engine power & propeller levers
9 Door to passenger cabin
10 Pulleys & cables – elevator & rudder tabs
11 Engine & propeller control cables
12 Airflow duct
13 Oil cooler
14 Air intake deflector
15 Hartzell constant speed, reverse pitch, fully feathering propeller
16 Pratt & Whitney PT6A-27 free-turbine powerplant
17 Engine exhaust nozzles
18 Engine air inlet
19 Engine oil tank filler
20 ADF loop antenna (two places, customer option)
21 Engine & propeller control cables
22 Engine & propeller control pulleys
23 Aileron control quadrant
24 Flap/elevator trim inter-connect screw jack
25 Wing flap actuator & control quadrants
26 VHF antennæ (two places, customer option)
27 ADF sense antennæ (two places, customer option)
28 Wing/fuselage attachment – FWD
29 Wing/fuselage attachment – AFT
30 Cabin door – right
31 Door to aft baggage compartment
32 Baggage compartment – aft
33 Passenger oxygen cylinder – customer option
34 Pulleys & cables – elevator & rudder trim tabs
35 Aft baggage compartment extension
36 HF antenna – customer option
37 Rudder control pulleys
38 Elevator control quadrant
39 Elevator control rod
40 Elevator torque tube
41 VOR/ILS antenna (customer option)
42 Anti-collision light & lightning protection horn
43 Rudder
44 Rudder attachment point
45 Rudder trim tab
46 Rudder trim tab screw jack
47 Rudder trim cables
48 Rudder geared tab
49 Elevator/flap interconnect trim tab
50 Elevator trim tab
51 Elevator trim tab screw jack
52 Elevator attachment point
53 Elevator
54 Rudder lever
55 Rudder geared tab gearbox
56 Rudder control pulleys
57 Tail bumper
58 Rudder & elevator cables
59 No. 1 & No. 2 static inverters
60 Aft baggage compartment door
61 Oxygen recharging point – (customer option)
62 Rudder & Elevator pulleys
63 28-volt battery
64 Air conditioning unit – (customer option)
65 Cabin door – left
66 Airstair door
67 Wing flap bellcrank – intermediate
68 Wing flaps – fore & trailing
69 Wing flap push-pull rod
70 Aileron geared tab
71 Wing flap bellcrank – outboard
72 Adjustable push-pull rod-wing flap
73 Aileron control pulley
74 Aileron push-pull rod
75 Aileron
76 Aileron trim tab actuator
77 Aileron trim tab – left wing only
78 Position light & lightning protection horn
79 Position light visual indicator
80 Long range fuel pressure pump & transfer valve (customer option)
81 Long range fuel tank (customer option)
82 Wing front spar
83 Wing fence
84 Reinforced upper skin
85 Aileron pulleys
86 Aileron cables
87 Lift transducer – left wing only
88 Engine power control pulleys
89 Landing light – both wings
90 Main landing gear leg
91 Main landing gear shock absorber
92 Wing strut attachment point at fuselage
93 Engine power & propeller control cables
94 Hinged leading edge
95 Emergency door – both sides
96 Engine attachment point – 3 places
97 Engine air intake
98 Fuel cells – 315 imp gallons (1432 l) usable fuel, or with long range tanks 392 imp gallons (1782 l)
99 Interconnecting fuel vent lines
100 Fuel filler

Left: A Twin Otter in service with NorOntair, one of six used by this company to fly an extensive network of scheduled flights to serve small communities in northern Ontario. Sales of the Twin Otter had passed the 600 mark by mid-1978.

Below: The cutaway drawing shows the de Havilland Canada Twin Otter in its Series 300 version. Typically seating 19 passengers, Twin Otters are used world-wide for commuter and third-level type services.

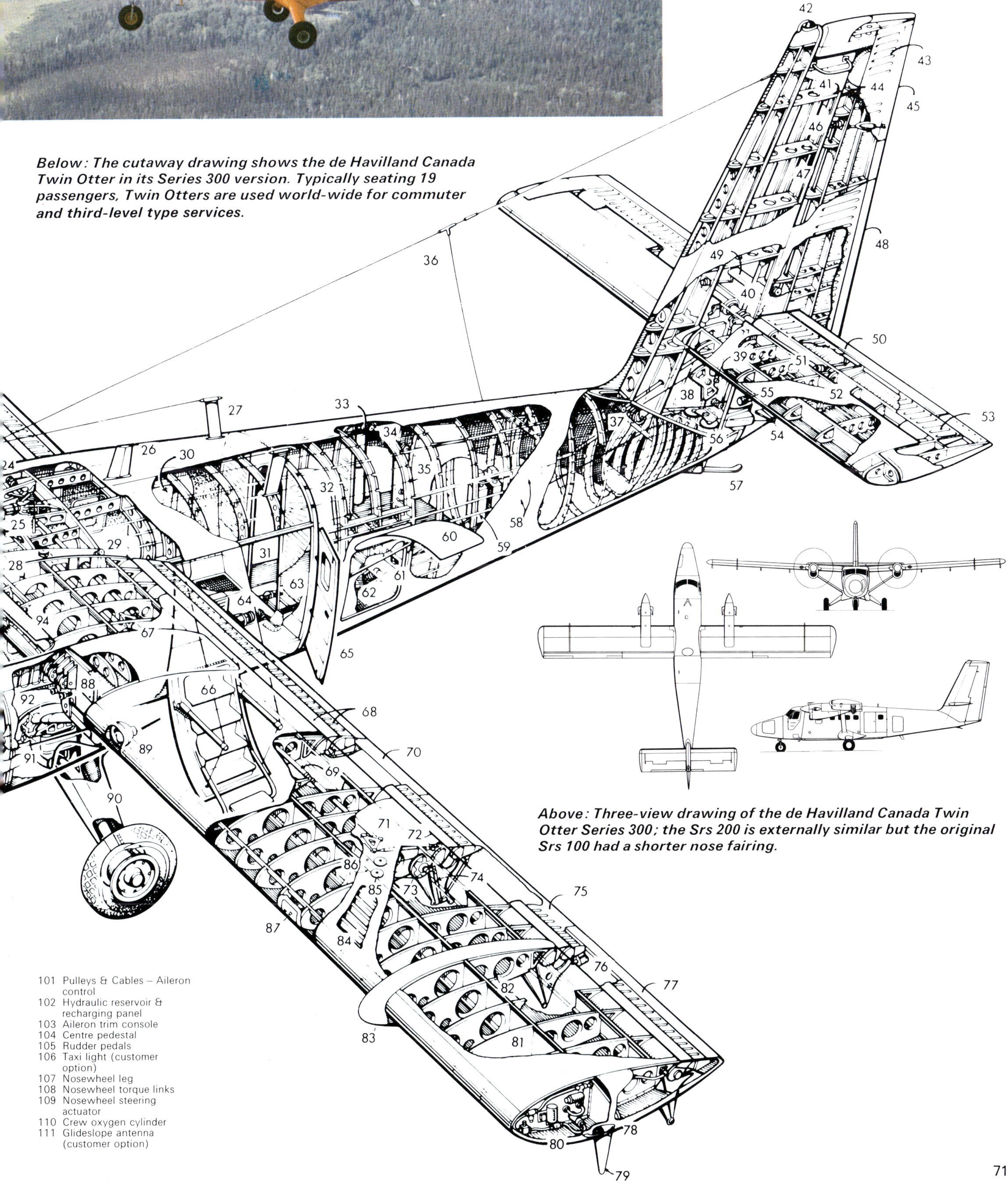

Above: Three-view drawing of the de Havilland Canada Twin Otter Series 300; the Srs 200 is externally similar but the original Srs 100 had a shorter nose fairing.

101 Pulleys & Cables – Aileron control
102 Hydraulic reservoir & recharging panel
103 Aileron trim console
104 Centre pedestal
105 Rudder pedals
106 Taxi light (customer option)
107 Nosewheel leg
108 Nosewheel torque links
109 Nosewheel steering actuator
110 Crew oxygen cylinder
111 Glideslope antenna (customer option)

De Havilland Canada DHC-7 Dash-7

Canada

Power Plant: Four 1,120shp Pratt & Whitney (UACL) PT6A-50 turboprops.
Performance (estimated): Max cruising speed, 281mph (452km/h) at 15,000ft (4570m); initial rate of climb, 1,310ft/min (6·51m/sec); service ceiling, 22,200ft (6770m); range with max payload, 935mls (1504km); range with max fuel, 1,425mls (2293km).
Weights: Operating empty, 25,860lb (11,730kg); max payload, 11,640lb (5280kg); max take-off, 43,000lb (19,504kg).
Dimensions: Span, 93ft 0in (28·35m); length, 80ft 4in (24·50m); height, 26ft 3in (8·00m); wing area, 860sq ft (79·9m^2).

The Dash-7 is the latest and largest in a series of specialized STOL aircraft originated by the de Havilland Canada company, being intended to make airline-standard flying possible from airfields with runways little more than 2,000ft (610m) in length. Its STOL performance is derived from an aerodynamic lift system using double slotted flaps operating in the slipstream from four large-diameter, slow-running, five-bladed propellers. These propellers, and the PT6A-50 turboprops, are also designed to minimize noise levels both externally and within the cabin, which provides accommodation for 48–54 passengers in four-abreast layouts.

Construction of two prototypes was launched in 1972 with backing of the Canadian Government, and this was followed by a full production decision announced on 26 November 1974. The prototypes made their first flights on 27 March and 26 June 1975 respectively and the flight test programme was continued with these aircraft throughout 1976. The first production aircraft of an initial batch of 50 approved by the Canadian government (which had acquired DHC from Hawker Siddeley in June 1974) flew early in 1977 and was one of a pair ordered by Rocky Mountain Airways. Two Dash-7s were ordered in 1977 by Wardair Canada and other orders followed from Emirate Air Services and Spantax. Other airlines that had held options for the Dash-7 included Air Alpes, Air West Airlines, Eastern Provincial, Ethiopian Airlines, Greenlandair, Nordair and Quebecair.

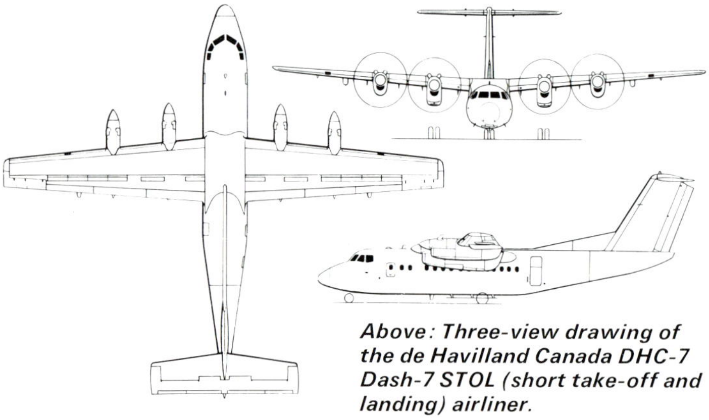

Above: Three-view drawing of the de Havilland Canada DHC-7 Dash-7 STOL (short take-off and landing) airliner.

Below: A prototype of the Dash-7 STOL airliner. First commercial services were flown by Rocky Mountain Airways early in 1978.

Dornier Skyservant

West Germany

Power Plant: Two 380hp Lycoming IGSO-540-A1E six-cylinder horizontally-opposed piston engines.
Performance: Max speed, 202mph (325km/h) at 10,000ft (3050m); cruising speed, 170mph (273km/h) at 10,000ft (3050m); initial rate of climb, 1,050ft/min (5·35m/sec); service ceiling, 25,200ft (7680m); range with max fuel, 1,830mls (2950km).
Weights: Empty equipped, 5,080lb (2304kg); max take-off, 8,853lb (4015kg).
Dimensions: Span, 51ft $0\frac{1}{4}$in (15·55m); length, 37ft $5\frac{1}{4}$in (11·41m); height, 12ft $9\frac{1}{2}$in (3·90m); wing area, 312·2sq ft (29·00m^2).

The Skyservant is a product of the famous German Dornier company, being the final development of a design that had its origins in the single-engined Do 27 – itself the first aircraft of indigenous design to be produced in Germany after World War II. From the Do 27, which was a 6–8 seat general-purpose monoplane, Dornier evolved the Do 28 using basically the same fuselage, a similar wing of extended span and two engines carried on cantilever stub wings off the fuselage sides. The first Do 28 flew on 29 April 1959 with 180hp Lycoming O-360 engines but 60 production-model Do 28A-1s had 250hp O-540 engines. A further 60 Do 28Bs had more powerful engines, higher weights and other changes. A number of Do 28As and Bs remain in service with civil operators for air taxi and general duties in various parts of the world.

The Do 28D Skyservant, first flown on 23 February 1966, differs from the earlier Do 28 models in many respects although it retains the same overall configuration. With a longer fuselage of greater cross section, the Skyservant can seat up to 14 passengers, and it has a large freight-loading door, adding to its utility. Production comprised seven Do 28Ds, after which the Do 28D-1 and Do 28D-2, with various relatively small refinements, were produced in series. Of total production of over 260, more than half are for military use; civil versions are operated by some small airlines for third level and air taxi services. A Turbo-Skyservant, with Lycoming LTP101-600 turboprops, made its first flight on 9 April 1978.

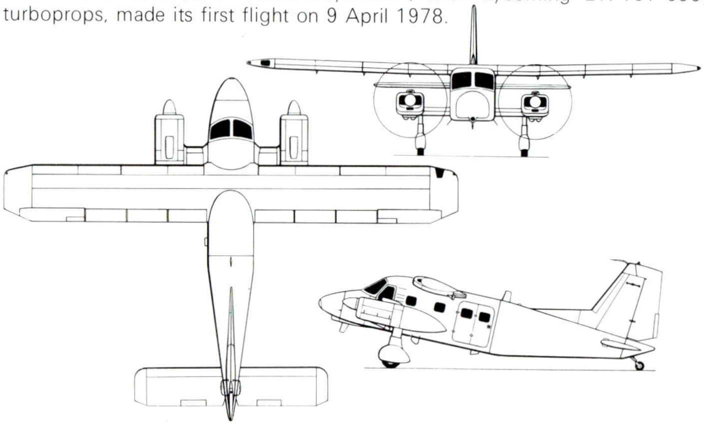

Above: Three-view drawing of the Dornier Do-28D Skyservant, sales of which had exceeded 240 by mid-1978.

Below: A Dornier Skyservant in the markings of Corsair. A prototype Turbo-Skyservant, with turboprop engines, flew in April 1978.

Douglas DC-3
USA

Power Plant: Two 1,200hp Pratt & Whitney R-1830-92 Twin Wasp piston engines.
Performance (typical post-war conversion of C-47): Max speed 215mph (346km/h); high speed cruise 194mph (312km/h); economical cruise, 165mph (266km/h) at 6,000ft (1829m); initial climb, 1,070ft/min (5·4m/sec); service ceiling, 21,900ft (6675m); range with max payload, 350mls (563km); range with max fuel, 1,510mls (2430km).
Weights: Operating weight empty, 17,720lb (8030kg); max payload, 6,600lb (3000kg); max take-off (US passenger), 25,200lb (11,430kg); max take-off (British C of A, freight), 28,000lb (12,700kg).
Dimensions: Span, 95ft 0in (28·96m); length, 64ft 6in (19·66m); height, 16ft $11\frac{1}{2}$in (5·16m); wing area, 987sq ft (91·7m^2).

Probably the most famous of all airliners, and certainly the most widely used, the DC-3 (Douglas Commercial 3) brought together in a brilliantly successful manner all the technical innovations in aeronautical engineering of the early 'thirties. Its configuration was similar to that of the DC-1 prototype and the production batch of DC-2s that entered service on 18 May 1934 – starting with TWA on the New York–Los Angeles route. Evolution of the Douglas twin-engined transport design had begun in 1932, primarily to meet a TWA requirement for an aircraft to compete with United Air Lines' Boeing 247s, and the DC-1 flew on 1 July 1933.

The DC-2 flew on 11 May 1934, and useful operational experience had been gained within a year when American Airlines asked Douglas to produce an improved and enlarged version of the transport, initially for use on a sleeper service across the US. The aircraft that emerged, to make its first flight at Santa Monica on 17 December 1935, was somewhat larger overall than the DC-2, with a wider fuselage, larger wing and tail areas and increased power and weights. It was intended to seat 24 passengers, or carry 16 sleeping berths, and was known initially as the DST (Douglas Sleeper Transport) as well as the DC-3.

American Airlines put the DST into service on 25 June 1936 between New York and Chicago, certification having been granted on 21 May. The initial versions had 920hp Wright GR-1820-G5 Cyclone engines but 1,000hp Pratt & Whitney R-1380 Twin-Wasps were soon offered as alternatives in the DST-A and DC-3A, and 1,100hp Cyclone G-102s distinguished the DC-3B. Up to the time that all transport aircraft production in the US was taken over for the US military services, 430 examples of the DC-3 had been delivered for civil use, of which nearly 100 were for export. Even before the USA became engaged in World War II, however, the potential of the Douglas transport had been realized by the USAAC, and after evaluation of prototypes, a production order for 545 military DC-3s was placed in September 1940. These were the first of the C-47 Skytrains; the name Dakota was applied later, by the RAF.

By the time the war ended and further production of the DC-3 was terminated, 10,655 examples had been built at three Douglas-operated factories; the original Santa Monica works and new facilities at Long Beach and Oklahoma. The total includes the pre-war civil production, and 28 aircraft delivered post-war by Douglas as DC-3Ds and assembled from parts of military airframes then in production. The C-47 (and other variants of the design designated C-53, C-117, R4D etc) and the Dakota had been deployed to every Allied war zone, and thousands became available for civil use overnight, in many different parts of the world. The Douglas transport then became the universal workhorse of the world's airline industry and few companies that have operated in the 1945–1965 period have not had at least one in their fleet at some time. In the early post-war years, DC-3s were used on many primary routes, and various efforts were made to improve the performance and the standard of passenger comfort, leading to some aircraft being known as Super DC-3s and by other names. Even as recently as 1977, one US company, Specialized Aircraft Co, was promoting a conversion of the DC-3 with three 1,174eshp Pratt & Whitney PT6A-45 engines, having previously converted one airframe to have two Dart turboprops.

Lacking a pressurized cabin, the DC-3 was soon outmoded as a first-line transport, but the sheer numbers available combined with the very low first cost, the sound engineering design, and ability to fly into and out of small, unimproved airfields, ensured that the type would not quickly disappear from the airline scene. In 1975, over 400 were reported to be still actively engaged in air transport operations – for the most part with smaller operators in North and South America, and in many cases for freighting rather than passenger carrying. Up to 28 passengers could be carried by the DC-3 in its post-war variants.

A licence for production of the DC-3 was obtained pre-war by the Soviet government, and these licence-built aircraft were designated Li-2, production being the responsibility of a team led by B Lisunov. They were powered by Shvetsov M-621R or M-63R engines and had numerous differences in detail from the US version. Some DC-3s purchased from Douglas by Aeroflot in 1937 were designated PS-84, and 707 US-built C-47s were supplied to the Soviet Union through lend-lease. The latter and the Li-2s have the NATO reporting name *Cab*, and some examples were reported to be still in use in the mid-seventies in the Northern, Polar and Far East Directorates of Aeroflot.

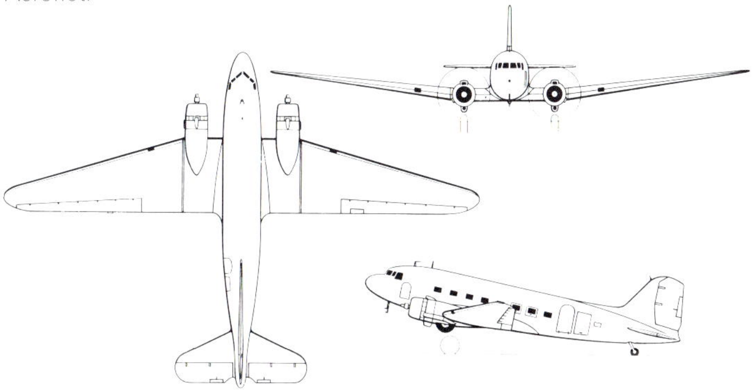

***Above:* The Douglas DC-3, all-time best-seller to the world's airlines, thanks to large-scale wartime production.**

***Below:* Florida Airlines, of Miami, was still using 15 DC-3s in 1978 to fly an extensive commuter and cargo network.**

Douglas DC-4 (and Carvair)
USA

The following specification refers to the DC-4:
Power Plant: Four 1,450hp Pratt & Whitney R-2000-2SD-13G Twin Wasp piston radial engines.
Performance: Max speed, 265mph (426km/h); cruising speed, 207mph (333km/h) at 10,000ft (3050m) at 65,000lb (29,484kg) mean weight; service ceiling, 19,000ft (5791m); range with max payload, 1,150mls (1850km); range with max fuel, 2,180mls (3510km).
Weights: Empty equipped, 46,000lb (20,865kg); max payload, 14,200lb (6440kg); max take-off weight, 73,000lb (33,112kg); max landing and max zero fuel weight, 63,500lb (28,800kg).
Dimensions: Span, 117ft 6in (35·82m); length, 93ft 5in (28·47m); height, 27ft 7in (8·41m); wing area, 1,462sq ft (135·8m^2).

The twin-engined, all-metal airliner of the mid-'thirties, of which the DC-3 was a prime example, brought about a revolution in air transportation, and the major US trunk airlines were the first to appreciate the full implications of that revolution. As early as mid-1935, with the DC-3 only just on the point of entering service, a consortium of five of these airlines – American, Eastern, Pan American, TWA and United – drew up specifications for a larger, long-range transport having the same advanced engineering features as the new twins. Out of this requirement grew the DC-4, which was to have as profound an impact upon air transport in the few years after the war as did the DC-3 in the years just preceding it.

Before the DC-4 emerged, however, Douglas made a false start with the DC-4E, a pressurized 52-seat airliner that was developed on a cost-sharing basis between Douglas and the airline consortium. It flew on 21 June 1938 and had a range of 2,000mls (3220km) cruising at 190mph (306km/h). Airline testing of the DC-4E led to demands for many modifications before production could begin, and with the worsening international situation casting a cloud over future planning, Douglas decided in 1939 to make a second, less ambitious, attempt to produce a four-engined airliner, this time with an unpressurized fuselage and only 42 seats, but still with enough range for transcontinental performance. Powered by four 1,450hp Pratt & Whitney R-2000 engines, this new model was known as the DC-4A and American Airlines and United Airlines both placed orders without waiting for a new prototype to be built.

Douglas laid down a batch of 24 DC-4As, but the entire production line was commandeered by the USAAF shortly after Pearl Harbor and the first of the new transports to fly – on 14 February 1942 – emerged in warpaint as a C-54 Skymaster. Over 1,000 military examples were built by Douglas by 1945, and the company then built 79 specifically for airline use; American Overseas Airlines became the first commercial operator of the type, in October 1945.

Many of the military C-54s were civilianized in 1946 and went into service as the initial long-haul equipment of airlines building up their operations in the austerity of the late 'forties. The excellent economy of the DC-4 was of particular significance at that time, helping airlines to make a profit out of which to finance the production of the new post-war generation of transports. The size of the DC-4 also made it suitable for high density layouts, eventually increased to a maximum of 86 seats, and for freighting, for which large side-loading doors could be fitted. Several dozen DC-4s were still in airline service in the mid-seventies, mostly for low-cost charter, freighting and other miscellaneous transport duties, and as recently as 1974 ex-USAF examples were still being offered for sale by the US government.

Another DC-4 derivative was the Carvair, developed by Aviation Traders in the UK to meet the needs of the associated company Channel Air Bridge for a vehicle ferry. First flown on 21 June 1961, the Carvair had an entirely new forward fuselage incorporating an hydraulically-operated sideways-opening nose door to permit up to five cars to be driven into the hold, and a new raised flight deck over the forward part of the cargo hold. The remainder of the DC-4 airframe was unchanged apart from increases in height and area of the vertical tail surfaces. A total of 21 DC-4s was converted and the Carvair entered airline service in March 1962. Examples were used in Luxembourg, Eire, Canada, France, Spain, Dominica and Australia but very few remained in service by the mid-seventies.

***Below:** The Douglas DC-4, built primarily for military use in World War II but much used commercially post-war.*

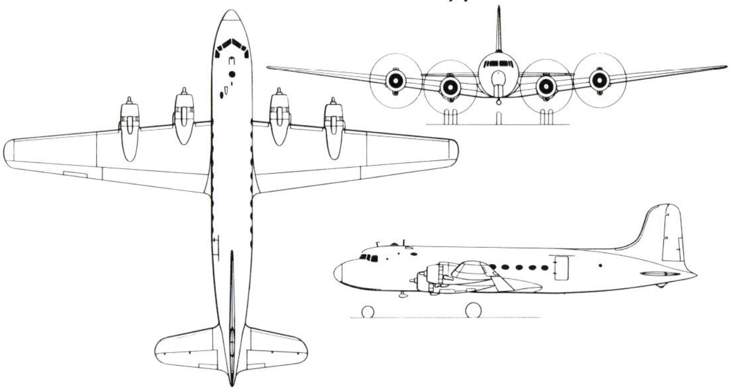

***Below:** Few DC-4s remained in civil use by 1978; this example is operated by Bergen Air Transport.*

Douglas DC-6
USA

The following specification relates to the DC-6B; the DC-6A is similar:
Power Plant: Four 2,500hp Pratt & Whitney R-2800-CB17 piston radial engines.
Performance: Typical cruising speed, 316mph (509km/h); initial rate of climb, 1,120ft/min (6·2m/sec); no reserves range with max payload, 3,000mls (4828km); no reserves range with max fuel, 4,720mls (7596km).
Weights: Basic operating, 58,635lb (26,595kg); max payload, 24,565lb (11,143kg); max take-off, 107,000lb (48,534kg).
Dimensions: Span, 117ft 6in (35·81m); length, 105ft 7in (32·2m); height, 29ft 3in (8·92m); wing area, 1,463sq ft (135·9m^2).

Like its arch-rival Lockheed, with the Constellation, the Douglas Aircraft Company acquired its preliminary experience of four-engined transport design and operation through the USAAF in World War II, which intervened to prevent the introduction of the commercial DC-4 (see previous page) as planned. Out of this experience, and with possible future military requirements as much in mind as the expected demand for such an aircraft by the airlines as soon as the war ended, Douglas set about developing an enlarged successor to the DC-4 during the war years. As the DC-6, it was destined to play a significant rôle in the evolution of air transport post-war.

Using the same wing as the DC-4, the DC-6 had a fuselage lengthened by 81 inches (2·06m) to increase the passenger capacity to a basic 52 – at the rather exaggereated seat pitches commonly used in the 'forties. The other major improvement was the introduction of pressurization, which the Constellation already offered; more powerful engines and system improvements were also featured. Construction of a prototype was ordered by the USAAF, which gave the new transport the designation XC-112; however, first flight was not made until 15 February 1946, by which time military requirements had evaporated, and only one other military example was purchased, as the C-118 *Independence* Presidential transport.

The first commercial order for the DC-6 was placed late in 1944 by American Airlines (for a fleet of 50) and United followed soon after, both airlines being faced by competition from TWA with the Constellation. The first production DC-6 flew in June 1946, deliveries to American and United began in November 1946 and the first commercial service was flown on 27 April 1947. Operating on the primary US transcontinental routes, the DC-6 offered coast-to-coast times of 10 hours eastbound and 11 hours westbound, and deliveries to other US and foreign operators quickly followed. The success of the DC-6 appeared to be in jeopardy when all examples were grounded (for four months) on 12 November 1947 following two accidents resulting from fuel venting into the intakes for the cabin heaters and causing fires. This set-back was overcome, however, and com-

Douglas DC-7
USA

The following specification refers to the DC-7C:
Power Plant: Four 3,400hp Wright R-3350-EA1 or EA4 piston radial engines.
Performance: Typical cruising speed, 345mph (555km/h); service ceiling, 21,700ft (6615m); range with max payload, 3610mls (5810km); no-reserves range with max fuel, 5,642mls (9077km).
Weights: Basic operating, 80,000lb (36,287kg); max payload, 21,500lb (9752kg); max take-off, 143,000lb (64,865kg).
Dimensions: Span, 127ft 6in (38·8m); length, 112ft 3in (34·23m); height, 31ft 8in (9·65m); wing area, 1,637sq ft (152·0m^2).

The success of the DC-6, and the continuing competitive pressure exerted by Lockheed with the Constellation, led Douglas to plan a further "stretch" of the DC-6 airframe in 1951, coupled with the introduction of the new Wright R-3350 turbo-compound piston engine with a big step-up in take-off and cruise powers. Retaining the same basic wing that had started on the DC-4 and had already been associated with three different fuselage lengths, Douglas designed a new fuselage that was 40in (1·02m) longer than that of the DC-6B, with passenger capacity increased to up to 95 in high density layouts. Apart from the new engines, the new aircraft had increased fuel capacity – sufficient to guarantee non-stop transcontinental operations in each direction. The designation DC-7 was logical – although it had been previously used when Pan American ordered a projected commercial version of the C-74 Globemaster I, which was not in the end built.

First flight of the DC-7 was made on 18 May 1953 and certification was completed by November, transcontinental service being started by American on 29 November 1953. Three other airlines, all US domestic operators, bought the DC-7, production of which totalled 105. Some of these passed eventually to other operators, together with the dimensionally similar DC-7B. The latter was a long-range version of the DC-7, with extra fuel carried in saddle tanks in the rear of the engine nacelles and within the wing. Structural modifications were made to permit operation at higher gross weights. The first DC-7B was flown on 25 April 1955 and Pan American was among the operators, using a fleet of seven to inaugurate, on 13 June 1955, the first non-stop New York–London service. Douglas delivered 110 aircraft as DC-7Bs (two others were built but not delivered), but not all these had the full range of B features and are sometimes included in the totals quoted for DC-7 production.

Although Pan American operated DC-7Bs between London and New York non-stop, this aircraft's ability to make the crossing under all conditions with a full payload was limited, and strong headwinds often led to intermediate landings or diversions to Gander. Douglas saw a clear demand for a DC-7 variant with greater range, but this could only be achieved by enlarging the airframe to provide additional fuel capacity. This led to development of the DC-7C Seven Seas, the last of the piston-engined Douglas Commercials and perhaps the peak of pre-jet airliner design.

The DC-7C had a 10ft (3·05m) increase in wing span, achieved by adding sections between the fuselage and the inner engine nacelles. Curtiss-Wright had offered a further increase in engine power, to 3,400hp in the Turbo Compound EA1, and Douglas designers were therefore able to increase the operating weights again, and the fuselage was lengthened by another 42in (1·1m) to give a maximum passenger capacity of 105. The first DC-7C flew on 20 December 1955 and production totalled 121. Pan American was the first of 13 airlines to buy the DC-7C from Douglas, starting service with it on 1 June 1956; so great was its impact on North Atlantic operation that BOAC was forced to join the queue for DC-7Cs as a stop-gap for the turboprop Britannia, development of which had slipped behind schedule. Another "first" for the DC-7C was its use for "over-the-pole" service between Europe and the Far East, inaugurated by SAS on 24 February 1957.

During 1959, Douglas offered a conversion scheme for DC-7 variants, to be fitted with double freight-loading doors, strengthened floor and other cargo features. These conversions were officially designated DC-7F regardless of basic model converted, but DC-7BF and DC-7CF designations were also used by some airlines. Other companies later made similar conversions as the original DC-7Cs came onto the second-hand market. They have remained in demand in many parts of the world for charter passenger flying and cargo operations, and were still being used in 1977 for scheduled passenger work on a few of the less competitive routes in some parts of the world.

Below: A Douglas DC-7, retired from regular airline service, flying in the markings of Ports of Call, a Denver charter company.

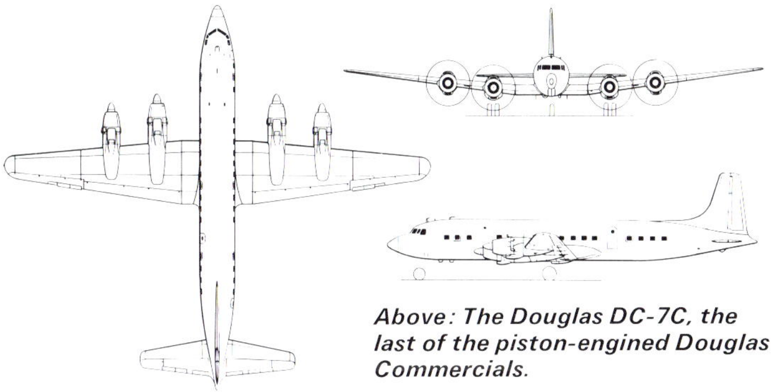

Above: The Douglas DC-7C, the last of the piston-engined Douglas Commercials.

mercial sales of the DC-6 eventually totalled 174, ending in 1951. A substantial number of DC-6s remained in use into the 'seventies, mostly for low-cost charters and freighting, in some cases having side-loading freight doors.

During 1948, Douglas began work on a further "stretch" of the DC-6 fuselage, made possible primarily by the availability of uprated R-2800 engines with water/methanol injection and by structural analysis that allowed the gross weight to be increased. The fuselage was lengthened by 5ft (1·5m), various improvements were made in systems engineering and all-freight and passenger versions were planned in parallel as the DC-6A and DC-6B. The prototype long-fuselage DC-6 flew in DC-6A configuration on 29 September 1949 and the first operator was Slick, starting on 16 April 1951. The DC-6B made its first flight on 2 February 1951, and American was the first to operate the new type, starting on 29 April 1951 on the transcontinental US route. Combining low operating costs with a high standard of comfort and outstanding mechanical reliability, the DC-6B was among the best of the generation of piston-engined airliners, and it saw service with many of the world's foremost airlines.

Production of the DC-6B totalled 288, ending in 1958; commercial deliveries of the DC-6A, ending about the same time, totalled 74 and included a few aircraft with convertible passenger/freight interiors and designated DC-6C. In addition, 166 DC-6As went to the USAF and USN as C-118As and R6D-1s respectively. As the DC-6Bs began to phase-out of front-line service, many were acquired by charter and freight operators, some being converted to DC-6A or similar standard with side-loading doors, but usually retaining the passenger windows and other features. Two DC-6Bs were converted (by Sabena) to swing-tail freighters. Many examples of the DC-6A and DC-6B remained in service in the mid-seventies, although no longer used on primary routes.

Left: Douglas DC-6Bs in their heyday, when these classic aircraft formed the main-line fleet of United Air Lines.

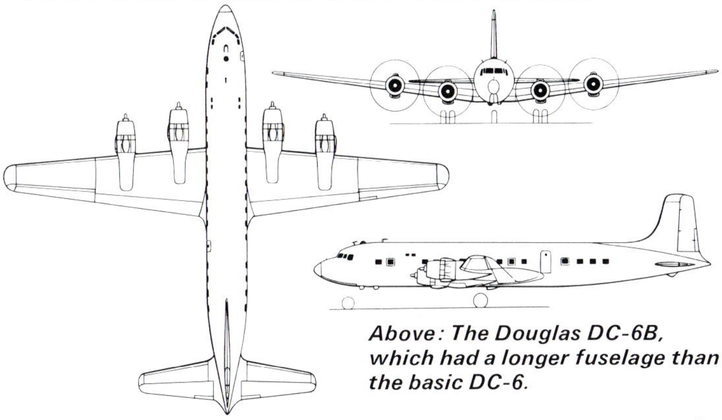

Above: The Douglas DC-6B, which had a longer fuselage than the basic DC-6.

Embraer EMB-110 Bandeirante
Brazil

The following data apply to the standard EMB-110C:
Power Plant: Two 680shp Pratt & Whitney (Canada) PT6A-27 turboprops.
Performance: Max cruising speed, 282mph (454km/h) at 9850ft (3000m); initial rate of climb, 1,970ft/min (10m/sec); single-engined rate of climb, 1,120ft/min (5·7m/sec); service ceiling, 27,950ft (8520m); single-engined ceiling, 11,810ft (3600m); take-off distance to 50ft (15·2m), 1,706ft (520m); landing distance from 50ft (15·2m), 1,312ft (400m); max range, 1,273mls (2050km) cruising at 9,850ft (3000m) with 30-min reserve.
Weights: Empty equipped, 7,054lb (3200kg); max take-off weight, 11,685lb (5300kg); max landing weight, 11,100lb (5035kg), max zero fuel weight, 10,360lb (4699kg).
Dimensions: Span, 50ft 3in (15·32m); length, 45ft 1in (13·74m); height, 13ft 6½in (4·13m); wing area, 312sq ft (29·00m²).

The Bandeirante (named after pioneering Brazilian explorers) emerged in 1968 as the first modern light transport of Brazilian origin, its design having been directed by the French engineer Max Holste (see also Aérospatiale/Nord 262) at the Institute for Research and Development. First flown on 26 October 1968, the Bandeirante met local needs for a third level airliner as well as a Brazilian Air Force requirement, and the EMBRAER organization (Emprêsa Brasileira de Aeronáutical) was set up at São Paulo during 1969 to handle production. Second and third prototypes flew on 19 October 1969 and 26 June 1970 respectively, all three having Pratt & Whitney PT6A-20 turboprops, circular windows and mainwheels partially exposed when retracted.

The production standard Bandeirante, first flown on 9 August 1972, featured PT6A-27 engines, a slightly lengthened fuselage with square cabin windows and redesigned nacelles that completely enclosed the main wheels when retracted. Early production deliveries were assigned to the Air Force, but the pressing needs of Brazilian airlines for a feeder-liner to replace DC-3s and similar elderly types led to deliveries being made to Transbrasil and VASP during 1973 before Air Force needs had been fully met. Typical airline layout provided accommodation for 15 passengers in single seats with a central aisle, this being the EMB-110C version that entered service (with Transbrasil) on 16 April 1973. Subsequently, a number of specialized variants has been developed to meet the needs of airline operators. Most important of these was the EMB-110P, designed to the requirements of third-level airlines in Brazil; with 18 passenger seats, this version entered service with TABA early in 1976. The EMB-110 and EMB-110F are, respectively, executive and all cargo versions; the EMB-110S is a geophysical survey version, the EMB-110K-1 has a slightly longer fuselage – 2ft 9in (0·84m) – with an enlarged cargo-loading door and the EMB-110P-2 is a similarly lengthened all-passenger variant.

Above: An EMB-110P Bandeirante. Originally developed for a Brazilian Air Force requirement, the EMB-110 has proved successful in several civil rôles, including business transport.

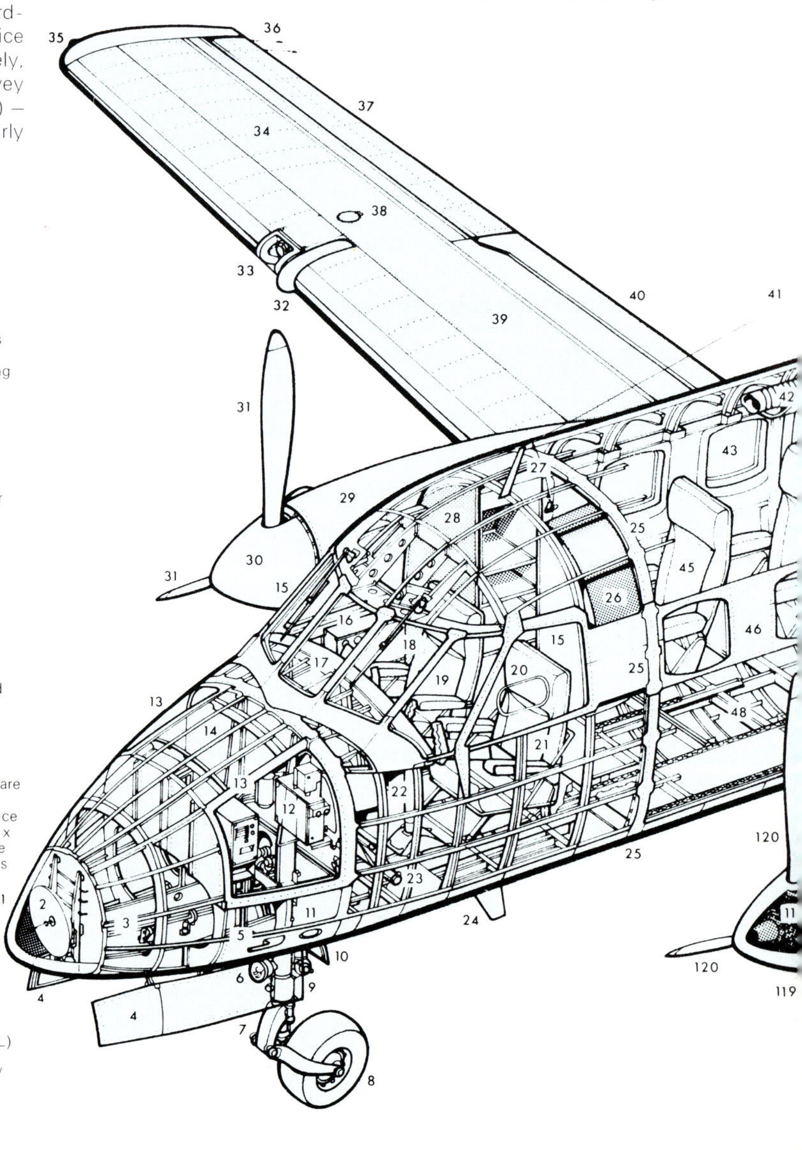

Embraer EMB-110 Bandeirante Cutaway Drawing Key:

1 Nose cone
2 Radar array (Bendix RDR-1200 or RCA AVQ-47)
3 Nosewheel well
4 Nosewheel doors (close after activation)
5 Pitot probe
6 250W taxi light
7 Nosewheel fork
8 Goodyear 6.50 x 8 nose-wheel tyre
9 Nosewheel oleo (by ERAM)
10 Nosewheel oleo flap
11 External power socket
12 Avionics bay
13 Avionics bay access doors (upward hinged)
14 Bulkhead
15 Plexiglass windscreen side panels
16 13-mm stressed acrylic windscreen centre panels
17 Instrument panel shroud
18 Variable speed wipers
19 Second pilot's seat
20 Clear vision panel
21 Pilot's adjustable seat
22 Control column
23 Rudder pedals
24 ADF antenna
25 Forward/centre fuselage join
26 Port-cloaks/stores
27 Aerial mast
28 Starboard equipment rack
29 Starboard nacelle
30 Spinner
31 Hartzell HC-B3TN-3C/T10178H-8R constant speed propeller
32 Leading-edge wing fence
33 Starboard 450 W shielded glare landing light
34 Riveted aluminium sheet wing skin
35 Starboard navigation light
36 Aileron static dischargers
37 Starboard statically-balanced aileron
38 Fuel filler cap
39 Two wing integral fuel tanks each side (total capacity 370 Imp gal/1690 l)
40 Double-slotted flap
41 Aerial
42 Starboard cabin-air trunking
43 Seven cabin windows (starboard)
44 Emergency exit window (starboard only)
45 Five-a-side cabin seating
46 Riveted aluminium sheet fuselage skin
47 Five cabin windows (port)
48 Floor support structure (stressed for cargo)
49 Front spar/fuselage steel join
50 Rear spar/fuselage steel join
51 Centre box structure
52 Main fuselage frames
53 Wingroot fairing
54 Entry door with integral steps
55 Three-place bench seat (C-95: optional cargo space)
56 Dorsal antenna
57 Cabin rear bulkhead (cargo compartment)
58 Port cabin-air trunking
59 Fin fairing
60 Cabin-air inlet
61 Front fin spar/fuselage join
62 Starboard tailplane
63 Elevator balance
64 Elevator static dischargers
65 Starboard elevator
66 All-metal cantilever fin
67 Fin leading-edge
68 Anti-collision beacon
69 Rudder balance
70 Rudder hinges
71 Rudder static dischargers
72 Rudder structure
73 Rudder tab (upper)
74 Rudder tab (lower)
75 Tail cone
76 Rear navigation light
77 Elevator tab
78 Port elevator
79 Elevator balance
80 All-metal cantilever tailplane
81 Tailplane centre-section structure
82 Tailplane/fuselage join
83 Angled fuselage frames
84 Air trunking
85 Aircycle air-conditioning plant
86 Aft cabin bulkhead
87 Aft window (port and starboard)
88 Rear single seat (C-95: optional cargo space)
89 Entry door frame
90 Door actuating cylinder
91 Handrails
92 Entry steps
93 Flap hinges
94 Front spar
95 Wing/integral tank construction
96 Double-slotted flaps
97 Fuel filler cap
98 Rear spar
99 Aileron tab (port only)
100 Aileron hinge
101 Port statically-balanced aileron
102 Moulded glass fibre wingtip
103 Port navigation light
104 Leading-edge ribs
105 Port 450 W shielded glare landing light
106 Leading-edge wing fence
107 Kleber-Colombes (670 x 210.12) mainwheel tyre
108 Mainwheel door (closes after activation)
109 Mainwheel fork
110 Mainwheel oleo flap
111 Mainwheel oleo leg (by ERAM)
112 Mainwheel well
113 Nacelle structure
114 Firewall
115 Engine bearers
116 Exhaust trunk
117 Pratt & Whitney (UACL) PT6A-27 turboprop
118 Propeller auto -feather/reverse pitch
119 Air intake
120 Hartzell three-blade propeller

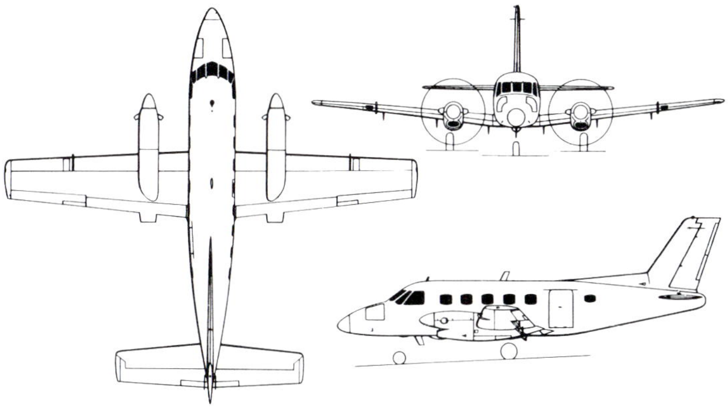

Above: Three-view drawing of the EMB-110 Bandeirante in its initial production form. Current production models for both the Brazilian Air Force and the commercial market are available with uprated engines and a slightly longer fuselage, designated EMB-110K and EMB-110P2 respectively.

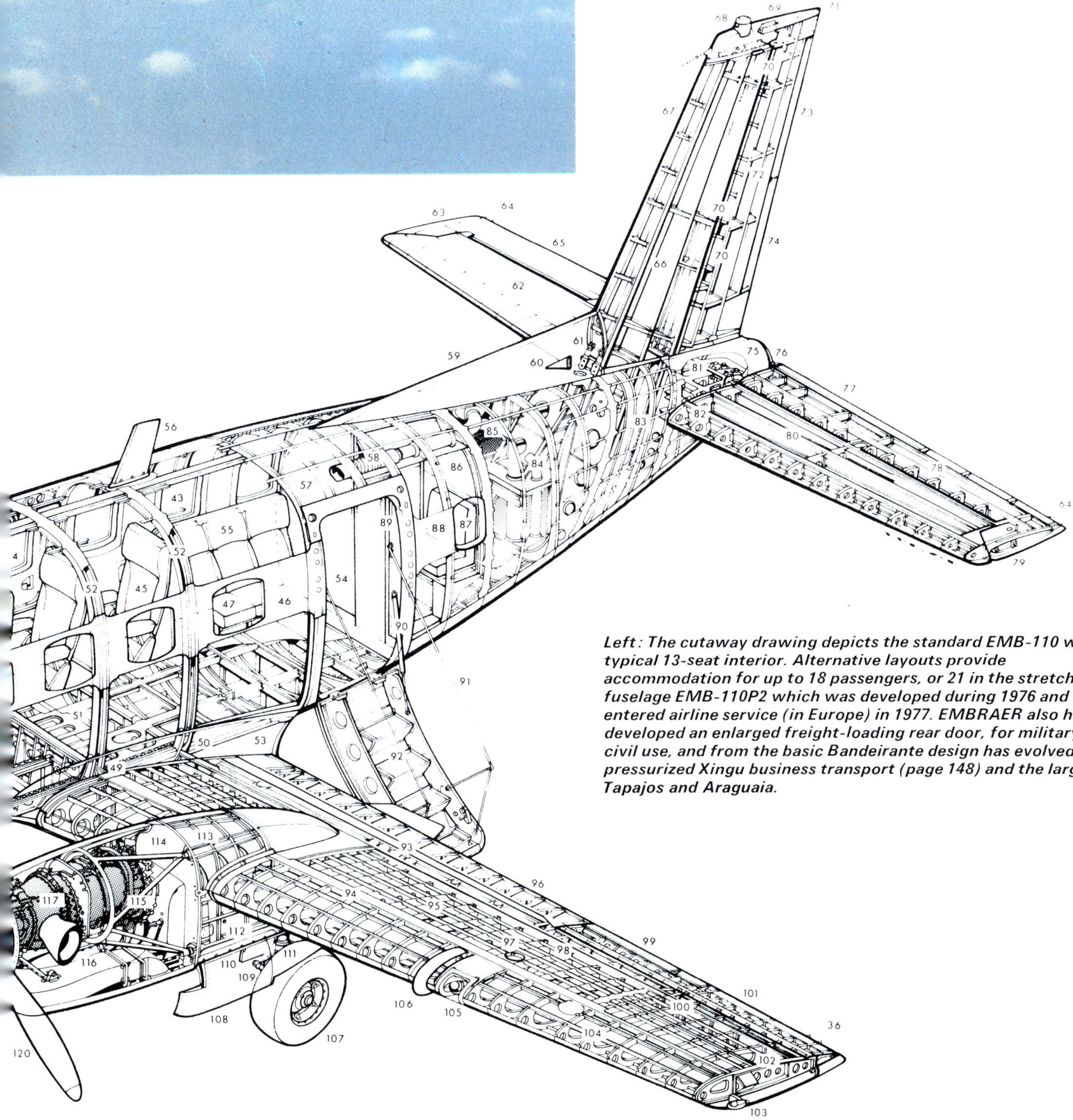

Left: The cutaway drawing depicts the standard EMB-110 with a typical 13-seat interior. Alternative layouts provide accommodation for up to 18 passengers, or 21 in the stretched-fuselage EMB-110P2 which was developed during 1976 and entered airline service (in Europe) in 1977. EMBRAER also has developed an enlarged freight-loading rear door, for military or civil use, and from the basic Bandeirante design has evolved the pressurized Xingu business transport (page 148) and the larger Tapajos and Araguaia.

Fokker F 27 Friendship and Fairchild FH-227

Netherlands

The following specification refers to the F.27 Mk 200:

Power Plant: Two 2,105eshp Rolls-Royce Dart 528 or 528-7E or 2,230eshp Dart 532-7 turboprops.

Performance: Cruising speed, 302mph (486km/h); initial rate of climb, 1,475ft/min (7·5m/sec); service ceiling, 29,500ft (9000m); range with max payload, 1,285mls (2070km); range with max fuel, 1,374mls (2211km).

Weights: Empty, 22,696lb (10,295kg), operating empty, 24,600lb (11,159 kg); max payload, 10,340lb (4690kg); max take-off, 45,000lb (20,410kg).

Dimensions: Span, 95ft 2in (29·00m); length, 77ft $3\frac{1}{2}$in (23·56m); height, 27ft 11in (8·51m); wing area, 753·5sq ft (70·0m^2).

The following specification refers to the FH-227E:

Power Plant: Two 2,300shp Rolls-Royce Dart 532-7L turboprops.

Performance: Max cruising speed, 294mph (473km/h) at 15,000ft (4570m); best economy cruise, 270mph (435km/h) at 25,000ft (7620m); initial rate of climb, 1,560ft/min (7·9m/sec); service ceiling, 28,000ft (8535m); range with max payload, 656mls (1055km); range with max fuel, 1,655mls (2660km).

Weights: Empty, 22,923lb (10,398kg); max payload, 11,200lb (5080kg); max take-off, 43,500lb (19,730kg).

Dimensions: Span, 95ft 2in (29·0m); length, 83ft 8in (25·50m); height, 27ft 7in (8·41m); wing area, 754sq ft (70·0m^2).

When the famous Fokker company resumed active work on aircraft design in the years following World War II, high priority was given to the development of a commercial transport, this having been one of the areas in which the company had excelled before the war. Since one of the activities at the Schiphol, Amsterdam, works from 1945 onwards was the overhaul and conversion of ex-military Douglas DC-3s, the company was already in close contact with many European and other airlines, and they were asked, during 1950, to outline their likely requirements for a "DC-3 replacement" aircraft. Out of this survey emerged a series of project studies, one of which, dated August 1950, was for a shoulder-wing, twin-Dart powered 32-seater known as the P.275.

Evolution of the P.275 led to the F.27 of 1952, with a circular-section pressurized fuselage seating up to 40 passengers and a range of 300mls (483km) with full payload. Double slotted flaps were to be used to obtain the required short-field performance. In 1953, Netherlands government backing was obtained for the construction of two flying prototypes and two structural test specimens and a marketing campaign began. First flights of the two prototypes were made on 24 November 1955 and 29 January 1957, respectively, the second of these introducing a fuselage extension of 3ft (0·91m) and having Dart 511s in place of the Dart 507s used temporarily in the first prototype. With the lengthened fuselage, adopted as the production standard, the basic seating capacity went up from 32 to 36, the initial gross weight being 35,700lb (16,193kg). Flight testing showed that the double slotted flaps were not needed and single-slotted flaps were adopted instead.

Fokker flew the first production F.27, which meanwhile had been named the Friendship, on 23 March 1958. Meanwhile, a licence agreement had been concluded with Fairchild in the USA and a production line had been laid down to meet a healthy demand from the local service operators, for whom the type offered an economic opportunity to introduce turbine engined equipment. Fairchild introduced a lengthened nose for weather radar (later adopted also by Fokker), increased the basic seating to 40, upped the fuel capacity and made various other changes. The first two F-27s off the

continued on page 80 ▶

***Right:** Fairchild developed the FH-227B, with lengthened fuselage, from the original Fokker Friendship design.*

***Below:** A Fokker F.27 Mk 200 Friendship in the markings of Air Anglia, the first British airline to fly the Dutch transport.*

Above: A Fairchild-built F.27A Friendship operated by Air Polynesie between the islands of French Polynesia.

Below: Three-view drawing of the Fokker F.27 Mk 200, a basic version of Europe's best-selling turboprop transport.

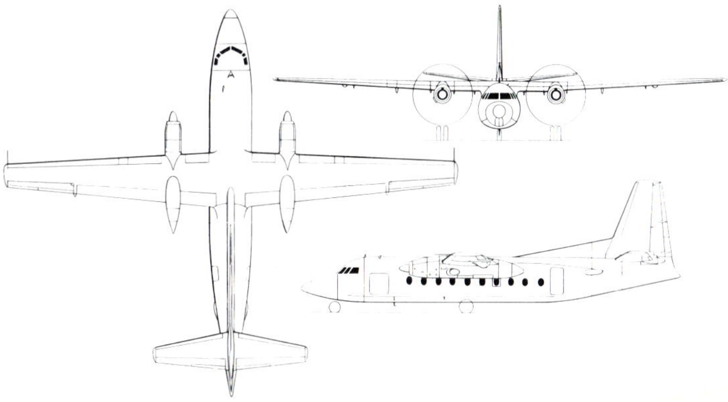

►Fairchild line at Hagerstown flew on 12 April and 23 May 1958, and after FAA Type Approval on 16 July 1958, the type entered service with West Coast Airlines on 27 September 1958. Initial services by Fokker-built F.27s followed in December, the operator being Aer Lingus.

Fokker has steadily improved the F.27, which is the world's best-selling turboprop transport with more than 650 sold by early 1977 (including Fairchild production), and identifies the variants by mark numbers (100, 200, etc) whereas Fairchild, which undertook its own evolution of the type in collaboration with Fokker, used letter suffixes (F-27A, F-27B etc). The first production batch by Fokker were F.27 Mk 100s, and the basic Fairchild aircraft were plain F-27s. In the F.27 Series 200 and the F-27A, more powerful Dart R.Da.7 Mk 528 engines provided improved cruising speeds and better airfield "hot and high" performance; both Fokker and Fairchild fitted the new engines in development airframes for certification during 1958, and subsequently the permitted maximum take-off weight went up to 45,000lb (20,410kg).

Sometimes referred to as the Combiplane, the F.27 Mk 300 and F-27B introduced a large freight loading door in the forward fuselage, plus a strengthened cabin floor, to permit mixed passenger/freight operations, being otherwise similar to the Mk 100. The first examples came from Fairchild, US certification being completed on 25 October 1958 and initial deliveries being made to Northern Consolidated. The F.27 Mk 400 (no Fairchild equivalent) was a Mk 300 with the Mk 528 engines, sold by Fokker primarily for military use. Some specifically military Friendships were known as F.27M Troopships, being based on the Mk 400. Fokker also found a requirement to produce a version of the F.27 with the large freight door but without the all-metal, watertight, freight floor of the Mk 300 and Mk 400. This emerged as the Mk 600 (with R.Da.7 engines) and provision was made for a quick-change interior to be installed. The designation Mk 700 was reserved for a similar version using the lower rated R.Da.6 engines of the original production standard.

Fairchild closed its Friendship line down in 1960 after meeting initial airline demand, but re-opened it in 1961, initially to produce the F-27F version for business users. This differed primarily in having Dart 529-7E engines rated at 2,190ehp, and was type approved on 24 February 1961. There were no airline buyers, and an F-27G variant, with cargo door, was not built. On 3 August 1965, Fairchild obtained type approval for the F.27J with Dart 532-7 engines and on 12 June 1969, for the F-27M with Dart 532-7N and larger diameter propeller; some examples of both these types went to airlines – 10 F-27Js to Allegheny and two F-27Ms to Lloyd Aero Boliviano. The last-mentioned brought Fairchild production of the F-27 to an end, with 128 built.

All versions of the Friendship from Mk 100 to Mk 400, plus the 600 and 700, had the same overall dimensions and maximum seating for 48 passengers. A long-fuselage variant was proposed in 1961 as the Mk 500, with a 4ft 11in (1·5m) stretch and forward freight door, but no orders were forthcoming until 1966, when the French government ordered 15 as DC-3 replacements, for use in the highly-developed Postale de Nuit mail delivery operation in France. The first Fokker F.27 Mk 500 flew on 15 November 1967 and deliveries began in June 1968. Meanwhile, however, Fairchild had taken up Fokker's idea and had introduced its own version of a stretched F.27 in the form of the FH-227. In this case, the fuselage stretch was 6ft (1·83m), and other special features were introduced to make the aircraft more specifically suited to the US market.

Fairchild flew the first of two prototypes on 27 January 1966 and then built 10 FH-227s for Mohawk, but later exchanged these on a one-for-one basis for FH-227Bs, which introduced higher weights and revised structure. Some FH-227s were later converted to FH-227C with some features of the B model but the original weights, or to FH-227E with uprated Dart 532-7L turboprops. The FH-227Bs became FH-227Ds when fitted with these same engines and other improvements. Production totalled 79.

With sales of the F-27 continuing in 1978, including a new version known as the Maritime for coastal reconnaissance, the Fokker transport has proved to be the best-selling of all turboprop airliners produced outside the USSR. Many Friendships have been sold for corporate and business use, but the type is also widely used by airlines for scheduled operations over feeder routes and routes on which traffic levels are low.

***Below:* First flown in 1955, the Fokker F27 had by 1978 become Europe's best-selling airliner, with production continuing.**

Fokker-VFW F28 Fellowship
Netherlands

The following specification refers to the F.28 Mk 1000:
Power Plant: Two 9,850lb st (4468kgp) Rolls-Royce Spey 555-15 turbofans.
Performance: Max cruising speed, 528mph (849km/h) at 21,000ft (6400m); best economy cruise, 519mph (836km/h) at 25,000ft (7620m); long-range cruise, 420mph (676km/h) at 30,000ft (9150m); max operating ceiling, 35,000ft (10,675m); range with max payload, 956mls (1538km); range with max fuel, 1,208mls (1945km).
Weights: Operating empty, 35,517lb (16,144kg); max payload, 19,700lb (8936kg); max takeoff, 65,000lb (29,480kg).
Dimensions: Span, 77ft $4\frac{1}{4}$in (23·58m); length, 89ft $10\frac{3}{4}$in (21·40m); height, 27ft $9\frac{1}{2}$in (8·47m); wing area, 822sq ft (76·4m^2).

The Fokker company announced plans in April 1962 for a new short-haul jet airliner that would complement its F.27 Friendship, which was destined to become, a few years later, the world's best-selling turboprop airliner when sales passed the Viscount's previous record-holding figure total of 444. At the time the jet project was first proposed – as the F.28, later to be named Fellowship – Fokker was still independent, but since 1969 the programme has been continued as one of the three short-haul transport aircraft marketed by the merged Fokker and VFW companies.

As originally conceived, the F.28 was to carry about 50 passengers over ranges of up to 1,000mls (1600km) and was to have a good short-field performance. The use of Bristol Siddeley BS.75 engines was studied but an early decision was made in favour of the Rolls-Royce RB.183 Spey Junior, a lighter and simpler version of the commercial Spey already committed to production for the Trident and BAC One-Eleven. Fokker had gained extensive experience of the potential airline market for an F.28-type aircraft through sales of the F.27, and planned development and production of the new aircraft on the assumption that sales would be made in small batches over a relatively long period, rather than in large fleets to airlines all wanting delivery at the same time, as tended to apply to the larger transport aircraft. In configuration, the F.28 followed the popular trend of the early 'sixties, with a low, slightly swept-back wing, T-tail and rear-fuselage mounted engines. The passenger capacity was set at 60 for the basic model.

Production was launched in July 1964 following completion of financing arrangements that included a loan from the Netherlands government, repayable from a levy on sales, and risk-sharing participation by Short Bros in the UK, the then-HFB (now MBB) and VFW companies in Germany and several equipment manufacturers in the UK and USA. Construction of three test and development airframes was put in hand at Schiphol, quickly backed up by the ordering of long lead-time items for production aircraft, the first of which was earmarked for the German IT operator LTU when it placed an order in November 1965.

First flights of the three prototypes were made on 9 May, 3 August and 20 October 1967, respectively, and the No 4 aircraft (first production and first for LTU) flew on 21 May 1968. Dutch certification was obtained on 24 February 1969, on which day the first delivery to LTU formally took place. The original production aircraft are known as Mk 1000, and are to the original specification for a 65-passenger (one-class, five-abreast) aircraft, the certificated gross weight having increased since 1969 from 62,000lb (28,123kg) to 64,000lb (29,510kg). A version of the F.28 Mk 1000 with a forward side freight loading door is available for mixed passenger/freight operations as the Mk 1000-C.

To provide an alternative for operators requiring more capacity over shorter ranges, Fokker developed the Mk 2000, with the fuselage stretched by 7ft 3in (2·21m). Started in 1970, this variant carries up to 79 passengers and the first prototype F.28 converted to the new standard first flew on 28 April 1971, being certificated in August 1972. The first production example was delivered to Nigeria Airways in October 1972.

Also in 1972, Fokker announced the first details of the Mk 5000 and Mk 6000, with improvements aimed at permitting the F.28 to operate from shorter runways. Respectively equivalent to the Mk 1000 and Mk 2000 in passenger accommodation, the Mk 5000 and the Mk 6000 have an increase of 6ft $11\frac{1}{2}$in (1·51m) in wing span, leading-edge slats, and improved versions of the Spey, designated Mk 555-15H, with additional noise reduction features. The original Mk 2000 prototype of the F.28 was fitted with the new wings and first flew in the guise of a Mk 6000 on 27 September 1973.

continued on page 83►

***Right:** Martinair Holland, which specializes in charter and IT flights from its Amsterdam base, operates this F28 Mk 1000.*

***Below:** A successful short-haul jet airliner, the Fokker F28 is also used as a transport by some air forces.*

► After obtaining certification of the Mk 6000 on 30 October 1975, Fokker went on to develop the Mk 3000 (short fuselage) and Mk 4000 (long fuselage) with the same increased wing span and the engine improvements, but without the leading-edge slats. A redesigned inter increases the seating capacity of the Mk 4000 to 85 and at a max gross weight of 71,000lb (32,200kg) it can carry this load a distance of 1,125mls (1814km). The Mk 3000 can carry 65 passengers for 1,725mls (2777km). Deliveries of the Mk 4000 (to Lingeflyg in Sweden) began at the end of 1976, and Garuda placed the first contract for the Mk 3000 in mid-1977, bringing the F-28 sales total to 128.

Above: The first operator to use the Mk 4000 high-density version of the Fokker F28 was Linjeflyg, flying domestic services in Sweden.

Fokker F28 Fellowship Mk 4000 Cutaway Drawing Key

1 Radome
2 Weather radar scanner
3 Front pressure bulkhead
4 Radar equipment mounting
5 Windscreen wipers
6 Windscreen frame
7 Instrument panel shroud
8 Back of instrument panel
9 Rudder pedals
10 Ram air intake
11 Cockpit roof control panel
12 Overhead window
13 Co-pilot's seat
14 Pilot's seat
15 Control column
16 Pilot's side console
17 Air conditioning plant
18 Nosewheel doors
19 Nose undercarriage leg
20 Twin nosewheels
21 Cockpit roof construction
22 Radio and electronics rack
23 Radio rack cooling duct
24 Galley
25 Stewardess' seat
26 Curtained doorway to passenger cabin
27 Handrail
28 Entrance vestibule
29 Entry stairway
30 VHF aerial
31 Main passenger door
32 Upper VHF aerial
33 Air conditioning duct
34 Forward cabin passenger seating
35 Seat rails
36 Freight and baggage hold door
37 ADF loop aerials
38 Fuselage frame and stringer construction
39 Soundproofing panels
40 Underfloor freight and baggage hold
41 Window panels
42 Cabin floor construction
43 Hot air duct
44 Wing centre section front spar
45 HF aerial fixing
46 Leading edge fence
47 Starboard wing integral fuel tank
48 Fuel filler
49 Starboard navigation light
50 Static discharge wicks
51 Starboard aileron
52 Aileron tab
53 Flap mechanism fairings
54 Starboard outer flaps
55 Outboard spoilers (open)
56 Starboard inboard flaps
57 Inboard spoilers (open)
58 Centre section main fuselage frames
59 Air distribution duct
60 Wing centre section construction
61 Emergency escape windows
62 Mainwheel well pre pressurised cover
63 Port mainwheel well
64 Cabin window-trim panels
65 Rear cabin seating
66 Passenger overhead service panels
67 Overhead luggage bins
68 Cabin rear bulkhead
69 Starboard engine cowling
70 Toilet
71 Wash basin
72 Air intake to APU
73 Fin root fairing
74 Fuselage sloping frames
75 De-icing air duct
76 HF aerials
77 Fin leading edge de-icing

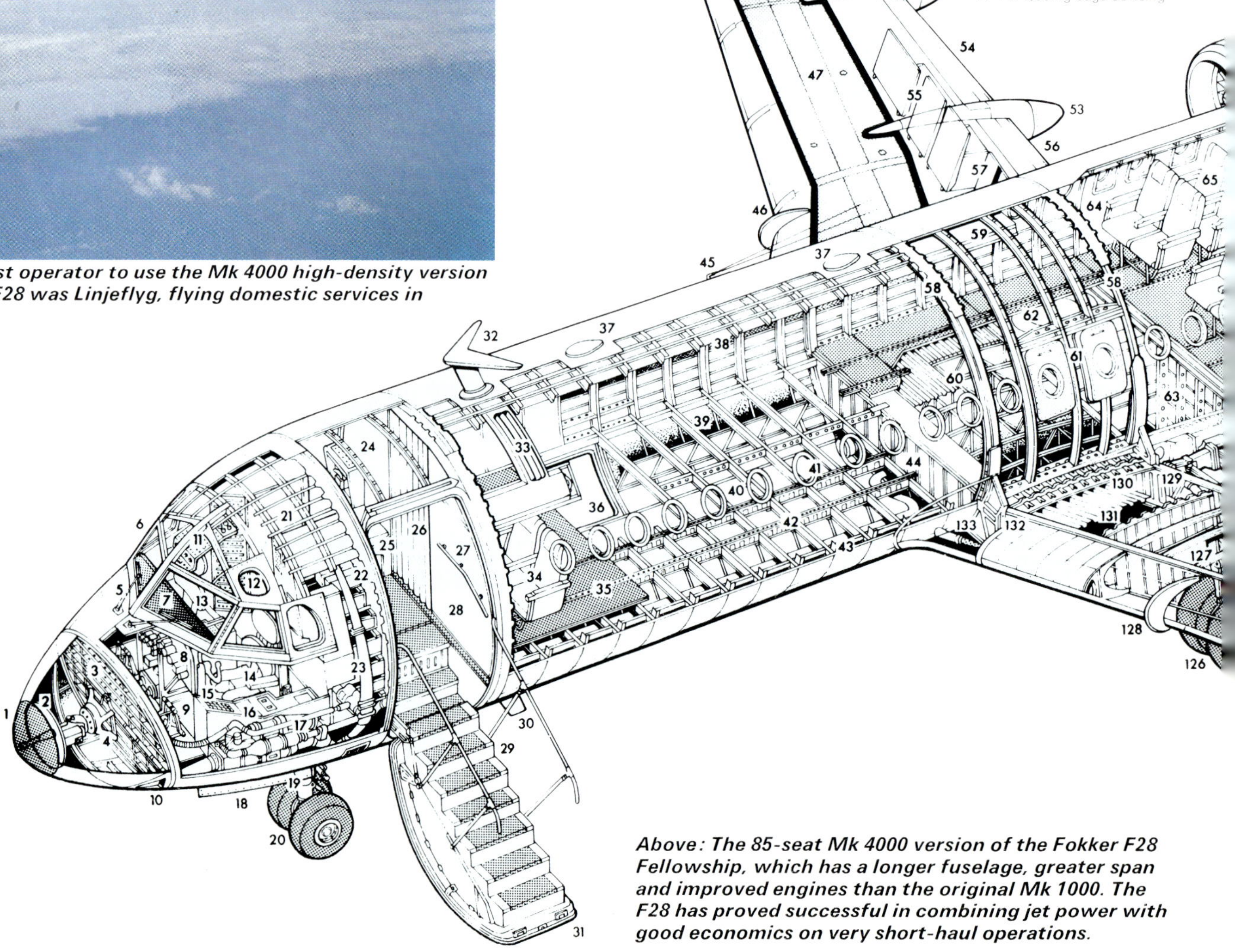

Above: The 85-seat Mk 4000 version of the Fokker F28 Fellowship, which has a longer fuselage, greater span and improved engines than the original Mk 1000. The F28 has proved successful in combining jet power with good economics on very short-haul operations.

78 Fin construction
79 Tailplane hydraulic jacks
80 Tailplane de-icing air duct
81 Anti-collision light
82 Starboard tailplane
83 Starboard elevator
84 Tailplane pivot fairing
85 Elevator hinge controls
86 Tailcone fairing
87 Tail navigation light
88 Port elevator
89 Tailplane construction
90 Leading edge de-icing
91 Tailplane pivot
92 Rudder
93 Rudder hydraulic jack
94 Port airbrake (open)
95 Airbrake jack housing
96 Rear fuselage construction
97 Hydraulic accumulators
98 Exhaust silencer nozzle
99 Engine pylon fairing
100 Bleed air ducting
101 Rolls Royce Mk 555-15 Spey Junior engine
102 Engine mountings
103 Engine cowlings
104 Auxiliary power unit (APU)
105 Engine mounting beam
106 Air intake
107 Five-abreast passenger seating
108 Underfloor air duct
109 Trailing edge wing root fairing
110 Inboard flap track fairing
111 Port inboard spoilers
112 Port flaps
113 Flap mechanism fairings
114 Port outboard spoilers
115 Flap construction
116 Aileron tab
117 Port aileron
118 Static discharge wicks
119 Port wingtip
120 Port navigation light
121 Outer wing rib construction
122 Leading edge de-icing air ducts
123 Leading edge construction
124 Lattice ribs
125 Wing integral fuel tanks
126 Twin mainwheels
127 Main undercarriage leg
128 Leading edge fence
129 Undercarriage retraction jack fixing
130 Wing panel bolted joint
131 Corrugated inner wing skin
132 Wing spar attachment frame
133 Leading edge de-icing air duct

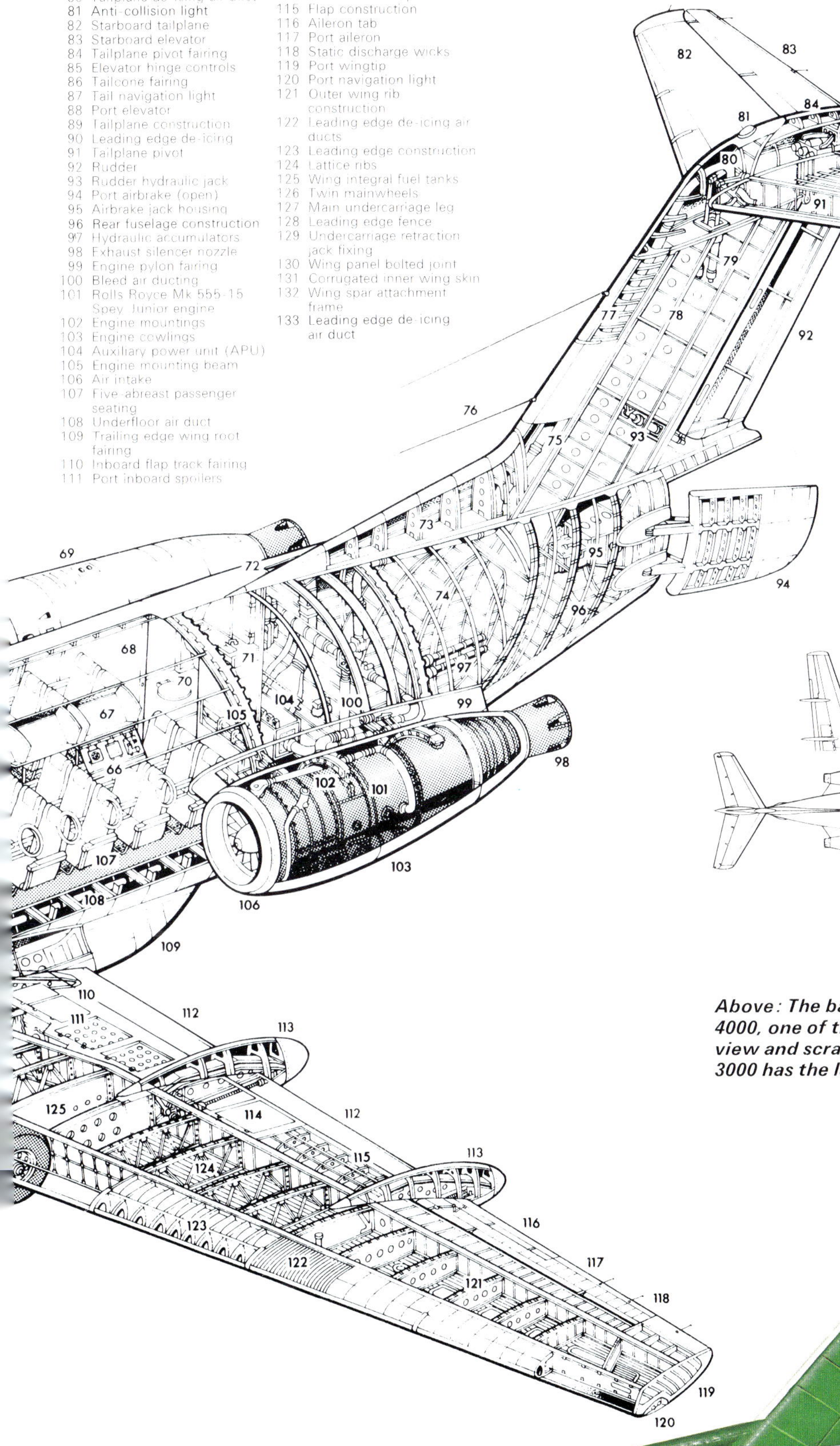

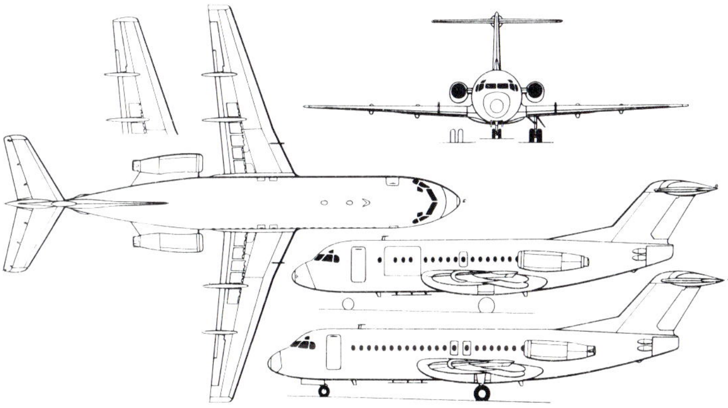

Above: The basic three-view drawing above depicts the F28 Mk 4000, one of the three production versions in 1978. The upper side view and scrap wing view relate to the original Mk 1000; the Mk 3000 has the latter's fuselage with the long span wing.

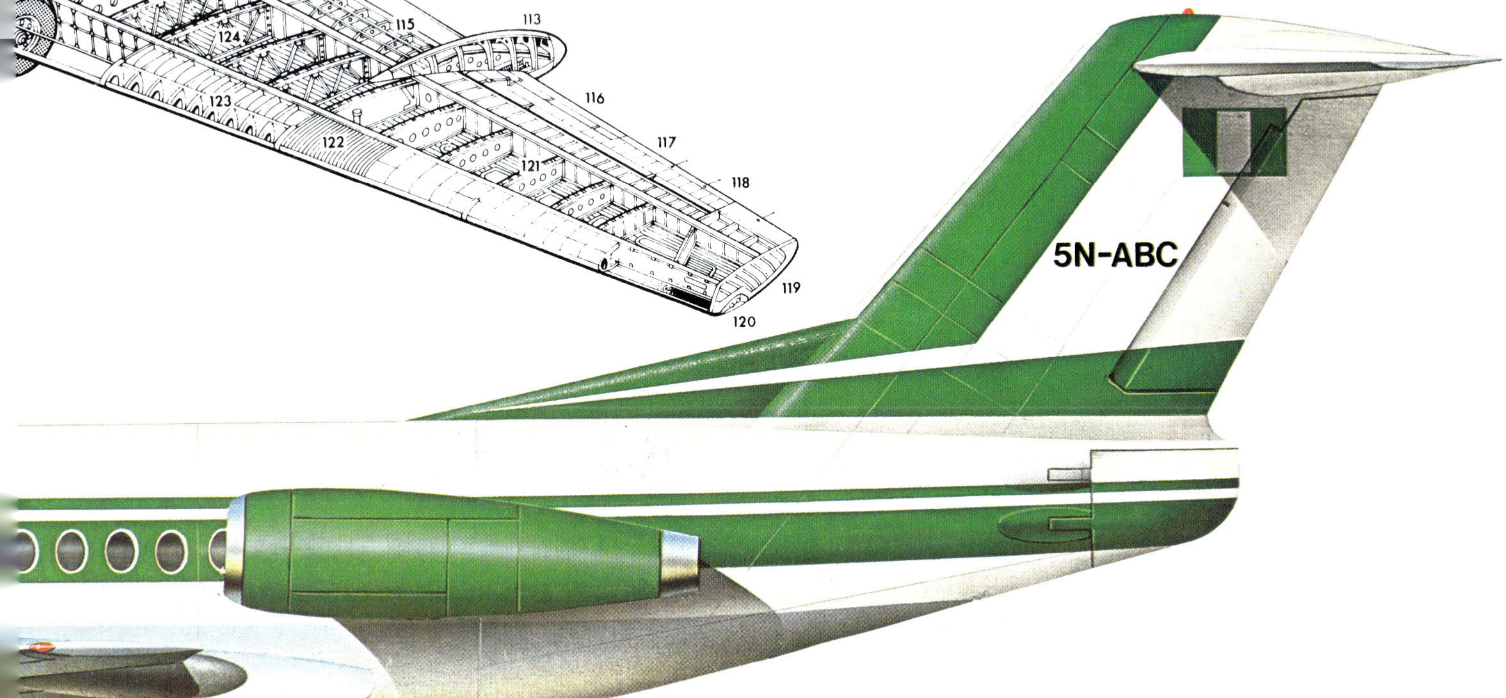

Above: Fokker F28 Mk 2000 in the colours of Nigeria Airways, the first airline to operate this stretched-fuselage version of the Dutch-built short-haul jet transport.

GAF Nomad
Australia

Power Plant: Two Allison 250-B17B turboprops, each rated at 400shp for take-off.
Performance: Normal cruising speed, 193mph (311km/h); initial rate of climb, 1,460ft/min (7·4m/sec); service ceiling, 22,500ft (6860m); max range, 840mls (1352km).
Weights: Operating weight empty, 4,666lb (2116kg); max take-off weight, 8,500lb (3855kg).
Dimensions: Span, 54ft 0in (16·46m); length, 41ft $2\frac{1}{2}$in (12·56m); height, 18ft $1\frac{1}{2}$in (5·52m); wing area, 324·0sq ft (30·10m^2).

With headquarters at Fishermen's Bend, near Melbourne, the Government Aircraft Factories is the principal aircraft production unit in Australia, and is operated by the Department of Industry and Commerce primarily as a source of defence supplies. During the mid 'sixties, the GAF began design of a small utility transport intended to provide a continuing production activity as well as meeting local military and civil needs. This type emerged in prototype form as the N2, the first two examples of which made their first flights on 23 July and 5 December 1971.

The N2 was of conventional high wing layout with an almost-square fuselage cross section, large side-loading doors, a retractable undercarriage and Allison 250 turboprop engines. After gaining Australian certification on 11 August 1972, the type entered production as the N22 for both military and civil use and, named Nomad, went into commercial service on 18 December 1975 with Aero Pelican. Although most N22s and N22Bs (the latter with increased gross weight) have so far been produced for military use, a few are used by civil operators for air taxi and third level services and for special duties such as aerial survey and mapping.

The Nomad N24, first flown in 1976, has the fuselage lengthened by 3ft 9in (1·14m), increasing the seating capacity from 12 to 15. Power plant and weights remain unchanged. The N24 is intended primarily for commercial use and one of the first customers is the Northern Territory Aeromedical Service, which has a fleet of six N24s equipped as air ambulances.

***Below:* Three-view drawing of the GAF Nomad N22, Australia's first recent attempt to design and produce a transport aircraft.**

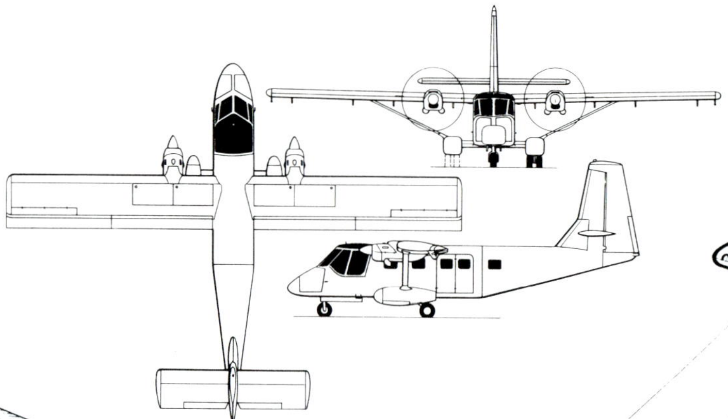

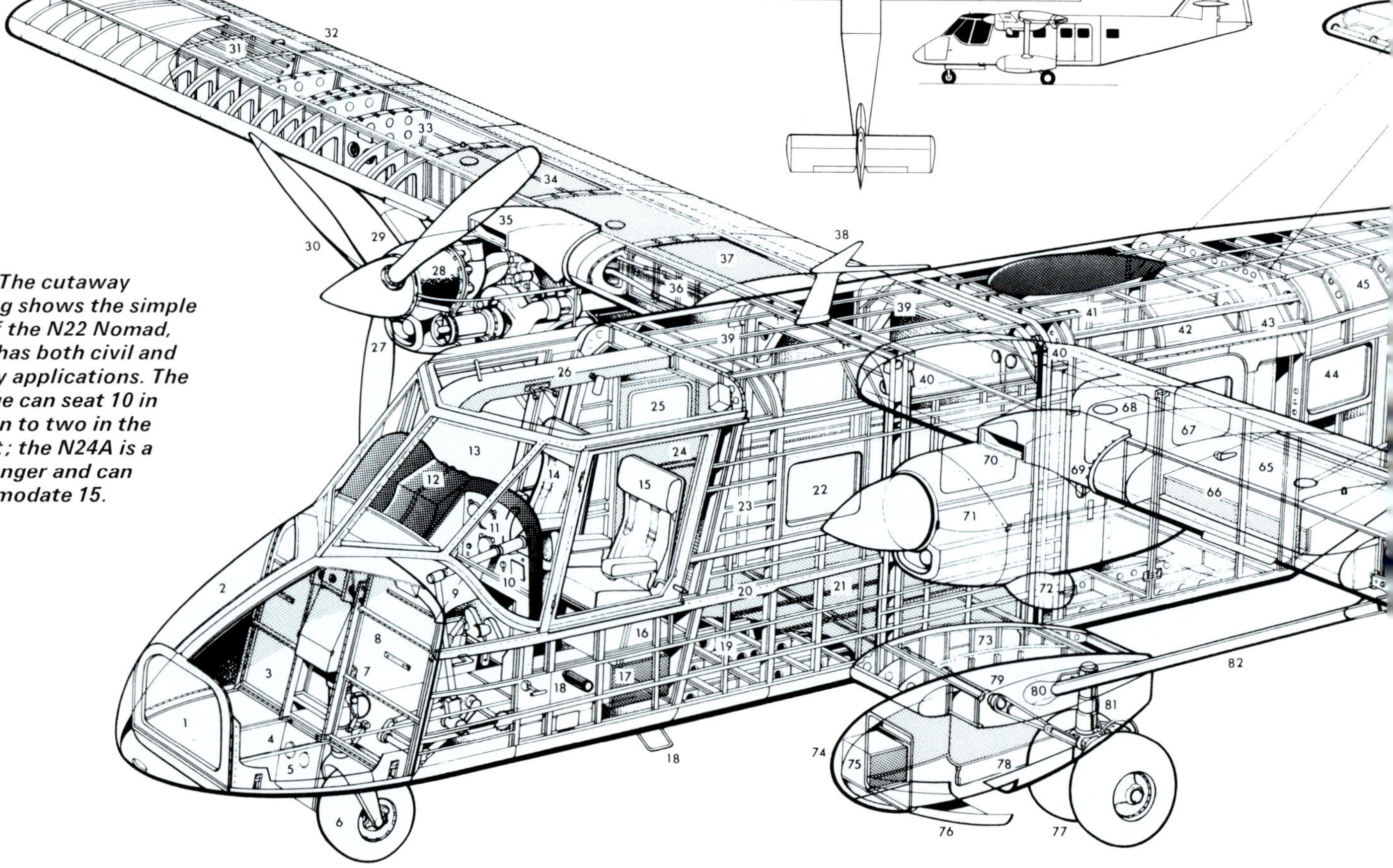

***Right:* The cutaway drawing shows the simple lines of the N22 Nomad, which has both civil and military applications. The fuselage can seat 10 in addition to two in the cockpit; the N24A is a little longer and can accommodate 15.**

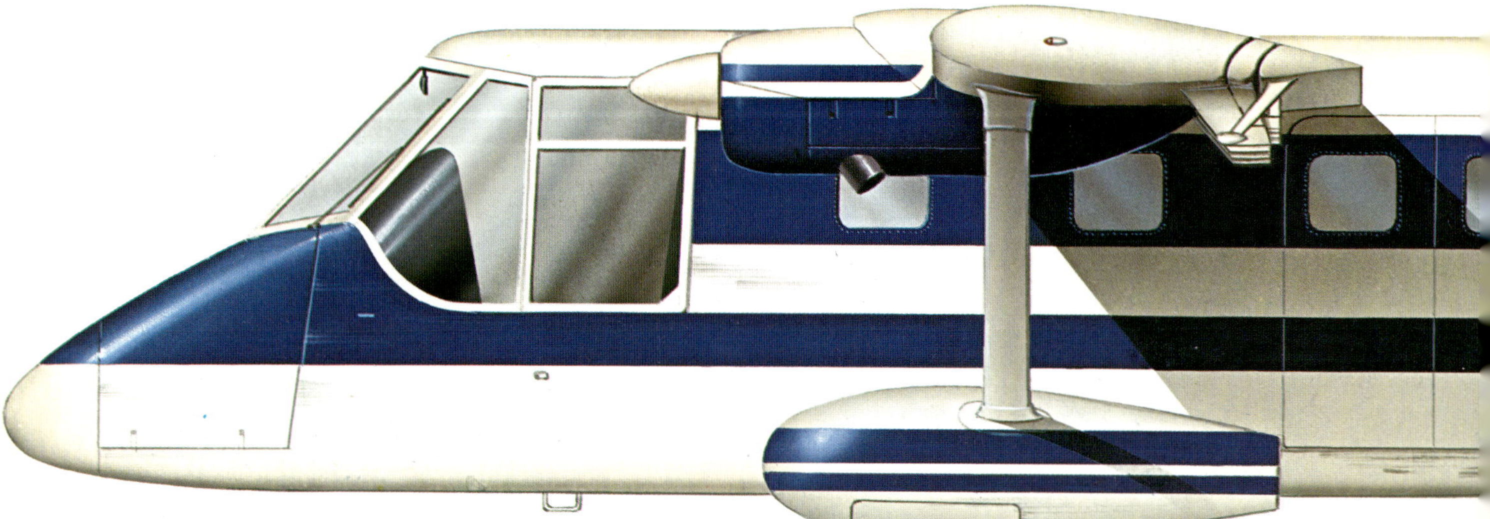

Government Aircraft Factories Nomad 22 Cutaway Drawing Key

1 Nose cone
2 Hinged baggage doors (port and starboard)
3 Nose baggage compartment (27cu ft/0·76m³)
4 Nosewheel door
5 Twin landing/taxying lamps
6 Nosewheel
7 Nosewheel pivot
8 Forward bulkhead
9 Port rudder pedals
10 Port instrument panel
11 Port control column
12 Instrument panel shroud
13 Windshield
14 Starboard pilot's seat
15 Port pilot's seat
16 Raised cockpit floor
17 Underfloor avionics bay (port and starboard)
18 Entry steps
19 Cabin underfloor structure
20 Fuselage longeron
21 Cabin floor (seat and freight tie-down rails)
22 Enlarged window area
23 Fuselage framework
24 Control runs behind cabin starboard wall
25 Starboard window
26 Overhead instrumentation (electrical and secondary controls)
27 Engine compressor air intake
28 Allison 250-B17 turboprop engine
29 Starboard wing strut
30 Hartzell three-blade propeller
31 Wing stringers
32 Starboard spoiler
33 Wing ribs
34 Starboard outer fuel tank
35 Engine intake
36 Hinged leading-edge (engine control access)
37 Starboard inner fuel tank
38 Antenna
39 Starboard wing/centre fuselage attachment points
40 Port wing/centre fuselage attachment points
41 Emergency exit (starboard only)
42 Cabin aft bulkhead position (7-passenger configuration)
43 Upper longeron
44 Additional aft window
45 Cabin aft bulkhead (12 passenger configuration)
46 Rear baggage compartment (27cu ft/0·76m³)
47 Control runs
48 Dorsal fin
49 Stub fin attachment point
50 Starboard tailplane
51 Elevator
52 Aerials
53 Fin forward spar
54 Anti-collision beacon
55 Rudder corrugated skin
56 Rudder post
57 Rudder tab
58 Elevator tab
59 All-moving tailplane
60 Rear navigation light
61 Rudder lower attachment point
62 Angled fuselage/stub fin frame
63 Aft fuselage construction
64 Fuselage skinning
65 Port outer fuel tank
66 Cabin step
67 Passenger/freight door (rear section)
68 Passenger/freight door (forward secton)
69 Nacelle attachment point
70 Glass-fibre laminate intake cowl
71 Glass-fibre laminate fixed nacelle panels
72 Exhaust stub (hinges with engine access panel)
73 One-piece machined stub wing
74 Port landing pod
75 Battery housing
76 Forward undercarriage door (closes after gear extension)
77 Dual-wheel main landing gear
78 Side-hinged rear undercarriage door
79 Retraction jack (electrically actuated)
80 Wing strut lower attachment
81 Mainwheel leg
82 Port wing strut
83 Wing-strut/main spar attachment point
84 Double-slotted flaps
85 Aileron tab
86 Control surface/flap actuating mechanism
87 Main spar
88 Rear spar
89 Port spoiler
90 Port aileron
91 Forward outer-section flap
92 Port navigation light

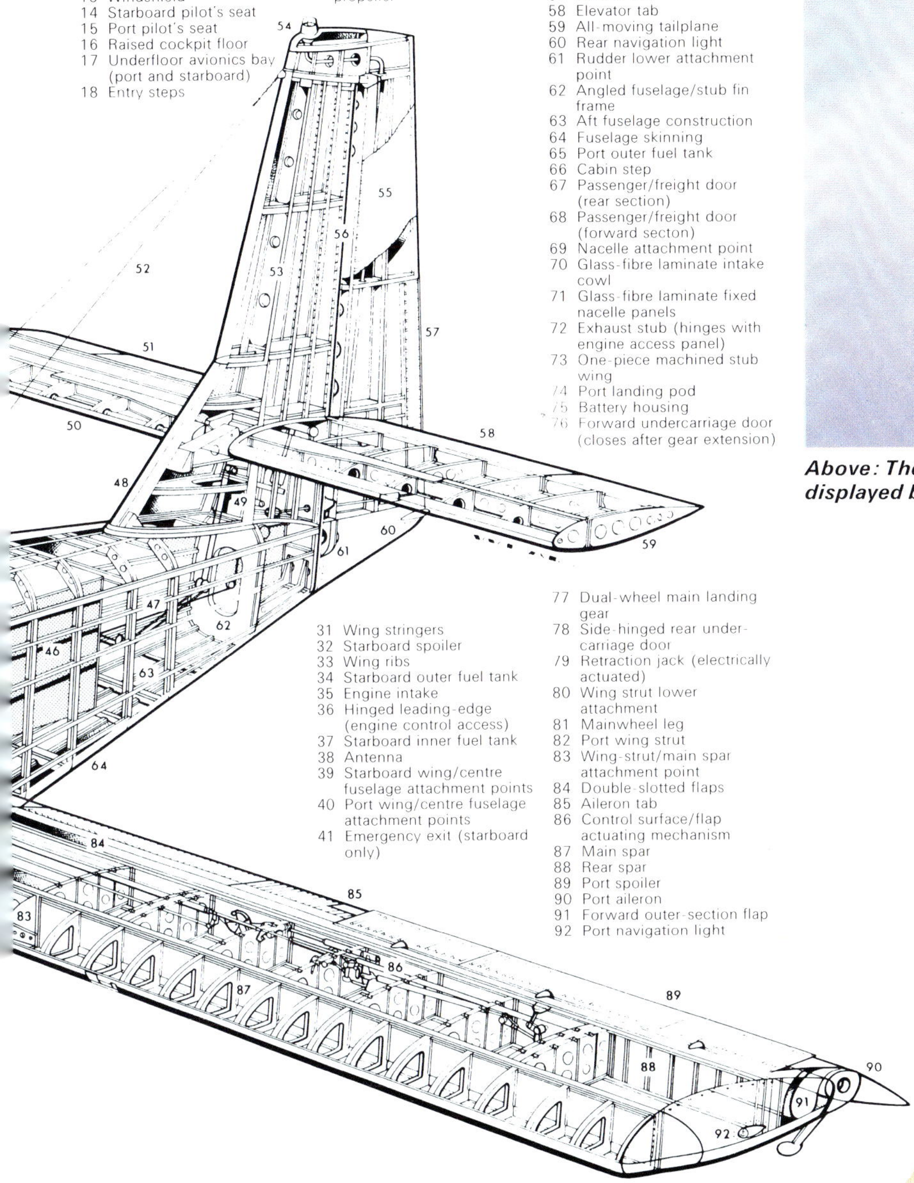

Above: The clean, functional lines of Australia's N22 are displayed by an N22B on a European demonstration tour.

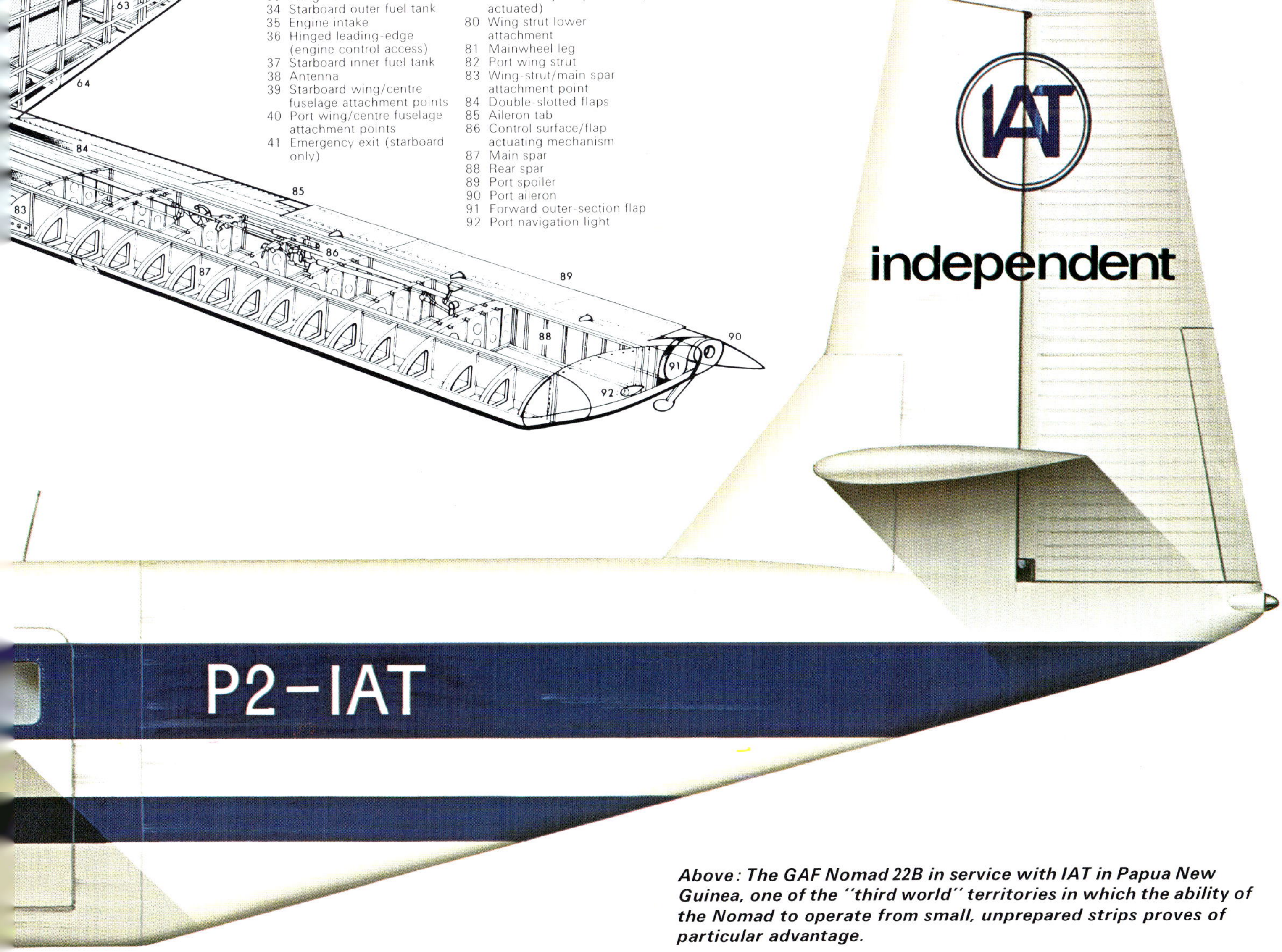

Above: The GAF Nomad 22B in service with IAT in Papua New Guinea, one of the "third world" territories in which the ability of the Nomad to operate from small, unprepared strips proves of particular advantage.

Grumman (McKinnon) Goose
USA

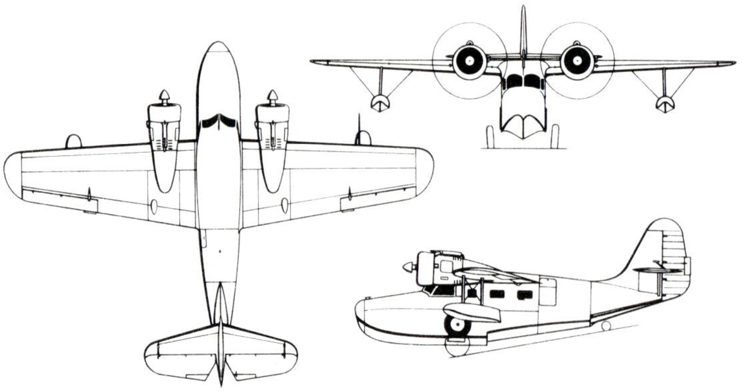

The following specification refers to the G-21G:
Power Plant: Two 715eshp Pratt & Whitney (UACL) PT6A-27 turboprops.
Performance: Max speed, 236mph (380km/h); cruising speed, 205mph (330km/h); service ceiling, 20,000ft (6096m); range with max fuel, 1,600mls (2575km).
Weights: Empty, 6700lb (3040kg); max take-off, 12,500lb (5670kg).
Dimensions: Span, 50ft 10in (15·49m); length, 39ft 7in (12·07m); wing area, 377·64sq ft (35·07m^2).

The Grumman G-21 Goose was first flown in June 1937 and received US Type Approval on 29 September that year, followed by the G-21A production model on 5 February 1938. These were commercial amphibians with up to eight seats (including the pilot) built primarily for private and business

***Below:** A Grumman G-21A Goose of Antilles Air Boats, one of the largest remaining users of the little amphibian.*

Handley Page Herald
United Kingdom

The following specification relates to the Herald 200:
Power Plant: Two 2,105ehp Rolls-Royce Dart 527 turboprops.
Performance: Max cruising speed, 274mph (441km/h) at 15,000ft (4572m); best economy cruise, 265mph (426km/h) at 23,000ft (7010m); initial rate of climb, 1,805ft/min (9·1m/sec); service ceiling, 27,900ft (8504m); no-reserves range with max payload, 1,110mls (1786km); no-reserves range with max fuel, 1,620mls (2607km).
Weights: Operating empty, 25,800lb (11,700kg); max payload, 11,242lb (5100kg); max take-off, 43,000lb (19,505kg).
Dimensions: Span, 94ft 9in (28·88m); length, 75ft 6in (23·01m); height, 24ft 1in (7·34m); wing area, 886sq ft (82·3m^2).

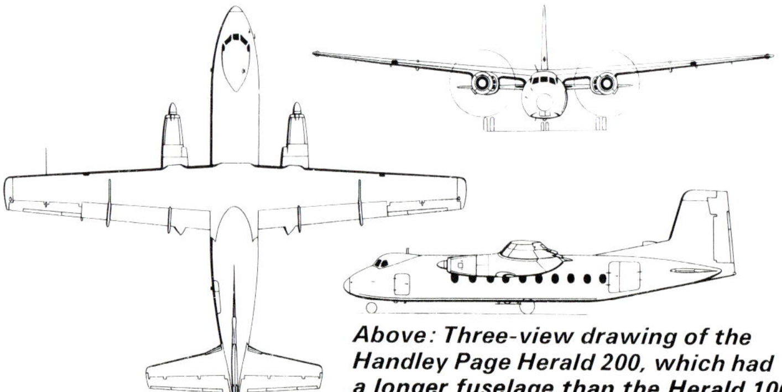

***Above:** Three-view drawing of the Handley Page Herald 200, which had a longer fuselage than the Herald 100.*

Like the Aérospatiale (Nord) 262 and the Short Skyvan, the Herald was designed around piston engines but went into production with turboprops. The design was started as the company's first post-war essay into the civil market since the Hermes, and after market study the decision was taken to build a feeder-line aircraft with about 44 seats in a pressurized fuselage, with a range of about 400 miles (644km) – or up to 1,400mls (2253km) with reduced payload. Design was made the responsibility of the Reading branch of the company, previously the Miles Aircraft organization. Details of the HPR 3 Herald were first published in 1954, at which time the aircraft was based upon the use of four Alvis Leonides Major piston radial engines.

By the time the first of two prototypes flew at Woodley on 25 August 1955, orders had been placed for a total of 29 Heralds by Queensland Airlines, Australian National Airways and Lloyd Aereo Colombiano. A second prototype flew in August 1956 and a production batch of 25 was put in hand, but by 1957 the success of the turboprop engine, particularly in the Viscount, made it apparent that future prospects for the Herald were bleak and even the initial customers were reluctant to proceed with their commitments. In May 1957, consequently, Handley Page announced plans to offer an alternative version of the Herald with two Dart turboprops in place of the four radials, and subsequently the original version was dropped altogether.

Both the Herald prototypes were converted to take the Dart engines, flying in their revised form on 11 March and 17 December 1958 respectively. Initially, the name Dart Herald was used, but the prefix was soon dropped. The first production aircraft flew on 30 October 1959 and was identified as a Srs 100, being used as a company demonstrator. Earlier in 1959, the UK government had ordered three Heralds for use by BEA on its Scottish Highlands and Islands routes, and the next three aircraft to appear were also of the Srs 100 type (specifically, Srs 101, individual numbers being adopted for each customer) for BEA. No more Srs 100s were built.

In September 1960, Jersey Airlines (now British Island Airways) placed an order for six of a lengthened and improved version of the Herald known as the Srs 200. The overall length increased by 3ft 7in (1·09m) and gross weight by 2,000lb (907kg); maximum passenger capacity increased from 47 in the Srs 100 to 56 in the Srs 200, although more usual arrangements were 40 and 44 respectively. The second prototype Herald/Dart Herald was converted to the new standard and flew as a Srs 200 on 8 April 1961. British certification was obtained on 1 June 1961.

Handley Page flew the first production Herald Srs 200 on 13 December 1961 and deliveries to Jersey Airlines began in January 1962, this airline eventually increasing its fleet to 12 after becoming part of the BUA group. Production of the Herald 200 continued at a very low rate until mid-1968, by which time the company had delivered 36 Srs 200s and eight Srs 400s, the latter being a military variant sold to the Royal Malaysian Air Force. At the time the Handley Page company collapsed, six more Heralds were in hand as speculative production but were not completed.

The Heralds were acquired by a variety of operators in small batches, and became the subject of much second-hand trading from an early stage. By early 1977, the major operators were British Island Airways with 12 and British Air Ferries with eight, based in the UK, and Europe Air Service in France with two.

use, and also during the war, for the USAAF and US Navy as general purpose transports. Post-war, the amphibious capability of the Goose was found to be particularly useful in certain airline applications especially in Alaska, parts of Canada, New Zealand, Scandinavia and other areas with lengthy coastlines.

Because of the lack of new amphibians to replace the Goose in this rôle, a market developed for reconditioned and improved versions of the original Grumman design, in which McKinnon Enterprises has specialized since 1958. The G-21C and G-21D had four 340hp Lycoming engines replacing the original two 450hp R-985 Wasp Juniors, the G-21D featuring a lengthened bow. The G-21E introduced 579eshp PT6A-20 turboprops and the G-21G had 715eshp PT6A-27s, with optional wing tip floats and accommodating up to 11 passengers.

Another conversion programme developed by Volpar Inc. comprised the installation of Garrett-AiResearch TPE331-2U-203 turboprops in a Goose, using the company's Package Power units as fitted also to the Volpar Turboliner and the Texas Aeroplane CJ600.

***Left:** The Grumman G-21 Goose in its original piston-engined form, as still used by several airlines.*

***Below:** A Grumman G-21A in the markings of Catalina Airlines (now Air Catalina), a small company that flies regular services from the Californian coast to the island of Catalina.*

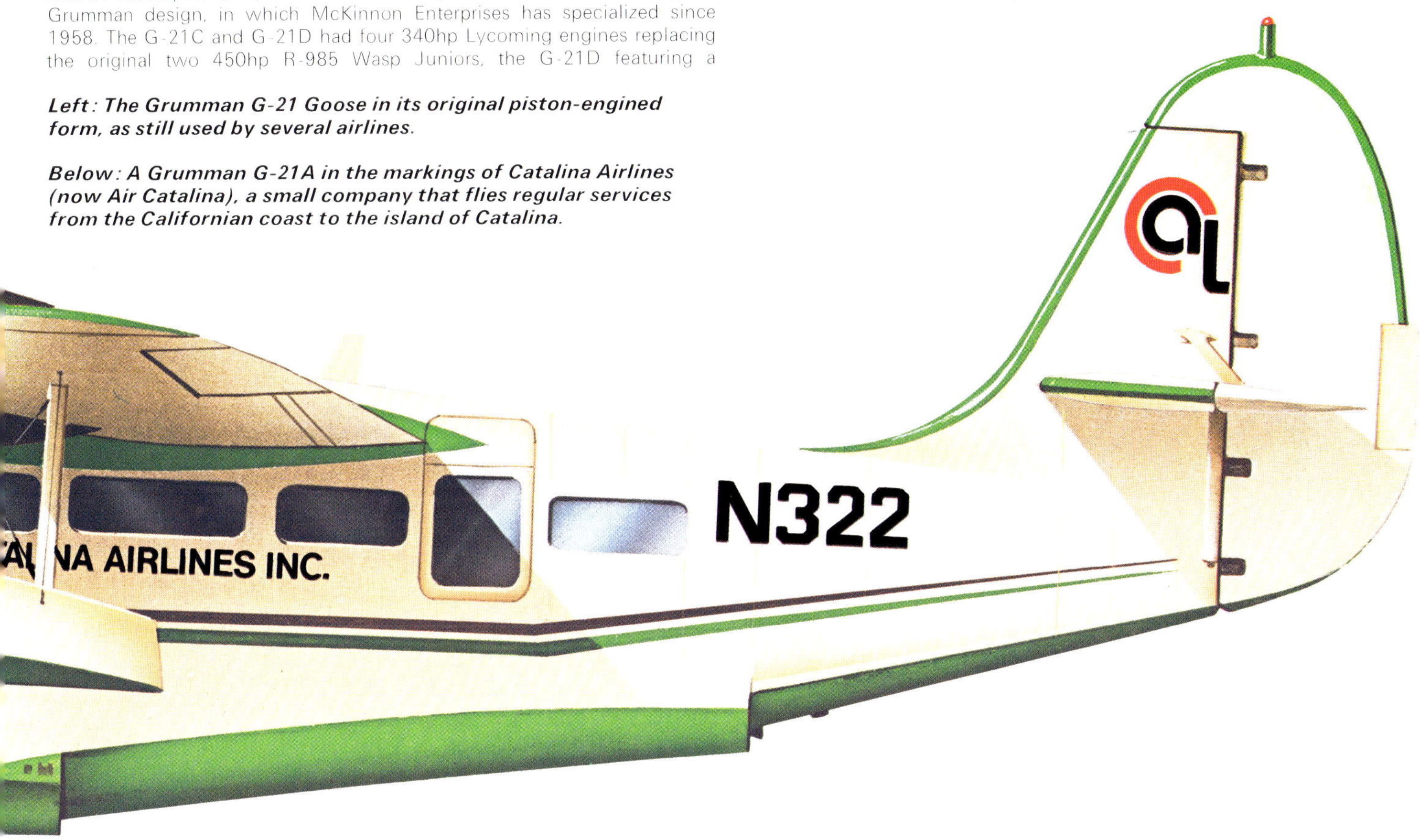

***Below:** A Handley Page Herald 200 in service with the former British United Airways, now used by its successor BIA.*

Handley Page Jetstream
United Kingdom

The following data refer to the basic version with Astazou engines:
Power Plant: Two Turboméca Astazou XIV turboprops each rated at 996shp for take-off.
Performance: Max speed, 298mph (480km/h); range, 745mls (1200km); service ceiling, 30,000ft (9270m).
Weights: Empty, 8,450lb (3835kg); max take-off, 12,500lb (5680kg).
Dimensions: Span, 52ft 0in (15·86m); length, 47ft 1½in (14·35m); height, 17ft 6in (5·30m); wing area, 270sq ft (25·05m²).

The last aeroplane to bear the respected Handley Page name, and the project that was largely responsible for the financial collapse and demise of that illustrious company, the Jetstream was designed in the mid-sixties to provide an 8/18-seat transport suitable for third level airline as well as executive use. Two Turboméca Astazou XIV engines were chosen to power the HP.137 Jetstream, as the new type was named, and by the time the first of four prototypes flew on 18 August 1967, full-scale production had already been launched. A fifth prototype was powered by Garrett AiResearch TPE331 engines and flew on 21 November 1968.

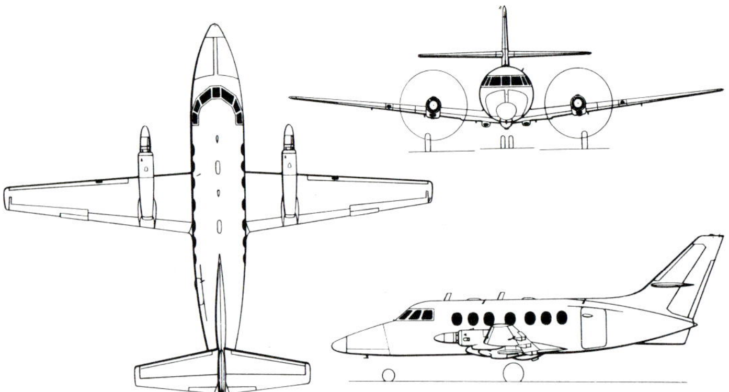

Above: Three-view of the Handley Page Jetstream, the last aircraft to bear the name of the famous British company.

Right: Produced initially as a business transport, the Jetstream has been used as a commuter-liner by several airlines.

Jetstreams with Astazou engines were in operation, both for business use and as airliners, by mid-1969, with the principal demand coming from the USA but when Handley Page ceased operating in 1970 only 38 Jetstreams had been delivered; another 10 were completed subsequently from components already manufactured. Many of the Jetstreams remained in service subsequently, although the Astazou engine proved unpopular among American operators and several alternatives have been offered. These include at least one conversion to have Pratt & Whitney PT6A-34 turboprops by Riley Aeronautics Corporation, and the Century Jetstream III featuring 904eshp Garrett AiResearch TPE331-3U-303s offered by Century Aircraft and engineered by Volpar Inc. The first Century Jetstream III flew in August 1976.

Hawker Siddeley AW 650 Argosy
United Kingdom

The following specification relates to the Argosy 220:
Power Plant: Four 2,230shp Rolls-Royce Dart 532/1 turboprops.
Performance: Max cruising speed, 282mph (455km/h); best economy cruise, 280mph (451km/h); initial rate of climb, 900ft/min (4·6m/sec); service ceiling, 21,000ft (6400m); range with max payload, 485mls (780km); range with max fuel, 1,760mls (2835km).
Weights: Empty equipped 48,920lb (22,186kg); max payload, 32,000lb (14,515kg); max take-off, 93,000lb (42,185kg).
Dimensions: Span, 115ft 0in (33·05m); length, 86ft 9in (26·44m); height, 29ft 3in (8·91m); wing area, 1,458sq ft (135·45m²).

The Argosy – produced by the Armstrong Whitworth subsidiary of Hawker Siddeley – was a private venture design aimed at the airline cargo market, but only 17 examples were built for commercial use, plus 56 specialized transports for the RAF. The first AW650 flew on 8 January 1959 and seven of the 10 Series 100s built were sold in the USA for use on Logair military contract freighting, BEA acquiring the other three. Primarily to meet BEA requirements, the Srs 200, first flown on 11 March 1964, incorporated uprated engines and operated at higher weights. Five similar Srs 220s were built for BEA, but were operated for only a few years before being sold abroad. Two of these were in service in 1977 with SAFE-Air in New Zealand; another was operating in Australia and a few were still in use in the UK with ABC (Air-Bridge Carriers) and by Rolls-Royce. Their nose and rear loading provisions facilitated cargo handling but imposed rather high operating costs and, for many airlines, their relatively short range with maximum payload limited their usefulness. Consequently, when the RAF withdrew its fleet of AW660 Argosies as an economy measure in 1975 and offered them for sale, little interest was aroused in the civil market and only one or two examples were acquired for special freighting tasks.

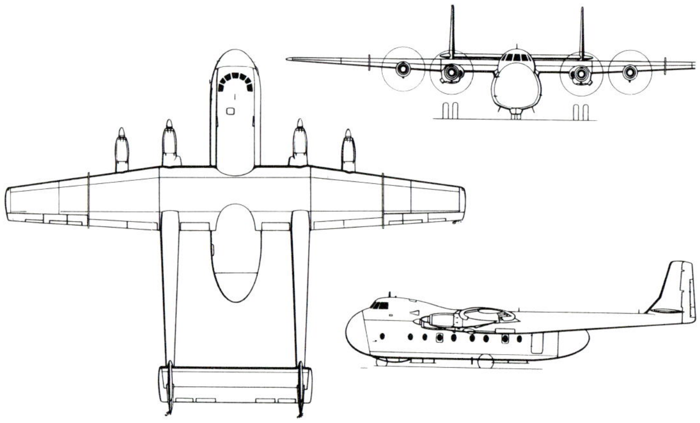

Above right: The AW 650 Argosy, an early attempt to produce a specialised air freighter that achieved only limited success.

Right: Civil Argosies have been operated by several airlines, one of the latest being Air Bridge Carriers (ABC) in the UK.

Hawker Siddeley DH 106 Comet
United Kingdom

The following specification refers to the Comet 4C:
Power Plant: Four 10,500lb st (4763kgp) Rolls-Royce Avon 525 turbojets.
Performance: Max cruising speed, 535mph (861km/h); best economy cruise, 526mph (847km/h); no-reserves range with max payload, 3,540mls (5697km); range with max fuel, 4,310mls (6936km).
Weights: Basic operating, 78,500lb (35,610kg); max payload, 28,950lb (13,130kg); max take-off, 162,000lb (73,482kg).
Dimensions: Span, 115ft 0in (35·05m); length, 118ft 0in (35·97m); height 29ft 5in (8·97m); wing area, 2,121sq ft (197·0m²).

The Comet's place in airline history is secure, for on 2 May 1952 a Comet 1 in service with BOAC operated the world's first service by jet transport, flying from London to Johannesburg via Rome, Beirut, Khartoum, Entebbe and Livingstone. Although the early success of the Comet 1 was marred by a series of accidents that led to it being withdrawn from service two years later, the design was subsequently developed into the long-serving Comet 4.

The concept of the Comet was first formulated as early as 1944, when the Brabazon Committee, set up to suggest the types of aircraft to be developed in Britain after the war, recommended that one such should be a pure-jet

continued on page 90 ▶

Right:* *The Comet celebrated its Silver Jubilee in 1977, having inaugurated the world's first commercial jet service in 1952, with BOAC.

Below:* *Prior to the Comet, nobody had any idea how to arrange the flight-deck of a jetliner (Nene jet engines fitted to a piston-engined Viking hardly counted). From the start de Havilland Aircraft, a talented and enthusiastic team at Hatfield, north of London, aimed high and planned with the proverbial clean sheet of paper for complete success (it was the only way, when so wholly treading in uncharted waters). Once having settled on a circular-section fuselage of 10ft in diameter, the next question was whether or not to have stepped windscreens for the pilots. The decision was to have a completely smooth streamlined nose, and this in turn led to substantial glazed panels in order to achieve the necessary pilot field of view. The unprecedented cabin pressure-differential of nearly 9lb/sq in required an extremely strong forged and machined frame, and the forward-facing panels were also new in having transparent electrically conductive films (Triplex GF) for anti-icing and Dunlop Maxivue wipers cleared for 500mph TAS. As the flight deck fitted so closely into a pointed nose it was quite compact, but a flight engineer was able to manage all the system panels on the right wall of the forward fuselage. In front of each pilot was a basic group of six primary flight instruments – vertical speed, airspeed, horizon, altimeter, directional gyro and twin/slip – with a completely new family of gas-turbine instruments in the centre. Large trim wheels and fuel cocks graced the central console, and the only completely new feature was a mass of controls for Red, Blue, Yellow and Green hydraulic systems, without which flight control was in peril. The French wisely picked up all this research in the Caravelle, whose flight deck differed only in having dual instead of quad engine controls and instruments.

►transport carrying 14 passengers and mail over short ranges. Subsequent discussions led to this basic idea being "stretched" to have transatlantic range and with BOAC showing positive interest, the de Havilland company (later to be absorbed by Hawker Siddeley) was given authority to proceed with design of an aircraft of this type in February 1945. Several different projects were studied in succession under the designation D.H.106, and on 21 January 1947, BOAC placed a preliminary order for eight aircraft (later, nine) which were to seat 24–32 passengers and, with a gross weight of 100,000lb (45,360kg), would cruise at 505mph (813km/h).

Two prototypes were put in hand and the first of these flew from Hatfield on 27 July 1949, followed by the second one year later to the day. The engines were four 5,050lb st (2290kgp) de Havilland Ghost 50s and the prototypes differed from subsequent production aircraft in having single main wheels instead of four-wheel bogies. The first production aircraft flew on 9 January 1951 and British certification was obtained on 22 January 1952. The nine Comet 1s for BOAC were followed by 10 Comet 1As, which had increased fuel capacity and gross weight. Orders were placed by Canadian Pacific, UAT, Air France and the RCAF. First services were flown by UAT on 19 February 1953 and by Air France on 26 August 1953; Canadian Pacific never put the type into service and all operations by Comet 1s and 1As ceased in April 1954.

Before the grounding of the original Comets, de Havilland had developed the Comet 2, with a 3-ft (0·91-m) fuselage stretch and 6,500lb st (2948kgp) Rolls-Royce Avon 502s and had projected the Mk 3 with an 18ft 6in (5·64-m) fuselage stretch to seat 58–78 passengers, 9,000lb st (4082kgp) Avon RA 16s and extra fuel in pinion tanks on the wings. A prototype Mk 2 flew on 16 February 1952, initially with Avon 501s, and orders for this type were placed by BOAC, Canadian Pacific, UAT, Air France, BCPA, JAL, LAV and Panair do Brasil. More significantly, Pan American ordered three Mk 3s with an option on seven more, orders also being placed by BOAC and Air India.

None of these orders was fulfilled, but after the reasons for the accidents to the Comet 1s had been fully explained, construction of a prototype Comet 3 was completed and this prototype flew on 19 July 1954. Comet 2s already in production for BOAC were eventually completed for the RAF, and the Comet 4 was evolved as the production form of the Comet 3, having 10,500lb st (4763kgp) Avon 524s and accommodation for 63–81 passengers. BOAC ordered the Comet 4 into production and the first flight was made on 27 April 1958. Commercial services by Comet were resumed on 4 October 1958 when BOAC flew the first London–New York jet service (stopping at Gander) by Comet 4. Eventually, 28 Comet 4s were built.

Primarily for BEA, de Havilland next developed the Comet 4B with the span reduced by 7ft (2·13m) and length increased by 3ft 4in (1·02m), to carry 92 passengers (five abreast) over shorter ranges. The Comet 3 prototype converted to Comet 3B flew in this form on 21 August 1958 and the first Comet 4B flew on 27 June 1959; 18 were built. The final production variant was the Comet 4C, first flown on 31 October 1959. This had the lengthened fuselage of the Comet 4B with the original wings of the Comet 4; 28 were built, ending in 1964; and two final Comet airframes were converted to become prototypes of the Nimrod maritime reconnaissance aircraft, thus ensuring that the final descendant of the design would continue in service until late in the century.

Comets of the 4, 4B and 4C series were flown by numerous airlines between 1962 and the early 'seventies, but by 1977 the only operator of the type was the UK charter and IT airline Dan Air, which had first acquired two ex-BOAC Comet 4s in 1966 and had gone on to purchase surplus 4s, 4Bs and 4Cs from operators all over the world, having had 49 Comets in its hands at one time or another and 15 still in service in 1977.

Above: By 1978, only Dan-Air was still using the Comet commercially. Its fleet included several 4Bs, with shorter wingspan, and examples of other Comet types.

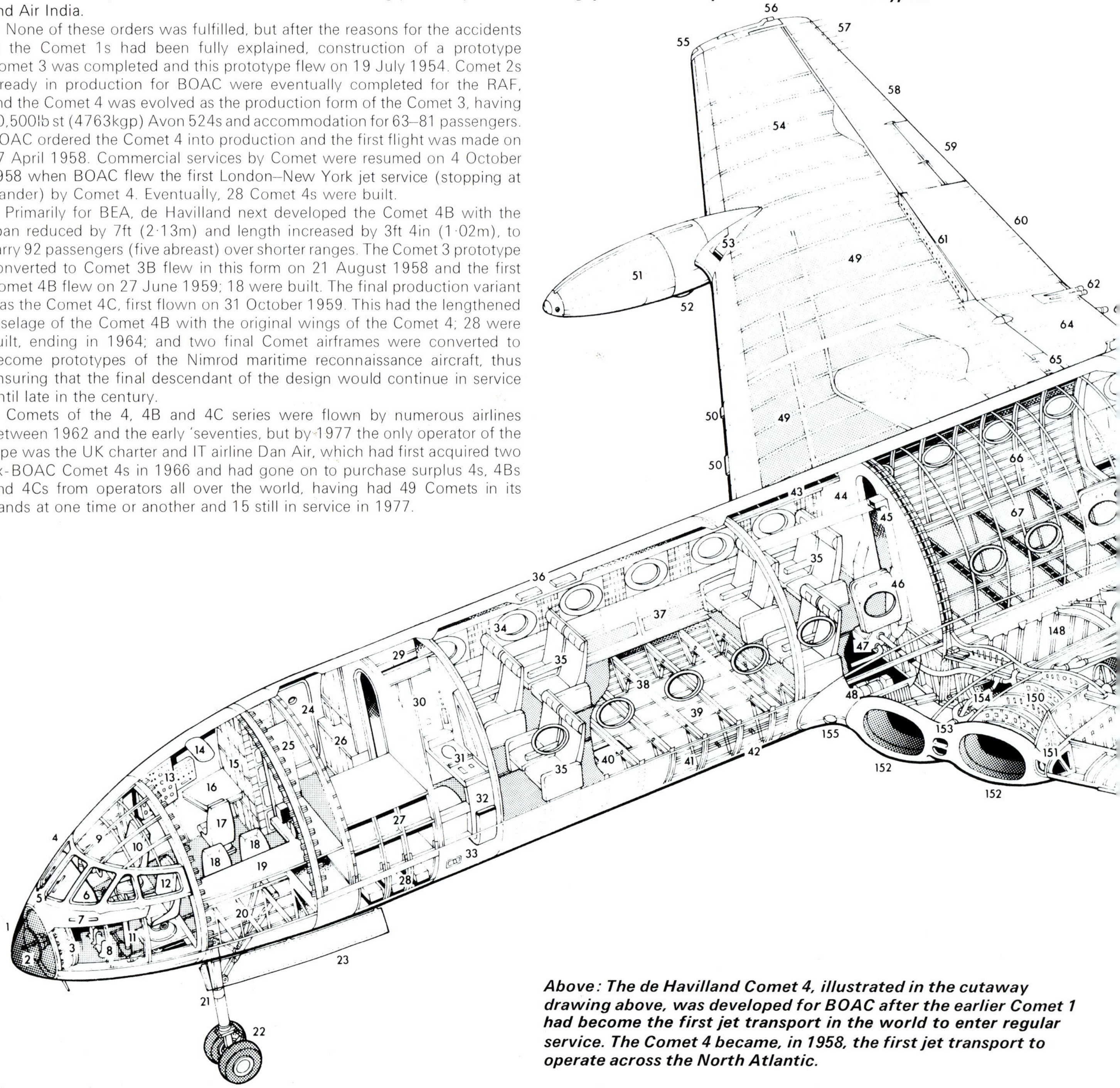

Above: The de Havilland Comet 4, illustrated in the cutaway drawing above, was developed for BOAC after the earlier Comet 1 had become the first jet transport in the world to enter regular service. The Comet 4 became, in 1958, the first jet transport to operate across the North Atlantic.

De Havilland Comet 4 Cutaway Drawing Key

1 Radome
2 Radar scanner
3 Front pressure bulkhead
4 Windscreen framing
5 Windscreen wipers
6 Instrument panel coaming
7 DME aerial
8 Rudder pedals
9 Cockpit roof construction
10 Co-pilot's seat
11 Control column
12 Pilot's seat
13 Engineer's control panel
14 Emergency escape hatch
15 Radio rack
16 Engineer's work table
17 Engineer's swivelling seat
18 Navigator's seats
19 Navigator's work table
20 Nosewheel bay construction
21 Nosewheel leg strut
22 Twin nosewheels
23 Nosewheel door
24 Crew entry door
25 Crew's wardrobe
26 Forward galley
27 Galley supplies stowage boxes
28 Radio and electrical equipment bay
29 Forward starboard toilet compartment
30 Forward port toilet compartment
31 Wash basin
32 Air conditioning duct
33 Toilet servicing panel
34 Cabin window panel
35 First class cabin seats
36 Twin ADF loop aerials
37 Air conditioning grilles
38 Floor beams
39 Forward freight and luggage hold
40 Freight hold door
41 Control cable runs
42 Fuselage keel construction
43 Overhead hat rack
44 Cabin dividing bulkhead
45 Air distribution duct
46 Emergency escape window
47 Air conditioning plant
48 Hydraulics bay
49 Starboard wing integral fuel tanks
50 Flow spoilers
51 External fuel tank
52 Tank bumper
53 Fixed slot
54 Outer wing fuel tanks
55 Navigation light
56 Wing tip fuel vent
57 Static dischargers
58 Starboard aileron
59 Aileron tab
60 Flap outer section
61 Airbrake (upper and lower surfaces)
62 Fuel dump pipes
63 Fuel vent
64 Flap inboard section
65 Inboard airbrake (upper surface only)
66 Fuselage frame and stringer construction
67 Wing centre section fuel cells
68 Emergency escape hatch
69 Aileron servo controls
70 Main fuselage frame
71 Aft tourist class cabin
72 Rear freight hold/luggage compartment
73 Floor beam construction
74 HF aerial cable (port and starboard)
75 Overhead hat rack
76 Tourist class cabin seats
77 Aft galley
78 Starboard service door
79 Aft starboard toilet compartment
80 Aft radio rack
81 Rear pressure bulkhead
82 Anti collision light
83 Dorsal fin fairing
84 Starboard tailplane
85 ILS aerial
86 Starboard elevator
87 Leading edge de-icing ducts
88 Fin construction
89 HF blade aerial
90 Rudder balance weight
91 Rudder
92 Elevator hinge controls
93 Elevator tab
94 Port elevator
95 Tailplane construction
96 ILS aerial
97 Leading edge de-icing
98 Tailplane attachment
99 Fuselage fin frame
100 Tail bumper/fuselage vent
101 Rudder and elevator control rods
102 Access hatch to control bay
103 De-icing air supply duct
104 Rear freight hold
105 Tailplane servo controls
106 Mail locker
107 Aft port toilet compartment
108 Passenger entry door
109 Door frame construction
110 Steward's seat
111 Tourist class passenger seating
112 Wing fillet construction
113 Life raft stowage
114 Inboard tailpipe duct
115 Exhaust silencer nozzles
116 Outboard tailpipe
117 Thrust reverser (outboard only)
118 Inboard flap section
119 Fuel vent
120 Fuel dump pipes
121 Flap jack
122 Flap connecting links
123 Port airbrake (upper and lower surfaces)
124 Outboard flap section
125 Flap construction
126 Aileron tab
127 Port aileron
128 Aileron hinge controls
129 Aileron construction
130 Static dischargers
131 Wing tip fuel vent
132 Port navigation light
133 Outer wing construction
134 Outboard fuel tank bays
135 Fuel tank access panels
136 Wing stringer construction
137 External fuel tank
138 Tank bumper
139 Fixed slot
140 Wing rib construction
141 Leading edge de-icing ducts
142 Four wheel bogie unit
143 Wing skin joint strap
144 Undercarriage well
145 Main undercarriage leg mechanism
146 Wing integral fuel tank
147 Rolls Royce Avon R.A.29 engine
148 Inboard engine bay (engine omitted)
149 Engine mounting frame
150 Intake duct construction
151 Landing lamp
152 Engine intakes
153 Ram air intake
154 Heat exchangers
155 Taxi lamp

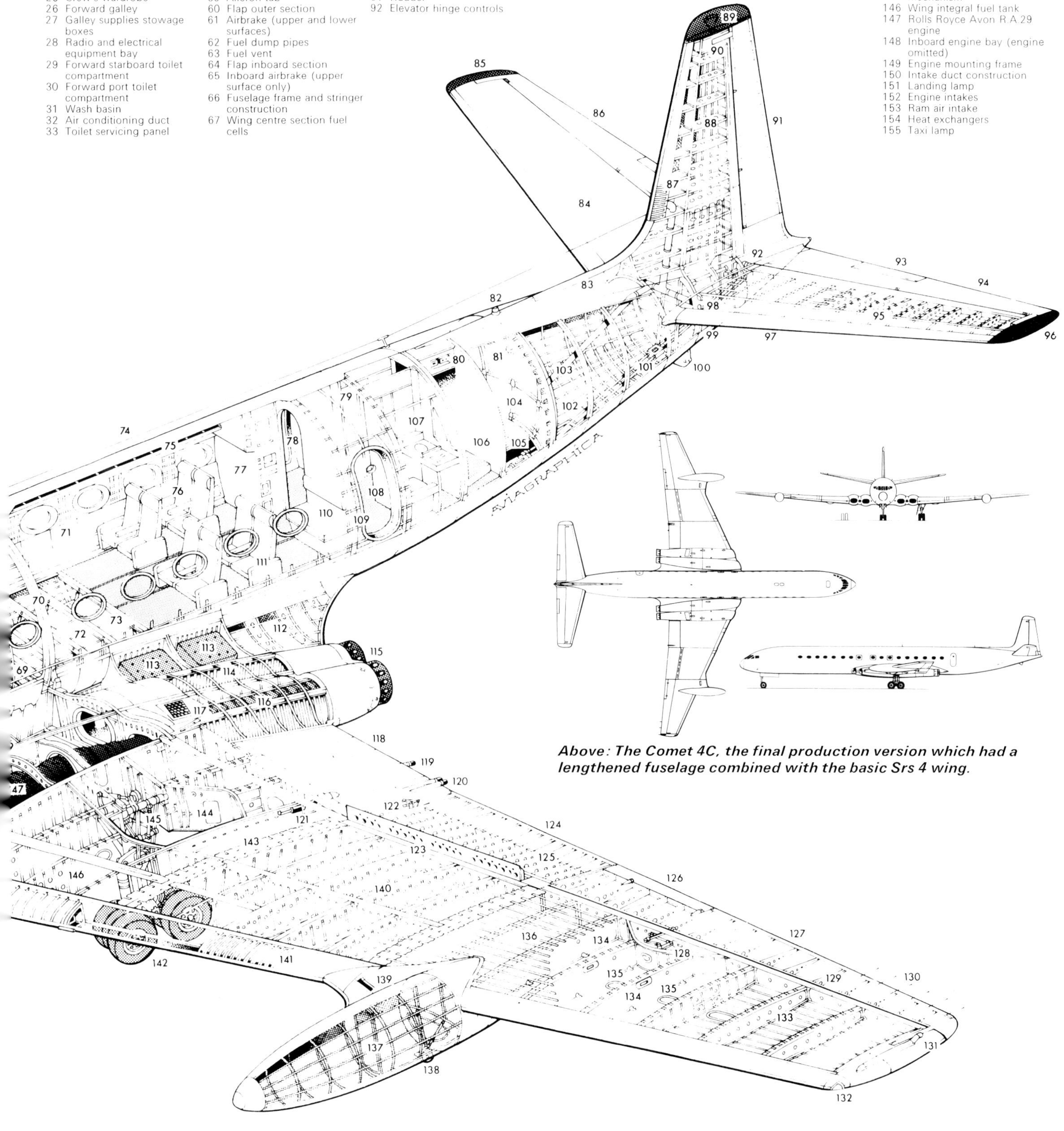

Above: The Comet 4C, the final production version which had a lengthened fuselage combined with the basic Srs 4 wing.

Hawker Siddeley HS. 748

United Kingdom

***Above:* Sales of the HS.748 had totalled over 300 by mid-1978, mostly to smaller airlines around the world.**

The following specification refers to the HS.748 Srs 2A:
Power Plant: Two 2,280ehp Rolls-Royce Dart 532-2L or -2S turboprops.
Performance: Max cruising speed, 278mph (448km/h) at 10,000ft (3050m); initial rate of climb, 1,320ft/min (6·7m/sec); service ceiling, 25,000ft (7600m); range with max payload, 530mls (852km); range with max fuel, 1,987mls (3150km).
Weights: Basic operating, 26,700lb (12,110kg); max payload, 11,800lb (5350kg); max take-off, 44,495lb (20,182kg).
Dimensions: Span, 98ft 6in (30·02m); length, 67ft 0in (20·42m); height, 24ft 10in (7·57m); wing area, 810·75sq ft (73·35m^2).

After concentrating upon military aircraft development for a decade after World War II, A V Roe and Co Ltd (Avro – now absorbed in Hawker Siddeley Aviation) decided to re-enter the commercial aircraft field in 1957, primarily as a result of the Sandys White Paper on Defence in that year, with its prediction that the RAF would have no more new manned aircraft. After a study of the market, the company elected to develop a twin turboprop transport for the short-haul market – in general terms, a replacement for the DC-3 and Viking. Thus, the new aircraft would inevitably be a competitor

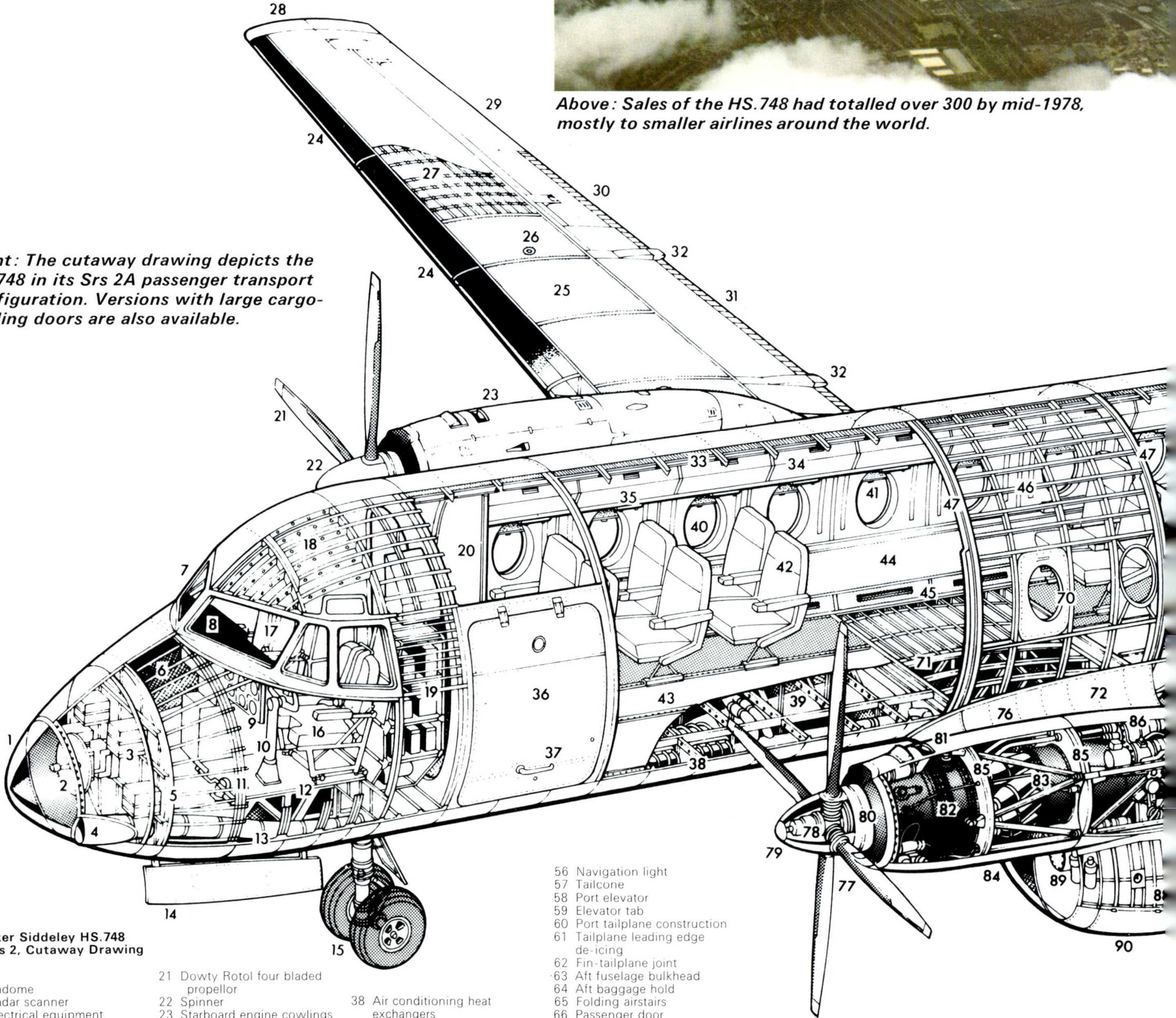

***Right:* The cutaway drawing depicts the HS.748 in its Srs 2A passenger transport configuration. Versions with large cargo-loading doors are also available.**

Hawker Siddeley HS.748 Series 2, Cutaway Drawing Key:

1 Radome
2 Radar scanner
3 Electrical equipment
4 Air intake
5 Front bulkhead
6 Nose structure
7 Windscreens
8 Instrument panel shroud
9 Instrument panel
10 Control column
11 Rudder pedals
12 Nosewheel bay structure
13 Air ducting
14 Nosewheel door
15 Twin nosewheels
16 Pilot's seat
17 Co-pilot's seat
18 Cabin roof structure
19 Radio rack
20 Forward baggage hold
21 Dowty Rotol four bladed propellor
22 Spinner
23 Starboard engine cowlings
24 Leading edge de-icing sections
5 Starboard wing fuel tank, capacity 720 Imp gal (3273l)
26 Fuel filler
27 Wing stringers
28 Starboard wingtip
29 Starboard aileron
30 Aileron tab
31 Starboard flap
32 Flap fairings
33 Fuselage frames
34 Overhead baggage lockers
35 Passenger service units
36 Freight and crew door
37 Door handle
38 Air conditioning heat exchangers
39 Cabin floor structure
40 Cabin windows
41 Window blind
42 Passenger seats
43 Floor fixing rails
44 Cabin trim panels
45 Air louvres
46 Centre fuselage construction
47 Wing beam carrying frames
48 Fin root fairing
49 Starboard tailplane
50 Fin construction
51 Fin leading edge de-icing
52 Anti-collision light
53 Rudder construction
54 Rudder tabs
55 Tab control rod
56 Navigation light
57 Tailcone
58 Port elevator
59 Elevator tab
60 Port tailplane construction
61 Tailplane leading edge de-icing
62 Fin-tailplane joint
63 Aft fuselage bulkhead
64 Aft baggage hold
65 Folding airstairs
66 Passenger door
67 Toilet compartment
68 Rear cabin seating
69 Window frame panel construction
70 Escape hatch
71 Centre wing construction
72 Wing root fillet
73 Water methanol boost tank, capacity 30 Imp gal (136l)
74 Filler cap
75 Trailing edge fairing
76 Port engine top cowling
77 Dowty Rotol four bladed propeller
78 Propeller pitch change mechanism
79 Spinner
80 Engine air intake
81 Oil cooler duct
82 Rolls-Royce Dart 535-2 turboprop
83 Engine mounting frame
84 Engine bottom cowlings
85 Fireproof bulkheads
86 Engine accessory equipment
87 Jet pipe
88 Undercarriage bay
89 Hydraulic equipment
90 Mainwheel doors
91 Mainwheel leg pivot
92 Leg fairing doors
93 Shock absorber strut
94 Twin mainwheels
95 Port wing fuel tank, capacity 720 Imp gal (3273l)
96 Front spar
97 Rear spar
98 Fuel tank bulkheads
99 Leading edge de-icing
100 Flap profile structure
101 Trailing edge flap
102 Flap fairing
103 Flap tracking
104 Leading edge construction
105 Outer wing construction
106 Port aileron
107 Aileron tab
108 Port wingtip
109 Port navigation light

for the Fokker F-27 which was already in flight test, and one of the design objectives set by Avro was to offer an aircraft that was cheaper and had a better performance.

One early study (mid-1958) under the Avro 748 designation was for a high wing design resembling the F-27 in general configuration but having only 20 seats and a gross weight of 18,000lb (8165kg). Airline reaction, however, led to a general scaling-up of the project to use two Rolls-Royce Darts, and to a decision to adopt a low-wing layout. In this form, with capacity for 36 passengers (four abreast) and a gross weight of 33,000lb (14,968kg), the project went ahead, the Hawker Siddeley board approving, in January 1959, construction of two flying prototypes and two test specimens. Special features of the design were the use of fail-safe principles in structural design, rather than the more usual (at that time) safe-life (this being the first medium-sized aircraft so designed) and the use of an unusual single-slotted flap to help provide a very good field performance.

The two prototypes made their first flights on 24 June 1960 and 10 April 1961 respectively. They had Dart R.Da.10 Mk 514 engines and were generally similar to the production Series 1 standard, the first example of which flew on 30 August 1961. The first customer for the Avro 748 was Skyways Coach-Air, which wanted three to use on its short cross-Channel routes, and following British certification on 7 December 1961, Skyways inaugurated services in 1962. Second operator of the type was Aerolineas Argentinas, the first overseas customer of many that were to sign up to buy the 748 in subsequent years.

After 18 Srs 1s had been built (plus the prototypes), production switched to the Avro 748 Srs 2, which introduced uprated Dart R.Da.7 Mk 531 engines and had a gross weight, eventually, of 44,495lb (20,182kg), compared with the 39,500lb (17,915kg) eventually approved for the Series 1. The prototype Srs 2 (a Srs 1 converted) flew at Woodford on 6 November 1961 and deliveries began after certification in October 1962, the first operator being BKS Air Transport. Improved performance was achieved with the introduction, from mid-1967, of the Dart Mk 532-2L or 532-2S, changing the designation to Srs 2A, and on 31 December 1971, a modified Srs 2A made its first flight, incorporating a large freight door in the fuselage aft of the wing. This door was offered together with a strengthened cabin floor and an optional air-transportable cargo hoist; sometimes referred to as the Srs 2C, this variant was of primary interest to military users.

In addition to production by the parent company in the UK, the HS.748 (the name Avro having been dropped in favour of HS for Hawker Siddeley) was assembled under licence by Hindustan Aeronautics Ltd at Kanpur, primarily for the Indian Air Force but also for Indian Airlines. The first Srs 1 assembled in India flew on 1 November 1961 and the first Srs 2 on 28 February 1964. By early 1978, some 320 HS.748s had been sold and the type was in widescale use, having been purchased by 64 operators in 39 countries, and had proved of special interest to smaller operators using airfields with limited facilities, as well as for feeder-line use by larger airlines on their secondary routes.

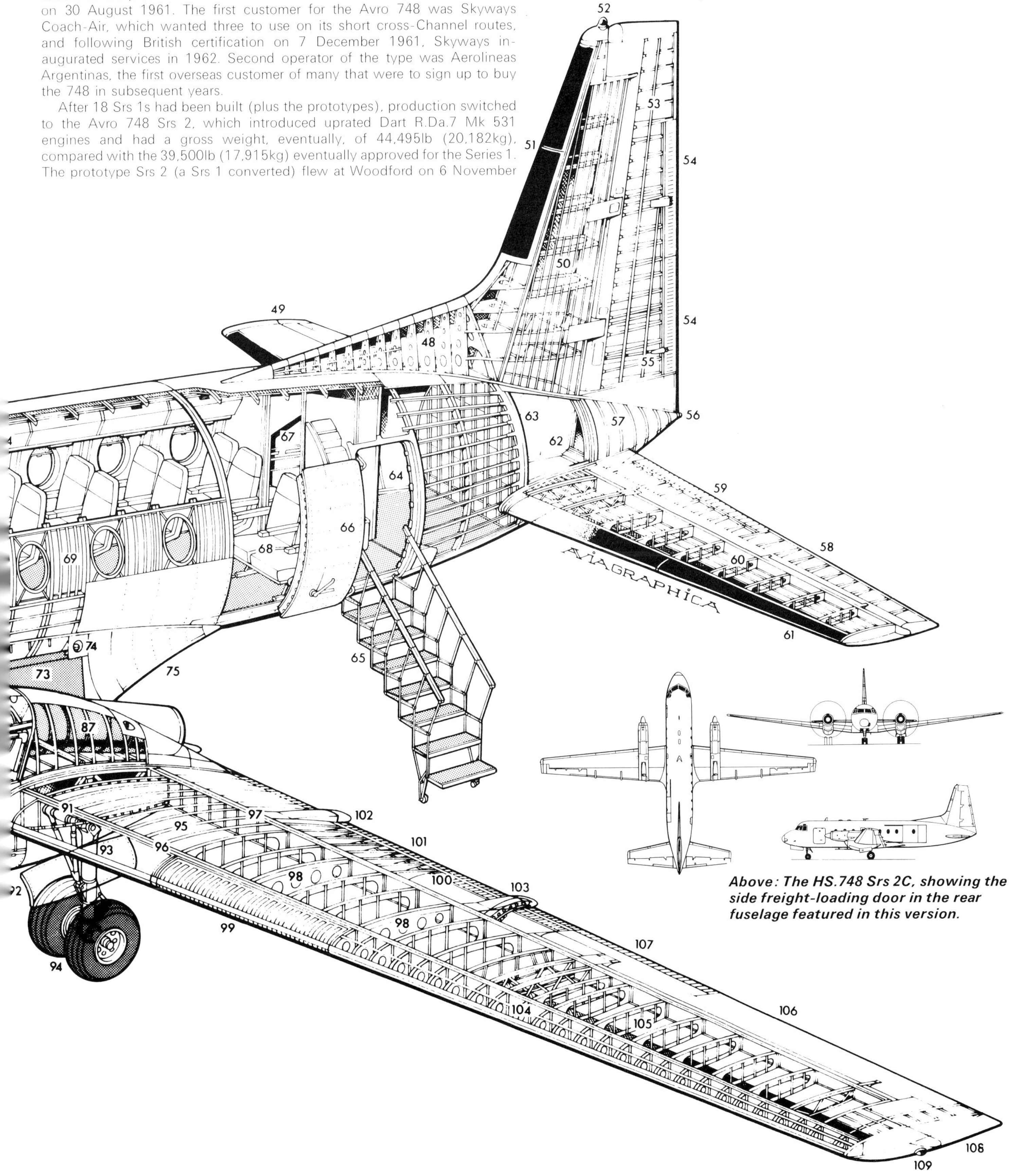

Above: The HS.748 Srs 2C, showing the side freight-loading door in the rear fuselage featured in this version.

Hawker Siddeley HS. 121 Trident

United Kingdom

The following specification refers to the Trident 2E:

Power Plant: Three 11,960lb st (5425kgp) Rolls-Royce Spey 512-5W turbofans.

Performance: Max cruising speed, 596mph (960km/h); long-range cruise, 505mph (812km/h); no-reserves range with max payload, 3,155mls (5078km); no-reserves range with max fuel, 3,558mls (5726km).

Weights: Basic operating, 73,250lb (33,250kg); max payload, 29,600lb (13,426kg); max take-off, 143,500lb (65,090kg).

Dimensions: Span, 98ft 0in (29·9m); length, 114ft 9in (34·98m); height, 27ft 0in (8·23m); wing area, 1,461sq ft (135·7m^2).

Although the Trident short-medium haul transport has achieved only modest success compared with that enjoyed by the Boeing 727 of similar concept and characteristics, it has provided a steady line of business for the Hawker Siddeley division at Hatfield for some 20 years. Like most commercial transports of the post-war period, the Trident suffered a somewhat involved period of conception and gestation before emerging in 1958 as BEA's first pure-jet transport.

The requirement for such an aeroplane to operate over BEA's routes, few of which were of more than 1,000mls (1610km) in length, was first drawn up in July 1956, and an initial de Havilland proposal was made as the D.H.119, using four Rolls-Royce Avon RA.29 engines. This was followed by the D.H.120, an attempt to meet with one aeroplane both the BEA requirement and BOAC's need for a long-haul jet (eventually met by the VC10). Concentrating again on the BEA requirement, de Havilland then evolved the D.H.121, which the airline chose on technical merit over the competing Avro 540 and Bristol 200. To meet political requirements at that time, de Havilland then set up the Airco consortium, with Fairey and Hunting, to produce the D.H.121, for which BEA placed a preliminary order for 24 in February 1958.

At that stage, the aircraft was to have been powered by three 13,790lb st (6255kgp) RB.141/3 Medway engines grouped in the rear fuselage, have 111 seats and a range of 2,070mls (3330km). In 1959, however, BEA scaled down its requirement and a smaller version of the design emerged, with three 9,850lb st (4470kgp) RB.163 Spey 505 engines, 97–103 seats and range of 930mls (1500km), and in this form production went ahead. The Airco consortium was dissolved later in 1959 when de Havilland joined the Hawker Siddeley Group, and the aircraft was named Trident 1.

No prototypes were built, and the first Trident 1 flew on 9 January 1962; the first revenue flight was made on 11 March 1964 in BEA service, with full scheduled operations starting on 1 April. From the start, the Trident was designed to have suitable equipment to permit its operation in very low weather minima, this equipment comprising the Smiths Autoland system. BEA Trident 1s were certificated in September 1968 to make autolands in Cat II weather condiditions.

In addition to the 24 Trident 1s, Hawker Siddeley built 15 Trident 1Es for other operators (Kuwait, Iraqi, Pakistan, Air Ceylon, Channel and Northeast). This version had 11,400lb st (5170kgp) Spey 511s, gross weight increased from 115,000lb (52,165kg) to 128,000lb (58,060kg), span increased from 89ft 10in (27·41m) to 95ft (28·95m) and accommodation increased to 140 (six abreast).

In 1965, BEA ordered 15 Trident 2s (maker's designation, 2E), which had the same fuselage as the Srs 1s but a further small increase in span to 98ft (29·9m) and more fuel; weights went up and 11,960lb st (5425kgp) Spey 512-5Ws were used. With internal re-arrangements, the Trident 2E could carry up to 149 passengers (six-abreast). First flight was made on 27 July 1967 and BEA operated the first scheduled service on 18 April 1968. Two Trident 2Es were sold to Cyprus Airways and in 1971 the Chinese Peoples' Republic selected this variant in a major re-equipment drive for CAAC, following initial experience with four Trident 1Es acquired from Pakistan International. Successive orders brought the total ordered by China to 33 by the end of 1974; the first was flown on 20 October 1972 and handed over on 13 November.

Third of the Trident variants for BEA was the Trident Three (maker's designation, 3B), which had the fuselage lengthened by 16ft 5in (5·00m) in order to accommodate up to 180 passengers (six-abreast) and operate on BEA's high-density short-haul routes. The wing span remained as on the 2E but changes were made in the control surfaces, and to improve the take-off performance at the higher operating weights, a fourth, "booster", engine was added, this being a 5,250lb st (2381kgp) Rolls-Royce RB.162-86 in the tail above the fuselage. The Trident Three first flew on 11 December 1969 and the first flight with boost engine operating was made on 22 March 1970. The first of 26 ordered by BEA entered service on 1 April 1971, and in December of that year, approval was given for autoland operations by the Trident Three down to 12ft (3·66m) decision height and 885ft (270m) runway visual range, plus take-offs in full Cat IIIA conditions, with an RVR of 295ft (90m). Operations to these standards were begun by BEA (now British Airways European Division) in May 1973.

Two other Trident Threes were ordered by CAAC in 1972, as Super Trident 3Bs, these differing from the BEA model in having higher fuel capacity and operating weights.

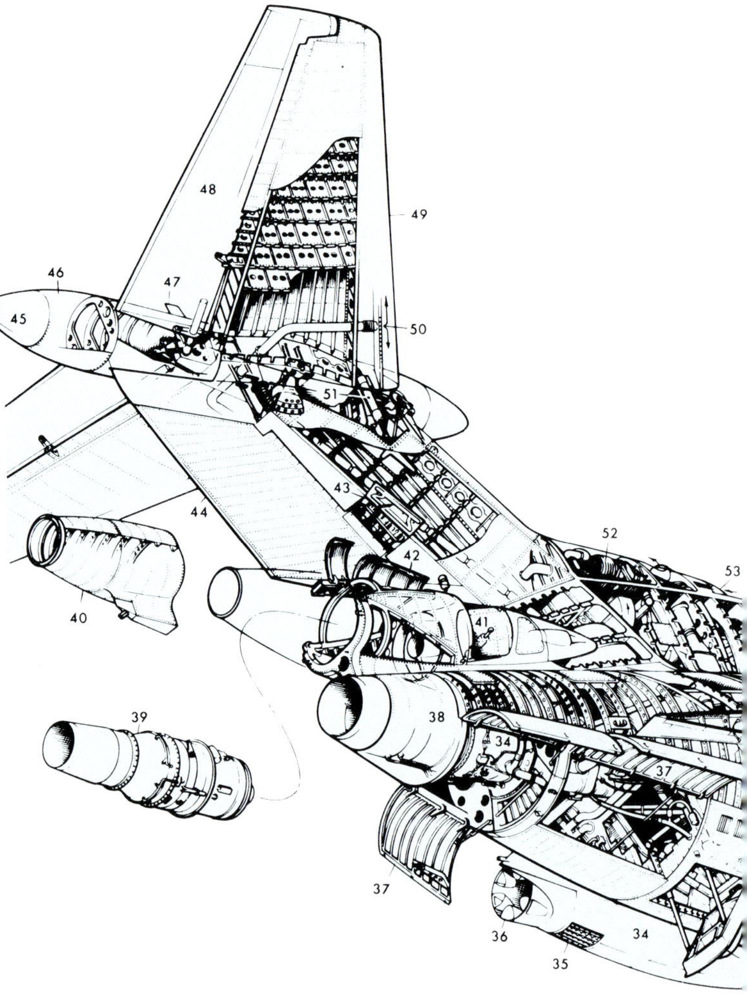

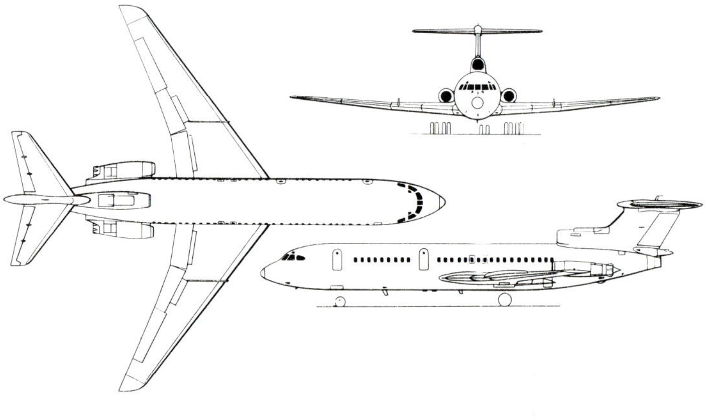

Above: The HS.121 Trident 2E, the principal production version of the tri-jet for British Airways and China's CAAC.

Above: A Trident 2E on a pre-delivery flight in the UK, in the markings of the Civil Aviation Administration of China.

Hawker Siddeley Trident 3B Cutaway Drawing Key

1 Captain's seat
2 Co-pilot's seat
3 Third crew member's seat
4 Folding seat for supernumerary crew member
5 Centre console
6 Control column
7 Rudder pedals
8 Nosewheel steering, port and starboard
9 Passenger windows
10 Forward cabin service door
11 Search radar
12 Upward hinged radome
13 Pitot heads
14 Offset nosewheel, retracting sideways
15 Unpressurised nose landing gear bay
16 Radio services bay
17 Static heads, port and starboard
18 Forward freight door, plug type
19 Forward freight hold
20 Seat attachment rail
21 Luggage racks housing passenger service panels
22 Emergency escape panels
23 Air conditioning duct
24 Leading edge Kruger flap
25 Centre passenger door
26 Main landing gear doors
27 Main landing gear, starboard (turned through 90 deg for retraction)
28 Main landing gear, port
29 Centre torsion box
30 Rear freight hold
31 Plug type rear freight door
32 Rear pressure dome
33 Equipment bay access door, with integral stairs and tail bumper
34 Rolls-Royce Spey engine
35 Thrust reverser cascades (outer engines only)
36 Exhaust silencers (outer engines only)
37 Centre engine access doors
38 Centre engine jet pipe fairing, fixed to engine
39 Rolls-Royce RB.162 boost engine
40 RB.162 jet pipe fairing
41 Air intake doors for RB.162
42 Access panels for RB.162
43 Access doors to rudder
44 One-piece rudder
45 Navigation lamp
46 Detachable tail cone
47 VHF aerials
48 Elevator
49 Variable-incidence tailplane
50 Tailplane anti-icing duct
51 Tailplane actuating jacks
52 AiResearch APU
53 Air inlet to APU
54 Air intake to centre Spey
55 Fixed portion of pod cowling
56 Rear toilet, port and stbd
57 Rear toilet servicing point
58 Rear cabin service door
59 Double slotted flaps, two sections each side
60 Lift dumpers, two sections each side
61 Main landing gear bays
62 Underwing access doors
63 Flap tracks (two per flap)
64 Air brake/spoiler (one each side)
65 No 1 fuel tank (port and stbd)
66 No 2 fuel tank (port and stbd)
67 Aileron
68 Retractable landing lamp
69 Kuchemann wingtip
70 Four-piece slat
71 Slat tracks
72 Slat screw jack
73 Telescopic supply pipes for slat anti-icing
74 Slat torque shafting
75 Leading edge anti-icing ducts

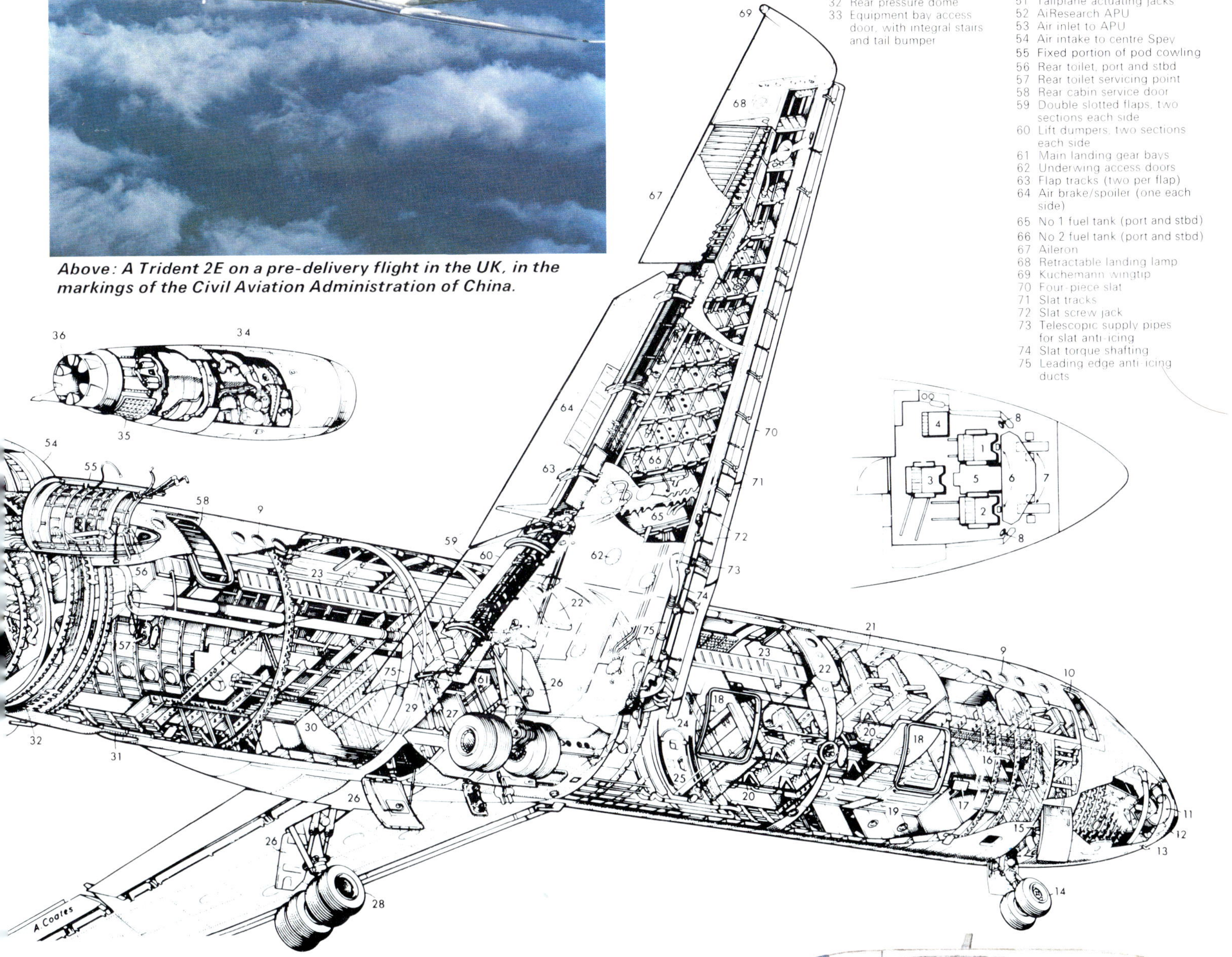

Above: A cutaway of the Trident Three, showing the extra (fourth) turbojet carried above the rear fuselage to boost take-off performance.

Below: The purchase of 33 Trident 2Es plus two Super Trident Threes gave CAAC its first experience of modern jet transport.

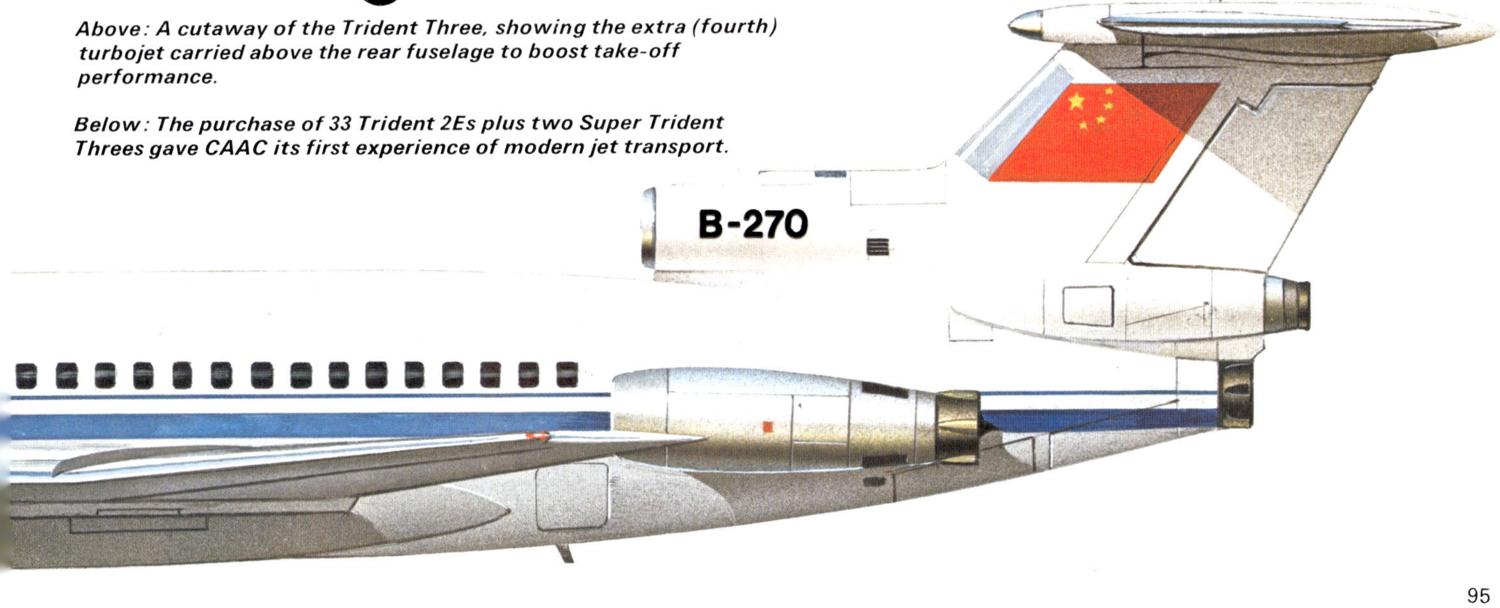

Ilyushin Il-14
Soviet Union

The following specification relates to the Il-14M.
Power Plant: Two 1,900hp Shvetsov ASh-82T 14-cylinder radial air-cooled engines.
Performance: Max speed, 259mph (417km/h); high-speed cruise, 239mph (385km/h); long-range cruise, 193mph (311km/h); initial climb, 1,220ft/min (6·2m/sec); service ceiling, 22,000ft (6705m); range with max payload, 810mls (1034km), with max fuel, 1,988mls (3202km).
Weights: Operational equipped, 27,776lb (12,600kg); max take-off, 39,683lb (18,000kg).
Dimensions: Span, 104ft 0in (31·69m); length, 73ft 2in (22·30m); height, 25ft 11in (7·90m); wing area 1,075sq ft (99·70m^2).

The Il-14 was the first post-WWII design from the bureau led by Sergei V

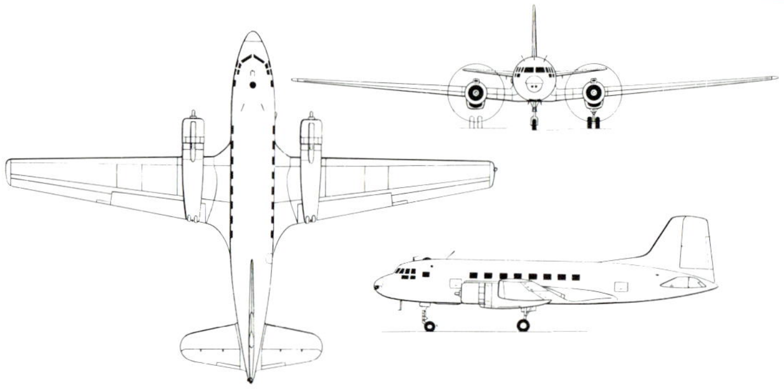

***Above:** Three-view drawing of the Ilyushin Il-14.*

***Right:** An Il-14 of CSA Czechoslovak Airlines, one of several Soviet Bloc airlines that used substantial numbers of the type.*

Ilyushin Il-18
Soviet Union

The following specification relates to the Il-18D:
Power Plant: Four Ivchenko AI-20M turboprops each rated at 4,250ehp.
Performance: Max cruise (at max take-off weight), 419mph (675km/h); economy cruise, 388mph (625km/h); operating altitude, 26,250–32,800ft (8000–10,000m); range (max payload and one hour's reserves), 2,300mls (3700km), (max fuel and one hour's reserves), 4,040mls (6500km).
Weights: Empty equipped (90-seater), 77,160lb (35,000kg); max take-off, 141,000lb (64,000kg).
Dimensions: Span, 122ft $8\frac{1}{2}$in (37·40m); length, 117ft 9in (35·90m); height, 33ft 4in (10·17m); wing area, 1,507sq ft (140m^2).

Numerically the second most important airliner in the Aeroflot inventory in the mid-seventies, the Il-18 entered service with the Soviet carrier on 20 April 1959, and was reported to have carried 60 million passengers by the spring of 1969, when it was being utilized on 800 international and domestic services. The prototype Il-18, which was known as the *Moskva*, was flown for the first time in July 1957, being followed by two pre-production examples. Series production aircraft, with accommodation for 75 passengers, were initially delivered with the Kuznetsov NK-4 or Ivchenko AI-20 turboprop providing optional power plants. The 21st and subsequent

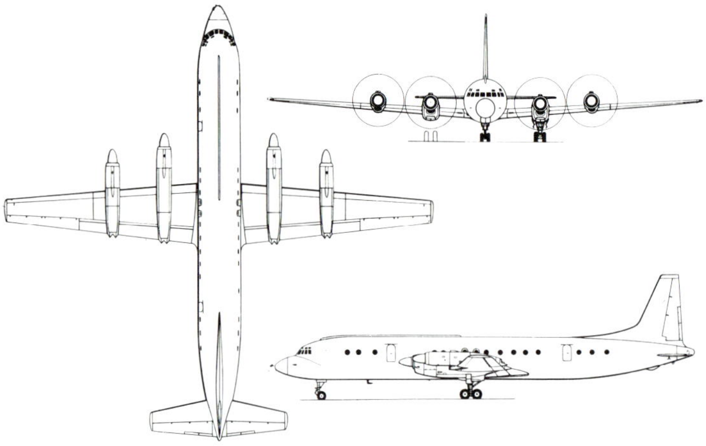

***Above:** Three-view drawing of the Ilyushin Il-18, one of the key types in the modernization of Aeroflot.*

***Right:** The Il-18 was produced in substantial numbers in the Soviet Union and was put into service by all the East European airlines as well as by Aeroflot.*

Ilyushin Il-76T
Soviet Union

Power Plant: Four Soloviev D-30KP turbofans each rated at 26,455lb st (12,000kgp) for take-off.
Performance: Typical cruising speed, 528mph (850km/h) at 42,650ft (13,000m); take-off run, unpaved runway, 2,790ft (850m); landing run, unpaved runway, 1,476ft (450m); typical range with max payload, 3,100mls (5000km).
Weights: Max payload, 88,185lb (40,000kg); max take-off weight, 346,125lb (157,000kg).
Dimensions: Span, 165ft 8in (50·50m); length, 152ft $10\frac{1}{2}$in (46·59m); height, 48ft 5in (14·76m); wing area, 3,229·2sq ft (300·0m^2).

The Ilyushin Il-76 was evolved in the Soviet Union in the early 'seventies primarily to meet Soviet Air Force requirements for a strategic freighter with a secondary flight refuelling tanker role, and the first of six prototype and development aircraft flew on 25 March 1971. Bearing civil markings and Aeroflot insignia, the prototype was displayed publicly at the Paris Air Show

***Below:** The Ilyushin Il-76, a specialized freighter that has also been produced for service with the Soviet Air Forces.*

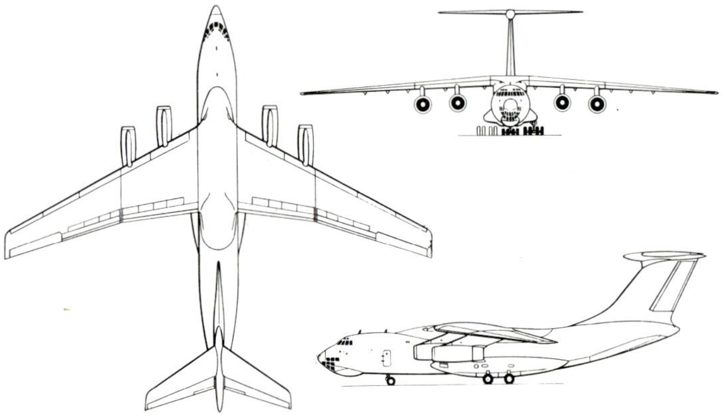

a month later, indicating that the Il-76 was also expected to have commercial applications.

Subsequently, Soviet sources reported that Aeroflot had a requirement for about 100 Il-76s, primarily for operation in Siberia and other under-developed areas of the Soviet Union, where it was able to use short un-

***Below:** The Il-76 entered service as an all-cargo carrier on internal routes in the Soviet Union early in 1978, later being introduced also on international flights.*

Ilyushin to achieve production status and, by comparison with its predecessor the Il-12, embodied a refined structure, improved aerodynamics and up-rated engines. Flown in prototype form in 1952, the Il-14 entered production for both military use and Aeroflot, the commercial version for the latter being designated Il-14P (*Passazhirskii*) and providing accommodation for 18–26 passengers.

A "stretched" variant, the Il-14M (*Modifikatsirovanny*), appeared in 1956, this having a 3ft 4in (1·0m) additional section inserted in the forward fuselage and accommodation being increased to 24–28 passengers. A substantial number of Il-14P and Il-14M airliners were later adapted as freighters under the designation of Il-14T (*Transportny*).

Production of the Il-14 in the Soviet Union reportedly exceeded 3,500 aircraft, 80 were built by the VEB Flugzeugwerke in East Germany and approximately 80 Il-14Ps were manufactured in Czechoslovakia where production continued with several different versions of the Avia 14.

The Il-14T remains in the Aeroflot inventory in steadily decreasing numbers; other airlines that were operating versions of the Il-14 in the mid-seventies were Balkan, CAAC, CSA, Cubana, Mongolian and Tarom.

aircraft standardized on the latter engine and the initial version was quickly supplanted by the Il-18B which had an increase in max take-off weight of 4,409lb (2000kg) from 130,514lb (59,200kg) and accommodated 84 passengers.

Further development resulted in the Il-18V in 1961, with accommodation for 89–100 passengers, this being followed three years later, in 1964, by the Il-18I with 4,250eshp AI-20M turboprops in place of the 4,000 eshp AI-20Ks of previous versions, accommodation for 110–122 passengers made possible by the lengthening of the pressurized section of the fuselage through deletion of the unpressurized tail cargo hold, and a 32 per cent increase in total fuel capacity as a result of the introduction of additional centre-section fuel tankage. Redesignated Il-18D, this model entered Aeroflot service in 1965, together with the Il-18Ye (usually referred to in Western circles as the Il-18E) which was similar apart from having the same fuel capacity as the Il-18V. Both the Il-18D and Il-18V were operated by a flight crew of five, and in their standard 110-seat high-density arrangement had 24 and 71 seats in six-abreast rows in the forward and main cabins respectively, and 15 seats five-abreast in the rear cabin.

Production of the Il-18 reportedly exceeded 800 aircraft of which more than 100 were exported for commercial and military use. Foreign commercial operators included Air Guinee, Air Mali, Air Mauritanie, Balkan, CAAC, CSA, Cubana, Egyptair, Interflug, LOT, Malev, Tarom and Yemen Airways. The small number of examples in military service as personnel transports were operated by the air forces of Afghanistan, Algeria, Bulgaria, China, Czechoslovakia, Poland and Yugoslavia.

prepared landing strips. The take-off run from unpaved runways has been reported to be as short as 2,790ft (850m), although it is not clear if this remarkable performance can be achieved at the max take-off weight of 356,125lb (157,000kg) or if it is related to a specific short-haul mission with reduced fuel.

The Il-76 is operated by a flight crew of four and the entire freight section, which includes a permanent station for the cargo master, is pressurized. A navigator's station is situated below and forward of the flight deck, to facilitate visual selection of landing sites. An internal overhead crane system is carried by the Il-76, comprising two hoists on rails running the length of the cabin, each with a 5,000-lb (2268kg) capacity.

The capabilities of the Il-76 were demonstrated in 1975 when no fewer than 24 records were claimed, and subsequently confirmed by the FAI, for a series of flights that included lifting a payload of 154,590lb (70,121kg) to an altitude of 6,560ft (2000m) and averaging a speed of 532mph (857km/h) with a 121,145-lb (55,000-kg) payload for a distance of 1,243mls (2000km). A version designated Il-76T appeared in 1977, with a gross weight of 374,450lb (170,000kg).

Ilyushin Il-62
Soviet Union

The following specification relates to the standard Il-62:
Power Plant: Four 23,150lb st (10,500kgp) Kuznetsov NK-8-4 turbofans.
Performance: Typical cruising speed, 528–560mph (850–900km/h) at 33,000–39,400ft (10,000–12,000m); initial climb rate, 3,540ft/min (18m/sec); take-off distance required (FAR, SL, ISA, max weight) 10,660ft (3250m); landing distance required (FAR, SL, ISA, max landing weight), 9,185ft (2800m); range with max payload, and 1-hr fuel reserve, 4,160mls (6700km); range with max fuel, 5,715mls (9200km).
Weights: Operating weight empty, 153,000lb (69,400kg); max payload, 50,700lb (23,000kg); max fuel load, 183,700lb (83,325kg); max take-off, 357,000lb (162,000kg); max landing, 232,000lb (105,000kg); max zero-fuel weight, 206,000lb (93,500kg).
Dimensions: Span, 141ft 9in (43·20m); length, 174ft $3\frac{1}{2}$in (53·12m); height 40ft $6\frac{1}{4}$in (12·35m); wing area, 3,010sq ft (279·6m^2).

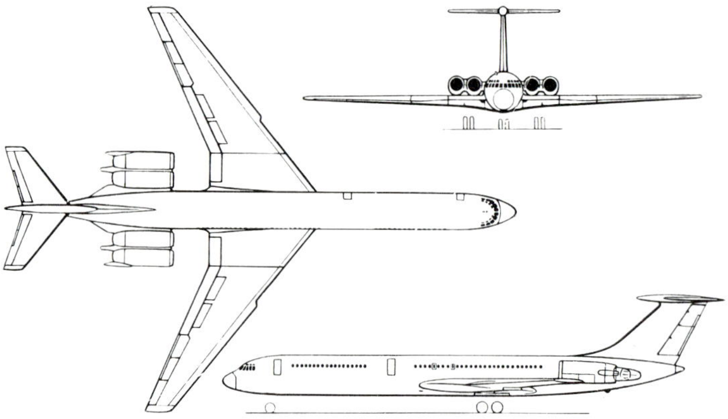

***Above:** Three-view drawing of the Ilyushin Il-62M, which shared its four engined rear-mounted configuration with the BAC VC10.*

Entering service with Aeroflot on 15 September 1967, the Ilyushin Il-62 was the first long-range four-engined jet transport developed in the Soviet Union for commercial use to achieve production status, and has become an essential component in the Aeroflot fleet in the 'seventies. The introduction into service – initially as a replacement for the Tupolev Tu-114 on the Moscow–Montreal transatlantic service – came almost exactly five years after the Il-62 had been publicly unveiled in Moscow.

The Il-62 design featured an all-manual flying control system, with a yaw damper in the rudder circuit, and an automatic flight control system that allowed it to operate in weather minima similar to those defined as Cat II by ICAO standards. Like many other aircraft with a rear-engined, high tail layout, the Il-62 was found to have slender control margins at low speed, and an extensive flight test programme was undertaken to refine the wing design, resulting in the adoption of a fixed, drooped extension of the leading edge over approximately the outer half of each wing. The first flight was made in January 1963, and this prototype was fitted with 16,535lb st (7500kgp) Lyulka AL-7 turbojets pending the development of a new turbofan unit by the Kuznetsov engine design bureau. This new engine, the 23,150lb st (10,500kgp) NK-8-4, became available in time to power some of the later trials aircraft, comprising a second prototype and three pre-production examples. Cascade-type thrust reversers were fitted on the outer engines only.

With six-abreast seating and a central aisle, the Il-62 accommodated 186 passengers in a high-density layout or 168 in a one-class tourist layout. A typical mixed-class layout had 20 seats four-abreast in the forward cabin and 102 six-abreast in the rear cabin, separated by a large galley amidships. Two passenger doors, one immediately aft of the flight deck and the other just ahead of the wing leading edge, gave access to the cabin.

Aeroflot was believed to have over 100 Il-62s in service by early 1974. Following its introduction on the Moscow–Montreal service, the Il-62 went into service on the Moscow–New York prestige route in July 1968, and subsequently replaced Tu-114s and Tu-104s on many of the longer international routes as well as the trunk routes within the Soviet Union. The first user of the Il-62 outside the USSR was Czechoslovakian Airlines CSA, which leased a single example from Aeroflot for its Prague–London service in May 1968. Subsequently CSA procured its own fleet of seven Il-62s, and most of the East European bloc airlines followed suit, with Interflug putting the first of six into service in 1970, LOT ordering three in 1972 with a fourth being delivered mid-1974 when a fifth was on order, and Tarom of Rumania acquiring two. Under a 1970 trade agreement, China procured five examples for use by CAAC, and United Arab Airlines (later Egyptair) acquired seven.

During 1970, the Ilyushin design bureau evolved an improved version of the basic design with increased seating and more range. Known as the Il-62M (and sometimes referred to as the Il-62M-200), this new version is powered by four Soloviev D-30KU turbofans rated at 23,350lb st (11,500kgp) each and with clamshell-type instead of cascade-type reversers on the outer engines. The extra power permits operation at a higher gross weight of 363,760lb (165,000kg) and additional fuel capacity was provided by a tank in the fin. These improvements give Il-62M a better payload-range performance, the max range increasing to 6,400mls (10,300km); internal redesign makes it possible to accommodate up to 198 passengers. The flight control system permits operation in Cat II weather minima and is capable of development for Cat III operation. Aeroflot introduced the Il-62M in 1974 and has subsequently been standardizing on this model for all its long-range subsonic operations.

***Right:** An Ilyushin Il-62 on final approach. Used in substantial numbers by Aeroflot, the Il-62 has had limited export success.*

***Below:** LOT Polish Airlines is one of several East European airlines operating small fleets of Ilyushin Il-62s on their long-range routes.*

Ilyushin Il-86
Soviet Union

Power Plant: Four Kuznetsov NK-86 turbofans each rated at 28,635lb st (13,000kgp) for take-off.
Performance: Cruising speed, 560–590mph (900–950km/h) at 30,000ft (9000m); range, 2,350mls (3800km) with full passenger payload.
Weights: Max payload, 92,500lb (42,000kg); gross weight 453,745lb (206,000kg).
Dimensions: Span, 158ft $6\frac{1}{2}$in (48·33m); length 191ft 11in (58·50m); height, 51ft 6in (15·70m); wing area, 3,444sq ft (320m^2).

The rapid growth of air transport within the Soviet Union has led Aeroflot to initiate the development of a whole range of new aircraft types for service during the 'seventies. Among this new generation of transports is the first wide-body "airbus" type designed in the Soviet Union. When the requirement for this type was formulated in the late 'sixties, design proposals were made by the Antonov, Tupolev and Ilyushin bureaux, the last-mentioned winning official backing for construction of what became known as the Il-86. As first projected, it had four rear-mounted engines, in an arrangement similar to that of the Il-62, but as design proceeded it became clear to the Soviet engineers that this layout incurred structure weight penalties that were unacceptable in so large an aircraft. Consequently, before construction began, the design was changed to have four engines in individual underwing Pods, making the Il-86 the first Soviet airliner to use this "classic" layout.

A unique feature of the Il-86 is the provision of entrance vestibules on a lower level beneath the main cabin floor, allowing passengers to embark and disembark by way of airstairs incorporated in the doors and making it unnecessary to provide complex ground handling equipment at every airport. Stowage space is provided in the vestibules for outer coats and carry-on luggage and passengers then proceed by internal stairways to the main deck.

Originally designed to be powered by Soloviev D-30KP turbofans, the Il-86 in fact makes use of Kuznetsov NK-86 engines of new design, flight testing of which began in 1975 beneath the wing of an Il-86. First flight of the prototype Il-86 was made on 22 December 1976 and deliveries to Aeroflot were expected to begin in 1980. Intended to be equipped to permit automatic landings to be made in Cat IIIa weather conditions, the Il-86 will be furnished to accommodate about 350 passengers.

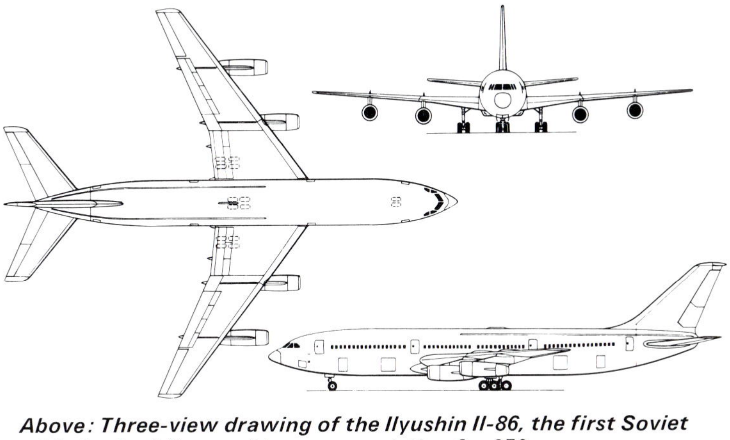

Above: Three-view drawing of the Ilyushin Il-86, the first Soviet wide-body airliner, with accommodation for 350 passengers.

Above: First flown in December 1976, the Il-86 prototype was shown at the Paris Air show six months later.

Let L-410 Turbolet

Czechoslovakia

The following specification refers to the L-410A with PT6A engines:
Power Plant: Two 715eshp Pratt & Whitney (UACL) PT6A-27 turboprops.
Performance: Max cruising speed, 230mph (370km/h) at 9,840ft (3000m); best economy cruise, 224mph (360km/h); initial rate of climb, 1,610ft/min (8·2m/sec); service ceiling, 23,300ft (7100m); range with max payload, 186mls (300km); range with max fuel, 807mls (1300km).
Weights: Basic weight empty, 6,834lb (3100kg); operating weight empty (cargo version) 7,275lb (3300kg); max cargo payload, 4,078lb (1850kg); max take-off, 12,566lb (5700kg); max landing, 12,125lb (5500kg).
Dimensions: Span, 57ft $4\frac{1}{4}$in (17·48m); length, 44ft $7\frac{3}{4}$in (13·61m); height, 18ft $6\frac{1}{2}$in (5·65m); wing area, 353·7sq ft (32·86m²).

The L-410 was developed by the Czech National Aircraft Industry at its Kunovice works, being the first indigenous design to emerge from that factory. It was intended to be used as a commuter or third-level airliner, seating 15 to 19 passengers in a 2+1 arrangement, and development of a suitable turboprop engine, the M-601, was put in hand in Czechoslovakia at the same time.

As the M-601 was not cleared for flight in time for installation in the prototype L-410, Pratt & Whitney PT6A-27s were fitted and with these the first flight was made on 16 April 1969. Production aircraft, similarly powered, began to appear in 1971 and had small increases in wing span and overall length. Initial deliveries were made to Slov-Air, which took over responsibility from CSA for some domestic air routes in Czechoslovakia and four were in service by the end of 1972. The L-410 was also reported to have been selected by Aeroflot after competitive evaluation with the Beriev Be-30, but deliveries to the Soviet Union were delayed until the L-410M version with M-601 engines became available, in 1975.

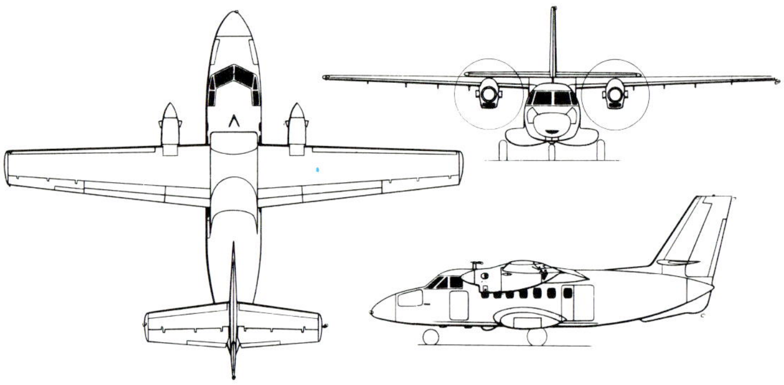

***Above:** Three-view drawing of the L-410, a baby airliner evolved during the sixties and put into production in 1972.*

Lockheed Hercules

USA

The following specification relates to the L-100-30:
Power Plant: Four 4,508eshp Allison 501-D22A turboprops.
Performance: Max cruising speed, 377mph (607km/h); initial rate of climb, 1,900ft/min (9·65m/sec); range with max payload, 2,130mls (3425km); range with max fuel, 4,740mls (7630km).
Weights: Operating empty, 71,400lb (32,386kg); max payload, 51,400lb (23,315kg), max take-off, 155,000lb (70,308kg).
Dimensions: Span, 132ft 7in (40·41m); length, 112ft $8\frac{1}{2}$in (34·35m); height, 38ft 3in (11·66m); wing area, 1,745sq ft (162·12m²).

The Hercules freighter was designed in 1951 to meet USAF requirements for a tactical airlift transport powered by turboprop engines, and development under USAF contract proceedings from July 1951 onwards at the company's California headquarters. Two prototype YC-130s flew at Burbank, the first on 23 August 1954, and the entire programme was then transferred to the Lockheed-Georgia Company at Marietta, near Atlanta, where the first production C-130 flew on 7 April 1955. The C-130 featured straight-in loading through doors and ramps in the rear fuselage, and could carry large freight loads.

The commercial potential of the Hercules was realized at an early stage in its development, but early efforts to market the type as the L-100 met with relatively little success. On 21 April 1964, however, Lockheed flew a civil demonstrator, based on the military C-130E and known as the Model 382-44K-20, the second and third cyphers in the designation indicating its specific configuration. FAA certification was obtained on 16 February 1965, and deliveries of commercial Hercules variants began later in 1965. Among the first users were Continental Air Services, which acquired two for use in its operations in Laos, Zambia Air Cargoes, which eventually acquired four and Alaska Airlines, which purchased three and which gave the Hercules a foretaste of what was to become a significant future rôle, supporting oil exploration activities on the Alaskan North Slope.

These Hercules and those delivered in 1966 and 1967 to Delta, Interior, Pacific Western and Airlift International were basically Model 382B. The designation L-100 was also used, specifically for Delta's Hercules which had a special cargo loading system, and the designation L-100-10 was applied to a proposed version with 4,500shp Allison 501-D22A turboprops in place of the usual 4,050shp 501-D22s.

During 1967, Lockheed embarked on development of a stretched version of the Hercules offering better operating economics by increasing the fuselage length by 8ft 4in (2·54m). The D22A power plant was adopted, although the maximum take-off weight remained unchanged at 155,000lb (70,307kg). The original commercial Hercules demonstrator was converted to the new standard as Model 382E or L-100-20 and flew in this guise on 19 April 1968, obtaining FAA Type Approval on 4 October that year. Several of the 382Bs already in use were converted to 382E standard and others were built from scratch; two with the lower-rated 501-D22s were delivered as Model 382Fs.

Another stretch of the Hercules was undertaken in 1969, producing the Model 382G or L-100-30. The primary requirement was raised by Saturn Airways, which wished to be able to ferry complete aircraft-sets of three Rolls-Royce RB.211 engines from the UK to the TriStar assembly line in Calfornia. The L-100-30 had various of the original military features deleted,

***Below:** Three-view drawing of the Hercules in its L-100-20 version, with a longer fuselage than the basic Hercules.*

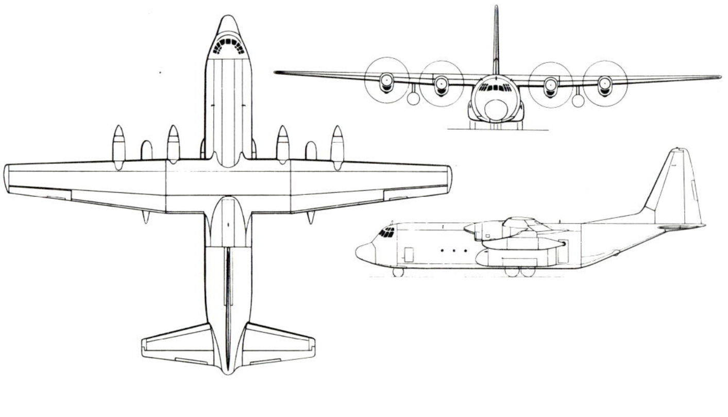

Above: The L-410 Turbolet 15-19 passenger feederliner is operated on domestic routes by CSA, which has a fleet of 12.

Below: Depicted in the colour profile below is an L-410 in the markings of Slov-Air, since taken over by CSA.

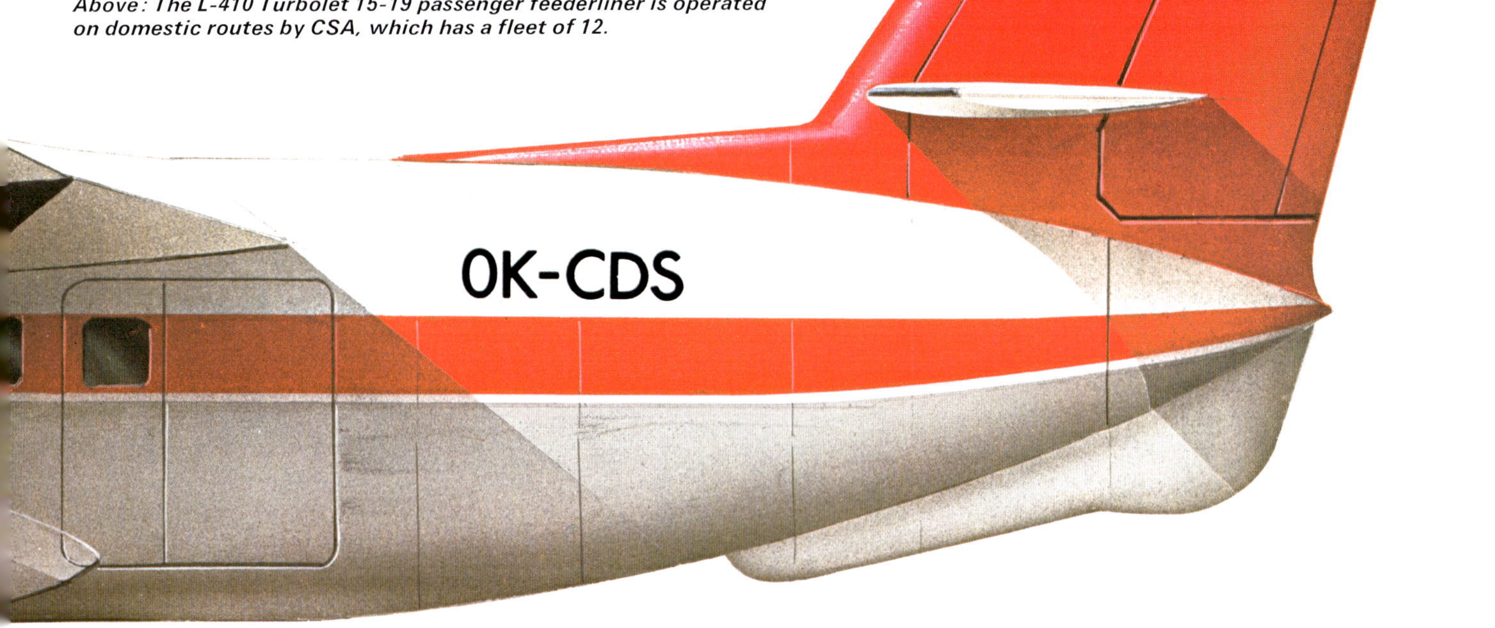

including the rear cargo windows, paratroop doors and rocket ATO provision and the first example flew on 14 August 1970. Type Approval was obtained on 7 October 1970 and in addition to a fleet of L-100-30s for Saturn (some as conversions of earlier models), Lockheed obtained orders for this model from Safair of South Africa, and Southern Air Transport. Further developments of the basic Hercules had been proposed for the civil market by 1977, including the L-100-50 with the fuselage lengthened by another 20ft (6·1m) from the L-100-30, and the L-400, a twin-engined derivative.

Below: One of four L-100-20 Hercules used by Philippine Aerotransport for scheduled domestic freight services and world-wide charters.

Lockheed Electra
USA

The following specification relates to the L-188A:
Power Plant: Four 3,750ehp Allison 501-D13A turboprops.
Performance: Max cruising speed, 405mph (652km/h) at 22,000ft (6700m); best economy cruise, 374mph (602km/h); initial rate of climb, 1,670ft/min (8·5m/sec); service ceiling, 27,000ft (8230m); range with max payload, 2,200mls (3540km); range with max fuel, 2,500mls (4023km).
Weights: Basic operating, 61,500lb (27,895kg); max payload, 22,825lb (10,350kg); max take-off, 116,000lb (52,664kg).
Dimensions: Span, 99ft 0in (30·18m); length, 104ft 6in (31·81m); height, 32ft 10in (10·0m); wing area, 1,300sq ft (120·8m^2).

The only major US airliner to make use of turboprop engines, the Lockheed Electra proved – like the Vickers Vanguard which was closely comparable in size, performance and timescale – to be an expensive venture for its manufacturer, being overtaken by the development of pure-jet transports before its expected sales potential could be realised. By the time the first Electra flew, orders had been placed for 144, promising a bright future for the type, but only 26 more were sold subsequently, leaving the production total far short of the break-even figure. The design did, however, provide the basis for the P-3 Orion maritime reconnaissance aircraft.

Design of the Electra began in 1954 primarily to meet requirements set out by American Airlines for a short-medium range transport for US domestic operation, with a larger capacity than was available in the Vickers Viscount or similar types. Both Vickers and Lockheed were among the companies that attempted – at first unsuccessfully – to meet the requirement, but in 1955 American Airlines re-issued the specification in modified form and Lockheed then succeeded in selling its revised L-188 design to American Airlines and, simultaneously, to Eastern Airlines.

The combined "launching" orders from these two companies, placed in June 1955, were for 75 aircraft and the design was for a 100 seat transport with a non-stop range of about 2,300mls (3700km). By the time the first Electra flew, on 6 December 1957, the gross weight had been established at 113,000lb (57,260kg); three further aircraft were flown in quick succession in 1958 and the fifth, to be the first for airline delivery, flew on 19 May 1958. FAA Type Approval for the Electra was obtained on 22 August 1958 and the type entered service with Eastern Airlines on 12 January 1959 and with American Airlines on 23 January 1959. The Electra thus became the first turbine-engined airliner of US design and production to operate regular services, and was to be the only US turboprop to achieve this status. The engines were Allison 501-D13s, commercial versions of the T56.

Once the Electra had been launched into production, orders accumulated rapidly – primarily from other US domestic airlines, but including several from Australasian airlines and one European order, from KLM. In this period, 1955–56, the Vickers Vanguard was competing for the same market, but with markedly less success. It was also the period of the so-called "jet buying spree" when major airlines all over the world were placing their first orders for pure-jet equipment, with the Electra being chosen in several cases as the complementary short-haul type. Ansett-ANA in Australia became the first non-US operator to introduce the Electra, in March 1959.

Within 15 months of the Electra's first service, two fatal accidents had occurred in similar circumstances and on 25 March 1960 the FAA introduced a speed limitation of 275 knots (510km/h) IAS, reduced further to 225 knots (417km/h) a few days later. Painstaking investigations revealed that the problem lay in the structural strength of the power plant mounting which could suffer damage in, for example, a heavy landing and this could then result in an oscillation of the engine and propeller being allowed to develop, with catastrophic structural failure following. Lockheed undertook a structural modification programme, flying a modified aircraft in October 1960, obtaining FAA certification on 5 January 1961 and then putting in hand a programme to modify all Electras delivered or in production.

For some customers – initially Northwest and Western – Lockheed developed the L-188C version of the Electra with additional fuel and higher gross weight. This was primarily an overwater variant, with a max fuel range increased to 3,020mls (4860km). Fifty-five of the 170 Electras built were of this model. By the mid-seventies, most Electras had been retired from front-line service but the type was still being used for secondary service, mostly in North and South America, a substantial number having been modified as pure freighters with large side-loading doors.

***Below:** Three-view of the Lockheed Electra, which was the only major airliner of American origin to use turboprop engines.*

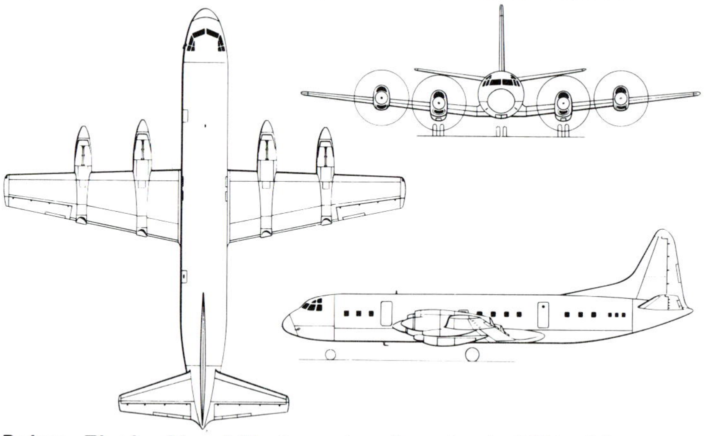

***Below:** The Lockheed Electra entered service in 1959 with Eastern Airlines, but it achieved only limited commercial success.*

Lockheed L-1011 TriStar

USA

The following specification refers to the L-1011-1:

Power Plant: Three 42,000lb st (19,050kgp) Rolls-Royce RB.211-22B or 43,500lb st (19,730kgp) RB.211-22F turbofans.

Performance: Max cruising speed, 575mph (925km/h) = Mach 0·85 at 35,000ft (10,670m); best range cruise, 544mph (875km/h) = Mach 0·82 at 35,000ft (10,670m); initial rate of climb, 2,800ft/min (14·3m/sec); service ceiling, 42,000ft (12,800m); range with max payload, 2,878mls (4629km); range with max fuel, 4,467mls (7189km) with payload of 40,000lb (18,145 kg).

Weights: Operating empty, 234,275lb (106,265kg); max payload, 90,725lb (41,150kg); max take-off, 430,000lb (195,045kg).

Dimensions: Span, 155ft 4in (47·34m); length, 178ft 8in (54·35m); height, 55ft 4in (16·87m); wing area, 3,456sq ft (320·0m²).

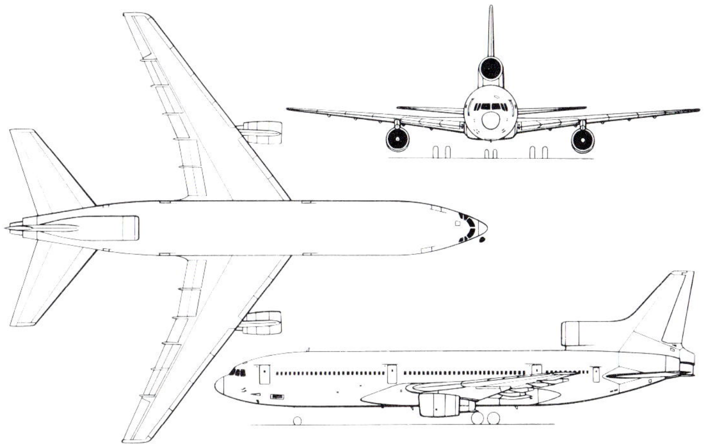

***Above:** The Lockheed TriStar in its initial L-1011-1 version; the later L-1011-100 and L-1011-200 differ only in gross weight and engine power.*

For the Lockheed company, the ending of production of the turboprop Electra in 1962 meant that for the first time since World War II it had no airliner in production at its Burbank, California, headquarters, and that its hard-earned expertise in the commercial field (gained particularly with the Constellation) was in danger of being lost. To fill the vacuum at Burbank, Lockheed mounted a major effort to re-enter the commercial market, setting in train a sequence of events that was to bring the company to the brink of bankruptcy as well as presenting the airlines with a family of advanced high capacity aircraft which they are likely to be operating well into the 21st century.

The trigger for Lockheed's design activities leading to production of the L-1011 TriStar came in 1966 when American Airlines (which had previously sponsored the Electra) drew up a specification for a large capacity, short-to-medium haul transport of the "airbus" type, using the new-technology turbofan engines then becoming available. Although American eventually decided, after months of intensive and competitive design effort by Lockheed and McDonnell Douglas, to order the DC-10, Lockheed was in a position to offer its L-1011 to other US domestic operators that were in the market for a similar aircraft, and on 29 March 1968, TWA and Eastern Airlines announced that they were placing contracts which, combined with a deal between Lockheed and the British Air Holdings company, promised the eventual production of 144 aircraft.

The name TriStar was adopted to continue Lockheed's stellar theme and to emphasize the three-engined layout. As launched, the TriStar was an aeroplane of 409,000lb (185,520kg) gross weight, with a Mach = 0·85 cruising speed, able to carry a 345-passenger payload and to be powered by three Rolls-Royce RB.211 engines. The choice of British engines was made easier by the arrangement for Air Holdings (parent company of BUA) to buy 50 TriStars for resale outside of the UK, and the decision was responsible for launching development of the RB.211, at a projected initial thrust rating of 42,000lb st (19,050kgp). The cost of this programme was to lead Rolls-Royce into bankruptcy on 4 February 1971, placing the whole TriStar future in jeopardy and having repercussions from which Lockheed had not fully recovered four years later.

The first L-1011 had flown on 17 November 1970, with the second flying a month later, the third on 17 May 1971, the fourth in September and the fifth on 2 December 1971 – with varying standards of RB.211. After intensive financial and political negotiations, a firm basis for continuing with the RB.211 and the TriStar was established in September 1971, and on 8 September engines of 42,000lb st (19,050kgp) were flown in the L-1011 for the first time.

Lockheed delivered the first TriStar (No 7 aircraft) to Eastern on 5 April 1972; FAA Type Approval was obtained on 14 April and the first revenue service was flown on 26 April; TWA flew its first TriStar service on 25 June. Thereafter, production and deliveries continued steadily, with initial service standard RB.211Cs being followed in due course by RB.211Bs, with the same rating but a wider range of ambient temperatures at which full power could be delivered. Following Lockheed custom, aircraft were identified by a "dash number" based on configuration: the full designation of the original version was L-1011-385-1, customer suffixes including 193A, Eastern; 193B, TWA; 193M, Haas Turner; 193E, Air Canada; 193K, Court Line; 193R, LTU; 193C, British Airways and 193P, All Nippon. Other customers for the

continued on page 104 ▶

***Below:** Air Canada was among the first non-US customers for the TriStar, with a dozen in service by 1978.*

▶type included Delta, Saudia and Cathay Pacific, and total sales by early 1977 stood at a little over 200.

Several developed versions of the TriStar were proposed by Lockheed from 1971 onwards, with fuselage "stretch", more fuel, and more powerful engines. None of these became firm, however, until 1974, when a go-ahead was confirmed for the RB.211-524 engine with an initial service thrust of 48,000lb st (21,772kgp), increasing to 50,000lb (22,680kg) after one year and perhaps to 55,000lb (24,950kg) eventually. The TriStar with these engines is known as the L-1011-200, and is available with two alternative fuel capacities and gross weights of 450,000lb (204,120kg) or 466,000lb (211,374kg). With these same weights and fuel capacities, but RB.211-22 engines, the TriStar is designated L-1011-100, the basic L-1011-1 having a gross weight of 430,000lb (195,045kg). First customer for the L-1011-200 was Saudia, and for the L-1011-100, Cathay Pacific. A TriStar prototype with RB.211-524s first flew on 12 August 1976 and the first -200 for Saudia followed before the end of the year, entering service in mid-1977.

Also in August, Lockheed launched the L-1011-500 when British Airways ordered six of this extended range version with 50,000lb st (22,700kgp) RB.211-524Bs, fuselage shortened by 13ft 6in (4·11m), extra fuel and still higher gross weight of 496,000lb (224,982kg). On offer or under development in 1977 were the L-1011-250, which has the original fuselage length of the TriStar with the wing, fuel capacity and engines of the -500; the long-fuselage -300; the -400A with a shortened fuselage and a new supercritical wing, and the -600 also with a new wing and shorter fuselage, but with only two engines. Delta Airlines became the second customer for the TriStar 500 in 1978 when ir ordered two with an option on three and Pan American also ordered 12 of this model in 1978.

Below: Cutaway drawing of the Lockheed TriStar in its initial production L-1011-1 form. Most later versions are similar but have uprated engines and increased operating weights, but the L-1011-500, ordered by British Airways, Delta and Pan American, has a shorter fuselage and reduced passenger accommodation.

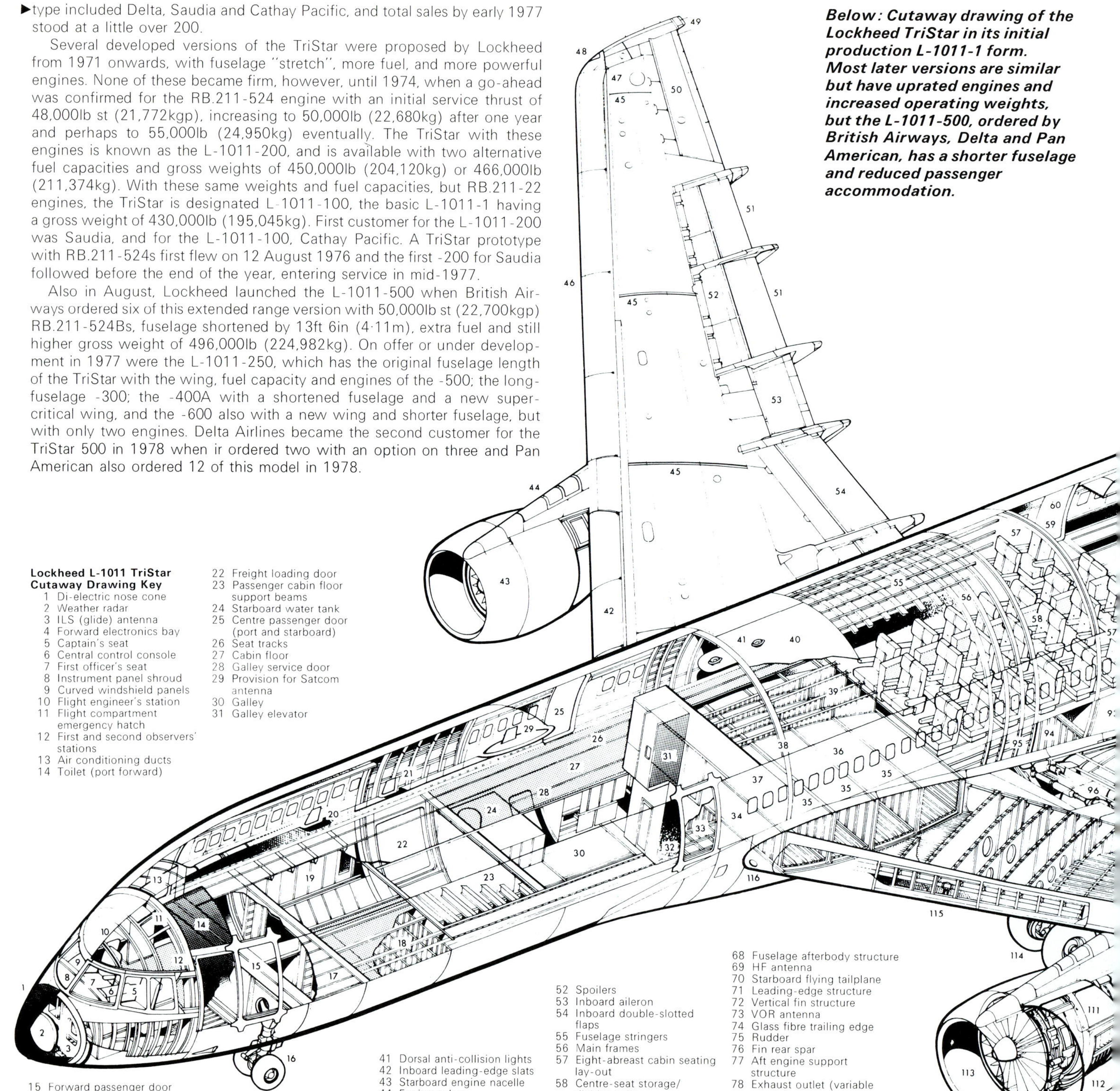

Lockheed L-1011 TriStar Cutaway Drawing Key

1 Di-electric nose cone
2 Weather radar
3 ILS (glide) antenna
4 Forward electronics bay
5 Captain's seat
6 Central control console
7 First officer's seat
8 Instrument panel shroud
9 Curved windshield panels
10 Flight engineer's station
11 Flight compartment emergency hatch
12 First and second observers' stations
13 Air conditioning ducts
14 Toilet (port forward)
15 Forward passenger door (port and starboard)
16 Nose landing gear
17 Passenger floor level
18 Freight hold support beam assembly
19 Forward freight hold (containerized cargo)
20 UHF antenna
21 Provision for second dorsal antenna
22 Freight loading door
23 Passenger cabin floor support beams
24 Starboard water tank
25 Centre passenger door (port and starboard)
26 Seat tracks
27 Cabin floor
28 Galley service door
29 Provision for Satcom antenna
30 Galley
31 Galley elevator
32 Central electronics bay
33 Keelson structure
34 Centre-section front spar
35 Intermediate spars
36 Centre-section wing box
37 Stringerless sidewalls
38 Forward main frame
39 Floor support members
40 Fuselage skin
41 Dorsal anti-collision lights
42 Inboard leading-edge slats
43 Starboard engine nacelle
44 Engine pylon
45 Fuel tank bulkheads
46 Outboard leading-edge slats
47 Fuel vent collector box
48 Starboard forward position light
49 Starboard rear position light
50 Outboard aileron
51 Outboard flaps
52 Spoilers
53 Inboard aileron
54 Inboard double-slotted flaps
55 Fuselage stringers
56 Main frames
57 Eight-abreast cabin seating lay-out
58 Centre-seat storage/divider units
59 Rear main frame
60 Rear passenger door (port and starboard)
61 Floor support beam
62 Rear freight loading door
63 Overhead storage racks
64 Emergency exit (starboard)
65 Coffee-bar area
66 Engine inlet
67 "S"-duct
68 Fuselage afterbody structure
69 HF antenna
70 Starboard flying tailplane
71 Leading-edge structure
72 Vertical fin structure
73 VOR antenna
74 Glass fibre trailing edge
75 Rudder
76 Fin rear spar
77 Aft engine support structure
78 Exhaust outlet (variable nozzle)
79 Rolls-Royce RB.211 turbofan
80 Glass fibre trailing edge
81 Port elevator
82 Static dishargers
83 Detachable tip assembly
84 Fixed leading-edge
85 Horizontal stabilizer box structure
86 Airgate fairing
87 Flying stabilizer actuators
88 Rear pressure dome
89 Pressure deck
90 Emergency exit (port)
91 Rear freight hold (bulk cargo)
92 Wing root/fuselage fairing

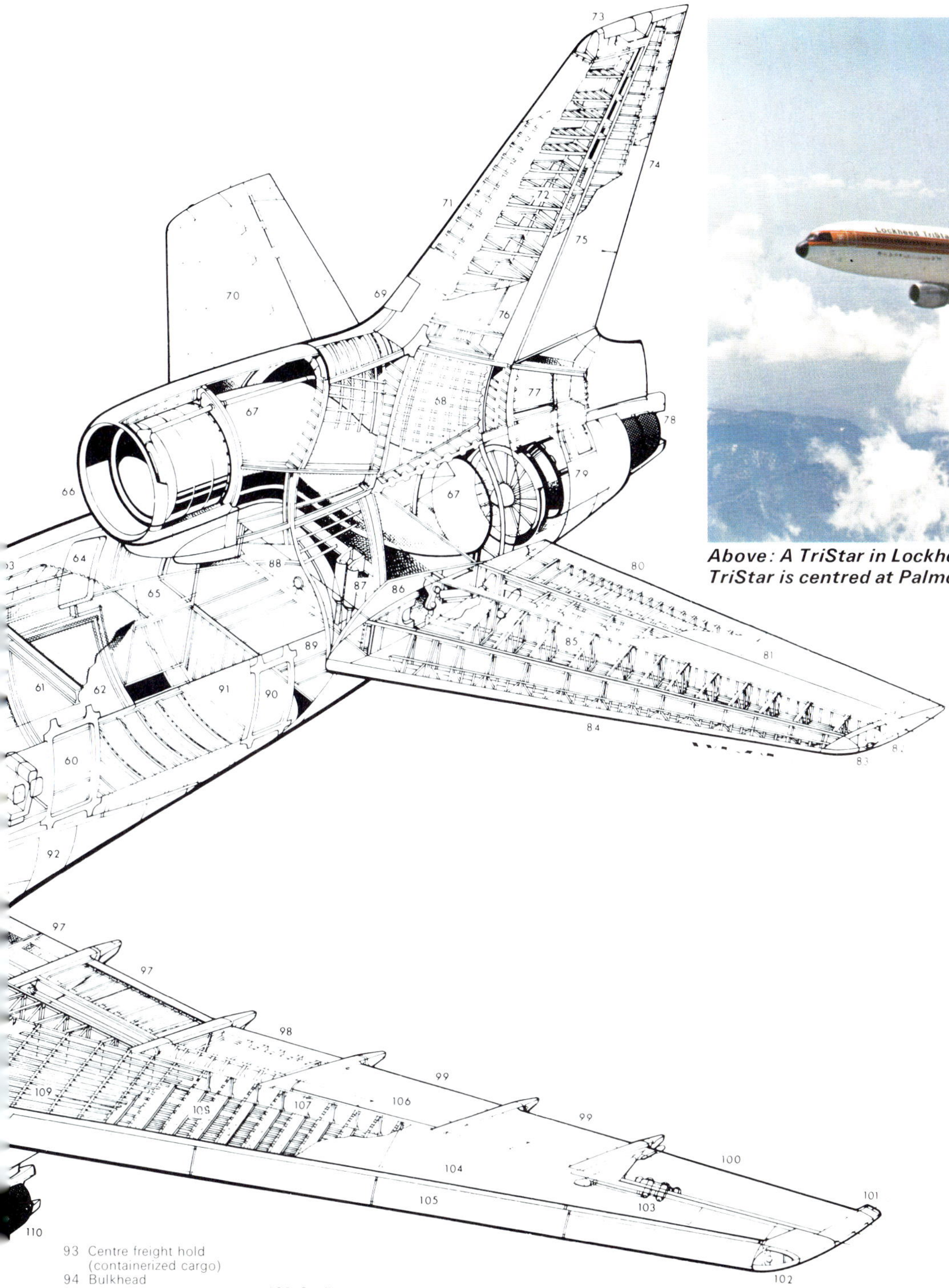

Above: *A TriStar in Lockheed company livery. Flight testing of the TriStar is centred at Palmdale, California.*

93 Centre freight hold (containerized cargo)
94 Bulkhead
95 Main landing gear well
96 Landing gear pivot point
97 Inboard double-slotted flap structure
98 Inboard aileron
99 Outboard flaps
100 Outboard aileron
101 Port rear position light
102 Port forward position light
103 Outboard aileron actuators
104 Wing skin
105 Outboard leading-edge slats
106 Spoilers
107 Rear spar
108 Wing box structure
109 Wing stringers
110 Exhaust outlet (variable nozzle)
111 Rolls-Royce RB.211 turbofan
112 Nacelle panel
113 Engine inlet
114 Four-wheel main landing gear
115 Inboard leading-edge slats
116 Landing light

Below: One of Gulf Air's fleet of Golden Falcons – Lockheed L-1011-100 TriStars that differ from the initial production version only in fuel capacity and gross weight. The Golden Falcons feature unusually luxurious interiors, in keeping with the status of the Arab states that own Gulf Air.

McDonnell Douglas DC-8
USA

The following specification refers to the DC-8 Srs 50:
Power Plant: Four 17,000lb st (7945kgp) Pratt & Whitney JT3D-1 or 18,000lb st (8172kgp) JT3D-3 or -3B turbofans.
Performance: Max cruising speed, 580mph (933km/h); no-reserves range with max payload, 6,185mls (9950km).
Weights: Basic operating, 132,325lb (60,020kg); max weight limited payload, 46,500lb (21,092kg); max take-off, 325,000lb (147,415kg).
Dimensions: Span, 142ft 5in (43·41m); length, 150ft 6in (45·87m); height 42ft 4in (12·91m); wing area, 2,868sq ft (266·5m^2).

The following specification refers to the DC-8 Srs 63:
Power Plant: Four 17,000lb st (7945kgp) Pratt & Whitney JT3D-1 or 18,000lb st (8172kgp) JT3D-3 or -3B or 19,000lb (8618kgp) JT3D-7 turbofans.
Performance: Max cruising speed, 583mph (938km/h); best economy cruise, 523mph (842km/h); initial rate of climb, 2,165ft/min (11·0m/sec); range with max payload, 4,500mls (7240km).
Weights: Basic operating, 153,749lb (69,739kg); max payload, 67,735lb (30,719kg); max take-off, 350,000lb (158,760kg).
Dimensions: Span, 148ft 5in (45·23m); length, 187ft 4in (57·12m); height, 42ft 5in (12·92m); wing area, 2,927sq ft (271,9m^2).

Above: The Douglas DC-8 closely resembled the Boeing 707 but was less successful, and production ended in 1972.

In the continuing effort to maintain its competitive position as a supplier of transport aircraft to the world airline industry (versus Lockheed and Boeing in particular), Douglas Aircraft Company began the search for a successor to the DC-7 in the early 'fifties. Like Boeing, Douglas concluded that the future lay with a turbojet-powered long-range airliner and projected designs along lines very similar to those chosen by Boeing for its military tanker/transport prototype, the Model 367-80. The first flight of the latter in July 1954 heightened Douglas' awareness that the large-scale adoption of jet transports was imminent and on 7 June 1955 the company took the decision to proceed immediately with construction and certification of the DC-8. Details were first published in August 1955, revealing a sleek, low-wing monoplane with 30deg of wing sweepback (less than the Boeing 707), four Pratt & Whitney J57 (JT3C) turbojets in underwing pods and a gross weight of 211,000lb (95,710kg) for domestic US operation (with trans-continental non-stop range) or up to 257,000lb (116,570kg) for projected overwater variants with greater range.

Pan American was the first airline to order the DC-8, placing orders with both Douglas and Boeing for 20 each of their new jet transports on 13 October 1955. United followed with a contract less than two weeks later, and before the end of the year National Airlines, KLM, Eastern, SAS and JAL had joined the queue. Douglas announced that the intercontinental version would have J75 (JT4A) engines, with Rolls-Royce Conways as an alternative, and the gross weights began to rise, to 265,000lb (120,200kg) for the domestic model and 287,500lb (130,410kg) in the intercontinental version – both these figures being increased still further after the aircraft entered service.

Series numbers were adopted for the DC-8 variants at the end of 1959, when the initial domestic model became the Srs 10, and a similar version with JT4A engines for improved take-off performance became the Srs 20. The intercontinental model with JT4As was Srs 30 and with Conway engines, Srs 40. A further variant was also in the planning stage by the time these designations were introduced, being the Srs 50 with JT3D turbofans. All these variants had substantially the same overall dimensions (although some changes in wing span and chord were introduced in the course of production) and provided accommodation for 117 passengers in a typical mixed-class layout or up to 189 in one-class high-density layouts, subject to suitable emergency exit provisions being made.

Flight testing of the DC-8 began on 30 May 1958, with a Srs 10, and the second aircraft to fly was a Srs 20, on 29 November 1958, two more Srs 10s flying in December – by which time the order book stood at 142. Certification of the Srs 10 was obtained on 31 August 1959 and initial services were flown by both United and Delta on 18 September, almost a year later than the commercial introduction of the Boeing 707.

The first DC-8 Srs 30 had flown meanwhile, on 21 February 1959, and Douglas introduced increased fuel capacity in this version, with the weight going up to 310,000lb (140,615kg) initially and 315,000lb (142,880kg) after entry into service. Extended wing tips and a new leading edge that added 4 per cent to the wing chord were also evolved during flight testing, and 17,500lb st (7945kgp) JT4A-11 or -12 engines became available in place of the 15,500lb st (7167kgp) -3 or -5 and 16,500lb st (7620kgp) -9 or -10 units used originally. The Srs 30 was certificated on 1 February 1960 and entered service with Pan American and KLM in April across the North Atlantic, although the first international services by DC-8 had been flown on 14 March 1960 with a United Air Lines Srs 20.

Douglas flew the first Conway-powered DC-8 on 23 July 1959 and obtained Type Approval for this version on 24 March 1960, TCA (now Air Canada) being the first operator, starting in April. Only two other airlines, Alitalia and Canadian Pacific, specified this variant.

The DC-8 Series 50 was essentially a fully-developed Srs 30 airframe with JT3D turbofan engines, these being derivatives of the JT3C with a front fan offering a considerable improvement in thrust and specific fuel consumption. The original DC-8 was re-engined and flew as the Srs 50 prototype on 20 December 1960 and initial certification was obtained on 10 October 1961 at a gross weight of 276,000lb (125,190kg), with 17,000lb st (7945kgp) engines; subsequently, weights up to 325,000lb (147,415kg) were approved, with 18,000lb st (8172kgp) JT3D-3 or JT3D-3B engines. Some earlier DC-8s were converted to Srs 50s, in addition to new-built aircraft.

In April 1961, Douglas announced the development of a passenger/cargo variant of the DC-8 Srs 50 called the Jet Trader. This had a side-loading freight door in the forward fuselage and a reinforced floor with built-in cargo handling provision, and used the same power plant and gross weights as the Srs 50 described above. The first production Jet Trader flew on 29 October 1962, being one of four ordered by TCA (Air Canada), and certification was obtained on 29 January 1963.

Sales of the DC-8 consistently lagged behind those of the Boeing 707, partly because of its later entry in the market but also because the family of DC-8s, all of the same capacity, was less flexible in meeting varying airline requirements than the variety of Boeing 707 models on offer. Production of the DC-8 Srs 10 to Srs 50 inclusive in fact totalled 293, comprising, in addition to one company prototype/demonstrator, 28 Srs 10 (of which 21 were first converted to Srs 20 and 11 later converted to Srs 50); 34 Srs 20;

Below: A McDonnell Douglas DC-8 Srs 62 in service with Air Jamaica. This is the very long range version of the DC-8.

Above: A DC-8 Series 63CF, one of the second "family" of DC-8s with greatly lengthened fuselages and other improvements.

57 Srs 30 (of which three later converted to Srs 50); 32 Srs 40; 87 Srs 50 and 54 Srs 50 Jet Traders.

To overcome the sales disadvantage resulting from the standardization on one size of fuselage, the Douglas company finally decided in April 1965 to offer three new models of the DC-8, to be known as the Sixty Series and providing different combinations of fuselage stretch and payload/range performance. Based initially on the JT3D-1 or JT3D-3 turbofans as used in the Series 50, the Sixty Series comprised the Srs 61 with the fuselage lengthened by 36ft 8in (11·18m) to provide accommodation for up to 259 passengers; the Srs 62 with a fuselage stretch of only 6ft 8in (2·03m) for up to 189 passengers combined with extra fuel and aerodynamic refinements to achieve a very long range; and the Srs 63 combining the long fuselage of the Srs 61 with various of the improvements developed for the Srs 62, including a 6ft (1·82m) increase in span, to give maximum flexibility of operation over medium-to-long ranges.

The first DC-8 Srs 61 flew from Long Beach on 14 March 1966 and was Type Approved by the FAA on 2 September 1966; the Srs 62 flew on 29 August 1966 and was certificated on 27 April 1967; and the Srs 63 flew on 10 April 1967, being approved on 30 June 1967. All three versions entered airline service in 1967 – respectively on 25 February, 22 May and 27 July. In addition to the full passenger variants, Douglas offered convertible and all-freight versions with a forward cargo door as used in the Jet Trader; these were identified by a CF suffix for the convertible (all three series) and AF for all-freight Srs 62s and Srs 63s. Some of the latter were built with the structural provision of the Srs 63CF, to permit subsequent modification and enhance the resale value, but did not have the freight door or floor fitted, and these were designated Srs 63PF.

The addition of the Sixty Series to the DC-8 range brought a spurt of new orders in the mid-sixties, and resulted in the sale of an additional 263 examples by the time production ended in May 1972. This total was made up of 78 Srs 61; 10 Srs 61CF; 52 Srs 62; 16 Srs 62CF and AF; 41 Srs 63 and 66 Srs 63CF, AF and PF, and brought the grand total of DC-8s produced to 556. By 1977, some of the early turbojet-powered versions had been retired and consideration was being given to ways in which others could be re-engined or modified to meet the latest noise requirements. Over 400 DC-8s were still in airline service and the manufacturers had embarked upon a programme to convert earlier DC-8s to full cargo configuration, with original engines or JT3D turbofans.

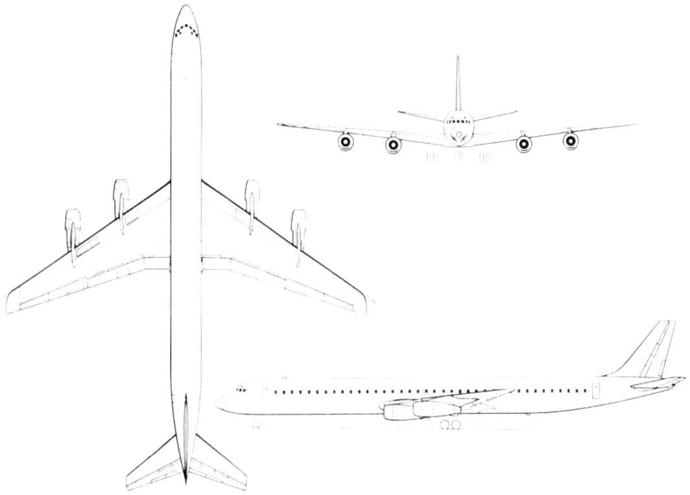

Above: The DC-8 Srs 61, with the longest of the three fuselage lengths applied to the different DC-8 variants.

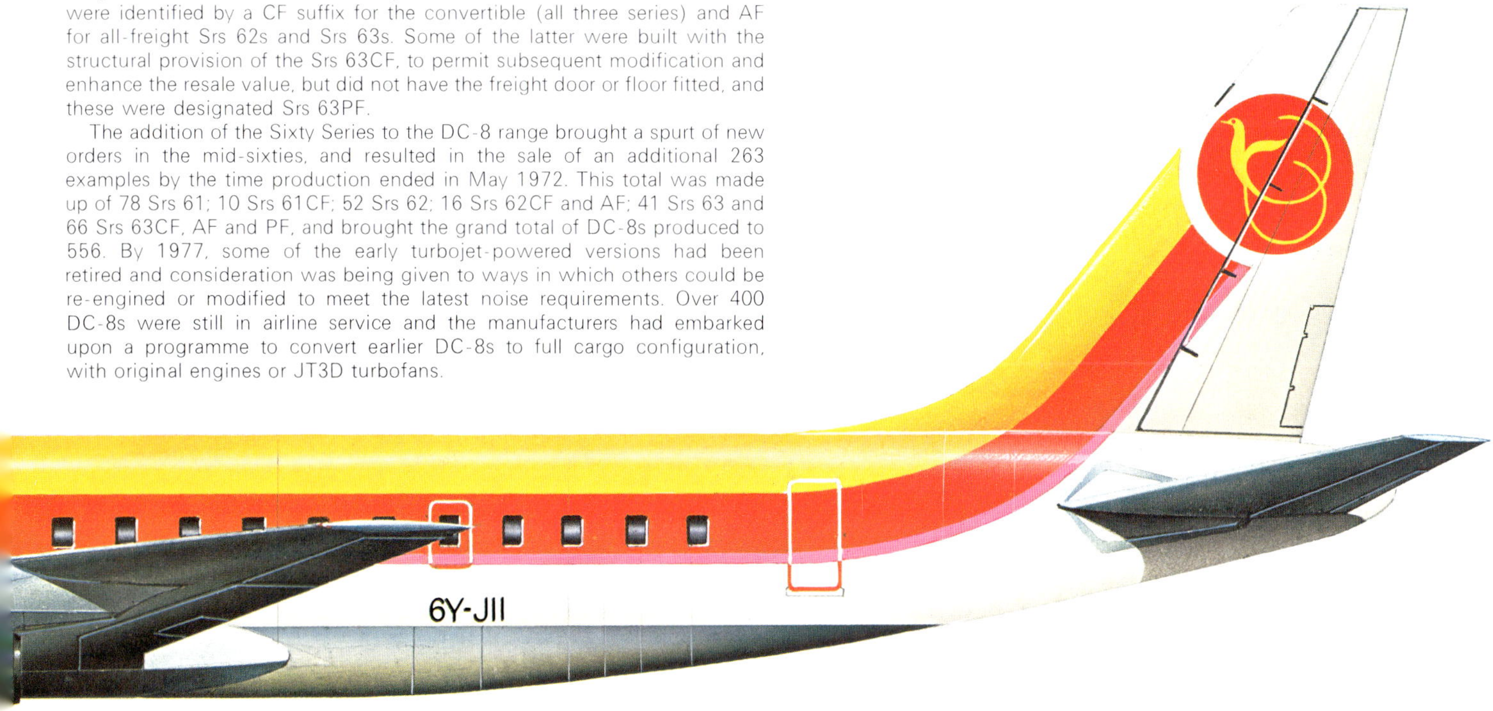

McDonnell Douglas DC-9
USA

The following specification refers to the DC-9 Srs 30:
Power Plant: Two 14,500lb st (6580kgp) Pratt & Whitney JT8D-9 or 15,000lb st (6800kgp) JT8D-11 or 15,500lb st (7030kgp) JT8D-15 turbofans.
Performance: Max cruising speed, 572mph (918km/h); long-range cruise, 496mph (796km/h); range with max payload, 1,100mls (1770km).
Weights: Operating empty, 58,500lb (26,535kg); max weight-limited payload, 29,860lb (13,550kg); max take-off, 108,000lb (49,000kg).
Dimensions: Span, 93ft 5in (28·5m); length, 119ft 4in (36·37m); height, 27ft 6in (8·38m); wing area, 1,001sq ft (92·97m^2).

The following specification refers to the DC-9 Srs 50:
Power Plant: Two 16,000lb st (7257kgp) Pratt & Whitney JT8D-17 turbofans.
Performance: Max cruising speed, 564mph (908km/h) at 27,000ft (82000m); economical cruising speed, 535mph (861km/h) at 33,000ft (10,000m); long range cruise, 509mph (819km/h) at 35,000ft (10,700m); no-reserves range with max payload, 1,470mls (2360km) at Mach = 0·80 cruise; no-reserves range with max fuel, 2,787mls (4480km) with payload of 21,400lb (9700kg).
Weights: Operating weight empty, 65,000lb (29,500kg); max take-off, 120,000lb (54,400kg); max landing, 110,000lb (49,900kg); max zero fuel, 98,000lb (44,400kg).
Dimensions: Span, 93ft 4in (28·40m); length, 132ft 0in (40·30m); height 28ft 0in (8·50m); wing area, 1,001sq ft (92·97m^2).

The following specification refers to the DC-9 Super 80
Power Plant: Two 18,500lb st (8400kgp) Pratt & Whitney, JT8D-209 turbofans.
Performance: Max cruising speed, 546mph (878km/h) at 31,000ft (9450m), range with 137 passenger load, 2,055st mls (3306km) at 35,000ft (10,668m).
Weights: Operating weight empty, 77,757lb (35,270kg) max take-off weight, 140,000lb (63,503kg), max landing weight, 128,000lb (58,060kg), max zero fuel weight, 118,000lb (53,524kg).
Dimensions: Span, 107ft 10in (32·85m); length, 147ft 10in (45·08m), height, 29ft 4in (8·93m); wing area, 1,279sq ft (118·8m^2).

The designation DC-9 was in use from the early 'fifties onwards to indicate the company's plans to develop a medium-range jet transport partner for the DC-8. At first, the idea was to produce what would essentially have been a scaled-down DC-8, of similar configuration and about two-thirds the capacity, but continuing contacts with airlines throughout the world in the late 'fifties and early 'sixties served to extend the timescale for launching the DC-9, and led eventually to a complete re-appraisal of the project and its development as a new design unrelated to the DC-8.

By 1962, Douglas had defined the potential market more clearly and was emphasizing the short rather than medium-range aspect, aiming, like BAC with the One-Eleven, to produce an aeroplane to replace the smaller, piston-engined and turboprop transports; and the project took shape along similar lines to the One-Eleven, with a T-tail and rear-mounted engines. The decision to proceed with development and production was announced by Douglas on 8 April 1963 without the backing of a firm airline order, but this followed less than three weeks later when Delta signed a contract for 15 with 15 more on option. The initial DC-9 variant was therefore aimed at the requirements of the US airlines, but the company planned from the start to offer a range of variants with differing passenger capacities and ranges, this being in contrast to the policy followed in respect of the DC-8 and giving Douglas a significant edge over BAC in the sales battles that were to follow in the mid-'sixties.

The first DC-9 flew at Long Beach on 25 February 1965, two more following in May, one in June and one in July to complete the test fleet. As for the DC-8, the DC-9 variants were distinguished by Srs numbers, all these early examples being Series 10 with Pratt & Whitney JT8D-5 engines rated at 12,000lb st (5443kgp), and having a gross weight of 77,000lb (34,930kg), or 83,000lb (37,650kg) when extra centre section fuel was carried. In typical mixed-class arrangements, the DC-9 Srs 10 carried 72 passengers, the maximum high-density accommodation being for 90 (five-abreast). FAA Type Approval was obtained on 23 November 1965 and Delta put the DC-9 into service on 8 December. Subsequently, some Series 10s were delivered with 14,000lb st (6350kgp) JT8D-1 or -7 engines and a gross weight of 90,700lb (41,140kg) was approved.

The first order for a "stretched" DC-9 was placed by Eastern Air Lines, on 25 February 1965, at which time it was referred to as the DC-9B or DC-9 Srs 20, the fuselage being lengthened by 9ft 6in (2·9m). However, the stretch was later increased to 14ft 11in (4·6m) and the designation changed to Srs 30; the Srs 20 designation was re-used subsequently for another version. To preserve performance at higher weights, the DC-9 Srs 30 was given extended wing tips – adding 4ft (1·21m) to the span – full-span leading edge slats and uprated engines. The first flight was made on

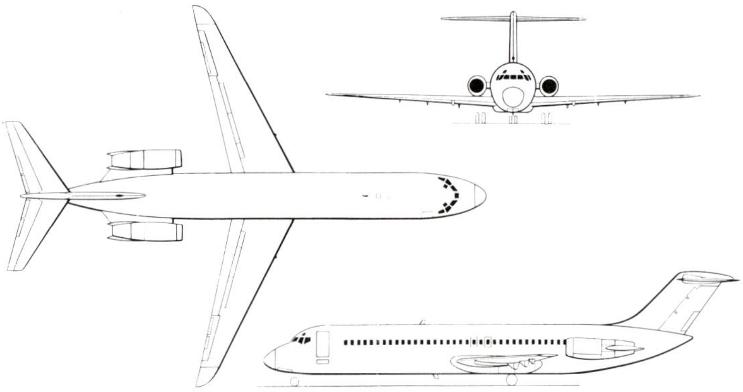

Above: The DC-9 Srs 30, one of the five dimensionally different versions of the twin-jet put into production by 1978.

Below: One of two DC-9 Srs 50s put into service by BWIA in 1978, showing the longer fuselage of this version.

1 August 1966, and after certification on 19 December, this variant entered service with Eastern early in 1967. Initially, with 14,500lb st (6580kgp) JT8D-9 engines, the gross weight was 98,000lb (44,444kg), but uprated JT8D-11 or -15 engines could also be used and the max permitted weight increased to 108,000lb (49,000kg). Accommodation varied from a typical mixed class layout for 97 up to a maximum of 115.

Sales of the DC-9 proceeded vigorously during the 'sixties, helped by the company's willingness to respond to specific airline needs by developing special versions. For SAS, the Srs 40 was developed as a further stretch of the Srs 30, having 6ft 4in (1·87m) more fuselage length to seat 107–125 passengers with improved payload/range performance. Using 15,500lb st (7030kgp) JT8D-15 engines, the Srs 40 had a gross weight of 114,000lb (51,800kg) and was flown on 28 November 1967; it entered service with SAS in 1968 and has also been used by Swissair (leased from SAS) and purchased by TDA of Japan.

Another SAS requirement resulted in the re-introduction of the Srs 20 designation at the end of 1966 for a "hot and high" version of the Srs 10. This had the Srs 30 wings and JT8D-9 or -11 engines, but the original fuselage length and capacity and a max weight of 100,000lb (45,360kg). The first Srs 20 flew on 18 September 1968 and was ordered only by SAS, which bought 10.

The fifth major variant of the DC-9 was announced in July 1973, when Swissair placed an order for 10 Srs 50s, several other airlines ordering this type subsequently. The major difference, once again, was in fuselage length, which grew by another 6ft 4in (1·87m) over the Srs 40, representing a total increase of 27ft 7in (8·41m) on the original length of the Srs 10. Offering a passenger capacity of 122–139, the Srs 50 was made possible by the availability of additional thrust from the JT8D engine, being based on the use of either the 15,500lb st (7030kgp) -15 or the 16,000lb (7257kgp) -17. Other changes included the introduction of Hytrol Mk IIIA skid control and canting the engine thrust reversers 17 deg from the vertical to avoid the risk of exhaust gas ingestion. With an initial gross weight of 120,000lb (54,400kg), the Srs 50 made its first flight on 17 December 1974 at Long Beach and entered service with Swissair on 24 August 1975.

Versions of the DC-9 were offered with a forward, side-loading freight door, for use in convertible or all-freight configuration. For certification purposes, these were identified by an F suffix to the series number, but the manufacturer used a C or RC (for rapid change) suffix in reference to these versions also. The first order for a convertible DC-9C, with freight door, was placed by Continental Airlines, in March 1965, and the first delivery was made on 7 March 1966, this being a Srs 10 aircraft; the first Srs 30 convertible was delivered in October 1967, to Overseas National. A few all-freight DC-9Fs have also been delivered, the first, a Srs 30F, going to Alitalia in May 1968.

On 9 January 1975, McDonnell Douglas flew a DC-9 fitted with JT8D-109 (refanned) engines in a programme to develop a quieter engine installation for retrofit to existing DC-9 models. As an outcome of this programme, a number of new DC-9 variants were studied between 1975 and 1977, including the DC-9 Srs 50 RS with the refanned JT8D-209 engines and an increase of 7ft 11in (2·41m) in fuselage length; the DC-9 Srs 60 with more powerful CFM-56 or JT10D turbofans and fuselage stretch of 17ft 4in (5·30m); the DC-9 Srs 50-17R, with JT8D-17Rs and 7ft 11in (2·41m) fuselage stretch and the DC-9SC, similar to the Srs 50RS but with an improved wing of supercritical design.

From these considerations, the DC-9 Srs 55 took shape in 1977 with JT8D-207s and a fuselage stretch of 12ft 8in (3·86m), but final negotiations with the prospective customers led to the stretch being increased to 14ft 3in (4·34m) and the thrust of the -207 engine being further increased to 18,500lb (8400kgp). In this guise, the new variant was renamed the DC-9 Super 80 and was given a go-ahead by the company in October 1977, at which time initial orders were announced by Swissair (for 15), Austrian Airlines (8) and Southern Airways (4), with others on option. First flight of a Super 80 was scheduled to be made in May 1979 with airline deliveries starting in March 1980.

By early 1978, McDonnell Douglas had sold 926 DC-9s, with some 30 more on option or conditional sale (this total including 32 for the USAF and USN). The type was being operated by some 50 airlines throughout the world.

Below: Turkish Airlines THY is one of the many European airlines operating DC-9s; the illustration shows a Srs 30.

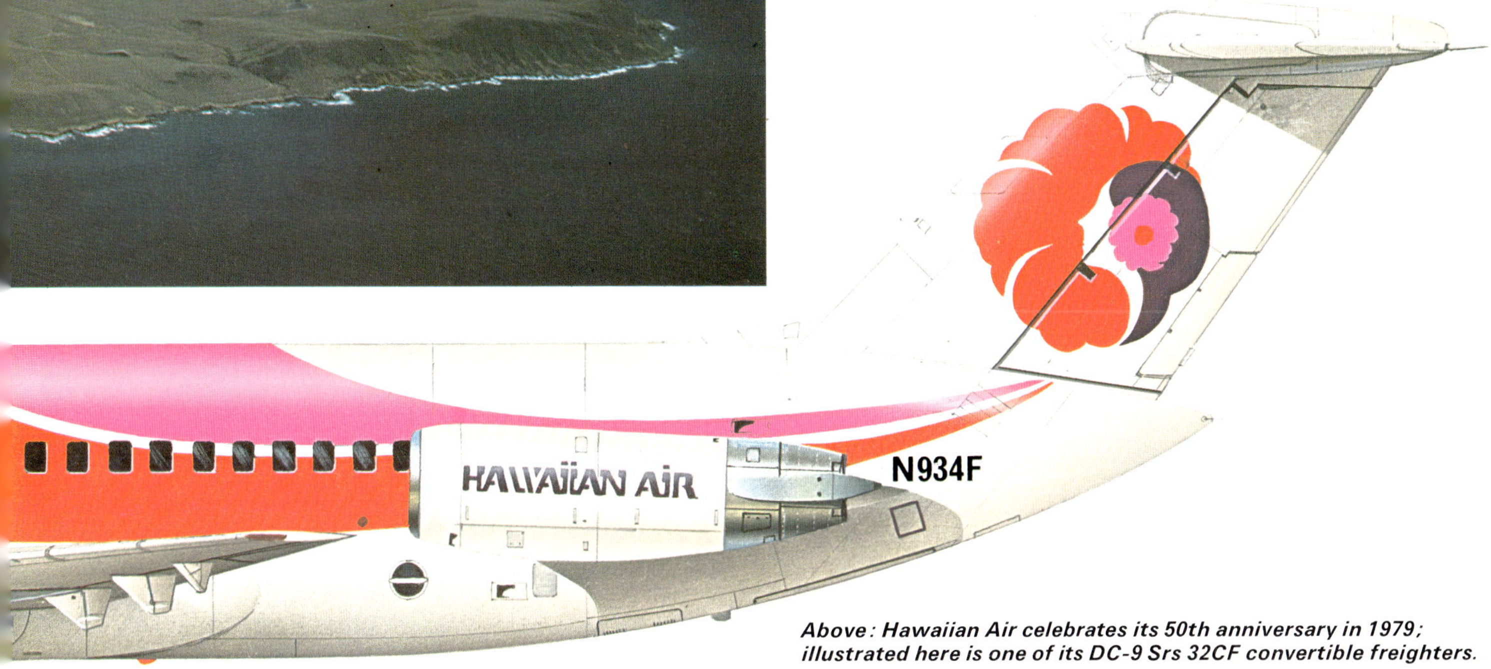

Above: Hawaiian Air celebrates its 50th anniversary in 1979; illustrated here is one of its DC-9 Srs 32CF convertible freighters.

McDonnell Douglas DC-10
USA

The following specification refers to the DC-10 Srs 30:
Power Plant: Three 51,000lb st (23,134kgp) General Electric CF6-50C turbofans.
Performance: Max cruising speed at 31,000ft (9450m), 570mph (917km/h); initial rate of climb, 2,320ft/min (11·8m/sec); service ceiling, 32,700ft (9965m); range with max payload, 4,272mls (6875km); range with max fuel, 6,910mls (11,118km).
Weights: Basic operating, 263,087lb (119,334kg); max payload, 104,913lb (47,587kg); max take-off, 555,000lb (251,744kg).
Dimensions: Span, 165ft 4in (40·42m); length, 181ft 7in (55·35m); height, 58ft 1in (17·7m); wing area, 3,921sq ft (364·3m²).

Spurred by an outline specification for a "Jumbo Twin" issued by American Airlines in March 1966, the Douglas Aircraft Company embarked upon a series of design studies for a possible addition to the Douglas Commercial series of airliners. By the middle of 1967, the company (which meanwhile

continued on page 112

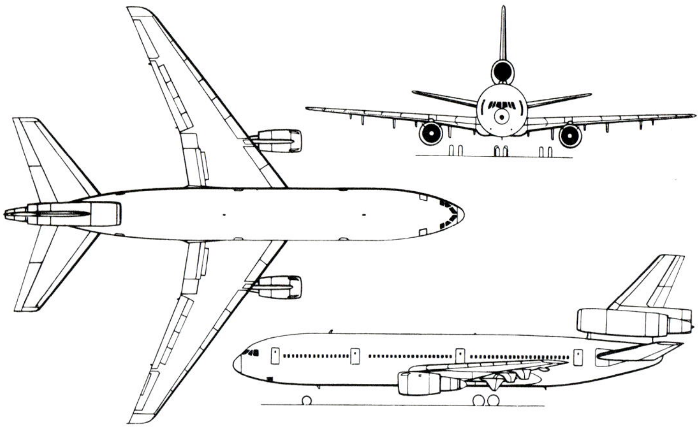

***Above:** The McDonnell Douglas DC-10 Srs 30, the principal production version of the wide-body trijet in 1978.*

McDonnell Douglas DC-10 Series 30 CF Cutaway Drawing Key
1 Weather radar
2 Windshield
3 Instrument console
4 Flight deck
5 Captain's seat (Aircraft Mechanics Inc)
6 First Officer's seat (ditto)
7 Flight Engineer's position
8 Supernumerary crew seat
9 Flight deck door
10 Forward starboard toilet
11 Forward port toilet
12 Crew and passenger forward entry door
13 Twin wheel nose gear (Abex or Dowty Rotol, Goodyear tyres)
14 Air conditioning access doors
15 Forward cargo bulkhead
16 Air conditioning bay (Garrett AiResearch equipment)
17 Forward lower galley area (used for containerized cargo)
18 Air conditioning trunking
19 Cargo deck lateral transfer area (omni-caster rollers)
20 Cargo deck pallet channels (rollers)
21 Main cargo door (fully open position)
22 VHF antenna
23 Frame-and-stringer fuselage construction
24 Main deck cargo (ten 88 x 125-in, 2·23 x 3·17m (pallets), capacity 4,958cu ft (140·4m³))
25 Passenger door
26 Forward lower compartment (five 88 x 125-in, 2·23 x 3·17-m pallets) capacity 1,890cu ft (53·5m³)
27 Centre section fuselage main frame
28 Centre-section front beam
29 Sheer-web floor support over centre-section fuel tank
30 Cargo/passenger compartment dividing bulkhead
31 Starboard engine pod (Rohr subcontract)
32 Engine intake
33 Nacelle pylon
34 Leading-edge slats
35 Integral wing fuel tank
36 Starboard navigation lights
37 Low-speed outboard aileron
38 Fuel ventpipe
39 Wing spoilers/lift dumpers
40 Double-slotted flaps
41 All-speed inboard drooping aileron
42 Passenger doors
43 Centre-section fuselage mainframe
44 Cabin air ducts
45 Centre undercarriage bay
46 Keel box structure
47 Fuselage wing attachment points
48 Wing torsion-box construction

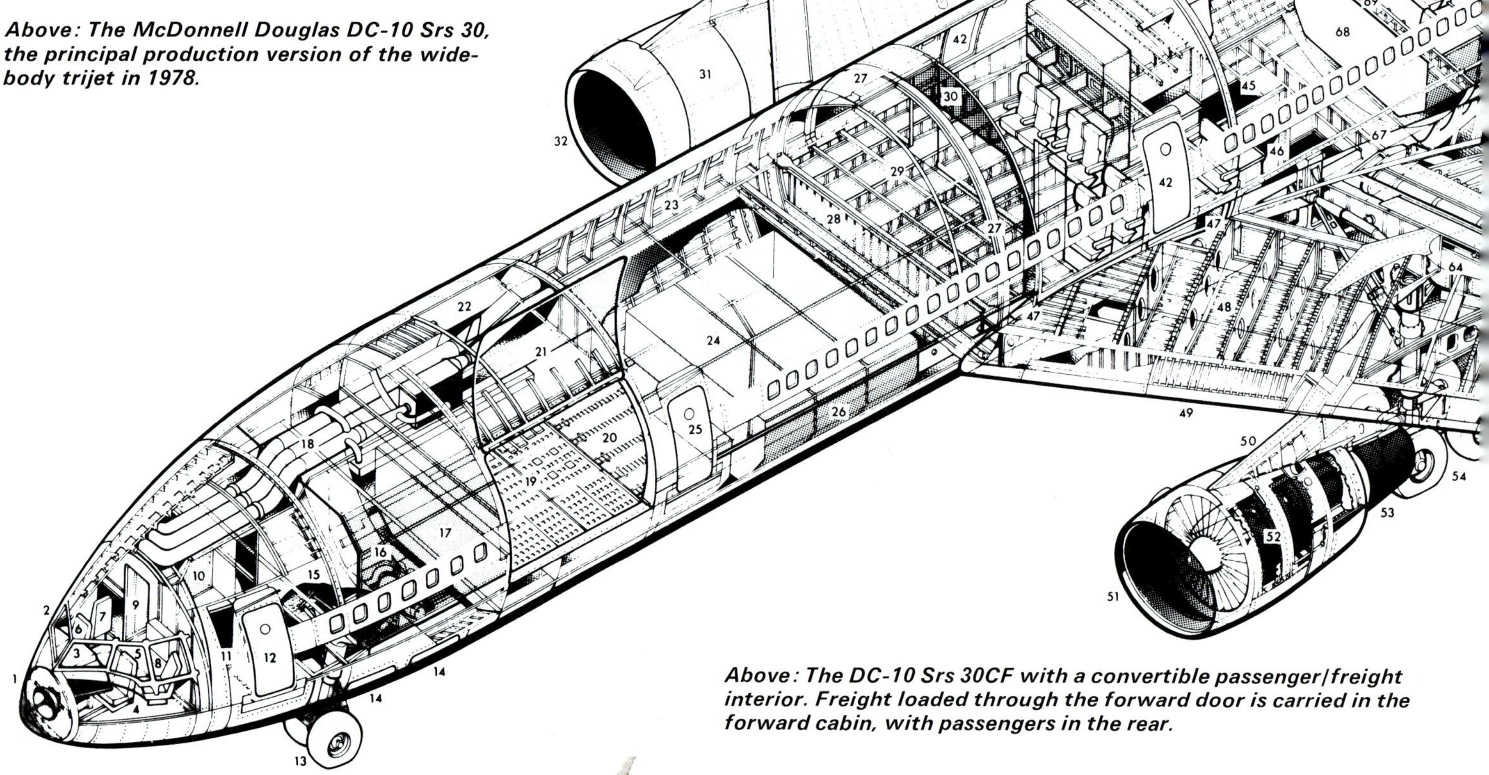

***Above:** The DC-10 Srs 30CF with a convertible passenger/freight interior. Freight loaded through the forward door is carried in the forward cabin, with passengers in the rear.*

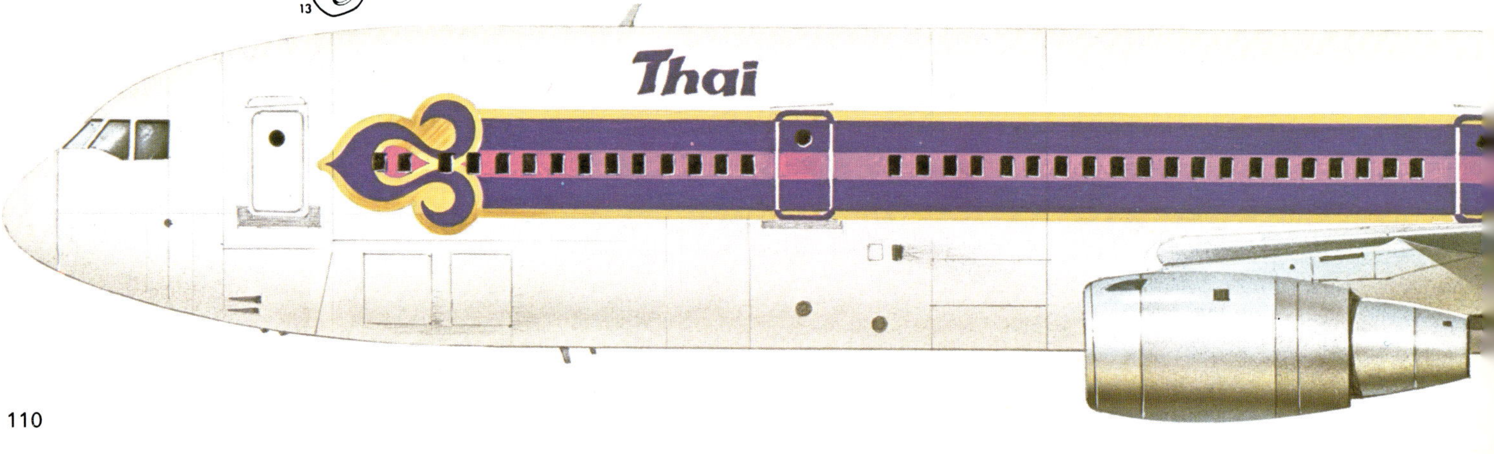

49 Leading edge structure
50 Nacelle pylon
51 Engine intake
52 General Electric CF6-50 turbofan
53 Exhaust outlet
54 Four-wheel main undercarriage (Menasco Manufacturing; Goodyear tyres and brakes)
55 Leading edge slats
56 Outboard slat extended
57 Port navigation lights
58 Low-speed outboard aileron
59 Fuel vent pipe
60 Outboard flap hinge fairings
61 Fuel pipes
62 All-speed inboard drooping aileron
63 Inboard flap hinge actuator and fairing
64 Undercarriage support structure
65 Flap construction

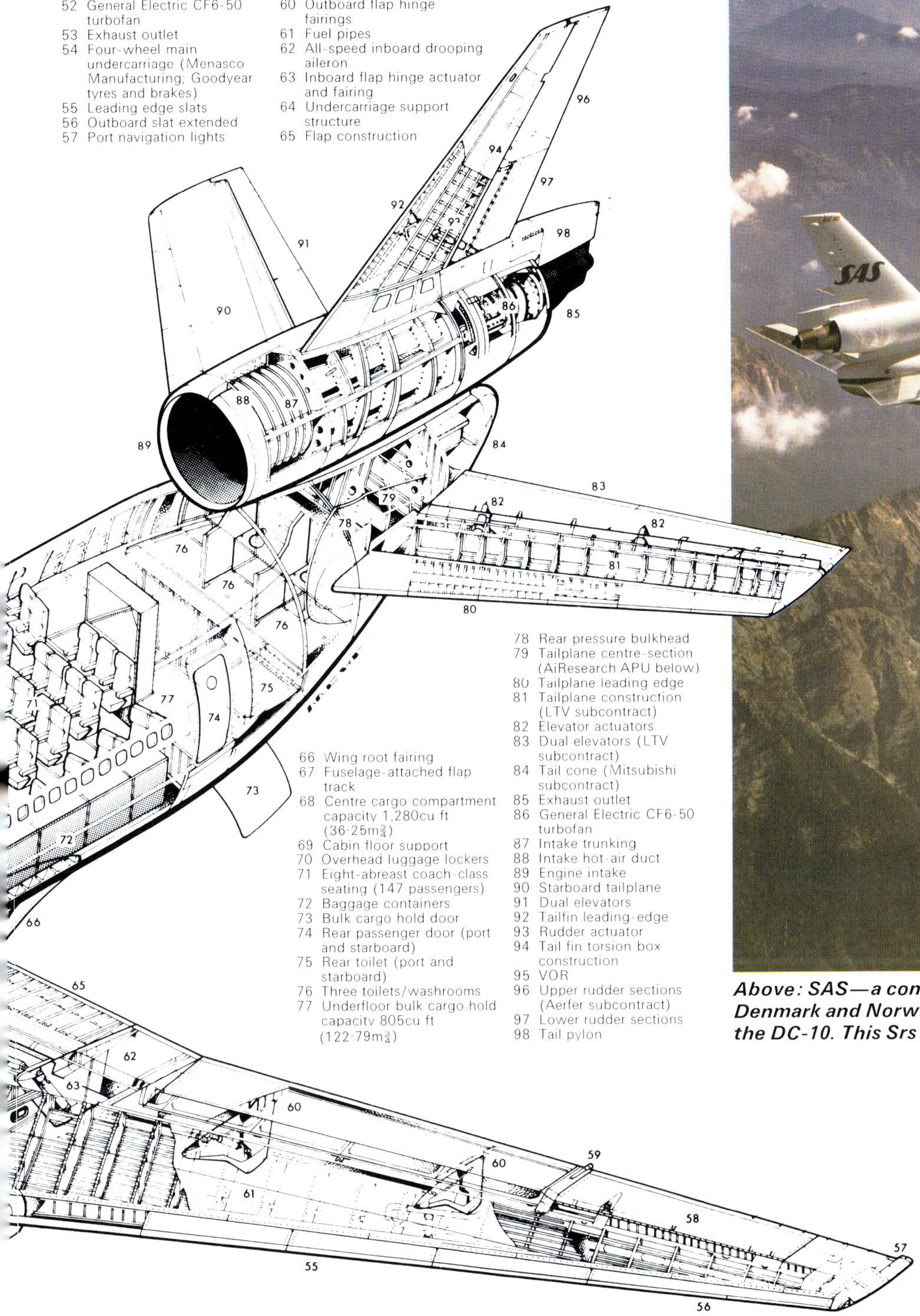

66 Wing root fairing
67 Fuselage-attached flap track
68 Centre cargo compartment capacity 1,280cu ft (36·25m³)
69 Cabin floor support
70 Overhead luggage lockers
71 Eight-abreast coach-class seating (147 passengers)
72 Baggage containers
73 Bulk cargo hold door
74 Rear passenger door (port and starboard)
75 Rear toilet (port and starboard)
76 Three toilets/washrooms
77 Underfloor bulk cargo hold capacity 805cu ft (122·79m³)
78 Rear pressure bulkhead
79 Tailplane centre-section (AiResearch APU below)
80 Tailplane leading edge
81 Tailplane construction (LTV subcontract)
82 Elevator actuators
83 Dual elevators (LTV subcontract)
84 Tail cone (Mitsubishi subcontract)
85 Exhaust outlet
86 General Electric CF6-50 turbofan
87 Intake trunking
88 Intake hot-air duct
89 Engine intake
90 Starboard tailplane
91 Dual elevators
92 Tailfin leading-edge
93 Rudder actuator
94 Tail fin torsion box construction
95 VOR
96 Upper rudder sections (Aerfer subcontract)
97 Lower rudder sections
98 Tail pylon

Above: SAS—a consortium of airlines representing Sweden, Denmark and Norway—is one of several European operators of the DC-10. This Srs 30 is the intercontinental version.

Below: A dramatically-marked DC-10 Srs 30 operated by Thai International on its "Royal Orchid" services to Europe. The DC-10 can accommodate up to 380 passengers; about 270 is typical.

►had become a division of McDonnell Douglas Corporation) had concluded that the requirement, and the potential future market, for such a type required the use of three engines and a larger capacity than American had originally indicated. American Airlines concurred, issuing an amended "Jumbo Trijet" specification in July 1967 and after further refinement of the Douglas proposal. American placed an order on 19 February 1968 for 25 DC-10s with options on 25 more and a forecast need for 100 by 1975.

This order gave the DC-10 first honours in the intensive sales battle versus the Lockheed TriStar, but was not sufficient evidence of an adequate market to allow the company to launch full production, that stage being reached only at the end of April 1968 when United Air Lines ordered 30 DC-10s and took an option on 30 more. The DC-10, as then defined, was a wide-body transport seating about 270 passengers in typical mixed-class layouts or up to 380 in one-class high density arrangements. Powered by four 40,000lb st (18,144kgp) General Electric CF6 turbofans, it shared with the TriStar the previously untried configuration of two underwing engine pods and a third engine in the rear – in the case of the DC-10, carried above the fuselage in an independent nacelle integrated with the fin. Aimed specifically at meeting the requirements of the US trunk airlines, the initial DC-10 had enough range for transcontinental non-stop operation with full payload. Longer-range versions were planned to be made available in due course however.

The first order for a range-extended variant came from Northwest Orient Airlines at the end of 1968. Extra fuel was carried in the wing centre section and fuselage tanks, and the gross weight increased from 386,500lb (175,000 kg) at which the original version had been launched, to 530,000lb (240,400 kg) – further increases in both these weights having been made subsequently. The higher weights required the use of a third main undercarriage unit to spread the load more evenly on the runway, this unit being added on the fuselage centreline; more engine power was also needed, and Northwest opted to use the Pratt & Whitney JT9D-15 to obtain standardization with its Boeing 747s. Designations were introduced by Douglas at this stage to differentiate between the variants, the initial version being the Srs 10, the Northwest variant being Srs 20 and a similar long-range version with CF6-50 engines being Srs 30. Both the Srs 20 and Srs 30 had a small increase in wing span and area, and the overall length varied slightly.

The DC-10 Srs 30 gained its go-ahead in June 1969 when it was selected by the KSSU consortium of European airlines; subsequently, three of the four ATLAS group airlines also chose the Srs 30, confirming its lead over the TriStar at least so far as Europe was concerned. For marketing reasons, the Srs 20 was later redesignated Srs 40, and its engines were redesignated JT9D-20. Later variants of both the CF6-50 and the JT9D have been evolved for introduction in the DC-10 in due course.

First flight of the DC-10 was made on 29 August 1970, with a second aircraft (in American Airlines finish) joining the test programme on 24 October and the third (in United colours) on 23 December. Full FAA Type Approval was obtained on 29 July 1971, and the DC-10 entered service with American Airlines on 5 August, operating a daily non-stop flight between Los Angeles and Chicago. The work of certificating the Series 40 began with the first flight of this version on 28 February 1972 and was completed on 27 October, with first delivery to Northwest on 10 November. The first Series 30 flew on 21 June 1972 and was certificated on 21 November.

***Left:** A DC-10 Srs 30 of the West German national airline Lufthansa at Frankfurt Main. The company had 11 DC-10s in service in 1978.*

***Below:** Laker Airways "Eastern Belle", one of the four DC-10 Srs 10s with which the company launched its popular transatlantic Skytrain service in 1977.*

Maximum weights approved for DC-10 operation have progressively increased and by the end of 1974, the Srs 10 was certificated at 430,000lb (195,045kg) and the Srs 30 and 40 at 555,000lb (251,744kg), these increases being made possible in part by the progressive growth in available engine thrust. Some of the Srs 10s for American Airlines were certificated at 440,000lb (199,581kg), with extra centre section fuel to operate the routes to Honolulu.

Extending the utility of the DC-10, Douglas offered a convertible freighter as the DC-10CF, featuring a side-loading cargo door ahead of the wing and provision for freight carrying in the forward part of the fuselage. The first convertible model, a DC-10 Srs 30CF, flew on 28 February 1973 and deliveries began on 17 April 1973, when both Overseas National and Trans International accepted their first examples. Pure freight versions were also on offer to airlines in 1974.

By early 1978, McDonnell Douglas had sold some 275 DC-10s to 42 operators and had conditional orders or options on nine more. In numbers of customers, the DC-10 had also proved to be the most popular of the wide-body airliners and is certain to figure prominently in airline fleets up to the end of the century, with additional versions or derivatives of the basic design likely to be launched in due course.

***Below:** The flight deck of the McDonnell Douglas DC-10 is the most modern illustrated in this book (though in other respects the L-1011 and A300B are even more advanced). Like most modern cockpits, it shows extreme ergonomic attention to detail, so that everything is correctly positioned for effortless functioning. Everything possible is done to minimise pilot workload and eliminate errors. Part of the credit rests with the manufacturers of instruments and systems, who have virtually eliminated any display or control that could result in confusion. One of the most advanced features of modern wide-bodies, and a customer option on the DC-10 (absent from this particular example), is an ACL (automatic check list). Instead of captain and co-pilot labouring with old-fashioned printed cards and manual checks through over 200 items at a time, they can press a button and have it all done automatically at great speed. Should any item fail to function correctly its name is flashed on a caption panel immediately above the triplets of engine instruments. Once the situation has been rectified the procedure continues until another item fault lights up. This automated system is doubly valuable during take-off and landing when workload is high and radio procedures make inter-pilot communication difficult.*

***Below:** The flight engineer's panel in the DC-10, which differs according to the sub-type (the Dash-30 and -40 have a larger fuel system), is in the usual place for a long-haul airliner on the right wall aft of the first officer. The DC-10 project team spent many hours testing crew seats, and arrived at models that are electronically driven along the floor and whose seat and back rake are variable (seen here at maximum recline). In the next generation of aircraft it is thought that flight engineers will depend on computer control of display panels to provide the sort of complex information the crew may require to make in-flight decisions.*

Martin 404
USA

The following sqecification refers to the Martin 404.
Power Plant: Two 2,400hp Pratt & Whitney R-2800-CB-16 Double Wasp piston engines.
Performance: Max speed 312mph (500km/h) at 14,500ft (4420m); typical cruise, 276mph (442km/h) at 18,000ft (5486m); initial rate of climb, 1,905ft/min (9·6m/sec); service ceiling, 29,000ft (8845m); range with payload of 10,205lb (4633kg), 310mls (500km); range with max fuel, 1,070mls (1715km).
Weights: Empty equipped, 29,126lb (13,223kg); max payload, 11,692lb (5263kg); max take-off, 44,900lb (20,385kg); max landing, 43,000lb (19,522kg).
Dimensions: Span, 93ft $3\frac{1}{4}$in (28·44m); length, 74ft 7in (22·75m); height, 28ft 2in (8·61m); wing area, 864sq ft (79·89m^2).

The Martin 404 was the final model in a series of twin-engined transport aeroplanes developed by the Martin company in an early post-war bid to provide a replacement for the DC-3. The first of the series was the Martin 202, which flew as a prototype on 22 November 1946 and was an unpressurized short-range transport with seats for 48–52 passengers. Forty-three examples were built for airline use, and a pressurized prototype, the Martin 303, flew on 20 June 1947. Further improvements were made in the Martin 404, first flown on 21 October 1950, and 103 examples of the latter were produced, starting in July 1951.

All but two of the Martin 404s entered airline service, initially with TWA on 5 October 1951, but the majority had been phased out by the mid-sixties, some then passing to executive use and others to smaller airlines. By the mid-seventies, fewer than 20 remained in airline service, the last major user being Southern Airways of Atlanta, Georgia. When this airline began to replace its Martin 404s at the end of 1977, the type was relegated to operating a handful of routes in the hands of small operators.

***Left:** The Martin 404 remained in limited airline service in 1978, with other examples in use as executive transports.*

***Below:** Three-view drawing of the Martin 404, the only civil aircraft produced post-war by a famous American manufacturer.*

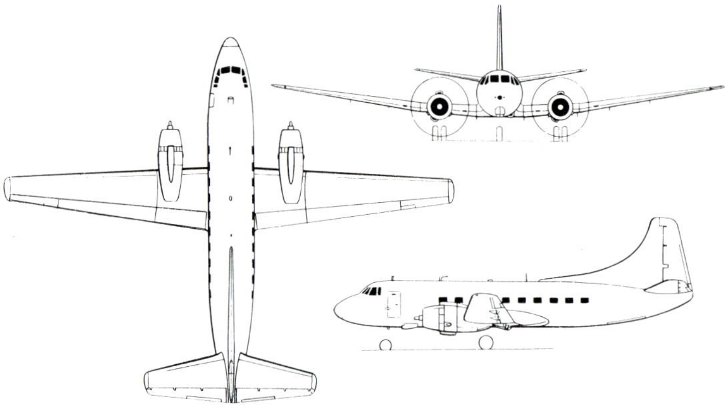

NAMC YS-11
Japan

The following specification refers to the YS-11A-200:
Power Plant: Two 3,060hp Rolls-Royce Dart 542-10K turboprops.
Performance: Max cruising speed at 15,000ft (4575m), 291mph (469km/h); best economy cruise at 20,000ft (6100m), 281mph (452km/h); initial rate of climb, 1,220ft/min (6·2m/sec); service ceiling, 22,900ft (6980m); no-reserves range with max payload, 680mls (1090km); no-reserves range with max fuel, 2,000mls (3215km).
Weights: Operating empty, 33,993lb (15,419kg); max payload, 14,508lb (6581kg); max take-off, 54,010lb (24,500kg).
Dimensions: Span, 104ft $11\frac{3}{4}$in (32·00m); length, 86ft $3\frac{1}{2}$in (26·30m); height, 29ft $5\frac{1}{2}$in (8·98m); wing area, 1,020·4sq ft (94·8m^2).

Although production of the YS-11 ended when only 182 examples had been built – substantially fewer than the manufacturers had hoped when the programme was launched – the type earned its place in aviation history as the first commercial transport of Japanese design and manufacture to achieve production status at all. The programme to develop a short-to-medium range civil airliner was launched in Japan in 1956 by the Ministry of International Trade and Industry, which encouraged the local aerospace companies to combine their resources to tackle what would be their most challenging project since World War II.

Initial project design activity was shared by six companies, comprising Mitsubishi, Kawasaki, Fuji, Shin Meiwa, Japan Aircraft Manufacturing and Showa, and these six later became participants in the Nihon Aircraft Manufacturing Co Ltd (NAMC), in which the Japanese government held the majority shareholding. Manufacturing activities related to the new transport were in due course shared by the six companies in proportion to their shareholding in NAMC.

The requirements of the Japanese domestic airline industry played a large part in defining the specification to which the new transport was to be built, and this led NAMC to make the aircraft somewhat larger than the turboprop twins already on the market, such as the Fokker F.27 and HS.748. Basic passenger accommodation was set at 60. Some early studies considered a high-wing layout similar to that of the F-27, but the more popular low-wing arrangement was eventually chosen, and an evaluation of the Allison 501, Napier Eland and Rolls-Royce Dart left the last-mentioned as the favoured power plant, in a version developed specially for the Japanese aircraft as the RDa.10/1.

The transport was designated YS-11 and work on four prototypes (two flying and two structural test) began following the creation of NAMC in May 1957. The two prototypes flew on 30 August and 28 December 1962 respectively and after more than 1,000hr of flight testing the YS-11 received

***Below:** An NAMC YS-11A-200, in service with Toa Domestic Airlines (TDA) on domestic routes in Japan in 1978.*

Saunders ST-27 (and De Havilland Heron)

Canada

The following specification relates to the ST-28:
Power Plant: Two 783eshp Pratt & Whitney (UACL) PT 6A-34 turboprops.
Performance: Max cruising speed, 232mph (373km/h) at 10,000ft (3050m); best economy cruise, 210mph (338km/h); initial rate of climb, 1,600ft/min (8·1m/sec); service ceiling, 25,000ft (7620m); range with max payload, 140mls (225km); range with max fuel, 970mls (1561km).
Weights: Operating empty, 9,284lb (4210kg); max payload, 4,216lb (6790kg); max take-off, 14,500lb (6576kg).
Dimensions: Span, 71ft 6in (21·79m); length, 58ft 10in (17·93m); height, 15ft 7in (4·75m); wing area, 499sq ft (46·36m²).

The ST-27 is derived from the de Havilland Heron, a four-engined light transport that was first flown on 10 May 1950 as "big brother" to the DH Dove. A total of 148 was built, in Srs 1 (fixed undercarriage) and Srs 2 (retractable undercarriage) versions. Saunders Aircraft in Canada acquired rights to produce a conversion of the Heron, designated ST-27, the principal new features of which were a lengthened fuselage to increase seating from 17 to a maximum of 23, and substitution of two Pratt & Whitney (UACL) PT6A-34 turboprops for the original four Gipsy Queen piston engines.

The prototype ST-27 first flew on 28 May 1969 and up to the end of 1974 the company modified 13 Heron airframes into ST-27s for sale to local service airlines, including operators in Canada and South America. One of the ST-27s was converted to ST-28 standard and first flew on 17 July 1974, this having more fuel, redesigned vertical tail surfaces, interior refinements and complying fully with FAR Part 25 airworthiness requirements for third level operations. Production of a batch of ST-28s was then launched by Saunders and the first aircraft flew on 12 December 1975, by which time the company held orders and options for 34 ST-28s. Early in 1976, however, the financial support for Saunders given by the Manitoba government was withdrawn, and further work on the ST-28 was halted.

***Below:** The Saunders ST-28, the final evolution in Canada of this twin-engined derivative of the de Havilland Heron.*

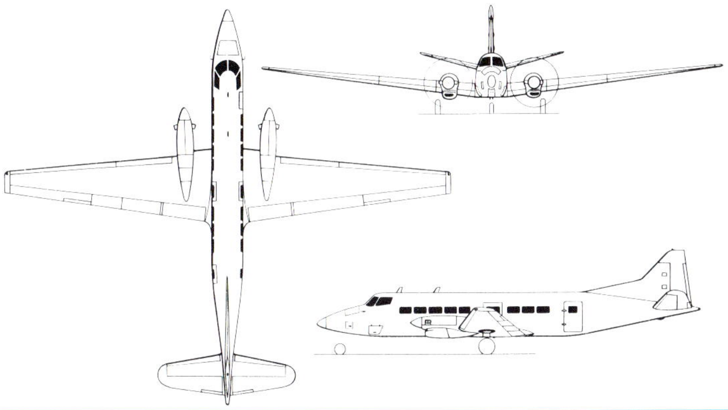

***Below:** One of the dozen ST-27s produced by Saunders Aircraft in Canada, using Heron airframes with major modifications.*

***Right:** NAMC YS-11 Srs 300/600, with the forward freight door that distinguished those versions of the Japanese transport.*

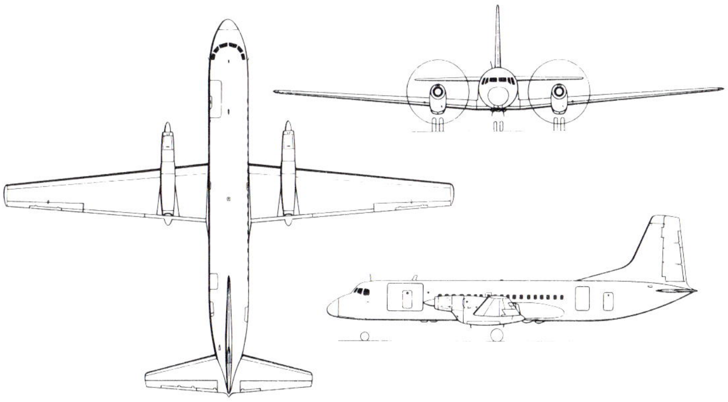

Japanese certification on 25 August 1964 followed by FAA Type Approval on 7 September 1965. The first production YS-11 had flown, meanwhile, on 23 October 1964 and this was delivered to the Japan Civil Aviation Bureau in March 1965. Airline use of the YS-11 began a month later, the first user being Toa Airways of Hiroshima (now TDA), followed by Japan Domestic in May and All Nippon in July.

Export sales of the YS-11 began only slowly, starting with the purchase of two by Filipinas Orient in September 1965, three by Hawaiian Airlines in 1966 and three by LANSA of Peru in 1967. A major effort to sell the YS-11 in the USA was then mounted, resulting in the appearance of the YS-11A which, with the same overall dimensions, had higher operating weights and an increase of 2,800lb (1270kg) in the payload. The YS-11A was offered in three sub-variants identified as the Srs 200, 300 and 400, of which the Srs 200 was the basic passenger variant with the same 60-passenger capacity (five abreast) as the original production variant, construction of which ended in October 1967 when 48 (plus the two prototypes) had been built.

A significant order was obtained from the US local service airline Piedmont for the YS-11A-200, the first example of which flew on 27 November 1967 and was FAA-approved on 3 April 1968. Deliveries to Piedmont began in 1968 and over 90 Series 200s were built in all, for some nine different airlines and for Japanese armed services and government agencies.

The Srs 300, flown in 1968, was a mixed-traffic version of the 200, with a forward cargo door and provision for 46 passengers plus 540cu ft (15·3m*)*) of cargo space. Some 16 were delivered, to several different airlines. The Srs 400, used only by military forces, was an all-cargo version, first flown on 17 September 1969. Three further variants, the Srs 500, 600 and 700, were designated, being respectively similar to the 200, 300 and 400 but having a 1,105-lb (500-kg) increase in max take-off weight. A few examples of these variants were included in the final batch of YS-11As produced.

Shorts 330
United Kingdom

Power Plant: Two 1,120shp Pratt & Whitney (UACL) PT6A-45 turboprops.
Performance (estimated): Max cruising speed, 228mph (367km/h) at 10,000ft (3280m); long-range cruise, 184mph (296km/h); initial rate of climb, 1,280ft/min (6·5m/sec); range with max payload 500mls (805km) with 30 passengers at long-range cruise speed, 870mls (1400km) with 20 passengers at long-range cruise speed.
Weights: Empty equipped weight, 12,685lb (5753kg); design max payload, 7,500lb (3400kg); max take-off, 22,000lb (9979kg).
Dimensions: Span, 74ft 9in (22·78m); length, 58ft $0\frac{1}{2}$in (17·69m); height 15ft 8in (4·78m); wing area, 453sq ft (42·1m^2).

This third-level/commuter airliner is an outgrowth of the Skyvan (see previous page). It features similar outer wing panels, with a new centre section; and a lengthened fuselage of the same cross section as the Skyvan. A switch was made from Garratt-AiResearch engines to Pratt & Whitney PT6A-45s driving five-blade propellers, these being similar to the engines developed for the de Havilland Canada Dash-7.

The SD3-30 was given official approval for go-ahead on 23 May 1973 with a UK government grant towards the launching costs. A primary objective of the design team was to achieve a selling price of not more than $1m (£400,000) in 1973 values, and a rapid prototype programme was established, with first flight achieved on 22 August 1974. A second prototype, first flown on 8 July 1975, was also used for certification flying, which was completed soon after the first flight of the first production SD3-30 on 15 December 1975. Initial contracts for the SD3-30 were placed by Command Airways and Time Air, respectively US and Canadian operators of third level airlines and the latter was the first to put the type into service, on 24 August 1976. Further orders had come, by mid-1978, from DLT in Germany and Golden West and Henson Aviation in the USA, from ALM Antillean Airlines and from Hawaiian Airlines.

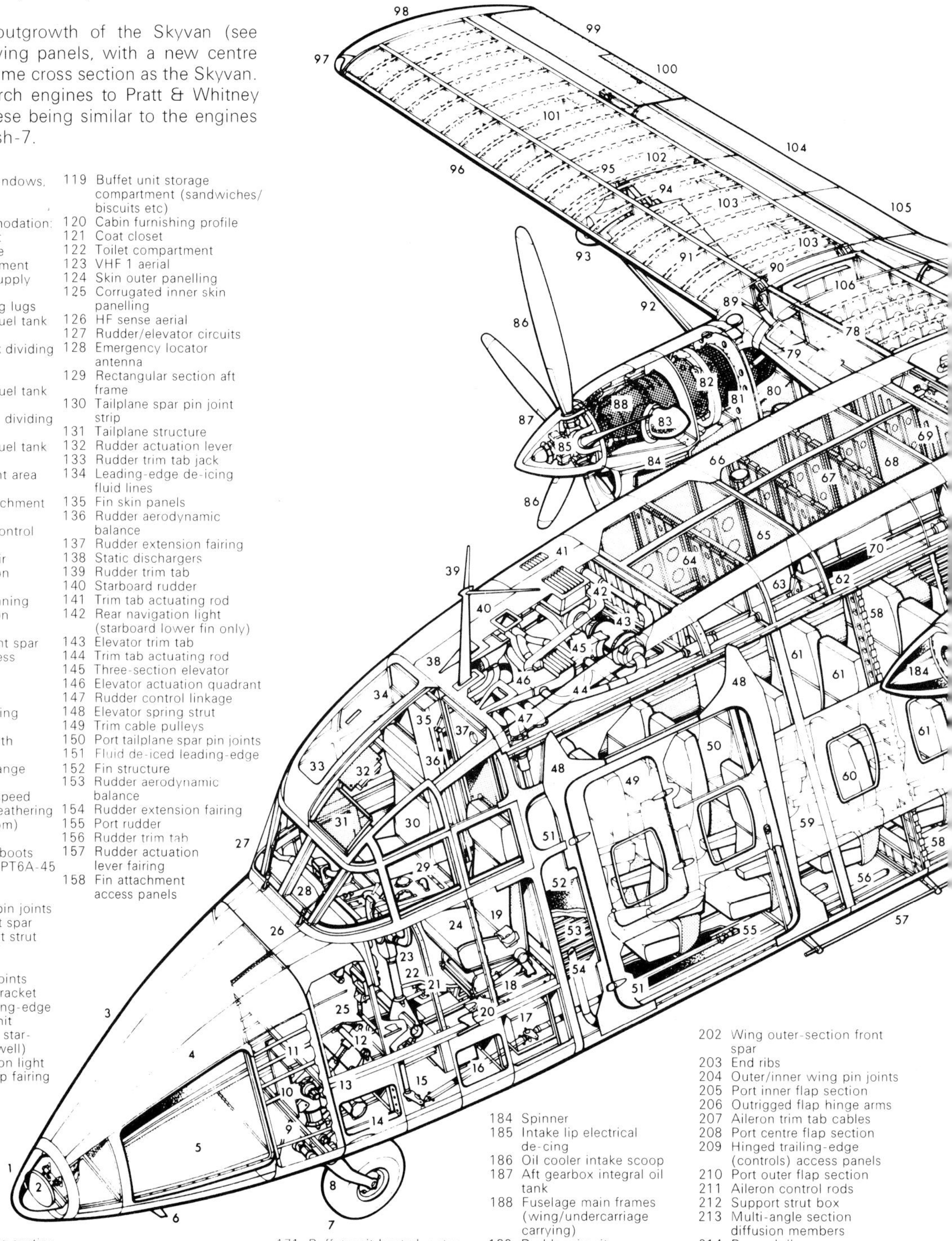

Shorts SD3-30 Cutaway Drawing Key
1 Glass-fibre nose cone
2 Weather radar installation
3 Nose skin panelling
4 Forward baggage compartment, 45cu ft/400lb (1·27m^3/181kg) max
5 Upward-hinged baggage door, 30·5in x 37·7 in (77·5cm x 95·8cm)
6 VHF 2 aerial
7 Hydraulically steerable rearward-retracting nosewheel
8 Nosewheel fork
9 Nosewheel oleo
10 Nosewheel pivot point
11 Nosewheel box
12 Nosewheel retraction mechanism and jack
13 Undercarriage emergency actuation accumulator
14 Hydraulics bay
15 Rudder circuit linkage
16 Avionics bay (port and starboard)
17 23 Amp/hr batteries (port and starboard)
18 Seat adjustment lever
19 Seat belt
20 Heated pitot head
21 Underfloor avionics equipment
22 Elevator circuit linkage
23 Control column
24 Pilot's seat
25 Rudder pedals
26 Windscreen wipers
27 Windscreen panels (electrically heated)
28 Instrument panel coaming
29 Central control console (trim wheels)
30 Co-pilot's seat
31 Overhead panel (AC/DC power supply)
32 Fuel cocks
33 Crew escape/ditching hatch
34 Flight deck/cabin sliding door
35 Aileron circuit linkage
36 Control cable conduit (rudder and elevator trim circuits)
37 Flight deck conditioned/heating/de-misting air supply
38 Ambient-air intake
39 Combined VOR/Localiser/ILS glide-slope aerials
40 Blow-in door (ground running)
41 Turbine-blower intake
42 Heat exhanger
43 Air cycle installation
44 Engine bleed-air supply
45 Pre-cooler
46 Pre-cooler intake
47 Cabin conditioned/fresh air supply
48 Doorway-surround doubler plate
49 Cabin forward emergency exits, port 37in x 24·5in (94cm x 62cm); starboard 42in x 27in (107cm x 68·6cm)
50 Forward freight door, 65·6in x 55·6in (167cm x 141cm)
51 Freight door hinges
52 Honeycomb-sandwich floor panels
53 Corrugated inner skin
54 Cabin air distribution duct
55 Seat mounting rails
56 Rudder circuit
57 ADF sense aerials (port and starboard)
58 Rectangular fuselage section frames
59 Chemically-milled window panel
60 12-a-side cabin windows, 18·5in x 14·4in (74cm x 36·6cm)
61 Passenger accommodation: 30 seats, 3-abreast (single port/double starboard) arrangement
62 Engine bleed-air supply duct
63 Fuel tank mounting lugs
64 Forward multiple fuel tank (Cell 1)
65 Class II sealed tank dividing bulkhead
66 Fuel gravity filler
67 Forward multiple fuel tank (Cell 2)
68 Class I sealed tank dividing bulkhead
69 Forward multiple fuel tank (Cell 3)
70 Sealed containment area (tank seepage)
71 Tank/fuselage attachment
72 Wingroot fairing
73 Engine-propeller control cable runs
74 Hydraulics reservoir
75 Wing centre-section
76 Chemically-milled centre-section skinning
77 Dorsal anti-collision beacon
78 Centre-section front spar
79 Leading-edge access panels
80 Oil cooler
81 Engine firewall
82 Engine mounting ring
83 Exhaust ducts
84 Air intake duct (with debris deflector)
85 Propeller pitch-change mechanism
86 Hartzell constant-speed five-bladed auto-feathering propeller, 9ft (2·75m) diameter
87 Propeller de-icing boots
88 Pratt and Whitney PT6A-45 turboprop engine
89 Oil filler cap
90 Outer/inner wing pin joints
91 Outer-section front spar
92 Outer wing support strut
93 Starboard landing/taxying lamp
94 Support strut pin joints
95 Strut attachment bracket
96 Fluid de-iced leading-edge (tank and pump unit mounted at rear of starboard mainwheel well)
97 Starboard navigation light
98 Glass fibre wing-tip fairing
99 Starboard aileron
100 Aileron trim tab
101 Aileron hinge rib
102 Support strut box
103 Flap hinge ribs
104 Starboard outer flap section
105 Starboard centre flap section
106 Centre section end rib
107 Starboard inner flap section
108 Flap actuating rod mechanism (mounted on spar rear face)
109 Water-methanol tank and pump
110 Gravity fuel filler
111 Aft fuel tank (Cell 4)
112 Sealed containment area (tank seepage)
113 Tank/fuselage attachment
114 Elevator circuit
115 Cabin concealed ceiling lighting
116 Fuselage (detachable) top fairings
117 Overhead passenger hand-baggage lockers
118 Service door/emergency exit, 56·5in x 28·4in (143·5cm x 72cm)
119 Buffet unit storage compartment (sandwiches/biscuits etc)
120 Cabin furnishing profile
121 Coat closet
122 Toilet compartment
123 VHF 1 aerial
124 Skin outer panelling
125 Corrugated inner skin panelling
126 HF sense aerial
127 Rudder/elevator circuits
128 Emergency locator antenna
129 Rectangular section aft frame
130 Tailplane spar pin joint strip
131 Tailplane structure
132 Rudder actuation lever
133 Rudder trim tab jack
134 Leading-edge de-icing fluid lines
135 Fin skin panels
136 Rudder aerodynamic balance
137 Rudder extension fairing
138 Static dischargers
139 Rudder trim tab
140 Starboard rudder
141 Trim tab actuating rod
142 Rear navigation light (starboard lower fin only)
143 Elevator trim tab
144 Trim tab actuating rod
145 Three-section elevator
146 Elevator actuation quadrant
147 Rudder control linkage
148 Elevator spring strut
149 Trim cable pulleys
150 Port tailplane spar pin joints
151 Fluid de-iced leading-edge
152 Fin structure
153 Rudder aerodynamic balance
154 Rudder extension fairing
155 Port rudder
156 Rudder trim tab
157 Rudder actuation lever fairing
158 Fin attachment access panels
159 Fin lower section
160 De-icing system access
161 Fluid de-iced leading-edge
162 Aft fuselage structure
163 Aft baggage door, 43in x 57in (109cm x 145cm)
164 Baggage door (open)
165 Baggage restraint net
166 Stepped aft baggage compartment, 100cu ft/600lb (2·83m^3/272kg) max
167 Bulkhead
168 Doorway-surround doubler plate
169 Passenger entry door, 56·5in x 28·4in (143·5cm x 72cm)
170 Cabin electrics and communications panel
171 Buffet unit heated water container/cup stowage/trash bin
172 Cabin attendant's tip-up seat (lowered)
173 Contoured inner window surrounds
174 Cabin seating rearmost row (port seat omitted for clarity)
175 Rudder circuit linkage
176 Damper strut
177 Flap actuating rod
178 Centre-section ribs
179 Centre-section front spar
180 Firewall/bulkhead
181 Engine support structure
182 Engine mounting ring (with four dynafocal resilient mounts)
183 Exhaust duct
184 Spinner
185 Intake lip electrical de-cing
186 Oil cooler intake scoop
187 Aft gearbox integral oil tank
188 Fuselage main frames (wing/undercarriage carrying)
189 Rudder circuit
190 Stub wing front and rear spars
191 Undercarriage mounting beam
192 Undercarriage retraction jack
193 Wing support strut attachment
194 Undercarriage pivot point
195 Undercarriage levered suspension leg
196 Port main landing-gear fairing
197 Retractable mainwheel
198 Shock-absorber strut
199 Port wing support strut
200 Port landing/taxying lamp
201 Hydraulic ground service panel (fairing hinged aft section)
202 Wing outer-section front spar
203 End ribs
204 Outer/inner wing pin joints
205 Port inner flap section
206 Outrigged flap hinge arms
207 Aileron trim tab cables
208 Port centre flap section
209 Hinged trailing-edge (controls) access panels
210 Port outer flap section
211 Aileron control rods
212 Support strut box
213 Multi-angle section diffusion members
214 Pressed ribs
215 Corrugated inner skin panels
216 Aileron actuating rod
217 Cable-operated trim tab jack
218 Trim tab actuating rod
219 Aileron trim tab
220 Port aileron
221 Outer-section rear spar
222 Aileron mass-balance weights
223 Wing skin outer panelling
224 Outer-section front spar
225 Outer-section leading-edge spar
226 End rib structure/tip attachments
227 Glass-fibre port wing-tip fairing
228 Port navigation light

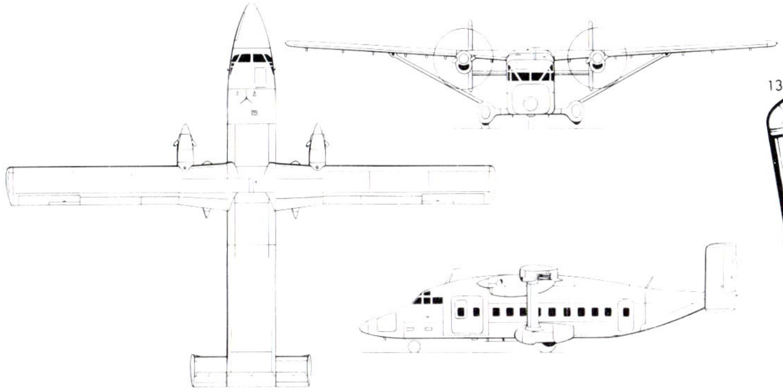

Above: Three-view of the Shorts 330 (originally known as the SD3-30), a commuter liner derived from the smaller Skyvan.

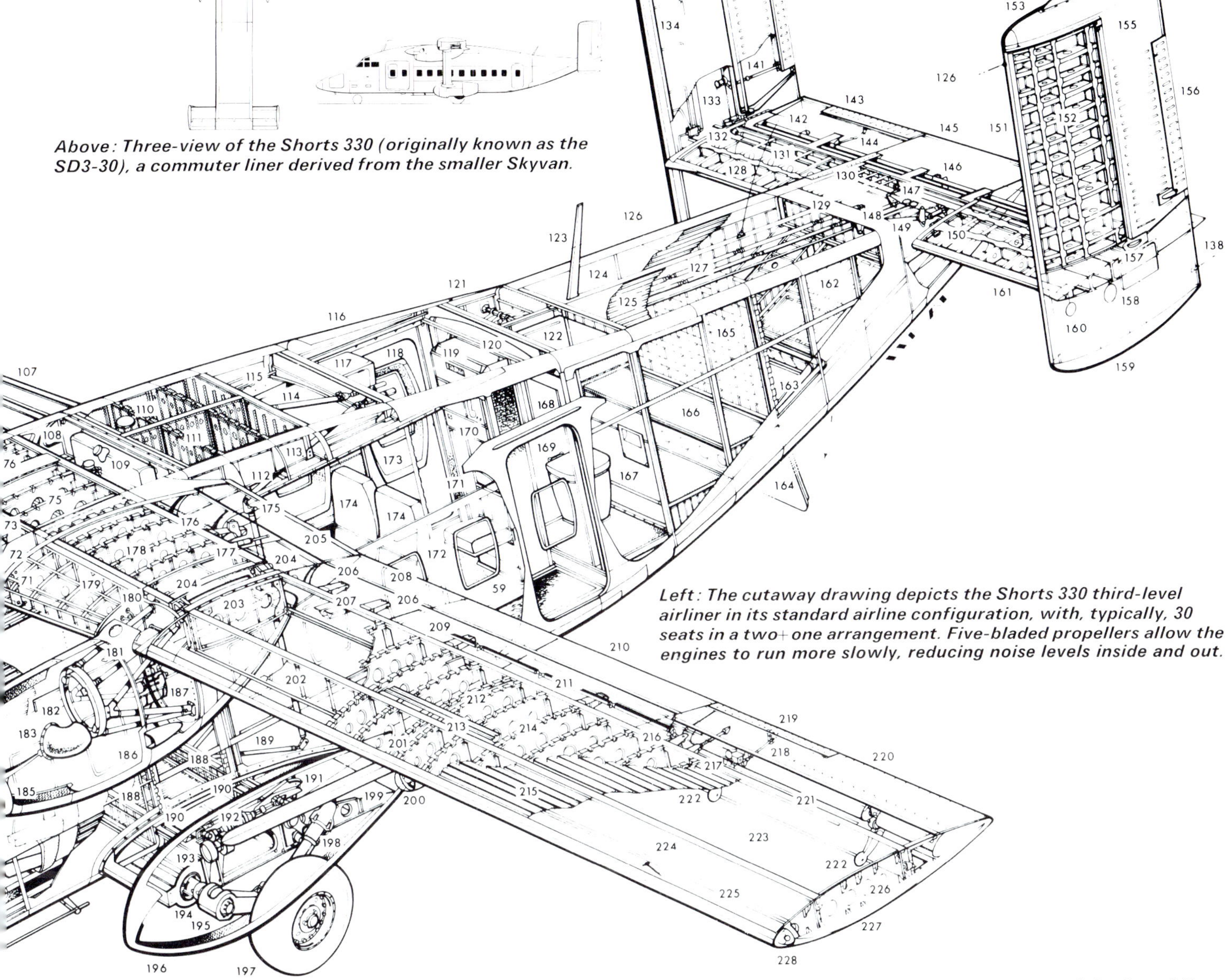

Left: The cutaway drawing depicts the Shorts 330 third-level airliner in its standard airline configuration, with, typically, 30 seats in a two+one arrangement. Five-bladed propellers allow the engines to run more slowly, reducing noise levels inside and out.

Below: Command Airways of New York is one of the first airlines to use the Belfast-built commuter.

Shorts Skyvan and Skyliner
United Kingdom

The following data refer to the Skyvan Srs 3:
Power Plant: Two Garrett-AiResearch TPE331-201 turboprops each rated at 715shp for take-off.
Performance: Max crusing speed, 203mph (327km/h); initial rate of climb 1,640ft/min (8·3m/sec); service ceiling, 22,500ft (6858m); range, up to 694mls (1115km); range with 4,000lb (1814kg) of freight, 187mls (300km).
Weights: Basic operating, 7,344lb (3331kg); max payload, 4,600lb (2086kg); max take-off weight, 12,500lb (5670kg).
Dimensions: Span, 64ft 11in (19·79m); length, 40ft 1in (12·21m); height, 15ft 1in (4·60m); wing area, 373sq ft (34·65m²).

First flown in 1963, the Shorts Skyvan set a fashion for small utility transports, featuring a high wing, fixed tricycle undercarriage and uncluttered box-section fuselage with provision for straight-in loading from the rear. The prototype was powered by two 300hp Continental piston engines but after an initial phase of flight testing which began on 17 January 1963, it was re-engined with 730shp Turboméca Astazou XII turboprops, flying in this guise as the Skyvan Srs 1A on 2 October 1963. Nineteen Skyvan IIs followed, with the same engines, the first of these flying on 29 October 1965, and these saw limited service in the hands of civil operators, carrying up to 19 passengers or about 4,000lb (1814kg) of freight.

The definitive production version of the Skyvan is the Srs 3 with 715shp Garrett AiResearch TPE331-201 turboprops. The first TPE331 installation flew on 15 December 1967 and deliveries began in mid-1968, some Srs 2s also being converted to this standard. The Skyvan Srs 3 has a gross weight of 12,500lb (5670kg) and is the basic version for use in various civil rôles including passenger transport, ambulance, aerial survey, freighting and

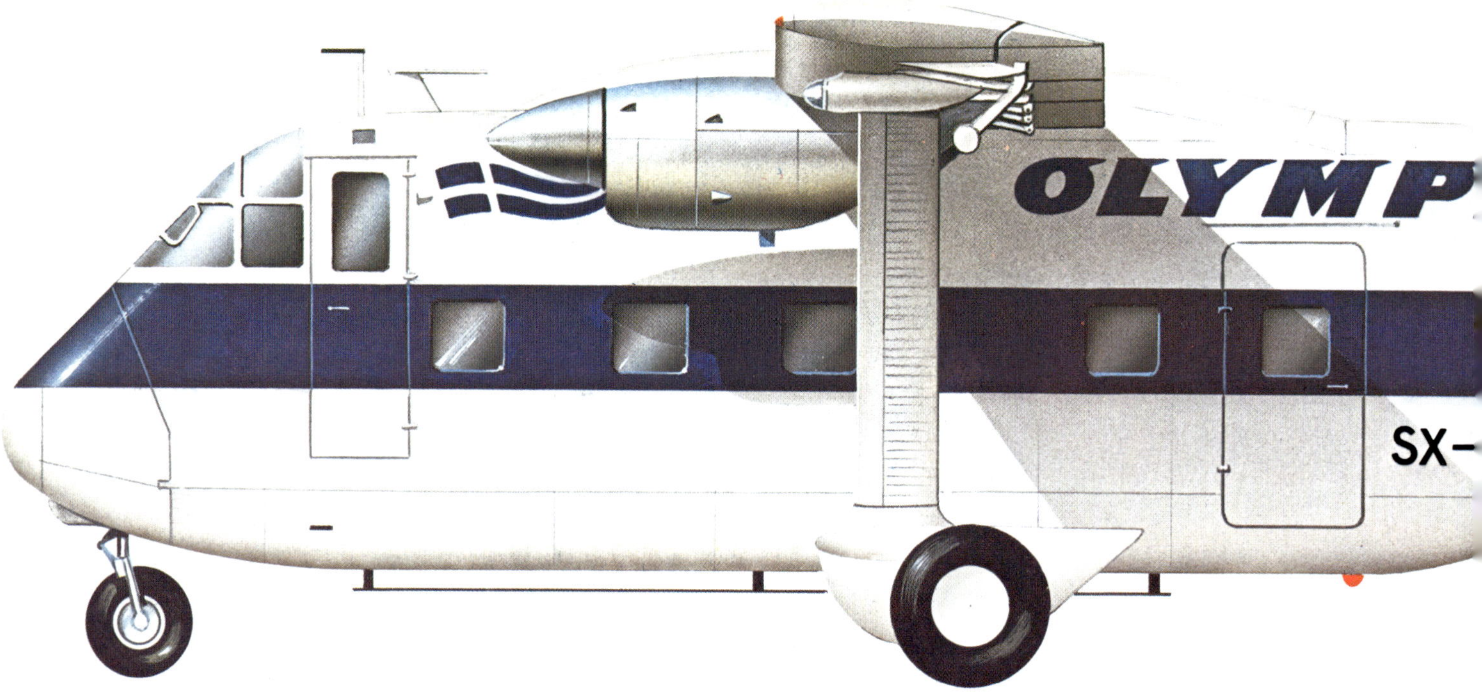

Sikorsky S-61
USA

The following specification refers to the S-61N:
Power Plant: Two 1,500shp General Electric CT58-140-2 turboshaft engines.
Performance: Max speed, 146mph (235km/h) at sea level; typical cruise, 138mph (222km/h); max inclined climb, 1,300ft/min (6·6m/sec); hovering ceiling (OGE), 3,800ft (1158m); max range, 518mls (833km).
Weights: Empty, 12,336lb (5595kg); max take-off 19,000lb (8620kg).
Dimensions: Rotor diameter 62ft 0in (18·90m); fuselage length, 58ft 11in (17·96m); height, 18ft 5½in (5·63m).

Helicopters have achieved only limited success in airline operations, although their contribution to air transport development in other ways has been dramatic, and has expanded rapidly in recent years because of the helicopter's special rôle in support of off-shore oil exploration operations. Of the few types of helicopter that have actually been adopted for regular airline service, the Sikorsky S-61 is the most used and most successful.

The basic S-61 was designed to meet US Navy requirements for an anti-submarine search and strike helicopter, and in this guise it is widely used as the SH-3 Sea King, having been built in the UK, Japan and Italy as well as the USA. The commercial variants, used by airlines and charter operators, are the S-61N, which has the same amphibious characteristics as the naval Sea King and first flew in 1962; and the S-61L which has the amphibious features deleted and first flew in 1961. Scheduled operators include British Airways Helicopters, New York Airways and Los Angeles Airways.

***Right:** A Sikorsky S-61N of Ansett Airlines of Australia. A boat-type hull and the outrigged floats make this version of the helicopter amphibious.*

***Left:** A Sikorsky S-61L at John F. Kennedy Airport, from which direct flights are operated to heliports in Manhattan.*

police duties; the Srs 3A operates at an increased gross weight of 13,700lb (6215kg) and complies with British airworthiness requirements in the Passenger Transport Category. The Skyliner is similar but is equipped to a higher standard exclusively as a passenger carrier for 19–22 passengers. By early 1977, Shorts had delivered about 120 Skyvans of all models, including some 60 Srs 3s, eight Skyliners and about 50 Skyvan 3M military models.

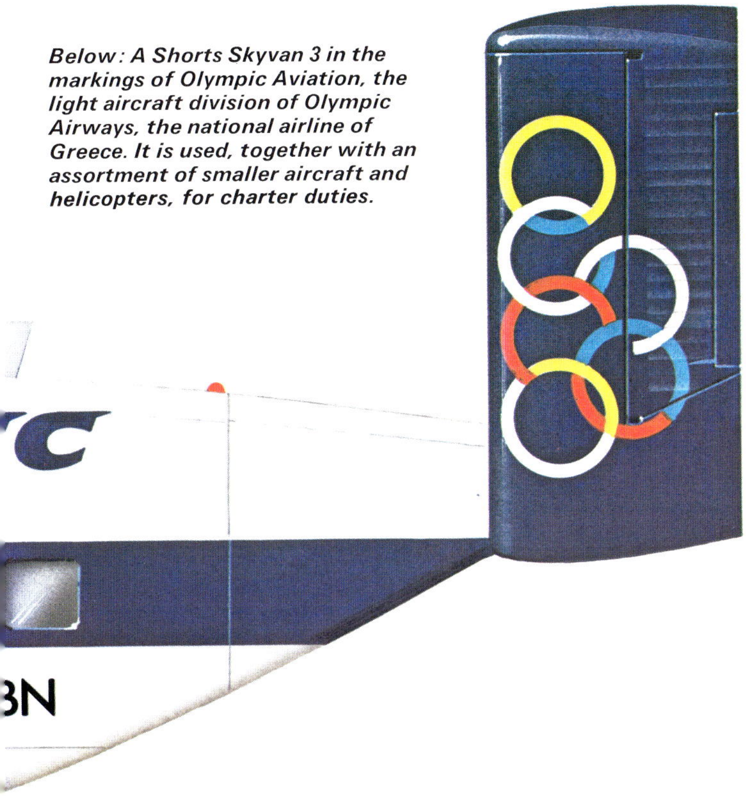

Below: A Shorts Skyvan 3 in the markings of Olympic Aviation, the light aircraft division of Olympic Airways, the national airline of Greece. It is used, together with an assortment of smaller aircraft and helicopters, for charter duties.

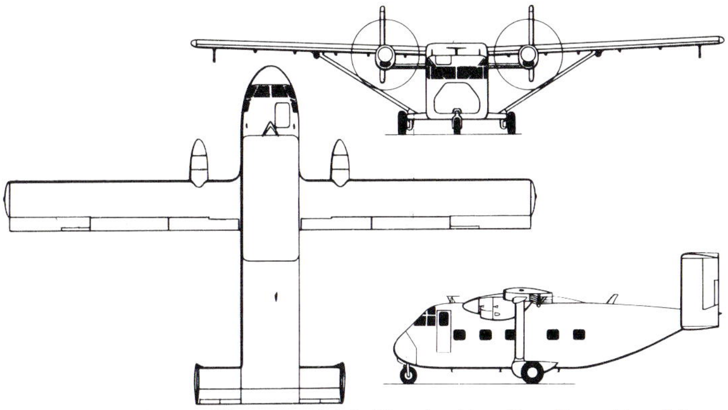

Above: The Short Skyvan, which like the Handley Page Herald began life with piston engines before acquiring turboprop power.

Right: A Short Skyvan on test prior to delivery to Venezuela. By 1978, over 120 of these Belfast-built transports had been sold.

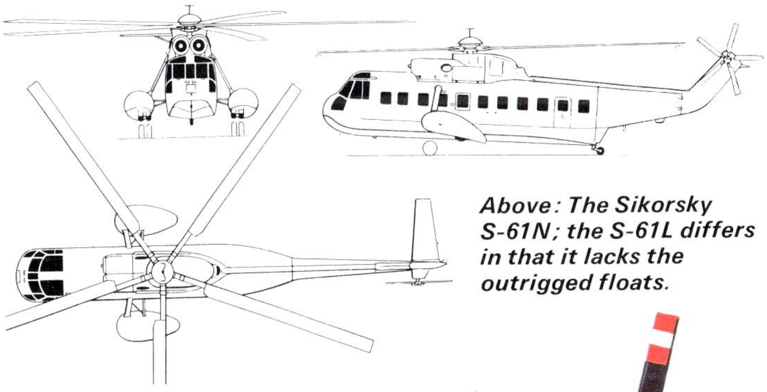

Above: The Sikorsky S-61N; the S-61L differs in that it lacks the outrigged floats.

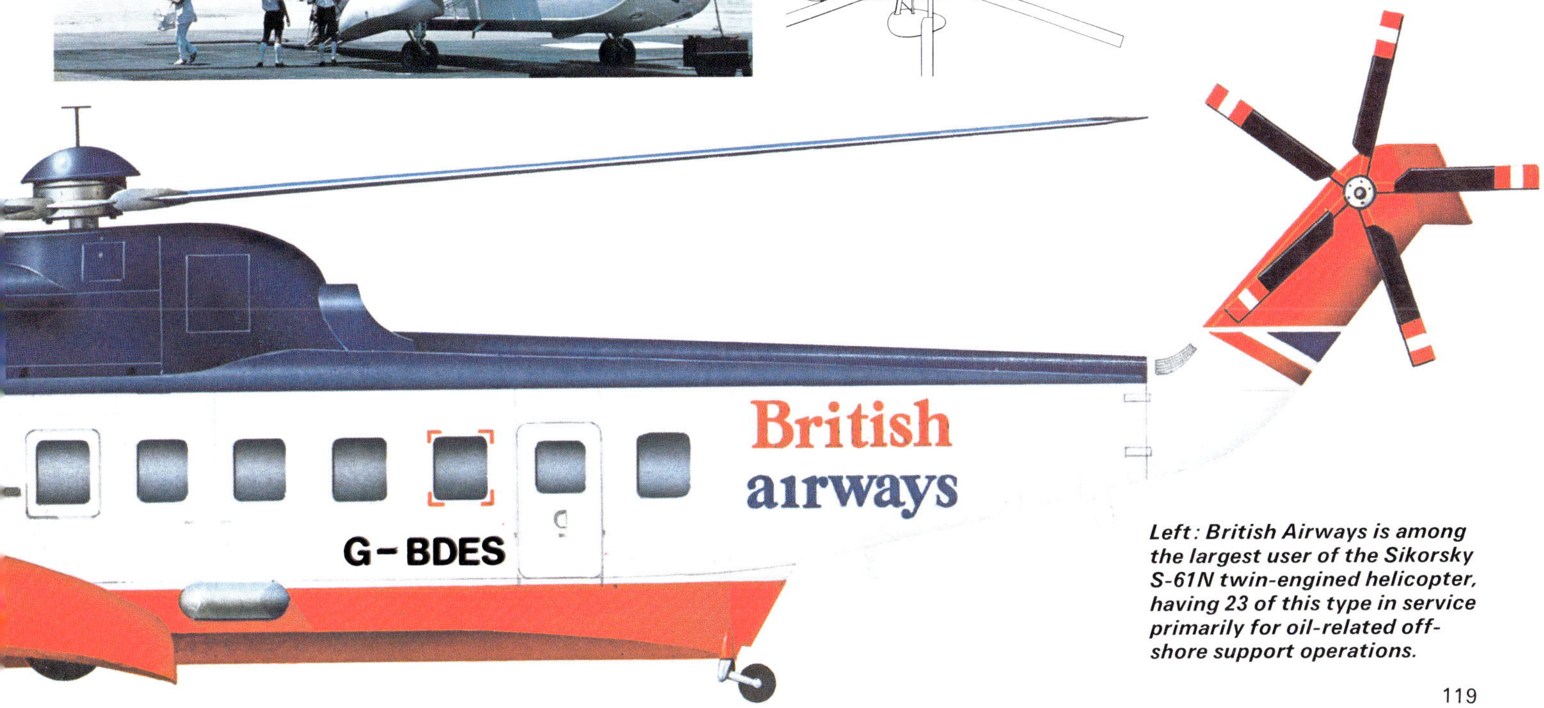

Left: British Airways is among the largest user of the Sikorsky S-61N twin-engined helicopter, having 23 of this type in service primarily for oil-related off-shore support operations.

Swearingen Metro (and Merlin IV)
USA

Power Plant: Two 940shp Garrett-AiResearch TPE 331-3UW-303G turboprops.
Performance: Max cruising speed, 294mph (473km/h) at 10,000ft (3050m); best range cruise, 279mph (449km/h) at 20,000ft (6100m); initial rate of climb, 2,400ft/min (12·2m/sec); max certificated altitude, 31,000ft (9450m); range with max payload, 100mls (161km); range with max fuel, 500mls (804km).
Weights: Empty, less avionics, 7,400lb (3356kg); max payload, 3,920lb (1778kg); max take-off, 12,500lb (5670kg).
Dimensions: Span, 46ft 3in (14·10m); length, 59ft $4\frac{1}{4}$in (18·09m); height, 16ft 8in (5·08m); wing area, 277·5sq ft (25·78m^2).

The Metro was designed by Ed Swearingen to meet the needs of the third level airlines, and was the first product of wholly original concept produced by the Swearingen company, which was acquired by Fairchild Industries as a subsidiary in November 1971. Up to 22 passengers can be carried by the Metro in single seats each side of a central aisle; the same airframe was offered in the business market as the Merlin IV with an executive interior seating up to 12.

First flown on 11 June 1970, the Metro entered service early in 1971 and the principal operators became Air Wisconsin, with a fleet of 10 by 1977; others were in service with a number of other commuter and third level operators, principally in the USA but also in Europe. During 1974, the Metro 2 was introduced, with square windows and some internal refinements, plus optional installation of a small rocket unit in the tail to improve take-off performance in hot and high conditions. A significant breakthrough for the Metro came in mid-1977 when Southern Airways, a US regional airline, ordered a fleet of seven to replace its elderly and much larger Martin 404s. Some 40 Metros had been sold by the end of 1977.

Swearington Metro II

1 Radome
2 Weather radar scanner
3 Oxygen bottle
4 Radio and electronics equipment
5 Nosewheel door
6 Baggage restraint net
7 Baggage doors, forward opening
8 Fuselage nose construction
9 Nose baggage hold
10 Landing and taxi lamp
11 Nosewheel leg
12 Twin nosewheels
13 Torque scissors
14 Pitot tube
15 Cockpit pressure bulkhead
16 Windscreen panels
17 Instrument panel shroud
18 Curved centre panel
19 Windscreen wipers
20 Rudder pedals
21 Control column
22 Co-pilot's seat
23 Cockpit roof construction
24 Cockpit bulkhead
25 Electrical panels
26 Pilot's seat
27 Pilot's side control panel
28 Passenger door
29 Airstairs
30 Handrails
31 Entry doorway
32 Cabin centre aisle floor
33 Air conditioning duct louvre
34 Forward fuselage frame construction
35 Starboard engine cowlings
36 Engine intake
37 Hartzell three-blade propeller
38 Propeller de-icing boot
39 Leading edge de-icing
40 Starboard wing fuel tank, capacity 324 US gal (1226 litres)
41 Starboard navigation light
42 Fuel filler cap
43 Starboard aileron
44 Static dischargers
45 Starboard flap
46 Tailpipe exhaust duct
47 Fuselage frames
48 Cabin interior trim panels
49 Passenger seats
50 Window side panel
51 Cabin floor construction
52 Seat rails
53 Air trunking
54 Cabin windows
55 Starboard emergency escape hatches
56 Main fuselage frames
57 Centre box construction
58 Port emergency escape hatch
59 Starboard seating, 10 passengers
60 Port seating, nine passengers
61 Cabin rear bulkhead
62 Toilet compartment door
63 Toilet
64 Rear cargo door
65 Door actuator
66 Rear cargo and baggage compartment
67 Fuselage frame and stringer construction
68 Fin root fillet
69 Tailplane electric trim jacks
70 Starboard tailplane
71 Leading edge de-icing
72 Elevator horn balance
73 Starboard elevator
74 Static dischargers
75 Fin construction

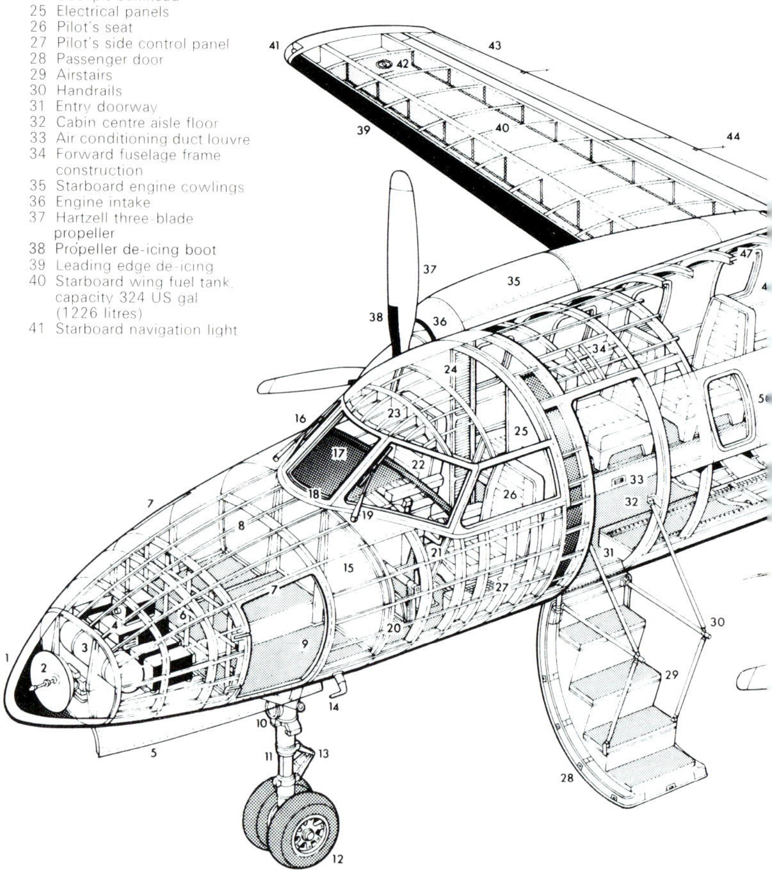

Below: Light twins, even ones as big as the Metro II, are designed so as to have all auxiliary (as well as flying) systems at the pilot's fingertips. There may be no cabin staff, and though all Metros have dual controls it is permitted in some circumstances to fly solo. Since any one of a vast range of instruments and controls might be needed at any moment by the pilot, he is likely to have more to do than the captain of a 747, and the general impression of the cabin to the uninitiated is one of total clutter. All engine and propeller instruments are grouped in a column just left of centre. Next comes the prominent column of avionics, which is a customer option. Though fully pressurized, the flight-deck windows are deep-set and give an excellent view without the need for roof windows. In commuter flying the pilot is expected to carry out duties usually performed by rear cabin staff, such as looking after the passengers and checking that the airstairs are locked. Most Metros have weather radar and autopilot, but some fly with neither and it will not be until the 1990s that commuter flight decks feature computerized displays instead of instruments.

76 Rudder balance
77 Antenna
78 Anti-collision light
79 Rudder trim tab
80 Trim tab control jack
81 Rudder construction
82 Elevator hinge control
83 Port elevator
84 Static dischargers
85 Tailplane construction
86 Tail navigation light
87 Ventral fin
88 Rudder hinge control
89 Tailplane control cables
90 Fin attachment frame
91 Cargo hold rear bulkhead
92 Baggage/cargo hold floor
93 Rear fuselage frames
94 Seat fixing rails
95 Trailing edge root fillet
96 Port flap
97 Fuel pumps
98 Wing main spar
99 Wing spar attachment
100 Air conditioning plant
101 Engine cowling construction
102 Tailpipe
103 Engine exhaust duct
104 Double slotted flap construction
105 Static dischargers
106 Aileron trim tab
107 Trim tab hinge control
108 Port aileron
109 Aileron hinge control
110 Port wing tip
111 Port navigation light
112 Fuel tank filler cap
113 Wing rib construction
114 Leading edge de-icing
115 Port wing fuel tank, 324 US gal (1126 litres)
116 Main undercarriage leg
117 Twin mainwheels
118 Retraction strut
119 Mainwheel door
120 Leading edge ice inspection light
121 Main undercarriage wheel bay
122 Hydraulic system reservoir
123 Engine oil tank, 4 US gal (15 litres)
124 Engine bearers
125 Detachable engine cowlings
126 Garrett AiResearch TPE 331-3UW-303G turboprop
127 Oil cooler
128 Oil cooler intake
129 Propeller gearbox
130 Engine intake
131 Propeller reversing and feathering hub mechanism
132 Spinner
133 Hartzell three-blade propeller
134 Propeller blade de-icing boots

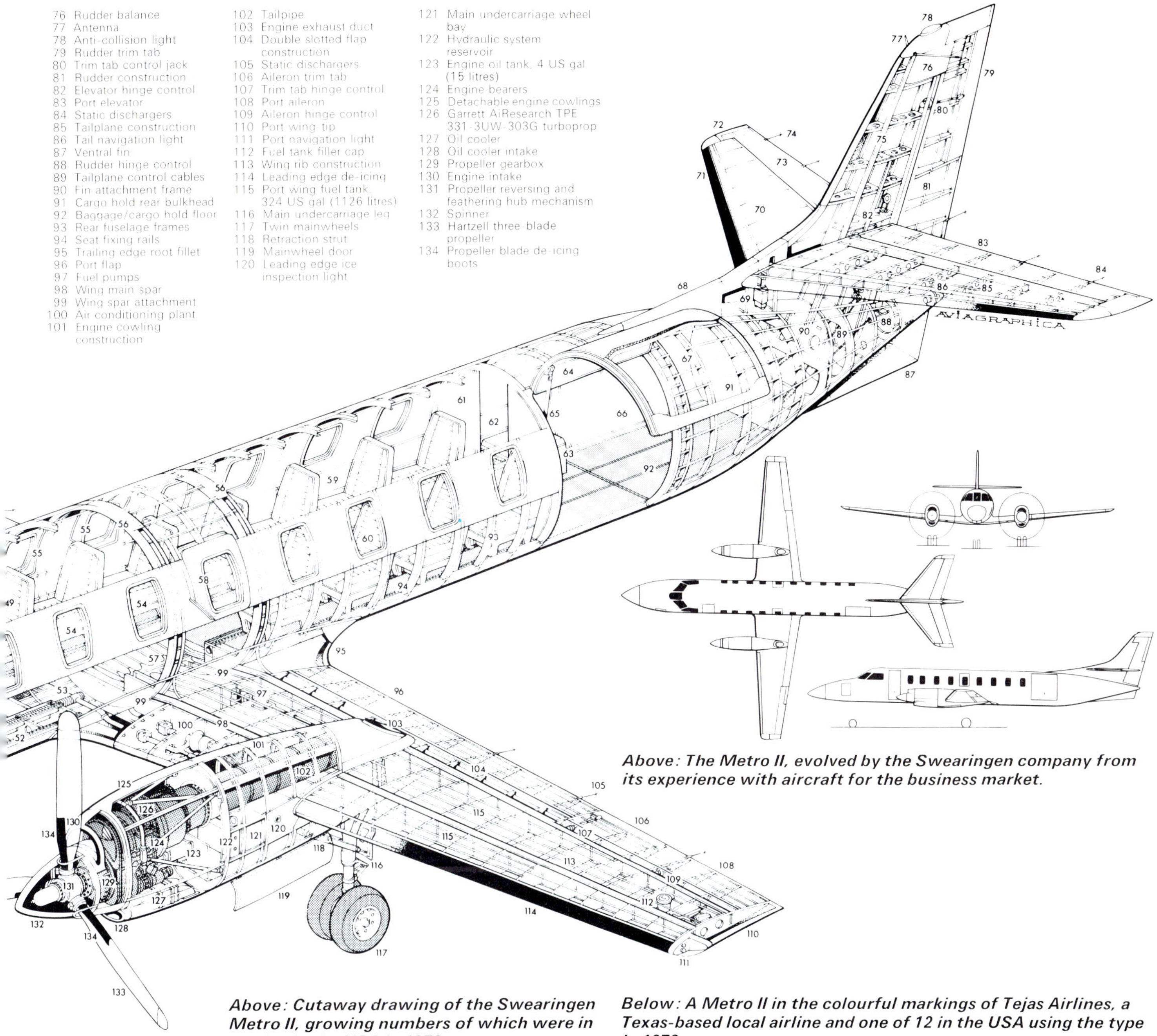

Above: The Metro II, evolved by the Swearingen company from its experience with aircraft for the business market.

Above: Cutaway drawing of the Swearingen Metro II, growing numbers of which were in service in the USA in 1978.

Below: A Metro II in the colourful markings of Tejas Airlines, a Texas-based local airline and one of 12 in the USA using the type in 1978.

Texas Airplane CJ 600 (and DH Dove)
USA/ United Kingdom

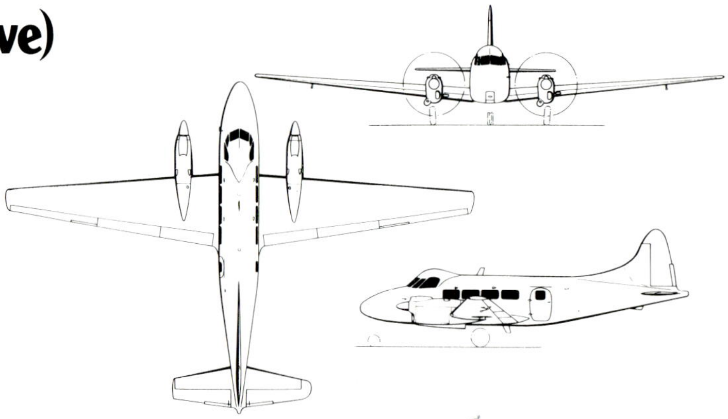

The following data refer to the CJ 600:
Power Plant: Two Garrett AiResearch TPE 331-101-E turboprops each rated at 575shp for take-off.
Performance: Max cruising speed, 288mph (463km/h); typical cruising speed, 265mph (426km/h); initial rate of climb, 2,800ft/min (14·3m/sec).
Weights: Empty, about 6,000lb (2721kg); max take-off, 10,500lb (4762kg).
Dimensions: Span, 57ft 0in (17·37m); length, 48ft 6in (14·17m); height, 13ft 4in (4·06m).

The CJ 600 is a heavily modified version of the de Havilland Dove, first flown on 18 December 1966 as the Carstedt Jet Liner 600 and subsequently marketed by the Texas Airplane Manufacturing Co. Using the Dove's wing, tail unit and undercarriage, it has a much lengthened fuselage able to seat 18 passengers in addition to the crew of two, and is powered by two 605hp Garrett AiResearch TPE 331 turboprops. The take-off weight is increased to 10,500lb (4762kg) and fuel capacity is increased to give a range of 500mls (805km) with the 18 passenger payload or up to 2,700mls (4340km) with reduced payload. A double cargo-loading door in the side of the fuselage is optional.

The original Dove, which was the first civil transport to fly in Britain after the end of World War II, was in production until 1964, some 540 being built and examples were still being used for third-level airline operations and as air taxis in some parts of the world in the mid-seventies. First flown on 25 September 1945, the Dove accommodated 8–11 passengers and was powered by 340hp or 380hp Gipsy Queen in-line piston engines. The gross weight was 8,950lb (4060kg) and the range was up to 880mls (1416km). Some Doves in the USA were modified to Riley Turbo-Exec 400 standard with 400hp Lycoming IO-720 engines and, optionally, a swept-back fin and rudder.

Above: Three-view drawing of the de Havilland Dove, the first post-war British civil transport.

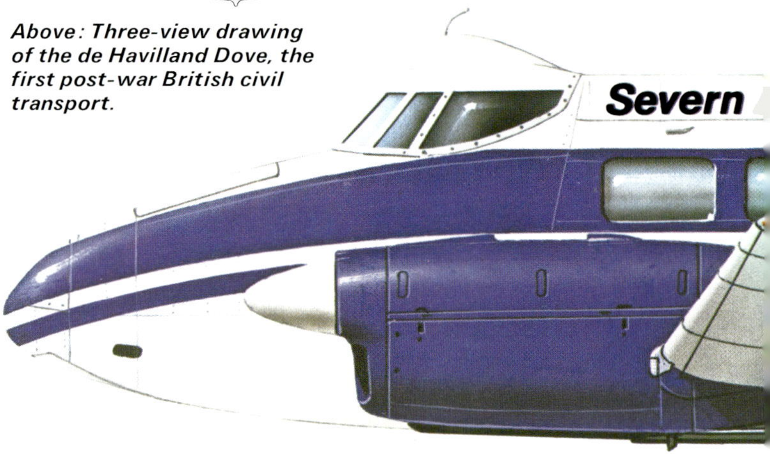

Transall C-160P
International

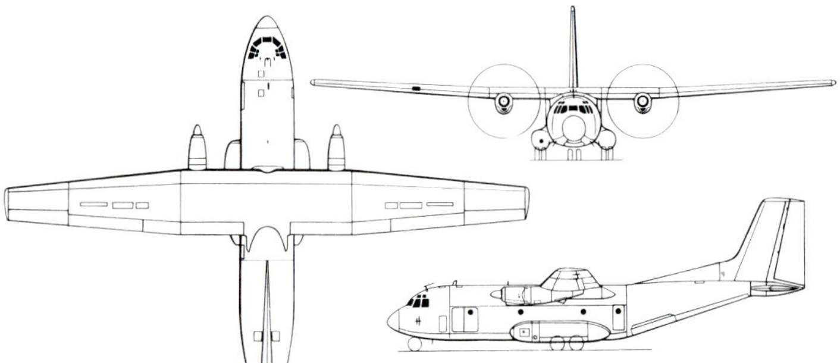

Power Plant: Two Rolls-Royce Tyne RTy 20 Mk 22 turboprops each rated at 6,200ehp for take-off.
Performance: Max speed, 367mph (592km/h) at 16,000ft (4875m); economical cruising speed, 282mph (454km/h) at 20,000ft (6100m); rate of climb, 1,300ft/min (6·6m/sec); service ceiling, 25,500ft (7770m); range, 2,982mls (4800km) with 17,637lb (8000kg) payload and 1,056mls (1700km) with 35,274lb (16,000kg).
Weights: Operating weight empty, 63,815lb (28,946kg).
Dimensions: Span, 131ft 3in (40·00m); length, 106ft $3\frac{1}{2}$in (32·40m); height, 40ft $6\frac{3}{4}$in (12·36m); wing area, 1,723sq ft (160·10m^2).

Above: Three-view drawing of the Transall C-160, a military transport with specialized civil application.

Four examples of the Transall C-160 – which is primarily a military tactical transport – have been in operation with Air France since 1973 on night mail services within France. The operation of these services, under contract to the Centre d'Exploitation Postal Metropolitan (CEPM), has long been an Air France speciality, and a formidable record of regularity and punctuality has been achieved despite the difficulties, in the early days, inherent in night flying in all types of weather. The DC-3s used at first gave way, eventually, to DC-4s and then Fokker F27 Mk 500s and the four Transall supplement the fleet of the last-mentioned type. For mail carrying, the C-160s were modified to allow 13·5tons of mail to be loaded or off-loaded in about 12 minutes. Operating between Paris and Bastia, Corsica (with two aircraft permanently stationed at each end of the route), the Transalls have been carrying an average of 1·8 million letters each night and in the first three years of service achieved a regularity of 98 per cent while flying a total of 10,000hrs.

The C-160 Transall was developed originally to meet the joint requirements of the *Luftwaffe* and the *Armée de l'Air*, with the AG Transall concern being set up to handle its production. Assembly lines were established in both France and Germany and these turned out three prototypes – the first of which flew on 25 February 1963 – six pre-production C-160s, 110 C-160Ds for the *Luftwaffe*, 50 C-160Fs for the *Armée de l'Air* and nine C-160Zs for the South African Air Force. Delivery of the military Transalls was completed by 1970 and the four C-160Ps for Air France were converted by SOGERMA from *Armée de l'Air* C-160Fs.

Left: Derived in the USA from the Dove, the Carstedt Jet Liner (later known as the Texas CJ600) featured turboprop engines and a lengthened fuselage.

Below: A de Havilland Dove of Severn Airways, a typical British air-taxi operator, for which the Dove's 8-11 seats made it of ideal size.

Above: One of the four Transall C-160Ps operated by Air France on the regular Aéropostale services between Paris and Corsica, with one flight in each direction nightly.

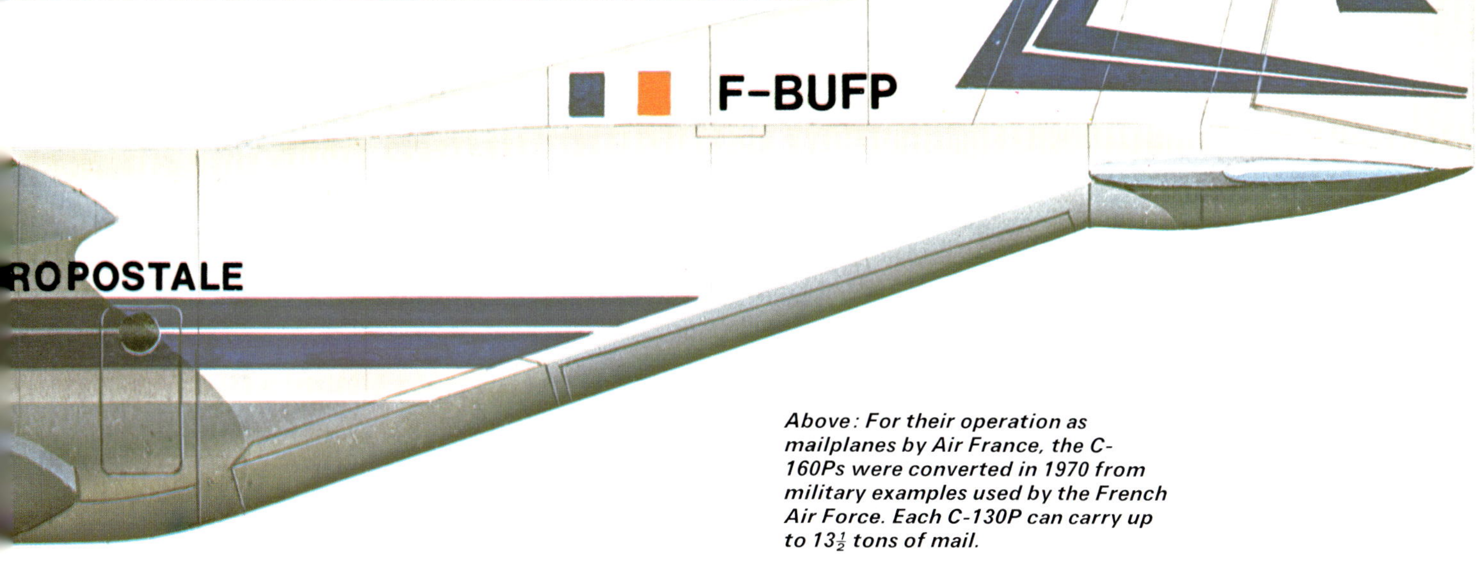

Above: For their operation as mailplanes by Air France, the C-160Ps were converted in 1970 from military examples used by the French Air Force. Each C-130P can carry up to $13\frac{1}{2}$ tons of mail.

Tupolev Tu-104
Soviet Union

The following specification relates to the Tu-104A:
Power Plant: Two 21,385lb st (9700kgp) Mikulin AM-3M 500 turbojets.
Performance: Max cruising speed, 560mph (900km/h); best economy cruise, 497mph (800km/h); service ceiling, 37,750ft (11,500m); range with max payload at 33,000ft (10,000m), 1,645mls (2650km); range with max fuel, 1,925mls (3100km).
Weights: Empty, 91,710lb (41,600kg); max payload, 19,840lb (900kg); max take-off, 167,550lb (76,000kg).
Dimensions: Span, 113ft 4in (34·54m); length, 127ft $5\frac{1}{2}$in (25·85m); height, 39ft 0in (11·90m); wing area, 1,877sq ft (174·4m^2).

Of the various Soviet aircraft design bureaux, that originally headed by the late Andrei Tupolev, and still bearing his name, has played the most significant rôle in the modernization of Aeroflot. This process began in 1956 when the Tu-104 entered service, becoming only the second jet airliner in the world to achieve this status (after the Comet). As the Soviet Union's first jet transport, the Tu-104 was of historic importance; five other commercial Tupolev designs have followed with "1×4" designations, making this bureau the nearest thing in the USSR to the Boeing Company with its "7×7" The following specification refers to the Tu-134:

The Tu-104 was, in fact, a simple adaptation of the Tu-16 bomber, using the same wings and a new fuselage. The first batch were 50-seaters, followed in 1958 by the Tu-104A, with improved engines and a 70-passenger interior. The final production version had a small fuselage "stretch", higher weights and up to 100 seats, and some earlier aircraft were later fitted with a similar interior and operated at the higher weights, in which guise they were designated Tu-104V.

At least 200 Tu-104s were reported to have been built, all but six being for Aeroflot; the only other user was CSA in Czechoslovakia. By 1977, those Tu-104s still operating in the Soviet Union had been relegated to secondary routes.

Right: The Tupolev Tu-104 in its original Aeroflot markings, as used to fly the Soviet Union's first jet services in 1956.

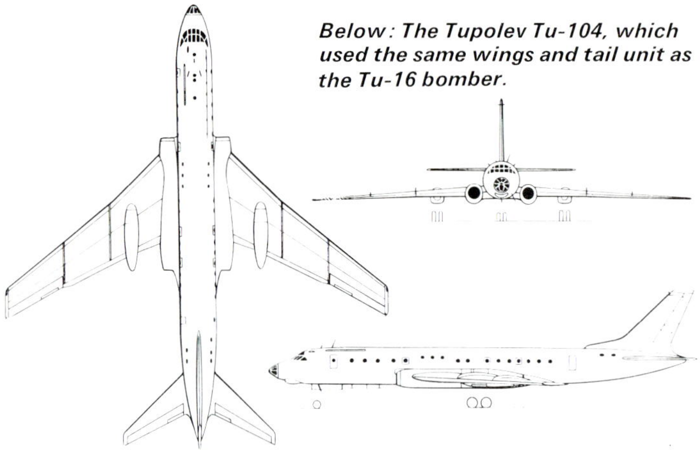

Below: The Tupolev Tu-104, which used the same wings and tail unit as the Tu-16 bomber.

Tupolev Tu-134
Soviet Union

The following specification refers to the Tu-134:
Power Plant: Two 14,490lb st (6800kgp) Soloviev D-30 turbofans.
Performance: Max cruising speed, 559mph (900km/h) at 28,000ft (8500m); economical cruise, 466mph (750km/h) at 36,000ft (11,000m); initial climb rate, 2,913ft/min (14·8m/sec); normal operating ceiling, 39,370ft (12,000m); take-off field length (FAR, SL, ISA, max weight), 7,152ft (2180m); landing field length (FAR, max landing weight), 6,726ft (2050m); range with 1-hr reserve, 1,490mls (2400km) with 15,430-lb (7000-kg) payload and 2,175mls (3500km) with 6,600lb (3000kg) payload.
Weights: Operating weight empty, 60,627lb (27,500kg); max payload, 16,975lb (7700kg); max fuel, 28,660lb (13,000kg); max take-off, 98,105lb (44,500kg); max landing, 88,185lb (40,000kg); max zero fuel, 77,600lb (35,200kg).
Dimensions: Span, 95ft $1\frac{3}{4}$in (29·00m); length, 112ft $8\frac{1}{4}$in (34·35m); height, 29ft 7in (9·02m); wing area, 1,370·3sq ft (127·3m^2).

With the Tu-104 and the Tu-124, the Tupolev design bureau allowed Aeroflot to take a major step forward and to enter the jet age, but in a number of respects both these types lagged behind the standards being established by contemporary products of western companies. Recognizing the need to overcome these discrepancies and to match the standards of the equipment of other airlines in all respects, Aeroflot established a new requirement for a short-haul medium capacity airliner almost as soon as the Tu-124 had entered service, and to meet this requirement the Tupolev bureau evolved the Tu-134. The design was undertaken at the time that "compact jets" such as the Caravelle, One-Eleven and DC-9 were receiving much publicity, and Tupolev adopted a similar rear-engined, T-tail layout.

Initially, an attempt was made to use the Tu-124 fuselage with minimum change, and the designation Tu-124A was applied, but a complete redesign was eventually found to be required, and the designation was then changed. The Tu-134 did retain, however, the short-field and rough-field capabilities of the Tu-124, with a similar undercarriage and high-lift features. Avionics and flight control system were suitable for operation in conditions approximately equivalent to those of ICAO Cat II, and an airbrake was fitted beneath the fuselage to permit steeper approaches to be flown.

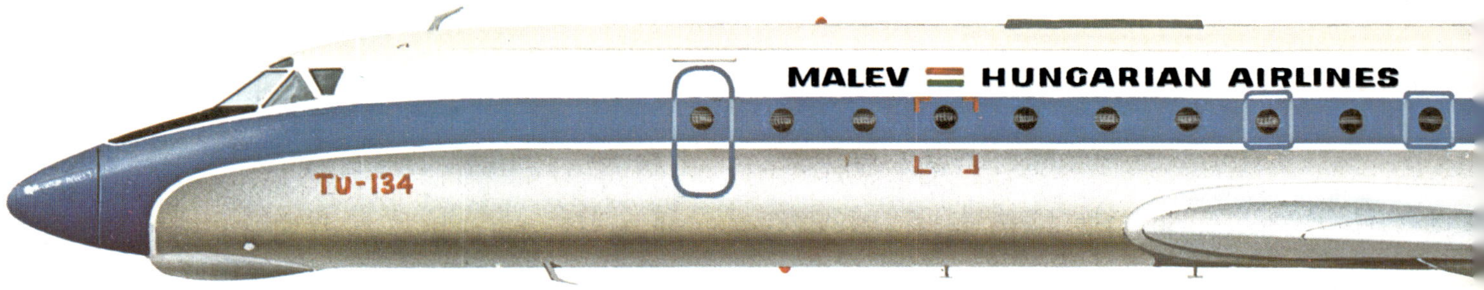

Tupolev Tu-124
Soviet Union

Power Plant: Two 11,905lb (5400kg) Soloviev D 20P turbofans.
Performance: Max speed, 603mph (970km/h); max cruising speed, 540mph (870km/h); economical cruising speed, 497mph (800km/h) at 33,000ft (10,000m) at a mean weight of 58,000lb (26,300kg); typical take-off run, 3,380ft (1030m); typical landing run, 3,050ft (930m); range with max payload and 1-hr reserve, 760mls (1220km); range with max fuel and 7,715-lb (3500-kg) payload, 1,305mls (2100km).
Weights: Empty, 49,600lb (22,500kg); max payload, 13,228lb (6000kg); max take-off weight, 83,775lb (38,000kg); max landing weight, 77,160lb (35,000kg); max zero-fuel weight, 52,400lb (23,770kg).
Dimensions: Span, 83ft 9½in (25·55m); length, 100ft 4in (30·58m); height 26ft 6in (8·08m); wing area, 1,281sq ft (119m²).

Second of the Tupolev jet transports was the Tu-124 (the Tu-114 being turboprop-powered). Although the Tu-124 was very similar in overall appearance to the Tu-104, it was some 25 per cent smaller and consequently was a completely new design insofar as structural detail was concerned.

The first Tu-124 was flown in June 1960, and following flight trials with a small number of prototypes, production was initiated in time for deliveries to be made to Aeroflot in mid-1962. The first commercial service was flown on the Moscow-Tallinn route on 2 October 1962, this being the first use anywhere in the world of an airliner with turbofan engines – specially developed by the Soloviev engine bureau. Originally, the Tu-124 was designed to carry 44 passengers in three separate cabins; seating was increased to 56, however, in the standard Aeroflot version, designated the Tu-124V.

Apart from Aeroflot, only two airlines operated the Tu-124, CSA Czechoslovakian Airlines having acquired three and East Germany's Interflug, two. Fewer than 200 were built and few remained in commercial service by 1977.

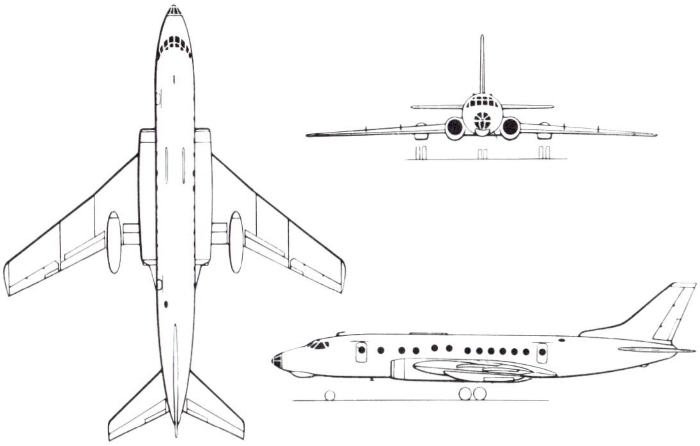

***Above right:** Three-view drawing of the Tupolev Tu-124, the smaller twin-jet based on the design of the Tu-104.*

***Right:** The Tupolev Tu-124 was produced in relatively small numbers for Aeroflot and a few examples were exported, including two to the East German Interflug (as illustrated).*

Prototype testing began in late 1962, and the test programme used a total of six aircraft. Production was launched in 1964 at the Kharkhov factory where the Tu-104 had also been built, and early production aircraft underwent a series of proving flights over Aeroflot routes before full commercial services were launched in September 1967, on the Moscow–Stockholm route. In its standard version, the Tu-134 seats 72, four-abreast in a single class layout, alternative arrangements seating 68 one-class or 64 (eight first-class and 56 tourist).

***Left:** A Tupolev Tu-134A twin-jet operated by the Czech national airline CSA, which had 10 in its fleet in 1978.*

***Below:** The Tupolev Tu-134A, which has a slightly longer fuselage and nose radar to distinguish it from the Tu-134.*

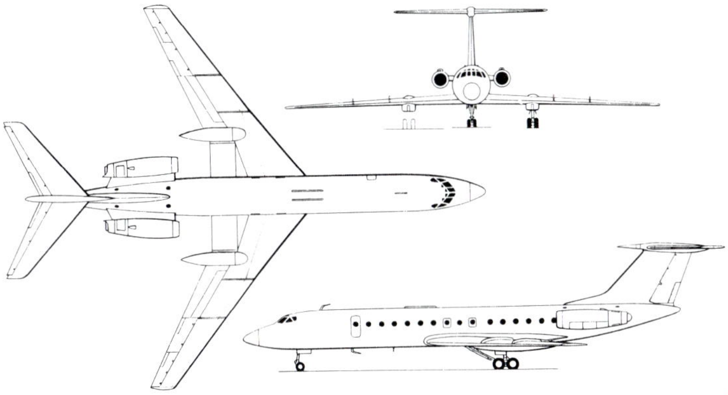

In the second half of 1970, Aeroflot introduced the Tu-134A into service, this version differing from the Tu-134 in having the fuselage "stretched" by 6ft 10½in (2·10m) and being fitted with Soloviev D-30 Series II engines and an APU. The standard layout in this version seats 76, with up to 80 seats at reduced pitch or 68 in a mixed-class layout (12 first class and 56 tourist). Although all early Tu-134s and some Tu-134As had the distinctive glazed nose of earlier Tupolev designs, containing a navigator's station, some later examples dispensed with this crew position and had a "solid" nose fairing containing radar.

The Tu-134 and Tu-134A have proved to be among the most popular of Soviet airliners for export, matching the earlier success of the Il-18, which in many instances the Tu-134 has been purchased to replace. Among the operators in the mid-seventies, in addition to Aeroflot, are CSA, with 11 Tu-134s and Tu-134As; Interflug, with 11 Tu-134s and 11 Tu-134As; Balkan Bulgarian, with six Tu-134s and seven Tu-134As; LOT, with 10 Tu-134s; Malev, with seven Tu-134s and Tu-134As; and Aviogenex, with five Tu-134As. Aeroflot was believed to have about 250 of the two types in service by the end of 1976.

***Above:** A Tupolev Tu-134A in the markings of Malev-Hungarian Airlines, one of the several Eastern European countries operating this Soviet twin-jet.*

Tupolev Tu-144
Soviet Union

Power Plant: Four 44,000lb st (20,000kgp) with reheat Kuznetsov NK-144 turbofans.
Performance: Max cruising speed, up to M = 2·35 (1,550mph/2500km/h) at altitudes up to 59,000ft (18,000m); normal cruise, M = 2·2 (1,430mph/2300km/h); typical take-off speed, 216mph (348km/h); typical landing speed, 150mph (241km/h); balanced field length (ISA, sl, max take-off weight), 9,845ft (3000m); landing run, 8,530ft (2600m); max range with full 140-passenger payload, 4,030mls (6500km) at an average speed of M = 1·9 (1,243mph/2000km/h).
Weights: Operating weight empty, 187,400lb (85,000kg); max payload, 30,865lb (14,000kg); max fuel load, 209,440lb (95,000kg); max take-off weight, 396,830lb (180,000kg); max landing weight, 264,550lb (120,000 kg); max zero-fuel weight, 220,460lb (100,000kg).
Dimensions: Span, 94ft 6in (28·80m); length overall, 215ft 6½in (65·70m); height (wheels up), 42ft 2in (12·85m); wing area, 4,714·5sq ft (438m²).

Holding a secure place in history as the world's first supersonic airliner to fly, the Tupolev Tu-144 has often been described in the popular press as the "Soviet Concorde" or the "Concordskii" – an appellation that underlines the similarity of the two types. There is little doubt that Aeroflot was led to initiate design of an SST by the launching of the Concorde by Britain and France in 1963, and the Tupolev design bureau, having been selected to undertake this prestigious programme, reached similar design conclusions to those of the Concorde's designers. The first public indication of the Tu-144's appearance came in May 1965, when a model was exhibited in Paris, revealing that it was a large ogival-wing transport with provision, like the Concorde, for the nose and visor to be hinged down ahead of the cockpit to improve the forward view in the nose-high approach angle. Unlike Concorde, the chosen engines were turbofans rather than turbojets, and were arranged side by side across the underside of the fuselage in a single large nacelle; the overall dimensions were also somewhat greater than those of its western counterpart and the design cruising speed a little higher, at M = 2·2 to 2·3.

The first of three prototypes of the Tu-144 to be assembled at the Zhukovsky works, near Moscow, made its first flight on 31 December 1968, and supersonic speed was achieved for the first time on 5 June 1969, followed by the first excursion beyond M = 2·0 on 26 May 1970. All these three events were world "firsts", but the rate of flight testing with the prototypes was relatively slow with only about 200hrs achieved in the first 3½ years after initial flight. During this period, and based on early flight test results, a major redesign of the Tu-144 was put in hand, the production configuration appearing early in 1973 in the Soviet Union and in May 1973 at the Paris Air Show. Compared with the prototypes, this production model had larger overall dimensions; a new wing; relocated engine nacelles; uprated engines; a new undercarriage and retractable noseplanes for improved slow-speed handling.

The wing of the Tu-144 has been changed from the original ogival form (with curved leading edges) to a compound delta, with straight leading edges and sweepback angles of about 76 deg on the inboard portions and 57 deg

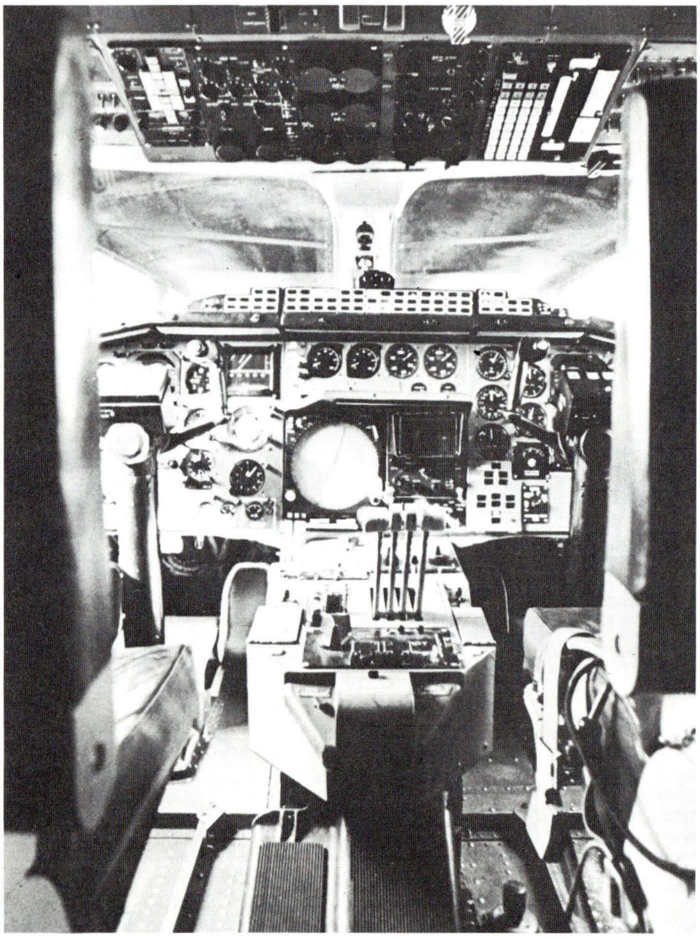

Above: Like most large Soviet jetliners the Tu-144 required a long period of development before it was judged ready for passenger service. Early prototypes were designed with military-type flight decks, and even included crew-escape systems. This photograph shows the production prototype flight deck (aircraft 77110), with the nose raised and vizor in place for high-speed cruising flight. The available width is fractionally greater than Concorde's, and the Russian version still retains something of its massive military origins, especially in the use of fully adjustable seats for two pilots and a flight engineer. The large boxes on the control yokes were officially claimed to be prototype instrumentation only; yet they significantly obstruct the pilot's view of the instruments. The centre panel contains engine speed and pressure-ratio indicators, exhaust gas temperature and inlet/nozzle indicators for the variable-geometry turbofan engines. It is thought by Western observers that the Russian designers intend to clear the Tu-144 for automatic blind landing.

Right: An early production Tupolev Tu-144, as used by Aeroflot to launch supersonic service between Moscow and Alma Ata in November 1977.

on the outer panels. The whole wing incorporates complex camber from leading to trailing edge, with anhedral towards the tips.

Addition of noseplanes to the production Tu-144 was an indication of the difficulties of achieving acceptable low-speed control, since they provide unwanted drag and weight penalties in cruising flight. The noseplanes are stowed in the upper fuselage just behind the flight deck, pivoting to open to an overall span of about 20ft (6·1km); they have anhedral when open, and incorporate fixed double leading edge slots plus double slotted trailing edge flaps.

Each pair of engines is housed in an individual nacelle (unlike the prototype arrangement) The engines have been improved since first being flown in the prototype to have a dry thrust rating of 33,000lb st (15,000kgp) and an afterburner thrust of 44,000lb st (20,000kg). The cruising technique called for about 35 per cent of maximum reheat boost to be maintained throughout the supersonic cruise, and the intakes incorporate fully-automatic movable ramps.

The Tu-144 was designed to be operated by a crew of three (two pilots and an engineer) and can carry up to 140 passengers. Typically, the forward cabin seats 11 at first-class standards and the centre and rear compartments, separated by galleys, toilets and cloakrooms, accommodate 30 and 99 passengers at tourist class standards, basically five abreast. There are no under-floor freight or baggage holds, but provision is made for containerized baggage in a compartment behind the cabin.

The first production Tu-144 is believed to have flown towards the end of 1972, and by mid-1974, four production models and two prototypes were reported to be under test. On 26 December 1975, Aeroflot began a regular service with Tu-144s between Moscow and Alma Ata (a distance of about 2,200mls/3500km) but only freight was carried in accordance with normal Aeroflot procedure for the introduction of a new type. This service was reported in 1976 to have encountered some technical difficulties as a result of the Tu-144s need to reheat for long periods to achieve its cruising Mach No; and passenger services with the type were not introduced by Aeroflot until November 1977, when a twice-weekly schedule was started on the same route.

***Below:* The production form of the Tupolev Tu-144, which differed in many details from the prototypes.**

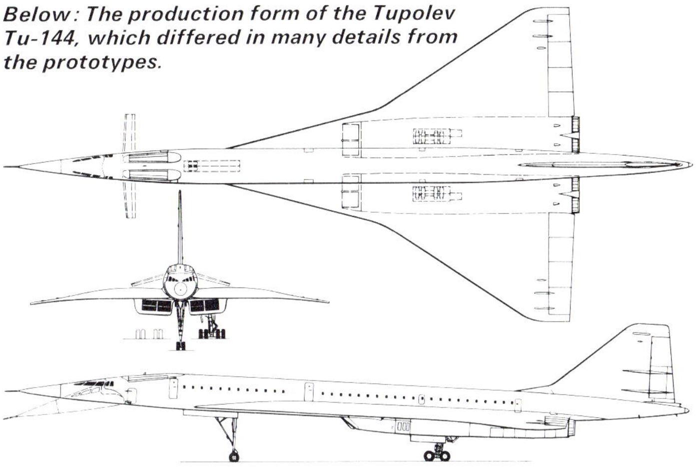

Tupolev Tu-154
Soviet Union

Power Plant: Three 20,950lb st (9500kgp) Kuznetsov NK-8-2 turbofans.
Performance: Max cruising speed, 605mph (975km/h) at 31,150ft (9500m); best-cost cruise, 560mph (900km/h); long-range cruise 528mph (850km/h); balanced take-off distance (FAR, ISA, SL, max take-off weight), 6,890ft (2100m); landing field length (FAR, ISA, SL, max landing weight), 6,758ft (2060m); range with max payload and 1-hr reserve, 2,150mls (3460km); range with max fuel and 30,100-lb (13,650-kg) payload, 3,280mls (5280km).
Weights: Operating weight empty, 95,900lb (43,500kg); max payload, 44,090lb (20,000kg); max fuel load, 73,085lb (33,150kg); max take-off weight, 198,416lb (90,000kg); max landing weight, 176,370lb (80,000kg); max zero fuel weight, 139,994lb (63,500kg).
Dimensions: Span, 123ft $2\frac{1}{2}$in (37·55m); length, 157ft $1\frac{3}{4}$in (47·90m); height, 37ft $4\frac{3}{4}$in (11·40m); wing area, 2,169sq ft (201·45m²).

The sixth and latest of the Tupolev bureau's commercial airliners, the Tu-154, can be considered as a direct counterpart of the Boeing 727-200/HS Trident Three transports, having a similar three-engined T-tail layout. Compared with its western contemporaries, however, the Tu-154 was designed to have a higher power-to-weight ratio, giving it a better take-off performance, and a heavy duty undercarriage suitable for use from Class 2 airfields with surfaces of gravel or packed earth. These features are common to most Soviet transports and indicate the importance of air transport in the Union's remoter areas, where airfield facilities are minimal. Lacking the characteristic glazed nose of the earlier Tupolev transports, the Tu-154 nevertheless retained the wing pods for main undercarriage stowage that are a feature of all the Tupolev series except the Tu-144.

First flight of the Tu-154 was made on 4 October 1968, and six prototype/pre-production models were used for flight development. Production was launched soon after first flight, the Tu-154 having been selected by Aeroflot as a replacement for the Tu-104, Il-18 and An-10 on domestic and international routes of medium length, in partnership with the Il-62 and Il-62M on longer stages. The first delivery was made to Aeroflot early in 1971 and there followed the customary period of route proving with freight and mail, plus a few passenger services on an *ad hoc* basis, from May 1971 onwards, but full commercial exploitation began only on 9 February 1972, initially on the route from Moscow to Mineralnye Vady. First international services were flown on 1 August 1972, between Moscow and Prague.

The Tu-154 was normally laid out to accommodate 158 or 164 passengers in a single-class layout, six abreast in two cabins separated by the galley. If a mixed-class layout was required, 24 seats could be provided four abreast in the forward cabin, with 104 tourist class seats in the rear cabin. Maximum high density seating was for 167. Standard avionics and flight control system permit operation to Cat II levels, with projected future development for fully automatic landings (Cat III). An improved version, the Tu-154A, was put into limited service by Aeroflot in April 1974, followed by large-scale introduction in 1975. Using uprated NK-8-2U turbofans of 23,150lb st (10,500kgp), the Tu-154A has increased fuel capacity and higher operating weights, up to 207,235lb (94,000kg) for take-off. Overall dimensions remain unchanged. A further increase in operating weight is offered with the Tu-154B, which has a max take-off weight of 211,650lb (96,000kg) changes in the control system and modifications to the interior allowing greater flexibility of loading.

Although the needs of Aeroflot in 1974 led to a temporary interruption in the export of Tu-154s, the type had already been specified by several airlines in the Soviet Bloc, with deliveries being made during 1973 and early 1974. These included; Balkan Bulgarian, 10, Malev six and Tarom, two. Over 100 Tu-154s have been delivered to Aeroflot.

***Below:** A Tupolev Tu-154 of the Hungarian state airline Malev comes in to land. Six were in the Malev fleet by 1978.*

Above: The Tu-154 was initially projected with a glazed "bomb-aimer" type nose such as had been incorporated in all earlier Tupolev gas-turbine transports (Tu-104, 110, 114, 124 and early versions of the 134). In the course of design it became evident that a normal opaque nose, with weather radar, was a better choice, because by the 1960s even Soviet aircraft could navigate by electronic means, as had been done in the West for almost 30 years. Accordingly the Tu-154 has a more conventional flight deck with no lower forward section; the navigator has likewise vanished, as in Western transports, and the only concession to Soviet conservative thinking is the presence of a full-time engineer. The pilots have panels more modern and neater than in any previous Soviet airliner, with white-outlined T-shapes of primary flight instruments, large groups of central warning panels and a moving-map display just to the left of the radar tube (which in this particular aircraft has a viewing hood, though bright tubes are now standard on Aeroflot routes). Again, the traditional Russian rubber-bladed fans of this 154 are today seldom seen. Flight controls, incidentally, are pure Trident: triplexed hydraulics.

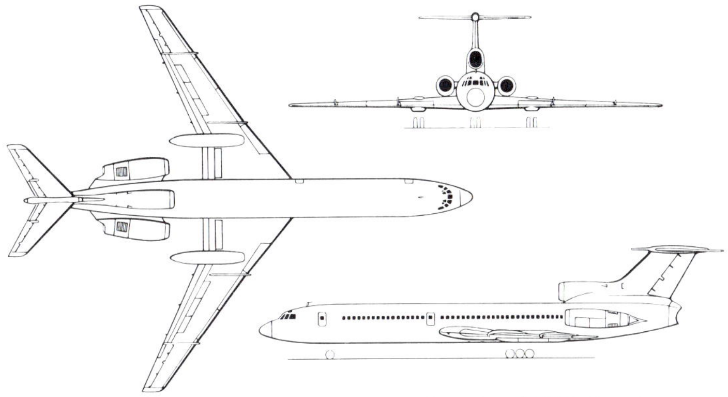

Left: The Tupolev Tu-154, which shares its trijet layout with the Boeing 727 and HS Trident and is of comparable size.

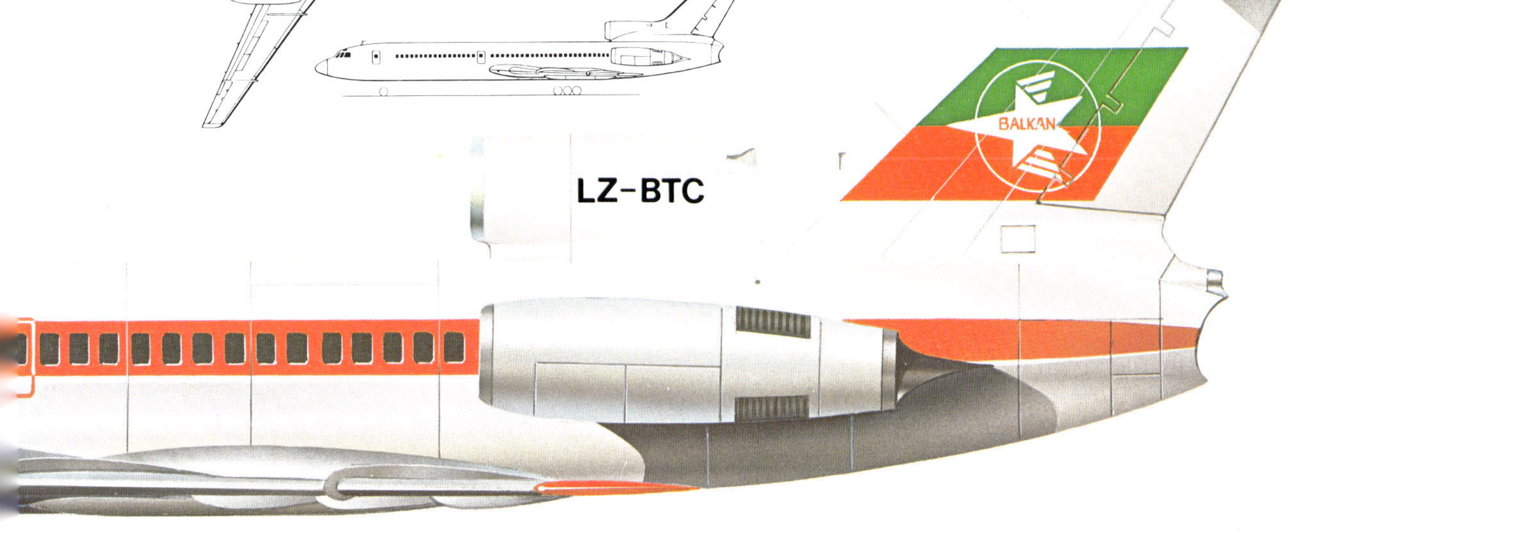

Below: Balkan Bulgarian Airlines (formerly TABSO) had a mixture of Tu-154, Tu-154A and Tu-154B models in service by 1978.

VFW-Fokker VFW 614
Federal Germany

Power Plant: Two 7,473lb st (3392kgp) Rolls-Royce/SNECMA M45H Mk 501 turbofans.
Performance: Max cruising speed, 457mph (735km/h) at 21,000ft (6400m); long-range cruise, 390mph (627km/h) at 25,000ft (7620m); initial rate of climb, 3,360ft/min (17·1m/sec); service ceiling 25,000ft (7600m); range with max payload, 700mls (1126km); range with max fuel, 1,553mls (2500km).
Weights: Operating empty, 26,900lb (12,200kg); max payload, 8,600lb (3900kg); max take-off, 44,000lb (19,950kg).
Dimensions: Span, 70ft 6in (21·50m); length, 67ft 6in (20·60m); height, 25ft 8in (7·84m); wing area, 688·9sq ft ($64{\cdot}00m^2$).

The VFW 614 was developed in Germany during the sixties as a potential "DC-3 replacement" and was notable for its unusual configuration with the engines in nacelles above the low-position wing. This arrangement made it possible to use a very short undercarriage, facilitating passenger and cargo loading, and also gave good protection against ingestion of debris by the engines if the aircraft was operating from rough fields or poor grade runways. As originally proposed in 1961 as the E.614, by the Entwicklungsring Nord (ERNO) group of Weser, Fock-Wulf and HFB, the aircraft was a 36–40 seater with Lycoming PLF1B-2 turbofans. It subsequently became the VFW 614 after regrouping of the German aircraft industry had taken place, and by the time the German government gave the project a go-ahead, contributing 80 per cent of the launching costs, it had grown in size to a 44–48 seater with Rolls-Royce/SNECMA M.45 engines.

A decision to launch full-scale production of the VFW 614 was made in June 1970, by which time the merger of VFW and Fokker had been effected, and risk-sharing agreements were concluded with SIAT in Germany (now part of MBB), SABCA and Fairey in Belgium and Short Bros in the UK (as a sub-contractor to Rolls-Royce). All these companies shared in production, as did the Fokker–VFW unit in the Netherlands, final assembly being at the VFW plant (originally Focke-Wulf) at Bremen.

A development batch of three flying prototypes and two test specimens of the VFW 614 was put in hand, but before the first of these could fly, the programme was jeopardized by the collapse of Rolls-Royce and although the first prototype flew on 14 July 1971, a new agreement confirming M45 engine availability was not concluded with the revised Rolls-Royce company until the end of the year. The second and third aircraft flew on 14 January and 10 October 1972 respectively but the loss of the first prototype (due to elevator flutter) on 1 February 1972 imposed a further delay on the programme. A full production go-ahead was finally given on 13 December 1972, by which time options had been taken on some 26 aircraft by nine customers. The first firm order was confirmed in May 1974, by Cimber Air of Denmark for two aircraft, and German cer-

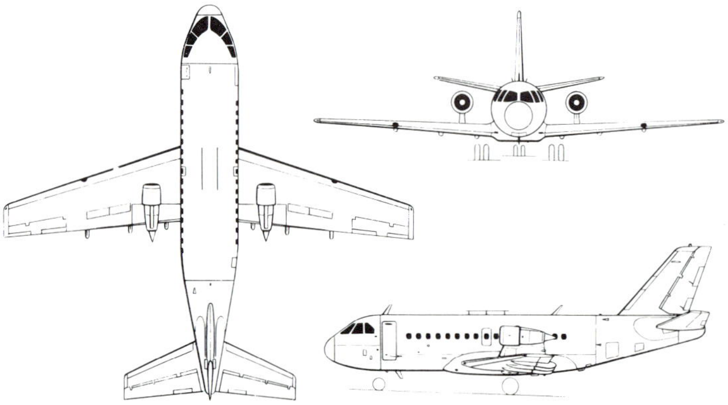

Above: Three-view drawing of the VFW-Fokker VFW-614, showing the unique overwing mounting for its M45 engines.

Right: A VFW 614 in the markings of Cimber Air, the first airline to operate the type. Production ended prematurely in 1977.

Vickers Vanguard
United Kingdom

The following specification refers to the Vanguard Type 952:
Power Plant: Four 5,545ehp Rolls-Royce Tyne 512 turboprops.
Performance: High speed cruise, 425mph (684km/h) at 20,000ft (6100m); long-range cruise, 420mph (676km/h) st 25,000ft (7620m); initial rate of climb, 2,700ft/min (13·7m/sec); service ceiling, 30,000ft (9145m); range with max payload (no reserves), 1,830mls (2945km) at 25,000ft (7620m); range with max fuel, 3,100mls (4990km) at 25,000ft (7620m).
Weights: Empty equipped 82,500lb (37,422kg); max payload, 37,000lb (16,785kg); max take-off, 146,500lb (66,448kg); max landing, 130,500lb (61,238kg).
Dimensions: Span, 118ft 7in (36·15m); length, 122ft 10½in (37·45m); height, 34ft 11in (10·64m); wing area, 1,529sq ft ($142{\cdot}0m^2$).

The Vanguard, first flown on 20 January 1959, was designed primarily to meet BEA requirements for a "big Viscount", of similar overall configuration and using turboprop engines. It was, however, overtaken by the advent of pure-jet airliners able to operate economically on medium stage lengths and initial sales were made only to BEA (now British Airways European Division) and to TCA (now Air Canada). The latter bought the Type 952 with Tyne 513 engines while BEA had a mixture of 951s and 953s with Tyne 506s, the 953 having increased weights. Up to 139 passengers could be carried in one-class layouts.

By 1974, Air Canada had retired all its Vanguards and two years later British Airways had in service only five, all converted to Merchantman freighting standard, with a large side-loading door. Several other operators had acquired Vanguards second-hand, however, including Air Bridge Carriers in the UK, Merpati Nusantara in Indonesia and Europe Aero Services in France, the last-named being the principal remaining user of the type with a fleet of 10.

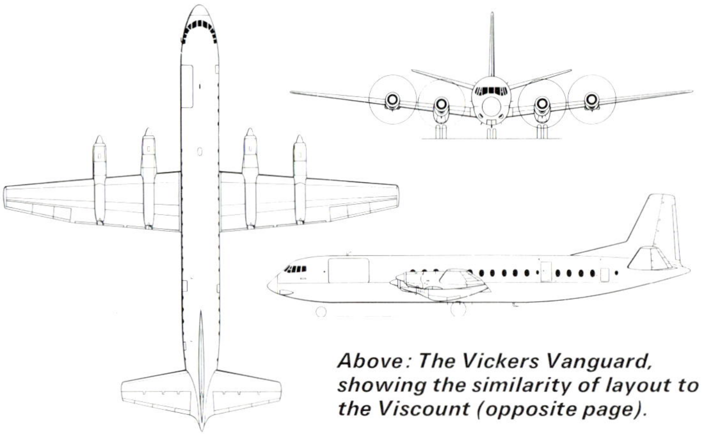

Above: The Vickers Vanguard, showing the similarity of layout to the Viscount (opposite page).

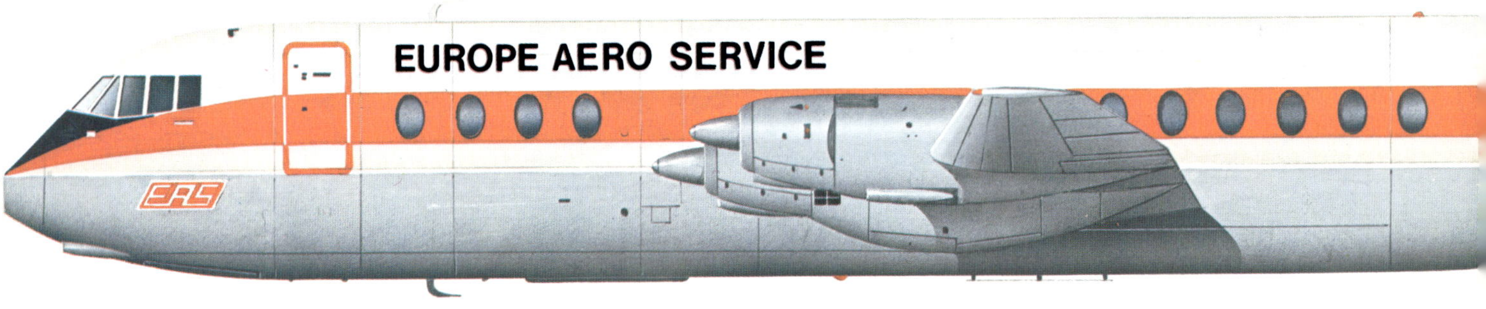

tification was obtained on 23 August 1974, clearing the way for production deliveries to begin in the middle of 1975 and entry into service with Cimber Air later in the year.

Subsequently, orders were obtained from Air Alsace for three and from Touraine Air Transport for eight, but only limited service by these two operators had been undertaken by the end of 1977, at which time VFW-Fokker decided to discontinue production of the VFW 614 in view of the poor sales and future market prospects. Although an agreement had been signed with the Romanian government earlier in the year providing for production of up to 100 VFW 614s in the latter country, this did not in itself provide the German company with sufficient work to justify continued production, and the Romanian deal was also cancelled, therefore, when the programme in Germany came to an end. Continued airline use of the few VFW 614s already in service in 1977 seemed unlikely.

Above: After giving reliable service with BEA and Air Canada, Vanguards have been acquired by a number of smaller operators.

Above left: Converted for all-freight duties, five V-953C Vanguards remained in service with British Airways in 1978, named Merchantmen.

Below: A Vanguard 952, originally of the fleet built for Air Canada and later operated by Europe Aero Service.

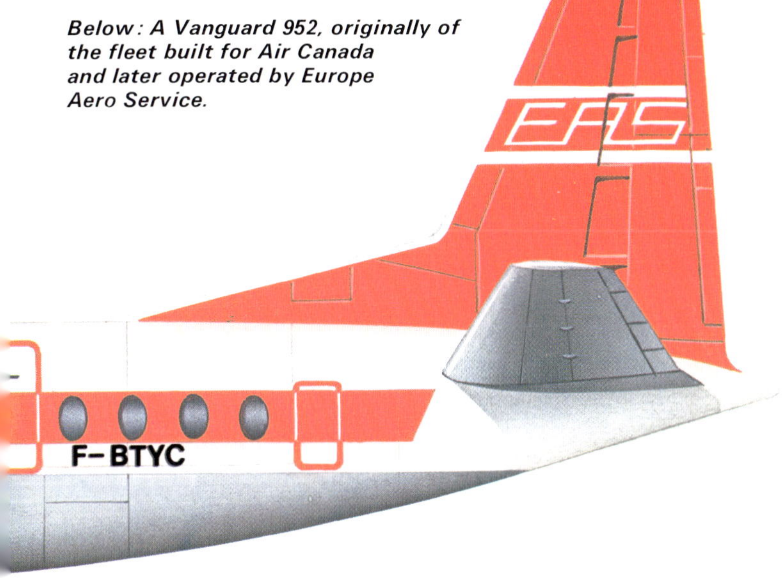

Vickers Viscount

United Kingdom

The following specification refers to the Viscount 810:
Power Plant: Four 2,100ehp Rolls-Royce Dart 525 turboprops.
Performance: Cruising speed, 350mph (563km/h) at 20,000ft (6100m); service ceiling, 25,000ft (7620m); no-reserves range with max payload, 1,725mls (2775km); no-reserves range with max fuel, 1,760mls (2830km).
Weights: Basic operating 41,565lb (18,753kg); max payload, 14,500lb (6577kg); max take-off, 72,500lb (32,886kg).
Dimensions: Span, 93ft $8\frac{1}{2}$in (28·50m); length, 85ft 8in (26·11m); 26ft 9in (8·16m); wing area, 963sq ft (89·46m^2).

An order confirmed by BEA on 3 August 1950 for 20 Vickers Viscounts ensured that production of this four-turboprop short-to-medium haul transport would go ahead, and thus put in train a sequence of events that would establish the Viscount as Britain's most-produced commercial transport to date and one that was to be the means of introducing gas turbine operations to a large proportion of the world's airlines. The event came more than six years after the first steps had been taken that were to lead to the design and production of the Viscount, during which time the future of the aircraft was at times in jeopardy.

The idea of developing a turboprop transport emerged late in 1944 in discussions between the Brabazon Committee and Vickers designers, who were already working on a transport derivative of the Wellington bomber as the VC1 Viking. By March 1945, Vickers had projected possible pressurized transports to seat 24–27 passengers, with a gross weight of 35,000lb (15,875kg) under the designation VC2 and in May the Brabazon Committee set out the requirements in greater detail as the Type IIB, specifying 24 seats, a 1,000 mile (1610km) range and a 7,500lb (3400kg) payload. By the end of the year, Vickers had chosen the Rolls-Royce Dart as the potential power-plant and on 9 March 1946 the company received a government contract to build two prototypes, one with Armstrong Siddeley Mamba engines and one with Rolls-Royce Darts. The name Viceroy was adopted, but was dropped after the partition of India and Viscount was chosen instead.

continued on page 132 ▶

Below: The Vickers Viscount 800, with longer fuselage and more power than the original 700 series.

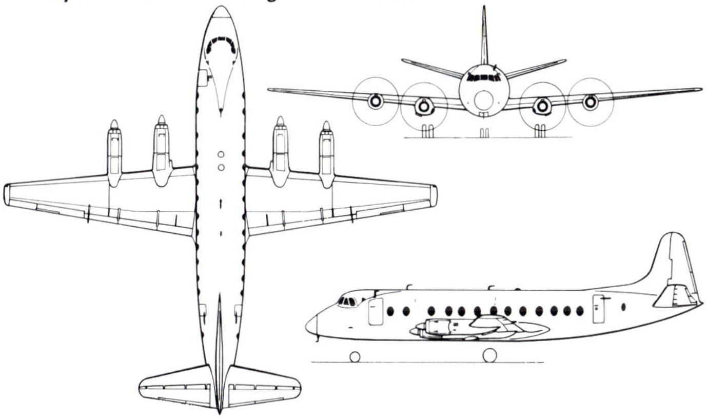

Below: About 130 Viscounts remained in commercial service in 1978, with British Airways still operating 25 on secondary routes.

► By the time the first Viscount prototype (with Dart R.Da.1 engines) was ready to fly, it had grown in size to seat 32 qassengers. First flight was made at Wisley on 16 July 1948, but airline interest remained lukewarm and progress on the other prototype was slowed down. When Rolls-Royce offered a new Dart variant, the R.Da.3, with 40 per cent more power, however, Vickers was able to redesign the Viscount with a 6ft 8in (2·03-m) fuselage stretch and 5-ft (1·52-m) increase of span, and seats for 40 passengers (four-abreast). The economics of this new variant, the Vickers Type 700 or Viscount 700, looked much more attractive to the airlines and once the BEA order had set the ball rolling, the order book for this version of the Viscount grew rapidly, helped by demonstration flights by the new prototype, which had made its first flight on 19 April 1950.

The first production Viscount flew on 20 August 1952, to BEA standard, having a gross weight of 53,000lb (14,040kg), 47 seats (five-abreast) and Dart 505s in place of the 504s in the prototype. A full certificate of airworthiness was granted on 17 April 1953 and BEA inaugurated Viscount services the next day, between London and Cyprus. This marked the inauguration of regular passenger services by a turboprop aircraft, although the original Viscount 630 prototype had been used in 1950 for a month-long trial on the London–Edinburgh route.

As the world's first, and for some time only, turboprop transport, the Viscount quickly gained a favourable passenger reaction and important airline orders were achieved, notably from TCA (now Air Canada) in November 1952 and from Capital Airlines of the USA in June 1954. The latter company eventually bought 60 Viscounts and TCA bought 51; other early sales were made to operators throughout the world. Each customer variant was distinguished, in accordance with Vickers practice, by an individual type number, ranging from 701 (BEA's first variant) to 798. Significant changes were introduced in the Type 724 for TCA, including a new fuel system, a two-pilot cockpit, US styling and a 60,000lb (27,215kg) gross weight. The Type 745 for Capital marked another stage in Viscount development, introducing uprated Dart R.Da.6 Mk 510 engines, full compliance with US regulations and a gross weight (eventually) of 64,500lb (29,256kg); FAA approval was obtained on 7 November 1955. Subsequent Viscounts fitted with the R.Da.6 engines were known generically as Type 700Ds.

To improve the payload/range performance of the Viscount and to take advantage of possible increases in engine power, Vickers developed a stretched-fuselage variant as the Type 800, the fuselage being 3ft 10in (1·17m) longer but the effective cabin length being 9ft 3in (2·82m) greater through relocation of the rear bulkhead. Passenger capacity therefore increased to 65 (or 71 high-density) and with Dart R.Da.6 engines the gross weight was 64,500lb (29,256kg). A prototype flew on 27 July 1956 and first delivery was made, to BEA, on 11 January 1957. In addition to 22 Viscount 802s, BEA bought 19 similar 806s, with Dart R.Da.7 Mk 520 engines.

A further stage in Viscount evolution came in 1957 with the Type 810, which was dimensionally the same as the 800 but with R.Da.7/1 engines and structural strengthening to allow the gross weight to increase to 72,500lb (32,885kg). A prototype flew on 23 December 1957 and most of the final production batch of Viscounts were of this type. The last order of all came from China, buying six as the first Western equipment ever acquired by CAAC. Deliveries of these aircraft were completed in 1964, bringing the total of Viscounts built to 444 (of which 438 were sold to customers, the others being prototypes or rebuilds). The only turboprop transports to have exceeded this sales record are the Fokker F27 and, within the Soviet Union, the Antonov An-24, the Ilyushin Il-18 and the Antonov An-10/12 family, many of which were for military use.

Since the beginning of the seventies, growing numbers of Viscounts of the earlier series have been withdrawn from service and scrapped, and few of any variant remain in use on primary routes. On secondary routes and in less developed areas of the world, however, over a hundred were still in regular airline service in 1977, and several dozen more were used for corporate transportation.

***Below:** Two classic transport aircraft—a Viscount (the world's very first turboprop airliner) and a DC-3 (the most widely used airliner ever produced).*

Yakovlev Yak-40
Soviet Union

The following specification refers to the standard 27-seat Yak-40 with AI-25 engines.

Power Plant: Three 3,300lb st (1500kgp) Ivchenko AI-25 turbofans.

Performance: Max speed, 373mph (600km/h) at sea level; max cruising speed, 342mph (550km/h) at 19,685ft (6000m); initial climb rate, 1,575ft/min (8·0m/sec); typical take-off run, 1,968ft (600m); typical landing roll, 1,804ft (500m); range with max fuel, 45-min reserve, 590mls (950km) at max cruise speed; max range, no reserves, 900mls (1450km) at 261mph (420km/h) at 26,247ft (8000m).

Weights: Empty, 20,140lb (9135kg); max payload, 5,070lb (2300kg); max fuel load, 6,614lb (3000kg); max take-off and landing weight, 32,410lb (14,700kg).

Dimensions: Span, 82ft $0\frac{1}{4}$in (25·0m); length, 66ft $9\frac{1}{2}$in (20·36m); height, 21ft 4in (6·50m); wing area, 753·5sq ft (70·0m^2).

First flown on 21 October 1966, the Yak-40 marked the first venture of the Yakovlev design bureau into the civil transport field, although several light transport designs had previously been produced under the Yakovlev banner in addition to its better-known fighters and trainers. The task confronting the bureau was to evolve a small, economic short-haul transport that could replace many of the Lisunov Li-2 (DC-3) transports still being used in the Soviet Union, and this requirement meant that the new aircraft had to be able to operate at Class 5 airfields, with grass runways.

The emphasis on good field performance led the design team to adopt a three-engined layout rather than the usual twin-engined configuration for aircraft of this size; this meant that take-off weights and runway lengths could be calculated on the basis of losing only one-third, and not one-half, of total power in the case of an engine failure. The 3,300lb (1500kg) turbofan engines were specially developed for the Yak-40 at the Ivchenko engine bureau, and the high thrust-to-weight ratio that they bestow on the aircraft is especially beneficial for operations at high-altitude airfields, of which there are many in the remoter regions of the USSR. The standard range of avionics and flight control system provided for operation down to Cat II standards, and future development for Cat III was projected.

The basic Yak-40 was designed as a 27-passenger short-haul feederliner, seating being three abreast (2+1) with an off-set aisle. A variety of alternative layouts has been evolved by the design bureau, including one with 33 seats at reduced pitch, mixed-class arrangements with 16 or 20 seats, and an executive model with 11 seats in two separate cabins. All versions have a ventral airstair as the main access to the cabin, and an APU is mounted above the rear fuselage, primarily for engine starting.

***Below:** The Yak-40, built in large numbers for use by Aeroflot but yet to achieve substantial export success.*

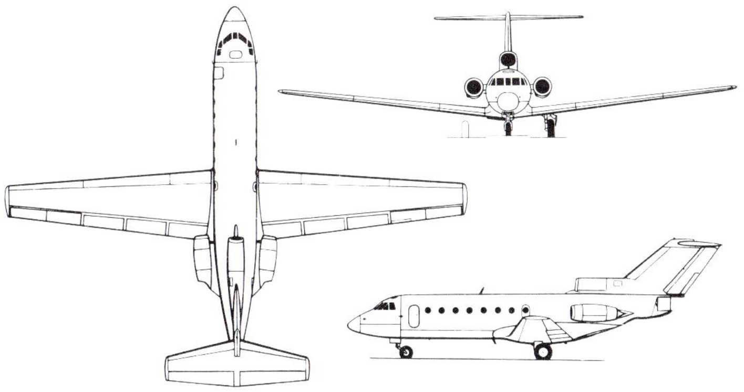

***Above:* The Yak-40, which applies the three-engined layout to a smaller airframe than in any contemporary airliner.**

Following construction of a batch of five prototypes, production of the Yak-40 was launched at a factory at Saratov, some 300 miles (500km) SE of Moscow, in 1967 and deliveries to Aeroflot began during the following year. Regular operations on scheduled services began on 30 September 1968, and production increased to eight a month by 1973 to meet the very large domestic demand. Over 700 Yak-40s have been built, primarily for service with Aeroflot, and the type has been the subject of a major export campaign by Aviaexport, the Soviet state aircraft marketing organization. To facilitate overseas sale, the Yak-40 has undergone full certification to western standards in Italy and Federal Germany, and a version with Collins avionics is available as the Yak-40EC. Among the users of the Yak-40 are Avioligure in Italy; General Air of Hamburg; Bakhtar Afghan; CSA in Czechoslovakia and its internal subsidiary Slovair. Other examples are used by government agencies and air forces within the Soviet Bloc, and the Yugoslav Air Force has two.

Since the Yak-40 entered service, it has undergone some modifications, the most noticeable of which are the addition of a clam-shell thrust reverser on the centre engine, and deletion of the acorn fairing at the fin/tailplane leading-edge junction. During 1970, a version with a lengthened fuselage was projected as the Yak-40M, to carry 40 passengers, but this apparently did not proceed. During 1974, the Yak-40V became available for export, this having 3,858lb st (1750kgp) AI-25T engines and fuel capacity increased from 6,614lb (3000kg) to 8,820lb (4000kg). This increased power permitted the gross weight to be raised from 34,410lb (14,700kg) for the original 27-seater to 35,274lb (16,000kg) with a similar layout or 36,376lb (16,500kg) with a 32-seat high-density layout, when the payload was 6,000lb (2720kg). To make the Yak-40 more acceptable in the North American market, a version with Garrett-AiResearch TFE731-2 turbofans has also been projected as the X-Avia, to be marketed by ICX Aviation in Washington.

Yakovlev Yak-42

Soviet Union

Power Plant: Three Lotarev D-36 high by-pass turbofans each rated at 14,200lb st (6440kgp).
Performance: Normal cruising speed, 510mph (820km/h); high speed cruise, 540mph (870km/h); range, 1,150mls (1850km) with 26,430lb (12,000kg) payload; airfield requirement, 5,900ft (1800m).
Weights: Max take-off, 114,535lb (52,000kg); max payload, 31,940lb (14,500kg).
Dimensions: Span, 112ft $2\frac{1}{2}$in (34·20m); length, 119ft 4in (36·38m); height, 32ft 3in (9·83m); wing area, 1,614·6sq ft (150m^2).

The Yak-42 is the second jet transport to emerge from a design bureau that has been famous for many years for its fighters serving with the Soviet Air Force. Resembling, in overall configuration, the Yak-40 (see previous page) with its three engines grouped in the rear, the Yak-42 was designed to replace the Tu-134 and Il-18 on the shorter-range trunk routes and An-24s on local routes operated by Aeroflot within the USSR. Its development began in the early 'seventies, a mock-up being displayed to Western correspondents visiting Yakovlev's works near Moscow in mid-1973, and the prototype made its first flight on 7 March 1975.

Two versions of the Yak-42 have been designed – a 100-seater for the local routes, with provision for passengers to stow carry-on baggage and outer garments as they board the aircraft (using the same concept adopted in the Il-86) and a 120-seater for the trunk routes with baggage preloaded into containers for stowage under the cabin floor. Like the Yak-40, the Yak-42 has a rear-loading integral stairway, but there is also a forward fuselage door. According to Soviet reports, the first and second prototypes of the Yak-42 have different degrees of sweepback – 11 and 25 respectively – for comparative flight testing, the latter having been adopted for the production aircraft.

The D-36 engines for the Yak-42 were developed at the former Ivchenko design bureau under the direction of V. A. Lotarev and are claimed to have a very low specific fuel consumption. Although the passenger capacity of the Yak-42 is about the same as that of the Douglas DC-9 Srs 40 or 50, it has almost 50 per cent more power, indicating the emphasis placed upon field performance to allow the aircraft to operate from relatively short airfields with only grass runways. Special attention has also been given to achieving long fatigue life and low maintenance man hours. A total Aeroflot requirement for up to 2,000 examples of the Yak-42 has been reported, with entry into service by the late 'seventies.

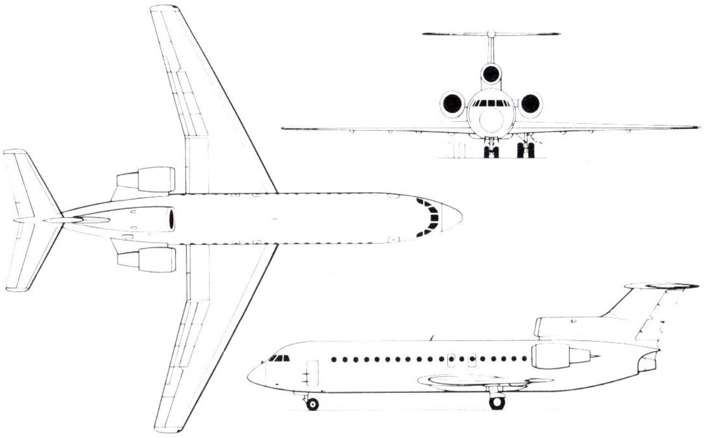

***Above:* Three-view drawing of the Yak-42, which has a similar configuration to that of the considerably smaller Yak-40.**

***Below:* The Yak-42, first flown in 1975, was nearing the end of flight testing in 1978.**

BUSINESS and EXECUTIVE AIRCRAFT

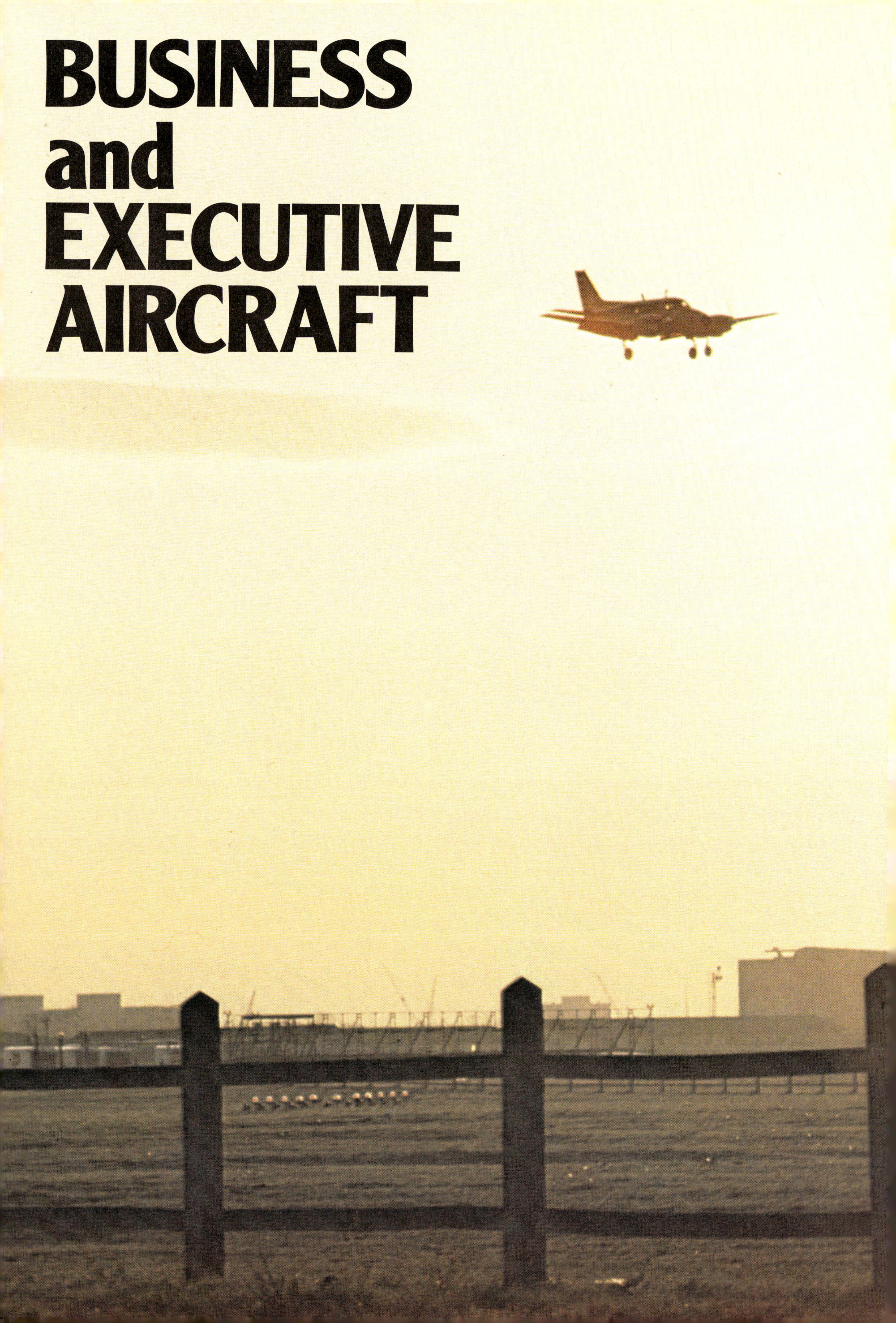

In this section are described aircraft which are mainly members of a family less than 20 years old: the executive or "biz-jet" (short for business jet) types. Also included are numerous light piston-engined and turboprop aircraft which are used for business rather than commercial airline purposes. The division between this and the previous section of the book is necessarily arbitrary, however, because hundreds of examples of the aircraft in this section do belong to airlines and are used on scheduled or air taxi services. In fact, one enterprising operator, Federal Express of Little Rock, Arkansas, built an entirely new kind of airline by buying a very large fleet of small so-called executive jets (Dassault-Breguet Falcons) and running a round-the-clock timetable carrying nothing but freight. On the other hand, many of the world's most important commercial operations are flown by the mainliners up to Jumbo size on a non-scheduled basis: some of the world's biggest passenger carriers run no regular scheduled services at all, but carry millions of people each year on what the trade calls ITX – for inclusive-tour excursion–flights; in other words, the package holiday. Such aircraft, of course, have been featured in the previous section.

All flying other than airline and military is known as General Aviation, or GA. The total GA fleet is almost a quarter of a million aircraft worldwide, of which 170,000 are in the United States; the fleet includes all sorts of aircraft types, from the personal Boeing 747 of the King of Saudi Arabia to helicopters, which are described in the next section, and small lightplanes and specialized machines, such as the growing fleet of Ag-planes used in agriculture, which are outside the scope of this book.

The main purpose of the aircraft described in this section is to carry passengers rapidly between points that are often off the scheduled airline map. Apart from extensive use in the business world, where biz-jets more than pay their way in terms of cost and efficiency, and personal use by the rich, these aircraft play an important role in the "third world", where the governments of many nations run a kind of airline with small transports serving communities which have no proper surface communications. These aircraft, used to navigate rough terrain, often have a much harder life than the jets of the scheduled airlines, which fly above the weather between first-class airports. In such operations, it is not uncommon for a flight to last only a few minutes of actual airborne time, though it may save hours of travel through jungle or across mountainous territory. Weather is often severe, and pilots may have to get acquainted with 20 new airstrips in a single week. And because these airstrips may lack facilities of any kind – the area may even be totally uninhabited – the aircraft have to be completely self-sufficient. The diversity of aircraft described here, and the numbers in which they have been built, show that the aircraft manufacturers have not been unsuccessful in meeting the special challenges posed by this kind of specialized operation.

American Jet Hustler 500
USA

Power plant: One Pratt & Whitney (Canada) PT6A-41 turboprop derated from 1,089hp to 850shp and one Pratt & Whitney JT15D-1 turbofan rated at 2,200lbst (1,000kgp).
Estimated performance: Max cruise, 460mph (740km/h) at 23,000ft (7,010m); economical cruise, 403mph (648km/h) at 40,000ft (12,192m); initial rate of climb, 4,950ft/min (25·1m/sec); operational ceiling, 40,000ft (12,192m); take-off distance to clear 50ft (15·2m), 1,500ft (457m); landing distance from 50ft (15·2m), 1,500ft (457m); range, 1,290–2,300mls (2,076–3,700km).
Weights: Empty, 4,681lb (2,125kg); max take-off, 9,500lb (4,313kg).
Dimensions: Span, 34ft 5in (10·49m); length, 41ft (12·49m); height, 13ft 1in (3·99m); wing area, 192·76sq ft (17·9m²).

Having entered the flight test stage on 11 January 1978 and expected to be available for service from 1979, the Model 500 Hustler is a new entry into the business transport field. American Jet Industries Inc announced its intention of developing such an aircraft during 1975; this being the first all-new aircraft to emerge from the company previously responsible for a number of specialized conversions of airline and business aircraft types by other manufacturers.

Features of the Hustler, which seats up to five passengers in addition to two pilots and has a cabin pressurized to "airline" standards with a differential of 8·0psi (0·56kg/cm²), include an advanced wing aerofoil section with supercritical characteristics, and the installation of a turbojet engine in the rear fuselage to provide twin-engine safety and performance. The prototype, known as the Hustler 400, has only the turboprop in the nose, and a Hustler 400A is projected with only an 800-lbst (363-kgp) turbojet in the tail.

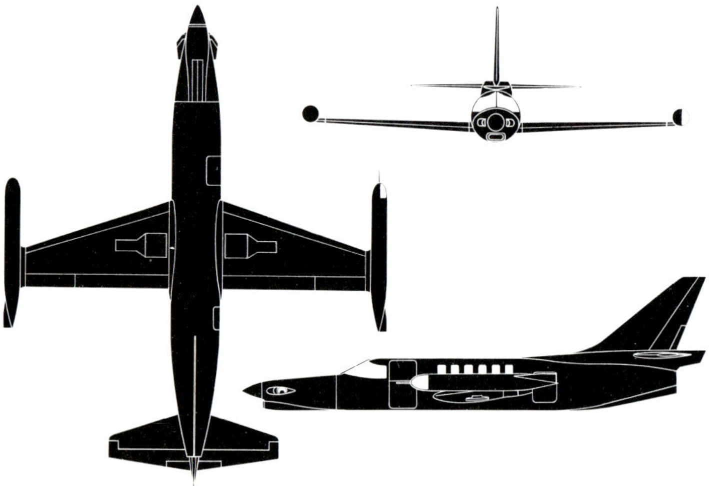

Above: Three-view drawing of the American Jet Hustler 500, the enlarged production derivative of the Hustler 400 prototype.

Below: The AJI Hustler 400 prototype, as first flown in January 1978 powered only by a turboprop in the nose. The production Hustler 500 also has a turbofan in the tail.

Beech Baron Model 55 and 58
USA

Power Plant: Two Continental IO-520-C flat-six piston engines each rated at 285hp for take-off.
Performance: Max speed, 242mph (390km/h) at sea level; economical cruising speed, 208mph (235km/h) at 12,000ft (3660m); initial rate of climb, 1,694ft/min (8·6m/sec); service ceiling, 17,800ft (5425m); take-off run, 1,403ft (428m); landing run, 1,044ft (318m); range, standard fuel, 1,212mls (950km).
Weights: Empty, 3,286lb (1490kg); max take-off, 5,400lb (2449kg).
Dimensions: 37ft 10in (11·53m); length, 29ft 10in (9·09m); height, 9ft 6in (2·90m); wing area, 199·2sq ft (18·50m²).

Beech Duke Model 60
USA

Power Plant: Two Lycoming TIO-541-E1C4 turbosupercharged flat-six engines each rated at 380hp for take-off.
Performance: Max speed, 286mph (460km/h) at 23,000ft (7010m); economic cruising speed, 205mph (330km/h) at 20,000ft (6100m); initial rate of climb, 1,601ft/min service ceiling, 30,000ft (9145m), take-off run, 2,006ft (611m); landing run, 1,318ft (402m); range, 1,157–1,413mls (1862–2274km) according to speed and altitude.
Weights: Empty, 4,275lb (1939kg); max take-off, 6,775lb (3073kg).
Dimensions: Span, 39ft 3¼in (11·97m); length, 33ft 10in (10·31m); height, 12ft 4in (3·76m); wing area, 212·9sq ft (19·78m²).

Added to the Beech range of business twins in 1968, following a first flight on 29 December 1966 and subsequent certification on 1 February 1968, the Duke is similar in size to the Baron but offers somewhat better performance through the use of more powerful engines and is therefore more expensive. Like the Baron, it seats four-six, but the standard Duke model is pressurized whereas this feature is offered only on the Baron 58P. About 400 Dukes were in service by early 1977, when the current production model was the B60, with specification as above.

Beech Queen Air
USA

Power Plant: Two 380hp Lycoming IGSO-540-A1D flat-six supercharged piston engines.
Performance: Max level speed, 248mph (400km/h) at 11,500ft (3500m); cruising speed, 225mph (362km/h) at 15,000ft (4570m) at 70 per cent power and 183mph (294km/h) at 15,000ft (4570m) for best range; initial rate of climb, 1,275ft/min (388m); service ceiling, 26,800ft (8168m); take-off run, 2,000ft (610m); landing run, 1,620ft (494m); range with max fuel, 1,100–1,517mls (1770–2440km) according to speed.
Weights: Empty, 5,277lb (2393kg); max take-off, 8,800lb (3992kg).
Dimensions: Span, 50ft 3in (15·32m); length, 35ft 6in (10·82m); height, 14ft 2½in (4·33m); wing area, 293·9sq ft (27·3m²).

The Queen Air was added to the Beech range of business twins in 1958, at which time it became the largest of the Beech twin-engined types (a distinction now held by the King Air). The prototype flew on 28 August 1958 and was produced as the Queen Air 65, distinguished by its unswept-back vertical tail surfaces. In the Queen Air A65, these surfaces took on the now familiar swept-back form, the engines in both these models being 340hp Lycoming IGSO-480-A1A6 flat sixes. The Queen Air 80, first flown on 22 June 1961, introduced 380hp IGSO-540-A1A Lycomings and in January 1964 the A80 appeared with these same engines but increased wing span and higher gross weight.

Further improvements were made in the B80, which was still in production

***Above:* The Baron 58, typical of the smaller piston-engined business twins operated in their hundreds, particularly in North America.**
***Left:* Three-view drawing of the Beech Baron 58, one of five variants in production in 1978.**

***Above:* The Baron is offered with several optional features, including pressurization and turbosuperchargers.**

The smallest of the Beech twins available in the business aircraft market, the Model 95-55 was developed as a successor for the Twin Bonanza and Travel Air series, flying as a prototype on 29 February 1960. A family of Baron designs is now available, some 4,000 examples in all having been built by early 1977. The basic 4-6 seat Barons are the 95-B55 with 260hp Continental IO-470-L engines and the Model E55 with 285hp IO-520-Cs. The Baron 58 was introduced at the end of 1969 with the same engines as the E55 but with a lengthened fuselage that provided more comfortable accommodation when the cabin was equipped to seat six. The range was later extended to include the Baron 58P, with a pressurized cabin and 310hp Continental TSIO-520-L engines and the Baron 58TC with the same powerplant but without pressurization. The specification above refers to the Baron 58.

***Above:* Three-view drawing of the Beech Duke, which is similar in size to the Baron but has a higher performance.**
***Right:* The Duke celebrated the 10th anniversary of its certification in 1978 but sales success has been only modest.**

***Left:* Three-view drawing of the Queen Air A80, the first version to introduce increased span.**

***Below:* The Queen Air with its roomy cabin has proved attractive to the air taxi and commuter airline operator.**

in 1977. Beech had also produced a number of Queen Air 70s, combining 340hp engines with the increased-span wing, but production of the Model 65 and 70 had ended by 1971, with some 450 built (including 71 for the US Army). Over 500 of the 80 series Queen Air had been built by 1977.

In its business transport role, the Queen Air usually seats four–six passengers in addition to the crew of two. Versions have also been built for the commuter airline market and these seat seven–nine passengers; they are known as Queen Airliners and have the same overall performance as the B80 executive model described above.

Beech King Air
USA

Power Plant: Two Pratt & Whitney (Canada) PT6A-21 turboprops each rated at 550ehp for take-off.
Performance: Max cruising speeds, 256mph (412km/h) at 12,000ft (3660m) and 249mph at 21,000ft (6400m); initial rate of climb, 1,955ft/min (9·9m/sec); service ceiling, 28,100ft (8565m); take-off distance to 50ft (15·2m), 2,261ft (689m); landing run, 1,075ft (328m); range with max fuel, 1,100–1,384mls (1773–2227km) according to altitude, with reserves; max range at economical cruising speed, 1,475mls (2374km) at 21,000ft (6400m).
Weights: Empty, 5,640lb (2558kg); max take-off, 9,650lb (4377kg).
Dimensions: Span, 50ft 3in (15·32m); length, 35ft 6in (10·82m); height, 14ft $2\frac{1}{2}$in (4·33m); wing area, 293·9sq ft (27·31m^2).

As its name suggests, the King Air is a derivative of the Queen Air (previously described), from which it differs primarily in having a pressurized cabin and turboprop power plant. Like the Queen Air, the type is used to a limited extent by small airlines for commuting and air taxi operations, but the great majority of King Airs built are for business use. Total production of all variants by the end of 1976 exceeded 1,000, including a few for military use.

Development of the King Air began with the installation of PT6A turboprops in a Queen Air airframe. This was followed by the first flight of a true King Air prototype on 20 January 1964 and initial production deliveries of the Model 90 later the same year. The Model 90 with PT6A-6 engines was superseded by the A90 and B90 with slightly more powerful PT6A-20s and the C90, current in 1977, with PT6A-21s and cabin improvements. All these variants had the same dimensions and provided accommodation for a crew of two and, typically, six passengers although arrangements were available for up to 15 seats in a high-density layout.

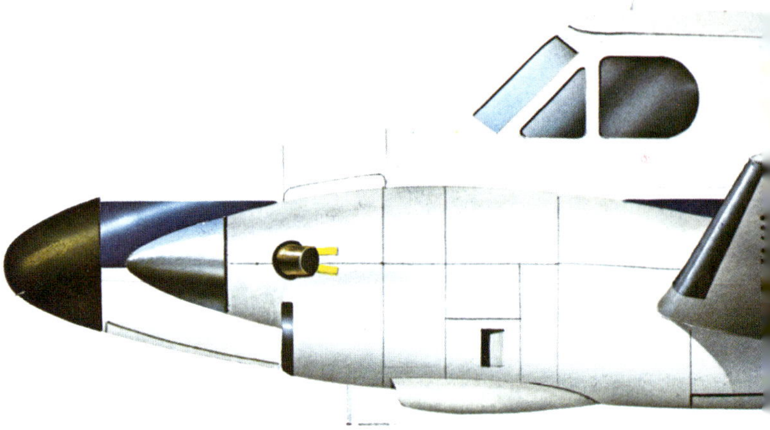

In 1969, Beech introduced the larger King Air 100, with more powerful PT6A-28 engines, cabin lengthened by 4ft 2in (1·27m), wing span reduced and other changes. Seating is normally for 6–8 passengers in the King Air 100, or up to 13 for commuter airline use. The A100 is similar with a series of refinements and the B100, also in production in 1977, uses 715shp Garrett AiResearch TPE 331-6-252B turboprops in place of the Canadian Pratt & Whitney units. By combining the uprated PT6A-28s of the King Air 100 with the smaller airframe of the King Air C90, Beech was able to offer the E90 from 1972 onwards, this having improved field performance. The data refer to the King Air C90.

Beech Super King Air 200
USA

Power Plant: Two Pratt & Whitney (Canada) PT6A-41 turboprops each rated at 850shp for take-off.
Performance: Max speed, 333mph (536km/h) at 15,000ft (4570m); economical cruising speed, 313mph (503km/h) at 25,000ft (7620m); initial rate of climb, 2,450ft (12·4m/sec); service ceiling, 31,000ft (9450m); take-off run, 1,942ft (592m); landing run, 1,760ft (536m); take-off run, 1,942ft (592m); landing run, 1,760ft (536m); range 1,370–2,000mls (2204–3218km) according to speed and altitude.
Weights: Empty equipped, 7,315lb (3318kg); max take-off and landing, 12,500lb (5670kg).
Dimensions: Span, 54ft 6in (16·61m); length, 43ft 10in (13·36m); height, 14ft 10in (4·52m); wing area, 303sq ft (28·15m^2).

The Super King 200 joined the Beech range of business twins during 1974 after a four-year period of development and the type is now in production as the largest of the Beech executive transports, for both commercial and

Canadair Challenger
Canada

Power Plant: Two Avco Lycoming ALF 502 turbofans each rated at 7,500lb st (3405kgp) for take-off.
Performance: Max cruising speed, 581mph (935km/h) above 36,000ft (10,980m); long-range cruise speed, 528mph (850km/h); time to climb to 40,000ft (12,200m), 15·5min; take-off distance required, 4,700ft (1434m); landing distance required, 4,400ft (1342m); range with 14 passengers and reserves, 3,220mls (5185km) at Mach=0·85 cruise.
Weights: Operating weight empty, 16,900lb (7673kg); max payload, over 3,000lb (1362kg); max take-off weight, 32,500lb (14,755kg); max landing weight, 31,000lb (14,074kg).
Dimensions: Span, 59ft 9in (18·22m); length, 63ft 10in (19·48m); height, 19ft $8\frac{1}{2}$in (6·01m); wing area, 420sq ft (39·02m^2).

Marking the Canadian entry into the business jet market, Canadair Ltd acquired during 1976 the production and marketing rights in a twin turbofan aircraft designed by William P ("Bill") Lear, who had previously been

Far left: Beech King Air Model 100. Five variants of the King Air were in production in 1978.

Left: Three-view of the Beech King Air A100. Versions with Pratt & Whitney and Garrett AiResearch turboprops are in production.

Below: A Beech King Air A90 in Lufthansa service; the German airline operates four of these aircraft for pilot training.

Left: The Super King Air 200, first of the Beech business twins to feature a T-tail.

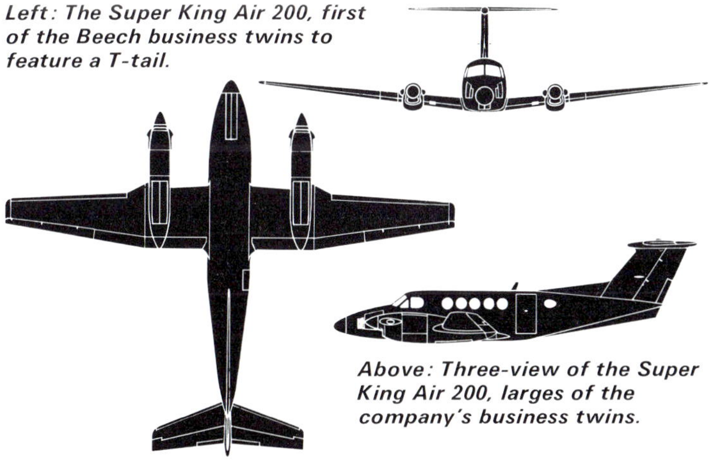

Above: Three-view of the Super King Air 200, larges of the company's business twins.

military use. Retaining the same basic fuselage cross-section and structural design as the King Air 100, the Super King Air has a longer fuselage, more powerful engines on a wider wing centre section (to reduce noise levels in the cabin) and a T-tail. The last-mentioned feature was adopted after careful investigation and has subsequently become something of a "trade mark" for newer Beech types such as the Model 76 light twin and the Model 77 single-engined trainer/tourer.

Initially identified as the Model 101, the prototype of the Beech Super King Air 200 first flew on 27 October 1972 and was followed by a second on 15 December the same year. FAA certification was obtained in December 1973 and production deliveries began immediately. By the end of 1975, Beech had delivered 100 Super King Airs for commercial use and 22 military versions for the USAF and US Army; a further 105 were delivered in 1976. As a business aircraft, the Super King Air 200 carries a crew of one or two with, typically, six seats in the cabin; up to 13 passengers can be carried in the third level/commuter airline version, a few examples of which are in service. Provision has been made for the Super King Air 200 to carry wing-tip fuel tanks to increase the endurance by one hour, the first examples with this feature having been delivered in 1977 to the French Institut Geographique National for air survey duties.

Left: The first Canadair Challenger on the occasion of its roll-out in Montreal on 25 May 1978.

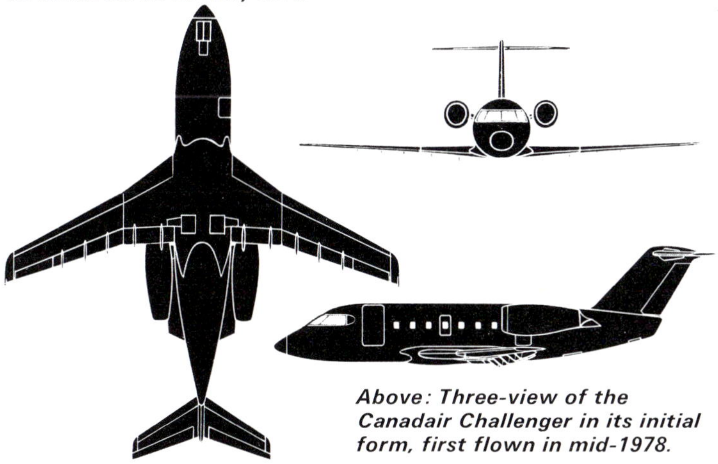

Above: Three-view of the Canadair Challenger in its initial form, first flown in mid-1978.

responsible for the initial design of the Learjet biz jets, described separately. The new design, larger than the Learjet family, was initially known as the LearStar 600 and was based from the outset upon a wing of supercritical design characteristics as evolved at the NACA by Richard T Whitcomb.

After a close analysis of the potential market and its own needs for a new manufacturing programme, Canadair confirmed an option to acquire the LearStar 600 design rights in the late summer of 1976, and then spent several months refining the design and confirming performance with the chosen power plant, in order to offer a guaranteed specification and price for the initial batch of aircraft. In addition to small changes in dimensions and detail design, a T-tail was adopted in this period, marking a major change from the original LearStar 600 project.

Construction of a pre-production batch of three Challengers was put in hand during 1977 with a target first flight date in 1978 to allow deliveries to begin in the second quarter of 1979. By the time the first aircraft flew, 102 Challengers were on order, plus an option on 25 in stretched configuration to be used by Federal Express in the USA on its extensive network of short-haul scheduled cargo services. In passenger configuration, the Challenger has a flight crew of two and, typically, 10–11 passengers for business use or up to 30 in third level/commuter type airline service.

Cessna Skymaster
USA

Power Plant: Two Continental IO-360-C flat-six piston engines each rated at 210hp for take-off.
Performance: Max speed at sea level, 206mph (332km/h); economical cruising speed, 147mph (237km/h); initial rate of climb, 1,100ft/min (5·7m/sec); service ceiling, 18,000ft (5490m); take-off run, 1,000ft (305m); landing run, 700ft (213m); range with standard fuel, 627–771mls (1009–1241km) according to speed.
Weights: Empty, 2,710lb (1229kg); max take-off, 4,630lb (2100kg); max landing, 4,400lb (1995kg).
Dimensions: Span, 38ft 2in (11·63m); length, 29ft 9in (9·07m); height, 9ft 2in (2·79m); wing area, 202·5sq ft (18·81m^2).

A unique twin-boom layout was adopted by Cessna for its Model 336 Skymaster business twin, introduced in 1963 after extensive studies to establish that the arrangement of two engines on the centre line of the aeroplane – one driving a tractor propeller, the other a pusher – offered particular advantages of safety, low cost and simplicity. The prototype flew on 28 February 1961 and certification was obtained in May 1962.

The Model 336 had a fixed tricycle undercarriage, but the Model 337, introduced in February 1965, has retractable gear together with numerous other changes and improvements. A version with turbosupercharged engines was subsequently offered as the Turbo-System Super Skymaster but this was in turn superseded by the Model P337 Pressurized Skymaster, which flew on 23 July 1971 and was first delivered in May 1972, becoming the cheapest twin-engined pressurized aircraft available in the commercial market.

By the end of 1976, well over 2,000 Skymasters of all types had been built, including a number by Reims Aviation in France under licence from Cessna. The specification refers to the standard Model 337 Skymaster.

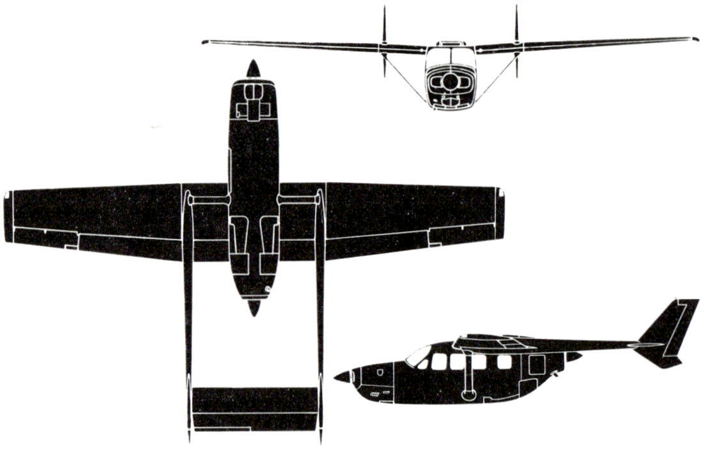

***Above:** Three-view of the Cessna Skymaster, which has a unique configuration for a twin-engined business aircraft.*

***Right:** Cessna Skymaster 337, carrying a freight "Speedpak" under the fuselage. A pressurized version is also produced.*

Cessna 340
USA

Power Plant: Two Continental TS10-520-N flat-six piston engines each rated at 310hp for take-off.
Performance: Max level speed, 278mph (448km/h) at 20,000ft (6100m); economical cruising speed, 214mph (344km/h) at 25,000ft (7620m); initial rate of climb, 1650ft/min (503m); service ceiling, 29,800ft (9085m); take-off run, 1615ft (492m); landing run, 760ft (232m); range, 1139–1481mls (1833–2383km) according to speed altitude.
Weights: Empty, 3868lb (1754kg); max take-off and landing, 5990lb (2717kg).
Dimensions: Span, 38ft 1in (11·62m); length, 34ft 4in (10·46m); height, 12ft 7in (3·84m); wing area, 184sq ft (17·09m).

First flown on 3 January 1953, the Model 310 was Cessna's first business twin, and it has remained in production ever since, some 4500 having been built by early 1977. Current versions seat up to six including the pilot and are powered by 285hp Continental IO-520-M or 285hp TSIO-520-B turbosupercharged engines. Primarily in use for executive transportation, the Cessna 310 is also operated as an air taxi by a number of small airline operators in various parts of the world.

In 1971, Cessna added the Model 340 to its range by combining features of the Model 310 and the larger Model 414, described separately. With 285hp TSIO-520-K engines, similar to those used to power the turbosupercharged T310, the Model 340 has a pressurized fuselage and the wing and landing gear are similar to those of the Model 414. The standard layout provides four seats in the cabin plus two pilots side-by-side. Adding to the utility of this and other Cessna twins is the provision of baggage lockers in the wing, with further capacity in the nose and the rear of the cabin.

The following data refer to the 1976-model Cessna 340A; total deliveries of the 340 series by the end of 1976 were approaching 500.

***Above:** Three-view of the Cessna 340, one of the numerous twin-engined business aircraft developed by Cessna since 1945.*

***Below:** A cruising Cessna 340. Relatively small windows in the fuselage are indicative of the use of a pressure cabin.*

Cessna 401, 402 and 411

USA

Power Plant: Two Continental TSIO-520-E flat-six piston engines each rated at 300hp for take-off.
Performance: Max speed, 261mph (420km/h) at 16,000ft (4875m); max cruising speed, 240mph (386km/h) at 20,000ft (6100m); initial rate of climb, 1,610ft/min (8·2m/sec); service ceiling, 26,180ft (7980m); take-off run, 1,695ft (517m); landing run, 777ft (237m); range, 1,156–1,417mls (1860–2280km).
Weights: Empty, 3,896lb (1767kg); max take-off, 6,300lb (2857kg); max landing, 6,200lb (2812kg).
Dimensions: Span, 39ft $10\frac{1}{4}$in (12·15m); length, 36ft 1in (11·0m); height, 11ft 8in (3·56m); wing area, 195·7sq ft (18·18m²).

***Above:* Three-view drawing of the Cessna 411, the largest of the company's range when introduced in 1962.**

Development of a "big brother" for the Model 310 series was launched by Cessna in the early 'sixties and led to the introduction of the Model 411, first flown on 18 July 1962. When deliveries began in February 1965 this was the largest of the Cessna twins, but production continued for only three years, with 301 built. Many are still in use in the mid-seventies.

Closely related to the Model 411, but lighter and cheaper, the Cessna 401 first flew on 26 August 1965 and was aimed specifically at the business market with up to eight seats including the pilot. The Model 402 was offered in parallel with the 401, and was intended specifically for the third level/commuter airline market, featuring a strengthened floor for light cargo carrying as an alternative to a 10-seat commuter interior. In 1971, the Model 402B appeared, with a lengthened nose and optional Utili-liner and Business-liner configurations, and production of the Model 401 ended. By the middle of 1977, nearly 1,000 Model 402s had been built, including a few for military use but primarily in business or airline configuration. The specification refers to the Model 402 Utililiner.

A turboprop conversion of the Model 402 has also been developed, by American Jet Industries, as the Turbo Star 402 with 400shp Allison 250B-17 engines.

***Below:* A Cessna 411 of TAM, a Brazilian air taxi operator. The wing-tip fuel tanks are a permanent feature.**

Cessna 414 Chancellor and 421

USA

Power Plant: Two Continental GTSIO-520-M flat-six engines, each rated at 375hp for take-off.
Performance: Max speed, 295mph (474km/h) at 20,000ft (6096m); max cruising speed, 276mph (445km/h) at 25,000ft (7620m); initial rate of climb, 1,940ft/min (9·8m/sec); service ceiling, 30,200ft (9205m); take-off run, 1,786ft (544m); landing run, 720ft (219m); range, 1,271–1,712mls (2045–2755km) according to speed and altitude.
Weights: Empty, 4,501lb (2041kg); max take-off, 7,450lb (3379kg); max landing, 7,200lb (3265kg).
Dimensions: Span, 41ft $1\frac{1}{2}$in (11·53m); length, 36ft $4\frac{1}{2}$in (11·09m); height, 11ft $5\frac{1}{2}$in (3·49m) wing area, 215sq ft (19·97m^2).

The Model 421 was first flown by Cessna on 14 October 1965, to become the company's largest twin and a replacement for the previously-described Model 411. The principal new feature of the Model 421 was that it had a pressurized cabin, permitting higher cruising altitudes to be achieved. With FAA approval obtained on 1 May 1967, deliveries began in the same month.

Successive improvements led to the introduction of the Model 421B, named Golden Eagle in its business transport version and Executive Commuter in a 10-seat variant for the third level/commuter airline, and then the Model 421C in 1976, with a new wing containing integral fuel tanks that made the tip tanks unnecessary. Over 1,200 Model 421s had been built by the end of 1976 and a number of these were in airline service. The specification refers to the Model 421C Golden Eagle.

On 1 November 1968, Cessna flew the prototype of another variant in the "400" family of business twins, this being the Model 414. This made use of the wing of the Model 401 combined with the pressurized fuselage of the Model 421; the engines were 310hp Continental TSIO-520-Ns, and up to five passengers could be carried in addition to the two pilots. Some 450 Cessna 414s had been built by early 1977, with production continuing.

In 1978, Cessna introduced a revised version of the Model 414 as the Chancellor, featuring the larger span wing, with integral fuel and without tip tanks, previously adopted for the Model 421C. The Chancellor also has a larger nose than the Model 414, with extra baggage capacity.

Right: A Cessna 421C in flight; a pressurized fuselage combined with a "wet wing" made tip tanks unnecessary.

Below: The Cessna 414, with a similar fuselage to the Model 421 but the older type of wing.

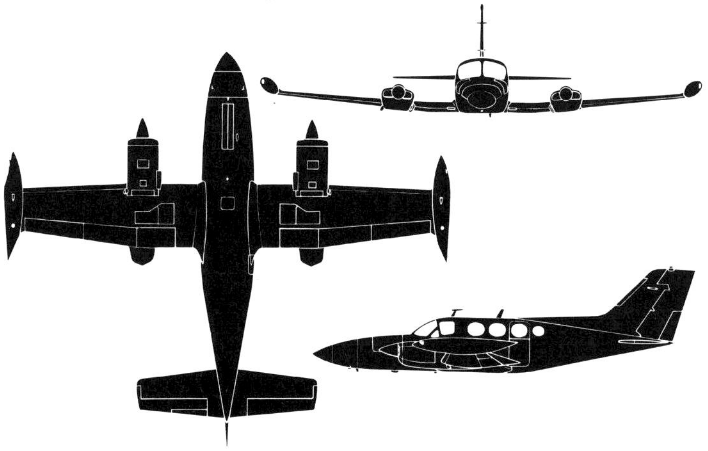

Cessna 404 Titan

USA

Power Plant: Two Continental GTSIO-520M flat-six piston engines, each rated at 375hp for take-off.
Performance: Max speed, 225mph (363km/h), at sea level and 269mph (433km/h) at 16,000ft (4877m); max cruising speed, 223mph (359km/h) at 10,000ft (3050m); initial rate of climb, 1,515ft/min (7·7m/sec); service ceiling, 22,200ft (6767m); take-off distance to 50ft (15·2m), 2,240ft (683m); range, 1,020mls (1641km) with 10 occupants; range, 2,060mls (3315km) with six occupants.
Weights: Empty, 4,754lb (2156kg); max take-off 8,300lb (3705kg); max landing weight, 8,100lb (3674kg).
Dimensions: Span, 46ft 0in (14·02m); length, 39ft 5in (12·04m); height 13ft 1in (3·99m); wing area, 242sq ft (22·48m^2).

Now the largest of the piston-engined twins offered by Cessna, the Titan was announced in July 1975 and deliveries began at the end of 1976, the

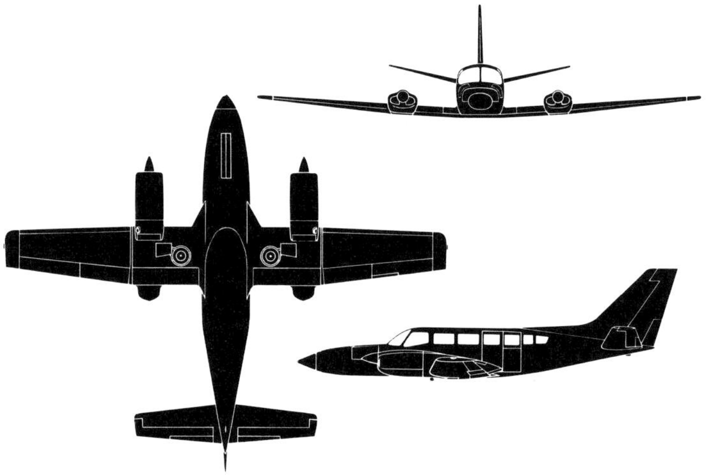

Cessna 441 Conquest

USA

Power Plant: Two Garrett-AiResearch TPE331-8-401S turboprops each flat rated to 635shp up to 16,000ft (4877m).
Performance: Max speed, 340mph (547km/h) at 16,000ft (4877m); max cruising speed, 328mph (528km/h) at 17,000ft (5182m); initial rate of climb, 2,435ft/min (12·435m/sec); service ceiling, 37,000ft (11,278m); take-off distance to 50ft (15·2m), 2,465ft (751m); landing distance from 50ft (15·2m), 1,875ft (592m); range with 11 occupants and reserves, at max cruise speed, 1,466mls (2383km).
Weights: Empty, 5,589lb (2535kg); max take-off weight, 9,850lb (4468kg); max landing weight, 9,360lb (4246kg).
Dimensions: Span, 49ft 4in (15·04m); length, 39ft $0\frac{1}{4}$in (11·89m); height, 13ft 1in (3·99m); wing area, 253sq ft (23·5m^2).

The success of its extensive family of piston-engined business twins and of the Citation twin-jet, all of which are described separately, served to delay Cessna's entry into the turboprop transport market. Following an initial announcement of plans to introduce a turboprop-engined business aircraft in November 1974, a prototype made its first flight on 26 August 1975 as the Model 441, subsequently named Conquest.

For the first series of test flights, the prototype had Garrett AiResearch TPE331-8-251 turboprops but these were replaced in mid-1976 with definitive TPE331-8-401S engines having a maximum output of 865shp but derated in the Conquest to give a constant 625shp at all altitudes up to 16,000ft (4877m). Flight testing also led to an increase in wing span, which allowed more fuel to be carried and improved overall performance by increasing the aspect ratio.

First production Conquests with the modified wing were flying in early 1977 and after certification by the FAA, deliveries began in mid-year. Typically, the Conquest seats up to 10 passengers in addition to the pilot and although developed primarily for the business market as a "step-up" aircraft for users of Cessna piston-twin, it is also expected to find applications in the third-level/commuter airline market.

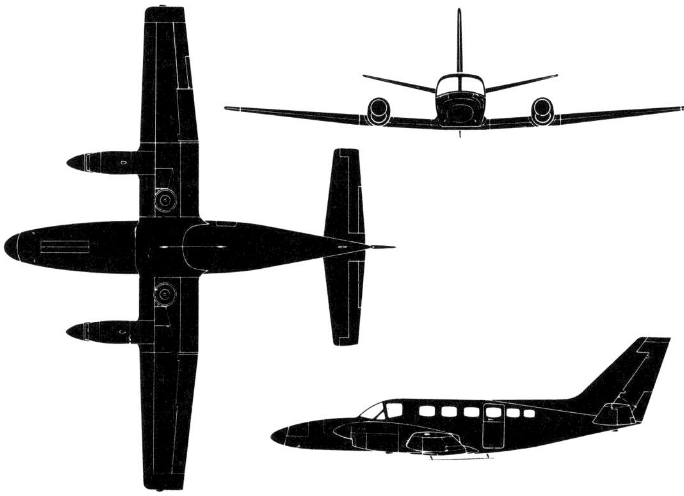

Above: Three-view of the Cessna 441 Conquest, the first of the company's business twins to feature turboprop power.

Right: One of the early production models of the Cessna Conquest, deliveries of which were under way during 1978.

prototype having flown on 26 February 1975. Like the Model 421, the Titan is offered in versions equipped specifically for the needs of the businessman and of the third-level/commuter airline. Its wing and landing gear are substantially the same as those of the Model 441 Conquest; the fuselage is new, offering substantially more capacity than available in the Model 402.

Versions of the Titan equipped for passenger-carrying are designated Titan Ambassador and seat, typically, six passengers in executive comfort. For the third level/commuter market, the Titan Courier can carry up to 10 occupants including the pilot and the cabin provides 284cu ft (8·04m*)*) of volume in a total cabin length of 18ft 9in (5·72m). An extra large cargo door is available as an option, and seat tracks along the whole length of the cabin allow the maximum of flexibility of layouts.

Deliveries of the Titan began in October 1976, totalling 17 by the end of the year and the type seemed likely to attract attention from the smaller airlines as well as business users.

***Left:** Three-view drawing of the Cessna Titan, a 6–8 seat twin with Cessna's ''wet wing'' and an unpressurized cabin.*
***Right:** The Titan in flight, showing the clean lines of the ''wet wing'' which has been introduced on successive Cessna models.*

Cessna Citation I and II
USA

Power Plant: Two Pratt & Whitney (Canada) JT15D-1A turbofans each rated at 2,200lb st (998kgp) for take off.
Performance: Maximum cruising speed, 404mph (650km/h) at average weight; initial rate of climb, 2,680ft/min (13·6m/sec); max certificated operating altitude, 41,000ft (12,505m); take-off distance to 35ft (10·1m), 2,750ft (839m); landing distance, 2,300ft (702m); range with six passengers and reserves, 1,535mls (2470km).
Weights: Typical weight empty, 6,464lb (2935kg); max take-off weight, 12,850lb (5834kg); max landing weight, 11,350lb (5153kg).
Dimensions: Span, 47ft 1in (14·36m); length, 43ft 6in (13·27m); height 14ft 4in (4·37m).

***Below:** Three-view of the Citation II, the slightly enlarged version of the original Cessna 500 Citation biz-jet.*

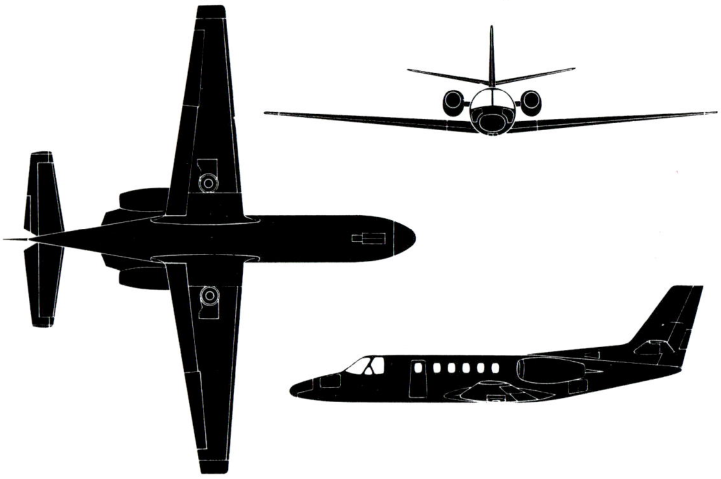

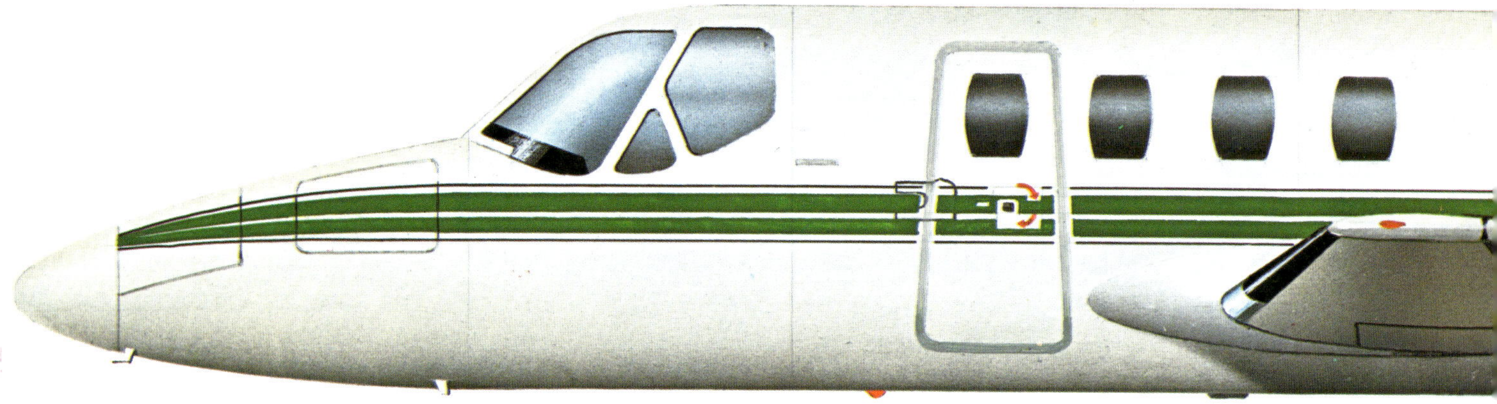

Cessna Citation III
USA

Power Plant: Two Garrett AiResearch TFE731-3 -100S turbofans each rated at 3,700lb st (1680kgp) for take-off.
Performance: Max cruising speed, 540mph (869km/h) at average weight; initial rate of climb, 5,325ft/min (27·1m/sec); max certificated operating ceiling, 50,000ft (15,240m); take-off field length, 3,900ft (1189m); landing distance, 3,100ft (945m); range with max payload and reserves, 2,760mls (4440km).
Weights: Typical empty weight, 9,441lb (4286kg); max take-off weight, 17,150lb (7786kg); max landing, 15,700lb (7128kg).
Dimensions: Span, 50ft 7in (15·43m); length, 51ft 7in (15·73m); height, 17ft 0in (5·19m).

After some three years of design activity to define a "big brother" for the Citation, featuring larger passenger capacity and greater range, the Cessna company finally announced details of the definitive Citation III towards the end of 1976. Earlier proposals had covered the Citation 600, which was an enlarged version of the basic Citation, and then the Model 700 Citation III, a three-engined, straight-winged project in 1974. As finally launched, the Citation III is twin-engined with a swept-back wing, the section of which is based upon NASA research into the application of supercritical technology to general aviation aircraft.

The Citation III was scheduled to make its first flight in March 1979, and provisional type certification was to be achieved by January 1981, by which time demonstration aircraft would be available. Customer deliveries were to begin in March 1981.

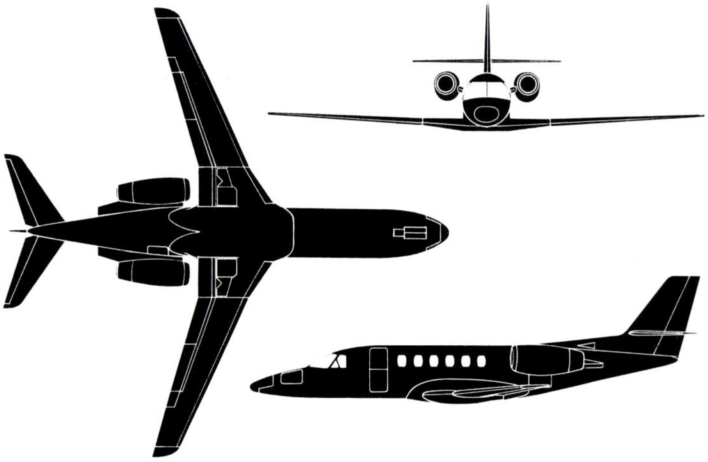

***Above:** Three-view drawing of the Cessna Citation III which, despite its name, is virtually a completely new design.*

The Cessna company, world leader in the production of piston-engined aircraft for general aviation, announced its plans to introduce a business jet in October 1968, under the name Fanjet 500. A prototype flew about a year later, on 15 September 1969, at which time the name was changed to Model 500 Citation. After a second prototype had flown on 23 January 1970 and the first production model had been launched, FAA certification was obtained on 9 September 1971, allowing deliveries to begin.

Successive increases have been made in the operating weights of the Citation during production of 350 examples up to the end of 1976. A switch was then made to the improved Model 501 Citation I which has uprated engines and an increase of 7ft 3in (2·21m) in wing span; the specification above refers to this variant, deliveries of which began at the beginning of 1977. The Citation and Citation I have the same size of fuselage and cabin, with provision for a maximum of eight seats including the two pilots; a version is also available certificated for single pilot operation, known as the Citation I/SP, and examples of this are used by American Airlines for its pilot training programme.

On 31 January 1977, Cessna made the first flight of its Citation II, a partner for the Citation I featuring uprated engines (2,500lb st/1135kgp JT15D-4s), lengthened fuselage, increased wing span and higher weights. Able to seat 10 passengers plus a crew of two, the Citation II has a range of over 2,000mls (3220km) and deliveries were to begin in February 1978. The Citation III, sharing the name of Cessna's first business jet, is in fact a totally new design, described separately below.

Left: The Cessna 500 Citation was the company's first business jet, over 400 having been sold by 1978.

Below: The Cessna Citation has the low-wing, rear-engined configuration of most biz-jets now on the market.

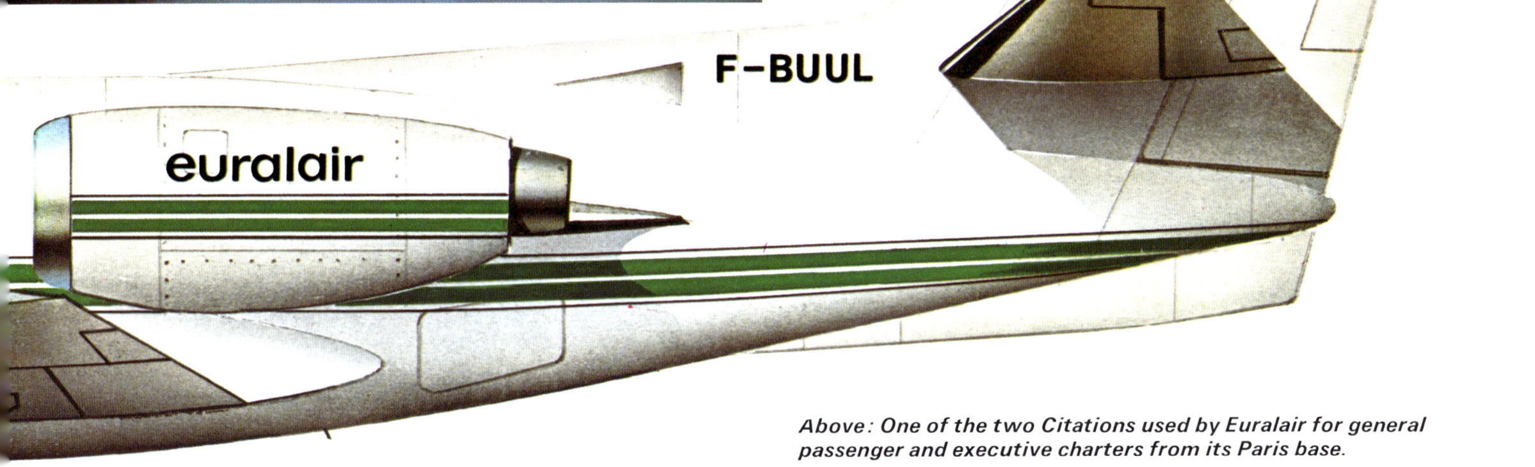

Above: One of the two Citations used by Euralair for general passenger and executive charters from its Paris base.

Above: An impression of the Cessna Citation III as first projected, with a third engine and a T-tail.

Above: The Cessna Citation III as launched in 1977, with a supercritical wing and conventional twin-engined layout.

Dassault-Breguet Falcon 10

France

Power Plant: Two Garrett-AiResearch TFE731-2 turbofans each rated at 3,230lb st (1466kgp) for take-off.
Performance: Max cruising speed, 568mph (915km/h) at 30,000ft (9145m) and 495mph or Mach 0·75 at 45,000ft (13,716m); take-off field length required, 4,100ft (1250m); landing run, 2,070ft (630m); range with four passengers and reserves, 2,210mls (3555km).
Weights: Empty equipped, 10,760lb (4880kg); max payload, 1,740lb (789kg); max take-off weight, 18,740lb (8500kg); max landing weight, 17,640lb (8000kg).
Dimensions: Span, 42ft 11in (13·08m); length, 45ft 5in (13·85m); height, 15ft 1½in (4·61m); wing area, 259sq ft (24·1m²).

The Falcon 10 (or Mystère 10) emerged in 1969 as a "baby brother" for the Falcon 20 previously described, with the same overall configuration but dimensions scaled down and less powerful engines. Standard layouts provide for 4–7 passengers with a crew of two.

Several engine options were considered by Dassault-Breguet, the Falcon 10 requiring about 6,600lb (2996kg) of thrust to achieve its designed performance. The prototype, first flown on 1 December 1970, had two General Electric CJ610 turbojets as a temporary expedient but by the time the second Falcon 10 flew on 15 October 1971, a decision had been made in favour of the Garrett AiResearch TFE731-2 turbofans and these have been used to power production aircraft to date. The French-designed Larzac turbofan was also considered as a potential engine for the Falcon 10, but has flown in only one example used as an engine test bed.

Like the Falcon 20, the Falcon 10 is marketed in North America by Falcon Jet Corporation, which placed an initial order for 54 with options on another 106. Deliveries began in November 1973 and 149 had been sold by the end of 1977.

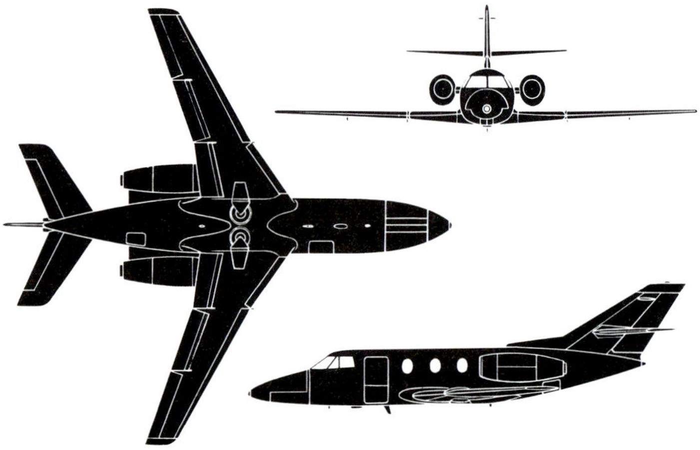

Above: Three-view of the Dassault-Breguet Falcon 10, the smallest of the company's range of biz-jets.

Above: The family of Dassault-Breguet business-jets in formation. Heading the flight is the first prototype of the Falcon 50, the long-fuselage, three-engined derivative of the Falcon 20 (right

Dassault-Breguet Falcon 20

France

Power Plant: Two General Electric CF700-2D-2 turbofans each rated at 4,315lb st (1960kgp) for take-off.
Performance: Max cruising speed, 536mph (862km/h) at 25,000ft (7620m); economical cruising speed, 466mph (750km/h) at 40,000ft (12,200m); absolute ceiling, 42,000ft (12,800m); take-off to 35ft (10·7m); 3,790ft (1155m); landing distance from 50ft (15·2m), 1,930ft (590m); range with max fuel, 2,230mls (3570km).
Weights: Empty equipped, 15,970lb (7240kg); max payload, 3,320lb (1500kg); max take-off weight, 28,660lb (13,000kg).
Dimensions: Span, 53ft 6in (16·30m); length, 56ft 3in (17·15m); height, 17ft 5in (5·32m); wing area, 440sq ft (41·00m²).

The Dassault company entered the biz-jet market in 1961 with the design of a typical "first generation" executive transport featuring rear-mounted engines, swept-back wings, a cruciform tail and cabin space for eight–ten passengers. Powered by Pratt & Whitney JT12A-8 turbojets, the prototype flew on 4 May 1963; subsequently, Dassault decided to use General Electric CF700 turbofans and the prototype re-engined with these units flew on 10 July 1964. Certification of the basic aircraft, known in France as the Mystere XX, was obtained on 9 June 1965, by which time the Business Jets Division of Pan American World Airways had become responsible for marketing the type in North America, under the name Fan Jet Falcon or just Falcon 20.

Sales of the Mystère/Falcon 20 totalled 437 at the end of 1977, with about two in every three going to the North American market where Falcon Jet Corporation, jointly owned by Dassault-Breguet and Pan American, is now responsible for sales. Successive production batches have introduced various improvements: uprated engines on the Falcon C, more fuel in the Falcon D, a further uprating of the engines for the Falcon E and then a major series of improvements including more fuel and new leading and trailing edge flaps in the Falcon F, which was 1977's standard production model.

In basic executive transport form, the Falcon F seats up to 10 passengers with a crew of two, but layouts are available for 12–14 passengers in a third-level/commuter rôle, for cargo carrying with a forward freight loading door (Falcon Cargo Jet, 33 of which serve with Federal Express Corporation in the USA), and for such duties as airline crew training and calibration.

Following the selection of a version of the Falcon by the US Coast Guard early in 1977 to meet its requirements for a maritime surveillance aircraft, the Falcon G is also to be offered commercially. It differs from the Falcon F primarily in having 5,050lb st (2293kgp) Garrett AiResearch ATF 3–6 turbofans, the lower sfc of which bestows upon this variant a greatly increased range. A prototype of the Falcon G flew on 28 November 1977. The new engine installation is also available as a retrofit on the Falcon F, to which the specification refers.

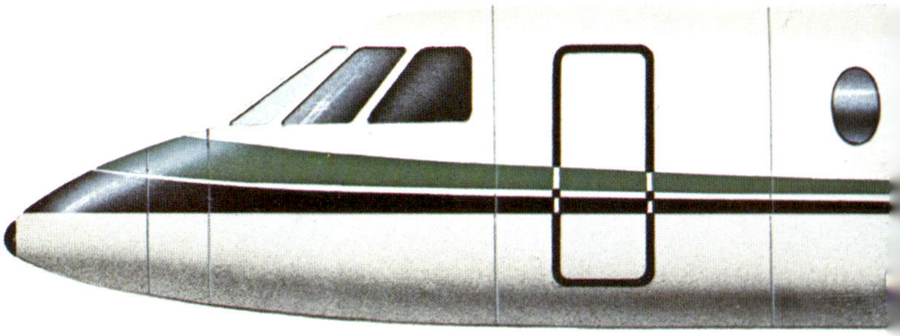

foreground), which was the company's original entry into the market. They and the smaller Falcon 10 (right background) have sold particularly well in the USA.

Dassault-Breguet Falcon 50

France

Power Plant: Three Garrett AiResearch TFE731-3 turbofans each rated at 3,700lb st (1680kgp) for take-off.
Performance: Max cruising speed, 540mph (870km/h); take-off run, 5,415ft (1650m); landing run, 3,280ft (1000m); range, 3,450mls (5560km) cruising at Mach 0·73 with four passengers and reserves.
Weights: Empty equipped, 19,840lb (9000kg); max take-off, 36,600lb (16,600kg); max landing, 34,855lb (15,810kg).
Dimensions: Span, 61ft $10\frac{1}{2}$in (18·86m); length, 60ft $5\frac{3}{4}$in (18·43m); height, 18ft $8\frac{1}{2}$in (5·70m); wing area, 495sq ft (46m^2).

Considerable design effort was expended by the Dassault-Breguet company in the early 'seventies to define a "big brother" for the Falcon 20 – an aircraft that would offer extended range and a greater degree of comfort for the executive passenger and would also have application in the third level/commuter airline market. The design eventually launched, in May 1974, is the Falcon (Mystère) 50, a prototype of which flew for the first time on 7 November 1976; after a short initial series of flight tests, a new wing was fitted and testing was resumed on 6 May 1977.

Using the same fuselage cross section as the Falcon 20, the Falcon 50 is able to incorporate certain common components, but the fuselage is longer, the tail surfaces are larger and the wing is based on the advanced aerodynamics used for the Dassault-Breguet Mercure, with double-slotted trailing edge flaps. The power plant arrangement is also significantly different, with a third engine added in the rear fuselage and fed by a dorsal intake.

The Falcon 50 is designed, like the Falcon 20, to carry 8–10 passengers and production deliveries were scheduled to begin at the end of 1978 following completion of further aircraft for the test programme in 1978. By the time the first aircraft flew, some 50 options had been taken on the Falcon 50, mostly in the USA where marketing is the responsibility of Falcon Jet Corporation, and firm sales totalled 71 by the end of 1977.

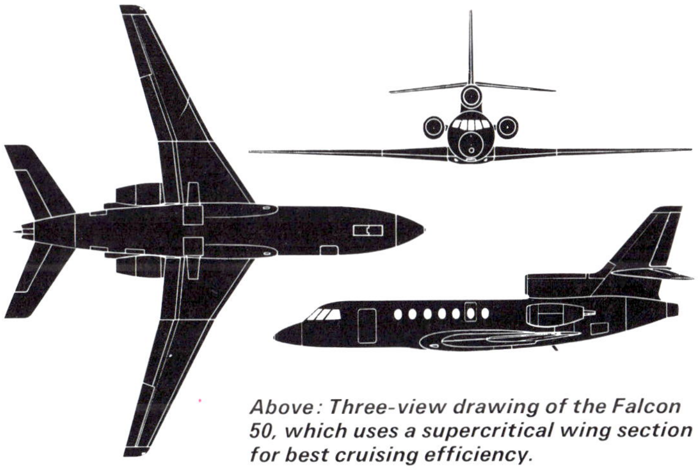

Above: Three-view drawing of the Falcon 50, which uses a supercritical wing section for best cruising efficiency.

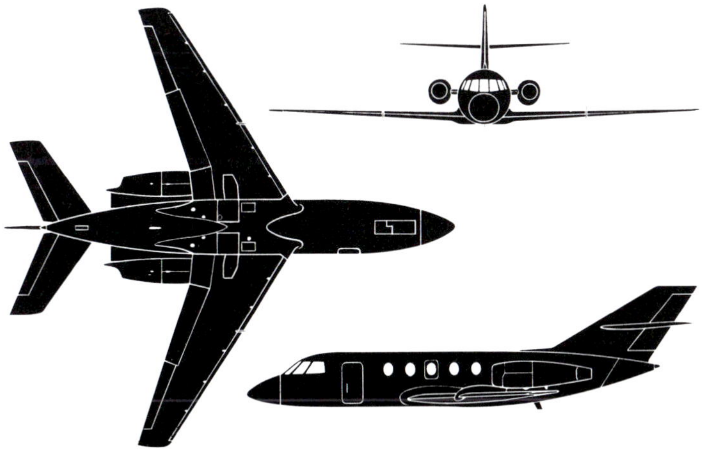

Left: Three-view of the Falcon 20. The name Falcon is used primarily outside Europe, as an alternative to Mystère.

Below: Business Jets Pty Ltd was founded in 1966 with a single Falcon 20 to operate executive charters, and has now added scheduled commuter services to its operations. The original Falcon 20 is illustrated.

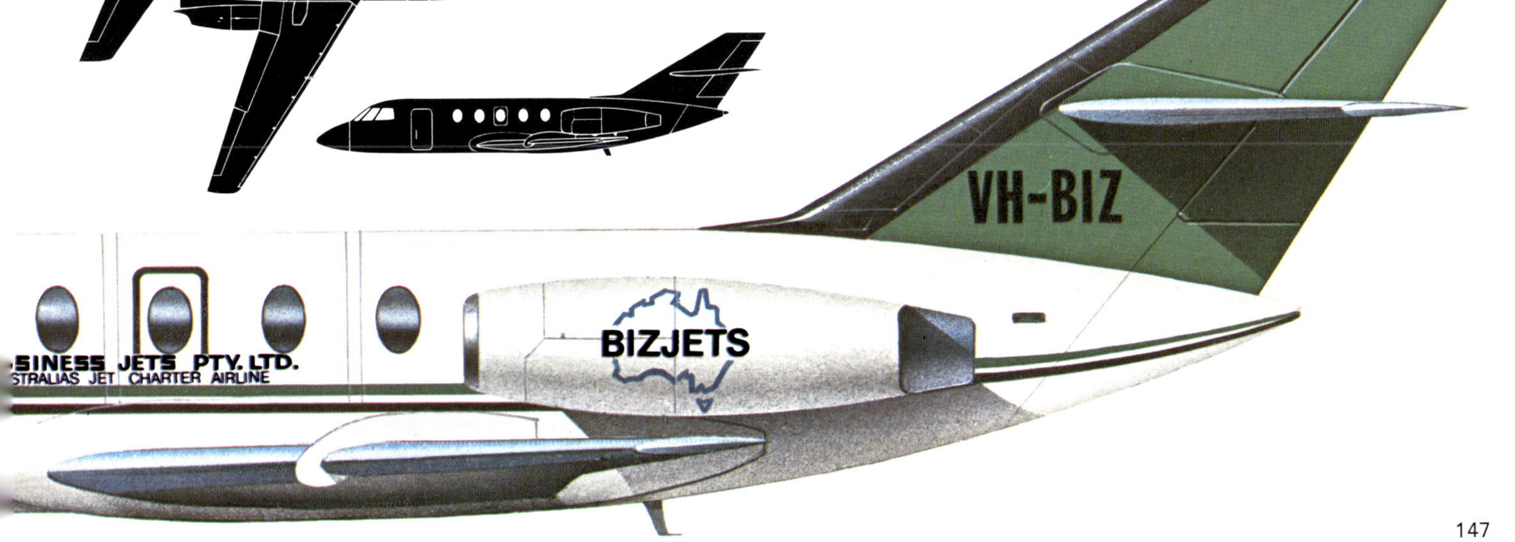

Embraer EMB-121 Xingu
Brazil

Power Plant: Two Pratt & Whitney (Canada) PT6A-28 turboprops each rated at 1,120shp for take-off.
Performance: Max speed, 290mph (467km/h) at 15,000ft (4575m); economical cruise, 242mph (389km/h) at 15,000ft (389km/h); initial rate of climb, 1,900ft/min (9·6m/sec); service ceiling, 27,000ft (8230m); take-off run, 1,706ft (520m); landing run, 1,033ft (315m); range, 1,497mls (2410km) with max payload.
Weights: Empty equipped, 7,000lb (3175kg); max take-off, 12,346lb (5600kg); max landing, 11,684lb (5300kg).
Dimensions: Span, 46ft 4¾in (14·14m); length, 40ft 5in (12·32m); height, 16ft 2½in (4·94m); wing area, 296sq ft (27·50m²).

With the Bandeirante general purpose short-haul transport established in production (as described in the Airliners section), the Brazilian state-owned company EMBRAER drew up plans in the early 'seventies for a series of derivatives of the basic design to meet various specialized requirements. After first considering a pressurized version of the Bandeirante itself, these plans were developed to embrace three distinct but related designs in the EMB-12X family, all with pressurized cabins.

The first of this trio to fly was the EMB-121 Xingu, aimed at the executive market. It has a circular fuselage cross section, and a shorter fuselage than the Bandeirante with a cabin designed to accommodate only six passengers. The wing is substantially the same as that of the Bandeirante but of reduced span, the engines are more powerful and a T-tail layout has been adopted. The prototype Xingu first flew in October 1976 and deliveries were to begin before the end of 1977. Specifications for this aircraft appear above.

The EMB-123 Tapajos, intended to follow the Xingu, has the same fuselage cross section but the fuselage is longer to allow up to 10 passengers to be carried in addition to the crew of two. The same tail unit is used, but a new wing is planned, with a supercritical aerofoil section and provision for tip tanks. To make available the same refinements in an aircraft of suitable size for the third level/commuter market, EMBRAER plan the EMB-120 Araguaia, with the fuselage lengthened for up to 20 passengers. Both the EMB-120 and EMB-123 are designed to use the 1,120shp Pratt & Whitney PT6A-45 turboprops.

Above: Three-view drawing of the EMBRAER EMB-121 Xingu, a derivative of the Bandeirante third-level transport (see page 76).

Below: The EMB-121 Xingu differs from the Bandeirante in having a smaller, pressurized fuselage and a T-tail.

Foxjet
USA

Power Plant: Two Williams WR44-800 turbofans each rated at 800lb st (363kgp).
Performance: Max speed, 410mph (660km/h) at 36,000ft (10,973m); best cruise speed, 330mph (531km/h); initial rate of climb, 3,400ft/min (17,3m/sec); single-engined climb rate, 1,000ft/min (5,1m/sec); service ceiling, 40,000ft (12,200m); single-engined ceiling, 25,000ft (7620m); take-off distance to clear 50ft (15,2m), 2,700ft (823m); landing distance from 50ft (15,2m), 1,860ft (567m), range (with typical reserves), 1,100mls (1770km) at best cruise at 36,000ft (10,973m).
Weights: Empty, 2,308lb (1047kg); max take-off, 4,449lb (2020kg).
Dimensions: Span, 31ft 7in (9,64m); length, 31ft 6in (9,60m); height, 10ft 3in (3,12m).

Below: Three-view drawing of the Foxjet ST-600 biz-jet in its optional three-engined version, for future development.

Gates Learjet 23/24/25
USA

The following specification refers to the Learjet 24F:
Power Plant: Two General Electric CJ610-6 turbojets each rated at 2,950lb st (1340kgp) for take-off.
Performance: Max operating speed, 545mph (877km/h) at 31,000ft (9450m); economical cruising speed, 481mph (774km/h) at 45,000ft (13,715m); initial rate of climb, 6,800ft/min, (34·5m/sec); service ceiling, 27,000ft (8230m); take-off run, 2,305ft (703m); landing run, 1,375ft (419m); range, 1,695mls (2728km) with four passengers, max fuel and reserves.
Weights: Empty equipped, 7,130lb (3234kg); max payload, 3,870lb (1755kg); max take-off weight, 13,500lb (6123kg); max landing weight, 11,880lb (5388kg).
Dimensions: Span, 35ft 7in (10·84m); length, 43ft 3in (13·18m); height, 12ft 3in (3·73m); wing area, 231·8sq ft (21·53m²).

As well as being one of the smallest and fastest of the "first generation" business twin jets, the Learjet is also the best selling. In 1976, Gates Learjet, manufacturers of the Learjet family of models, sold 84 of the assorted types then in production to mark the 12th consecutive year in which it had led the industry, world-wide, in biz-jet sales. By July 1977, more than 700 Learjets of all types had been delivered.

The Learjet was designed in Switzerland under the direction of William

Below: Three-view of the Learjet Model 24, representative of the initial production version of the world's best-selling biz-jet.

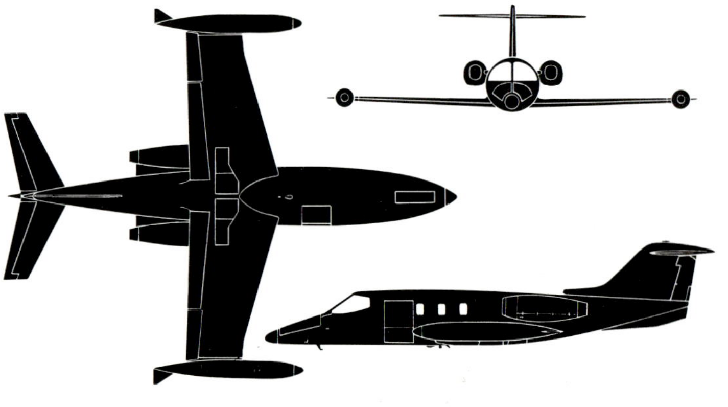

The Foxjet emerged in mid-1977 as an unexpected entry in the biz-jet market, projected by an "unknown" name in aviation circles. The smallest jet-powered business aircraft projected to date, the Foxjet is developed by Foxjet International, a company set up by Tony Team Industries under its president Tony Fox, and designed by Emerson W. Stevens.

The ST-600 is designed to accommodate only three passengers, in addition to the pilot and is expected to be marketed for about $500,000 (256,500). It is to be capable of operating from grass fields and other soft surfaces, and will carry a self-propelled tow bar that works by friction on the nosewheel and allows the aircraft to be manoeuvred on the ground by one man. Hence, the aircraft is expected to be independent of ground services and will be able to operate at army airfields not available at present to the larger biz-jets.

Early in 1978, Foxjet International announced that it had concluded a deal whereby Aeronca Inc – a former aircraft producer that had more recently specialized in component sub-contracting – would be responsible for production of the Foxjet. A prototype was to be built by the end of 1978, with two more for the certification programme in 1979 and full-scale production starting in 1980.

Below: A mock-up of the Foxjet 600 as originally designed; larger engines and overall dimensions have since been adopted.

P Lear as the SAAC-23 and was put into production in Wichita in 1962 by a company founded by Lear and later sold to Gates Rubber Co. The prototype Learjet 23 flew on 7 October 1963 and deliveries began a year later, with 104 being sold before production switched to the Model 24, incorporating a series of design refinements, increased weights and uprated CJ610-4 engines. Successive models have introduced further engine upratings, increased fuel and higher weights to account for models 24B, 24D, 24E and 24F.

The Learjet 25, first flown on 12 August 1966, has a lengthened fuselage (by 4ft 2in/1·27m) to allow up to eight passengers to be carried in executive comfort, whereas the Model 24 seats only six passengers. Increases in fuel capacity and operating weights, plus small structural changes, again accounted for the successive introduction of Models 25B, 25D and 25F. On 24 August 1977, the company flew the prototype of a new Learjet known as the Longhorn and available from late 1978 in two versions, Model 28 and Model 29. The Longhorn has a modified wing of increased aspect ratio and incorporating upturned NASA-type winglets for improved cruising efficiency. Model 29 has a shorter cabin than the Model 28, but increased fuel capacity.

Below: A Learjet Model 24. Originally designed by William Lear, it is now built by the Gates Learjet Corporation.

Gates Learjet 35/36
USA

The following data refer to the Model 35A:

Power Plant: Two Garrett AiResearch TFE 731-2 turbofans each rated at 3,500lb st (1590kgp) for take-off.

Performance: Max cruising speed, 534mph (859km/h); economical cruise, 481mph (774km/h); initial rate of climb, 5,100ft/min (25·9m/sec); service ceiling, 42,500ft (12,955m); take-off to 50ft (15·2m), 4,300ft (1310m); landing distance from 50ft (15·2m), 2,860ft (872m); range, 2,775mls (4466km) with four passengers, max fuel and reserves.

Weights: Empty, 9,110lb (4132kg); max payload, 3,990lb (1810kg); max take-off, 17,000lb (7711kg).

Dimensions: Span, 39ft 6in (12·04m); length, 48ft 8in (14·83m); height, 12ft 3in (3·73m); wing area, 253·3sq ft (23·53m²).

The Model 35 and 36 version of the Learjet were developed during 1973 to take advantage of the improved performance and low sfc of newer turbofan engines and thus to offer aircraft with a greater range than the Learjet 24 and 25, previously described.

To obtain initial flight test data, a Learjet 25 airframe was fitted with Garrett AiResearch TFE 731 engines and, as the Learjet 26, made its first flight on 4 January 1973. For marketing purposes, the designation of this version was changed to Model 36 when production aircraft began to appear, and the Learjet 35 was introduced in parallel, with reduced fuel but greater payload and the same overall dimensions. Compared with the Model 25, both types have a slightly longer fuselage with an extra cabin window each side, and increased wing span through an extension at the tips.

FAA certification was obtained, using one development aircraft of each type, in July 1974 and customer deliveries began later in that year. A series of aerodynamic refinements was introduced on all Learjets in 1976 under the title of Century III, including a new wing leading edge contour to reduce stall and approach speeds and the balanced field lengths required. With these changes, the Model 35A and 36A were in production in 1977, by which time about 100 of the two types had been built.

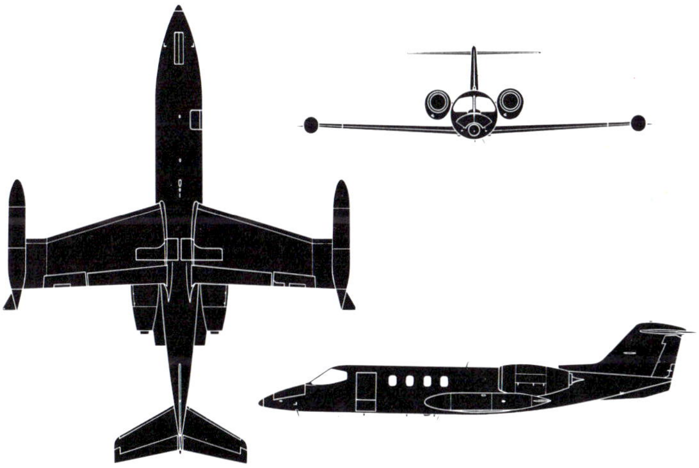

Above: Three-view drawing representing both the Learjet Model 35 and 36, which are externally identical.

Below: The Learjet 35 in flight. The Model 36 differs internally, with differences including fuel capacity and passenger accommodation.

Gates Learjet 54/55/56

USA

The following data refer to the Model 55 Longhorn; the Model 54 and 56 have the same speeds and ceilings, the Model 54's range being 2,486mls (4000km) with 1,200lb (545kg) payload:

Power Plant: Two Garrett TFE 731-3-100B turbofans each rated at 3,650lb st (1657kgp) for take-off.

Performance: Max speed, 550mph (885km/h); max certificated ceiling, 51,000ft (15,550m); take-off distance required, 3,900ft (1189m); initial climb, 5,020ft/min (25·5m/sec); landing distance required, 2,480ft (756m); range, 2,475mls (7478km) with 1,200lb (545kg) payload.

Weights: Empty, 10,216lb (4638kg); max take-off, 18,500lb (8400kg).

Dimensions: Span, 43ft $9\frac{1}{2}$in (13·34m); lenth, 55ft $1\frac{1}{2}$in (16·79m); height, 14ft 8in (4·47m); wing area, 264·5sq ft (24·57m²).

During 1977, Gates Learjet announced that it would add a new 50-series model to its range of Learjet biz-jets, offering greater comfort for passengers in a deepened cabin that offers "stand-up" headroom. Cabin height had been, in the Learjet 20-series and 30-series, somewhat restricted and although this had not prevented the earlier Learjets from becoming the best-selling of all the biz jets, competition from other newer designs led to the evolution of this bigger model for delivery from 1980 onwards.

Apart from the deepened cabin, the new Learjet retains the same configuration as the earlier models, using the TFE 731 turbofans of the Model 35/36, and the improved wing, with tip winglets, of the Model 28/29 Longhorn. The name Longhorn also applies to the new 50-series, having been coined by Gates Learjet to stress the extra range capability bestowed by the use of winglets.

Three variants of the 50-series Longhorns are proposed, all with the same overall dimensions, but having different cabin lengths and fuel capacities. Thus, the Model 54 has a cabin length of 17ft 10in (5·43m) and fuel capacity of 825 US gal (3122 l), the Model 55 has a length of 16ft $2\frac{1}{2}$in (4·93m) anc capacity of 985 US gal (3728 l) and the Model 56 has a length of 14ft 4in (4·36m) and capacity of 1,194 US gal (4520 l). All models can be furnished to carry up to 10 passengers but have different ranges with their maximum payloads; the Model 56 also is designed to operate at a higher gross weight of 20,000lb (9080kg), to achieve a range of 3,660mls (5890km) with an 800lb (363kg) payload.

***Right:** The prototype Learjet Model 28/29 Longhorn, with the winglets featured in the larger Model 54/55/56 Longhorn.*

***Below:** Three-view of the Learjet Model 54/55/56 Longhorn (all three are dimensionally similar) showing the deeper fuselage.*

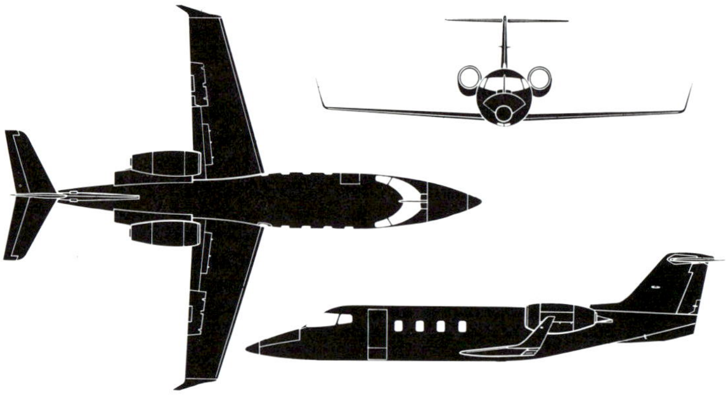

Grumman Gulfstream I

USA

Power Plant: Two Rolls-Royce Dart R Da 529-8 turboprops, each rated at 2,210eshp for take-off.

Performance: Max cruising speed, 348mph (560km/h) at 25,000ft (7625m); economical cruise, 288mph (483km/h) at 25,000ft (7625m); initial rate of climb, 1,900ft/min (9·6m/sec); service ceiling, 33,600ft (10,240m); range with max fuel, 2,540mls (4058km).

Weights: Empty equipped, 21,900lb (9933kg); max payload, 4,270lb (1937kg); max take-off weight, 35,100lb (15,920kg).

Dimensions: Span, 78ft 6in (23·92m); length, 63ft 9in (19·43m); height, 22ft 9in (6·94m); wing area, 610·3sq ft (56·7m²).

Grumman began the design of a turbine-engined business aircraft under the company designation G-159 in 1956, choosing to use turboprops rather than the turbojets that were then just coming into fashion for air transport.

***Right:** A Grumman Gulfstream I business twin with Rolls-Royce Dart engines. Production of 200 ended in 1969.*

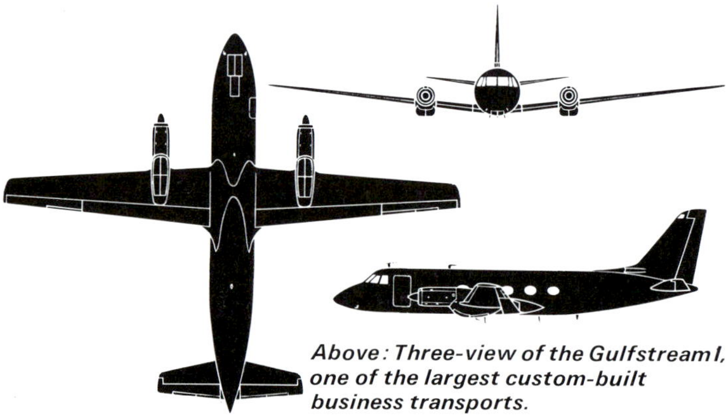

***Above:** Three-view of the Gulfstream I, one of the largest custom-built business transports.*

Grumman Gulfstream II

USA

Power Plant: Two Rolls-Royce Spey Mk 511-8 turbofans each rated at 11,400lb st (5175kgp) for take-off.

Performance: Max cruising speed, 581mph (936km/h) at 25,000ft (7620m); economical cruising speed, 495mph (796km/h) at 43,000ft (13,105m); initial rate of climb, 4,350ft/min (22·1m/sec); service ceiling, 43,000ft (13,100m); take-off field length required, 5,700ft (1737m); landing field length required, 3,190ft (972m); range with max fuel, 4,275mls (6880km) with reserves.

Weights: Operating weight empty, 36,900lb (16,737kg); max take-off, 65,500lb (29,711kg); max landing, 58,500lb (26,535kg).

Dimensions: Span, 68ft 10in (20·98m); length, 79ft 11in (24·36m); height, 24ft 6in (7·47m); wing area, 809·6sq ft (75·21m²).

The Gulfstream II was launched by Grumman Aerospace in May 1965 as a successor for the Gulfstream I, previously described, being of similar size with a fuselage suitable for the accommodation of 19 passengers in a maximum high density layout or 10 in a typical executive arrangement. It was

***Below:** Three-view of the Grumman Gulfstream II, evolved as a jet-powered derivative of the Gulfstream I.*

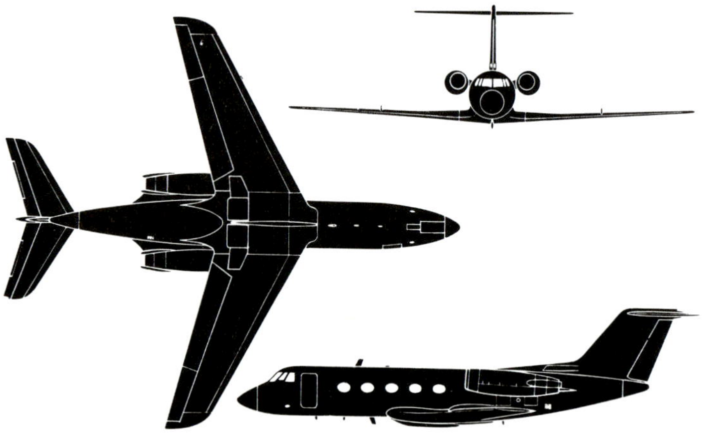

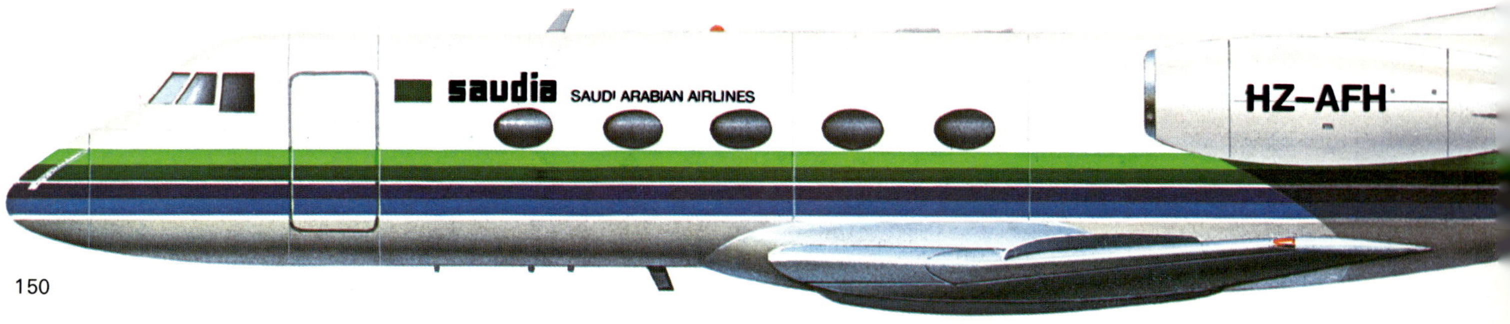

First projects were based on the TF-1 Trader, itself a transport version of the S-2 Tracker anti-submarine aircraft then in production by Grumman, with Rolls-Royce Darts replacing the piston engines. These studies gave way to a series of completely original project designs, out of which evolved the Gulfstream I as the largest aircraft of its time produced for the executive market.

Based on extensive market research, Grumman set out to produce a large long-range transport capable of operating to airline standards to replace the large number of DC-3s and similar elderly piston-engined types serving as corporate transports, primarily in the USA. Designed to operate wholly independently of external services and equipment at airfields around the world, the Gulfstream I found favour with a number of large business corporations and 200 were built by the time production ended in February 1969; the majority of these were still in use in 1977.

The first Gulfstream flew on 14 August 1958 and was joined by two others for the certification programme, completed in May 1959, when deliveries began. Typical executive layouts provide for 10 passengers plus a flight crew of two; high density commuter-type airline interiors were designed for 19 passengers but the Gulfstream did not find application in this role.

aimed, like the Gulfstream I, specifically at the upper end of the executive market, providing facilities and standards of comfort and performance comparable with full international airline standards.

The long range of the Gulfstream II put it in a class of its own when it was first offered, and made it particularly attractive to the larger companies with international operations: thus, some 97 per cent of Gulfstream II operators in 1973 each had an annual turnover in excess of S100m (£56m).

No prototype of the Gulfstream II was built, the first production model entering flight test on 2 October 1966. Certification was obtained on 19 October 1967 and customer deliveries began in December of that year. About 200 Gulfstream IIs had been delivered by early 1977. Aircraft from No 166 onwards, delivered in July 1975, incorporated hush-kits on the Spey engines and also during 1975 Grumman began flight testing wing-tip tanks on a Gulfstream II, which added 3,120lb (1415kg) of fuel and extended the range by some 14 per cent for a 3 per cent reduction in cruising performance.

***Below:** The 1978 version of the Gulfstream II, which introduces tip tanks to increase the fuel capacity and range.*

***Left:** One of Saudia's three Gulfstream IIs, used for executive transport and crew training.*

Hawker Siddeley HS. 125

United Kingdom

Power Plant: Two Garrett AiResearch TFE731-3-1H turbofans each rated at 3,700lb st (1680kgp) for take-off.
Performance: Max level speed, 368mph (592km/h) at sea level; max cruising speed, 502mph (808km/h) at 27,500ft (8380m); service ceiling, 41,000ft (12,500m); take-off run, 4,180ft (1275m); landing run, 4,040ft (1231m); range with max payload, 2,210mls (3556km).
Weights: Empty, 12,670lb (5747kg); max payload, 2,355lb (1068kg); max take-off, 24,200lb (10,977kg); max landing, 22,000lb (9979kg).
Dimensions: Span, 47ft 0in (14·33m); length, 50ft 8½in (15·46m); height, 17ft 7in (5·36m); wing area, 353·0sq ft (32·8m²).

Among the most successful of the first generation biz-jets in the "standard" configuration of low, swept-back wing, rear-mounted engines and cruciform tail, the HS 125 originated as a de Havilland project before that company became part of the Hawker Siddeley organization. The prototype, as DH 125, flew on 13 August 1962 and by early 1977, sales had reached a total of 372, with production continuing. A substantial proportion of the total was made up of sales in the North American market, and aircraft destined for the USA carried an "A" suffix to their designations while those for other parts of the world, marketed from the UK had a "B" suffix.

The first eight DH.125s were Series 1 with Viper 520s and a 20,000-lb (9070-kg) gross weight, followed by 77 Srs 1A/1B with uprated engines and higher weights. The Srs 2 was a military version for the RAF and the civil Srs 3A/3B had a gross weight of 21,700lb (9843kg) and other refinements: 29 were built. For longer ranges, the 3A-R and 3B-R incorporated extra fuel in a tank faired into the underside of the rear fuselage; 36 were built. A further series of refinements marked the introduction of the Srs 4, marketed as the HS.125-400A/400B, of which 116 were built.

With the Srs 600, first flown on 21 January 1971, Hawker Siddeley introduced a lengthened fuselage, increasing the standard executive seating from six to eight, in addition to the crew of two; high density layouts for up to 14 passengers were possible. Other changes included the use of 3,750lb st (1700kgp) Viper 601-22 turbojets, a taller fin, extended ventral fin, fuel tank in lengthened dorsal fin and numerous detail refinements. The Srs 600 was certificated in 1971 and was the principal production variant until 1976.

On 28 June 1976, Hawker Siddeley flew the prototype 125 Srs 700, which introduces TFE 731 turbofans in place of the Viper turbojets to achieve significant savings in fuel consumption and therefore greatly increased range. The Srs 700 was certificated in April 1977, by which time 14 were on order, and production of the Srs 600 had terminated in favour of the improved model, to which the specification refers. By the end of 1977, 33 Srs 700s had been sold, bringing the HS.125 sales total to 391.

Hawker Siddeley H. S. 125-700 Cutaway Drawing Key:

1 Radome
2 Radar scanner
3 Nose equipment bay
4 VOR localiser aerial
5 Nose undercarriage bay
6 Nosewheel doors
7 Windscreen
8 Instrument panel shroud
9 Back of instrument panel
10 Rudder pedals
11 Nosewheel steering jack
12 Twin nosewheels
13 Control column
14 Second pilot's seat
15 First pilot's seat
16 Safety harness
17 Electrical distribution panel
18 Baggage compartment
19 Avionics racks
20 Vestibule
21 External doorhandle
22 Entry steps
23 Handrail
24 Galley
25 Galley storage locker
26 ADF aerial
27 HF aerial
28 Wardrobe
29 Fuselage stringer construction
30 Rearward facing passenger seats
31 Cabin windows
32 Folding table
33 Emergency exit window
34 Fuselage main frame
35 Starboard wing fuel tank
36 Wing fence
37 Starboard navigation light
38 Static dischargers
39 Starboard aileron
40 Trim tab
41 Geared tab
42 Aileron fence
43 Airbrake
44 Starboard flap
45 Window blind
46 Rear cabin seats
47 Ram air intake
48 Passenger service unit
49 Cabin window panel
50 Three seat settee
51 Magazine rack
52 Starboard engine cowling
53 Intake duct to heat exchangers
54 Water tank
55 Air conditioning supply
56 Wash basin
57 Toilet compartment
58 Pressure bulkhead frame
59 Dorsal fuel tank
60 Heat exchanges
61 Air conditioning plant
62 Auxiliary power unit
63 APU intake
64 Rear equipment compartment
65 Fin spar attachment
66 Fin root fairing
67 Fin construction
68 Control cable ducting
69 Aerial attachment
70 Starboard tailplane
71 Starboard elevator
72 Static dischargers
73 Elevator tab
74 Overfin
75 Anti collision light
76 VHF aerial
77 Fin bullet fairing
78 Tail navigation light
79 Port elevator
80 Tailplane construction
81 Leading edge de-icing
82 Elevator hinge control
83 Rudder construction
84 Rudder tab
85 Tailcone
86 Ventral fin
87 Rudder hinge control
88 Oxygen bottles
89 Batteries
90 Engine pylon fairing
91 Fire extinguisher
92 Garrett AiResearch TFE-731 engine
93 Detachable cowling
94 Engine intake
95 Ventral fuel tank
96 Main undercarriage well
97 Flap hinge control
98 Undercarriage leg pivot fixing

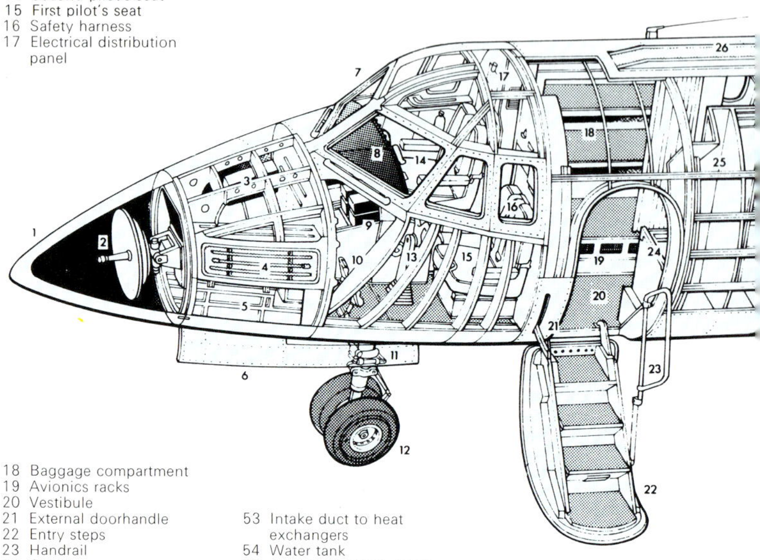

***Right:** There is no such thing as a standard HS.125 cockpit. Most business jets have cockpits that could be called flight decks, for they seat two pilots side-by-side, have a central console and a door to isolate them from the passenger accommodation. The 125 is a comfortable aircraft which has always been popular with businessmen.*

Each major new family is distinguished by major flight-deck improvements, and within these families there is wide scope for customer options in avionics and even in the selection and positioning of instruments and controls. The biggest single change came with the HS.125-600 which had a completely new electronics and annunciator panel in the roof, as illustrated. In 1970–71 Beech of the USA, then associated with Hawker in what was designated Beechcraft Hawker BH-125, further "streamlined" the cockpit and fitted a roof panel full of neatly styled rocker switches and the whole panel at the centre of the coaming (glare shield) filled with warning captions.

***Below:** The prototype of the Series 700 version of the HS.125, the only production variant in 1978.*

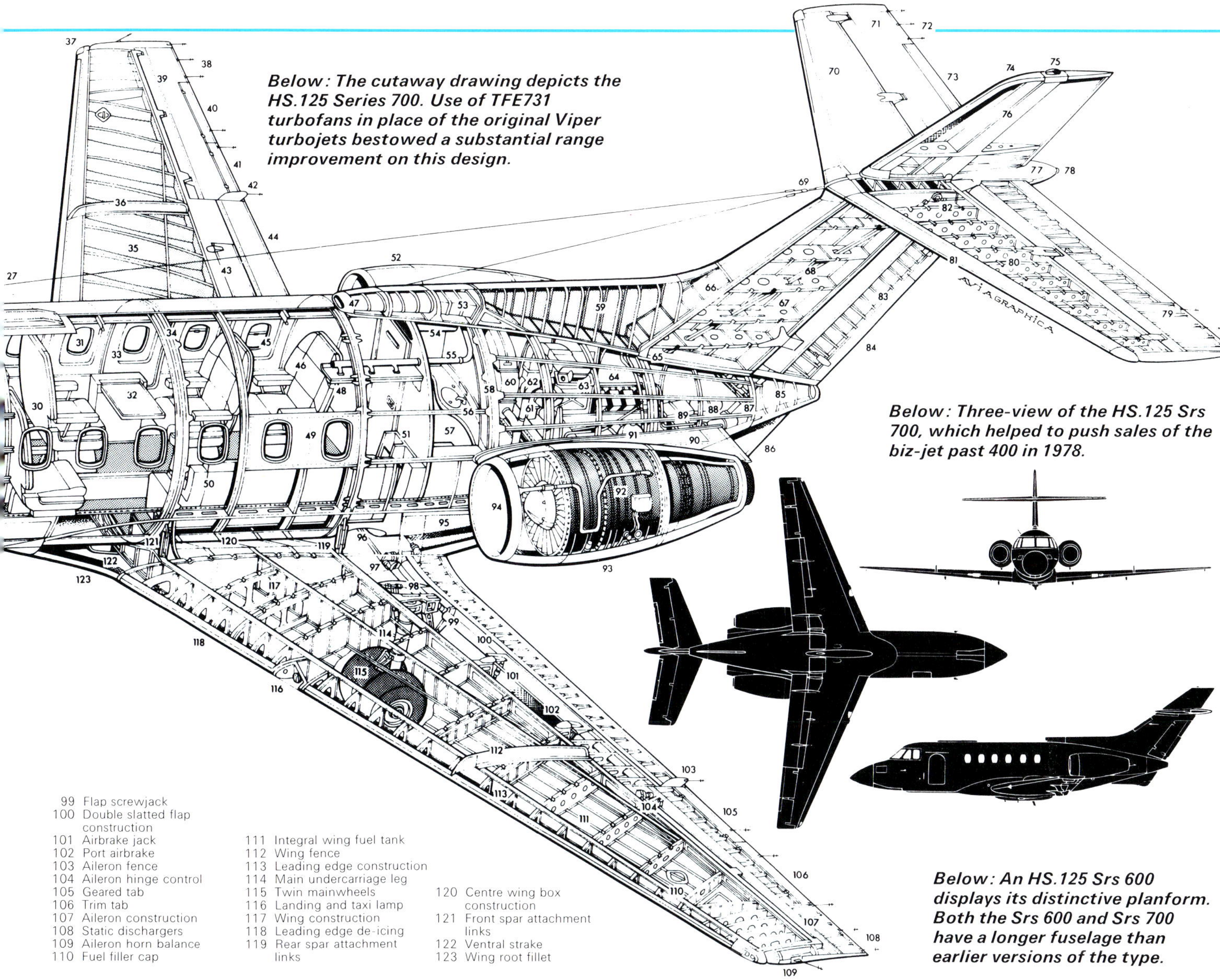

Below: The cutaway drawing depicts the HS.125 Series 700. Use of TFE731 turbofans in place of the original Viper turbojets bestowed a substantial range improvement on this design.

99 Flap screwjack
100 Double slatted flap construction
101 Airbrake jack
102 Port airbrake
103 Aileron fence
104 Aileron hinge control
105 Geared tab
106 Trim tab
107 Aileron construction
108 Static dischargers
109 Aileron horn balance
110 Fuel filler cap
111 Integral wing fuel tank
112 Wing fence
113 Leading edge construction
114 Main undercarriage leg
115 Twin mainwheels
116 Landing and taxi lamp
117 Wing construction
118 Leading edge de-icing
119 Rear spar attachment links
120 Centre wing box construction
121 Front spar attachment links
122 Ventral strake
123 Wing root fillet

Below: Three-view of the HS.125 Srs 700, which helped to push sales of the biz-jet past 400 in 1978.

Below: An HS.125 Srs 600 displays its distinctive planform. Both the Srs 600 and Srs 700 have a longer fuselage than earlier versions of the type.

IAI Westwind

Israel

Power Plant: Two Garrett AiResearch TFE 731-3 turbofans each rated at 3,700lb st (1680kgp) for take-off.
Performance: Max speed, 542mph (872km/h) at 19,400ft (5900m); service ceiling, 45,000ft (13,725m); take-off field length required, 4,840ft (1475m); landing distance required, 2,400ft (732m); range with seven passengers and reserves, more than 2,765mls (4448km).
Weights: Basic operating, 12,800lb (5806kg); max take-off, 22,850lb (10,364kg); max landing, 19,000lb (8618kg).
Dimensions: Span, 44ft 9½in (13·65m); length, 52ft 3in (15·93m); height, 15ft 9½in (4·81m); wing area, 308·3sq ft (28·64m²).

Marketed by Israel Aircraft Industries as the Westwind since 1973, this biz-jet began life in the USA in the early 'sixties as a product of the Aero Commander company, which was already producing a range of piston-engined business transports (see Rockwell Commander 685, described later). Two prototypes of the Aero Commander Model 1121 were flown,

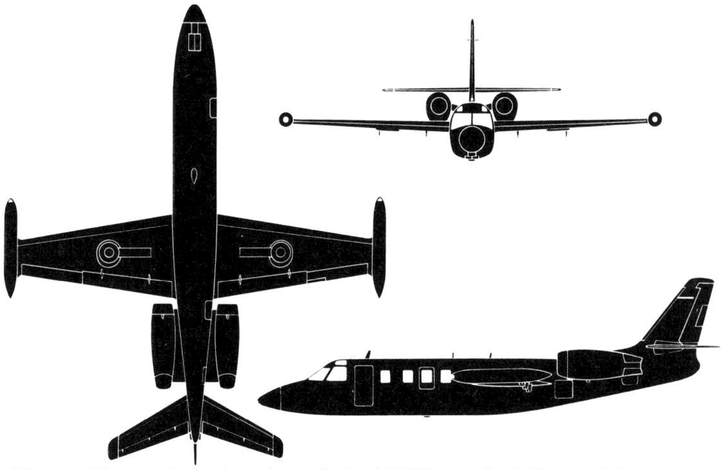

Above: Three-view drawing of the IAI Westwind Eleven-23, designed in the USA and later acquired for production in Israel.

Lockheed JetStar

USA

Power Plant: Four Garrett AiResearch TFE731-3 turbofan engines each rated at 3,700lb st (1680kgp) for take-off.
Performance: Max cruising speed, 547mph (880km/h) at 30,000ft (9145m); economical cruising speed, 508mph (817km/h) at 35,000ft (10,670m); initial rate of climb, 4,200ft/min (21·3m/sec); service ceiling, 38,000ft (11,580m); take-off to 50ft (15·2m), 5,250ft (1600m); landing from 50ft /15·2m), 3,900ft (1·189m) range with max payload and reserves, 2,994mls (4818km).
Weights: Basic operating weight, 24,178lb (10,967kg); max payload, 2,822lb (1280kg); max take-off, 43,750lb (19,844kg); max landing, 36,000lb (16,329kg).
Dimensions: Span, 54ft 5in (16·60m); length, 60ft 5in (18·42m); height, 20ft 5in (6·23m); wing area, 542·5sq ft (50·40m²).

The JetStar originated at the Lockheed California Company in 1956, when the USAF had indicated an interest in buying small jet transports "off the shelf" if suitable designs were developed by industry at private expense. Both the JetStar and the North American Sabreliner resulted from this

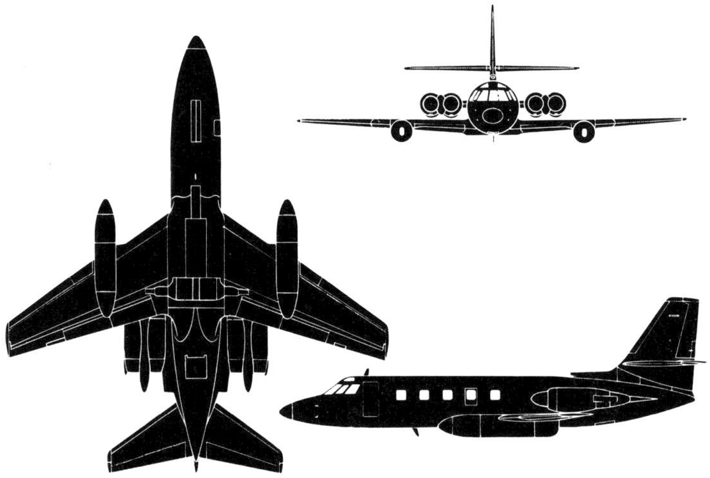

Above: Three-view drawing of the Lockheed JetStar II, the revised and uprated version that re-entered production in 1976.

Partenavia P.68 Victor

Italy

Power Plant: Two Lycoming 10-360-A1B6 flat-four piston engines each rated at 200hp for take-off.
Performance: Max level speed, 199mph (320km/h) at sea level; max cruising speed, 188mph (302km/h) at 5,500ft (1675m); cruising speed at 168mph (270km/h) at 10,500ft (3206m); initial rate of climb, 1,390ft/min (7·0m/sec); service ceiling, 20,000ft (6100m); take-off run, 912ft (278m); landing run, 820ft (250m); max range, 1,045mls (1681km).
Weights: Empty, 2,778lb (1260kg); max take-off, 4,321lb (1960kg); max landing, 4,100lb (1860kg).
Dimensions: Span, 39ft 4½in (12·00m); length, 30ft 8in (9·35m); height, 11ft 1¾in (3·40m); wing area, 200sq ft (18·60m²).

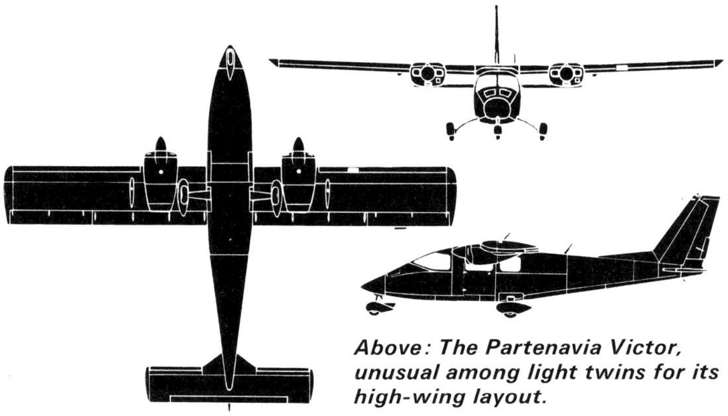

Above: The Partenavia Victor, unusual among light twins for its high-wing layout.

Piaggio P.166

Italy

Power Plant: Two Avco Lycoming LTP-101-600 turboprops each rated at 587shp for take-off.
Performance: Max speed, 259mph (417km/h) at 10,000ft (3050m); economical cruising speed, 186mph (300km/h) at 10,000ft (3050m); initial rate of climb, 2,080ft/min (10·6m/sec); service ceiling, 26,000ft (7925m); take-off to 50ft (15·2m); 1,640ft (500m); landing distance, 984ft (300m); range (with wing-tip fuel tanks), including reserves, 1,364–1,657mls (2195–2668km/h) according to speed.
Weights: Empty weight, 4,688lb (2126kg); max take-off weight, 9,480lb (4300kg); max payload, 2860lb (1306kg); max landing weight, 8377lb (3800kg).
Dimensions: Span, 48ft 2in (14·69m); length, 39ft 0in (11·90m); height, 16ft 5in (5·0m); wing area, 285·9sq ft (26·56m²).

The P.166 light transport has been in production and service for almost 20 years, deliveries having started in 1958 following a first flight by the prototype on 26 November 1957. Developed initially for the civil market, the

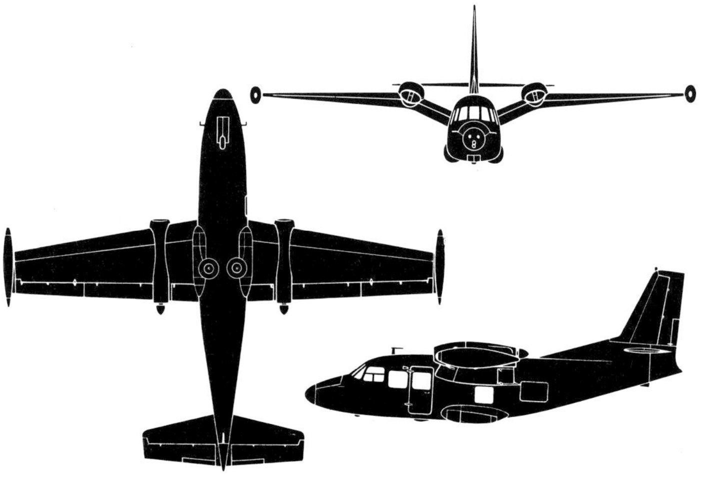

Above: The Piaggio P.166, which was influenced by the earlier P.136 amphibian. Pusher engines are an unusual feature.

respectively, on 27 January 1963 and 14 April 1964, and the first production example flew on 5 October 1964 and was delivered in January 1965.

Powered by General Electric CJ610-1 turbojets of 2,850lb st (1293kgp), the Model 1121 Jet Commander seated up to seven passengers plus a flight crew of two and enjoyed a steady sales success up to the time that Aero Commander was acquired by North American. Because of a marketing conflict between the Jet Commander and the Sabreliner, North American disposed of the entire Model 1121 programme to IAI in 1967 and the Israeli company assumed responsibility for the sale of the final 49 Jet Commanders of a total of 150 built by Aero Commander.

After testing two interim Model 1122s, IAI developed the 1123, at first known as the Commodore Jet and then as the Westwind Eleven-23; this features a lengthened fuselage to seat up to 10 passengers and was first flown on 28 September 1970. The engines are 3,100lb st (1406kgp) CJ610-9 turbojets, and 36 aircraft were built by mid-1976, when production ended in favour of the Westwind Eleven-24.

Differing from the 1123 primarily in having turbofan engines, the 1124 Westwind made its first flight on 21 July 1975 and production began in 1976. A number of detail improvements were made in addition to substitution of the improved engines, and the specification at the top of the opposite page refers to this model.

Above: Built in Israel, the Westwind Eleven-23 and Eleven-24 biz-jets have found their principal market in the USA.

initiative but military sales of the JetStar were, in the event, fewer than had been expected and Lockheed's major marketing effort was directed at the executive market, in which the JetStar proved a steady seller.

Two prototypes were each powered by a pair of 4,850lb st (2200kgp) Bristol Siddeley Orpheus turbojets but production aircraft used four Pratt & Whitney JT12A-6s. The first prototype flew on 4 September 1957 and the first production example on 2 July 1960, production being centred at Lockheed's Georgia Company. Between 1960 and 1973, this production line turned out 162 JetStars which, in typical executive layouts, seated 10 passengers in addition to a crew of two.

During 1973, the AiResearch Aviation Company developed a conversion kit for the JetStar, substituting TFE731-1 turbofans for the older turbojets, and introducing certain aerodynamic refinements. A prototype of this JetStar 731 flew on 10 July, 1974 and the first production conversion on 18 March 1976, with conversions continuing on a production line basis in 1977. Following the AiResearch lead, Lockheed adopted the same engines and a similar range of aerodynamic modifications for a new production version, the JetStar II, the first example of which flew on 18 August 1976, with deliveries starting early in 1977. The overall dimensions were unchanged and the specification refers to the production JetStar II.

Right: The prototype Lockheed JetStar II, powered by Garrett TFE 731 turbofans in place of the original turbojets.

The Victor light twin transport, designed by Prof Ing Luigi Pascale and put into production by Partenavia in 1972, has applications as a business transport, air taxi and for specialized rôles such as aerial survey and meteorlogical research. The prototype flew on 25 May 1970 and Italian and US type approval was obtained at the end of 1971. A pre-production batch of 10 P.68s had slightly shorter fuselages than the P.68B, which entered production at the company's new Naples factory in 1974 and seats six in its standard transport version.

About 100 Victors had been built by the end of 1976, at which time Partenavia began flight testing the P.68R variant with a retractable undercarriage. Also planned for future development was a turboprop version, a floatplane/amphibian version and the P.68T with turbosupercharged TIO-360 engines. The specification refers to the standard P.68B.

Right: Successful marketing of the P68 Victor led to the development of new versions including the P68R and the P68T.

P.166 has found rather more application in military rôles, but a number of examples are used as company transports and for third-level/commuter airline services.

Some 110 P.166s had been built, in several versions, by the time production ended in the early 'seventies, all these versions having piston engines. They included the initial P.166 (32 built) with 340 hp Lycoming GSO-480 engines and gross weight of 8,113lb (3680kg); the P.166B Portofino of 1962 with 380hp IGSO-540s and 8,377-lb (3800-kg) gross weight and the P.166C high-density commuter version with weight increased to 8,708lb (3950kg). Typically, these aircraft carried 6–8 passengers in addition to the crew of two; maximum accommodation was for 10.

In May 1975 Piaggio flew a prototype P.166-BL2 with improved systems, and this aircraft was then converted to the P.166-DL3 configuration with turboprop engines, increased weights and other changes. First flown on 3 July 1976, the P.166-DL3 was offered with a wide range of alternative interiors for roles including 10-seat business transport, environmental control, geophysical survey, aero-photogrammetry, aerial fire fighting etc. A batch of five was in production in 1978.
The data left refer to the P.166-DL3.

Right: A Piaggio P.166 operating in Nigeria as a light transport; it also serves in several specialized roles.

Mitsubishi MU-2

Japan

Power Plant: Two Garrett AiResearch TPE 331-6-251M turboprops each rated at 724ehp for take off.
Performance: Max cruising speed, 365mph (587km/h); economical cruising speed, 310mph (499km/h) at 28,000ft (8535m); initial rate of climb, 2,840ft/min (14·5m/sec); service ceiling, 32,200ft (9815m); take-off to 50ft (15·2m); 1,800ft (548m); landing distance from 50ft (15·2m); 1,600ft (488m); max range with reserves, 1,680mls (2705km).
Weights: Empty equipped, 6,864lb (3113kg); max take-off, 10,470lb (4750kg); max landing, 9,955lb (4515kg).
Dimensions: Span, 39ft 2in (11·94m); length, 33ft 3in (10·13m); height, 12ft 11in (3·94m); wing area, 178sq ft (16·55m²).

The MU-2 was the first original design of the famous Mitsubishi Aircraft company to enter production in Japan in the post World War II period. Designed as a general purpose light transport with special attention to field performance, it has been sold in several military versions to the Japanese Self-Defence forces, but is marketed primarily as an executive transport. Special marketing arrangements were made for the MU-2 in North America, at first through the Mooney company and subsequently through a Mitsubishi subsidiary, and a major share of the total sales of over 500 by mid-1978 had been made in the USA.

Mitsubishi MU-2J Cutaway Drawing Key

1 Nose cone
2 Hinged nose doors (left and right)
3 Hinged landing and taxi lamps (left and right)
4 Nosewheel doors
5 Forward-retracting twin nosewheels
6 Nosewheel leg
7 Landing gear access panel
8 Forward electronics compartment
9 Forward battery
10 Bulkhead
11 Control column
12 Rudder pedals
13 Windshield wiper
14 Instrument console shroud
15 Windshield de-icing installation
16 Two-piece curved windshield
17 Control yoke
18 Second pilot's seat
19 First pilot's seat
20 Seat adjustment mechanism
21 Circuit breaker panel
22 Floor support structure
23 Main undercarriage fairing
24 Underfloor control runs
25 Main passenger cabin floor
26 Three-a-side cabin windows
27 Strengthened anti-ice panel
28 Frame and longeron fuselage construction
29 Fuselage skinning
30 Aerial mast
31 Wingroot fairings
32 Leading-edge relay panel
33 Fuselage/front spar attachment points
34 Emergency escape window (right-hand rear)
35 Wing carry-through surface
36 Centre-section fuel tank
37 No 1 right-hand fuel tank
38 Fuel lines
39 Garrett AiResearch TPE331-6-251M turboprop
40 Intake
41 Airscrew spinner
42 Three-blade Hartzell propeller
43 Pneumatic leading-edge de-icer
44 Leading-edge ribs
45 No 2 right-hand fuel tank
46 Auxiliary tip tank
47 Tip tank fin
48 Spoilers (extended)
49 Trim aileron section
50 Flap track fairing
51 Aerial
52 Inner section double-slotted flap
53 Centre-section anti collision beacon
54 Spoiler mechanism
55 Fuselage/rear spar attachment points
56 Flap actuator mechanism
57 Wingroot fillet
58 Cabin entry door
59 Air-conditioning ducts
60 Dorsal fillet
61 Pneumatic fin leading-edge de-icer
62 Aerial (to right-hand tailplane)
63 Fin main spar
64 Rudder tab mechanism
65 Antenna
66 Anti-collision beacon
67 Static dischargers
68 Rudder hinge fairing
69 Rudder construction
70 Rudder tab control
71 Rudder post main beam
72 Rudder tab
73 Tail cone
74 Rear navigation light
75 Elevator tab
76 Tab mechanism
77 Port elevator
78 Tailplane construction
79 Pneumatic leading-edge de-icer
80 Tailplane fillet
81 Control runs
82 Ventral strake (left and right)
83 Electronics access panel
84 Air-conditioning and pressurisation installation
85 Aft electronics compartment (main junction box and batteries)
86 Aft cabin coat closet space
87 Door handle
88 Door hinges
89 Fuel dump line (left and right)
90 Undercarriage retraction mechanism
91 Mainwheel door
92 Mainwheel leg
93 Axle
94 Port mainwheel
95 Wing ribs
96 Outer-section flap profile
97 Port auxiliary tip tank
98 Wingtip lights (navigation and strobe)
99 Tip tank fin
100 Tip tank strake

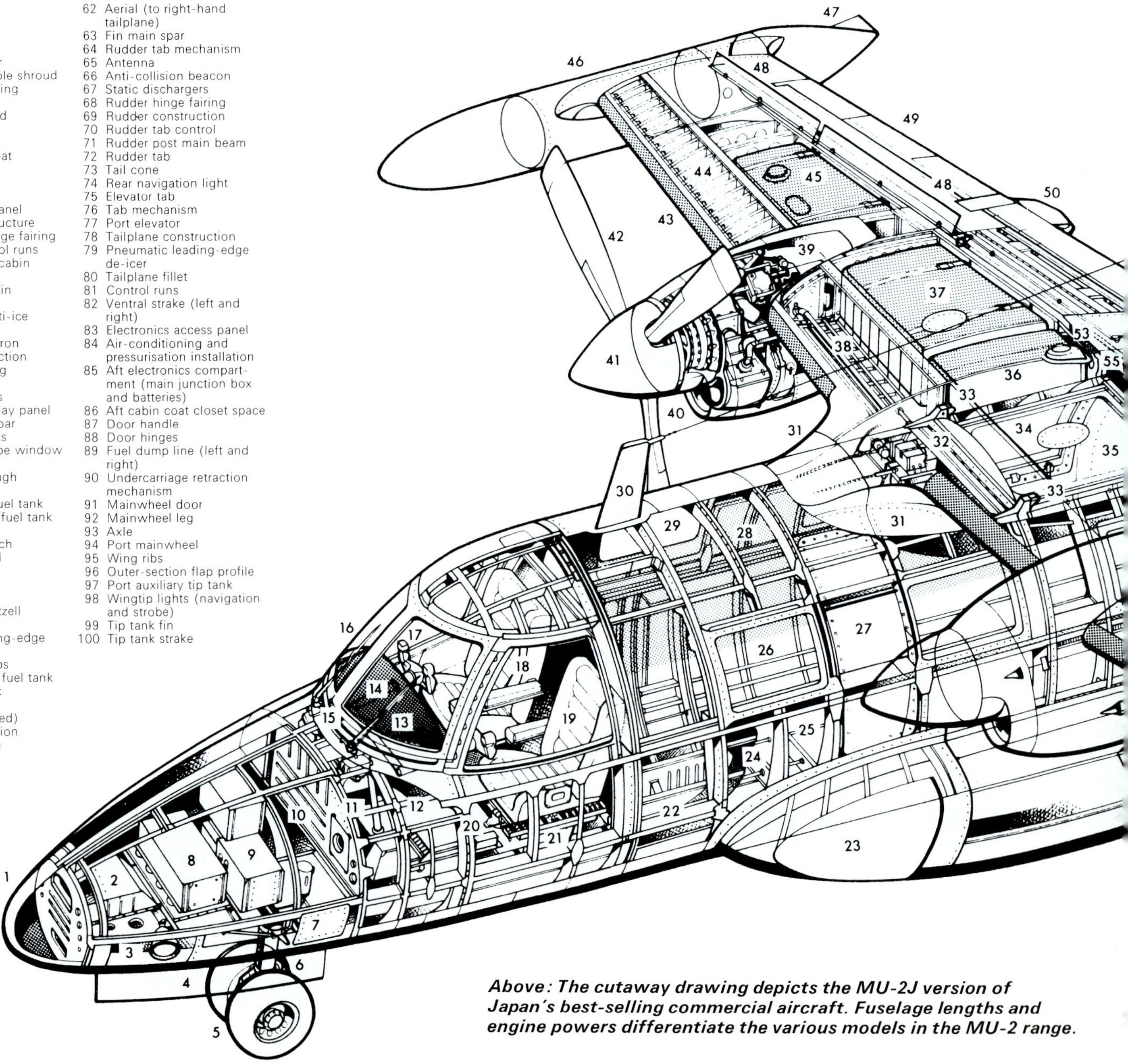

***Above:** The cutaway drawing depicts the MU-2J version of Japan's best-selling commercial aircraft. Fuselage lengths and engine powers differentiate the various models in the MU-2 range.*

The prototype MU-2 (with Turboméca Astazou engines) flew on 14 September 1963 and the first MU-2B – the initial production version with TPE 331 engines – flew on 11 March 1965. All initial variants had the same overall dimensions and seated up to seven passengers in addition to the flight crew of two, the cabin being pressurized in all commercial versions. Changes of gross weight, power plant rating and rôle accounted for successive changes of designation, the business transports being the MU-2B, MU-2D, MU-2F, MU-2K, MU-2M and MU-2P.

A "stretched" version of the basic aircraft appeared in 1969, when the prototype MU-2G made its first flight on 10 January. This had a lengthened fuselage to accommodate up to nine passengers and has been followed in production by the MU-2J, MU-2L and MU-2N, with changes of engine rating and gross weight. The data refer to the MU-2M.

Left: A Mitsubishi MU-2 climbs away at the start of a demonstration flight. Sales of the MU-2 totalled over 500 by mid-1978.

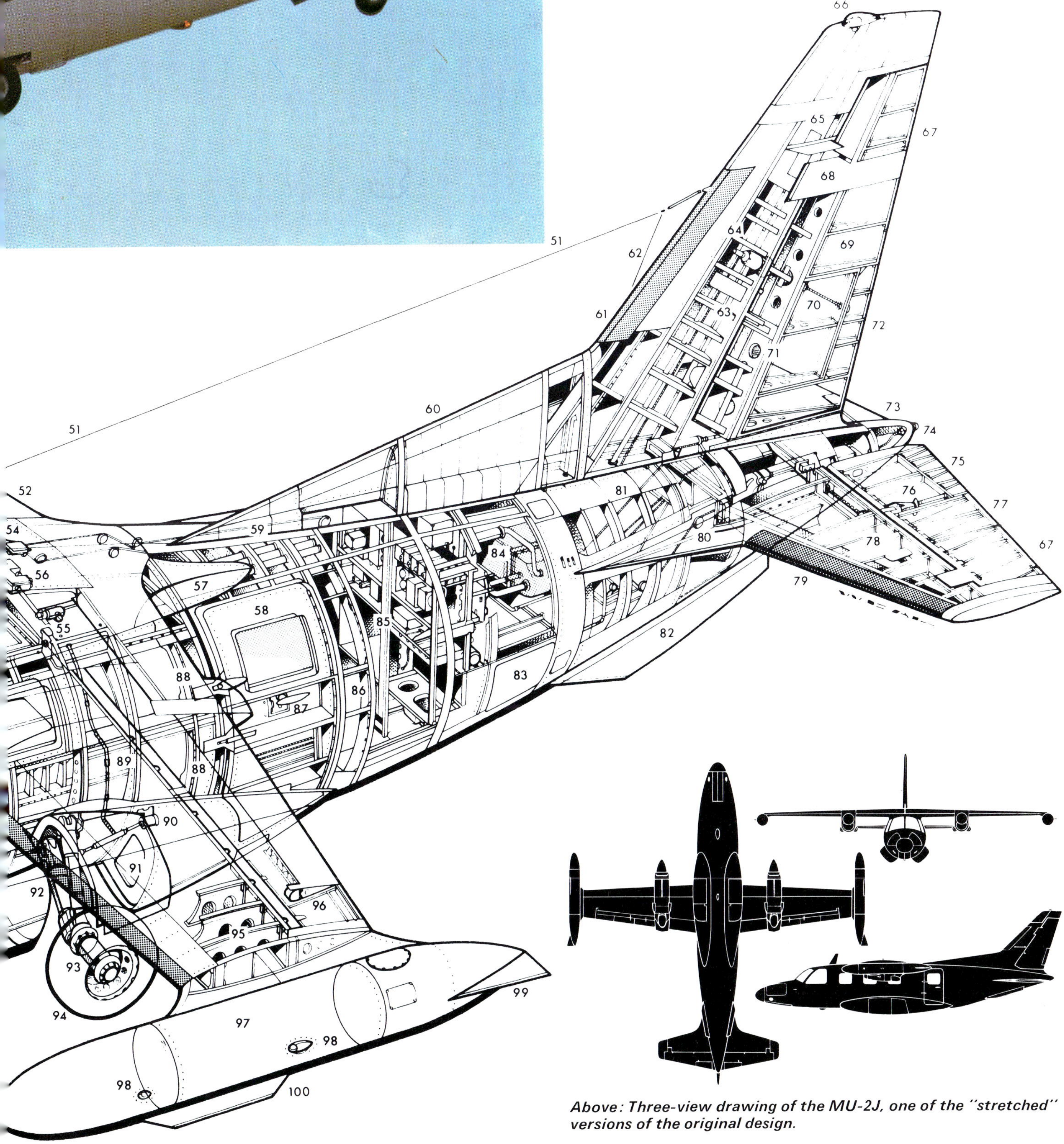

Above: Three-view drawing of the MU-2J, one of the "stretched" versions of the original design.

Piper PA-23 Aztec
USA

Power Plant: Two Lycoming IO-540-C4B5 flat-six piston engines rated at 250hp for take-off.
Performance: Max speed, 215mph (346km/h); economical cruising speed, 192mph (309km/h); initial rate of climb, 1,400ft/min (6·1m/sec); absolute ceiling, 18,950ft (5775m); take-off run, 945ft (288m); landing run, 1,310ft (400m); range, 1,012–1,519mls (1630–2445km) according to speed.
Weights: Empty, 3,180lb (1442kg); max take-off and landing, 5,200lb (2360kg).
Dimensions: Span, 37ft $2\frac{1}{2}$in (11·34m); length, 31ft $2\frac{3}{4}$in (9·52m); height, 10ft 4in (3·15m); wing area, 207·6sq ft (19·28m^2).

***Below:** Three-view of the PA-23 Aztec, a derivative of the Apache, differing in shape of tail unit and other detail.*

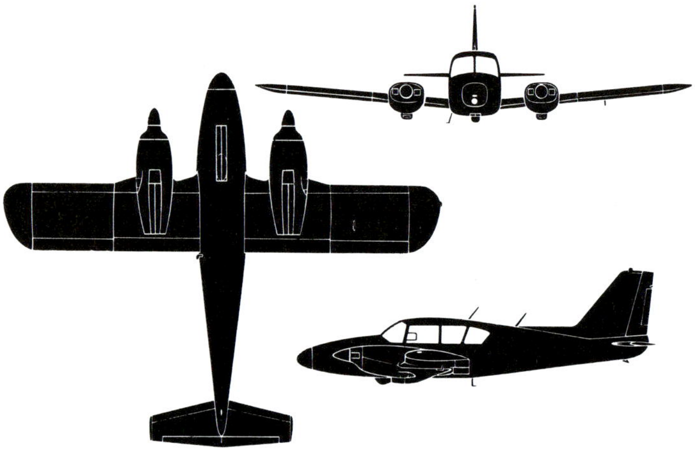

Piper's first twin-engined aircraft, known in prototype form as the Twin Stinson in March 1952, entered production as the 4-5 seat Apache, with deliveries starting in 1954. The Apache was in turn evolved into the Aztec, with enlarged cabin to seat six, changed fin and rudder shape, lengthened nose, uprated engine and other refinements.

The Aztec continued in production into 1977, by which time over 4,000 of the Piper twins had been delivered, to become one of the most-used business aircraft in many parts of the world. The latest version was then designated Aztec F, with a version also available with 250hp TIO-540-C1A turbosupercharged engines. The data refer to the basic model.

***Below:** A highly decorated example of the Aztec; most users of business aircraft prefer a more restrained (and less costly!) finish.*

Piper PA-31 Navajo
USA

Power Plant: Two Lycoming TIO-540-J2BD flat-six turbosupercharged engines each rated at 350hp for take-off.
Performance: Max level speed, 270mph (435km/h) at 15,000ft (4575m); economical cruising speed, 246mph (396km/h) at 20,000ft (6100m); initial rate of climb, 1,390ft/min (7·0m/sec); service ceiling, 27,200ft (8290m); take-off to 50ft (15·2m), 2,490ft (759m); landing distance from 50ft (15·2m), 2,725ft (831m); range, 1,060–1,270mls (1706–2044km) according to speed.
Weights: Empty, 4,114lb (1866kg); max take-off and landing, 7,000lb (3175kg).
Dimensions: Span, 40ft 8in (12·40m); length, 34ft $7\frac{1}{2}$in (10·55m); height, 13ft 0in (3·96m); wing area, 229sq ft (21·3m^2).

Piper introduced its PA-31 as an addition to its range of business twins in 1964, the prototype making its first flight on 30 September in that year. With the name Navajo, it had 300hp Lycoming IO-540-M1A5 engines and provided accommodation for six in standard layouts, or up to eight. Primarily sold in the business market, it also found applications as a third level airliner and for air taxi duties.

A version of the basic Navajo with turbosupercharged 310hp TIO-540-A engines became known as the Turbo Navajo and continues in production in 1977, by which time more than 2,000 Navajos of all types had been delivered. In 1970, the range was extended with the addition of the PA-31P Pressurized Navajo, the prototype of which had flown in March 1968. With 425hp Lycoming TIGO-541-E1A flat-six turbosupercharged engines, it has a pressurized cabin and normally seats six.

A further addition to the Navajo family in 1972 was the PA-31-350 Navajo Chieftain, with 350hp TIO-540-J2BD turbosupercharged engines (rotating in opposite directions to cancel out engine torque) and the fuselage lengthened by 2ft 0in (0·61m) to seat 6–10 according to role. The counter-rotating feature was later adopted on the PA-31-325 Turbo Navajo CR, with 325hp TIO-540-F2BD engines. The specification refers to the Navajo Chieftain.

***Below:** Three-view drawing of the Piper Navajo; the Navajo Chieftain has a longer fuselage.*

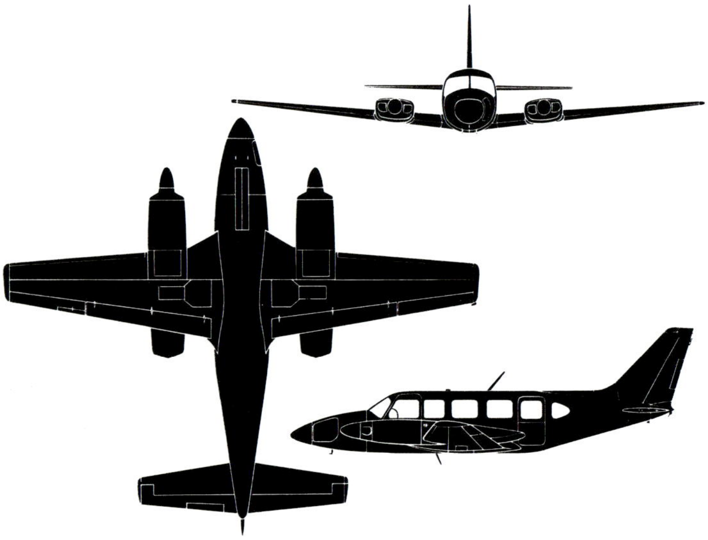

***Below:** A Navajo Chieftain. Its capacity of up to nine passengers has made it attractive to air taxi operators.*

Piper PA-31T Cheyenne

USA

The following data refer to the Cheyenne II:

Power Plant: Two Pratt & Whitney (Canada) PT6A-28 turboprops each rated at 620eshp for take-off.

Performance: Max cruising speed, 326mph (525km/h) at 11,000ft (3355m); economical cruising speed, 244mph (393km/h) at 25,000ft (7620m); initial rate of climb, 2,800ft/min (14·2m/sec); max operating altitude, 29,000ft (8840m); take-off to 50ft (15·2m), 1,980ft (604m); landing distance from 50ft (15·2m), 1,860ft (567m); range, 1,621–1,702mls (2608–2739km) according to speed, with reserves.

Weights: Empty, equipped, 4,870lb (2209kg); max take-off and landing, 9,000lb (4082kg).

Dimensions: Span, 42ft $8\frac{1}{4}$in (13·01m); length, 34ft 8in (10·57m); height, 12ft 9in (3·89m); wing area, 229sq ft (21·3m²).

The following specification refers to the Cheyenne III:

Power Plant: Two 680hp Pratt & Whitney PT6A-41 turboprops.

Performance: Typical cruising speed, 346mph (558km/h) at 20,000ft (6100m); initial climb, 2,450ft/min (12·4m/sec); service ceiling 30,500ft (9296m); take-off distance, 2,320ft (707m); landing distance, 2,610ft (796m); typical range, nine occupants and reserves, 1,318mls (2121km).

Weights: Standard empty, 5,621lb (2550kg); max take-off, 10,500lb (4763kg); max landing weight, 9,975lb (4525kg).

Dimensions: Span, 47ft 8in (14·53m); length, 38ft 0in (11·6m); height, 11ft $9\frac{1}{2}$in (3·60m); wing area, 293sq ft (27·2m²).

First flown on 20 August 1969, the Cheyenne is in effect a turboprop-powered version of the previously-described Pressurized Navajo, as indicated by the common PA-31 type number. Certificated on 3 May 1972, the Cheyenne was added to the Piper range in 1974 as the company's first turbine-engined business aircraft, and was still the only turboprop Piper in production in 1977.

With substantially the same fuselage as the Navajo, the Cheyenne seats six–eight including pilots. Apart from the turboprop engines, its most obvious point of difference from the Navajo is the use of tip tanks to obtain extra fuel capacity and allow a greater range to be offered. The first production Cheyenne flew on 22 October 1973 and during 1976 a Cheyenne was the 100,000th Piper aeroplane to be produced – a record that no other manufacturer in the world has approached.

At the end of 1977, Piper increased its range of Cheyenne models by offering a low-cost version as the Cheyenne I and an enlarged and improved version as the Cheyenne III. The original model, as described above, then became the Cheyenne II, all three models being offered in 1978. The Cheyenne I has the same airframe as the original PA-31T, but uses the lower-rated 500hp Pratt & Whitney PT6A-11 engines, and use of tip tanks is optional.

The PA-42 Cheyenne III has been extensively redesigned and features a lengthened fuselage that allows two more occupants to be carried in the cabin, for a maximum of 10 (including two pilots). Piper also adopted a T-tail, making the Cheyenne immediately distinguishable from the earlier models. The engines, which are uprated versions of the PT6A, are located farther outboard on the centre section to reduce cabin noise levels, and redesigned nacelles incorporate baggage lockers and provide space for optional long-range fuel tanks.

***Left:** Piper Cheyenne painted as a "flying blueprint" to draw attention to this aircraft's special features.*

***Below:** Three-view of the PA-31T Cheyenne in the version subsequently designated as Cheyenne II; the Cheyenne III is larger.*

Piper PA-34 Seneca

USA

Power Plant: Two oppositely-rotating Continental TSIO-360-E flat four piston engines each rated at 200hp for take-off.

Performance: Max level speed, 228mph (367km/h) at 14,000ft (4265m); economical cruising speed, 187mph (301km/h) at 24,000ft (7315m); initial rate of climb, 1,340ft/min (6·8m/sec); max operating altitude, 25,000ft (7620m); take-off to 50ft (15·2m), 1,460ft (445m); landing distance from 50ft (15·2m); 2,090ft (637m); range with standard fuel and reserves, 626–701mls (1007–1128km) according to speed.

Weights: Empty, 2,788lb (1264kg); max take-off, 4,570lb (2073kg); max landing, 4,342lb (1969kg).

Dimensions: Span, 38ft $10\frac{3}{4}$in (11·85m); length, 28ft $7\frac{1}{2}$in (8·73m); height, 9ft $10\frac{3}{4}$in (3·02m); wing area, 208·7sq ft (19·39m²).

***Below:** A Seneca in flight; one of Piper's most successful business twins in the late 'seventies.*

The Seneca, among the lightest of the six-seat business twins on the market, was derived from the single-engined PA-32 Cherokee Six, of which it is in effect a twin-engined version. The tail unit, rear fuselage and cabin of the two types are substantially identical, and the wing incorporates a new centre section on which the two engines are mounted, and a new nose cone is provided, incorporating a baggage compartment.

First flown in 1970, the PA-34 Seneca was certificated on 7 May 1971 and production deliveries began in 1971. In 1975, a series of refinements led to the designation being changed to Seneca II, production of which was running at an annual rate of 350–400 in 1976. Normally seating six in three rows of paired seats in the cabin, the Seneca can have a larger freight loading door in the fuselage side.

***Below:** Three-view of the PA-34 Seneca, a twin-engined derivative of the PA-32 Cherokee Six.*

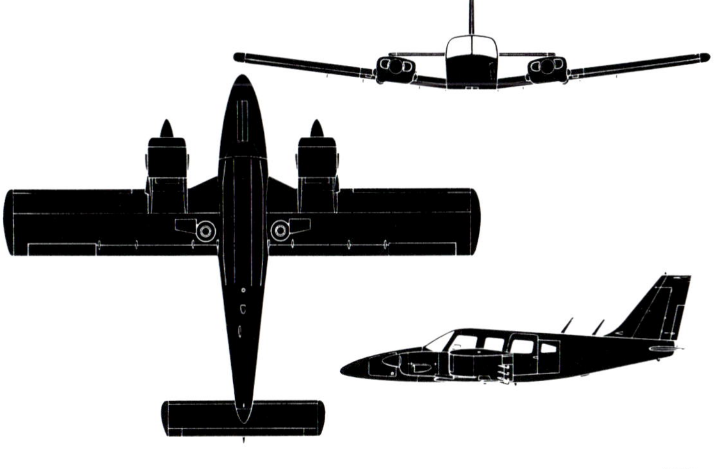

Rockwell Commander 685 and Shrike Commander

USA

Power Plant: Two Continental GTSIO-520-F flat-six piston engines, each rated at 435hp for take-off.
Performance: Max speed, 279mph (449km/h) at 20,000ft (6100m); economical cruising speed, 175mph (281km/h) at 14,000ft (4265m); initial rate of climb, 1,490ft/min (7·5m/sec); service ceiling, 27,500ft (8380m); take-off to 50ft (15·2m), 2,711ft (826m); landing from 50ft (15·2m), 2,312ft (705m); range, 976–1,320mls (1570–2124km) according to speed, with reserves.
Weights: Empty equipped, 6,021lb (2731kg); max take-off and landing, 9,000lb (4082kg).
Dimensions: Span, 46ft 6½in (14·19m); length, 42ft 11¾in (13·10m); height, 14ft 11½in (4·56m); wing area, 266sq ft (24·7m²).

***Right:** A Rockwell Shrike Commander, one of the later production versions of the original Aero Commander.*

Rockwell Turbo Commander

USA

Power Plant: Two Garrett AiResearch TPE 331-5-251K turboprops each rated at 700ehp for take off.
Performance: Max speed, 328mph (528km/h) at 12,000ft (3660m); economical cruising speed, 289mph (465km/h) at 31,000ft (9450m); initial rate of climb, 2,849ft/min (14·5m/sec); service ceiling, 33,000ft (10,060m); take-off to 50ft (15·2m), 2,216ft (675m); landing from 50ft (15·2m), 1,606ft (490m); range, with max payload, 850mls (1370km) with reserves.
Weights: Empty, 6,126lb (2778kg); max take-off, 10,250lb (4649kg); max landing, 9,600lb (4364kg).
Dimensions: Span, 46ft 8in (14·22m); length, 44ft 4¼in (13·52m); height, 14ft 11½in (4·56m); wing area, 266sq ft (24·7m²).

A turboprop version of the original Aero Commander was first flown on 31 December 1964 as the Model 680T Turbo Commander, and production was continued in the Model 680V version with increased gross weight and Model 680W with improved engines. After the Aero Commander take-over by North American, further improvements were offered in the Model 681 Hawk Commander but the name Turbo Commander was restored for the Model 681B in 1971.

On 3 March 1969, the prototype of an improved Turbo Commander 690 had flown and this was certificated in July 1971. A year later, the Turbo Commander 690A appeared, with increased cabin pressure differential, better performance and many detail improvements. Still in production in 1977, the Turbo Commander 690A is described in the specification above. In common with other models in the same design family, it seats six passengers in addition to the pilot, and is widely used as a business transport and utility twin.

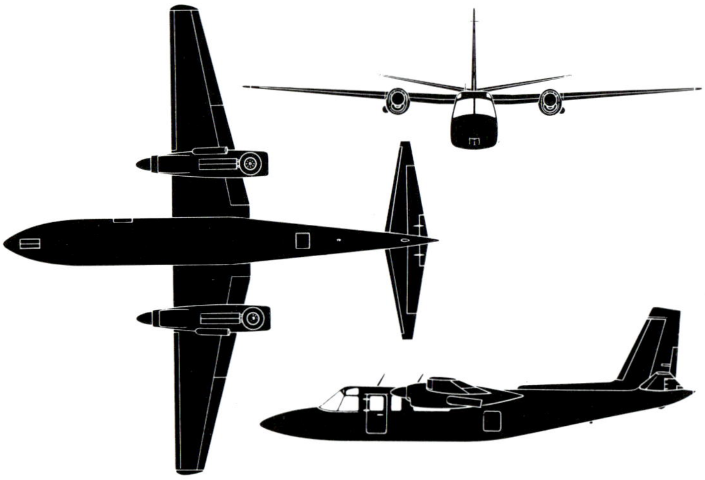

***Above:** Three-view of the Rockwell Turbo Commander 690. The high-wing layout is relatively unusual among business twins.*

***Below:** The Rockwell Turbo Commander, which combines the basic Commander airframe with turboprop engines.*

Above: Three-view of the Rockwell Shrike Commander. Some earlier Aero Commander versions had longer fuselages but were otherwise similar.

Rockwell International still had in production during 1977 a range of piston-engined high-wing business twins derived from the original Aero Commander L-3805 design by Ted Smith. That design went into production as the Commander 520, a six/seven-seat light transport with 240hp Lycoming GO-435-C2 engines and a gross weight of 5,500lb (2495kg). The Model 560 followed, with 260hp GO-480 engines, swept tail and 6,000lb (2720kg) weight. Model 500 versions had 260hp Continental IO-470-M or 250hp Lycoming O-540-A2Bs, with progressive increases in gross weight and engine power in later variants. After Aero Commander became part of North American (now Rockwell International), names were given to the series of light aircraft then in production and Model 500 became the Shrike Commander. The version in production in 1977 has 290hp Lycoming IO-540-E1B5 engines and 6,750-lb (3062-kg) gross weight.

Larger and more powerful versions of the basic Aero Commander high-wing twin-engined design appeared as the Model 680 and 720, some with pressurized fuselage. With longer fuselage, the Grand Commander later became known as the Courser Commander. By 1977, the only piston-engined variant in production in addition to the Shrike Commander was the Commander 685, data for which are given above. This had the same pressurized fuselage as the Turbo Commander (see following entry) and standard accommodation for six passengers in addition to the pilot.

Rockwell Commander 700 (and Fuji FA-300)

USA/Japan

Power Plant: Two Lycoming TIO-540-R2AD flat-six piston engines each rated at 325hp for take-off.
Performance: Max speed, 266mph (428km/h) at 20,000ft (6100m); max cruising speed, 252mph (405km/h) at 24,000ft (7315m); initial rate of climb, 1,460ft/min (7·4m/sec); service ceiling, 30,400ft (9265m); take-off to 50ft (15·2m), 2,420ft (738m); landing from 50ft (15·2m), 2,080ft (634m); range at max cruising power, 810mls (1303km).
Weights: Empty, 4,400lb (1995kg); max take-off and landing, 6,600lb (2993kg).
Dimensions: Span, 42ft $5\frac{1}{2}$in (12·94m); length, 39ft $4\frac{1}{2}$in (12·00m); height, 12ft $9\frac{1}{2}$in (3·90m); wing area, 200·2sq ft (18·60m^2).

To add a small twin-engined business aircraft to its range of products for the general aviation market, Rockwell International concluded an agreement with Fuji in Japan during 1974 for the joint development and production of an aircraft already designed by Fuji. As the FA-300, this had first been projected in 1971 as a twin of conventional low-wing layout, seating 6–8 including the pilot and powered, in the first version, with piston engines.

Following completion of the Fuji-Rockwell agreement, the new type was given the name Commander 700 for the North American market and a batch of six aircraft was laid down for certification to proceed, with three to be completed in the USA. The first FA-300 flew in Japan on 13 November 1975 and the first Commander 700 assembled by Rockwell flew on 25 February 1976. Production deliveries of this initial version, for which data appear above, were to begin during 1977. A second version, the FA-300-Kai or Commander 710, made its first flight on 22 December 1976 and differs in having 450hp engines.

Above: Three-view of the Rockwell Commander 700, designed basically by Fuji in Japan and also in production as the FA-300.

Below: A prototype Rockwell Commander 700. Testing shared between Japan and the USA led to certification in 1977.

Rockwell Sabreliner

USA

The following data refer to the Sabreliner 75A:

Power Plant: Two General Electric CF700-2D-2 turbofans each rated at 4,500lb st (2043kgp) for take-off.

Performance: Max cruising speed, 563mph (906km/h); economical cruising speed, 480mph (773km/h) above 39,000ft (11,895m); initial rate of climb, 4,500ft/min (22·9m/sec); max operating altitude, 45,000ft (13,715m); take-off balanced field length, 4,380ft (1336m); landing distance required, 4,283ft (1305m); range with five passengers and reserves, 1,960mls (3156km).

Weights: Empty, 13,000lb (5896kg); max take-off, 23,300lb (10,580kg); max landing, 22,000lb (9988kg).

Dimensions: Span, 44ft 8in (13·62m); length, 47ft 0in (14·34m); height, 17ft 3in (5·26m); wing area, 342·05sq ft (31·78m²).

The prototype Sabreliner was built as a private venture by North American Inc to meet USAF requirements for a small trainer/transport that could be bought "off the shelf" (as was also the Lockheed JetStar previously described). The gamble proved successful and nearly 200 Sabreliners had

continued on page 164 ▶

***Below:** The cutaway drawing depicts the Rockwell Sabreliner 75A, one of several versions of this original North American Aviation design being produced in 1978. It is distinguished by a deeper fuselage, with better headroom in the cabin, than earlier models of the Sabreliner.*

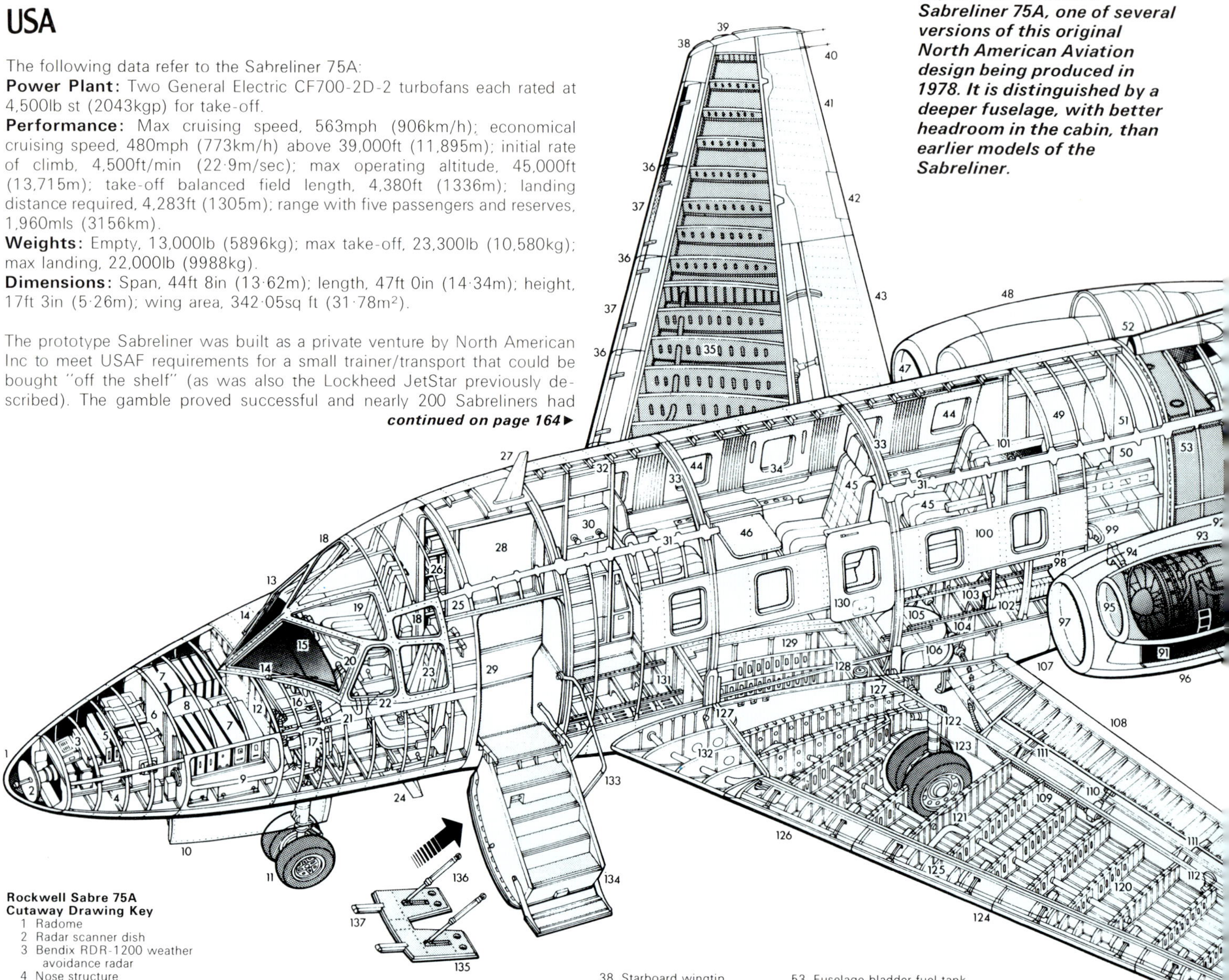

Rockwell Sabre 75A Cutaway Drawing Key

1 Radome
2 Radar scanner dish
3 Bendix RDR-1200 weather avoidance radar
4 Nose structure
5 Electrical equipment compartment
6 Batteries
7 Avionics compartment (Collins flight director and autopilot)
8 Nosewheel well
9 Equipment access doors
10 Nosewheel door
11 Twin steerable nosewheels, Goodrich Type VII
12 Fuselage front bulkhead
13 Windscreen panels
14 Windscreen wipers
15 Instrument panel shroud
16 Back of instrument panel
17 Control linkages
18 Cockpit roof windows
19 Co-pilot's seat
20 Throttles
21 Control column
22 Opening side window
23 Pilot's seat
24 Lower VHF aerial
25 Flight deck bulkhead
26 Electrical equipment rack
27 Upper VHF aerial
28 Forward baggage and coat locker
29 Passenger door
30 Buffet and bar locker
31 Fuselage top longeron
32 Cabin roof structure
33 Fuselage main frames
34 Starboard escape hatch
35 Starboard integral wing fuel tank, capacity 452 US gal (1710 l)
36 Leading edge slat segments
37 Leading edge de-icing
38 Starboard wingtip
39 Navigation light
40 Static dischargers
41 Starboard aileron
42 Aileron trim tab
43 Starboard flap
44 Cabin windows
45 Three-a-side seating
46 Folding table
47 Starboard engine intake
48 Starboard nacelle
49 Rear baggage and coat locker
50 Toilet compartment
51 Cabin rear bulkhead
52 Air system intake
53 Fuselage bladder fuel tank, capacity 199 US gal (753 l)
54 Air trunking
55 Air cycling and air conditioning plant
56 Auxiliary power unit
57 Fuel dump pipe
58 Fin root fairing
59 Fin spar fixing
60 Fin structure
61 Leading edge de-icing
62 Pressure and temperature sensors
63 Starboard tailplane
64 Starboard elevator
65 Fin VHF navigation aerial
66 Anti-collision light
67 Static dischargers
68 Rudder structure
69 Trim tab mechanism
70 Rudder trim tab
71 Tailcone
72 Fuel jettison
73 Port elevator
74 Elevator hinge connection

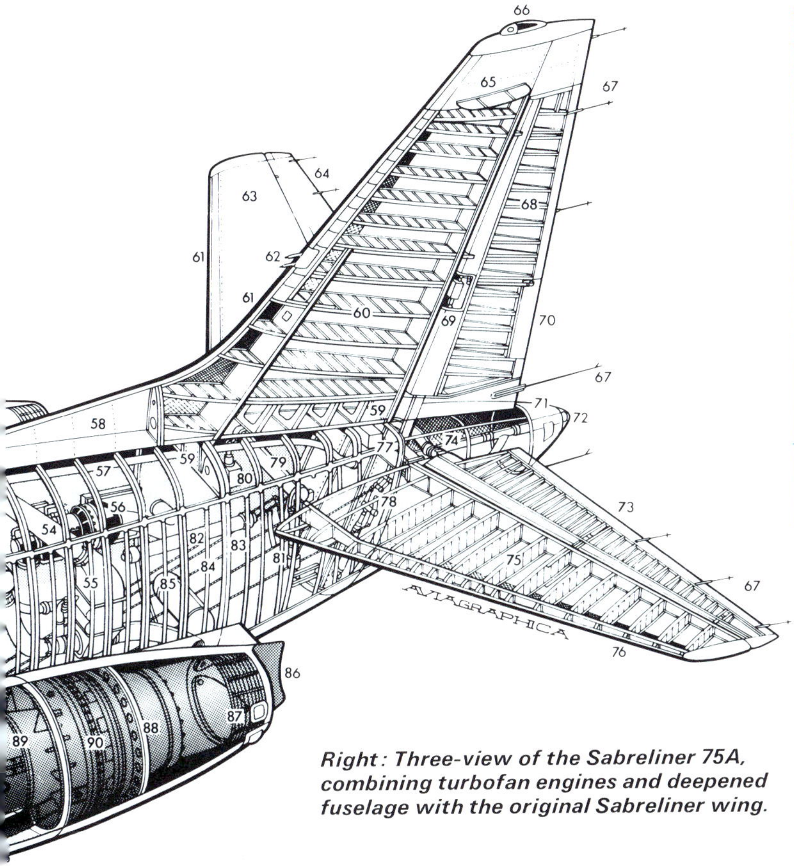

Above: Under development in 1978, the Rockwell Sabreliner 65 introduces fuel-efficient Garrett TFE731 turbofans and an improved wing.

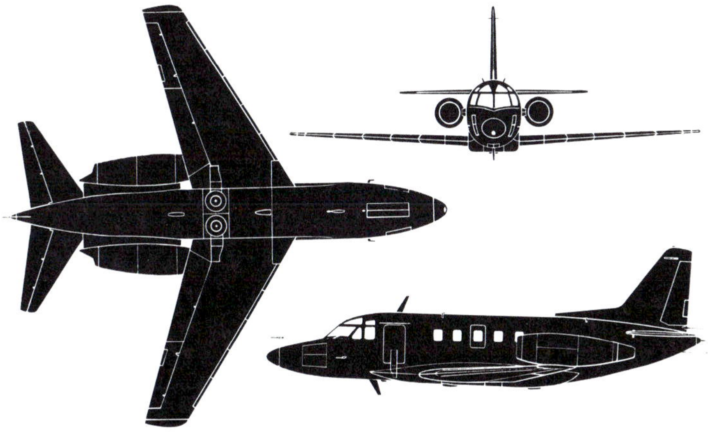

Right: Three-view of the Sabreliner 75A, combining turbofan engines and deepened fuselage with the original Sabreliner wing.

75 Port all-moving tailplane structure
76 Leading edge de-icing
77 Autopilot rudder servo control
78 Elevator controls
79 Tailplane interconnection
80 Autopilot tailplane servo control
81 Moving tailplane jack
82 Hydraulic pressure accumulator
83 Rear fuselage structure

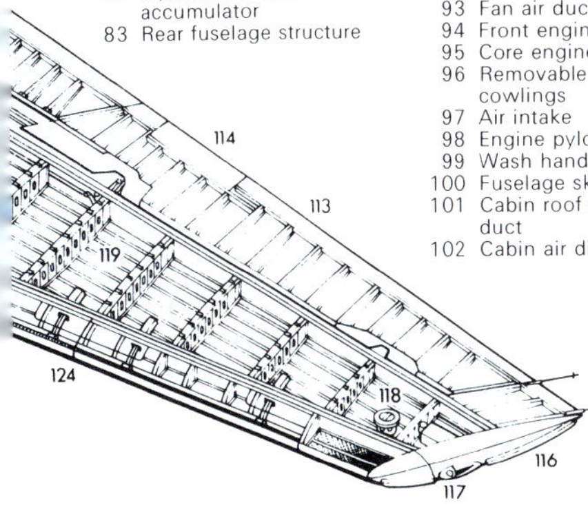

84 Control cables
85 Hydraulic reservoir
86 Port jet efflux
87 Cascade-type vertically-orientated thrust reverser mechanism
88 Nacelle fireproof bulkhead
89 General Electric CF700-2D-2B engine
90 Aft fan casing
91 Engine gearbox and equipment
92 Rear engine mounting
93 Fan air duct
94 Front engine mounting
95 Core engine intake
96 Removable engine cowlings
97 Air intake
98 Engine pylon fairing
99 Wash hand basin
100 Fuselage skin panel
101 Cabin roof air and lighting duct
102 Cabin air distribution duct
103 Fire extinguisher
104 Flap electric motors
105 Seat rails
106 Port mainwheel well
107 Fuselage lower fairing
108 Port flap
109 Flap drive shaft
110 Flap control jack
111 Flap rails
112 Aileron controls
113 Port aileron
114 Aileron trim tab
115 Static dischargers
116 Port wing tip strakes
117 Navigation light
118 Fuel filler
119 Wing structure
120 Port wing fuel tank, capacity 452 US gal (1710 l)
121 Fuel system pipes
122 Port main undercarriage leg
123 Twin mainwheels, Goodrich 10-ply tyres
124 Leading edge slat sections
125 Leading edge structure
126 Leading edge de-icing
127 Spar root fixing
128 Fuel pump
129 Centre box structure
130 Port escape hatch
131 Cabin floor structure
132 Fuel in inboard leading edge (part of main wing integral tank)
133 Handrail
134 Folding entry steps
135 Under fuselage airbrake
136 Twin airbrake jacks
137 Airbrake hinges

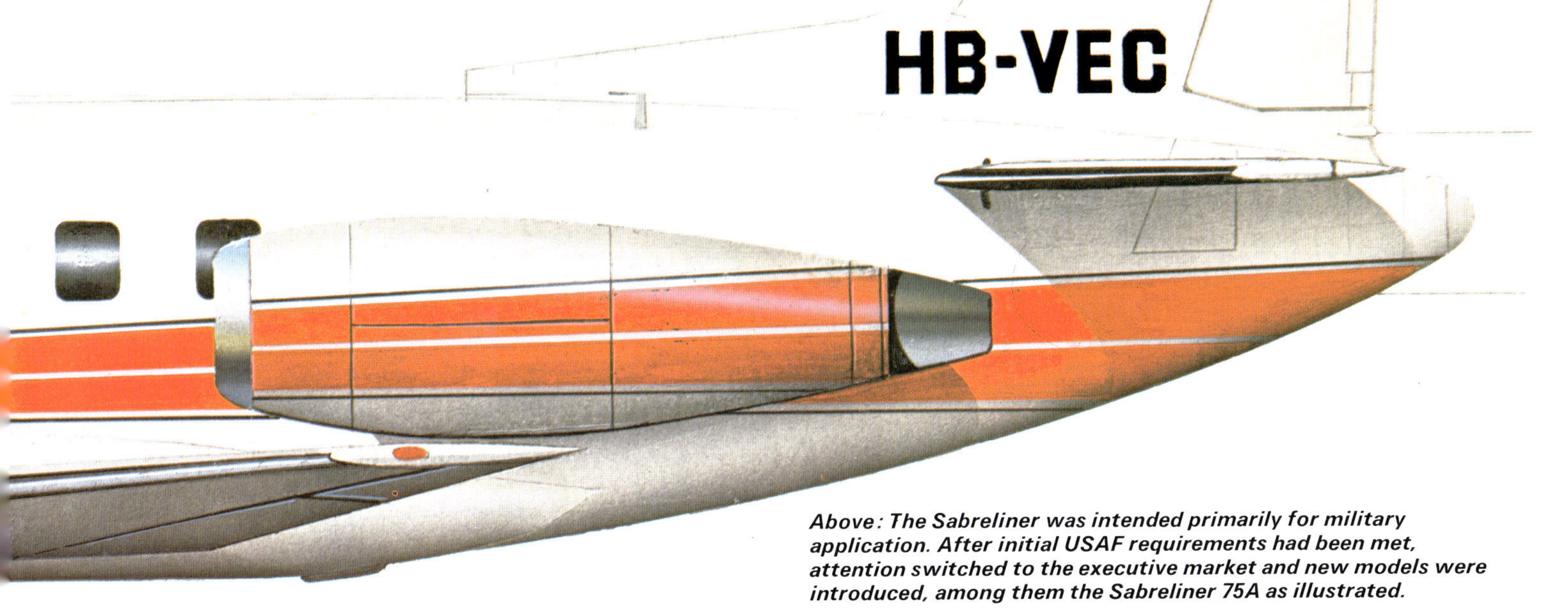

Above: The Sabreliner was intended primarily for military application. After initial USAF requirements had been met, attention switched to the executive market and new models were introduced, among them the Sabreliner 75A as illustrated.

►been built to USAF and USN orders by 1977. A version similar to the military trainer was offered for commercial use as a business transport as the Sabreliner 40, powered by 3,000lb st (1360kgp) Pratt & Whitney JT12A-6A turbojets and over 125 were built by the time production of this variant ended in the early 'seventies.

In 1967, the Sabreliner 40 was joined by the Sabreliner 60 with a longer fuselage and 3,200lb st (1497kgp) JT12A-8 engines, and in 1970 the Sabreliner 70 appeared, with the same engines and a deepened fuselage to give more headroom in the cabin. Whereas the Sabreliner 40 seated up to seven passengers in addition to the flight crew of two, the Models 60 and 70 carried up to nine passengers.

After the North American-Rockwell merger, the name of the Sabreliner 70 was changed to Sabre 75 for a time, then reverting to Sabreliner 75, and in 1973 the Model 75A appeared with CF700-2D-2 turbofan engines. Data for this model appear below. While production of both the Sabreliner 60 and 75A continued in 1977, Rockwell was working on the development of the Sabreliner 65, using a wing evolved by the Raisbeck Group under the title of Mark Five System. This wing allows more fuel to be carried and has supercritical characteristics, giving an overall improvement in performance. While Raisbeck was offering retrofits of this wing for existing Sabreliners, Rockwell adopted TFE 731-3-1D engines for the Sabreliner 65, a prototype of which flew in 29 June 1977 with production deliveries to begin in March 1979. Data appear below.

The following specification refers to the Sabreliner 65:

Power Plant: Two 3,700lb st Garrett AiResearch TFE 731-3-1D turbofans

Performance: Max cruising speed, Mach 0·80, 528mph (849km/h); initial rate of climb, 3,540ft/min (17·9m/sec); max operating altitude, 45,000ft (13,716m); max range, four passengers, with reserves, 2,774mls (4460km); take-off distance, 5,250ft (1600m); landing distance, 4,270ft (1301m).

Weights: Operating weight empty, 13,730lb (6227kg); max take-off, 23,800lb (10,805kg); max landing, 21,755lb (9877kg).

Dimensions: Span, 50ft 5in (15·37m); length, 46ft 11in (14·3m); height, 16ft 0in (4·88m).

***Below:* The Sabreliner 75, which introduced the deepened fuselage but retained the original JT12A turbojets.**

Swearingen Merlin III
USA

Power Plant: Two Garrett AiResearch TPE 331-3U-303G turboprops each rated at 840shp for take-off.

Performance: Max cruising speed, 325mph (523km/h) at 16,000ft (4875m); economical cruising speed, 288mph (463km/h) at 28,000ft (8535m); initial rate of climb, 2,530ft/min (12·9m/sec); service ceiling, 28,900ft (8810m); take-off field length required, 3,050ft (930m); landing distance from 50ft (15·2m), 1,570ft (479m); range with max fuel, 1,968mls (3167km).

Weights: Empty equipped, 7,400lb (3356kg); max take-off, 12,500lb (5670kg); max landing, 11,500lb (5217kg).

Dimensions: Span, 46ft 3in (14·10m); length, 42ft 2in (12·85m); height, 15ft 9½in (5·12m); wing area, 277·5sq ft (25·78m²).

The Swearingen range of business twins derives from the original specialized conversion designed by Ed Swearingen and making use of Beech Queen Air wings and power plant, twin Bonanza undercarriages and new, pressurized fuselages. With turboprop engines replacing the piston power plant, these evolved into the Merlin IIA and Merlin IIB with, respectively, Pratt & Whitney PT6A-20 and Garrett AiResearch TPE331-1-161G engines. Over 100 of these two types were built by Swearingen.

The Merlin III is a refinement of the IIB with uprated engines and small improvements. After Swearingen became part of the Fairchild group of industries, it remained in production alongside the Merlin IV/Metro, described in the airliner section. Data for this model, which usually seats six passengers, or a maximum of eight, in addition to the crew of two, are given above.

***Above right:* Three-view of the Swearingen Merlin III, derived initially from components of the Beech Queen Air.**

***Right:* A Swearingen Merlin II in flight. Pressurization of the fuselage and turboprop engines are featured by all variants of the Merlin business twin.**

Ted Smith Aerostar
USA

Power Plant: Two Lycoming TIO-540-SIA5 flat-six piston engines, each rated at 290hp for take-off.
Performance: Max level speed, 296mph (476km/h) at 25,000ft (7620m); cruising speed, 261mph (420km/h) at 20,000ft (6100m); initial rate of climb, 1,800ft/min (9·15m); 1,680ft (512m); landing distance from 50ft (15·2m), 2,180ft (664m); range, 1,455mls (2341km) with reserves.
Weights: Empty, 4,000lb (1814kg); max take-off and landing, 6,000lb (2721kg).

height, 12ft $1\frac{1}{2}$in (3·70m); wing area, 178sq ft (16·54m^2).

The Aerostar was the last design by the late Ted Smith, who had earlier been responsible for the series of Aero Commander business twins, described under the Rockwell heading above. Known as the Aerostar 320, the prototype flew in November 1966, with 160hp engines and later (as Model 360) with 180hp Lycoming IO-360-E1As. Model 400 had 200hp IO-360-D1As and entered production as Model 600 with 290hp IO-540-G1B5s.

In 1970/71, Aerostars were built by Butler Aviation but Ted Smith's own Aerostar Corporation re-acquired production rights in 1972 since which time production has continued steadily with the rate reaching 100 a year by 1976. In addition to the basic Model 600, the company offers Model 601 with turbosupercharged TIO-540-S1A5 engines and the 601P with pressurized cabin and increased wing span. All provide basic seating for six including the pilot. The Ted Smith company was acquired in 1978 by Piper, with production continuing in the original Ted Smith facilities.

The specification refers to the Model 601P.

***Left:** Three-view of the Aerostar 601, showing the mid-wing location which made the design unique among business twins.*

***Below:** A Smith Aerostar; production of the Model 601 and 601P was continued after Piper had acquired the company in 1978.*

Volpar Turboliner
USA

The following data refer to the Turboliner:
Power Plant: Two Garrett AiResearch TPE331-1-101B turboprops each rated at 705ehp for take-off.
Performance: Max cruising speed, 280mph (451km/h); economical cruising speed, 256mph (412km/h); rate of climb, 1,520ft/min (7·7m/sec); service ceiling, 13,000ft (3960m); range with max payload, 346mls (556km).
Weights: Empty, 5,900–6,600lbs (2676–2993kg) according to version; max take-off weight, 11,500lb (5216kg).
Dimensions: Span, 46ft 0in (14·02m); length, 44ft $2\frac{1}{2}$in (13·47m); height, 9ft 7in (2·92m); wing area, 374sq ft (34·75m^2).

Volpar Inc is one of several companies that have developed improved versions of the Beech 18 for the third-level airline and taxi operator, and between 1960 and 1977, four distinct stages of development had evolved. The first comprised simply a tricycle undercarriage kit for any model of the Beech 18; this was certificated by the FAA in 1960, since which time more than 400 sets have been produced for application to existing Beech 18s.

The second Volpar/Beech conversion comprised the substitution of 705hp Garrett-AiResearch TPE331-1-101B turboprops for the usual Wasp Jr piston radials, plus the tricycle undercarriage. A number of changes were also introduced to the wing and the equipment and a large cargo-loading door was offered as an option. This Turbo 18 was certificated in February 1966 and Volpar was continuing to produce kits against orders from standard Beech users 10 years later.

With all the features of the Turbo 18, the Volpar Turboliner introduced in addition a lengthened fuselage, to allow up to 15 passengers to be carried. A prototype flew on 12 April 1967 and about 30 have been delivered since then, for use by various small airlines in different parts of the world. In 1970, the Turboliner II variant was certificated to conform with the requirements of FAR Part 23, changes primarily being concerned with items of equipment.

The fourth development in the Volpar/Beech series was the Centennial, which has many changes from the original Beech 18. The fuselage was lengthened still further, compared with the Turboliner, to seat 19 passengers, and 750shp Pratt & Whitney PT6A-34 turboprops replaced the TPE331s. A new wing was adopted with improved fail-safe characteristics, and a single fin and rudder replaced the familiar Beech 18 twin unit. Construction of a prototype was put in hand in 1977.

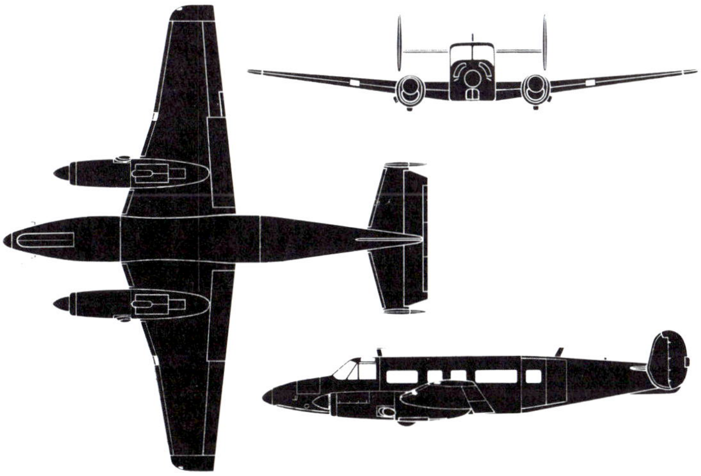

***Above:** Three-view of the Volpar Turboliner. The wing planform and the tail unit are substantially unchanged from those of the original Beech 18 on which the type are based.*

***Below:** The Turboliner, showing TPE331 turboprops and the Volpar-developed nosewheel undercarriage.*

It is well over 30 years since British European Airways formed a pioneer helicopter unit to see where rotary-winged aircraft might fit into the civil air transport scene. For many years, despite bold and determined attempts by others, such as Sabena in Belgium and New York Airways and Los Angeles Airways in the United States, the answer seemed to be that it did not fit in at all. Nothing proved profitable, and many of the services did not even look sensible at the time. One by one nearly all the early routes were abandoned, and the few helicopter airlines, or helicopter divisions of larger fixed-wing airlines, either ceased trading or hung on by odd-jobbing or with subsidies. Gradually, in the 1960s, the situation changed. The chief reason was the development of basic helicopter technology. By far the most important single factor was the emergence of the turbine engine, giving much greater power, much higher reliability and lower costs than those of the piston engines used formerly. This turned the large transport helicopter into a practical and efficient vehicle, able to operate arduous services round the clock with much greater loads. A second factor was that the turbine engine allowed even quite small helicopters to have more than one engine, and thus enjoy a measure of multi-engine safety on a par with that of fixed-wing airliners. A third advance was the development of helicopters with night and IFR (instrument flight rules, ie bad-weather) capability, so that they could at last operate a timetable that could be reliably offered to the

HELICOPTERS

public in summer and winter alike. A very important by-product of these developments was that turning the helicopter into a reliable all-weather transport vehicle dramatically lowered the insurance premiums, which had previously been several times higher than for fixed-wing aircraft of similar size.

While these developments were transforming the helicopter, the global search for oil, allied with dozens of other duties, emerged to give the helicopter operator much more work. Such tasks as forest patrol and firefighting, pipeline construction and patrol, erection and patrol of remote electric power lines, and shuttling to ships at sea, added to mushrooming growth in mercy flights, casualty evacuation from disasters, sea rescue and diverse other kinds of work. But the oil industry is in many areas the No 1 helicopter user today, for the obvious reason that drill rigs, work platforms and even many on-shore oilfields generally cannot be reached quickly by any other means of transport. The North Sea oil and gas fields are served around the clock by over one hundred large helicopters shuttling between the rigs and up to nine base airfields, carrying everything except the heaviest or least-urgent supplies (and "least urgent" usually does not apply to the oil industry). Similar helicopter fleets are found around the United States, Alaska, Siberia and many other areas. These intensive services help underpin scheduled and taxi operations for the general public and provide a basis for the development of more efficient helicopters in future.

Aérospatiale SA 341 Gazelle
France

The specification refers to the SA 341G.
Power Plant: One Turboméca Astazou IVA turboshaft rated at 590shp for take-off.
Performance: Max cruising speed, 164mph (264km/h); economical cruising speed, 144mph (233km/h); initial rate of climb, 1,770ft/min (9·0m/sec); hovering ceiling (in ground effect), 9,350ft (2850m); range with typical load, 223mls (360km).
Weights: Empty, 2,022lb (917kg); max take-off, 3,970lb (1800kg).
Dimensions: Rotor diameter, 34ft 5½in (10·50m); fuselage length, 31ft 3¼in (9·53m); height, 10ft 2½in (3·15m); main rotor disc area, 931sq ft (86·5m²).

The second of the Aérospatiale helicopters included in the Anglo-French package deal of 1967, the Gazelle was developed as a general purpose lightweight helicopter for military and civil use and has been produced in large numbers by both Aérospatiale and Westland, as well as being assembled in Yugoslavia. The Gazelle is basically a five-seater, with two side-by-side in the front of the cabin and a bench seat for three in the rear. Folding the latter seat down leaves the cabin unobstructed for the carriage of cargo. The SA 340 prototype first flew on 7 April 1967, with an Astazou III engine and the first production SA 341 on 6 August 1971. Initial versions up to the SA 341F were for military use; the civil SA 341G was certificated on 7 June 1972 and later became the world's first helicopter authorised for one-pilot operation in IFR conditions. About 500 Gazelles had been built by early 1977, including military models. During 1977, Aérospatiale began delivery of the SA 342J variant, with 870shp Astazou XIVH engine and 4,190lb (1900kg) gross weight.

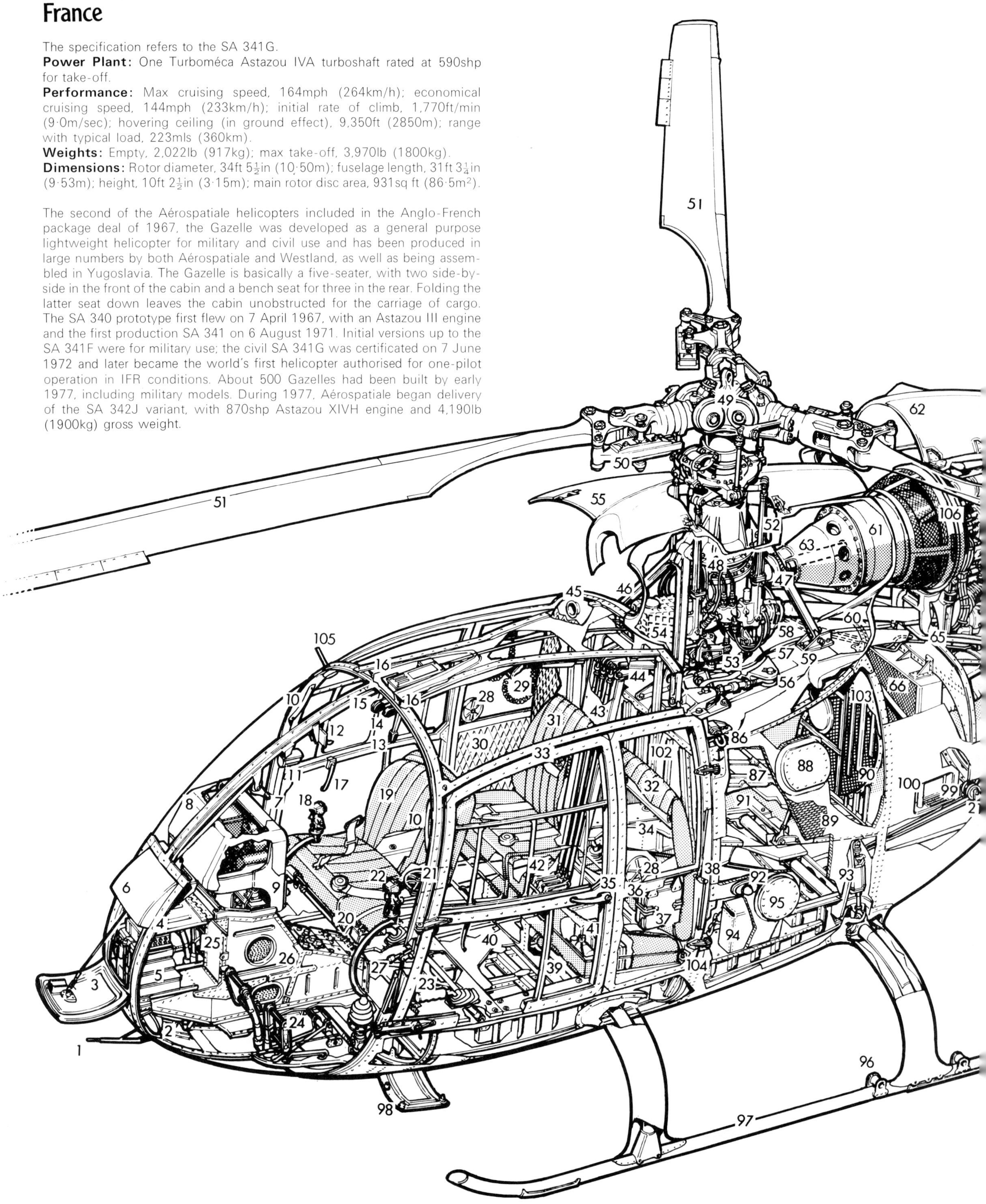

Above: The commercial version of the Aérospatiale Gazelle is depicted in the cutaway drawing; military versions are similar apart from special equipment provision.

Right: A civil Gazelle with emergency flotation equipment attached to the skid undercarriage. This is one of a dozen civil Gazelles delivered from the Westland assembly line in the UK.

Westland/Aerospatiale SA.341 Gazelle Cutaway Drawing Key

1 Pitot head
2 Landing light
3 Battery access panel (open)
4 Circuit breaker panel
5 Battery
6 Cabin ventilating air intake
7 Cabin ventilating air control lever
8 Instrument panel shroud
9 Instrument panel
10 Handgrip (assisting entry/exit)
11 Standby compass
12 Rear view mirror
13 Transmission brake control lever
14 Fuel flow control lever
15 Fuel shut-off lever
16 Cabin heating system ducts
17 Door pull (both forward doors)
18 Pilot's cyclic pitch stick
19 Pilot's seat
20 Collective lever with control box
21 Tail-rotor control cable relay
22 Co-pilot's cyclic pitch stick
23 Co-pilot's collective pitch stick
24 Co-pilot's directional control assembly
25 Pilot's directional control assembly
26 Control pedestal and radio control panel
27 Left hand front door jettison lever
28 Ventilator with rotational adjuster
29 Roof mounted intercom connectors
30 Padded interior trim
31 Single passenger seat
32 Double passenger seat
33 Circuit breaker panel
34 Cargo compartment access (seat squab can be raised and seat base/cushion hinged forward into floor recess)
35 Left hand front door
36 Left hand rear door
37 First aid kit stowage (inner face of door)
38 Left hand rear door jettison linkage
39 Hinged passenger seat base/cushion
40 Passenger seat floor recess
41 Dynamotor and transmitter/receiver
42 Mixing unit (rotor controls)
43 Main rotor controls and guard panel
44 Transmission platform main rotor control linkage
45 Stale air extractor duct
46 Main gearbox mounting 'V' strut
47 Engine to main gearbox coupling
48 Main gearbox
49 Main rotor head (semi-articulated)
50 Friction type drag damper
51 Bolkow-type rotor blades
52 Pitch change control assembly
53 Control linkage to pitch change assembly
54 Hydraulic pack (master hydraulic pump)
55 Right hand main gearbox cowling (open for access)
56 Mounting plate damper (main gearbox)
57 Transmission platform
58 Transmission disc-brake
59 Main gearbox mounting rear strut
60 Transmission shaft (main gearbox to intermediate gearbox)
61 Reduction gear housing
62 Starboard engine cowling (open for access)
63 Clutch and free-wheel unit
64 Fuel flow control assembly
65 Engine mounting strut with rubber dampers
66 Oil cooler
67 Intermediate gearbox
68 Oil cooler warm air extraction duct
69 Transmission shaft to tail-rotor gearbox
70 Hydraulic lines to tail-rotor gearbox
71 Tail boom
72 Transmission shaft bearing
73 Tail rotor control rod
74 Tail rotor gearbox
75 Tail rotor gearbox filler cap (lubricant)
76 Tail rotor hub
77 Tail rotor blades
78 Main stabilizer ventral fin
79 Stabilizer/tailplane
80 Tail rotor hub/fairing support strut
81 Tail beacon
82 Upper UHF aerial
83 Navigation light
84 Conduit for tail electrics leads
85 Lower UHF/VHF aerial
86 Securing (anchorage) ring
87 Fuel tank (upper compartment of centre section)
88 Fuel tank access panel
89 Honeycomb sandwich centre section structure
90 Oil cooler compartment air intake mesh grill
91 Distribution box
92 Port side navigation light
93 Landing gear damper (hydraulic)
94 Medical kit container with securing hook
95 Port access panel to cargo compartment
96 Attachment lug for wheel (towing)
97 Landing gear
98 Access panel to under-floor section
99 Foot hold with anti-slip surface (to aid access to cowling/transmission platform)
100 Hand hold (to aid access to cowling/transmission platform)
101 Main stabilizer fin (heavily cambered to offload rotor)
102 Forward bulkhead
103 Aft bulkhead
104 Passenger safety belt anchorage point
105 Air temperature (exterior) gauge
106 Turbomeca Astazou III turboshaft
107 Honeycomb and wood end plate fin structure (metal skinned)
108 Honeycomb structure of main rotor blade(s)
109 Adjustable weights assembly (fine balance dynamically) in tip of each main rotor blade
110 Tab on main lift area of main rotor blade(s)
111 Polyurethane band on leading edge of main rotor blade(s)

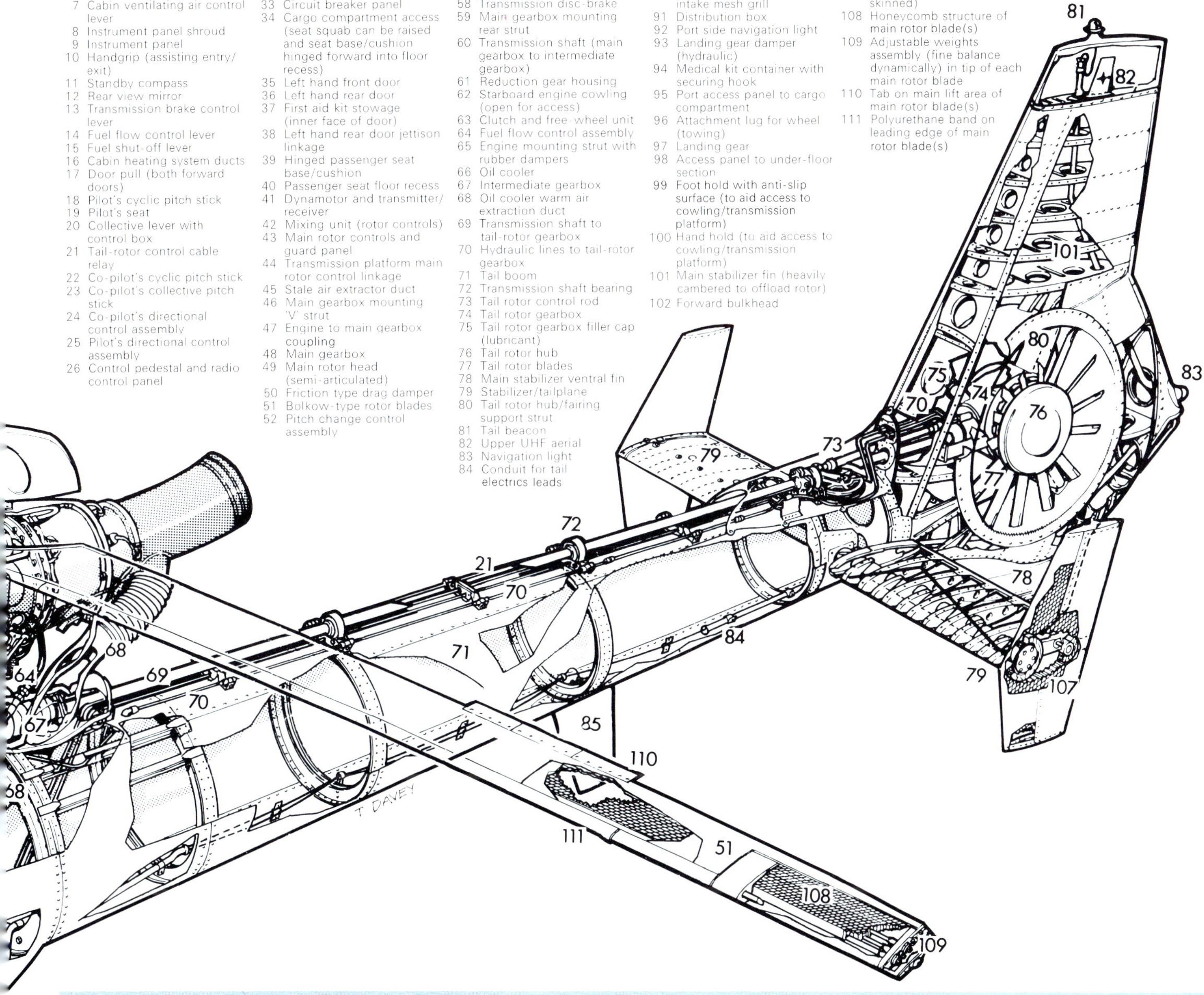

Aérospatiale SA 316/319 Alouette III
France

Power Plant: One Turbomeca Astazou XIV turboshaft derated to 600shp.
Performance: Max speed, 136mph (220km/h) at sea level; max cruising speed, 122mph (197km/h) at sea level; initial rate of climb, 885ft/min (4·5m/sec); hovering ceiling (in ground effect), 10·70ft (3100m); range with six passengers, 375mls (605km).
Weights: Empty, 2,513lb (1140kg); max take-off, 4,960lb (2250kg).
Dimensions: Rotor diameter, 36ft $1\frac{3}{4}$in (11·02m); overall length (rotors folded), 32ft $10\frac{3}{4}$in (10·03m); height, 9ft 10in (3·00m).

To date the most successful of an extensive range of helicopters developed by the national Aérospatiale company in France, the Alouette had its origins in the Sud-Est SE.3101 prototype flown on 15 June 1948. First to bear the Alouette name were the SE.3120 prototypes, the first of which flew on 31 July 1951. A switch was made from piston engine to turboshaft power in the Alouette II, which entered production in 1956; about 1,300 were built. The Alouette III – originally SE.3160 and then SA 316 and SA 316B – first flew on 28 February 1959 and introduced a more refined fuselage with a cabin seating up to six passengers in addition to the pilot. The current SA 316B has an 870shp Turboméca Astouste IIIB engine and gross weight of 4,850lb (2200kg). Also in production since 1968 has been the SA 319B version with an Astazou engine, offering improved performance. Including military sales, some 1,400 Alouette IIIs of these two types had been built by early 1977, and the Alouette was in service in 70 countries. The data refers to the SA 319B.

***Below:** The Aérospatiale Alouette, one of Europe's best-selling helicopters, is widely deployed throughout the world, in its several variants.*

Aérospatiale SA 330 Puma
France

***Below:** Developed originally for military use, the Puma fulfils several civil roles, notably that of oil field support operations.*

Power Plant: Two Turboméca Turmo IVC turboshafts each rated at 1,575hp for take-off.
Performance: Normal cruising speed, 160mph (258km/h); initial rate of climb, 1,200ft/min (6·1m/sec); hovering ceiling (in ground effect), 7,545ft (2300m); max range, no reserves, 341mls (550km).
Weights: Empty, 7,800lb (3540kg); max take-off and landing, 16,315lb (7400kg).
Dimensions: Rotor diameter, 49ft $2\frac{1}{2}$in (15·00m); fuselage length, 46ft $1\frac{1}{2}$in (14·06m); height, 16ft $10\frac{1}{2}$in (5·14m); main rotor disc area, 1,905sq ft (177·0m²).

Aérospatiale SA 360/SA 365 Dauphin
France

Power Plant: One Turboméca Astazou XVIIIA turboshaft rated at 1,050shp for take-off.
Performance: Max cruising speed, 172mph (278km/h); economical cruising speed, 152mph (245km/h); initial rate of climb, 1,770ft/min (9m/sec); hovering ceiling (in ground effect), 7,380ft (2250m); range with max fuel, 405mls (650km).
Weights: Basic operating, 3,428lb (1555kg); max payload (internal), 2,500lb (1150kg); max take-off, 6,613lb (3000kg).
Dimensions: Rotor diameter, 37ft 8¾in (11·50m); fuselage length, 36ft 0in (10·98m); height, 11ft 6in (3·50m).

As a replacement for the widely-used Alouette, previously described, the Dauphin first flew on 2 June 1972, when the prototype was powered by a 980shp Astazou XVI turboshaft. An Astazou XVIIIA and certain small modifications were introduced for a second phase of flight tests which began on 4 May 1973 and this power plant is used in the production version, deliveries of which began in 1976 following certification on 18 December 1975. The SA 360 has a fully enclosed cabin for up to 10 occupants including the pilot and a number of alternative layouts are offered, for 13 seats in a high density transport version, six seats and 88-cu ft (2·50-m) of cargo space, four stretchers plus attendant and crew or four–five seats for VIP transport. A cargo sling can carry 2,755lb (1250kg) externally. Data for the standard SA 360 appear above; also available from 1978 is the SA 365 twin-engined variant of the Dauphin, first flown on 24 January 1975 with two 650shp Turboméca Arriel turboshafts.

***Below:** SA 360. The Aerospatiale Dauphin, like the Bell 214, is available in single- and twin-engined versions.*

Development of the SA 330 began in the early 'sixties to meet a French Army requirement for a medium lift helicopter and the type subsequently became one of a trio of helicopters included in an Anglo-French coproduction deal. With a crew of two, the Puma normally carries 16 troops in its military versions or a similar number of passengers in a typical commercial layout; VIP arrangements provide 8–12 seats, and in cargo or utility rôles, up to 6,600lb (3000kg) can be slung beneath the fuselage from an internally mounted cargo sling. The SA 330 prototype first flew on 15 April 1965 and the first civil version, the SA 330F, was flown on 26 September 1969 and certificated in October 1970. The SA 330G is the civil cargo-carrying version, and the SA 330J and SA 330L are respectively passenger and cargo versions with main rotor blades of composite construction and 16,315lb (7400kg) gross weight. Of 525 Pumas sold by early 1977, 72 were for civil or government agency use. The specification refers to the SA 330J.

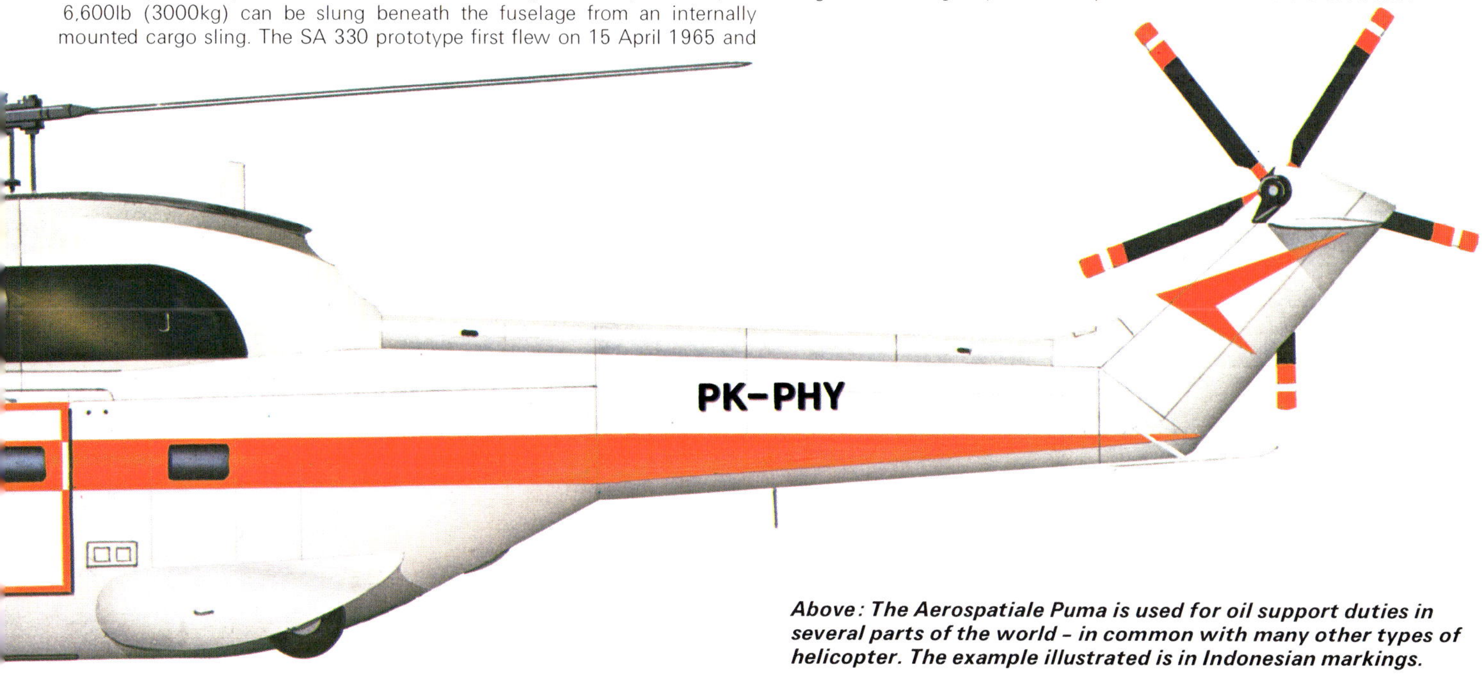

***Above:** The Aerospatiale Puma is used for oil support duties in several parts of the world – in common with many other types of helicopter. The example illustrated is in Indonesian markings.*

Agusta A-109A
Italy

Power Plant: Two Allison 250-C20B turboshafts each rated at 420shp for take-off.
Performance: Max cruising speed, 165mph (266km/h); best cruising speed, 143mph (231km/h); initial rate of climb, 1,620ft/min (8·2m/sec); hovering ceiling (in ground effect), 9,800ft (2987m); max range, 350mls (565km).
Weights: Empty, 3,120lb (1415kg); max take-off, 5,400lb (2450kg).
Dimensions: Rotor diameter, 36ft 1in (11·00m); fuselage length, 35ft 1¾in (10·71m); height, 10ft 10in (3·30m); main rotor disc area, 1,022·5sq ft (95·00m²).

The Agusta company (Costruzioni Aeronautische Giovanni Agusta SpA) is Italy's oldest surviving aircraft manufacturer, having been founded in 1907. Since 1952, it has specialized in helicopter production, and has held a series of licences for the construction of Bell and Sikorsky types. Several helicopters of original Agusta design have reached the prototype stage but the first to enter series production is the A-109, a high-speed general purpose type the prototype of which flew on 4 August 1971. Basic accommodation in the civil A-109A version is for eight, with two side-by-side at the front of the cabin and two bench seats for three each. Mixed passenger-cargo loads can be carried by removing one of the seat rows. The A-109A was certificated on 1 June 1975 and deliveries – initially of the military variant – began in 1977.

***Right:** An Agusta A109 demonstrator flies over the familiar skyline of downtown Los Angeles. Commercial deliveries began in 1978.*

***Above:** The first helicopter of original design to be put into production by Agusta, the A109 has both civil and military applications. Previously, Agusta had built large numbers of American helicopters under licence.*

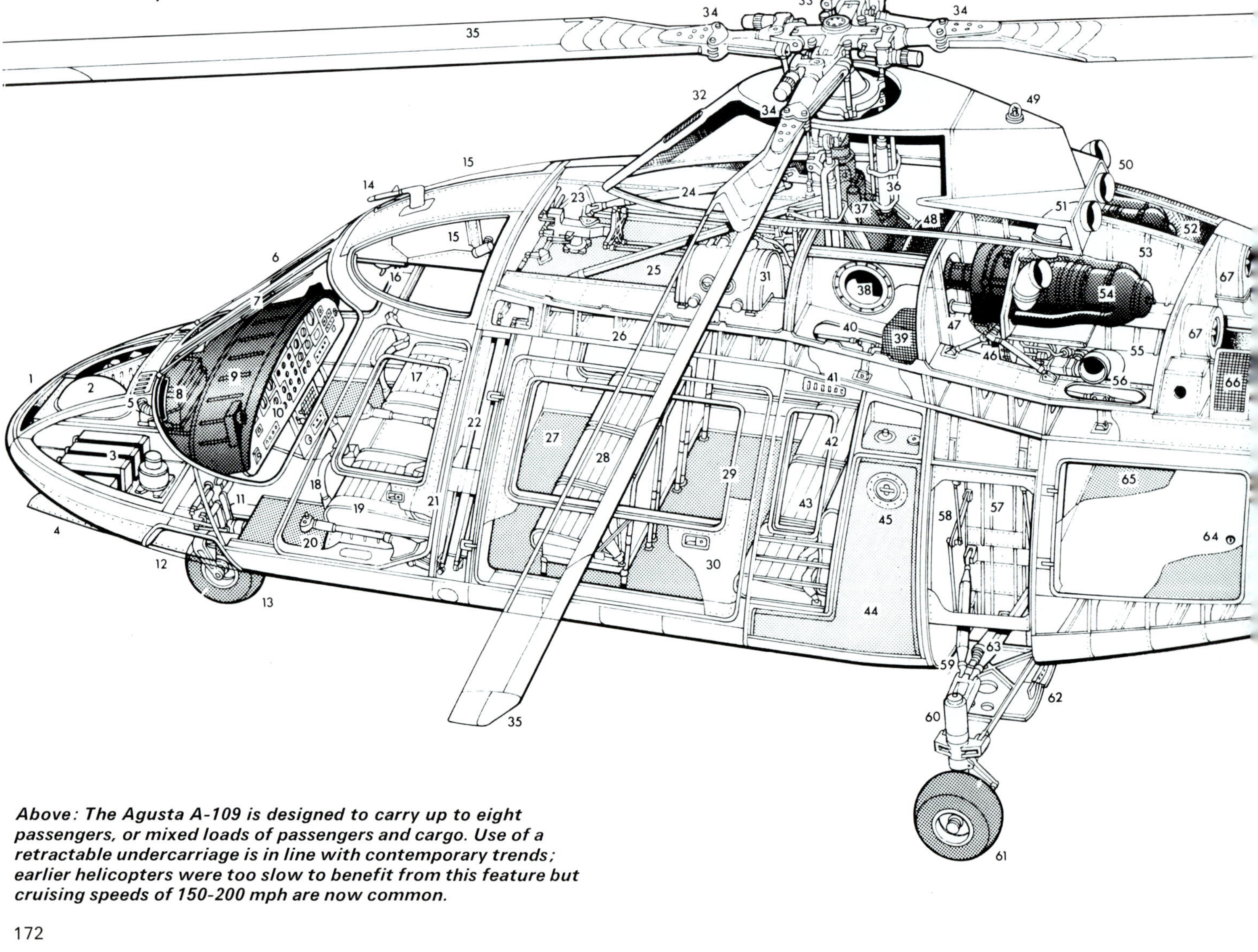

***Above:** The Agusta A-109 is designed to carry up to eight passengers, or mixed loads of passengers and cargo. Use of a retractable undercarriage is in line with contemporary trends; earlier helicopters were too slow to benefit from this feature but cruising speeds of 150-200 mph are now common.*

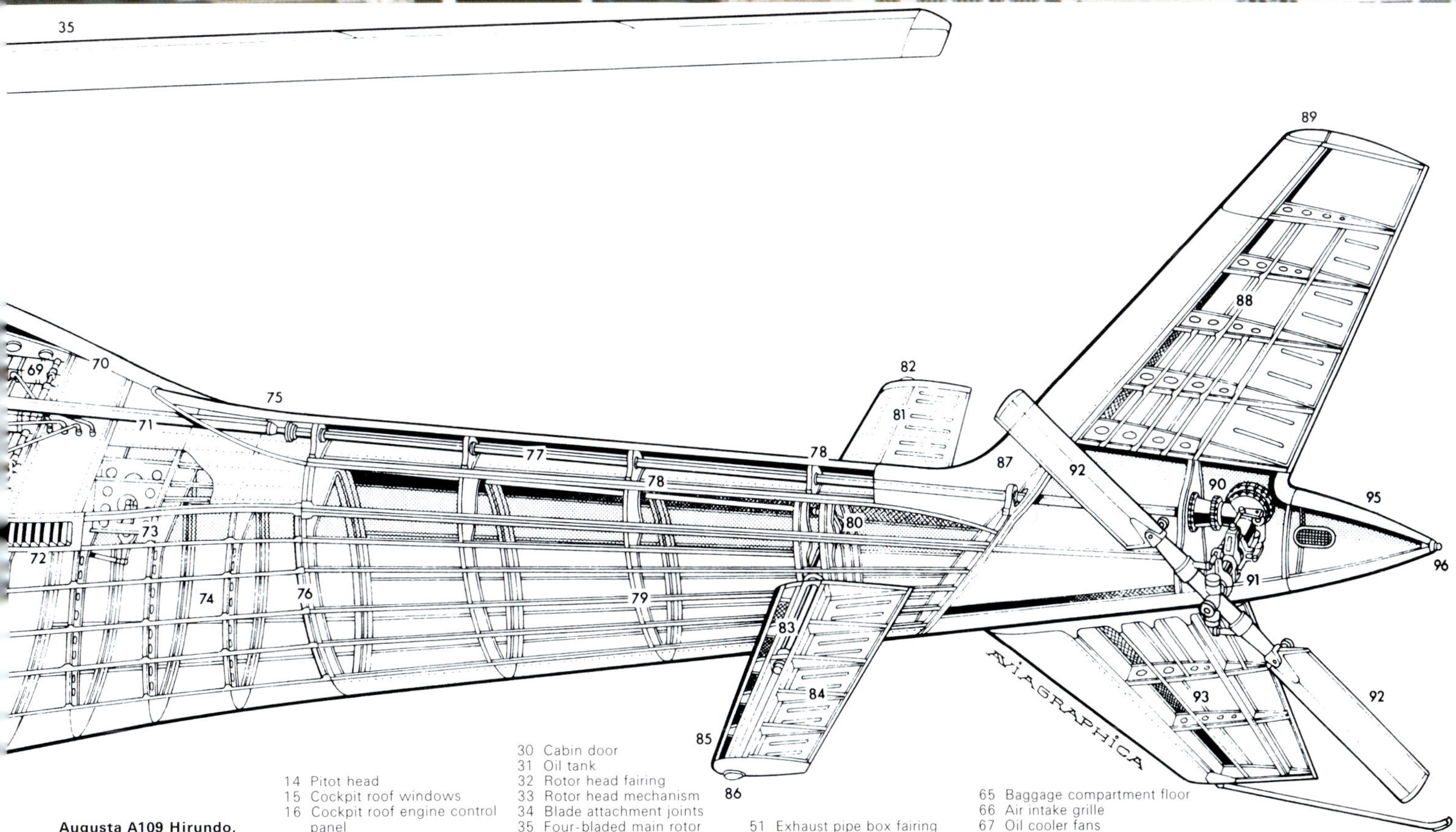

Augusta A109 Hirundo, Cutaway drawing key

1 Nose compartment
2 Nosewheel well
3 Radio and electronics rack
4 Nosewheel door
5 Ventilation duct
6 Windscreen
7 Windscreen wipers
8 Battery
9 Instrument panel shroud
10 Instrument panel
11 Rudder pedals
12 Downward vision window
13 Nosewheel
14 Pitot head
15 Cockpit roof windows
16 Cockpit roof engine control panel
17 First pilot's seat
18 Collective pitch control column
19 Second pilot's seat
20 Cyclic pitch control
21 Cockpit door
22 Control rod duct
23 Pitch control linkage mechanism
24 Gearbox mounting struts
25 Cabin roof
26 Roof beam construction
27 Passenger cabin floor
28 Passenger seats, front row
29 Cabin side window
30 Cabin door
31 Oil tank
32 Rotor head fairing
33 Rotor head mechanism
34 Blade attachment joints
35 Four-bladed main rotor
36 Pitch control jacks
37 Rotor gearbox
38 Engine air intake
39 Air intake grille
40 Push-pull control rods
41 Cabin air vent
42 Cabin rear window
43 Passenger seats, rear row
44 Port fuel tank
45 Fuel filler cap
46 Engine mounting struts
47 Engine transmission shaft
48 Engine combining gearbox
49 Anti-collision light
50 Engine exhaust pipes
51 Exhaust pipe box fairing
52 Starboard engine bay
53 Engine compartment firewall
54 Allison 250-C20B turboshaft engine
55 Port engine bay
56 Generator cooling duct
57 Main undercarriage bay
58 Undercarriage door mechanism
59 Undercarriage leg top forks
60 Main leg strut
61 Mainwheel
62 Mainwheel doors
63 Retraction jack
64 Baggage compartment door
65 Baggage compartment floor
66 Air intake grille
67 Oil cooler fans
68 Engine oil cooler
69 Transmission oil cooler
70 Fuselage top fairing
71 Tail rotor drive shaft
72 Oil cooler air vent
73 Control rod hinge joint
74 Rear fuselage frame construction
75 Spine shaft housing
76 Tailcone joint
77 Tail rotor transmission shaft
78 Transmission shaft bearings
79 Tailcone construction
80 Elevator hinge control
81 Starboard elevator
82 Starboard navigation light
83 Elevator hinge shaft
84 Elevator construction
85 Port elevator
86 Port navigation light
87 Fin foot fairing
88 Fin construction
89 Fin tip fairing
90 Tail rotor gearbox
91 Tail rotor control mechanism
92 Two-bladed tail rotor
93 Ventral fin construction
94 Tailskid
95 Tailcone fairing
96 Rear navigation light

Bell Model 204/205/214

USA

Power Plant: One Lycoming T5313A turboshaft derated to 1,250shp for take-off.
Performance: Max level speed, 127mph (204km/h) at 3,000ft (915m); max cruising speed, 111mph (179km/h) at 8,000ft (2440m); initial rate of climb, 1,680ft/min (8·5m/sec); hovering ceiling (in ground effect) 10,400ft (3170m); range, 344mls (553km) cruising at 8,000ft (2440m).
Weights: Empty equipped, 5,197lb (2357km); max take-off (with external load), 10,500lb (4763kg).
Dimensions: Rotor diameter, 48ft 0in (14·63m); length of fuselage, 41ft 10$\frac{3}{4}$in (12·77m); height overall, 14ft 6in (4·42m); main rotor disc area, 1,809 sq ft (168·06m^2).

First flown on 22 October 1956, the prototype Bell Model 204 was one of three ordered by the US Army (designated XH-40) after Bell had won a design competition for a new utility helicopter. Subsequently put into production as the HU-1 Iroquois (and, unofficially, Huey) the Model 204 gave rise to a family of subsequent variants that collectively have accounted for greater production numbers than any other type of helicopter to date, many thousands being built for US Army, Navy, Air Force and Marine Corps use – especially in Vietnam – and for export. The commercial Model 204B, with a 1,100hp Lycoming T5309A turboshaft, was certificated on 5 April 1963; seating up to 10 including the pilot, it was built by Bell in the USA, Fuji in Japan and Agusta in Italy. The Model 205 was an enlarged derivative of the original helicopter, having more power and a longer fuselage which, in the civil Model 205A version, seats up to 15. Rapid conversion for other duties is possible, including cargo carrying, flying crane (with 5,000-lb/2268-kg external load), ambulance, rescue or executive transport. The Model 205A has also been built in Italy, Japan and Taiwan and large numbers are in service throughout the world; data are for the 205A-1 variant, still in production in 1977. A further derivative, first flown as the Model 214 Huey Plus in 1970, is the Model 214B BigLifter, with a 2,250shp Lycoming T5508D turboshaft, a gross weight of 16,000lb (7257kg) and a rotor diameter of 50ft 0in (15·24m).

***Above:** A Bell 205 flies above a crowded motorway, demonstrating the attraction of the helicopter as a business transport.*

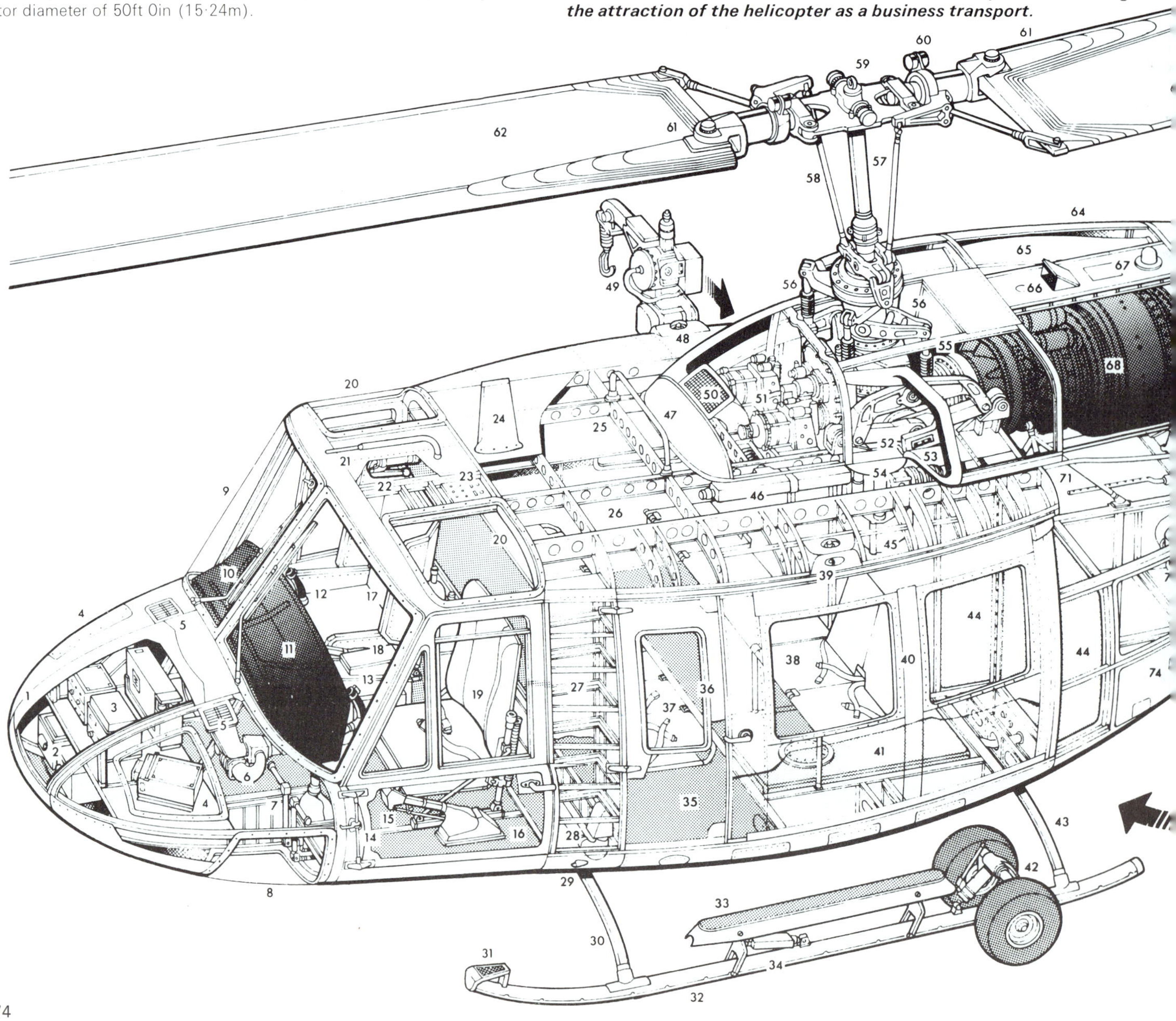

Above: The ability of the helicopter to operate into restricted areas and to lift awkward loads is another of its advantages.

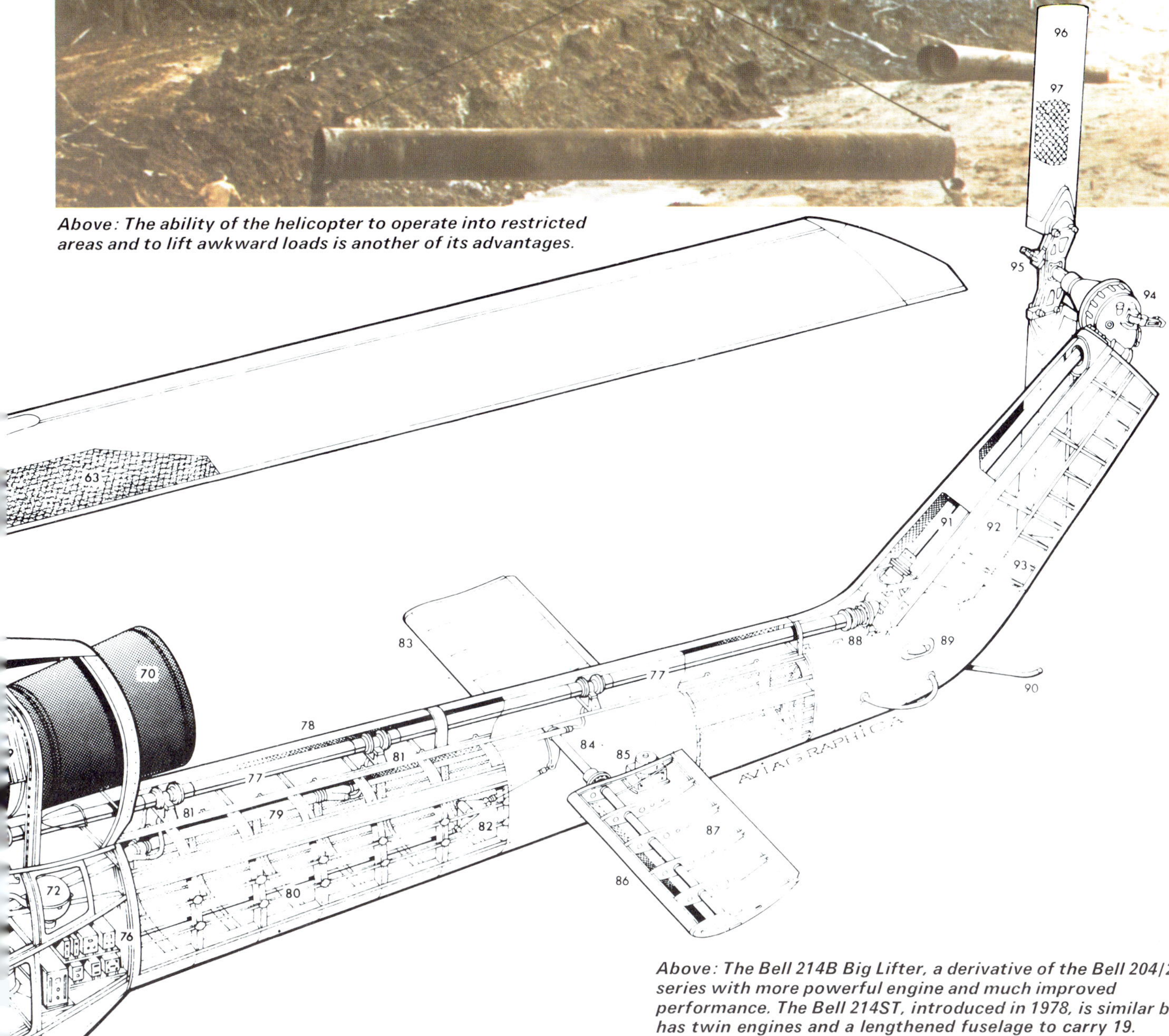

Above: The Bell 214B Big Lifter, a derivative of the Bell 204/205 series with more powerful engine and much improved performance. The Bell 214ST, introduced in 1978, is similar but has twin engines and a lengthened fuselage to carry 19.

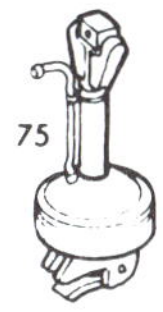

Bell 214B, Cutaway Drawing Key

1 Nose compartment access panel
2 Batteries
3 Radio and electronics compartment
4 Access doors
5 Air grilles
6 Air conditioning system
7 Yaw-control pedals
8 Downward-vision window
9 Windshield panel
10 Windscreen wipers
11 Instrument panel shroud
12 Pilot's control column, cyclic pitch
13 Co-pilot's control column
14 Cockpit door hinge release mechanism
15 Collective pitch control
16 Cockpit floor
17 Pilot's seat, military armoured type
18 Centre console
19 Co-pilot's seat, commercial type
20 Cockpit eyebrow windows
21 Pitot tube
22 Rotor brake control
23 Overhead control panel
24 Antenna
25 Cabin roof construction
26 Main passenger/cargo compartment
27 Fuselage side panel construction
28 Heater duct
29 Position light
30 Landing skid front strut
31 Cockpit step
32 Landing skid
33 Cabin entry step
34 Step jack
35 Cabin floor
36 Hinged forward cabin door
37 Rearward facing seats
38 Forward facing seat row
39 Port navigation lights
40 Main cabin sliding cargo door
41 Underfloor fuel tank
42 Ground handling wheels (removeable)
43 Landing skid rear strut
44 Main fuel tanks
45 Gearbox oil tank sump
46 Cabin air duct
47 Antenna
48 Starboard navigation lights
49 Rescue winch/hoist
50 Air intake grille
51 Hydraulic equipment compartment
52 Nodal beam gearbox mounting
53 Port engine intake
54 Gearbox (main and tail rotor drives)
55 Engine reduction gearbox
56 Rotor blade control hinge links
57 Main rotor shaft
58 Blade control rods
59 Pivoted rotor head mounting
60 Rotor blade counterweight
61 Laminated blade attachment straps
62 Main rotor blade
63 Honeycomb construction
64 Engine cowlings
65 Intake duct particle separator
66 Ventilating intake
67 Anti collision light
68 Lycoming T5508D turboshaft engine
69 Intake particle separator exhaust duct
70 Engine exhaust pipe
71 Engine mounting struts
72 Fire extinguisher bottle
73 Oil cooler fan
74 Rear equipment compartments
75 Cargo hook
76 Rear radio and electronics racks
77 Tail rotor drive shaft
78 Spine shaft housing
79 Bearing cooling air duct
80 Tailboom construction
81 Tailshaft bearings
82 Elevator hinge control
83 Starboard elevator
84 Elevator cross shaft
85 Radio compass
86 Port elevator
87 Elevator construction
88 Intermediate gearbox
89 Rear navigation light
90 Tail skid
91 Tail rotor transmission shaft
92 Fin construction
93 Cambered section fin (directional stability)
94 Tail gearbox
95 Tail rotor pitch control
96 Two-blade tail rotor
97 Honeycomb blade construction

Bell Model 206 JetRanger
USA

Power Plant: One Allison 250-C20 turboshaft rated at 400shp for take-off. **Performance:** Max speed, 140mph (225km/h) at sea level; max cruising speed, 136mph (219km/h) at 5,000ft (1515m); economical cruising speed, 138mph (222km/h) at 5,000ft (1525m); initial rate of climb, 1,260ft/min (6·4m/sec); hovering ceiling (in ground effect), 11,300ft (3445m); range with max payload, 388mls (624km) at 5,000ft (1525m) with no reserves. **Weights:** Empty, 1,455lb (660kg); max take-off, 3,200lb (1451kg). **Dimensions:** Rotor diameter, 33ft 4in (10·16m); fuselage length, 31ft 2in (9·50m); height, 9ft 6½in (2·91m); main rotor disc area, 873sq ft (81·1m^2).

Like the Model 204/205/214 series of helicopters previously described, the Model 206 had its origins in a military development programme but subsequently proved to have major applications in the civil market. More than 5,000 Model 206s had been delivered by early 1977 for military and civil use; one commercial operator, Petroleum Helicopters Inc, alone had a fleet of 135 JetRangers in service. As the OH-4A, the prototype Model 206 first flew on 8 December 1962 and for US Army service the helicopter entered production as the OH-58 Kiowa. The commercial Model 206A first flew on 10 January 1966 and deliveries began in 1967, the type subsequently being built also by Agusta in Italy. An uprated engine and other improvements distinguish the Model 206B JetRanger II, delivered from 1971 onwards, both types seating five in normal passenger layouts, but the Model 206L Long Ranger, first flown on 11 September 1974 and in production since 1975, has a cabin 2ft 1in (0·6in) longer than the original Jet Ranger and seats up to seven. The Long Ranger has a gross weight of 4,000lb (1814kg) and a 420shp Allison 250-C20B engine; the same power plant was offered with other improvements, in the Model 206C JetRanger III in 1977. The specification refers to the Model 20 B JetRanger II.

***Top right:* A Bell 206B JetRanger II, the basic commercial model until 1978, when the uprated JetRanger III became available.**

***Right:* A Bell 206L Long Ranger, showing the extra cabin length of this version of the popular helicopter.**

***Below:* A British-registered Bell 206A JetRanger, showing the optional high-skid landing gear that adds to this helicopter's versatility.**

Bell Model 212

USA

Power Plant: One Pratt & Whitney (Canada) PT6T-3 Twin Pac turboshaft flat-rated at 1,250shp for take-off.
Performance: Max level speed, 126mph (203km/h); initial rate of climb, 1,745ft/min (8·8m/sec); hovering ceiling (in ground effect), 14,700ft (4480m); max range, no reserves, 273mls (439km).
Weights: Empty, 5,550lb (2517kg); max take-off, 11,200lb (5080kg).
Dimensions: Rotor diameter, 48ft 2¼in (14·69m); fuselage length, 42ft 4¾in (12·92m); height, 14ft 4¾in (4·39m).

Utilising the same configuration and same basic dynamic components as the Model 205 previously described, Bell developed a twin-engined version of its basic UH-1 helicopter during 1968, initially to meet the requirements of the Canadian Armed Forces and the US armed forces. The principal difference in this new version, known as the Model 212, was the use of Canadian Pratt & Whitney PT6A engines, paired in a Twin Pac arrangement to drive into a common gearbox. A commercial version was certificated in October 1970 and received approval in Transport Type Category A in June 1971, since which time nearly 300 Model 212s have been delivered for commercial use, notably in the off-shore oil exploration market, where the twin-engined arrangement offers a useful safety margin. The Model 212 seats 14 passengers plus the pilot, or can carry 220cu ft (6·23-m³) of cargo internally or a 5,000-lb (2268-kg) externally-slung load.

***Below:** The Bell 212 is one of several derivatives of the highly successful Model 204/205 Iroquois, differing in having twin engines.*

Bell Model 222

USA

Power Plant: Two Lycoming LTS 101-650C turboshafts each rated at 600shp for take-off.
Performance: Max speed, 180mph (290km/h); normal cruising speed, 150mph (240km/h); hovering ceiling (in ground effect), 16,200ft (4940m); range, with reserves, 425mls (685km).
Weights: Empty equipped, 4,035lb (1830kg); max take-off, 6,700lb (3039kg).
Dimensions: Span, 38ft 11½in (11·87m); fuselage length, 39ft 9in (12·12m); height, 11ft 1½in (3·39m).

Development of the Bell Model 222 began in 1974 with the principal objective of producing a light transport helicopter to meet the requirements of the commercial operator and the off-shore oil industry in particular. Unlike other Bell helicopters, the Model 222 has, in the first instance, no military backing, although schemes for military and government agency rôles had been prepared by Bell while flight development of the prototypes proceeded, following a first flight on 13 August 1976. The standard high density layout provides for nine passengers in addition to the pilot; in executive rôle, the Model 222 seats six, and as an ambulance, two stretchers with attendants. Deliveries were to begin in 1978.

***Right:** The Model 222, entering service late in 1978, is Bell's first helicopter developed solely for commercial use from the outset.*

Hughes 500
USA

Power Plant: One Allison 250-C20B turboshaft rated at 420shp for take-off.
Performance: Max cruising speed, 160mph (258km/h); economical cruising speed, 150mph (241km/h); initial rate of climb, 1,700ft/min (8·6m/sec); hovering ceiling (in ground effect), 9,000ft (2745m); range, no reserves, 300mls (482km).
Weights: Empty, 1,320lb (598kg); max take-off, 3,000lb (1360kg).
Dimensions: Rotor diameter, 26ft 5in (8·05m); overall length, 30ft 6in (9·30m); height, 8ft 3½in (2·53m); main rotor disc area, 548sq ft (50·9m²).

Like the Bell Model 206 previously described, the Hughes Model 500 had its origins in a US Army requirement for a light observation helicopter. Hughes won the initial Army production contracts to fulfil this requirement with its Model 369, produced as the OH-6 Cayuse. During 1968, Hughes launched a commercial version as the Model 500, seating pilot and four passengers and several hundred have now been built, including licence production by Breda-Nordi in Italy, RACA in Argentina and Kawasaki in Japan. The original Model 500 had a 278shp Allison 250-C18A engine; the Model 500C has the -C20 engine, derated to the same output but with a bigger reserve margin for hot and high operations; and the Model 500D has the -C20B engine, a small T-tail and numerous other improvements. In production since 1976, the Model 500D is the subject of the specification above.

***Below:** An example of the Hughes 500C in commercial use. The later 500D has a new T-tail and much improved performance.*

Kamov Ka-26
Soviet Union

Power Plant: Two Vedeneev M-14V-26 piston engines each rated at 325hp for take-off.
Performance: Max speed, 105mph (170km/h); economical cruising speed, 56–68mph (90–110km/h); hovering ceiling (in ground effect) 4,265ft (1300m); range with seven passengers, 248mls (400km).
Weights: Operating weight empty, 4,300lb (1950kg); transport payload, 1,985lb (900kg); take-off weight, 7,165lb (3250kg).
Dimensions: Rotor diameter, 42ft 8in (13·00m); fuselage length, 25ft 5in (7·75m); height, 13ft 3½in (4·05m).

The late Nikolai I Kamov was one of two Soviet designers who specialised in the development of rotary wing aircraft, a specialisation continued by the bureau that bears his name. In addition to helicopters for military use, the Kamov bureau has been responsible for the general-purpose Ka-26 light helicopter, widely used by Aeroflot and in East European countries. First flown in 1965, it was designed to have the minimum necessary fuselage structure, comprising a two-seat cockpit, the rotor/power plant system and twin booms carrying the tail unit. When used to carry passengers (six) or cargo, a detachable pod is fitted behind the cockpit; in its place, special-purpose pods can be attached for agricultural duties (spraying or dusting); an open platform can be used to carry bulky freight loads or the aircraft can fly as a crane with a slung load of up to 2,425lb (1100kg). Several hundred Ka-26s have been built.

***Below:** A Kamov Ka-26 in service with Interflug, the East German agency responsible for agricultural work and other duties.*

***Below:** The Ka-26 carrying an insecticide hopper in place of the fuselage "pod", and with spray bars beneath the tail booms.*

MBB BO 105/106
Federal Germany

Power Plant: Two Allison 250-C20 turboshafts each rated at 400shp for take-off.
Performance: Max cruise speed, 144mph (232km/h) at sea level; initial rate of climb, 1,378ft/min (7·0m/sec); hovering ceiling (in ground effect), 8,900ft (2715m); range with standard fuel, 408mls (656km) at 5,000ft (1525m).
Weights: Empty, 2,469lb (1120kg); max take-off, 5,070lb (2300kg).
Dimensions: Rotor diameter, 32ft $2\frac{3}{4}$in (9·82m); fuselage length, 28ft $0\frac{1}{2}$in (8·55m); height overall, 9ft $9\frac{1}{2}$in (2·98m).

The most successful German helicopter to date, the BO 105 was developed by the Bölkow Entwicklungen (now part of the Messerschmitt-Bölkow-Blohm concern) under government contract and became the first light twin-turbine helicopter to enter production. The prototype BO 105 was first flown with Allison 250-C18 engines and a conventional rotor; a second prototype flown on 16 February 1967 introduced the Bölkow rigid rotor with glass-fibre blades. A pre-production BO 105 flew on 1 May 1969 and the Allison 250-C20 was subsequently offered in the BO 105C, which has been the standard version since 1973. Over 320 BO 105s had been delivered by early 1977, including military models, with some being assembled in the Philippines by PADC. In the USA, the BO 105, which seats five in the standard version, is marketed by Boeing Vertol, which also offers a variant known as the Executaire with lengthened rear cabin compartment to improve the comfort or allow up to six persons to be accommodated. First flown on 25 September 1973, the BO 106 is similar to the BO 105 but has a wider cabin to allow up to seven occupants to be carried. It is powered by the 420shp Allison 250-C20B and has performance similar to that of the BO 105C, which is the subject of the specification.

***Above:** One of Europe's most successful helicopters of recent years, the MBB BO-105 was an original Bölkow design.*

Mil Mi-4
Soviet Union

Power Plant: One Shvetsov ASh-82V piston engine rated at 1,700hp for take-off.
Performance: Max speed, 130mph (209km/h); economical cruising speed, 99mph (160km/h); ceiling, 16,000ft (4877m); max range, 250mls (400km) with eight passengers.
Weights: Payload, 2,645lb (1200kg); normal gross weight, 17,200lb (7800kg).
Dimensions: Rotor diameter, 68ft 11in (21·00m); fuselage length, 55ft 1in (16·80m); height, 17ft 0in (5·18m).

An early product of the design bureau headed by Mikhail Mil, one of two leading rotary-wing designers in the Soviet Union, the Mi-4 appeared in 1952 and was built in very large numbers for both military and civil use. Powered by a 1,700hp Shvetsov Ash-82V piston engine, it is no longer in production but still serving both in the Soviet Union and in Eastern European countries, for utility duties. The non-military versions comprised the Mi-4P (*Passajirskii*) transport helicopter for Aeroflot with 10 passengers and the Mi-4S agricultural version.

***Above:** An Mi-4 in East German operation. Strikingly similar to the Sikorsky S-55, the Mi-4 was one of the first Soviet successes.*

Mil Mi-8
Soviet Union

Power Plant: Two Isotov TV2-117A turboshaft engines each rated at 1,500shp for take-off.
Performance: Max speed, 161mph (260km/h) at 3,280ft (1000m); max cruising speed, 112mph (180km/h); hovering ceiling (in ground effect) 6,233ft (1900m); range, passenger version with fuel reserves, 264mls (425km); ferry range, 745mls (1200km).
Weights: Empty, 16,007lb (7261kg); max take-off weight, 28 passengers, 25,508lb (11,570kg).
Dimensions: Rotor diameter, 69ft $10\frac{1}{4}$in (21·29m); fuselage length, 60ft $0\frac{3}{4}$in (18·31m); height, 18ft $6\frac{1}{2}$in (5·65m); main rotor disc area, 3,828sq ft (355m^2).

Using the same configuration and similar dynamics system to the previously-described Mi-4, the Mi-8 introduced turbine power – a prototype in 1961 having a single 2,700shp Soloviev turboshaft but later aircraft, starting with a second prototype flown on 17 September 1962, have a twin-turbine power plant, feeding into a single gearbox to drive the main rotor. A five-bladed main rotor replaced the four-bladed rotor used on the first production batch. The basic Mi-8 passenger version seats 28–32, or carries 12 stretchers when used as an ambulance. A utility version, usually used for cargo carrying, internally stowed or slung externally (6,614-lb/3000-kg), is designated Mi-8T and a de luxe version is known as the Mi-8 Salon, with provision for 11 passengers.

***Above:** The Mi-8, derived from the smaller Mi-4 with turbine engines and a larger fuselage, seats 32.*

Mil Mi-6/Mi-10
Soviet Union

Power Plant: Two Soloviev D-25V turboshaft engines each rated at 5,500shp for take-off.
Performance: Cruising speed (empty), 155mph (250km/h); max cruising speed with slung load, 125mph (202km/h); service ceiling, 9,850ft (3000m); ferry range with auxiliary external tank, 494mls (795km).
Weights: Empty, 54,410lb (24,680kg); max slung load, 24,250lb (11,000kg); max take-off weight with slung cargo, 83,776lb (38,000kg).
Dimensions: Rotor diameter, 114ft 10in (35·00m); fuselage length, 107ft 9¾in (32·86m); overall height, 25ft 7in (7·80m).

The Mi-6 emerged from the Mil design bureau in 1957 as the world's largest helicopter (since surpassed by the Mi-12), designed for heavy transport duties, primarily of a military nature but including some civilian activities. With stub wings to off-load the massive five-bladed rotor in cruising flight, the Mi-6 has demonstrated – in record-breaking flights – the ability to lift payloads of up to 44,350lb (20,116kg) and to achieve speeds of 211mph (340km/h) over short ranges. The fuselage can accommodate 65 passengers. Several hundred Mi-6s are reported to have been built, of which about 30 are believed to be operated by Aeroflot in connection with construction activities in the more remote areas of the Soviet Union. The Mi-6 can carry a slung load of 19,840lb (9000kg), but the full load-carrying potential of the basic design was realised in the Mi-10 flying crane, first flown in 1960, with a "slenderized" fuselage and a long, stalky undercarriage allowing outsize loads to be carried on an open platform between the wheels. A few years after the Mi-10, the Mi-10K appeared, with the same fuselage but a more conventional short undercarriage; intended to carry its load slung beneath the fuselage, the Mi-10K featured a supplementary aft-facing control position beneath the cockpit, from which a crewman could control the lifting and positioning of slung loads with great accuracy. The specification refers to the Mi-10K; the Mi-10 and Mi-6 have the same power plant/rotor system.

***Above right:** The Mil Mi-6, the largest helicopter in the world when introduced in the Soviet Union in 1957.*
***Right:** The Mi-10, based on the Mi-6 dynamic components, demonstrates its ability to lift a prefabricated building.*

Sikorsky S-64
USA

Power Plant: Two Pratt & Whitney JFTD12-4A turboshafts each rated at 4,500shp for take-off.
Performance: Max level speed, 126mph (203km/h) at sea level; max cruising speed, 105mph (169km/h); initial rate of climb, 1,330ft/min (6·7m/sec); hovering ceiling (in ground effect), 10,600ft (3230m); range with reserves, 230mls (370km).
Weights: Empty, 19,234lb (9724kg); max take-off weight, 42,000lb (19,050kg).
Dimensions: Rotor diameter, 72ft 0in (21·95m); fuselage length, 70ft 3in (21·41m); height overall, 25ft 5in (7·75m); main rotor disc area, 4,070sq ft (378m²).

The largest helicopter adapted for commercial use to date outside of the Soviet Union is the Sikorsky S-64 Skycrane, a flying crane developed for military use and built in quantity for the US Army. The prototype first flew on 9 May 1962 and the design provided for a "minimum fuselage" carrying the power plant, rotor system and three-seat cockpit including an aft-facing seat with provision for piloting the aircraft in crane operation. A special pod could be attached under the fuselage, with up to 45 seats but in commercial use the S-64 operates as a heavylift crane for logging and oil drilling support. Two S-64As were delivered in April 1969 followed since 1972 by about a dozen improved S-64Es, to which the data refer.

***Below:** The Sikorsky S-64 is one of the few genuine "flying crane" helicopters produced, and is the nearest US equivalent to the Mi-10 shown above.*

Sikorsky S-58

USA

see **Airliners** section page 118

Power Plant: One Pratt & Whitney (Canada) PT6T-6 Twin Pac rated at 1,875shp for take-off.
Performance: Max speed, 138mph (222km/h) at sea level; cruising speed, 127mph (204km/h). Hovering ceiling (out of ground effect), 6,500ft (1980m); range, with reserves, 278mls (447km).
Weights: Empty, 8,354lb (3789kg); max take-off, 13,000lb (5896kg).
Dimensions: Rotor diameter, 56ft 0in (17·07m); fuselage length, 47ft 3in (14·40m); height, 15ft 11in (4·85m); main rotor disc area, 2,460sq ft (228·5m^2).

The Sikorsky company has produced a long series of commercial and military helicopters since Igor Sikorsky achieved the first practical helicopter in the USA in 1939. Following the success of the S-55, the similar but somewhat larger S-58 emerged in 1952 to meet US Navy requirements for an anti-submarine helicopter and the prototype flew on 8 March 1954. Certification of a commercial version was obtained on 2 August 1956, the production variants being the general purpose S-58B with seats for 5–7 passengers and the 12-seat S-58C, which was used by several airlines for scheduled services in the USA. By the time production ended in January 1970, Sikorsky had built 1,821 examples of the piston-engined S-58 for military and civil use and numbers remain in service, together with Westland-built examples with turboshaft engines, known as the Wessex 60 in civil guise. In January 1970, Sikorsky launched a programme to convert S-58s to turbine power and a prototype of this S-58T version flew on 19 August 1970. A substantial number of conversions has been completed since 1973, at first with 1,800shp Pratt & Whitney PT6T-3 Twin Pac engines and now, as S-58T Mk II, with uprated PT6T-6 engines; the specification refers to the latter version, which carries 10–16 passengers in addition to a crew of two and is in both military and civil use.

Sikorsky S-61

USA

Above: A Sikorsky S-58T of Bristow Helicopters, one of Europe's largest operators, specializing in North Sea oil support flying.

Sikorsky S-76

USA

Power Plant: Two Allison 250-C30 turboshafts each rated at 650shp for take-off.
Performance: Max speed, 180mph (289km/h); economical cruising speed, 144mph (231km/h) at sea level; hovering ceiling (in ground effect) 5,000ft (1555m); range with standard fuel, 460mls (740km/h) with reserves.
Weights: Standard empty, 4,942lb (2241kg); max gross 9,700lb (4400kg).
Dimensions: Rotor diameter, 44ft 0in (13·41m); fuselage length, 44ft 1in (13·44m); overall height, 14ft 6in (4·41m).

Development of a new medium-size helicopter for the commercial market, and in particular the oil drilling industry, was launched by Sikorsky early in 1975. Benefiting from design, research and development conducted by the company on its S-70 UTTAS military helicopter, the S-76 is nevertheless exclusively for civil use in the first instance, and is designed to seat 12 passengers plus a crew of two, or fewer in executive layouts. The prototype S-76 flew on 13 March 1977, by which time the company had a back-log of 92 orders. Deliveries were to begin in mid-1978.

Above: The Sikorsky S-76, in the final stages of development in 1978, was already backed by more than 100 orders.

WSK-Swidnik (Mil) Mi-2

Poland/Soviet Union

Power Plant: Two Polish-built Isotov GTD-350P turboshaft engines each rated at 400shp or (later aircraft) 450shp for take-off.
Performance: Max speed, 130mph (210km/h) at 1,640ft (500m); economical cruising speed, 118mph (190km/h) at 1,640ft (500m); initial rate of climb, 885ft/min (4·5m/sec); hovering ceiling (in ground effect), 6,550ft (2000m); range with max payload, 105mls (170km).
Weights: Basic empty, 5,213lb (2365kg); max take-off, 8,157lb (3700kg).
Dimensions: Rotor diameter, 47ft $6\frac{3}{4}$in (14·50m); fuselage length, 39ft 2in (11·94m); height, 12ft $3\frac{1}{2}$in (3·75m); main rotor disc area, 1,791sq ft (166·4m^2).

Developed in the Soviet Union by the Mil design bureau in the early 'sixties as a derivative of the Mi-1 – first of the Mil helicopters to achieve production – the Mi-2 is basically a turbine-engined version of the earlier type. After flight testing had confirmed the basic configuration details, production of the Mi-2 was launched exclusively in Poland at the WSK-Swidnik factory, where several hundred examples have been built for military and civil duties, and the type has been further developed. The basic Mi-2 is designed to be flown by one pilot only and accommodates 8–10 passengers in the cabin; alternatively, 1,543lb (700kg) of cargo can be carried, and special rôle versions have been developed for ambulance use, agricultural duties, training, aerial survey, television transmission and so on. On 1 July 1974, the WSK works flew the first Mi-2M, which differs in having a retractable nosewheel and a wider cabin to seat nine passengers. Deliveries began in 1975, including passenger/cargo, ambulance and agricultural versions. The specification refers to the standard Mi-2.

Right: An early example of the Mi-2, developed in the Soviet Union but built primarily in Poland by the WSK factory.

Index

All figures in bold type represent subjects mentioned in captions.

Picture Credits

The Publishers would like to sincerely thank the following airlines and aircraft manufacturers who have supplied photographs for this book:

Aérospatiale
Agusta
Air France
Air Mahe
Air New Zealand
Air Polynésie
Airbus Industrie
Alitalia
Allegheny Airlines
American Jet Industries
Ansett Airlines
Antonov
Beech Corporation
Bell Helicopter Textron
Boeing Company
British Aerospace Corporation
British Airways
Canadair
CASA
Cessna
Cimber Air
Cruzeiro Airways
Czechoslovakian Airlines
Dassault-Breguet
De Havilland Canada
Dornier
Embraer
Fokker-VFW
Foxjet International
Gates Learjet
Grumman Aerospace
Hawker Siddeley
Icelandair
Interflug
Iraqi Airways
Israel Aircraft Industries
Japan Air Lines
Lockheed Aircraft Corporation
Loganair
Lufthansa
Kamov
McDonnell Douglas Corporation
Malev
Mil
Mitsubishi
NorOntair
North Central Airlines
Pan-Am
Partenavia
Piper
Rockwell International
Shorts
Sikorsky
Southwest Airlines
Spantax
Swearingen
Swissair
Tupolev
Votec
Zambia Airways

We would like to particularly thank Arthur Gibson for the photographs appearing on: Jacket front/Jacket back (inset right)/Endpapers/Business and Executive Aircraft introduction spread/Helicopters introduction spread.

Other photographs have been credited by page number; references are made from left to right and from top to bottom, unless otherwise directed.

Page 6: (Main pic) M. B. Passingham
8: M. B. Passingham.
9: (Middle and below) M. B. Passingham.
10: (Centre) J. Bowdler.
12: M. Hooks.
13: (Above right) P. Jarrett.
15: (Bottom) R. J. Wiseman.
27: J. Bowdler, Air Portraits.
25: C. Ballantyne.
26: (Top) Austin J. Brown.
28: R. Wright.
33: Austin J. Brown.
38: Air Portraits.
40: Air Portraits.
49: R. Wright.
64: (Both) Air Portraits.
65: R. Kosys, D. Kuhn.
67: Austin J. Brown.
73: R. Kosys.
74: (Top) R. Kosys.
75: R. Wright.
85: Air Portraits.
87: Air Portraits.
88: Air Portraits, R. Wright.
89: (Top) J. Gilbert.
90: Air Portraits.
96: C. Ballantyne.
97: C. Ballantyne.
99: (Both) Austin J. Brown.
113: R. Wright.
114: (Both) R. Kosys.
118: R. Kosys.
124: (Top) Austin J. Brown.
125: C. Ballantyne.
130: Air Portraits.
131: (Middle and below) Air Portraits.
132: Austin J. Brown, R. Wright.
133: R. Wright.
153: G. Finch.
155: (Bottom) J. Bowdler.
165: Austin J. Brown, R. Wright.
169: Austin J. Brown.
176: Air Portraits.
178: (Top) R. Wright/(Below left) C. Ballantyne.
179: Air Portraits, C. Ballantyne, Austin J. Brown.
180: J. Gilbert.
181: (Top) Austin J. Brown.

PRINTED IN proost Turnhout (Belgium)

Range with full payload: 100 200 300 400 500 1000 1500

Aircraft	max pax	max payload lbs	max payload kgs	Range with full payload
Aérospatiale Caravelle	99	18000	8200	1430mls
Aérospatiale (Nord) 262 Frégate	26	7000	3200	600mls (965kms)
Aérospatiale/BAC Concorde	144	25000	11340	
Airbus A300 B2	336	67500	30620	
Airbus A300 B4	336	77200	35020	
Antonov An-22	freight	176300	79970	
Antonov An-24	50	12100	5490	340mls (550kms)
Antonov An-28	19	3750	1700	620mls (1000kms)
BAC (Vickers) Super VC10	187	60300	27350	
BAC One-Eleven 500	119	26400	11970	1500mls
Boeing 707-320	189	91000	41280	
Boeing 727-200	189	43000	19500	
Boeing 737-200	130	35700	16200	
Boeing 747-200	498	165000	74840	
Boeing 747 SP	360	99600	45180	
Bristol 175 Britannia 310	139	34500	15650	
Canadair CL-44D	178	63300	28700	
Convair 640	52	15800	7170	1230mls
Convair (General Dynamics) 990	106	26500	12020	
Dassault-Breguet Mercure	155	35300	16010	470mls (750kms)
De Havilland Canada Dash-7	54	11000	4990	730mls (1170kms)
Embraer EMB-110 Bandeirante	22	3400	1540	200mls (320kms)
Fokker F27 Friendship Mk 200	48	12900	5850	1200mls
Fokker-VFW F28 Fellowship Mk 400	85	20000	9072	1100mls
Hawker Siddeley DH 106 Comet 4	106	20300	9200	
Hawker Siddeley HS 748	58	11700	5300	850mls (1370kms)
Hawker Siddeley HS 121 Trident Two	149	29600	13430	
Ilyushin Il-18	122	29750	13500	
Ilyushin Il-62	186	50700	23000	
Ilyushin Il-86	350	92600	42000	1460mls
Lockheed Hercules L-100-30	freight	51400	23310	
Lockheed Electra	99	22800	10340	
Lockheed L-1011 TriStar-1	345	84600	38370	
Lockheed L-1011 TriStar-500	300	97800	44360	
McDonnell Douglas DC-8 Srs 63	259	68000	30840	
McDonnell Douglas DC-9 Srs 30	125	28000	12700	
McDonnell Douglas DC-9 Srs 50	139	34500	15650	
McDonnell Douglas DC-9 Super 80	172	35500	16100	
McDonnell Douglas DC-10 Srs 10	380	98500	44680	
McDonnell Douglas DC-10 Srs 30	380	106500	48300	
NAMC YS-11-200	60	14500	6580	450mls (725kms)
Shorts 330	30	5900	2680	1000mls (1600kms)
Tupolev Tu-134A	80	18075	8200	1240mls
Tupolev Tu-144	140	33000	14970	
Tupolev Tu-154	167	44000	19960	
Vickers Viscount 810	71	14500	6580	1300mls
Vickers Vanguard	139	37000	16780	1400mls
Yakovlev Yak-40	32	6000	2720	1100mls
Yakovlev Yak-42	120	32000	14515	620mls (1000kms)

500 1000 1500 2000 2500